N. ZHIROV

ATLANTIS

ATLANTOLOGY: BASIC PROBLEMS

University Press of the Pacific
Honolulu, Hawaii

Atlantis:
Atlantology - Basic Problems

by
N. Zhirov

ISBN: 0-89875-591-3

Copyright © 2001 by University Press of the Pacific

Reprinted from the 1970 edition

University Press of the Pacific
Honolulu, Hawaii
http://www.universitypressofthepacific.com

All rights reserved, including the right to reproduce
this book, or portions thereof, in any form.

CONTENTS

	Page
Editor's Foreword	5
Author's Note	6
Author's Note to the English Edition	8
Introduction	9

THE ATLANTIS OF PLATO

Chapter One. The Plato Legend 19
Chapter Two. Criticism of Descriptions of the Culture of Plato's Atlanteans 43
Chapter Three A Criticism of Plato's Texts on Atlantis 53
Chapter Four. Atlantis, Scheria and Tartessos 70
Chapter Five. Atlantis and the Mediterranean 82
Chapter Six. Esoteric Legends About Atlantis 99

NATURE AND ORIGIN OF OCEANS

Chapter Seven. Basic Geophysical and Geological Notions 109
Chapter Eight. Modern Views of the Origin of Oceans 129
    The Pacific Ocean and Atlantology (146)
Chapter Nine. Some Features of Oceans 156
    A. Submarine Valleys and Canyons (157). B. Guyots (160). C. Deep-Water Sand and Turbidity Currents (160). D. Bottom Currents and Submarine Erosion (170). E Mid-oceanic Mountain Ridges (171). F. Theory of the Anthropogen Global Transgression (182)

ATLANTIC

Chapter Ten. The Atlantic Ocean 186
    A. Oceanic Islands (186). B. Currents and Winds of the North Atlantic (191). C. The Sargasso Sea and the Spawning of Eels (195). D Distribution of Foraminifera (197). E. Diatoms and Pteropods (199)
Chapter Eleven. Makaronesia 201
    The Riddle of the Guanches (211)
Chapter Twelve. Topography of the Atlantic Floor 216
    Mythical Islands of the North Atlantic as a Problem of Atlantology (250)
Chapter Thirteen. North Atlantic Floor 258
    A. Seismic and Gravimetric Investigations (258). B. Studies of Bedrock Samples (265). C. Bottom Soil and Sediments (275)

Chapter Fourteen. Geological History of the Atlantic Ocean 287
  A. Views on the General Geological History of the Ocean (287). B. Origin of the Mid-Atlantic Ridge (292). C. Geological History of Scandicus (298). D. Geological History of Poseidonis (303). E. Geological History of Archhelenis (306)

ATLANTIS AS A REALITY

Chapter Fifteen. Atlantis as a Biogeographical and Geological Reality . . 309
  A. Geological Atlantis (309). B. Paleobotanical Data (311). C. Paleofaunistic Data (314). D. Soviet Scientists on the Reality of Atlantis (317). E. Geological History of Atlantis (318). F. Atlantis and Man (323)
Chapter Sixteen. Atlantis, the Arctic and the Ice Age 326
  A. Causes and Time of Glaciation in the Anthropogen (326). B. Atlantis, the Gulf Stream and the Ice Age (335). C. Geomorphology and Geological History of the Arctic (342). D. Arctic Climate (348). E. The Lomonosov and Mendeleyev Ridges and the Problem of Arctis (350). F. Settlement of America in Connection with Glaciation and Atlantis (351)
Chapter Seventeen. Location, Causes and Date of the Destruction of Atlantis 357
  A. Principal Variants of the Location of Atlantis (357). B. Our Reconstruction of Atlantis (359). C. Possibility of Geological Catastrophes and Atlantis (367). D. Cosmic Theories of the Destruction of Atlantis (371). E. Date of the Sinking of Atlantis and Ancient Calendars (374). F. Possibility of Later Dates of the Final Subsidence of Atlantis (379). G. Chronology of Events of the Last Glaciation and the Holocene and Establishment of the Most Probable Date of the Destruction of Atlantis (381)
Conclusion 386
Appendix 1 389
Appendix 2 401
References 403

EDITOR'S FOREWORD

The fascinating age-old riddle of the legendary continent of Atlantis is a challenge to any investigator for it would be hard to name a problem of longer standing or one that has given rise to sharper controversies and differences of views and opinions. Some investigators have rejected the problem as not worth attention. Others regarded it as a key to an ancient riddle throwing light on many aspects of human history and civilisation. Thousands of books and papers have been devoted to the thrilling problem of Atlantis, and a new scientific trend, *atlantology*, studying Atlantis has emerged.

Atlantology cannot advance without the aid of geomorphology and marine geology, which are relatively new spheres of human knowledge. Indeed, the problems linked up with Atlantis can be approached successfully only by drawing upon the latest achievements of world science in the study of the geological structure and relief of the ocean bed, only in the light of the new ideas about the youth and active development of oceans.

Not everything in N. F. Zhirov's book has been worked out and scientifically substantiated with equal profundity. It contains many controversial points, surmises, scientific hypotheses and preliminary conclusions. Nonetheless, it gives us an insight into a complex, creative process, many of whose elements remain to be ascertained.

The author believes that Atlantis existed and uses a great number of facts to back up his arguments. His work sums up much on what we know about atlantology. This book will unquestionably serve as the basis for elaborating on many aspects of one of the world's most dramatic problems.

Rostov-on-Don

Professor D. G. PANOV
Doctor of Geographical Sciences

AUTHOR'S NOTE

Anybody undertaking serious research in atlantology will find that he has to study closely and apply the findings of the most diverse sciences. He will always be faced with the difficult task of expounding and tying together a vast range of factual data and of dealing with and interpreting theories and hypotheses. Many of the conclusions drawn by one atlantologist or another, who interprets facts and theoretical notions from a non-canonical standpoint, are questioned and give rise to bitter arguments. Some atlantologists fail to study primary sources, frequently concentrating on second-hand material. I have, therefore, made a point of quoting a sufficiently large number of primary sources and supplementing my propositions with verbatim quotations.* Regrettably, for one reason or another, I have, in a number of cases, been unable to find the pertinent source or utilise the latest and more accurate translations of ancient texts and historical documents. This was noted by the adversaries of atlantology in their criticism of my first book on Atlantis. Some fundamental errors have been taken note of in the writing of the present book and a reply has been given to moot questions and tendentiously selected points.

There are three aspects to the problem of Atlantis. The first is the *geological and geographical* aspect, i.e., elucidating if a more or less considerable land area existed in the Atlantic Ocean in the past. This part of the problem has been studied the least. The second is the *historical and ethnical* aspect, which is linked up with the possibility of man having lived in Atlantis and the role that continent might have played in the history of human settlement and development. A huge number of books offering the most diverse arguments have been written on this immense part of the problem. In many of these books the authors allowed themselves to be carried away with the subject and for that reason much of what they write is open to question. Small wonder that throughout the ages this part of the problem has been most heavily attacked.

---

* References to the list of literature are given in round brackets (the numerator referring to the number of the list, and the denominator giving the page number). The page numbers of the works of foreign authors translated into the Russian language are given according to the Russian edition. References to antique authors are given in square brackets

The third aspect is *historical atlantology*, which studies views on various facets of the Atlantis problem that had developed in the course of more than two millennia. There is a prodigious quantity of raw material for historical atlantology and its inclusion in this book would have unjustifiably lengthened it. Historical atlantology, the author believes, must be the object of a special investigation that would read as a fascinating novel about the delusions in human thinking.

This book deals mainly with the most important—geological and geographical—part of the problem. The other aspects, which I felt I could not ignore completely, are subordinated to the main theme. My prime objective is to raise atlantology to the status of a recognised science. This can be done only by producing geological and geographical proof that Atlantis really existed, and that is what I have attempted to do in this book.

It is quite possible that I have overlooked some essential data, and I shall be grateful if this is pointed out to me.

In conclusion, I must express my profound gratitude to the many Soviet and foreign scientists, writers, atlantologists and others who rendered me invaluable assistance by sending me books, illustrations and comments.

Moscow, 1959-63

N. F. ZHIROV
Doctor of Chemical Sciences

AUTHOR'S NOTE TO THE ENGLISH EDITION

As compared with the Russian edition, the following amendments have been made in the English edition. Data that I feel will not interest the foreign reader have been omitted. On the other hand, the English edition contains some new data from works published in 1963-67, and reference tables, which due to technical reasons, were not included in the Russian edition. In the case of some hypothetical land areas and topographical features the author has taken the liberty of coining names for them.

The Author

January 1968
Moscow

INTRODUCTION

The Greek philosopher Plato (427-347 B.C.) was the first to tell the world about Atlantis, and ever since then, for more than two thousand years, human minds have been trying to fathom the mystery.

According to Plato, a huge island existed in the Atlantic somewhere near the Straits of Gibraltar some twelve thousand years ago. With abundant natural wealth it was inhabited by a numerous and mighty people, Atlanteans, whose rulers waged wars of conquest in the West and East. The Atlanteans had large towns with magnificent buildings, and their rulers possessed vast treasure. In the course of a single day and night, soon after a war against the forefathers of the Athenians, in which the Atlanteans suffered a crushing defeat, Atlantis and its entire population sank to the bottom of the ocean.

The Atlantis legend, born in Ancient Greece, attracted considerable interest throughout the world. It would be safe to say that more has been written about it than about any other problem. A huge number of scientific treatises and works of fiction have been devoted to it. A bibliography compiled by J. Gattefossé and C.C. Roux (3) as far back as 1920 lists nearly 1,700 books and papers.

The aura of fantasy and tragedy surrounding the Atlantis legend has attracted writers and poets. The Russian poet Valery Bryusov (1873-1924) whose interest in Atlantis went beyond poetry, was a prominent atlantologist. He delivered a cycle of lectures on the subject at the People's University in Moscow and, on Maxim Gorky's (15) recommendation, wrote a thought-provoking review of the historical and ethnical aspect of the problem. Konstantin Balmont (1867-1942) was another Russian poet who believed Atlantis existed. He devoted his poem *City of Golden Gates* to it. In his quest for facts he went to Central America, where he studied relics of ancient civilisations, whose origin he linked up with the existence of Atlantis. His book *Snake Flowers*, published in 1910, deals with the subject.

Alexei Tolstoi (1882-1945) has an episode about Atlantis in his novel *Aelita,* while Alexander Belayev (1884-1942), author of many works of science fiction, used factual material for the narrative *The Last Man From Atlantis.* Abroad, the Atlantis enigma was not overlooked by Jules Verne (1828-1905). In the novel *20,000 Leagues Under the Sea,* the hero visits the capital of Atlantis on the bed of the ocean (111). In the novel *Atlantis,* which caused a sensation at the time of its publication, the French writer Pierre Benoît advanced the idea that the lost continent was somewhere in the Sahara. Arthur Conan Doyle was likewise attracted by the Atlantis problem and used it as the subject of the short narrative *The Maracot Deep* (21). A major poem, *Atlantis,* was written by the Spanish poet Jacinto Verdaguer (1845-1902). Plays, operas and films have been devoted to the subject (33, 110, 121).

The attitude of scientists to the Atlantis problem has been extremely contradictory ever since antique times. Some scholars believed Plato, accepting his legends with little criticism. Others, wishing to evade difficulties, used only what they liked in Plato's legend, and many of them let their imaginations get the better of them. But the overwhelming majority, beginning with Plato's pupil, Aristotle (384-322 B.C.), were sceptical about the existence of this baffling island, believing that Plato had invented it with the purpose of popularising and substantiating his social, economic and political views. This idea is predominant in linguistics and literary criticism to this day. L. Zajdler (119/52) draws special attention to this, writing: "Mark the unusually sharp wording of this accusation: not 'use the myth he heard to express his ideas', but 'invented' it." Aristotle, for instance, not only said that the Atlantis story was false, but in the same breath accused Plato of vile deceit. If Aristotle was right, then Plato abused the name of Critias, his relative and friend, from whose lips we know the famous dialogue. Moreover, this would mean that he also abused the name of Solon, the "wisest of the seven sages and the pride of Greece". Zajdler adds: "However, to this day nobody has brought such a violent accusation as Aristotle. Even contemporary sceptics of the Atlantis story do not accuse Plato of lying." Here the riddle evidently lies in bitter differences both in philosophical and political views. Plato was an ardent Athenian patriot. That much cannot be said of Aristotle, who was a retainer of Alexander the Great, and when the latter died he feared persecution and fled to Euboea. Besides, throughout Aristotle's residence in Athens he never held Athenian citizenship. A criticism of Plato's writings about Atlantis is given in Chapter Three.

Two circumstances giving the entire problem a touch of fantastic improbability lie behind the sceptical attitude to Plato's legend about Atlantis. The first is the siting of Atlantis in the Atlantic Ocean, always regarded as a body of water where no major geological upheavals have taken place in the period embraced by the memory of man. The second is the claim that Atlantis was populated by people with a high level of economic and cultural development at a time when the rest of mankind were primitive savages who were just beginning to learn to use the bow and arrow. Propositions of this kind have no precedent in human history and do not fit into any canons. That is why, in their desire to prove that Atlantis really existed, many atlantologists preferred to evade difficulties, thereby abandoning the very essence of Plato's legend: they declined to accept the date of the destruction of Atlantis, or its siting in the Atlantic Ocean, or both these circumstances. Frequently they offered completely alien considerations, and it is not surprising that diverse locations are given for Atlantis, ranging from one pole to the other. T. H. Martin (167) aptly put it when he said that the authors of these pseudo-Atlantises used the compass of their own imagination.*

A fact to be borne in mind is that among the enormous output dealing with the Atlantis mystery, there are many pseudo-scientific works—fantastic, semi-fantastic and simply untrustworthy. Most of the early atlantologists (18th-first half of the 20th century) were dilettantes, enthusiastic amateurs who worked in isolation; they were very uncritical of their source material and had blind faith in doubtful documents. For that reason they tackled various aspects of the problem at their own peril. No serious scholars touched the Atlantic mystery: the epithet "liar", which Aristotle had hurled at his teacher, was more than enough to drive them away. Besides, the problem has acquired a not very pleasant hue because it interested mystics, occultists and even racists.

The abundance of pseudo-scientific literature devoted to Atlantis has led to the appearance of "exposures" in the forms of reviews, papers and even fat volumes, most of which, however, suffer from lack of scientific objectivity. Among these works are a review of the author's first book by Y. V. Knorozov (22) and a popular article (22a) in which Knorozov rehashed the initial review. Of serious works mention must be made of a book by L. Sprague de Camp (102), in which an effort is made to keep to the fringe of objectivity, and also a book by R. Wauchope (177a). Translated into the Russian under the editorship of Knorozov, it offers a quite interesting and at times deserved criticism of the founders of atlantology. Regrettably, much of what Wauchope says is couched in much too sharp a tone and is not always objective. He gives it "hot" not only to "deluded" atlantologists, but also to a noted ethnographer like Thor Heyerdahl. A curious point is that although Heyerdahl's attitude to Atlantis is negative, he found himself, by the irony of fate, in the same boat with atlantologists.

In atlantology today the situation is that, with few exceptions, scholars either adopt a negative attitude to the Atlantis problem or they simply ignore it. First and foremost, this concerns scholars in

---

* The list of pseudo-Atlantises and their authors given by L. Sprague de Camp (102/314-318) is far from complete.

foreign countries, where in the majority of cases a positive approach to the problem costs a scholar his reputation. A typical example of this is the review by a US critic (179) of a treatise on Atlantis by the Colombian anthropologist H. Daniel (55). The critic expressed surprise that a serious scientist let himself be carried away by a flippant subject which could only discredit him.

A similarly curious review was published by the Soviet geologist Vladimir Saks (in the magazine *Priroda*, No. 11, 1949, p. 91) on *Geology of the Sea*, a book written by Professor M. V. Klenova. He wrote: "It was quite superfluous to mention the mythical Atlantis in connection with the recent (post-glacial) submersion of the Thompson Ridge between Greenland, Iceland and Europe." Typical of the negative attitude to the Atlantis problem are the statements of scientists working in sciences that have a direct bearing on the problem but, evidently, approaching it one-sidedly, solely from the standpoint of their science. The well-known English student of historical geography J. O. Thomson (146/141) wrote that for the ancients it was more excusable to succumb to the mystifications of authors of utopias. R. Hennig (158/15), another prominent investigator of ancient traditions and legends, offered the opinion that the Plato report was nothing more than a figment of the imagination, for it was not backed up by incontrovertible facts. The Soviet linguist Y. V. Knorozov (290/249) flatly asserts: "In reality Atlantis never existed." His emphatically negative attitude to the problem is strikingly expressed in an article (22), in which he writes: "Lately, among other pseudo-scientific problems, the problem of Atlantis has attracted a great deal of undeserved attention in our newspapers and magazines." Obviously, he brackets atlantology with such pseudo-sciences as magic, astrology, alchemistry, chiromancy and so forth, assuming that the problem had long ago been settled negatively and that the publication of works proving the existence of Atlantis was intolerable.

It should be noted that the attitude of oceanologists and geologists to the Atlantis problem is likewise negative. For example, Doctor M. Ewing, the eminent US oceanologist, who took part in a series of oceanological expeditions in the area where Atlantis might have submerged, who, so to say, stood virtually on its threshold, had nothing better to say than: "There is no reason to believe that this mighty underwater mass of mountains (investigated by an expedition on the ship *Atlantis* with Ewing's participation—*N.Ž.*) is connected in any way with the legendary lost Atlantis, which Plato described as having sunk beneath the waves" (520/616). Another well-known US geologist, Francis P. Shepard (673/167), wrote in a similar vein: "The legend of the lost Atlantis, made famous by Plato, has been endorsed by some romantic geologists and archaeologists on the basis of obscure evidence from the Mid-Atlantic Ridge. A little serious study of the source of the legend will show that it is not even supported by the classics. The Atlanteans, according to the

Greek writings, lived somewhere beyond the Pillars of Hercules, meaning the Strait of Gibraltar. Any of the islands or even the African coast would do for the legend. The supposed disappearance (of Atlantis—*N.Z.*) may mean that the early navigators failed to find the area in their attempt to return to it. Furthermore, the ridge has so far yielded no acceptable evidence of having been above water for at least millions of years."

The result of the absence, among geologists, of a common viewpoint on the history and origin of oceans was that some leading Soviet geologists ruled out the possibility of Plato's Atlantis ever having existed. One of them, Academician A. L. Yanshin (31), wrote: "However, it must be said that the evidence of a recent existence of land in place of the submarine Atlantic Ridge does not stand the test of strict scientific criticism. All the facts produced in favour of this may be explained differently. . . . Thus, we have no weighty proof of any recent existence of land in the middle of the modern Atlantic Ocean. On the contrary, convincing arguments may be offered to show beyond a shadow of doubt that *in that area there has been a land area* (my italics—*N.Z.*) which submerged very long ago and could not have been the Atlantis described by Plato."

Incidentally, Academician Yanshin believes the Atlantis legend sprang from the Phoenician reports of ancient African civilisations in the region of the Gulf of Guinea.

To a reader not initiated in the subtleties of modern geology, it may seem that the opinion of such authoritative Soviet and foreign geologists and oceanologists very nearly shatters the geological aspect of the Atlantis problem. Luckily, things are not as black as all that. In recent years many facts have been produced that would be hard to explain without accepting the surmise that Atlantis existed, although in almost every case these facts are explained differently, frequently by drawing upon the most fantastic hypotheses. There is a large group of geologists whose opinion is diametrically opposed to that of the geologists named above. One of them is Academician Vladimir Obruchev, doyen of Soviet geological science. His views and detailed criticism of the notions of the US school are expounded below.

In our opinion there are two reasons for the above-mentioned negative attitude to Atlantis legend. Examined closely they appear to be either a manifestation of conservatism or hypercriticism, or founded on a narrow range of data and theoretical notions of some one science or even some one school of investigators. Very frequently in researches or conclusions of this kind facts that could contradict the views or hypotheses of the opponents of the Atlantis problem are ignored deliberately or involuntarily. Doctor René Malaise, the Swedish biogeographer and a prominent representative of modern scientific atlantology (76/198), wrote: "Marine geologists and oceanographers are just as conservative, and this makes it extremely difficult, not to say impossible, for them to interpret most of their recent discoveries."

A good example of biased criticism by oceanologists and geographers of the American school is the criticism levelled at this book (756) and a book by L. Zajdler (119, in the Afterword).

With regard to the significance of narrow specialisation, the eminent Norwegian scholar Thor Heyerdahl (416) wittily wrote: "Modern science requires that every special branch should dig in its own hole. It's not usual for anyone to sort out what comes up out of the holes and try to put it together." In this context, the atlantologist must always bear in mind the school or scientific trend producing a work that negatively examines the Atlantis problem. In most cases the reason for the negative attitude is to be found in this and not in the facts, which in many cases are used tendentiously or selectively.

What is atlantology? *It may be regarded as a department of the biogeography of the modern, Quaternary period (Anthropogen) of the Earth's geological history, a department chronologically relating to the period of the emergence of intelligent man, a period directly preceding our historical epoch beginning with the last glaciation.* Therefore, when we study the Atlantis problem we must take into account not only geological but also paleobiological factors, to say nothing of data provided by comparative mythology. The task of scientific atlantology is, first and foremost, to deduce hard facts from historical sources and myths, including the Plato legend, and find corroboration of these facts and considerations in the data obtained from different fields of science (127). One may take a broader view of this task by not confining it to the objective of studying the single problem of Atlantis. It is both the point of departure and the key to the whole problem. On a larger scale *atlantology seeks to establish the relationship between the possibility of large land areas and even continents having existed and been destroyed and the problem of human settlement and development.* In this context atlantology may be regarded as a department of anthropology. Atlantis is atlantology's principal sphere of investigation, but there are other objectives, namely, Hawaiis, West and East Pacifis in the Pacific Ocean and Lemuria in the Indian Ocean,* whose remains probably sank in a period embraced by the memory of man and whose submersion most certainly affected the settlement of tribes in remote antiquity. In this light, the well-known archaeologist Jacques de Morgan (333/278) seemed to be looking into the crystal ball when he wrote: "Unfortunately, the conclusions to which a study of the earth's crust lead us are far from being comprehensive because we know nothing of continents that have vanished and very little of the modifications in the outlines of our seaboards."

---

* Geological Lemuria, mentioned here, should not be confused with the Lemuria of the mystics, who describe it as being in the Pacific Ocean (103). See Chapter Six for occult pseudo-myths.

In tackling the problems facing it, atlantology draws upon data provided by geology, oceanology, history, astronomy, anthropology, ethnography and other sciences. *A feature of atlantology is that it is a synthetic, composite science.* The rise of such sciences is typical of the present stage of scientific development, when sciences specialising in a narrow field are superseded or complemented by new, compound sciences that synthetise and collate the facts and theoretical notions of a series of sciences, some of which are remote from each other. Cybernetics, which employs the data and experience of psychology, biology and radio engineering, may be cited as a good example of one of these synthetic sciences.

Obviously, *an atlantologist's range of knowledge must be encyclopaedic* to enable him to compare and generalise the data of various sciences. The same concerns the critics of the Atlantis problem. *The frequently practised indiscriminate rejection of everything relating to Atlantis or one-sided criticism stemming from not only inadequate knowledge of all aspects of the problem but also from preconception cannot be called scientific,* (22, 102, 122). Naturally, nothing could be easier than to brush aside everything linked up with the Atlantis problem or to interpret favourable facts from the standpoint of one or another school of thought or doctrine or give them a misleading slant. This is not only easier but also more convenient and safer for the scientific reputation of the critic.

In this book the author uses circumstances and facts that bear out the reality of Atlantis if they are founded on the postulate that Atlantis existed and, consequently, that there is a grain of truth in Plato's legend. Let us, therefore, try to assemble all the facts as well as the hypotheses and notions of modern science which could be interpreted in favour of the one-time existence of Atlantis and its geologically recent destruction. And after that let us see what happens.

I am firmly convinced that Atlantis must be examined primarily as a geological problem and that *only a knowledge of the geological history of the Atlantic Ocean, particularly in the glacial and postglacial periods, and thorough-going, objective oceanographic investigations will help to solve the age-old riddle of Atlantis.* But if geology's final answer is negative, it will put an end to this fascinating legend, because *the experience of many centuries has shown that historical, ethnical and literary research cannot solve the problem.*

The question of whether Atlantis was populated can be tackled only after we have facts establishing the geological reality of Atlantis, all the more so that the Atlantis legend is unprecedented in human annals. There is a unique time gap of twelve millennia between the Atlantean civilisation and modern times. A wide time gap also exists between the Atlantean civilisation and the most ancient of the world's dated civilisations (for example, the Sumerian and the Egyptian civilisations), which cover a period of several millennia. If we accept that in those days there was a civilisation such as Plato describes, we must also accept the hypothesis that in Atlantis mankind must, for some reason, have developed at a much faster rate than in other parts of the world. Generally speaking, this is not altogether improbable (18/102-106; 240), but it would be simpler to surmise that in reality the Atlantean civilisation was not at the level described by Plato because of the likelihood of embellishment, exaggeration and fantasy in that description. We must, therefore, carefully analyse Plato's narrative about the material culture of the Atlanteans; such an analysis is made in Chapter Two.

Many atlantologists who have studied the Atlantis problem from the historical and ethnical standpoint were inclined to credit the Atlanteans with a high level of cultural development and arrived at the surmise that Atlantis might have been the source of a number of known ancient civilisations, a source from where peoples borrowed much of their culture as well as plants and even domestic animals. Myths telling of the arrival of gods and civilisers from across the sea are used as the foundation for this surmise.

The most clear-cut idea in this direction was expressed by V. Y. Bryusov (15/200): "The community of sources underlying the most diverse and remote civilisations of 'early antiquity', such as the Aegean, Egyptian, Babylonian, Etruscan, Japhetic, early Indian, Mayan and, perhaps, the Pacific and South American civilisations, cannot be satisfactorily explained by reciprocal influences and imitation, by one people emulating the culture of another. Underlying all ancient cultures there must be a single influence, which alone can explain the remarkable analogy between these cultures. Beyond the framework of 'early antiquity' there must have been an unknown quantity, a cultured world as yet unascertained by science, which gave the first impetus to the development of all the civilisations known to us. The Egyptians, Babylonians, Aegeans, Hellenes and Romans were our teachers, the teachers of modern civilisation. Who were their teachers? Whom can we call by the lofty name of 'teachers of teachers'? Tradition answers that question—Atlantis."

It must be noted that *peoples who in the course of many millennia developed in isolation (in the absence of migration and diffusion), without contact with other, more cultured, peoples remained at a very low level of social and cultural development for a very long time*. A classical example of this are the aborigines of Australia and, in particular, of Tasmania. While their closest neighbours, the Melanesians learned navigation and to till the soil, and the Indonesians, who lived farther north, were at a stage where, in addition to navigation and farming, they worked metals, the Australians and Tasmanians were primitive hunters and gatherers of roots and herbs at the time they were discovered by Europeans. Thus, the culture of the Tasmanians was at the level of the Upper Paleolithic (Late Mousterian), i.e., at the level of the late Neanderthals of Europe, who lived 30,000-50,000 years ago. Grain was not grown in Australia and Tasmania, and the aborigines could get it only from without.

"Complete isolation from the outside world is the only explanation for the extraordinarily low level of development of the Tasmanians up until the time they were exterminated by the English early in the 19th century," writes P. P. Yefimenko (251/301), a leading Soviet authority on the history of primitive society.

Even if we assume that no civilisation as described by Plato existed in Atlantis, and that the people inhabiting it were at the same stage of primitive savagery as the rest of mankind, the very fact of the existence of Atlantis as a geologically-recent geographical entity is of tremendous scientific importance. Moreover, even if Atlantis existed in the epoch when intelligent man was only just emerging (30,000-100,000 years ago), it played a considerable role in human migration as a bridge between the Old and the New World.

Although I had no possibility of dealing comprehensively with historical atlantology, I found it necessary to mention some obviously fantastic, unscientific hypotheses, as well as modern pseudo-myths linked up with Atlantis and created for various purposes. I felt I had to mention them to show how much pseudo-scientific scum had settled on this captivating problem. In this connection it would be useful to quote Susemihl (144), a prominent investigator of Plato's works, who wrote: "The catalogue of statements about Atlantis is a fairly good aid for the study of human madness." These words were written long before modern pseudo-myths became widespread. It may be said that *at its present stage atlantology is going through a transitional period of development, a period characterised by its formation into a science and departure from fantasy and pseudo-scientific fabrications.*

Pseudo-atlantological works include the numerous books published abroad in the past few decades on the subject: Atlantis—Golden Age of Mankind. This literature is permeated with a mystical, idealistic spirit and has nothing in common with a scientific approach to the problem. In the history of atlantology there have been cases when the lure of Atlantis abroad acquired ugly shape. Bristling with mysticism, it reached a sort of hysteria and led to the rise of what may be termed as atlantomania. A great deal of interesting material on atlantomania is to be found in the works of A. Bessmertny (39/155), J. Bramwell (49/22) and G. Poisson (86/13). I should like to note that the interference of the atlantomaniacs has greatly harmed science, for it discredited the Atlantis problem in the eyes of many scientists.

The most popular pseudo-myths include primarily a so-called *esoteric* legend about Atlantis concocted by modern occultists—theosophists and anthroposophists—who give the history of Atlantis in great and, therefore, suspect detail. They maintain that hundreds of thousands of years before our era the Atlanteans reached a level of development that matched modern civilisation. Serious scholars studying the Atlantis problem usually either reject the esoteric legend or, like Bessmertny (39/163) and Bramwell (49/212), examine it from the psychological standpoint. The most serious criticism of this legend is given by L. Sprague de Camp (102/54). B. L. Bogayevsky (13/231), a prominent Soviet historian, assessed the esoteric legend as follows: "The 'edifices' erected by the occultists and theosophists may be completely swept away because there is not an iota of plausibility in them." In my opinion, this legend, nonetheless, deserves to be critically examined primarily because it has had an impact on the works of many foreign atlantologists and popularisers. If we closely study the influence of this legend, we shall find that it is much more considerable than one at first imagines. For example, some unsophisticated popularisers of atlantology, who utilise the materials of pseudo-atlantology uncritically, frequently refer to some enigmatic early Indian sacred writings and traditions (which are nothing more than the pseudo-myths of the occultists) and to the works, data and other "documents" of Paul Schliemann and many other fabrications. These fabrications are analysed in Chapter Six. On the whole, it must be said that *the Atlantis problem is frequently utilised for purposes remote from science, and that it is still cluttered up with pseudo-scientific rubbish, which it is vital for scientific atlantology to clear away. Atlantology will grow out of its infancy and win the trust of the scientific world only when it is cleansed of this rubbish.*

In conclusion it would be useful to quote a statement by Henri Lhote (144/116), the well-known French archaeologist: "If we dismiss certain far from naive and sometimes simply false theories, it must be admitted that there is much in Plato's idea that is positive. It has prompted many scientists to undertake serious investigations that have enriched oceanography, geology, anthropology and ethnology, to mention a few from a long list. The problem of Atlantis is an intricate one and our enthusiastic atlantophiles must approach it with caution."

THE ATLANTIS OF PLATO

Chapter One

THE PLATO LEGEND

Plato regarded the Atlantis legend as belonging to his family, claiming he heard it from Solon (638-559 B.C.), the Athenian lawgiver, who was related to his mother. He speaks of this legend twice: in the *Timaeus* and in the *Critias*. This repetition of the subject was not accidental, being most probably due to the fact that Plato himself attached great importance to the legend itself and to what he linked up with it.

In the *Timaeus* the story of Atlantis begins with a conversation between four of the personages, the narrator being Critias the Younger, poet, historian, sophist and atheist, who subsequently became the leader of the extreme oligarchs and head of the Thirty Tyrants of Athens. The other participants in the conversation were the philosopher and naturalist Timaeus of Locris, the Syracusan general Hermocrates and the celebrated Greek philosopher Socrates (470-399 B.C.), who was Plato's teacher.

In this dialogue the story of Atlantis is included only as an episode. Critias the Younger speaks of it to Socrates. In the beginning, addressing Socrates, Critias emphasises not only the marvel of the legend but also its authenticity: "Then listen, Socrates, to a tale which, though strange, is certainly true, having been attested by Solon, who was the wisest of the seven sages."

During his travels, which took him ten years, Solon went to Egypt, which, according to Herodotus [I, 30], was ruled by Amasis II of the XXVIth dynasty. V. S. Struve (395), however, points out that Amasis seized the throne in 569 B.C., while Solon travelled in the period 593-584 B.C. Consequently he could not have met Amasis. This is also borne out by Plutarch, who tells us that Solon went to Egypt as the first stage of his travels. This means he was in Egypt in the year 593 B.C. Moreover, neither Plutarch nor Diodorus [I, 96] mentions Amasis in connection with the story of Solon's life. Struve believes this disparity sprang from Herodotus' error of 25 years in chronologising the events of the 3rd century B.C. due to the inaccurate dating of a solar eclipse forecast by Phalesis, which served as the point of departure for a chronology of that epoch (395). At any rate, there is no doubt that Solon was in Egypt at a period bordering on the reign of the XXVIth dynasty.

As we shall see further, the date of Solon's Egyptian visit is vital in dating the destruction of Atlantis. But so far we have not been able to establish the date of his visit exactly. If we accept the error of 25 years, Solon was in Egypt not in 593 B.C. but in approximately 570 B.C.

In those days the capital of Egypt was the ancient town of Sais in the western part of the Nile delta (for which reason the dynasty ruling the country in that period is frequently called the Saite dynasty). The kings of that dynasty fought wars of conquest. Egypt did not have the manpower for these wars and the Saite kings gladly hired mercenaries, particularly Greeks. This explains why Solon was treated as an honoured guest. In *Parallel Lives* [XXVI] Plutarch informs us that Solon "'spent some time in study with Psenophis of Heliopolis, and Sonchis the Saite, the most learned of all the priests; from whom, as Plato says, getting knowledge of the Atlantis story, he put it into a poem, and proposed to bring it to the knowledge of the Greeks".

Plato writes that in the temple of the goddess Neith Solon had a long talk about ancient times with the priests. One of them, a man of venerable age, told him there were no records of remote antiquity. "And I will tell you why. There have been, and will be again, many destructions of mankind arising out of many causes; the greatest have been brought about by the agencies of fire (volcanic eruptions—*N.Z.*) and water (floods), and other lesser ones by innumerable other causes." Knowledge of history and relics of antiquity perished in these disasters, but more has been destroyed by wars than by elemental calamities (155/37).

At this point it would be appropriate to mention Neith in some detail. One of the most ancient goddesses of Egypt, her cult was typical of the matriarchal epoch and was in some way connected with Thoth, god of science and writing. Subsequently Neith was adopted by Libyan invaders, who were predominant in Egypt for some time. The ancient Greeks identified this goddess with their Athena. There must have been some grounds for this not only because of the similarity between the names (Neith—NTH; Athena—THN) but also because according to ancient Greek theology the cult of Athena originated in Libya* and Lake Triton (whose location has not been accurately established). There are some facts which indicate that this identification is quite realistic (51/4).

Inasmuch as Neith was a Libyan goddess, her priests could have

---

* In antique times Libya was the name of the whole of Northwest Africa, i e , the territory now occupied by Marocco, Algeria, Tunisia and modern Libya, including the part of the Sahara adjoining it. The countries lying to the south were known collectively as Ethiopia.

known myths, legends and traditions not only of Egypt herself but also of Libya, i.e., of the area embracing the whole of Northwest Africa, possibly up to the shores of the Atlantic from where, according to the legend, the Libyan tribes fanned out.

The Sais priest informed Solon that according to sacred writings the Egyptian state system was 8,000 years old, as old as the town of Sais. In the opinion of the priest, the Greeks had only vague memories of history that differed little from tales for children. "The fact is that wherever the extremity of winter frost or of summer sun does not prevent, mankind exists, sometimes in greater, sometimes in lesser numbers. And whatever happened either in your country or in ours, or in any other region of which we are informed—if there were any actions noble or great or in any other way remarkable, they have all been written down by us of old, and are preserved in our temples. Whereas just when you and other nations are beginning to be provided with letters and the other requisites of civilised life, after the usual interval, the stream from heaven, like a pestilence, comes pouring down, and leaves only those of you who are destitute of letters and education; and so you have to begin all over again like children, and know nothing of what happened in ancient times, either among us or among yourselves."

Ancient Egyptian goddess Neith. This statuette is part of a collection at the State Hermitage, Leningrad

Continuing his story the priest said that a mighty state existed in Athens 9,000 years before Solon visited Egypt. However, its social system was suspiciously similar to the ideal state conjured up by Plato in his *Republic*. Plato gives a detailed description of this pre-Athenian state in the dialogue *Critias*.

The priest promised to show Solon ancient writings relating to that epoch. There are some grounds for presuming that some writings were shown to Solon, but it is not known if these documents had any relation to the Atlantis problem—undoubtedly Solon did not speak the Egyptian language and communicated with the priest through an interpreter. Then in his story the priest spoke of what interests us most, namely, that in this period there was a huge island in the Atlantic beyond the Pillars of Hercules. Apropos of this, Plato himself writes: *"In those days the Atlantic was navigable; and there was an island situated in front of the straits which are by you called the Pillars of Heracles; the island was larger than Libya* [Northwest Africa] *and Asia* [Asia Minor] *put together, and was the way to other islands, and from these you might pass to the whole of the opposite continent* [on the far side of the Atlantic] *which surrounded the true ocean; for this sea* [the Mediterranean] *which is within the Straits of Heracles* [Strait of Gibraltar] *is only a harbour, having a narrow entrance, but that other is a real sea, and the land surrounding it on every side may be most truly called a boundless continent."*

This is a most vital excerpt enabling us to understand the legend. First and foremost, *it states that the island of Atlantis was in the Atlantic Sea (ocean) in front of the Strait of Gibraltar*. For that reason to transplant Atlantis to some other, even nearby, location would be an unjustified and arbitrary deviation from the sufficiently exact and direct text of the legend. Similarly, it is obvious that the Atlantic Sea mentioned by Plato is indeed the Atlantic Ocean and not part of the Mediterranean as many commentators and atlantologists, who have located their Atlantises in other places, would like us to believe. The problem of what the Greeks of Plato's and Solon's day took for the Atlantic Sea will be analysed in more detail in chapters Four and Five. *Plato's unambiguous point that the sea where Atlantis was located was a "real sea", i.e., an ocean as we understand it and not an inland sea ("harbour") like the Mediterranean incontrovertibly indicates that his Atlantic Sea is the Atlantic Ocean*. In addition, we are told that from Atlantis navigators reached some other islands, and from them a continent (on the far side of the Atlantic). This plainly shows that *Plato knew of the existence of a very large continent—America—situated farther to the west, beyond Atlantis*. This continent was reached by seafarers, who sailed from Atlantis in many directions (i.e., north, west and south), getting there easily by moving from one island to another. Indeed, in the west, likewise located meridionally and lying parallel with Atlantis, there was the continent (on the far side of the Atlantic) of America, which arched somewhat eastward (18/23) north and south of Atlantis.

This gave grounds for speaking of a continent on the far side of the Atlantic "surrounding" Atlantis. *The affirmative, even emphatically affirmative, tone of the narration makes it clear that Plato knew of the existence of America as a well-established fact, but we have not pin-pointed the source of his information.* It is astonishing that despite this precise indication many of Plato's critics refuse to regard this communication as the oldest of our records of the existence of America. This is obviously a matter of principle and not of facts.

But perhaps the most ancient record of a continent beyond the Atlantic dates from the days of Sargon of Akkad (2369-2314 B.C.), King of Sumer and Akkadia in Mesopotamia. He united these territories into a single state, which later emerged as the Babylonian Kingdom. The records of the deeds of this king contain an interesting point, namely that he "sailed across the sea to the west, spent three years in the west, where he conquered and united the country, set up his statues and brought captives across sea and land" (180/66). Sargon returned to Mesopotamia in the eleventh year of his reign, and we can therefore safely date the beginning of his campaign (to be more exact, piratical raid) to approximately the year 2361 B.C. The most cautious scholars consider that Sargon went only as far as Cyprus or, at the most, Crete. But these hypotheses are refuted by the absence of traces of an invasion on these islands. Bolder scholars surmised that Sargon reached Spain (146/38), basing their conclusion on finds and names that seem to mirror traces of Sumerian influence. Generally speaking, not even a trace of a Sargon statue or anything relating to his campaign has been found in the Mediterranean area, Europe, Africa or the eastern seaboard of the Atlantic. A. H. and Ruth Verril (696/293-97) propound the seemingly semi-fantastic theory that Sargon landed in America, in Peru to be exact, and in support of this theory speak of many similarities between the Sumerian and Peruvian civilisations, summarising them in a table of 42 points. Furthermore, they draw attention to the legends of many Indian tribes about bearded men who came from the east across the sea (696/310-15; 211/226; 559). The American Indians have a very sparse growth on their faces.

On the Atlantis island, the priest said, continuing his narrative, there was once a great and powerful federation of kings, who ruled not only Atlantis but also many other islands and countries both on the ("opposite") continent on the far side of the Atlantic (once more an exact reference to it) and "on this side" (*i.e., Mediterranean—N.Z.*). They ruled the whole of Libya up to Egypt, and Europe up to Tyrrhenia (the land of the Etruscans in Italy). The interesting point here is that the Etruscans did not submit to their rule.

According to the priest this federation mustered all its forces and invaded the territories of the pre-Athenian and Egyptian kingdoms (once again there is no mention of the Etruscans—they had not yet settled on pre-Athenian territory). *The purpose of this reference to the invasion was most likely to show that there was a military alliance between Athens and Egypt in those remote times.* The several tens of thousands of pre-Athenian warriors completely routed the numerically superior enemy, displaying miracles of bravery and valour. They smashed the Atlantean forces and liberated the Mediterranean countries from Atlantean tyranny.

Concluding his story of this war, the priest said that later there were earthquakes and floods and that in one day and night the pre-Hellenic tribes inhabiting Greece disappeared and the island of Atlantis sank into the sea.

Let us note the following salient points in the priest's narrative:

a) he spoke of earthquakes and floods in the plural, declaring that they preceded the disappearance of both states;

b) he did not say exactly that Atlantis disappeared on the same day as the pre-Athenian kingdom;

c) we do not know how much time elapsed between the defeat of the Atlanteans and the catastrophe; as G. Amato (69/68) notes, Plato gives the date of the war and not of the disappearance of Atlantis;

d) there is no record whatever of the disappearance of the continent on the far side of the Atlantic or of the other islands.

However, the most interesting and unexpected conclusion is that *actually Plato does not say when Atlantis disappeared.* The sequence of events is as follows: first there was a war, then there was a period of earthquakes and floods and, finally, after the disappearance of the pre-Athenian kingdom, Atlantis sank into the sea. We do not know how much time passed between the war and the destruction of Atlantis, and there are no additional indications that might have helped us to determine the length of this interval. Thus, *there is no data to help us establish when Atlantis was lost.* Atlantology tacitly accepts the hypothesis that Atlantis disappeared shortly after the end of this war.

Most atlantologists are inclined to date the disappearance of Atlantis to approximately the time of the rise of the pre-Athenian kingdom (plus the date of Solon's stay in Egypt), i.e., roughly 9,000+570=approximately the year 9570 B.C. On the face of it there is confirmation of this date in the next dialogue of Plato's *Critias*: "Let me begin by observing first of all that *nine thousand* was the sum of years which had elapsed since the war that was said to have occurred between those who dwelt outside the Pillars of Heracles and those who dwelt within them." However, O. Muck (80/381) and L. Zajdler (119/254) reasonably remark that according to the *Timaeus* Atlantis possibly disappeared at a considerably later date. The crux of the matter is that if we accept the evidence in the *Timaeus*, Sais was founded a thousand years later than Athens. Consequently, the Egyptians could have had direct contact with the pre-Athenians not earlier than the date of the founding of Sais, i.e., about the year 8570 B.C. Muck and Zajdler do not believe that the war lasted for a whole millennium. Yet, on the other hand, it is not improbable that the legend of the war (if it was true) might have reached Sais after the end of the war, after the disappearance of both adversaries.

Farther on in the *Timaeus* the priest says that where Atlantis was located the sea was (i.e., up to the time of the dialogue) unnavigable. Word for word, the record states: "...and the island of Atlantis in like manner disappeared in the depths of the sea. For which reason the sea (i.e., the Atlantic—*N.Z.*) in those parts is impassable and impenetrable, because there is a shoal of mud (pumicestone?) in the way; and this was caused by the subsidence of the island." Hence, it follows, firstly, that *Plato once again indicates that Atlantis was located in the Atlantic Ocean*. Secondly, it is clearly stated that *Atlantis vanished and that in its place there was the Atlantic Ocean and not land. To transfer Atlantis to some other land area (say the Iberian Peninsula or some other part of present-day Europe or Africa) would mean completely to ignore Plato's evidence*. This would be anything but the Atlantis of Plato.

The reference to the impenetrability of the Atlantic, which is today navigable, is explained and substantiated by events of the recent past. There have been periods when powerful volcanic eruptions covered the sea with a layer of ash and pumice so thick as to render navigation difficult. For example, in 1783 an eruption in Iceland covered the sea with a layer of ash and pumice over a radius of 150 miles and, to all practical purposes, navigation ceased for a time.

A volcanic eruption on Sumbawa Island, Indonesia, in 1815 covered the sea with a two-foot layer of ash for many miles along the shore, day turned into night and ships had great difficulty negotiating the mud. After the Krakatau eruption in 1883, there were whole islands of pumice several metres thick floating on the sea. A Dutch warship was trapped in one of these islands for a whole week, and it took a storm to free it (381/40). The report that the sea was unnavigable must be taken as a reference to shallow water with a large number of reefs and shoals that, according to the notions of the narrator, consisted of "mud", but were, evidently, the result of changes caused by volcanic eruptions and the accompanying accumulations of ash, pumice and discharges of lava. Thus, we believe *that initially Atlantis did not sink very deep; the modern depth is evidently the result of not one but a series of subsidences* (18/26).

We frequently come across the opinion that the myth of the Atlantic having been unnavigable was created by the Phoenicians and then kept alive by the Carthaginians, who replaced them in this region, to maintain a monopoly on navigation. That, we are told, was why all sorts of fantastic, disconcerting myths were spread about this ocean. But this, unquestionably, is an exaggeration, for the maritime power of the Carthaginians was great enough to lock all the exits from the Mediterranean. Indeed, as R. Hennig

(419/1,155) points out, in the course of nearly 300 years, from 509 to 214 B.C., there was not a single case of the ban on the passage through the Strait of Gibraltar having been violated. Naturally, this was not due to any fear of the dangers of navigation. On the other hand, the belief that the Atlantic was unnavigable existed for many centuries after the maritime power of Carthage was broken. The legend of "dead waters" in the west is to be found in the Sumerian Gilgamesh Epic (180/117) written long before the appearance of the Phoenicians. There must have been some foundation of extremely ancient origin for this legend.

The above-mentioned data are all that we can glean about Atlantis from a small part of the *Timaeus*. In the next dialogue, the *Critias*, which deals specially with Atlantis, the narrator (Critias the Younger) informs us that Solon recorded the Atlantis legend and that these records passed to his grandfather, Critias the Elder, and then to him and that he read them when he was a child. It is not known what happened to these records afterwards.

The story of Atlantis as recorded by Solon begins with some mythology and then says that when the Universe was divided between the gods, Athena and Hephaestus received Attica and Egypt, and Poseidon got Atlantis. The dialogue gives a detailed description of the pre-Athenian state (its location, political system and so forth). As V. V. Bogachev (14) remarks, *it is quite probable that Plato's description of this kingdom and other details are a piece of patriotic fantasy devised by him with the object of popularising his social and political views*. Some of these data are analysed in Chapter Three.

Plato writes that half-way from the sea, in the very heart of Atlantis there was a beautiful and fertile plain with a hill towering over it. This hill was 50 stadia (about 9.25 kilometres)* from the coast. One of the people, who had come directly from the earth, a man named Aevinor and his wife Leukippa, lived on this hill. This hints at the semi-divine origin of the inhabitants of Atlantis (according to Greek mythology, the Earth was the mother of the gods) and that *the forefathers of the Atlanteans evolved independently of the rest of mankind*. This is extremely interesting.

Aevinor and Leukippa had an only daughter named Clito (or Cleito). When she became a maiden and her parents died, Poseidon, god of the seas, married her. At an equal distance from the centre of the hill Poseidon surrounded it with two earthern ramparts and three moats, *making it inaccessible to mortals, who had not yet learned the art of navigation. This is an essential point proving the great antiquity of the event*. We know that primitive coastal navigation, connected with fishing, was developed only in the Mesolithic, i.e., about 10,000-12,000 years ago.

On the islet thus formed in the middle, Poseidon caused two

---

* Attic stadium equals 185 metres.

springs to flow from the earth—one with hot and the other with cold water—and provided the islet with luxuriant, edible vegetation. The hot spring is, perhaps, an indication of the proximity of a volcanic region.

Clito was the first queen of Atlantis. Johann Bachofen (39/158) believes this to be evidence that initially, in remote antiquity, Atlantis was a matriarchy. Clito bore Poseidon five pairs of twins. The number and the fact that all the twins were male is, undoubtedly, symbolical, but its significance has not been established. *Perhaps the circumstance that ALL of Poseidon's sons were twins should be taken to symbolise that all the kingdoms ruled by them were situated on EITHER side of the present-day meridional submarine North Atlantic Ridge, which is the most likely location of lost Atlantis* (124).

When his sons attained manhood Poseidon divided Atlantis into ten parts. The elder of the first pair of twins, Atlas (or Atlante) received his mother's kingdom (the hill), to which was added the largest and richest region. He thus held sway over his nine brothers. The whole country was named after him. The other Atlantean kingdoms were, possibly, relatively small and, perhaps, mountainous. Although Plato gives us the names of the other Atlantean kings they tell us practically nothing of the kingdoms themselves.

Plato's mythology does not conform to the classical Greek mythology, for example as propounded by Hesiod. According to the latter, Atlas (Atlante) was not the son of Poseidon but a Titan and the son of the Titan Iapetus. The Titans belonged to the older group of Greek gods, who were overthrown by Zeus. Atlas was a herdsman-king, an authority on ocean depths (!), the owner of the garden of the Hesperides in the extreme west (!). He was later turned into a boulder or mountain. His name is usually associated with the myth that he upholds the heavens. M. S. Bodnarsky (206) believes the Atlas myth was borrowed by the Greeks from North-west African legends.

Eumelus, the second of the first pair of twins, was given the easternmost part of Atlantis. In view of the importance of this passage and the controversy that rages over its interpretation, here is the text in full: "To his twin brother, who was born after him, and obtained as his lot the *extremity of the island towards the Pillars of Heracles, as far as the country which is still called the region of Gadeira* [Gades, now Cadiz] in that part of the world, he gave the *name* which in the Hellenic language is Eumelus, in the language of the *country which is named after him, Gadeirus*." A superficial and inaccurate interpretation of this passage by some critics led them to identify Atlantis with Spain. Let us try to prove that this is not true. This passage, which says that the extremity of Atlantis stretched from the Pillars of Hercules to Gades, may be interpreted in two ways. Either this extremity was the eastern part of Atlantis lying to the west in the ocean, or it was the southwestern part of Spain,

if Spain really was Atlantis. However, the next line of the passage—
"as far as the country which is still called the region of Gadeira
[i.e., after the Gades region of Spain] in that part of the world"
[i.e., the extremity of Atlantis]—specifically states that the extremity
of Atlantis was not Gades but that it only got its name from the
region. These were two distinct regions, but apparently they comprised Eumelus' kingdom. If we take into consideration the text from
the *Timaeus*, which we have already mentioned, the text which says
that Atlantis was situated in the Atlantic Ocean *IN FRONT of the
Pillars of Hercules*, i.e., to the west of them, *Eumelus' kingdom
must be regarded as the eastern (or north-eastern, or south-eastern)
and not the northern or southern extremity of the confederation of
Atlantean kingdoms.*

*Further, according to Plato, we find that the king of this region
was called Gadeirus, and the name was given to the Gadir region
of Spain and the kingdom as a whole.* It is quite a different matter
when we examine how correct Plato was to identify the names Gadeirus and Eumelus, because the Phoenician word "Gadeira" means
"fortress", while the Greek word "Eumelus" means "owner of fine
sheep". But, on the other hand, we have no grounds for assuming
that Plato knew the Phoenician language and could translate from
it. Also of quite a different issue is the question of whether the
eastern part of Atlantis was sufficiently close to the coast of Spain
and whether south-western Spain was ruled by Eumelus. On the
grounds of the text we have analysed, it may be assumed that both
questions may be answered in the affirmative.

The analysed texts of the dialogues show that *the principal kingdom of Atlantis was not as close to the shores of Europe as the kingdom of Eumelus and that it was probably situated on a more southerly latitude than Gades.* Confirmation of this is offered below.
Further, *it is established that Atlantis was situated independently of
Spain and, consequently, we cannot combine the location of both
these countries.*

Thus, if we credit Plato's texts with any truth at all, it may be
said that:

a) he was well aware of the geographical location of the Pillars
of Hercules, the town of Gades and Spain;

b) he showed exactly where the principal kingdom of Atlantis
was situated: in the Atlantic Ocean west of Gades and the Pillars
of Hercules;

c) he made it plain that in his day Atlantis was no longer in
existence.

In this light, the assertion of some atlantologists that in Plato's
writings the Pillars of Hercules symbolised nothing more than a
temple. that they were not a geographical entity, is clearly farfetched.

According to Plato, the Atlas family was the most numerous and
famous and held supreme power in the course of many generations.

It accumulated more wealth than any other dynasty in the world; we are told that all sorts of ores and metals, both hard and soft (the latter, obviously, implies tin and lead) were mined in Atlantis. Among the metals we find mention of an enigmatic "mountain brass" (orichalcum). We are told that it was a precious metal second only to gold. In the dialogue it is stated that it was no longer mined in Solon's day and was known only by its name.

Further, in the dialogue, we get a general description of the abundance of vegetation, but the individual species are not named. Mention is made of fodder grasses, grain, fruit and vegetables. A noteworthy point is that nothing is said of the olive tree, which is so beloved of the Greeks. Mention of the tree would have been appropriate if Atlantis was situated in the region of the Iberian Peninsula. As Diodorus Siculus [V, 16] points out, the olive tree came from the Pityusae Islands and Gadir region. But there is a reference to a mysterious tree "which yields a beverage, food and oil". G. V. Malevansky (140/18), Apelt (45) and some other Plato scholars consider that the description best fits the *coconut palm** (*Cocos nucifera*), which indeed yields a beverage (milk), food (the meat of the nuts) and oil (semi-liquid coconut oil). It would be safe to say that this description does not fit any other tree, although L. Frobenius (39/33), who sited his pseudo-Atlantis in the region of the Gulf of Guinea, identified Plato's mysterious tree with the oil palm (*Elaeias guineensis*). We feel, however, that the tree described by Plato is most likely a coconut palm. It is worth recalling that in Plato's day the Greeks knew of this palm, because Scylax of Caryanda accomplished his voyage in the Indian Ocean (249 18-21) in 518-516 B.C. It is, therefore, not surprising that Plato mentions the tree. But if it was indeed a coconut palm, the implication would be that *some of the Atlantean kingdoms might have been situated south of the 25th parallel* (18/30), because the coconut palm does not grow north of that parallel. Generally, Plato's phrase that the island produced "everything living under the sun" is interpreted by some atlantologists (51/88) as an indirect indication of Atlantis' location in the region of the subtropics or even in the tropics.

Plato says the lost continent had an abundance of domestic and wild animals among them large herds of elephants. *The mention of elephants on Atlantis is further evidence that the legend is based on fact.* We feel that the considerable meridional elongation of Atlantis (allowing that it was situated in the region of the modern submarine North Atlantic Ridge and on the adjoining spaces of the ocean floor) due to which its northern regions were covered with glaciers (during that period Europe and North America were in the grip of the Ice Age), brings us round to the assumption that mammoths lived in the northern part of the continent. An animal like the mastodon might have been extant in its southern regions.

---

* Venezuela and Indonesia are now considered the home of the coconut palm.

This, undoubtedly, was due to the fact that as a continent Atlantis was completely encircled by the sea, thus making the conditions on it favourable for the survival of many relic animals. It may be noted that the isolation of the American continent led to similar results. It has now been established beyond doubt that in America man at one time lived side by side with the now completely extinct elephants (*Elephas columbe, Elephas imperator*), mammoths (*Elephas primigenus*), mastodons (*Mastodon americanus*) and also horses and camels, remains of which have been found together with human remains or the remains of man-made implements (199). At the time of the submergence of Atlantis and, evidently, somewhat later* all these animals were still inhabiting the American continent. They might have existed in Atlantis as well.

Further, the dialogue gives a description of the Acropolis of the capital city of Atlantis. The water-filled moats around the ancient capital were interconnected, with the passages in the earthern ramparts wide enough for a ship. The gaps in the ramparts were roofed, and the ships went through them as through tunnels. Bridges connected the ramparts. A canal led from the capital to the sea. It was 300 Attic feet (about 75 metres) wide, 100 feet (about 25 metres) deep and 50 stadia (about 9,250 metres) long. This enabled ships to sail from the sea up to the third moat. The large, external moat, which was directly linked up with the sea, was three stadia (about 550 metres) wide; the adjoining moat had the same width. The next, middle moat was two stadia (about 370 metres) wide as was the second earthern rampart, while the inner moat encircling the central islet with the royal acropolis had a diameter of five stadia (about 925 metres). This islet and all the moats were surrounded with stone walls, and the bridges had towers and gates. Locally-quarried white, black and red stone was used for the walls. The hollows of the quarries were later turned into marine arsenals. I. Donnelly (56/36) points out that stone of all these colours occurs on the Azores and consists of easily worked volcanic tufa.

The wall of the external rampart was covered with copper, the middle with silvery tin and the inner with orichalcum, which "shone like fire". The geometric symmetry of the structure attracts attention. This should not cause any surprise because Plato was fascinated by the mysticism of numbers. As regards the symmetry of the layout, despite the repeated arguments of critics that this was nothing but fantasy on Plato's part, it should not excite astonishment because a symmetrical lay-out was by no means rare in ancient times. Evidently, a classical example is Mohenjo-Daro in the valley of the Indus, one of the oldest cities in the world, having been built in about 3000 B.C. or even earlier. The streets are arranged in the

---

* With the help of radiocarbon analyses it has been established that in Michigan, North America, the mammoths became extinct about 8,000 years ago and the mastodons died out later. about 6,000 years ago (504a, 674a).

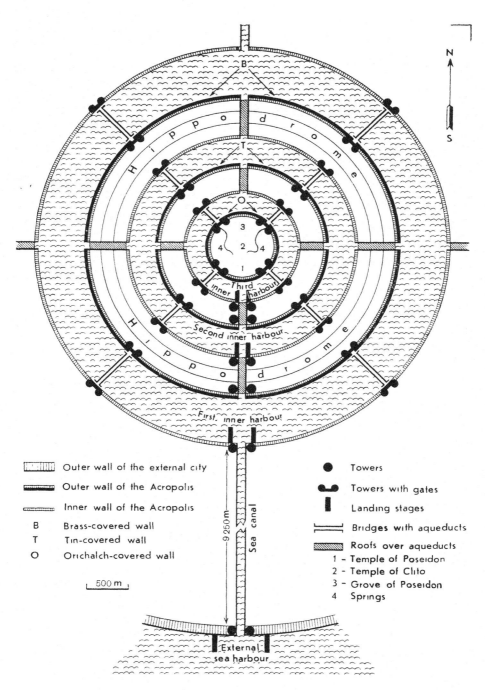

Acropolis of the capital of Plato's Atlantis

direction of the cardinal points of the compass and even had rounded corners at the crossings, apparently, for the convenience of traffic (315/410-12). Some investigators claim to see a similarity between the lay-out of the Atlantean capital and ancient Carthage (in our opinion, the similarity is quite remote) and use this as a basis for the theory that Plato had borrowed his lay-out, surmising, not without grounds, that he had visited Carthage (102). Other investigators, Y. Rudberg (84/21), for example, found a similarity with Syracuse, where Plato lived for a fairly long time. L. Spence (101), on the other hand, considers that, on the contrary, the lay-out of Carthage was borrowed from the Atlantis legend. Similar views are held by G. J. Bryant and E. Sykes (51/104). E. V. Andreyeva (135/70) finds that the Atlantean capital had the same lay-out as Tenochtitlan (now Mexico City), the Aztec capital situated on an island in the middle of a lake and surrounded by rings of canals with several dams interconnecting them. According to tradition, this city was modelled after Aztlan, the capital of the Aztecs' original homeland, from where they were forced to flee. After centuries of wandering they finally settled in the Anahuac Valley, where they built their capital; for a description of Tenochtitlan see G. Vaillant (211/159-68). It is believed that the building of Tenochtitlan was started at the close of the 14th century.

It is our opinion *in remote times the tradition of ringed towns was most likely linked up with the Sun cult.* Some cities sprang up round temples of the Sun (for example, Peking), in other cases temples had nothing to do with towns, for example, Stonehedge in Britain.

But let us return to the Atlantean capital. The royal palace in the Acropolis, as we learn from the *Critias*, consisted of several buildings. In the centre was an inaccessible temple dedicated to Poseidon and Cleito. It had a gold wall around it. This was where Cleito bore her sons. The temple of Poseidon was one stadium (about 185 metres) long and three plethra (about 75 metres) wide. Its outer walls were covered with silver, and the edges—with gold. On the inside the dome was covered with orichalcum and ivory with golden and silver ornaments. Here was a gold statue of Poseidon himself and around it the golden statues of 100 Nereids astride dolphins (instead of the 50 round the Greek Poseidon). Poseidon is portrayed driving six winged horses. He appeared majestic and formidable ("barbaric"). The head of the statue reached the dome. The royal palace stood nearby, but we are not given any details about it.

The golden statues of kings and their wives and descendants towered round the temple. This ensemble strikingly resembles the temples of the Sun and Moon in Cuzco, the Inca capital. These temples likewise had golden statues of Inca kings and their wives.

The two springs—one cold and the other hot—had trees growing round them. The water for open and closed reservoirs (where people bathed in the winter) came from these springs. The surplus water was channelled to the Poseidon grove, which had a huge variety of

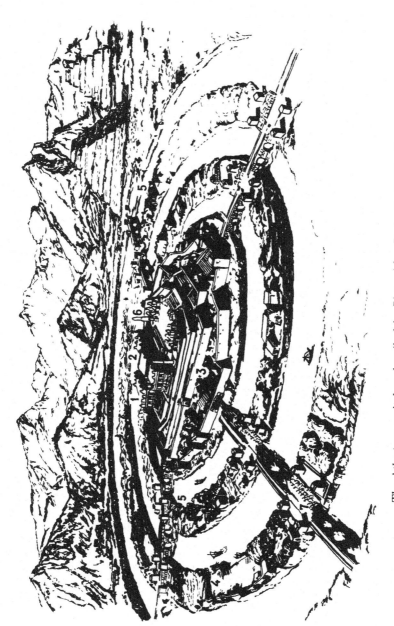

The Atlantean capital as described by Plato After R Avotin (32/No 9)

magnificently beautiful, tall trees. Canals carried water from the springs to the external moats. The walls held temples of different deities, gardens, gymnasiums, riding rings. A hippodrome with a width of one stadium (about 185 metres) ran along the middle of the largest wall. On either side were the dwellings of the royal guards; the most trusted courtiers resided in the Acropolis. There were three harbours along the sea canal (apparently where it was crossed by the moats). Plato speaks of triremes as ships of the Atlanteans, evidently being unable to conceive of seafarers sailing in any type of vessel, particularly, if it was a warship. As a matter of fact, triremes were first introduced in Greece in about the year 700 B.C. by Ameinocles of Corinth (102/7).*

A huge wall standing 50 stadia (about 9,250 metres) from the first moat began at the sea. In a gap in the wall was the mouth of a canal leading to the Acropolis. The space between the external wall and the Acropolis was densely populated, while the large harbour at the entrance to the sea teemed with ships and traders, who were so numerous that the noise of the bustle was heard constantly, day and night.

The seaboard was a vast, very high and steeply rising plateau: "The whole country was said by him to be very lofty and precipitous on the side of the sea, but the country immediately about and surrounding the city was a level plain, itself surrounded by mountains which descended towards the sea...."

Interesting surmises about the size and shape of the plateau in the main Atlantean kingdom are offered by A. Rousseau-Liessens (88/44). He starts with a literal translation of the pertinent passage in the *Critias*: "Elongated, its centre was more than 2,000 stadia (about 370 kilometres) from the sea on one side and more than 3,000 stadia (about 555 kilometres) away on the other...." Farther on, he writes: "Generally speaking, we feel that the conclusion about the plain having been a rectangle with sides of 2,000 and 3,000 stadia respectively is not accurate: the 2,000 stadia mentioned are the distance from the centre of the plain to the sea, which is half the real length. We thus know for certain that the two opposite sides were about 3,000 and 4,000 stadia long." This also implies that the plain faced the sea along one of its long sides and was an irregular rectangle. Taking into consideration the statement in the dialogue that the plain had a circumference of 10,000 stadia, Rousseau-Liessens comes to the conclusion that the ratio of the sides of the principal Atlantean kingdom was 1:2:3:4 (Plato's mysticism with regard to numbers?), which corresponded to 184, 368, 552 and 736 kilometres respectively. Hence, the principal Atlantean kingdom had a territory of a little over 160,000 square kilometres, which is equal to the territory of Czechoslovakia and the Netherlands taken together.

---

* Excavations of proto-Indian towns (642b) produced evidence that large, ocean-going vessels were known at least 5,000 years ago.

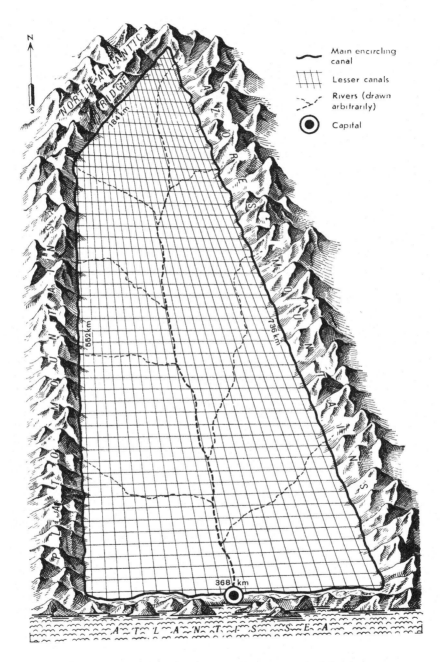

Map of the principal kingdom of Plato's Atlantis

Rousseau-Liessens' considerations concerning the size of the principal Atlantean kingdom merit attention, because his siting conforms quite well to the direction of the mountain ranges on the submerged Azores Plateau, which fan out south-east of the North Atlantic Ridge. This is discussed at length in Chapter Twelve.

We consider that inasmuch as the plateau in which the principal Atlantean kingdom was situated was high and steep, the canal running to the capital from the sea either had locks, which is unlikely in those remote times, or that the capital and the hill on which it stood were situated in a valley of a dried-up river (125) and, most probably, on an ancient, eroded volcanic cone. This locality, Plato writes, faced the south and was protected from winds on the north. "The surrounding mountains were celebrated for their number and size and beauty, far beyond any which still exist...."

J. Spanuth (100/58), however, contests the translation of this passage from the *Critias*. He maintains that the word *"kataborros"* means "in a northerly direction", for *"kata"* means "there, in the direction" and *"borros"*—"northern wind". Thus, according to Spanuth, the plain was situated north of both Egypt and Greece. But there are no grounds for using this for the theory (see Spanuth, p. 100) that Atlantis was situated near Heligoland.

The country abounded in rivers, lakes, forests and meadows. There were numerous settlements. The kings of Atlantis did much to introduce improvements. A huge canal (one plethron deep [about 25 metres], one stadium wide [about 185 metres] and 10,000 stadia long [about 1,850 metres] was built round the plain. It received the water running down the mountains, evidently acting as a storage lake, communicating with the sea via the moats round the capital. At intervals of about 100 stadia (about 18.5 kilometres) there were 100-foot-wide transversal canals in the plain. This dense network of waterways allowed transporting timber and other materials from the mountains to the capital at any time of the year.

We feel there may be some connection between the Atlantean Grand Canal and the present-day relief of the Atlantic floor. The submarine North Atlantic Ridge, which is the northern part of the vast Mid-Atlantic Ridge, runs across the middle of the ocean. This ridge is a chain of tall mountains with a series of deep, parallel valleys and stepped terraces on either side. The main chain of mountains is split by the deep and narrow Median Valley, which is hemmed in on either side by mountain chains towering several kilometres over its floor (560, 689).

When the mountain chain was subaerial, this valley was, unquestionably, an enormous natural storage lake. This made large-scale irrigation imperative not only for the purpose of watering the land but also for protection against floods, the washing away of soil and erosion on the mountain slopes. The latest data about the relief of the Atlantic floor indicates that *the huge Atlantean canal system* was built not only for irrigation but also for the purpose of reclaiming land (125).

According to Plato the Atlanteans had two harvests a year: in winter the fields were watered by rain, and in summer by the system of canals. This implies that the winters were mild, that the canals did not freeze but that the temperature was subject to sharp drops (this being borne out by the reference to closed swimming pools). Judging from what Plato says, the country was situated in the south but it had a cool climate due to the elevation of the plateau. Evidence of this kind and the reference to a coconut palm squashes the theory that Atlantis was situated in the northern latitudes.

The fact that there was a need for irrigation shows that the climate was dry. This is easily explained. The Mid-Atlantic Ridge acted as a barrier to humid westerly winds and, in addition, a cold, northern current, which in those days followed a different course and had a much larger mass than the modern Canary Current, flowed past the eastern shore of Atlantis. This last point is convincingly proved by R. Malaise (76). We therefore, hold that *the Atlantean climate resembled that of the present-day islands of Makaronesia* (Azores, Madeira, Canary and Cape Verde islands), but was colder.

Plato's information about the other nine Atlantean kingdoms is extremely meagre and scrappy. All he says about them is *that the descendants of Poseidon's sons settled the different islands in the open sea* (i.e., some of the kingdoms, including the kingdom ruled by Eumelus, were probably islands), that each kingdom had its own capital and its own, different military organisation. Virtually in a single phrase he informs us that the other kingdoms likewise had temples, royal palaces, harbours and wharves.

Plato's description of the war between the Atlanteans and the pre-Hellenes is much too imaginary to allow us to trust his data about the Atlantean armed forces. Nevertheless they are interesting because they give us an estimate of the Atlantean population. We must, however, make the reservation that these estimates do not give the real picture inasmuch as all of Plato's descriptions of the Atlanteans are controvertible.

On the basis of what Plato says we can roughly estimate that the principal Atlantean kingdom had a population of 5,000,000 or 6,000,000 (18, 31).

Many atlantologists suggest much larger figures. V. Y. Bryusov (15), for example, thinks the population was around 20-25 million. The point of departure taken by J. Imbelloni and A. Vivante (69/248) was that one-tenth of the population served in the army. This brought them to the fantastic figure of 138 million with a population density of more than 862 per square kilometre.

According to Plato, each of the ten Atlantean kings had autocratic powers. The state administration was purely despotic.

It differed substantially from the Greek, being closer to the Aztec confederation under Montezuma. The Atlantean military organisation was likewise unlike that of the Greeks. The latter had no war chariots like the Egyptians or the Persians. The description given by Plato smacks of a report by a military spy, and in that light it is not surprising that it contains many vital details.

A curious point is that Plato does not mention the Atlantean priests as a special caste. Judging by the sacrificial rites, the kings held the office of high priest as well.

Plato says nothing about the intellectual life of the Atlanteans. He mentions inscriptions on temple monuments and records of decisions of the royal councils made on golden plaques. This indicates that the Atlanteans had a written language.

T. H. Martin (167) emphasises that throughout his description Plato sets the Atlanteans off against the pre-Athenians, considering the former barbarians and their system tyrannical. In this light it would be absurd to side with zealous atlantologists in regarding the Atlantis of Plato as the ideal of mankind, as a "Golden Age".

In conclusion, the extant part of the *Critias* states that in the end the Atlanteans degenerated, losing their purity through inter-breeding with other peoples. Their divine nature was dissipated among the human race. They became corrupt and there was no restraint on lawlessness and violence. "Then Zeus, calling the gods together and determined to punish the inhabitants of Atlantis, spoke as follows:...." Here the *Critias* breaks off.

None of the antique authors, before or after Plato, give us any additional details about Atlantis or what happened to it.* Although many of them speak of islands in the Atlantic, the name "Atlantis" is very rarely used in reference to these islands. With extremely few exceptions, Plato is mentioned as the source of all information. These exceptions attract attention, because they show that antique authors had some supplementary information about Atlantis and the continent on the far side of the Atlantic Ocean.

In *Historia naturalis* [XV, 2], Aelian (2nd century A.D.) says that according to a legend then current among the inhabitants of the Atlantic seaboard, the Atlantean kings, in token of their descent from Poseidon, wore a headgear consisting of strips from the skins of "marine rams", while their wives wore headgear made from the skins of "marine ewes". By "marine rams" Aelian means some enigmatic large marine mammals, which were no longer extant in his day.

In another work (*Variae historiae* [III, 18]) he refers to a story

---

* On December 15, 1961, the French newspaper *Paris Jour* reported that the papers left behind by the noted author Pierre Benoît (who wrote the sensational novel *L'Atlantide*) included a hitherto unknown manuscript of the Greek mythographer Dionysius of Miletus entitled *A Journey in Atlantis* (112).

No confirmation of this report has been received by the author of the present work and it must be regarded only as a newspaper canard.

narrated by Theopompus of Chios, a 4th century B. C. Greek historian, who lived at the same time as or a little later than Plato. The interesting thing about this story is that it mentions a continent on the far side of the Atlantic. To understand where this story came from, we ought, as G. J. Bryant and E. Sykes (51/10) note, perhaps take into consideration the fact that shortly before his death Theopompus lived in Egypt.

The Theopompus story tells us of a conversation between the Phrygian king Midas and the demigod Silenus, mentor of the god Dionysus. Silenus told Midas that *Europe, Asia and Africa (Libya) were islands surrounded by an ocean. But, in addition, there was a continent situated beyond this world.* It was a vast continent and was inhabited by very large animals and human beings. There were many towns, the most noteworthy of which were Maximos (warlike town) and Eusebius (peaceful town). The inhabitants of Eusebius lived in peace and abundance. The soil yielded bounties without having to be ploughed. On the other hand, the inhabitants of Maximos were very warlike and their town ruled many nations. There were at least 2,000,000 people in Maximos. Mostly they died in war, not from wounds but from blows struck with stones or clubs—such were the weapons of these countries. They had much gold and silver, but had no knowledge of iron. At one time they wanted to invade our continent, transporting up to 10 million (!) men across the ocean and reaching the land of the Hyperboreans, whom they believed to be the happiest people on earth. But to the invaders the Hyperboreans looked so miserable that they renounced their intention and returned home.

Farther on, Silenus gives still more astonishing details. At the very edge of that country, in Meropides, there was a people called Meropians. Two rivers, a river of happiness and a river of sorrow, flowed across their land. Tall trees grew on the banks of both rivers. Along the river of sorrow the trees bore fruit which, if eaten, made people weep and finally die of sorrow. The fruit of the trees growing along the river of happiness made people younger until finally they found themselves in their second childhood and likewise died.

Although Theopompus was considered a writer of fables even in antiquity, we feel that what he writes is strongly reminiscent of a grotesquely distorted fabulous description of ancient America. For example, compared with the inhabited world as known to the Greeks, it was truly a vast land, stretching from one polar circle to the other. Its fauna differed essentially from the fauna of the known world.

Many Indian tribes, the Patagonians, for example, were noted for their gigantic proportions, being the tallest people in the world. In Theopompus' day there were fairly large towns in Central America and Peru; although the Indians had no knowledge of iron, they skilfully worked silver and gold. In farming they did not use ploughs and oxen, which were unknown in America prior to the arrival of

Europeans.* Their weapons were quite primitive, consisting of bows, clubs and stones. The action of the fruit of the trees growing along the river of happiness and the river of sorrow is suggestive of an exaggerated and garbled description of the action of some American plants containing alkaloids such as mescaline or cocaine.

We owe our most arresting information to the Greek writer Marcellus. It is given in his *Ethiopic History*, which has not survived to our day. Some of this information is used by the Greek Neoplatonist Proclus (410?-485) in his *Commentaries on the "Timaeus" of Plato* [translated by A. E. Taylor, London, 1820 (102/310)]. He writes: "That such and so great an island once existed, is evident from what is said by certain historians respecting what pertains to the external sea [the Atlantic—*N.Z.*]. For according to them, there were seven islands in that sea, in their times, sacred to Persephone [this probably refers to the Canary Islands], and also three others of immense extent, one of which was sacred to Pluto, another to Ammon, and the middle (or second) of these to Poseidon, the magnitude of which was a thousand stadia. They [the historians] also add that the inhabitants of it preserved the remembrance of their ancestors, or the Atlantic island that existed there, and was truly prodigiously great; which for many periods had domination over all islands in the Atlantic Sea, and was itself likewise sacred to Poseidon. These things, therefore, Marcellus writes in his *Ethiopic History*."

Nothing is known about when Marcellus lived. Most historians believe that he lived in the 1st century B.C., but A. Bescherelle and G. Devars state in their *Dictionary* (69/163) that they believe Marcellus wrote about Atlantis long before Plato.

So far as we can judge, the *Proclus-Marcellus story confirms Plato's legend about Atlantis. Moreover, according to Proclus and Marcellus, Atlantis existed in the Atlantic Ocean.*

Another thought-provoking report comes from the Byzantine traveller Cosmas Indicopleustes (102/311). In *Topographia Christiana* (547 A.D.) he points out that according to Timaeus (a Greek historian, 345-250 B.C.), whose source of information, as Cosmas himself declares, is unknown, the first ten kings of Chaldea (as confirmed by Berossus, a Babylonian priest who wrote a history of Babylonia in about 280-270 B.C.) came from a land on the island of Atlantis on the far side of the ocean.

Also exciting is a Hurrite myth (given in Hettish) about a giant stone pillar called Ulli Kummi. When this pillar grew to the sky in the middle of the Great Sea (Atlantic Ocean?), the sea flooded the land. Ulli Kummi was destroyed by the god of thunder, and its fragments sank to the bottom of the sea (94/108; 749).

The origin of the names "Atlas" and "Atlantis" merits attention. I. Donnelly (56/202) was attracted by the similarity of these words,

---

* According to some sources, the Incas of Peru had ploughs, and because they had no draught animals they harnessed people to them

which, allegedly, had no roots in the Greek language, with words in the Nahua language (the Aztecs were a Nahua tribe). Thus, in the Nahua language *"atl"* means "water", and *"atlan"* means "in the middle of the water". We feel that the most convincing interpretation is given by Y. G. Reshetov (25), who points out that in Phoenician the word *"atlath"* means "darkness" or "night", and that the name Atlat was given by the Phoenicians to their goddess of the night and also to the countries in the west.

Some atlantologists find vague responses to very ancient events, dating from the close of the Ice Age and in the period immediately following it, in Scandinavian mythology, particularly *in the Ragnarok or "Twilight of the Gods"* (174, 175). *It is assumed that the events described in the Ragnarok are an echo of the destruction of Atlantis.*

The most comprehensive Norse mythology was recorded by Snorri Sturluson (1178-1241). It has become known as the *Edda of Snorri Sturluson*. There are two variants of the *Edda*: one is a detailed prose work (the *Gylfaginning*) and the other a poetic chronicle (the *Voluspa*). The Frisians (*Oera Linda Boek*), Finns and Esths have similar myths. Moreover, there is some interesting data for atlantologists in Snorri Sturluson's *Inglingesaga*, particularly in the part headed *Heimskringla*.

According to Norse mythology, the Universe was created from the corpse of the giant Ymir. Initially the earth was round and encircled by a deep sea. The giant Jotuns settled on the coast at Jotunheim (or Utgard). The opposite side, Alftheim, was inhabited by dwarfs, who were expert smiths and potters. The citadel of Midgard was built as a barrier to the Jotuns. Half of the citadel lay in a region of snow and ice (Nifelheim), which was the home of the giants of hoarfrost, who were ruled by Loki, god of evil and destruction. The other half of Midgard lay in the south, in the region of fire and light (Muspelheim), which was the home of the giants of fire, who were ruled by Sutr, god of subterranean heat. Midgard was surrounded by a huge snake (Jormungard), daughter of Loki who protected the town from invasion by the sea. Odin, the chief god of the Norse pantheon, created the first mortals from wood and settled them in Midgard.* For themselves the gods built a new abode, Asgard, which towered over Midgard. In this new citadel they lived in magnificent palaces. There were four sacred rivers, while Asgard itself was surrounded by a massive wall. It was situated in the southwest, while the giants lived in the east (68).

The *Ragnarok* opens with a description of times reminiscent of the Ice Age. The ice-river Elivagar, rising in the north from the source Gvergelmir, gradually moved south, towards the land of the

---

* It is worth noting that according to the mythology of the Quiche, a Mayan tribe, the first race of man was likewise made from wood, but it was wiped out by a flood (470)

Aesir, bringing cold and darkness and widening the great yawning hollow Ginnungagap. Then there were three winters without a single summer, and then another three winters, during which there was a war of the elements that gripped the entire world. In a desperate attempt to save their country the Aesir fought their last battle against the forces of evil in the Vigritr plain. The wicked wolf Fenrir swallowed the sun, the moon was extinguished by another monster, the stars fell and disappeared from the sky, and the earth shook so violently that the mountains rocked. During the battle, Loki, who led the forces of evil, was assisted by his daughter, the snake, who released the subterranean waters that flooded Midgard and Asgard. The furious battle ended with the death of the Aesir, the gods, and their enemies, but before dying Sutr, the god of subterranean fire enveloped the earth in a sea of flame. The fire was finally extinguished by the Deluge. Only some of the younger gods and a very small number of mortals survived the battle. Modern mankind descended from the latter.

As regards the Frisian chronicle *Oera Linda Boek*, it is believed to have been written in the year 1256. It states that 3,449 years before it was written (i.e., 2193 B.C.), *Aldland* or *Atland* ("ancient land"), a country in the ocean, was destroyed by a geological upheaval. The disaster embraced other countries as well (119/144-48).

Here is what this chronicle says about the cataclysm (83a/49): "A bad time began. All that summer the sun hid behind the clouds as though it were reluctant to gaze down on the earth. The wind rested in the caves, and vapour rose from the ground, enveloping the houses as in a bog. The air was heavy and people forgot the meaning of happiness. In the very middle of this silence the earth began to tremble as though its end were near. The mountains burst open and spouted flames. Some began to sink and form fields, while new mountains grew out of the ground.

"Aldland or Atland, as the land was called by seafaring people, was swallowed by the waves together with its mountains and valleys, and everything else was covered by the sea. Many people were buried in the ground and others, who escaped, died in the water. The mountains breathed fire not only in the land of the Finda but also in Mosland (Twiskaland). The forests were burned to a cinder, and the wind bore the ash which covered the entire earth. New rivers took shape and the sand in their mouths formed new islands. For three years the land groaned, and when it recovered, its wounds could be seen. Many countries had disappeared and others had been rent asunder by the sea, and Mosland had been cut in two. Large numbers of the Finda came and settled in these empty spaces. Those of our people who were not exterminated became the allies of the invaders." Investigations have failed to establish what countries are meant. The description is reminiscent of the records in Egyptian temples about the invasion of Egypt by "people of the sea" (see p. 379.).

Chapter Two

CRITICISM OF DESCRIPTIONS OF THE CULTURE OF PLATO'S ATLANTEANS

There is, as we shall show later, a relative abundance of factual data supported by hypotheses for a study of the geological aspect of the Atlantis problem, but in our investigations of the historical and ethnographical aspect myths and legends comprise our only source of information. No material relics of the Atlantean culture have been found in the region where Atlantis is assumed to have submerged. We cannot accept as a relic the copper ring found on the ocean floor near the Azores by the *L'Hirondelle* expedition (84/60), although modern science could easily have established the origin of the copper from which the ring was made; or the mysterious belt of silver rings of unknown origin (108); or the gold Scythian buckle (at the State Hermitage, Leningrad) with a portrayal of a sabre-tooth tiger (138a/155). Interest is aroused by the "sea biscuits", about a ton of which was raised by a drag from a depth of 330 metres off the peak of Atlantis Seamount south of the Azores. These puzzling formations are calciferous discs (pteropodan limestone) with a depression in the middle of the external side giving them the shape of plates. The surface of these discs is relatively smooth, but in the depressions they are rough. Their average size is about 15 centimetres, and they are something like four centimetres thick. *It is hard to tally their astonishing and strange shape with the possibility of their being of natural and not of artificial origin. Besides, it has been established that they are approximately 12,000 years old. In addition, it has been proved that the material from which they are made was in subaerial conditions and that Atlantis Seamount was an island not very long ago* (474, 549, 689; see Chapter Thirteen). The shape of these discs brings to mind the plates on which in the past some Caucasian peoples used to carry sacrifices to their gods; these plates were set on the peaks of mountains or placed simply in hollows carved into rocks.

At the time Atlantis sank, most of mankind was at the Mesolithic stage. This corresponds to the age of the Azilio-Tardenoisean culture, while in North Africa to the Capsian culture of wandering hunters and gatherers of wild-growing edible plants and mollusks. True, by that time man was already using bows and arrows and was sailing in simple fishing boats near the shore. The Mesolithic was followed by the Neolithic and the Chalcolithic; in the latter epoch man learned to obtain and work natural metals. There is a span of several millennia between the Mesolithic and the Chalcolithic.*

---

* See Table 7, in Appendix 1.

So far Plato's legend is the only source for recreating a picture of Atlantean material culture. If we attach weight to what Plato tells us about Atlantean culture we must accept the hypothesis that it was far ahead of its age. But first we must establish its real level by eliminating exaggeration from Plato's legend (132).

Another thing we must bear in mind is that usually people overlook the fact that Plato was neither a historian nor an archaeologist, that he knew nothing of the methods of comparative investigation that have now become widespread in history and archaeology. Archaeology as we understand it was non-existent in his day, while history was only emerging and was closely intertwined with mythology. Plato possibly had data about the latest stages of Atlantean culture (4th-2nd millennia B.C.) and, without differentiating, he considered that the same culture existed unchanged 12,000 years ago, i.e., at the time of the main cataclysm. He could not have acted in any other manner, for it was the natural thing to do in his day.

A superficial reading of Plato's legend brings out a description of the splendours of the Acropolis, the wealth of the adornments of the Poseidon Temple, the abundance of metals and so forth. This, so to say, ostentatious aspect of the legend was accepted by some atlantologists as grounds for asserting that the Bronze Age was well advanced in Atlantis and that, evidently, the Atlanteans could be credited with inventing this alloy. This view is enthusiastically upheld, for example, by R. Devigne (17). Other researchers looked for an echo of the Atlantean bronze culture in the *Bronze Town* legend from the *Arabian Nights* and other similar traditions and legends (46, 104). But, as we shall show later, it is generally doubtful if bronze was known in Atlantis.

First and foremost, *it is natural to surmise that Atlantis' metal wealth and the magnificence of the temple ornaments were an exaggeration either by Plato himself or by his informants*. Indeed, the existence of a town whose inhabitants had some, even a small, store of metals in the shape of ornaments or for religious purposes could not have failed to command the respect of the surrounding population, which was still in the Stone Age and had no knowledge of how to work metals. Perhaps, in reality the Atlantean rulers did not have such immense wealth as Plato describes, but to the rest of the population, who did not use metal at all, this wealth seemed to be fabulous. Mostly, the demand for metal was still extremely small and the market, if it can be so called, was limited to domestic consumption in the town.

Plato's legend (the *Critias*) clearly says that gold, silver, copper, tin, the mysterious orichalcum, and probably lead and even iron were known to the Atlanteans. Iron, however, is mentioned only once—in a description of a sacrificial rite at the council of kings. Moreover, let us note that Plato says nothing of iron weapons (swords, daggers, and so forth), but simply mentions weapons. There might have been so little iron that there was not enough of it to make large objects. This forces us to assume that the iron used in Atlantis was of meteorite origin, as was the iron of the earliest finds in ancient Egypt and Sumer.

As a matter of fact, it is quite possible that Plato's words "without weapons" only mean that in Atlantis the rite of catching the sacred bull differed from the Greek ritual in that no barbed or cutting weapons were used. In this context, the question of whether iron was known to the Atlanteans remains open.

No doubt is aroused about the native origin of the gold and silver mentioned by Plato, but with regard to copper this question requires close study. Here the trouble is that the ancient Greeks had only one word for copper and bronze—*"chalkos"*. Generally speaking, this word was first used for copper, but later it also meant bronze. Gladstone (650/168) insists that *"chalkos"* meant only copper; he sees confirmation of this in Homer, who calls this metal *(chalkos)* "red", which can only be ascribed to pure copper and not to bronze. But in Plato's legend we find the assertion that what the Atlanteans used was pure copper and not bronze. In describing the walls of the Acropolis, Plato says that the "entire circuit of the wall, which went round the outermost zone, they covered with a coating of brass...." This passage may have two interpretations: either the Atlanteans "coated" the wall with copper, or they used the metal as a material for cementing the blocks of stone. We feel that the first variant is improbable; by a flattening process copper can be reduced to a powder, to a so-called bronze paint, but it is unlikely that the Atlanteans knew the technology for this, although cold forging is an ancient method of working metals. This makes the second variant more likely, especially as in the prehistoric Peruvian ruins at Tiahaunaco holes into which metal was poured were found in the blocks of stones. This metal held the blocs together. But in both cases only malleable, soft metal, i.e., pure copper, could have been used. Possibly, with a view to strengthening the binding, there were copper clamps along the entire circuit (i.e., the top) of the wall.

Plato further declares that the middle wall of the Acropolis was covered with silvery tin. Seemingly, this supports the surmise that bronze was known to the Atlanteans. But it is a far cry from knowing how to smelt tin to the manufacture of bronze. For example, the Aztecs of Central America did not know how to make bronze but tin was known to them. In a letter to the King of Spain, Hernando Cortes reported that they used T-shaped pieces of pure copper and pure tin as coins (650/683). Thus, the Atlanteans' ability to smelt tin cannot be offered as proof that they could manufacture bronze.[*]

There have been many arguments about the mysterious metal called orichalcum. The word itself means "mountain brass". But inasmuch as the ancient Greeks used the word *"chalch"* to denote metal generally, this word may be interpreted to mean "metal of the moun-

---

[*] For prehistoric methods of smelting tin see Y. M. Pokrovsky (369/11, 26)

tains" or simply "ore". Plato says that in Atlantis orichalcum was second only to gold in value, and that in his day this metal was not known. Orichalcum, Plato writes, "had the colour of fire". Consequently, it was a shining dark-yellow or reddish-yellow metal.

The word orichalcum was not coined by Plato. It was known to Homer, who used it as the name of a golden metal in the hymn of Aphrodite. Hesiod, too, knew about it. In *De mirabilibus auscultationibus* [62] pseudo-Aristotle speaks of orichalcum or mountain brass as of a shining metal obtained during the smelting of copper with the addition of some kind of earth found on the shores of the Black Sea. This earth was called "calmia", the name subsequently given to zinc oxide. Later the Romans transformed the word "orichalcum" into "aurichalcum" (gold copper) and as such it is used by Pliny, who says it was no longer mined because the ore reserves were exhausted [XXXIV, 2]. *Orichalcum is mentioned by many antique authors, all of whom agreed that it was a copper alloy*. We can, thus, eliminate as unfounded J. Spanuth's (100/98) view that orichalcum was amber. Similarly, there are no grounds for assuming that orichalcum is another name for electrum, a natural alloy of gold and silver (usually one part silver and three parts gold). This assumption is refuted by antique authors, who state that orichalcum was a darker yellow, while electrum was white or faintly yellowish and contained no copper.

All of which indicates that orichalcum might have been a copper alloy. Unquestionably, it was not bronze with an admixture of tin. Some investigators contend that it was the name for beryllium bronze, i.e., an alloy of copper and beryllium (116). Chemical and thermochemical computations show that beryllium cannot be introduced into copper by any of the processes involving carbon, the only powerful reducing agent known to prehistoric metallurgy. The method requires a vacuum and high temperatures, which cannot be obtained by simply burning coal even with the aid of blasting. By following the same line of reasoning we can eliminate the second, semi-fantastic variant, that orichalcum was an aluminium bronze (15).

There is yet another assumption, put forward by G. J. Bryant and J. Sykes (51/85), who think that orichalcum might have been phosphoric bronze. However, phosphoric bronze is virtually a variety of stannic bronze with a small quantity of phosphorus. The technology of producing this bronze is linked up with special phosphorous alloys (with copper or tin) and was absolutely unattainable by prehistoric metallurgy.

Thus, orichalcum might have been an alloy containing copper and a metal more or less easily reduced by carbon at not very high temperatures.

We are left with only one realistic assumption, namely *that orichalcum was a bronze-zinc alloy, in other words, simply brass (or tombac)*. This was the conclusion arrived at by B. Neumann (621) after a searching study of the history of this problem and of the prehistoric metallurgy of brass. Almost the same view is held by T. A. Rickard (650/155-57). Brass is yellow and contains from 20 to 50 per cent zinc. Below 18 per cent the colour of the alloy is red and above 50 per cent it is white. Alloys with 18 per cent and less zinc are called tombac, which lends itself to cold forging, flattening and drawing.

Zinc occurs in tetrahedrite as well. When copper is smelted from this ore, a small quantity of zinc may also be found. In this case there is very little zinc in the metal, most of it disappearing because of its volatility. Yet this method was used to produce brass in India in prehistoric times.

In addition to tetrahedrites there occur two independent minerals, which may be called a copper-zinc ore with a sufficiently large content of zinc: these minerals are aurochalcite and brass bloom (621). Aurochalcite is a basic copper zinc carbonate, with up to 28 per cent of the zinc oxide replaced by copper oxide. Brass bloom contains only 18 per cent copper oxide.* Most of the metallic zinc obtained when these ores are reduced usually evaporates, and only a small quantity is trapped in the copper. For that reason, despite the small content of copper oxide in aurochalcite, when metal is smelted from it we obtain a brass with only a small percentage of zinc, i.e., reddish tombac "of the colour of fire". Alloys similar to tombac may be obtained from aurichalcite by the same direct reducing smelting as pure copper. Aurichalcite occurs rarely and that made it an extremely costly metal (18, 29).

The most ancient relic made of brass is, evidently, the bracelet from a tomb of the IInd or IIIrd dynasty of ancient Egypt, which corresponds to the third-fourth millennium B.C. In that period bronze was not widespread in Egypt** and copper was regarded as a valuable metal. The Egyptian kings waged fierce wars to consolidate their rule over the copper mines in the Sinai Peninsula. D. G. Reder (374) is inclined to believe that this bracelet came from the Caucasus, considering that Georgia was the only place where copper-zinc ore was mined. It is not quite clear what he means by copper-zinc ore. It is hardly possible that in those days brass was obtained from an artificial mixture of copper and zinc ores. As regards aurichalcite, A. S. Uklonsky (406/339) says it was found in Tajikistan, Kazakhstan and the Altai Mountains but does not mention the Caucasus. The Caucasian origin of the bracelet is, therefore, open to doubt. Possibly, it is of Indian origin.***

---

* The possibility of obtaining orichalcum from brass bloom is mentioned also by P. Borchardt (44).

** R. Hennig (419/1, 119) believes that in Egypt, Crete and Lesbos the Bronze Age began in about the year 2750 B.C, but that in Asia Minor bronze remained unknown almost to 2050 B.C. Agreeing with H. Quiring, he assumes that initially Egypt and Asia Minor received their bronze as a finished product from the Iberian Peninsula.

*** P. Borchardt (44) mentions deposits of brass bloom in the north of Spain (Guipuzcoa, Santander).

We can now try to answer the question of the place occupied by the culture of Plato's Atlanteans in the universally recognised relay of human cultures. Quite many metals were known to the Atlanteans, first and foremost because theirs was a mountainous country. We may assume that native metals (gold, silver, copper and, perhaps, iron of meteorite origin) and metals obtained directly from ores (tin, orichalcum and, probably, copper) were known to them. *But alloys, including bronze, were not known to them, and they did not know how to smelt them from a mixture of ores or free metals. It is also unquestionable that they had no knowledge of the metallurgy of iron with its fairly intricate processes. This corresponds to the period of transition from the Stone to the Bronze Age, a period usually known as the Aeneolithic or the Chalcolithic.* In ancient Egypt this stage of culture was reached in the so-called pre-dynastic period, i.e., in the epoch preceding the union of Upper and Lower Egypt under Menes (fourth millennium B.C.). When the first Europeans came to America they found the Aztecs and the Mayas of Central America at the same stage of cultural development.

Interesting in this connection is the discovery of artifacts made of native copper, a feature of the early Chalcolite, in burial mounds near Oconto, Wisconsin, USA. By radiocarbon analysis it has been found that the burial ground dates back to about 5500 B.C. This, apparently, is the oldest dated metal relic (471, 194, 262).

At first glance, the problem of the Atlantean culture may appear in a quite different light if confirmation is found for the Malaise theory that the remains of Atlantis disappeared as late as the 13th-12th century B.C. (73, 74).

It would seem that the Malaise dating fits best of all with the Plato legend that Atlantis was a land of metals. Indeed, this dating fully accords with the period when bronze became widespread in human culture, and in this case there would be nothing incredible about the level reached by Atlantean culture. However, we can say quite definitely that Atlantis could not have been rich in precious metals and copper and that even if the Malaise dating is correct Atlantis could not have had a Bronze Age culture. It is common knowledge that *there is very little precious metal and copper to be found on volcanic islands consisting of basalt rock. It is hardly possible that Atlantis was an exception.* All that we can assume is that these metals were brought to Atlantis from South America or Spain. In itself this is not incredible, but even if we accept the Malaise dating it gives us no grounds for considering that Atlantis had a Bronze Age culture.

We may, with full justification, assume that in their everyday life the Atlanteans used articles made chiefly of stone. This is typical not only of the Stone Age but also of the period of transition from stone to metal. But since Plato says nothing of the use of brick and binding materials (cement, asphalt, lime, gypsum and so forth) and speaks of the utilisation of copper for fastening blocks of stone, there is good reason to suppose that the Atlanteans built cyclopean structures like those of Sacsahuaman and Tiahuanaco in pre-historic Peru. In our opinion, Atlantis was rather in the Stone Age, a land of cyclopean structures and megalithic edifices.

G. Poisson (86/170-174) believes there was a link between Atlantis and the megalithic structures in Western Europe. *Megaliths* are enormous edifices of huge natural, rough-hewn slabs of stone, either solitary slabs (*menhirs*), a row or circle of monoliths (*cromlechs*), or three or more slabs arranged to form a chamber (*dolmens*). They are to be seen all over the world.

A curious point is that megaliths occur mainly along the seashore. It is usually considered that the megalith culture arose independently among different peoples and that it marked a stage of development. But this does not explain the siting of megaliths in maritime regions. Poisson reasonably believes that megaliths are the remains of the culture of the so-called "people of megaliths or dolmens", of seafaring peoples. G. F. Debets, T. A. Trofimova and N. N. Cheboksarov (245/434) do not exclude the possibility that the presence of megaliths in Western Europe may be linked up with the settlement of West-Mediterranean tribes along the Atlantic coast.

It took many long centuries before the dolmen people stopped spreading, and for that reason the megalithic structures cannot everywhere be attributed to one and the same period. Moreover, science has not established where these people came from. But one thing is certain, and it is that the largest number of megaliths are on the Atlantic coast of Western Europe and that eastward their number gradually declines. Thus, on the Iberian Peninsula, the largest number of dolmens is to be found in Portugal, and there is not a single one in the middle of the peninsula (330/74).

An extremely interesting megalithic culture was discovered in 1952 by Dr. Daniel Ruzo (171-173) in the Marcahuazi Plateau about 50 miles from Lima, Peru. In this small plateau he found a series of gigantic sculptures hewn from natural cliffs. Some of them are sculptures of animals that have long been extinct in America (camels, glyptodons) or had never inhabited it (lions, cattle). Others resemble ancient Egyptian divinities, which are portrayed as having heads of animals or birds. In addition to sculptures there are cyclopean structures. Obviously, this plateau was once a sanctuary.

It is not known when this culture, called Mazma after a village near the plateau, emerged. In any case, the sculptures of animals that have died out in South America long ago show that the Mazma culture dates back to remote times. It must have been widespread in America because similar structures have been discovered in Mexico, Brazil and elsewhere (48/144; 159/52; 639).

Incidentally, it must be noted that some atlantologists, for example, D. Saurat (94), link up the problem of Atlantis and the megalithic and cyclopean structures with a hypothetical extinct race of giants. Ancient tribes of giants are mentioned in many myths of different peoples (Greeks, Scandinavians, Phoenicians, Amerindian and others) and in the Bible. These legends probably have a dual foundation. On the one hand, they are recollections of a race of powerfully built people—Cro-magnon man—who were nearly two metres tall. On the other hand, the myths and legends about wicked giants are perhaps vague recollections of prehistoric gigantic anthropoids—the meganthropus and the gigantopithecus, which coexisted with man at his earliest stages of evolution.

We feel that *the culture of Atlantis and of its successors and heirs who were closest to it in time was characterised by an inclination towards gigantism and cyclopeanism.* At first glance there seem to be insufficient grounds for this, but in reality it is the closest to the truth. *Atlantean architecture and sculpture had to be, first and foremost, earthquake-proof.* There are weighty grounds for assuming that Atlantis was subject to frequent, devastating earthquakes. In such a country life had to teach people, even if they were at the earliest stages of civilisation, to adapt themselves to local features.

S. A. Bashkirov (189/67-68), who studied the quake-resistance of prehistoric structures, found methods of anti-earthquake architecture in many cases and drew particular attention to cyclopean structures: "During earthquakes and tremors the irregularly placed slabs allow for an irregular distribution of the movement of the masonry. This irregularity creates the necessary organised lack of rhythm to offset the force of tremors." He discovered many elements of earthquake resistance in a number of prehistoric structures in Egypt and Mesopotamia.

We consider that *the Atlantean temples had nothing in common with the splendour of the temple described by Plato.* He Hellenised the Atlantis legend, and could picture the Poseidon Temple only after the Greek model. It is our opinion that *the Atlantean temples had no roofs and that natural conditions were used to create the corresponding religious atmosphere.*

Let us now analyse the possibility of there having been town-type settlements in or about the time of Plato's Atlantis. The most ancient known town-type settlement was situated near modern Jericho, west of the River Jordan. It had walls and even towers built of rough-hewn slabs of stone, and the houses were built of unburnt clay. There were no ceramics and, instead, stone vessels were used. Radiocarbon measurements give the date of this settlement as 6840 B.C. It existed until 5000 B.C., when pre-ceramic culture gave way to a new culture that probably came from the north, and brought handmade pottery. The new culture had nothing in common with the culture it replaced, and the reason for its accession is unknown (576).

A walled town of approximately the same age (about 6500 B.C.) has been recently discovered at Chatal Kuyuk in Anatolia, Turkey (825). The houses had flat roofs which served as entrances inasmuch as there were no doors. The inhabitants were farmers and herders. Also unearthed were tombs and sanctuaries decorated with frescoes, bas-reliefs and statuettes. The most noteworthy find consisted of ceramics dating from the 8th millennium B.C. Excavations brought to light beads made of various material—the town possibly had broad (evidently trade) relations reaching as far as the Mediterranean seaboard. Although artifacts made of copper and lead were found, the basic implements were made of stone.

Another point of interest is that Rumanian and Yugoslav archaeologists discovered recently and almost simultaneously Neolithic settlements with an ancient pictographic type of writing dating back to beyond the 5th millennium B.C.

A. Evans (365) had good reason to believe that the Knossos Palace in Crete was built in the eighth-ninth millennium B.C. (the time of the formation of the cultural layer beneath it), but this date frightened archaeologists and they made haste to reduce it. Some archaeologists are inclined to believe that the most ancient megalithic structures and the mysterious tracks discovered in Malta (cut in stone with sidings and "marshalling yards") date back to the sixth-seventh millennium B.C. (503). A remote Indian culture discovered at Mohenjo-Daro near the River Indus (315) evidently goes back to the fourth-fifth millennium B.C. (642b). It was a developed urban culture of a seafaring people, who, evidently, had known metals for a long time. The Cocle culture urban settlement in Panama was investigated by A. H. Verril (626/126). There the cultural layer is at least 10-12 feet (about 3.5 metres) thick and this, in Verril's opinion, corresponds to several millennia B.C. The great antiquity of the site is borne out by the clear portrayals of elephants, which died out in America long before our era. If this evidence is true, the Cocle settlement in Panama is the oldest town in America. Taking into consideration the slow rate of the development of prehistoric cultures, the gap of several millennia between the destruction of Atlantis and the date of the most ancient urban settlements does not seem to be either wide or incredible. Besides, it is extremely questionable if the Atlantean capital was a city after the usual prehistoric model. Perhaps (and most likely) *it was limited to the territory of the Acropolis, around which the primitive dwellings of the rest of the population stood.* Plato probably had a reason for describing only the Acropolis. Perhaps there was nothing else to describe. Town-type settlements of this kind have been discovered in many places (ancient Jericho, Knossos, the pre-historic capital of Crete, many Mayan towns, and so forth).

Many atlantologists, including I. Donnelly, assume that to some extent the existence of Atlantis was linked up with the rise and spread of cultivated crops. There is some substantiation for this idea. Academician P. M. Zhukovsky (255/10) reasonably points out that the prehistoric farming civilisations situated in river valleys were of secondary importance. The primary civilisations were situated in mountainous regions. Thus, the Sumer culture of Mesopotamia was created by invaders from a mountainous locality. The Chinese farming and the Indian civilisations were likewise founded by tribes of mountain-dwellers. The most highly developed cultures of both Americas (Maya, Toltec, Aztec, Inca) arose in mountainous regions and highland plateaus.

M. O. Kosven (277/57, 62) raised an interesting point when he advanced the theory that agriculture evidently emerged as long ago as the Aurignac-Solutrean epoch*, i.e., at the first stage of the evolution of man, and that, possibly, it was developed by women.

A study of the origin of cultured plants shows that the overwhelming majority have been cultivated since time immemorial. In most cases it is even impossible to state when, where and by whom they were evolved from wild-growing plants.

Academician P. M. Zhukovsky (255/29) writes: "The origin of maize provides us with our greatest enigma. It is unknown in its wild state even in the oldest archaeological finds. Modern maize cannot revert to its wild state primarily because it cannot shed its ripe seeds, and therefore self-sowing is excluded. The seeds sit tight in their cob cells, are covered with leaves, and the cobs themselves do not fall off." P. B. Sears (434/65) also notes maize's complete dependence upon man: "We have no data to show that maize can grow without human assistance, and geneticists agree that its pollen is not carried over long distances. Moreover, nothing is known about the time and place of the origin of maize." Further on he gives interesting data on the results of drilling in the region of present-day Mexico City.

Maize pollen was discovered in a cultural layer at a depth of nine metres, which means that it is about 4,000 years old. F. Reiney (377) has dated the earliest finds of maize as 2500 B.C. Sears has made the extremely interesting report that maize pollen has been found at a depth of 70 metres; stratigraphically this should give its age as more than 30,000 years. The intervening 61-metre layer is characterised by traces of volcanic activity and climatic changes.

From the above it is clear that *in view of the huge number of cultured plants of unknown origin there is a certain degree of probability in the surmise that some of them might have originated in Atlantis (i.e., that they had been bred by the Atlanteans) and spread to the continents on either side of the Atlantic* (57/49-50, 59-61). *It is possible that maize was bred in Atlantis, from where it was taken to America and Africa.* In recent years it has been established that *maize was grown by the peoples of Nigeria in remote antiquity, long before the arrival of Europeans. But in its wild state it was unknown in Africa as well.*

I. Donnelly (56/68) believed that the banana, which is today reproduced only vegetatively, might also have originated in Atlantis. The generally recognised theory is that Indonesia is the homeland of the banana and that it was brought to America in 1516 from the

---

* About 30,000-20,000 years ago.

Canary Islands. However, as long ago as at the turn of the 19th century Humboldt found that the banana was grown along the Orinoco and the Beni long before these areas were visited by the first Europeans. Later, banana seeds were discovered in Oligocene sediments in Colombia. This lends weight to the surmise that South America, too, might have been the home of the banana (222). A curious point is that in the tomb of Tutankhamen (266) the portrayal of stone goats with large dark spots on their skin was found on a bow-case. These goats are unknown in Asia, Africa and Europe.

Chapter Three

A CRITICISM OF PLATO'S TEXTS ON ATLANTIS

A study of the Atlantis problem must begin with an examination of the authenticity of the Plato legend, which is the most comprehensive and, perhaps, only historical record of Atlantis to have survived to our day. Moreover, we must ascertain what sources were available to Plato. In giving the legend, we have, in the preceding chapters, analysed some aspects of the problem chiefly from the standpoint of how far various statements are to be trusted. Let us now analyse both dialogues from the standpoint of the authenticity of the literary materials given by Plato and examine the principal objections to the authenticity of these texts.

First a few words about Plato himself. He was born in Athens, probably in the year 427 B.C., in an aristocratic family. It is interesting that Plato himself traces his family through Codrus, the last king of Athens, and the Homeric hero Nestor to Poseidon, god of the sea. His mother, Perictione, was related to Solon, the Athenian law-giver, from whom, Plato says, he learned the Atlantis legend.

As a philosopher, Plato was greatly influenced by Socrates, whom he first met in about the year 408 B.C. He was associated with Socrates until the latter's death in 399 B.C. and regarded himself as one of the philosopher's disciples. When Socrates died Plato went to Megara and then travelled in Cyrenaica, Egypt and Lower Italy, where he studied the philosophy of the Pythagoreans. He also visited Sicily and was, it is said, sold for a time into slavery by the Syracuse tyrant Dionysius the Elder, who grew tired of his philosophical tutelage. According to Strabo [XVII, 806], Plato travelled for 13 years. In Egypt he visited the Sun Temple at Heliopolis. But nowhere in Plato's dialogues is there any mention of his visit to Egypt or to the priests in Sais. Generally, Plato does not figure as a personage in the dialogues. However, some authors agree with Proclus that Plato had been to Sais and had had personal contact with a priest named Pateneith (102/10).

At the age of 40 Plato returned to Athens where he founded a philosophical school that later became known as the Academy. He made two more journeys to Sicily, where in Syracuse, after the death of Dionysius the Elder, he unsuccessfully tried to build his ideal state. According to legend, he died on his birthday in 347 B.C. His most celebrated pupil was Aristotle, whose philosophical views differed markedly from those of his teacher.*

Many students of Plato's works (22,102, 169, 170) consider that he cannot be trusted at all and that his dialogues are full of pseudo-myths which he himself had invented. The end of the dialogues *Republic, Phaedrus* and so on are cited as examples. When he read the *Lysis*, which was one of his first dialogues, before an audience, Socrates, who was present, voiced his dissatisfaction over the exaggerations. The Sophist Gorgias was likewise dumbfounded by Plato's talent for misinterpreting other people's words and ideas. It is well known that even in the dialogue *Socrates*, dedicated to his teacher, he greatly exaggerated and distorted reality.

Generally speaking, Plato is regarded as a person who made no effort to convey oral legends accurately, as nothing more than a Sophist. He loved to compose allegories and to present them to his contemporaries as truths (102/5; 208).

In this connection Y. V. Knorozov (22/214) writes: "Plato was never a historian and by no means tried to record any traditions. As a philosopher, he was extremely interested in devising a state system that would ensure internal prosperity and be powerful enough to resist its enemies. His attraction for this problem can be appreciated if we take into account the defeat sustained by Athens in the Peloponnesian War, during which the administration in Athens was changed repeatedly." "In publicising his philosophical views, Plato developed a literary genre in the shape of dialogues between several persons, who expounded these views.... These dialogues are not records of actual conversations but literary works. Even the dates of the conversations are given. Naturally, this is purely a literary method skilfully used by Plato to make his ideas sound more convincing."

We feel that although most of the above assessments of Plato as a personality are justified, there are no grounds for regarding him as a consummate liar and spinner of yarns. In the *Timaeus* he appeals to his listeners (not in his own name!) to believe his story about Atlantis. The reason for this appeal may have been that he knew of the prejudice of his contemporaries to some of his stories. To give more weight to his narrative he links the Atlantis legend up with the name of Solon. *In no other dialogue does Plato so insistently assure his listeners of the truth of his narrative. Obviously there must have been a reason for this. On the other hand, not everything that Plato reports can be trusted.*

With the exception of the *Critias*, all of Plato's compositions and many of his letters have survived in full. This was probably due to

---

* It is not the author's purpose to give a detailed biography of Plato or to analyse his philosophical views (176, 687).

the fact that as a philosopher he was extremely popular in antiquity. According to Diogenes Laertius, the *Timaeus* and the *Critias* were written by Plato shortly before his death. The same conclusion is arrived at by Lyutoslavsky (602), who made a stylistic analysis of these works. However, it is generally accepted that the *Laws* were the last of Plato's dialogues. As A. E. Taylor (176, 687) points out, this dialogue has the hallmarks of grammatical polishing, while the *Critias* gives the impression that it was only a rough draft. Developing this argument, Taylor holds that it was never finished. But L. Young (712) questions this argument and considers that the *Critias* was the last of the dialogues. It is believed that Plato wrote his last dialogues in about the year 355 B.C. (102/3).

With regard to the *Timaeus* a rumour was current, even in antiquity, that it was not written by Plato. The first to question Plato's authorship was Timon the Pyrrhonist, who claimed that Plato based his *Timaeus* on a book that somebody had given him. Timon lived in the century after Plato and it is, therefore, quite probable that he knew some details, later forgotten, of the philosopher's life. Many antique authors offer various points of view about the origin of the *Timaeus*: some attribute it to Ocellus Lucanus, others to Timaeus of Locri, and still others wrote that Plato was a member of a Pythagorean fraternity but was later expelled from it for claiming as his own the knowledge he had received. Yet another group considered that Plato had paid somebody to write this dialogue. Hermippus of Smyrna assumed that the *Timaeus* was the work of Philolaus (a contemporary of Socrates), who headed the Pythagorean fraternity after the death of Pythagoras, and that it was obtained by Plato from his relatives (102/210). Some later authors add that the book was bought for 10,000 dinars (145/353).

Indeed, with the exception of the Atlantis story, much in the *Timaeus* undoubtedly bears the stamp of the Pythagorean teaching, particularly in those places where Plato is carried away by the mysticism of numbers. It is interesting that when Timon speaks of the *Timaeus*, he does not mention the *Critias*, drawing attention only to the philosophical part of the dialogue and ignoring Atlantis (102/210).

On the other hand, it is true that for a long time Pythagoras studied under the Druids, Plato might have got his information about Atlantis from the Pythagoreans. The Druids were the higher priest caste of the Celtic tribes. They had extensive scientific knowledge, a written language and a written literature, of which nothing is extant because when Julius Caesar captured Alesia, capital of a Gallic state, he caused a huge Druid library to be burned (155/37). Subsequently, the entire Druid corporation was destroyed by the Romans in their campaign to put down the Druid-led liberation struggle. Very scanty information about the Druids and their sciences has been preserved.

G. Poisson (86/178) names the Druids among the possible successors of the Atlanteans. There are abundant grounds for this assumption. For example, the Greek historian Timagenes wrote that one-third of the Gauls were descended from peoples who came from distant islands situated in the Atlantic Ocean. He could not have meant the British Isles because after the campaigns of Julius Caesar they were quite well known to the Romans.

In the form that we know it, *Critias* became known very late, in the 4th century A.D., after Chalcidius translated the *Timaeus* into Latin and included the *Critias* in his commentaries. Could some of the text of the *Critias* been written by Chalcidius? Socher bluntly stated that the name of Plato should be taken off such a purposeless and vapid (from the point of view of philosophy) piece of writing. He was particularly indignant about the story of Atlantis. But G. F. Karpov (145/493) disagrees with Socher and advances a number of arguments defending Plato's authorship.

It may be considered as established that Plato made wide use of the literature of his day, including literature that is no longer extant. Karpov (145/352) writes: "There can be no doubt that Plato had access to the extensive researches of other philosophers." This viewpoint is shared by Y. V. Knorozov (22/215), who declares that "in writing his dialogues Plato utilised the most diverse material, including, probably, some vague records about the Minoan kingdom".

The *Critias* has come down to us as an unfinished work. It has been repeatedly surmised that its end was lost. But G. F. Karpov (145/495) writes that none of the ancient authors mentions the lost ending. Besides, we have the testimony of Plutarch, who writes in his *Parallel Lives*: "Plato inherited the materials for Atlantis by right of kinship from Solon, but they were as a piece of wasteland, and he set out to cultivate it as best he could. To the foundation that had been laid before him he added a spacious passage, a wall and doors such as no story and no poem ever had. But even he began the work much too late and died before he could finish it, and the more we admire what he has written the more we regret that he left it unfulfilled. Like the Athenians who left the Olympian temple unfinished, Plato's wisdom left unfinished only Atlantis."

The opinion of antique authors about Atlantis is interesting. It must be admitted that in antiquity Plato's Atlantis was not particularly popular. In most cases the attitude to it was one of scepticism. In Plato's works the ancients were interested only in his philosophical views and not in Atlantis.

Herodotus, Diodorus Siculus and other antique historians, whose works have survived to our day, contain no mention whatsoever of Atlantis, but speak of an Atlantean people in Libya, Africa. However, *there are serious grounds for believing that the Atlanteans of Herodotus and the Atlanteans of Diodorus were different peoples living in different regions of Libya*. The Atlanteans of Herodotus [IV,184] lived near Mount Atlas; this was not the modern Moroccan Atlas but rather the Ahaggar Mountains in Central Sahara (144/119).

Plato, originally known as Aristocles (427-347 B.C.) Bust from the Vatican Museum, Rome

R. Hennig (419) says that generally there was utter confusion about the location of Mount Atlas in the accounts of ancient authors; several Mount Atlases were known, and there was one even on an island in the ocean.

Diodorus [III, 52-62] says that the Atlanteans were a civilised people living on the African coast of the Atlantic. Their capital was the coastal town of Cerna, which was later identified with the Carthaginian colony of Cerna founded in the 6th century B.C. by Hanno. The history of Diodorus' Atlanteans is closely intertwined with the history of the African Amazons,* who came from the oceanic islands of Gorgad, overran the kingdom of the Atlanteans and then set out eastward across Egypt and Syria on a war of conquest. Myrina, their queen, is mentioned in the *Iliad* as well.

A noteworthy fact is that the legend about the Amazons was also current among the Indian tribes living along the Amazon in South America. H. Lhote (144/188) reasonably notes that *"in reality there are two problems: the problem of the Atlanteans and that of Atlantis"* and *"it would be the greatest mistake to site it [Atlantis] in Morocco on the basis of what is said by Herodotus"*.** It is somewhat surprising that Herodotus, who was in Egypt long before Plato, says nothing about Atlantis. In this connection, it has been surmised that his guides and interpreters told him only what was usually told to distinguished travellers. But Herodotus mistrusted such sources of information.

Aristotle, who was a pupil of Plato's, regarded Atlantis sceptically, saying: "He who created it destroyed it" (see Strabo [XIII, 598]). This attitude, H. Pettersson (84/22) points out, was the reason why in the period of ruthless Church oppression, when Aristotle enjoyed indisputable authority, nothing was heard about Atlantis up to the Renaissance. Besides, even in antiquity, Strabo [2, 3] was the first to mention Atlantis directly. He retold the words of Posidonius, a Greek geographer of the 2nd century B.C., who wrote about Atlantis in his *Geography*, which has not survived to our day. Strabo accuses Posidonius of gullibility for mentioning Atlantis. Pliny sceptically mentions Atlantis [2,92]. Ptolemy, the 2nd century A.D. geographer, says nothing about Atlantis. However, it is worth noting that in a geographical map compiled in Strabo's day and restored in the 9th-11th century there is an island beyond the Pillars of Hercules. It is bigger than Crete, being almost equal in size with Italy (311/48).

As for the Neoplatonists, some of them, for example Longinus, regarded Atlantis solely as a literary adornment of Plato's ideas and attached no importance to the legend. The Neoplatonist Porphyrius (232-304), like Origenes, one of the fathers of the Christian Church, regarded Plato's legend as an allegory in which the war

---

* J. O. Thomson (146/270) says disparagingly that the Amazons of Diodorus were nothing but the "fruit of unbridled fantasy".
** My italics. — *N. Z.*

between the Atlanteans and the pre-Athenians symbolised the struggle between the spirit and matter. Two other Neoplatonists, Iamblichos and Proclus, were of the opinion that the legend was true but was only of literary and symbolic importance. On the whole, classical Alexandria, where Neoplatonism flourished, was a hotbed of notions on allegorisation. It is, therefore, not surprising that the Alexandrian philosopher Philo Judaeus and the early fathers of the Christian Church (including Tertullian and Arnobius) held similar views. Let us note that Plato's doctrines were popular among the early apologists of Christianity and later served as the basis for the rise of a series of so-called heresies of the Gnostics.

According to Proclus, Krantor, who was one of Plato's first pupils, went to Egypt to check up on the Atlantis story. In Sais, the priests pursued inquiries, which, it is claimed, confirmed the story of their predecessors and even showed Krantor steles with inscriptions giving an account of the history of Atlantis. I. Imbelloni and A. Vivante (69/239-240) believed that the priests might have informed Krantor of an invasion of Egypt by a "people of the sea", which actually took place in the 13th-12th centuries B.C. These people apparently came from the western Mediterranean seaboard and overran Egypt jointly with the Libyans and other tribes from the western shore of the Atlantic (see Chapter Seventeen).

Sharing this belief, other atlantologists (74,100), including Knorozov (22/215), think that Plato himself might have known about the records of these invasions inscribed on the walls of the Karnak and Medinet-Habu temples near Thebes. However, the location of these inscriptions excludes the possibility of their having been shown to Solon or Krantor in Sais. Yet Plato might have learned about them during his travels in Egypt. Poisson reasonably notes (86/26) that no steles with inscriptions even remotely concerned with the history of Atlantis have been found near Sais. True, the absence of such records is not proof that these steles never existed.

The following points are, in our opinion, important:

1) Proclus does not say whether Krantor brought the end of the *Critias* from Egypt, which would have been natural if his purpose was to obtain confirmation of Plato's legend. This silence is strange or perhaps the end of the *Critias* existed in Krantor's day and was lost later? In any case, even if it existed it was probably only a rough draft and was lost soon after Plato's death.

2) The Sais priests would hardly have taken any step to discredit their corporation by admitting any deception on the part of their predecessors even if that, indeed, was the case.

3) It is generally unknown what the priests showed Krantor and more than doubtful that he could have read what was shown to him.

4) It is improbable that the history of Atlantis, which, properly speaking, had little to do with the history of Egypt, was inscribed on a temple stele. The inscriptions on steles were usually of a quite different nature (religious hymns, laudations of pharaohs, and so

on). Most likely, the record of Atlantis, if it existed, was written on papyrus—remember, the Sais priest promised to show Solon a "record". Therefore, quite probably, the priests were forced to trick Krantor by showing him steles with inscriptions about a "people of the sea". The fact that accurate documents about Atlantis have not survived in Egypt is evident from Proclus' report that the Atlantis problem was hotly debated in the Alexandrian library. In other words, the Academy did not have the pertinent documents.

Yet it is possible that the Sais legend contained some measure of truth and that Plato, in the end, decided to look for confirmation in other sources, after the manner of ancient logographers. We feel *it is quite probable that some legend obtained by Solon from the Sais priests and passed on, as an inheritance, to Plato was used by the latter first as a basis for part of the "Timaeus" and later, reinforced with data from other sources, it became the content of the "Critias"*. The argument in favour of this is that *Greek mercenaries were vital to the Egyptian kings of the Saite dynasty, and the Egyptian priest, therefore, flattered Solon with an invented legend about a military alliance in remote antiquity between the pre-Hellenic and the Egyptians and about a war between the pre-Hellenic and the Atlanteans*. This invention evidently achieved its object because Greek mercenaries poured into Egypt. If we approach the history of Egypt of those days realistically we must admit that the above sounds plausible.

On the other hand, *the war between the pre-Hellenic and the Atlanteans, as invented by the priests, served as a gratifying outline for Plato, who attributed all the features of his ideal kingdom to the non-existent pre-Hellenic state with the purpose of popularising his political ideas*. Here Plato gave full rein to his imagination and the account of this kingdom was coloured with so many details that even the vivid description of Atlantis itself is eclipsed. It seems to us that *without some records of Egyptian origin at his disposal Plato would have found it difficult to cope with his task*. However, many historians and linguists who studied Plato's compositions reject the reference to Solon and, consequently, the Egyptian origin of the legend, feeling, as S. Y. Lourier summed it up, that it was the "wrong address". A. E. Taylor (176, 687) calls the reference to Solon a fabrication, a literary method such as is used by present-day novelists. He sees proof of this in the fact that prior to the appearance of the *Timaeus* and the *Critias* no ancient Greek writer made any reference to Atlantis. However, L. Young (712) reasonably objects to this on the grounds that with the exception of the poems of Homer and Hesiod and the works of Herodotus, almost none of the works of the logographers of the 7th-5th century B.C. have come down to us, while only fragments exist of the works of Hellanicus and others.

T. H. Martin (167) and P. Couissin (54) are of the opinion that the Egyptian priests simply duped Solon. Some commentators assume that the Atlantis legend was brought from Egypt by Plato himself and that he attributed it to Solon to lend it more weight. But, perhaps, Plato was also humbugged by the priests, like his pupil Krantor, when he went to Egypt to check up on the veracity of his family tradition. That, probably, is why he destroyed Solon's main records and also the end of the *Critias,* which was devoted to the war, after he had studied all available sources and found that dust had been thrown into his eyes.

All these problems remain unanswered. On this score G. F. Karpov (145/493) writes: "We are coming round to the conclusion that Plato got the Atlantis legend from an Egyptian priest and used it as the basis for his composition. *Critias* is made to expound it with deviations and amendments to make it fit Plato's purpose in the dialogue."

A close examination of Plato's legend of Atlantis has brought many investigators round to the conclusion that the entire material is artificial and deliberately built up with no other purpose than to illustrate or popularise Plato's theories. This idea is not new. It has been propounded without any essential changes since ancient times. J. O. Thomson (146/139) has summarised the age-old scepticism with regard to Atlantis most precisely. After briefly recounting the legend, he wrote: "Obviously the date is fantastic, and the whole is a 'noble lie': Atlantis is a bad Utopia, called from the vasty deep to test a good one, and consigned there again as plausibly as possible. Of course, as not even Utopias are created in a vacuum, some local colour is used." But, as we shall demonstrate, the Atlantis legend is anything but Utopian, and Thomson's remarks are directed to the wrong quarter. Further, he goes on to say: "It is the continent which is the most striking feature for geography. On the globe, as the earth was now thought to be, the known world round 'our sea' was beginning to look small, and there was ample space for another 'inhabited world'. In a sense Plato may be said to have invented America."

It seems incredible to Thomson, as it does to most of Plato's critics, that the Greek philosopher possessed even the haziest knowledge about America. The reason for this is that the geographic knowledge of the ancient Cretans is underrated, as we shall show in detail in Chapter Four. In connection with the question, touched upon by Thomson, of a continent on the far side of the Atlantic it would be useful to cite V. Bryusov's (15) reasonable statement: "If Plato felt he had to invent an island in the Atlantic solely to depict a fantastic land with an ideal state system there was no need whatsoever to concoct a western continent as well. Obviously, the description was based not on a play of the imagination but on definite facts." Indeed, *if Atlantis was a fabrication, an absurdity, why should Plato have found it necessary to pile up one absurdity on another, especially when his contemporaries were satisfied that his was a rich imagination. Besides, his geography differs essentially from the geographical notions of his day, and the same may be said about his mythology.*

Some spokesmen of the extreme views on this subject reject as preposterous everything that Plato writes about Atlantis, considering that he invented the legend by borrowing all he could from the world around him. They regard the *Critias* as the prototype of the modern novel. This point of view is upheld by many commentators of Plato's works and by literary critics who have studied the history of ancient Greek literature, for example E. Rhode (169) and A. Rivaud (170).

Rivaud considered that Plato got all his elements for a description of Atlantis from the Greek world or from reminiscences of the Cretan-Aegean civilisation. In his opinion, the mythology in the *Critias* scrupulously conveys Greek traditions, while the deviations are attributed to Plato's knowledge of versions unknown to us (!). Further, Rivaud points out that the Poseidon Temple resembles many Greek temples, and that the only difference is that it is larger than the temple of Artemis in Ephesus and the temple of Zeus in Athens. The statue of Poseidon resembles the Zeus statue in Olympia; the temple is more ornate but the style of the decorations is the same. Some data, for example, the sacrificial ritual, bull-fighting and the cult of the bull (?) were borrowed from a knowledge of Cretan civilisation.

The extraordinary similarity between the Atlantean and Cretan civilisations has been noted by many authors (27, 50, 154). As we can judge from the data given in the preceding chapters, these elements of similarity do not go beyond the community of religious cults of many prehistoric civilisations and are far from being identical. Rivaud sees nothing original in the description of Atlantean flora and fauna. He is not amazed even by the elephants, because they were known in North Africa since the first centuries of our era, while in Syria, let us add, they were known since the time of the Ancient Kingdom of Egypt. On the other hand, Rivaud overlooked the mention of the coconut palm, which is the most interesting element of Atlantean flora.

He finds much in common between the geometrical lay-out of the Atlantean capital and the projects of Hippodamus of Miletus, a Greek architect of the first half of the 5th century B.C., who is considered as the originator of the symmetrical lay-out of towns. But the idea of a symmetrical lay-out does not by any means belong to Hippodamus. It was applied in remote antiquity. But the ring arrangement with canals in the Atlantean capital has no analogy among the ancient Greek towns. As we can see from the critical analysis of the Atlantean material culture described in the preceding chapter, after exaggeration is removed from the description it becomes clear that the Atlantean culture was original and by no means a carbon copy of the Greek culture. It is, therefore, very difficult to speak, as Rivaud does, of an identity between the Greek and Atlantean cultures.

Knorozov (22/215) adopts a sharply negative attitude to Atlantis. He writes: "Thus, no tradition, founded on legend of Atlantis exists. The story of a model barbarian Atlantean kingdom is no more 'historical' than the story of an ideal Athenian state, which is a component of the former. And both are no more 'historical' than the conversation itself between four philosophers, which, naturally, was invented. In his dialogues, which are literary and not historical works, Plato did not have to limit himself to the choice of the materials he required and utilised every device to make his story more convincing, interesting and true-to-life without, however, as we have stated above, going beyond certain boundaries. Both Athens and Atlantis are synthetic artistic images illustrating his philosophical ideas, as is frankly stated in the dialogues." This denotes that Knorozov adheres to the views of the linguists of the 19th and early 20th century (Martin, Rhode, Rivaud, Susemihl, Taylor and others), who completely reject the possibility of there being any truth in the Atlantis legend. However, *there is some portion of truth in any, even a primitive, literary narration that includes geographical and historical information, and it is this truth that must be ascertained.*

We are satisfied *that the "Hellenisation" of the whole legend is natural and should not cause surprise and that it is by no means the result of Plato simply distorting Greek reality to suit his purposes.* Plato was a man of his time and people and regarded and expounded facts as applied to the concepts, knowledge and views of his day. Moreover, he regarded some of his dialogues as didactic material, and by "Hellenising" facts he made them understandable to his pupils (18/32). *Perhaps in the "Critias", aiming to create a new epic, he followed the example of Homer, who completely Hellenised the Mycenaean epic in the "Iliad" and an ancient tradition of unknown origin in the "Odyssey".*

Up until the recent past it was in any analysis of the Atlantis problem impossible to side-step the *"biblical theory"*, which was current for a long time. This theory was most fully expounded by P.C. Baer (36) in a monograph published in 1762. In Russia it was championed by A. S. Norov (23, 83), who cited Greek and Arab sources to back up his view that Plato borrowed much from the Bible and that in writing the Atlantis legend he retold ancient Hebrew traditions. Norov's views are sometimes wrongly interpreted but we can judge them from his statement that "the Bible is the only luminary in the history of primitive times". Inasmuch as the Bible existed in Plato's day and he could have been familiar with it, Norov considers that he got his Atlantis legend from it despite the fact that it contains no direct reference to this legend. Furthermore, Norov draws attention to the fact that both the *Critias* and the *Bible* are incomplete; the sixth book, probably the *Book of the Wars of Jehovah*, has been lost. Various grounds were offered for the biblical theory, but most of them boiled down to the legend of the tribulation of the Jews in Egypt, to the claim that the Jews passed their legends on to the Egyptians and that Plato borrowed them from the latter. In reality, as archaeological excavations have demonstrated, the opposite was the case, for there was considerable Egyptian influence in Palestine and it lasted for many centuries, long before the Jews settled there.

Adherents of the biblical theory usually locate Atlantis in the stretch of the Mediterranean from Egypt to Asia Minor adjoining

Palestine. Some of them think it was situated farther to the west, linking it up with the problem of Crete and the adjoining parts of the Mediterranean. All these hypotheses disregard Plato's precise siting of Atlantis. Assumptions of this kind were made by A. Karnozhitsky (20), L. S. Berg (12), A. G. Galanopoulos (61, 62) and others. *The theory of the biblical origin of the Plato legend does not hold water and there are no grounds whatever for resurrecting it in any modernised or camouflaged form.*

Some researchers find some elements of independence in the Plato legend. True, they make the reservation that it is a limited independence. For example, T. Moreux (79) believes that like all legends, the Atlantis legend must have been founded on some facts—the cataclysm remembered by mankind through the centuries and taken by Plato from the Egyptian priests to adorn his narration; the reality has remained but by no means the morals and manners of the Atlanteans nor the description of their towns, monuments, palaces, institutions and everything else that Plato invented to expound his philosophical views and the ideas of his *Republic.* Thus, the proponents of this trend agree that there might have been some geological disaster but dispute the reality of Atlantis. Poisson (86/43) takes a somewhat broader view of the Plato legend: "There are grounds for taking the *Timaeus* into account, while the *Critias* must undoubtedly be dismissed." Consequently, Poisson accepts only the fact of the existence and sinking of Atlantis and of the war of the Atlanteans against some European people. This war interests him more than anything else, and he devotes his book chiefly to an analysis of this part of the legend, seeing in it an echo of a struggle between tribes in prehistoric Europe.

In the previous chapters we have cited many interesting facts contained in the *Critias* which contradict the views of Poisson, Moreux and Rivaud. The crux of the matter is that *in our opinion the "Critias" must be viewed as a compilative work of Plato's in which he drew upon a number of sources that we know nothing about.* This is stated directly or indirectly by many commentators.

Some of the data given by Plato, the superfluous and even incongruous numerical accuracy for such a cursory description of the Acropolis and some other places and the extreme scarcity and sometimes complete lack of the most vital information for a brief description of the country as a whole arouses a certain suspicion with regard to the veracity of the narration. In Plato's love of figures one can perceive the influence of the mysticism of numbers that was preached by the Pythagoreans and which had little to do with reality. On the other hand, this method of serving up material stems from the purpose of the *Critias,* namely, to give the history of the war between the Atlanteans and the pre-Hellenes. For that reason Plato laid emphasis on details of a military nature.

J. Bramwell and other researchers (42/61: 69/161; 102/209) point out certain textual incongruities in both dialogues. For instance, at the end of the section of the *Timaeus* which deals with Atlantis Critias relates he is not sure of everything he spoke of and in the course of the night he had thought and tried to fit in what was missing; then he stated that he clearly remembered his conversations with his grandfather. When he was ten Critias heard the story of Atlantis from his 90-year-old grandfather, who had heard it from his father Dropides (the great-grandfather of the narrator). But in the *Critias* the narrator refers to some notes; these notes were in the possession of Critias' grandfather and Critias had read them as a child. Nonetheless, at the beginning of the dialogue Critias found it necessary to invoke Mnemosyne, the goddess of memory. If there had been documents why had it been necessary to invoke the goddess of memory? And, in that case, where did the mass of detail in the description of the capital and the numerical data come from? A boy of ten could hardly have remembered them all. Apparently at the time of the narration Critias did not have these notes and therefore invoked Mnemosyne.

We consider that *the role played by Critias in the story was most likely invented. If Plato possessed any of Solon's manuscripts they could only have been fragments of the originals*, because Solon died more than two hundred years before Plato was born. Most probably Plato tells the story himself on the basis of oral legends and, partially, other sources, and in this part he is sparing of details. For those places where, perhaps there were fragments of Solon's manuscripts to draw upon, we find more detail, and Plato supplements them with his own imagination.

In conclusion we must examine an objection which is frequently made by the adversaries of the Atlantis problem and which is most succinctly expressed by Knorozov (22/215-216): "In N. F. Zhirov's opinion only one thing is not invented in the dialogues—the description of Atlantis. This approach to the dialogues is amazing for its extreme tendentiousness. If Zhirov does not believe that Athens existed nine thousand years ago why does he believe in a similar antiquity of the Atlanteans? If the description of Greece is the work of fantasy, why is the description of Atlantis not a similar fantasy? If it is not true that the Athenian hosts were swallowed by the earth, why must we believe that Atlantis sank in the sea?" The reply to this is that the experience of many linguists and literary critics has shown that an analysis of the Plato legend has never led to its outright rejection. This is also clearly confirmed by the attempt made by Knorozov, who followed a well-trodden path and, it should be noted, with similar success. For a study and objective analysis of the legend we must by-pass the more than a century-old canon* and

---

* One of the first commentaries expounding this canon was published in 1841 by T. H. Martin (167) and served as the foundation for modern notions about Atlantis among literary critics.

apply some other method. As we have pointed out, such an analysis must rest first on the hypothesis that the *legend with its historical and geographical elements may contain a grain of truth as any other narration (or even myth) of the same nature despite the profusion of elements of a lively imagination.* In our analysis we employed the *method of successive elimination,* which is well known in the applied sciences and in mathematics: all improbable variants are eliminated one after another until only the most probable data or surmises remain. Knorozov, evidently, never used this method in his work and it, therefore, seems "extremely tendentious" to him.

What do we get when we apply the method of successive elimination to Plato's dialogues about Atlantis? When we review the dialogues we find, first and foremost, two parallel pivots of narration: one about the pre-Hellenes and the other about the Atlanteans. First let us try to eliminate what has the least bearing on reality, i.e., the question of the pre-Hellenes and their kingdom. *Nobody questions the assumption that the description of the pre-Hellenic kingdom is an accurate reflection of Plato's political and social views. It is a Utopia created by Plato himself.* On the basis of all that we know of the development of human society we cannot conceive of a kingdom existing 12,000 years ago and uncannily satisfying Plato's ideas of an ideal state. In this context one can understand why *the greatest doubts are raised precisely by the pre-Hellenic kingdom. This logically brings one round to the conclusion that everything Plato connects with this kingdom likewise raises the greatest doubts.*

Let us now examine the problem of the legendary war between the pre-Hellenes and the Atlanteans. This gives rise to similar doubts not only because it is linked up with the pre-Hellenic kingdom but also because of the reasons behind this legend, namely, the political situation in Egypt at the time of Solon's visit and the demand for Greek mercenaries. *The Egyptian priests who spoke with Solon had to convince him that there had been a military compact between Egypt and Athens even in remote times. To gain their end they might have utilised historical data about ancient ties between Minoan Crete and Egypt.* Perhaps to impress Solon they showed him some records.

Lastly, the question arises of the destruction of the pre-Hellenic kingdom. Inasmuch as none of the ancient Greek myths and legends dealt with the war between the pre-Hellenes and the Atlanteans, thus making the existence of a pre-Hellenic kingdom doubtful, it had to be "removed in time". Plato could do this quite easily because the mythology of ancient Greece had suitable myths, and it was, therefore, not difficult to force the pre-Hellenic kingdom to be "swallowed by the earth".

And now let us turn to Atlantis. Even here there are two facets to the problem: the description of the Atlantean kingdom and the description of Atlantis itself. The description of the Atlantean kingdom, which Plato sets off against the pre-Hellenic kingdom, raises considerable doubt. It contains deliberate distortions, embellishments and pure inventions, at which Plato was so adept, and also elements of propaganda. However, it must be noted that *it is much more difficult to invent a verisimilar Atlantean kingdom than a pre-Hellenic state, for which Plato had everything up to the unsuccessful attempt to implement it in Syracuse.* For the Atlantean kingdom he had to have some *model* that differed markedly from the kingdoms known to the ancient Greeks, otherwise the borrowed elements would give away the author of the narration. Indeed, in speaking of the pre-Hellenic kingdom Plato gives many details about its social system, but in the case of the kingdom of the Atlanteans he limits himself to a description of the Acropolis and the council of kings. *Elements of a Utopia prevail in the description of the pre-Hellenic kingdom, but the Utopian element is virtually non-existent in the Atlantean kingdom,* and it can be found only by exercising one's imagination.

Lastly, there remains the question of Atlantis as a geographical entity. There is plenty of food for thought in this problem, and it may serve as the object of a closer discussion and investigation, especially if the data provided by geologists and oceanologists can lead us up to the assumption, even a modest one, that there once was land—an island or part of a submerged continent—beyond the Strait of Gibraltar. In this case, if we manage to show that there really existed such a land in the places where Plato says his Atlantis was situated and in the period that he mentions, the question of whether man might have lived in Atlantis and of how he lived there becomes real. At precisely this stage the information that the legend gives about the Atlanteans and their culture is critically analysed. Here we must ascertain what served as the model for Plato's Atlantean kingdom, and try to find out the real level of Atlantean civilisation.

This analysis brought us to the general conclusion, which may seem to be paradoxical at first glance, *that of the mass of historical and geographical material in the "Timaeus" and the "Critias" the account of Atlantis is the closest to reality.*

It may be useful to note that several years ago when the author of the present work started studying the problem of Atlantis, his initial, superficial review of the problem led him to views that hardly differed from those being expressed by Knorozov. Subsequently, after a deeper study of the problem and as a result of the accumulation of facts from many branches of sciences and of generalisations based on these facts the author of this book came round to the belief that there is a grain of truth in the Plato legend. This required a thorough-going study of the data provided by various sciences, and it was here that the major difficulty of atlantologists lies.

Thus, we are in a position to sum up some results. A careful examination of all the materials at our disposal leads us to the following conclusions:

1) *For a study of the Atlantis problem both dialogues—the "Timaeus" and the "Critias"—are of equal value but require that the facts in them should be critically weighed.*

2) We may agree with some critics that the main thread of the Atlantis legend is in the *Timaeus*, which was evidently, written before the *Critias*. However, in the *Timaeus* the Atlantis legend is secondary, serving only to illustrate material to which at the time of writing Plato did not attach any special importance. This is exactly one of the reasons for suspecting that Atlantis really existed. Possibly, the legend was based on some accounts of Egyptian origin or which were obtained by Plato himself during his travels in Egypt, or they were fragments of a tradition left by Solon, or that both the former and the latter assumptions are valid.

3) In the legend, which might indeed be of Egyptian origin, the Egyptian priests, motivated by political considerations, introduced the war between the Atlanteans and the pre-Hellenes. For this part of the legend they probably utilised quite different facts about some different war, for example, a war against a "people of the sea". G. F. Karpov (145/386) assesses this part of the legend as follows: "However, we shall not defend that part of the story where it mentions the valour of the ancient Athenians; this entire section is either a pure fabrication or, perhaps, a tradition that really existed but which was completely revised to suit the objective of the composition". Yet there are grounds for assuming that inasmuch as the "people of the sea" included Cretans, who in Egypt might subsequently have been identified with the ancestors of the Hellenes, the surmise of some commentators and atlantologists that they are the pre-Hellenes of Plato's story seems improbable to us.

4) *We feel that when Plato started writing the "Critias" he pursued a different object than in the "Timaeus", namely to create a didactic epic, which, although expounding the author's political views, would surpass Homer's epic and thus be accepted as the heroic epic of the Greek people,* as Plutarch unambiguously pointed out. Plato wrote the *Critias* after he had become disillusioned about the realisation of his ideal state, following the failure of his Syracuse experiment. For that reason this idea begins to fade into second place, and mystical elements and materials from Pythagorean sources seeped into the dialogue. But by that time Greek mythology had been put in relative order (Homer, Hesiod), and material for a new epic had to be found outside the Greek world. Plato already had the outline for such an epic—the Egyptian legend. But while it sufficed for an episode in the *Timaeus* there was too little of it for a long narration.

5) It may be considered as quite probable that *the legend given in the "Critias" was drawn not from a single source but from a considerable number of mythological, historical and geographical data obtained by Plato from various sources which we know nothing about.* It is our belief that part of the data might have been remains

of what the Cretan-Aegean civilisation knew of the continent on the far side of the Atlantic and even of what survived of Atlantis. Perhaps R. Hennig (158/38) is justified in thinking that Plato used the data on Scheria in the *Odyssey*. These data might have been supplemented with material of Etruscan and Carthaginian origin, which Plato could have obtained during his travels in Italy and Sicily.

6) *Plato's choice of Atlantis as the object of his epic was not accidental. It was his only possible choice and it did not depend upon the existence of an Egyptian legend.* He conceived the idea possibly while he wrote the *Timaeus*, but at that time he did not have all the materials he needed. He was reluctant to make the epic the fruit of nothing but fantasy for he wished to present his ideas in the most convincing form. He therefore had to select a place whose existence was linked up with some tradition. On the other hand, this place had to be unknown and inaccessible, for that enabled the author to colour up the epic with his own additions. He could not have chosen a better place than an island in the Atlantic.

G. F. Karpov (145/493) stresses this point: "The more indefinite the reports (about the islands in the Atlantic—*N. Z.*) were, the greater was the possibility for remembering and inventing all sorts of things about the affairs of these kingdoms and their institutions. Plato evidently took advantage of the vastness of the subject to apply it in detail to his purpose." *The existence of the Egyptian tradition and the reference to Solon likewise facilitated transferring Plato's social and political views to the state system of the pre-Hellenic kingdom.*

7) *It seems highly probable that the rough draft of the "Critias" was completed, but that before his death Plato destroyed the end when he found that the basis of his subject—the war between the Atlanteans and the pre-Hellenes—had never existed, that this part of the legend had been invented by the Egyptian priests.* For that reason, fearing ill-wishing criticism for this fabrication and finding no confirmation in Greek myths and legends, Plato, shortly before his death, saw the collapse of his epic, which was founded on a war that never was, on a war that proved to be nothing but fiction. He therefore destroyed the part of the dialogue beginning the description of this war. *But at the same time he could not part completely with his brainchild—the pre-Hellenic kingdom—and left the entire initial text unchanged.*

8) Moreover, *it is quite likely that Plato wanted to rewrite the dialogue and turn it into a real historical novel, setting himself quite different objectives in the Pythagorean spirit, i.e., to write a mystical, edifying work. For that reason the "Critias" ends with Zeus' decision to call a council of gods. Here not a word is said about the war between the Atlanteans and the pre-Hellenes; the text speaks only of the punishment being prepared for the impious Atlanteans, who had lost their original divinity.* Many commentators of Plato's works

have upheld the view that the *Critias* is the prototype of the historical or utopian novel. Karpov (145/493) writes: "... the dialogue written in the name of Critias seems to us to be a kind of historical novel, which, it must be surmised, is based on some truth." V. V. Bogachev (14) believed that had the *Critias* been finished it would have been similar to subsequent Utopias: the Icaria community of Etienne Cabet, the *Utopia* of Thomas More, or the *New Atlantis* of Francis Bacon. However, we feel that the notion about the *Critias* being the predecessor of the historical novel is closer to the truth. Besides, *we find a vital difference when we draw a comparison with subsequent Utopian novels: the action in Plato's novel does not take place in an arbitrarily selected locality, while the Utopian element exists only in that part of the dialogue where the pre-Hellenic kingdom is described. We do not think there are any grounds for seeing elements of a Utopia in the description of Atlantis and the Atlantean kingdom because this description lacks elements of idealisation: the Atlanteans were a warlike, barbarian people.*

Naturally, these conclusions are nothing more than hypotheses, but we feel that this interpretation is highly plausible.

Chapter Four

ATLANTIS, SCHERIA AND TARTESSOS

The peoples who inhabited or who are inhabiting the continents on either side of the Atlantic had or still have many myths, legends and traditions that might, in one degree or another, have something to do with the Atlantis problem. Atlantologists have been particularly attracted by myths about deluges and cataclysms. Among the indigenous peoples of both Americas, every single tribe had myths telling of a deluge or cataclysm (653). Indeed, *it is quite reasonable to assume that gigantic, super-tsunamis, started by the sinking of Atlantis, might have flooded a number of places along the Atlantic coast and this, in its turn, might have given rise to myths about a deluge* (18/40). However, this interpretation of the deluge myths usually meets with sharp objections. A debate on this subject would considerably and without purpose enlarge the volume of this work, for it would not achieve its object because the adversaries of atlantology maintain that convincing proof has not been produced to back up the assumption that there were pre-Columbus relations between the New and the Old World (22/217). "A feature of historical research is that it underestimates remote relations or simply the search for new land, which is a primordial human urge stemming directly from man's biological adaptation, that of a seeker of food. Fascinated by the achievements of construction, many historians overlook proof of distant journeys" [I. A. Yefremov (32)]. However, to some extent the critics are, possibly, right because the direction of the prevailing winds and currents in the North Atlantic makes it possible to reach the shores of America quite quickly, but for the return journey to Europe sailing vessels have to follow an enormous arc across the Azores. The fastest and shortest route lies along the very equator, but this route is fraught with difficulties.* Therefore, although it was not impossible to obtain information about America in antiquity, there were many obstacles to the flow of this information, making it extremely casual.

Hence, in this book we shall confine ourselves to the myths, legends and traditions of the Mediterranean peoples that may have a direct bearing on Plato's story of Atlantis.

A great deal of the information interesting us may be drawn from Greek myths and legends. It should be noted that the value of these myths and legends is that the ancient Greeks borrowed much from the other Mediterranean peoples, primarily from the Cretan-Aegean civilisation, which is also known as the *Minoan* civilisation (254a). In our view the *Minoan, which was the most brilliant civilisation of prehistoric Europe, should be given a special place in the Atlantis problem because it evidently had a wide sphere of contact with numerous peoples in both the east and the west, in this respect surpassing even the Phoenician and Carthaginian civilisations*. Thus, indisputable archaeological data prove that the influence and trade relations of Crete embraced not only the entire Mediterranean basin but also the British Isles, the Iberian Peninsula, the Canary Islands and Senegal in the west and India in the east. Let us recall that tin bars in the shape of swallow tails, traditional in Crete, have been found in the south of England (419/I, 121). R. Hennig (419/I, 72) writes that ample data is available to show that in about 3000-2700 B.C. the Cretans worked the mines in the Iberian Peninsula. He writes: "Convincing conclusions have now been arrived at that the most important islands of the Canary and Madeira groups were discovered not by the Phoenicians but by the Cretans. The seemingly proud glory of the Phoenicians is steadily fading." Generally, he reasonably considers that Phoenician trade flourished only in the period 1200-500 B.C., i.e., after the fall of the Minoan power, but that it was unlikely that the Phoenicians penetrated far beyond the Strait of Gibraltar. At the same time Cretan frescoes provide incontestable proof that the Cretans brought Negro mercenaries from Africa and imported monkeys from Senegal (365/214, 218). The portrayal on Cretan vases of flying fish, which are typical of oceans, favours, as I. A. Yefremov (32) points out, the assumption that Cretan navigators frequently sailed not only in the western part of the Mediterranean but also in the equatorial zone of the Atlantic. The finding of Cretan beads at Mohenjo-Daro (315/137) is an indication that Cretan trade relations reached as far as India.

The Minoan civilisation was discovered only in the first decades of

---

* See p. 195.

the 20th century. This, apparently, explains the circumstance that data on the achievements of that civilisation have not yet been fully appreciated by many modern historians, who continue to cling to 19th-century notions that assess everything linked up with Greece and Greek culture without taking into account the possibility that a Minoan civilisation existed.

Evidently, *the Minoans were not only intrepid navigators but also excellent geographers.* There is outward evidence that they might have been the authors of the first geographical maps (146/70). We feel that this assumption commands attention because it is difficult to picture regular travel in the western part of the Mediterranean and in the Atlantic without written guides and at least primitive maps.

There is no doubt that the ancient Greeks obtained much of their geographical information from what remained of Minoan culture in their day. Archaeological finds on some of the islands in the Mediterranean show that the Mycenaeans, who were the first successors of the Minoans, obtained a great deal of knowledge from their predecessors but, subsequently, after the Dorian invasion and the destruction of the Mycenaean kingdom, this knowledge was lost. We consider that we have ample grounds for supposing that *the Minoan power and its metropolis, Knossus, were destroyed with the active participation of the Phoenician navy.* It seems to us that in the fading of the Minoan power into oblivion the Phoenicians played the same role that was later played by their successors, the Carthaginians, in the destiny of the mysterious town of Tartessos, which we shall deal with in some detail below (113; 133; 719).

Furthermore, we hold that *the discrepancies in the information later collected by the Greeks are due to the geographical and political changes which took place after the destruction of the Minoan kingdom.* That introduced confusion in many legends and myths. An example is the geographical knowledge which the ancient Greeks had of the west: this territory, well known to the Cretans in 3000-2000 B.C. and later to the Mycenaeans, became known to the Greeks only in the 1st millennium B.C. Besides, this knowledge was gained gradually. For that reason, side by side with the extensive geographical knowledge of remote times there existed the naive and limited knowledge of a later period. This is strikingly brought to light by a study of Homer and Hesiod. J. O. Thomson (146/53) points out that much of Homer's seemingly meaningless information is simply a poor delivery of the once more extensive information available to the Minoans. R. Hennig (419/I, 74) is more emphatic on this point: *"In the course of many centuries (and frequently up to our day) students of antiquity considered that the geographical knowledge of the ancient Hellenes of Homer's epoch did not reach farther westward than Corfu or, at best, Sicily. This notion, in itself improbable, may now, without fear of contradiction, be called a prejudice. Research into prehistoric times has put an end to such erroneous notions* (my italics—*N. Z.*). It has now been proved that as long ago as the Mycenaean epoch (1650-

1200 B.C.), i.e., in the course of many centuries before Homer, the Hellenes had firm cultural and trade relations not only with Sicily but also with Western Italy. Moreover, the influence of Mycenaean culture can be traced right up to modern Portugal." However, to this day one still encounters assertions that the Greeks learned of the West much later (25).

In myths there is an extremely interesting reference to a mysterious land called Lyktonia, which Poseidon destroyed in anger. This mythical kingdom is mentioned in an Orphic hymn in which the Orphic Argonaut relates: "The dark-haired Poseidon grew angry at the father of Kronos and crushed Lyktonia with a blow of his golden trident." We know nothing about this kingdom, but from the above phrase we can only draw the conclusion that it was the kingdom of Kronos and was swallowed by the ocean. Greek and Italian (Roman) *myths link the name of Kronos (the Roman Saturn) up with a large island or continent in the ocean far in the west.* According to Roman myths this was a happy land which annually marked the festival of Saturn. H. Muller (620/470) *identifies Lyktonia directly with Atlantis.*

By and large, Greek mythology speaks of several islands in the distant west, in the ocean. These included the *Isles of the Blest with their Elysium,* where spring reigned eternally and the refreshing zephyr constantly blew. It was where Zeus' favourite immortals dwelt. Later these islands were identified with the *Fortunate or Makaros Isles* (Melcarthes as they were known to the Phoenicians), which were usually taken to mean the Canary Islands (249/53-57). Somewhere in the far west were the *Hesperides* with their miraculous apple orchard: the procuring of apples from this orchard was one of the labours of Hercules. Some investigators maintain that the golden apples of the Hesperides were citrus fruit, others, for example, A. Schulten (419/I,67), consider that they were the fruit of the strawberry tree (*Arbutus canariensis*), which grows on the Canary Islands. Farther away from the Hesperides were the *Gorgada Isles,* the homeland of the Amazons. Sometimes it is assumed that they are the Cape Verde Islands. On the whole, the Fortunate Isles are mentioned in different variants by antique writers: Pseudo-Aristotle [*De mirabilibus auscultationibus*] [84], Diodorus Siculus [V, 19], Plutarch Sertorius) Pliny [VI, 36], and Pomponius Mela [III, 10] to name a few.

Among the surviving Greek legends there is one in which some of the details amazingly coincide with much of the data about Atlantis as given by Plato. It is that part of Homer's *Odyssey* which describes the adventures of Odysseus in *Scheria,* land of the Phaeacians. Hennig (158) emphatically identifies both these countries as well as Tartessos, a metropolis that we shall deal with below. Indeed, *the fact that many of the details coincide gives us grounds for assuming that, in any case, for the "Critias" Plato might have used Homer's account of Scheria, particularly for his description of the Atlantean capital.* This assumption is backed up by the fact that Homer's *Odyssey* was undoubtedly well known to Plato.

First, a few words about the possible origin of the *Odyssey*. I. M. Trotsky (237/XIX) writes in his commentaries: "In the pattern of Greek mythology there is only one major legend which does not spring from the seats of Mycenaean culture. It is the legend of Odysseus, king of Ithaca. The entire group of northwestern islands, to which Ithaca belongs, was inhabited as early as the Neolithic, but remained a distant outskirt, and excavations have not brought to light any traces of Mycenaean culture. The setting of the legend in Ithaca, an exception from the general rule, shows that *the story of Odysseus is founded on material of a different type than the Mycenaean saga* (my italics.—*N. Z.*) and re-emphasises the originality of these legends. Other mythological seats have led archaeologists to the discovery of ancient cultures, which made it possible to establish the historical basis of the saga; Ithaca proved to be a false trail. It did not lead to any historically important reality." Consequently, *the Ithaca in the "Odyssey" is not one of the Ionian Islands but some outlying island in the west and not necessarily inhabited by Greeks.* Trotsky goes on to point out that *Odysseus himself is a strange and probably pre-Hellenic personality*. The Etruscans likewise knew of Odysseus by the name of Uthsta, whose meaning remains a puzzle. S. A. Kovalevsky, who has studied the portrayals on Greek vases, drew the conclusion that Odysseus was a circumcised Ethiopian. The following statement by I. M. Trotsky (p. XX) is extremely significant: "Very probably, therefore, the *story of Odysseus contains echoes of a more ancient historical reality than the culture of the Mycenaean period*" (my italics.—*N.Z.*).

It is obvious that *all this shows, firstly, that certain parts of the "Odyssey" date back to great antiquity and that the legend was threaded together by Homer from several historically and geographically different legends and applied by him to the history of the Trojan war and, secondly, that the most important parts of the "Odyssey" are of purely Western, non-Greek origin.* This hypothesis is indirectly borne out by the exceptional vagueness of how Odysseus got to the ocean. This brings out that the history of the wanderings of a western hero, merged into a single personality with the Odysseus of the *Iliad*, was artificially linked up with the myth about the Trojan war.

Properly speaking, there are two distinct parts in the travels of Odysseus: first by some incomprehensible route (perhaps via the Black Sea, Manych, the Caspian, the Volga and the post-glacial Lake Marimarussa, as S. A. Kovalevsky assumes) he reaches the Extreme North where he sees Aurora Borealis ("dances of the goddess Eos"), gives an account of some Northern peoples and then goes on to the ocean. The part of the journey interesting for us begins as follows. To avenge the slaughter by Odysseus' companions of the sacred bulls of Helios, the sun god, on the island of Trinacria, lightning strikes and sinks the ship as it sails southward. Odysseus loses all his companions, and nine days later the current brings him to Ogygia, the island of the sea nymph Calypso, daughter of Atlas (according to Hesiod she was the daughter of Oceanus), and lived a carefree life with her in a high cave for seven years.

Ogygia was thickly wooded; it was watered by four parallel streams. Nearby was an enigmatic abyss, the navel of the sea, possibly some whirlpool.* Hennig (555/46-47) considers that this was nothing more than an indication that Ogygia was situated far in the open sea, somewhere near the centre of the ocean as it was known in prehistoric times. Homer likewise indicates that Ogygia was the home of Atlas, who supported the columns on which the sky rested, i.e., evidently the implication being that there was a range of tall mountains. The flora on Ogygia, mentioned in the *Odyssey*, is interesting; it included pines, cypresses, alder-trees, olive-trees, lemon-trees, thujas, vine and celery. The cypresses, vine and lemon-trees are an indication that Ogygia was undoubtedly situated in the warm latitudes.

There were several points of view with regard to the location of Ogygia. Proponents of the Mediterranean version believed it was in the Aegean Sea or that it was the Island of Malta. Hennig (555/42) reasonably points out that the Mediterranean was too small if we take into account the fact that Odysseus' voyage took eighteen days. Even if his ship sailed at one-third of the speed of a sailing vessel of antique times it would have covered about 1,000-1,200 kilometres. According to Pliny [XIX, 1], with a fair wind behind it, a sailing vessel travelled 1,000 stadia (about 185 kilometres) in 24 hours. *From what Homer says, namely that Calypso was the daughter of Atlas, it may be inferred that Ogygia was situated in the Atlantic Ocean.* As Hennig (158/40) points out, in view of the custom of the ancients to personify geographical data, this indication is quite sufficient. U. von Wilamowitz-Mollendorf (700) emphasises that according to Homer Ogygia was an island in the ocean and was frequented by the gods because it was situated far from the known world. Indeed, Hermes who was sent to rescue Odysseus [V,100] reluctantly undertook the task, pointing to the boundlessness of this sea and asking if there were towns around it. Regarding Ogygia's location in the Atlantic, there are three assumptions. The first is that the island must have been situated in the northwestern part of the ocean. This viewpoint is based on the passage in the *Odyssey* [V, 227] where it states that on his return voyage from Ogygia Odysseus had the constellations Auriga, Pleiades and Ursa Major constantly on his left and the latter "revolved" overhead, never descending to the horizon. On these grounds O. Rudbeck (90) sited Ogygia between the 51st and the 64th parallel. However, A. Breusing (473), whom Hennig regards as extremely competent where navigation is concerned, considers that this passage of the *Odyssey*

---

* This has something in common with Ginungagap, the great whirlpool mentioned in ancient Norse sagas

only means that the images of the stars were in the front left side, an indication that Odysseus travelled from the south-west to the north-east. Agreeing with Breusing and taking into account Ogygia's warm climate, Hennig (158/42) believes that it was situated in the south-west and identifies it with Madeira, thus concurring with Humboldt. Hennig (555/45) points out that on the basis of computations given to him by Erpelt and Villiger, who analysed what Homer said about the location of the constellations, *Ogygia must have been situated between the 30th and 35th parallels* and that the voyage was accomplished in October. We feel that the weak points of this hypothesis are, first, that the date of Odysseus' voyage is not known (knowledge of the date would have enabled us to determine the location of the constellations); second, after eighteen days at sea Odysseus reached the island of Scheria, which was, evidently, situated east or north-east of Ogygia. *At present there is no island north or north-east of Madeira that might be identified as Scheria.** Besides, Madeira does not have a tall enough mountain that could have been the Atlas of the ancients; Pico Ruivo is only 1,860 metres above sea level. According to the third variant, suggested by E. Sykes (109), Ogygia was situated in the region of the Azores; perhaps it was Corvo, which has numerous caves. True, the Azores lie farther north than Erpelt and Villiger calculated (between the 35th and 40th parallels), but this difference may possibly be explained by the fact that the dating of the events was different from that accepted by these authors.

Ogygia is also mentioned by Pseudo-Plutarch in the 1st-2nd century A.D. [*De facia in orbe lunae*] (367). He related an interesting legend that is, possibly, of Carthaginian origin. According to Pseudo-Plutarch, Ogygia was situated five-days' journey west of Britain. If we accept Herodotus' [IV, 36] calculation that in the course of one day a ship sailed from 1,000 to 1,200 stadia, i.e., 185-200 kilometres, this would be a journey of about 1,000 kilometres. In addition, there were three other islands situated at equal distances from Ogygia.** One of these interests us because over it every year in the course of 30 days the sun sets for only one hour. O. Rudbeck (90) locates this island on the 66th parallel, which corresponds to Iceland.

With respect to Ogygia these three islands were situated primarily in the direction of the summer sunset (i.e., WNW). According to the legend, Zeus imprisoned his father Kronos on one of these islands, and the sea around it became known as the Kronos Sea. At a distance of some 5,000 stadia (about 1,000 kilometres) from Ogygia there was a large continent, which could be reached only by row-boats from Ogygia or, better still, from the other islands. Sailing vessels

---

* In these places oceanographical expeditions have discovered the Horseshoe Archipelago, which sank in the recent geological past.
** The report of three islands in the Atlantic probably has some connection with the Marcellus Islands mentioned by Proclus. It may be assumed that there were grounds for mentioning them.

could not negotiate the sea because of the silt brought by the continent's numerous rivers. This pollution gave rise to the belief that the sea looked as though it were frozen. This indicates that the shelf was shallow, like the off-shore tidal marsh in the North Sea, which may be linked with recent subsidences. The coast of the continent, we are told, was inhabited by Hellenes, who lived round a gulf larger than the Palus Maeotis (Sea of Azov) and almost equal in size to the Caspian. These Hellenes claimed descent from the Greeks who came with Hercules, settling there and inter-breeding with the people of Kronos. For that reason they paid more homage to Hercules than to Kronos. Every thirty years, when the star Kronos Niktur, or Phaenon, joined the constellation Taurus, an expedition with an embassy was sent to "our continent". C. Brasseur de Bourbourg (470) points out that on that day (end of the 19th century) this planet (Saturn), which symbolises the beginning of the spring equinox, was in the constellation Pisces, and that it was in the middle of the constellation Taurus in the year 3096 B.C.

Generally, depending on the precession of the equinoxes, which has a cycle of 26,000 years, the spring equinox in the different epochs conforms to the different points along the ecliptic. Professor M. M. Kamensky (574) offers the following table:

Sign of the Zodiac	Arc of the ecliptic	Era
Aquarius	300—330°	1950 A D.—4100 A D.
Pisces	330—360°	200 B.C.—1950 A.D.
Aries	0—30°	2350 B C.—200 B C.
Taurus	30—60°	4500 B C —2350 B C
Cancer	90—120°	8800 B C.—6650 B C
Leo	120—150°	10950 B.C —8800 B.C.
Virgo	150—180°	13100 B C —10950 B.C.
Libra	180—210°	15250 B.C.—13100 B.C.
Scorpius	210—240°	17400 B.C.—15250 B.C.
Sagittarius	240—270°	19550 B.C.—17400 B.C.
Capricorn	270—300°	21700 B.C.—19550 B.C.

Consequently, the epoch dealt with in the legend corresponds to events of great antiquity and not to the time described by Pseudo-Plutarch.

Let us return to Odysseus when he reaches the island of Scheria on the 18th day of his journey (after travelling a distance of approximately 3,000 kilometres).

Scheria was a wooded and mountainous island with steep banks surrounded by sharp reefs and cliffs. The shipwrecked Odysseus found it possible to reach land only in the mouth of a large river, where he spent the night in an olive grove and complained of the morning hoar-frost and the cold mist. *Scheria was inhabited by Phaeacians, evidently, a dark-skinned sea-faring people* (158/49), who had once lived in Hyperia ("Distant" or "Upper" land), and their neighbours were the wild and warlike Cyclopes with whom they were continually at war. As Homer further tells us, they were resettled by Nausitous, son of Poseidon, on Scheria, which was far from all the trade routes. They were the best sailors in the world and had fabulously swift ships, but they were suspicious of foreigners. They made only one journey to Greece, taking to Euboea the Cretan hero Radamantus, who subsequently lived permanently on the Fortunate Isles, and also visited Tityus, son of Gaea. *Consequently, the Phaeacians were western seafarers, whose existence was known in pre-Hellenic Crete.*

This, in our opinion, makes it probable that the *Scheria story is of Cretan origin and that, perhaps, the Fortunate Isles were situated near Scheria (550/50, 59).* With the help of the Phaeacians, Odysseus returned home to Ithaca; during the journey he was half-asleep.

Poseidon, who kept venting his wrath on Odysseus, now turned on the Phaeacians for accompanying the latter on his journey to Ithaca. On the homeward voyage the ship of the Phaeacians hit a rock near the shore and was itself turned into a rock. Long before that happened Poseidon caused a tall mountain to rise near the capital of Scheria, and Alcinous was afraid that in his anger the god would enclose the town with rocks as his (Alcinous') father Nausitous had prophesied. However, it is not known if that prophesy came true because Homer does not mention it again. But one thing is clear, namely that the appearance of a large rock near the capital and the formation of new rocks along the shore permit us to suppose that *there was a great deal of tectonic activity in Scheria. Moreover,* this implies that *some accounts about Scheria seeped through to the Mediterranean area after Odysseus' journey.*

Hennig (158/162), who identifies Atlantis as Scheria, has reduced some of the elements of similarity between them into a single table. Given the desire, one could compile a table of discrepancies whose number would likewise be large. It is, therefore, impossible to say that the identity is indisputable. However, Plato might have used much of Homer's information, which he undoubtedly knew, as supplementary material for the "Hellenisation" of his *Critias*. It is also possible that he might have known the original source of the *Odyssey*, the so-called "periplus of Odysseus". *In the final analysis it is not known where and when Scheria existed or what sort of island it was except that it was situated in the Atlantic. The description of Scheria does not fit any of the islands in the Atlantic today, so perhaps in the days of the Minoans the remains of Atlantis were still to be seen.*

We think *there are grounds for assuming that Odysseus' travels in the western ocean may be a partial rehash or continuation of a more ancient legend, in particular, of the Sumerian Gilgamesh epic* (443). Closely intertwined in this cycle of myths are an account of a king of the same name who reigned in Uruk, Mesopotamia, some time between 2800 and 2700 B.C., and the myth of a more ancient hero, unquestionably a traveller, who "saw everything up to the edge of the world, who sailed the seas and crossed all the mountains". Here is how the hero of the epic describes himself: "I have wandered for many years, travelled across all countries, climbed difficult mountains and sailed across all the seas" (443/70). According to V. I. Avdiyev (181/118), the main part of the epic dates back to extremely remote antiquity, the 4th millennium B.C., at least.

The part that interests us most describes Gilgamesh's journey to Utnapishtim, the ancestor of the Sumerians. This hero of Sumerian-Babylonian mythology was the only human survivor of a world-wide deluge, and the gods made him immortal. He was taken to an island situated beyond the confines of the inhabited world, from which the island was separated by a Great River (Oceanus) with "waters of death" (443/102, 193). His journey took him across deserts, "mountain passes guarded by lions", to the edge of the world, to the Mashu Mountains, "which the sunset and the sunrise guarded daily" (443/57). Monsters who were half-men and half-scorpions kept watch over these mountains. Further, Gilgamesh journeyed through a garden of the gods where the ground was strewn with precious stones, and found himself on the shore of an ocean, where he met the goddess Siduri-Sabitu: "Mistress of the gods, Siduri lives deep in the sea" (443/63). Like Calypso in the *Odyssey*, Siduri wanted Gilfamesh to live with her, promising him all the blessings of life, but he refused. He found the ferryman Urshanabi, who had once ferried Utnapishtim, "and they accomplished a six weeks' journey in three days, and Urshanabi headed his boat into the 'waters of death' " (443/68). Instead of oars, they used poles, to the number of 120, which they threw away one after another. Upon his arrival at Utnapishtim's Gilgamesh learned that the tree of life (immortality) had perished in the deluge. On the advice of Utnapishtim he found the grass of immortality on the floor of the ocean, returned with it to the shore, but there it was stolen from him by a snake. This myth, undoubtedly, *tells of Gilgamesh's travels in the west.* This is borne out by the following words of the hero: "I wandered about the mountains on a distant journey away from the rising sun"(443/66).

A group of German scholars—O. Jessen (70), R. Hennig (158) and A. Schulten (662)—advanced and energetically upheld the theory that in the Atlantis legend Plato actually described *Tarshish* or *Tartessos*, an ancient town in Western Europe (16; 330/202-220). Schulten writes: "It is difficult to understand why Atlantis was looked for everywhere, even on Spitzbergen and in America, except in Tartessos. This was extremely illogical, because anyone attributing any reality to the myth, should have looked for Atlantis not in unknown but in known places." A similar view was held by A. V. Mishulin (330/25), who pointed out that the "impression conveyed by the Greeks about Tartessos as far back as the journeys of the Phaeacians might indeed have served as material for a much later myth, which Plato related in his story of Atlantis". This theory has received backing from Y. V. Knorozov as well (22).

Under the name Tarshish this town was known to the ancient Hebrews and is mentioned in some of the books of the Bible. The earliest mention of it dates back to the year 730 B.C., while Ezekiel [27/12] (about 580 B.C.) notes that silver, tin, lead and iron were brought from Tarshish. The ancient Hebrews traded with Tarshish through the Tyrian Phoenicians, who founded a colony—Gades, called Gadir by the Greeks (according to legend, in about the year 1100 B.C.)—somewhere near it.

The origin of the name "Tartessos" is interesting. A. Rousseau-Liessens (88) assumes that the name "Tarshish" derived from the Berber word "tarsets", meaning "columns of stone". He associates this name with the legend of the Pillars of Hercules. Obviously, the Greek *name "Tartessos" with its "ss" suffix indicates that the Cretans knew of this town.* J.D.S. Pendlebury (365/285) maintains that in many geographical names the "ss" suffix is a survival of Cretan names.

Many ancient writers and later researchers identified Tartessos with Gades. However, this is rejected by Macrobius, the Latin grammarian of the late 4th and early 5th centuries A.D., whose *Saturnalia* [I, 20, 12] contains an account of a sea battle between the Tartessians and Gadesians, in which the latter were victorious. True, we must make the reservation that Macrobious does not mention the Tartessians directly. He only speaks of the navy of Feron, king of Outer Spain. A. Schulten (662/76), I. S. Shifman (435) and other researchers identify this Feron with the king of Tartessos.

The Greeks knew of Tarshish by the name Tartessos. The identity of these names is vouched for by Polybius [III, 24], the Greek historian. According to Herodotus [IV, 152], the Greeks learned of the existence of Tartessos in about the year 660 B.C., when a storm carried Koleus past the Pillars of Hercules to Tartessos. Herodotus [I, 163] writes that Tartessos was ruled for 80 years by the king Arganthonius, who died at the age of 120. Koleus was received hospitably by this king and when he returned home he took with him a ton and a half of silver. But after the naval battle at Alalia in 537 B.C., when the Phaeacians were defeated by the combined navies of the Etruscans and the Carthaginians, the passage through the Strait was closed to the Greeks for three centuries. According to Pseudo-Scylax, who quotes the Greek historian Ephorus, Tartessos was situated at a distance of a two days' journey (about 400 kilometres) from the Pillars of Hercules (98).

What we have mentioned on these pages and the mention in myths that Zeus' last battle with the Titans[*] took place near Tartes-

---

[*] It seems to us that this myth is, perhaps, a mythologised echo of a tectonic subsidence, accompanied by a devastating earthquake, in the region of Tartessos.

sos is, properly speaking, almost all we know about Tartessos from ancient sources.

On the strength of this fragmentary data, Schulten (662) made a bold attempt to recapture the history and prehistory of Tartessos, and in this connection he suggested a number of intriguing hypotheses. Thus, he considers that Tartessos was subjugated by the Tyrians in about the year 800 B.C., but soon after Tyre's fall (about 750 B.C.), it became free. However, this freedom was shortlived, for in about 530 B.C. it was conquered by the Carthaginians, and by 500 B.C. completedly destroyed by invaders and ceased to exist altogether.

Among other surmises, Schulten assumes that Tartessos may also be identified with the legendary island of *Erytheia* in the myth about Hercules. Following in the footsteps of Stesichorus, the Greek lyric poet, who in about the year 600 B.C. wrote the lost epic *Heroneida*, which eulogises Tartessos and its king Heron, Schulten identifies this king with the mythical Herion, King of Erytheia. According to the myth, Hercules sailed across the ocean to the island of Erytheia, where he slew Herion near the River Antemus and took his bulls to Spain. Solinus writes that *the island of Erytheia was situated opposite Lusitania, Portugal.* Avienus (181/738) adds that Erytheia was inhabited by Ethiopians and Cyclops, and says that it was located somewhere near Gades.

We feel that by telling us that Hercules sailed to Erytheia not only by day but also by night, using something in the nature of a compass (a gift from the god Helios), the myth implies first and foremost that *Erytheia could not have been an island off the shore of Spain but was situated so far away it could not be seen from the continent, and therefore Hercules had to use the compass given him by Helios and sail for at least a day and a night.* But for a voyage of more than one or two days he would have had to have a large ship to carry a stock of food and water for the bulls. *Evidently, Erytheia was about 100 kilometres from Spain (or Portugal)* (129).

As we can see, no data can be produced to support Schulten's assumption that Tartessos was Erytheia and that it was one of the islands in the delta of the Guadalquivir. Taking this into account, Hennig (419/1,71) considers that attention should be given to J. Schoo's opinion that the myth about Herion may be linked up with some volcanic upheaval: in Greek the very name "Herion" derives from the words meaning "I am wailing". Schoo identifies Ortu, Herion's dog, with the maw of a roaring volcano. Hennig thinks it quite probable that Tenerife, one of the Canary Islands, was the very same island of Erytheia. He feels that this is confirmed by a legend which says that Herion was buried beneath trees from which blood dripped. Trees yielding a red resin, called dragon trees *(Dracena drago)*, are also known to have grown on the Madeira and other islands of the same area.

Schulten has some grounds for identifying the later Tartessians with the Turdetans, an Iberian tribe which was subsequently subjugated by the Romans. The Turdetans had reached a quite high level of political development. On the strength of a whole series of clever but not always sufficiently convincing suppositions, Schulten built up a harmonious concept, on whose foundation he localised Tartessos on an island in the mouth of the Guadalquivir. However, extensive excavations in that area yielded practically nothing. R. Meyer (419/1,77) recently made an attempt to identify Tartessos with Asta (now Jerez de la Frontera), but, as Hennig (419/1,456) pointed out, the excavations conducted there in 1948 were likewise barren.

It seems to us that all these failures in the search for Tartessos in Spain were not accidental. In our opinion the search was conducted in the wrong places. It should be identified not with Atlantis as a whole but only with the kingdom of Eumelus, Poseidon's second son, which, evidently, included a region in Spain adjoining Gades. This kingdom sank later than the others and, apparently, was still in existence as late as the 6th century B.C. To be more exact, only a small part of it, namely, the little island of Tartessos (129), remained in existence.

We believe that *at one time the route from Atlantis to Europe passed through the island of Tartessos and that the town of Tartessos was the capital of the new kingdom. From this standpoint it is quite logical to regard Tartessos as the direct successor of Atlantis and that this town was built not very long after Atlantis was destroyed.* Let us recall that according to Strabo [III, 1, 6], the Turdetans, who were identified with the Tartessians, had a recorded chronicle that went back to 6,000 years before his day. Besides, the Tartessians were probably not Iberians, because the earliest literary sources, as Schulten (662/78) deduces, regarded them as composed of different peoples. He reasonably notes that the ruling class was evidently a foreign people.

Chapter Five

ATLANTIS AND THE MEDITERRANEAN

While a comparison between Plato's Atlantis and the mythical Scheria or the legendary Tartessos may be justified on the grounds that they were situated in the Atlantic, it is extremely doubtful, as we have pointed out at the beginning of the book, if Plato's Atlantis was in the Mediterranean, particularly in its eastern part. Yet the surmise that Atlantis was somewhere in the Mediterranean (in contradiction to Plato's geographical data, as we have repeatedly stated) continues to be advanced now and then to this day. It would be worth while to take a close look at some of these theories.

I. A. Yefremov (32) gives the general foundation for these views: "There, on both shores and on the islands of the Mediterranean we must look for the cradle of all the great civilisations of antiquity such as those of Egypt and Atlantis. Where must we look for Atlantis—in the east or in the west of this great zone of Mediterranean cultures? The reply is given by the remains of the ancient civilisations of South and Central America, which have much in common with that of Egypt and which, evidently, owe their existence to contact with the western tip of the zone of Mediterranean cultures. I feel it is not at all necessary to consider that the existence of an island in the Atlantic explains the continuity between the Mediterranean and American cultures."

First and foremost, let us note the premise of E. M. Wishaw (118), who identifies his Pseudo-Atlantis with Andalusia in the same way as, much later, Y. V. Knorozov (22) identified Atlantis with Spain. Wishaw assumed that exploitation of the ancient ore mines began 8,000-10,000 years ago, in the Neolithic, and that the hydrotechnical structures at Niebla and Ronda were built even earlier, 12,000 years ago. The labyrinth-temple of the Sun, excavated at Seville, whose architecture resembles that of the royal tower in Niebla (49/125) evidently dates back to the same epoch. However, it should be noted that this dating is highly questionable and has not yet been checked by radiocarbon analysis, although there is every possibility (by the poppy heads in the tomb) to use this method to date the burial of the Amazon queen discovered in a cave near Granada and attributed to the same cultural cycle (49/155-156).

To varying degrees many atlantologists have linked up the location of their Pseudo-Atlantises with various regions of the Mediterranean, primarily those regions that were once subaerial.

A. Rousseau-Liessens (88) situated his Pseudo-Atlantis closer to the Pillars of Hercules than any of this group of atlantologists. He believed that the main kingdom of Atlantis occupied the western extremity of the Mediterranean, between the most southerly shore of Spain and North Morocco. He based himself on the notions, developed by E. le Danois, that in the Miocene there was land west of the Bethia-Riff Mountains and that in those days in place of the present-day Guadalquivir-Segura Valley there were the North Bethia Straits. South of the Riff Mountains in Morocco were the South-Riff Straits. These straits linked the Atlantic up with the Mediterranean (the Strait of Gibraltar was as yet non-existent). Rousseau-Liessens believed that these straits existed as far back as the Atlantis epoch. This opinion does not have sufficient grounds and is, generally speaking, implausible from the geological point of view.

The Mediterranean is fairly shallow between Sicily and Tunisia. There are vast sand banks and shoals. It may be considered as beyond all doubt that this region subsided recently and that there was a broad isthmus between Sicily and Tunisia. This isthmus existed as late as the Quaternary period. On the strength of these data and being an advocate of the view that the extreme west, as known to the Greeks in Homer's day, did not stretch beyond Tunisia and Sicily, F. Butavand (53) advanced the theory that Atlantis was situated in this region. In favour of his theory he quotes Marcellus's report of three islands in the Atlantic, considering that when the ancient Greeks referred to the Atlantic they really meant the Western Mediterranean, and that the island of Pluto was situated between Sicily and Tunisia; the island of Neptune (Atlantis) lay east of the island of Pluto, near the shores of the latter in the direction of Malta, while the Atlantean capital was situated near the present small island of Kerkennah off the coast of Tunisia. Possibly, in this region there were land, islands and even ancient settlements (incidentally, the report that divers had discovered submerged towns between Sicily and Tunisia (503) proved to be false), but the Atlantis of Butavand is not the Atlantis described by Plato. His theory has been comprehensively criticised by G. J. Bryant (52).

A similar concept has been built up by N. Russo (91), who linked up the Atlantis problem with the fate of Tyrrhenia, a land mass that once existed between Italy, Corsica and Sardinia but which is now the Tyrrhenian Sea. Russo regarded the enigmatic Etruscans, who created a brilliant civilisation in Western Italy in the 1st millennium B.C., as descendants of the Atlanteans. In support of this theory he quoted fragments of the work of Philochorus, a little known Greek historian who lived in the 3rd century B.C. M. Guignard (157/192) likewise believes that the Etruscans might have come from Atlantis and quotes the following Etruscan text, which he claims to have deciphered: "Rao [an augur] is sailing in the direction of Attarland-hit (land of ancestors), the island of giant women". The *Oera Linda Boek* (83a/59) likewise indicates that the Etruscans had originally come from Atlantis: "When Atland perished, they [the Etruscans] came to the shore of the Mediterranean." These views clash with the generally accepted theory that the Etruscans came from Asia Minor, from the east.

In passing it should be noted that many atlantologists believed that Atlantis was situated not in the Western Mediterranean, now covered by water, but in North-West Africa, in the territory now occupied by Morocco, Algeria and Tunisia.

E. F. Berlioux (38) was one of the first to expound the African variant. He considered that Atlantis occupied the area from Tunisia to Morocco and was separated from the Sahara by a shallow sea, which subsequently dried up and became a zone of impassable salt marshes. He attached extremely great importance to his Pseudo-Atlantis as a link between the Old and the New World.

C. Roux (89) also held similar views. He believed that during the Upper and Lower Quaternary there were, south of the Atlas Mountains, shallow, elongated salt-water lagoons stretching towards the Mediterranean and towards the Atlantic, and that these lagoons transformed North Africa into a flowering peninsula. He held that the Atlantean epoch occupied the span of time from the end of the Neolithic to the beginning of the Bronze Age, after which the lagoons dried up and the desert advanced.

A. Rutot (93), too, went back to the Moroccan variant. He considered that the Atlantean capital was situated six or seven kilometres from the mouth of the River Sousse.

An interesting point is that near Goulimine, south of Agadir, there live a tribe that have an intensely blue skin. S. Hutin (161/94) believes that this colour comes from the bright blue fabric worn by these people. However, a colour photograph* at our disposal belies this opinion—there is no hint in it of blue clothes. Moreover, taking into consideration that the ancient Egyptians gave their idols a blue or green skin, some atlantologists ventured the opinion that *the Atlanteans might have been a blue-skinned people* (35). Generally speaking, this possibility should not be ruled out because to this day there are tribes of blue-skinned Indians in the Andes of South America. The blue colour is due to oxygen hunger (cyanosis caused by high altitudes). On the other hand, a person's skin may be blue as a result of a change of the conditions under which melanin—dark pigment—is bedded.

Later P. Borchardt (44, 45), A. Herrmann (67) and other atlantologists came out in support of the African variant of Pseudo-Atlantis.

Like many other investigators before him, Borchardt maintained that the Atlantic of the ancients was part of the Mediterranean, and that the Pillars of Hercules were nothing more than the columns of a temple. Thus, these investigators followed the trail blazed by A. S. Norov, A. Karnozhitsky, A. Paniagua and others.

Herrmann, too, was inclined to think that in Solon's day neither Spain nor Morocco was known to the Greeks. This viewpoint, however, does not conform to reality, as we have already pointed out. Herodotus [IV, 152] wrote that Koleus sailed past the Pillars of Hercules and visited Tartessos (according to Hennig, about the year 660 B.C. [419/1,73]) long before Solon was born. Hennig (p. 80) says that the latest archaeological excavations made by Garcia Belido have proved that the Greeks had contact with Spain long before the time of Koleus. Moreover, on the problem of whether the Greeks knew of the existence of the Atlantic Ocean, he says (419/1,69): "I fully side with Schulten when he declares: 'The fundamental question of whether the Greeks of the time of Homer and Hesiod knew of the existence of the western ocean must surely be answered in the affirmative, in the same way as it was answered in antiquity.'" Consequently, *the latest findings show that the opinion formely held by most historians, linguists and students of literature that the Atlantic*

---

* A colour photograph of a blue-skinned Moroccan woman was published by the Polish journalist Marian Marzinski in the magazine *Dookola Swiata*, No. 295, August 23, 1959.

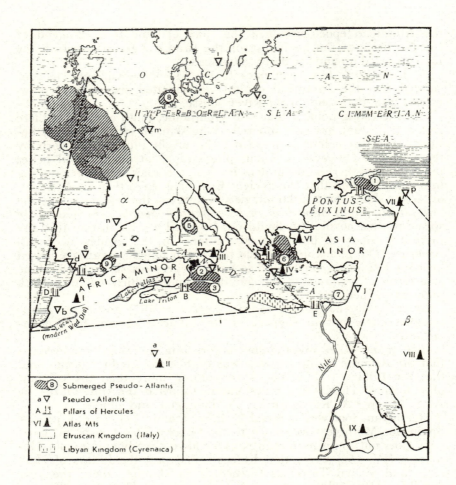

Localisation of Pseudo-Atlantises, Pillars of Hercules and Atlas Mountains in Europe and in the Mediterranean by different atlantologists; mainly after J. Imbelloni and A. Vivante (69/294), with additions by the author.

Submerged Pseudo-Atlantises

1. In the Sea of Azov, after M de Junnes and A. Paniagua; 2. in the Gulf of Syrtis (Gabes), after F. Butavand, 3 ditto, after L. Joleaud, 4. near the British Isles, after C. Beaumont, F. Gidon, P. Russo and F. Wilford; 5. in the Tyrrhenian Sea, after N. Russo, 6. in the Aegean Sea, after L. S. Berg and A. G. Galanopulos; 7. in the eastern Mediterranean, after A. S. Norov, A. Karnozhitsky and Mardo; 8. in the North Sea at Heligoland, after J. Spanuth; 9. in the western Mediterranean, after A. Rousseau-Liessens

Pseudo-Atlantises on Land

a. In the Ahaggar Mountains (central Sahara), after P. Benoît, D. A. Godron, B. Khun de Prorok; b. in Morocco, after E. F. Berlioux, Bruteau, L. Gentil, G. Lagneau, A. Rotot, and other authors; c on Tartessos, after E. Bjorkman, O. Jessen, A. V. Mishulin, R. Hennig and A. Schulten; d. in Gades (Cádiz), after V. Berard; e. in Spain, after Y. Knorozov, C. Cotte and E. M. Whishaw; f. in Tunisia, after P. Borchardt and A Herrmann; g. on Crete, after W. Brandenstein,

of the ancient Greeks was the Western Mediterranean is obsolete and conflicts with reality.

On the basis of notions similar to those of Herrmann, P. Statsenko lately suggested a new variant of Pseudo-Atlantis, namely that since the ancient Egyptians, from whom the Atlantis legend was obtained, knew nothing about the Atlantic Ocean, Sicily must be the Atlantis of that legend. By the Atlantic Ocean the ancient Egyptians, like the Greeks, meant the Western Mediterranean between Tunisia and the Strait of Gibraltar. On this point Statsenko is at one with Knorozov (22/215), who wrote: "Sicily lay beyond the world as it was known to the Egyptians." This is erroneous because by the time not only Plato but also Solon travelled in Egypt, the Egyptians knew of the existence of the Atlantic Ocean and the Pillars of Hercules. Herodotus [IV, 42] informs us that the pharaoh Nekho sent a Phoenician fleet on a voyage round Africa along the route Indian Ocean-Red Sea and Mediterranean-Strait of Gibraltar-Atlantic Ocean. Hennig (419) gives the date of this voyage as 596-594 B. C. and offers convincing arguments to show that it really took place. Such a voyage could not have been undertaken if the Egyptians knew nothing of the oceans and of the lanes of communication between them. Moreover, at the time Solon travelled in Egypt, there were Greeks and Phoenicians in the country and that could not but have extended the Egyptians' knowledge of geography. *There are, therefore, no grounds for believing that in the day of Solon and Plato the Egyptians were so illiterate geographically as to confuse the Western Mediterranean with the Atlantic. At this time, like the Greeks, the Egyptians unquestionably knew of the existence of the Atlantic.*

In connection with the invasion by "peoples of the sea" (507), the Egyptians could have had more or less exact information about a large sea in the west. Earlier, this information could have come

---

W Leaf, R. V. D. Magoffin, S. Uzin K. T. Frost; h. on Sicily, after P. Statsenko; i in Sweden, after O. Rudbeck; j. in Palestine, after F. C. Baer, C. M Olivier. J. Serranus and Eurenius; k. on Malta, after J. Bosco and Wasseau; 1. in central France, after J. L. Courseille-Seneuil; m in the Netherlands and Belgium, after C. J. Gravet and M Pollet; n. in Catalonia, after J. Verdaguer; o Kuursh Bay (Baltic), after Hafer; p. in the Caucasus, after J. B. C. Delisle de Sales and R. A. Fessenden.

Pillars of Hercules
A—classical, at the Strait of Gibraltar; B—near the Gulf of Gabès; C—in the Kerch Straits; D—coast on Morocco, E—in the Nile Delta; F—in Peloponnesos.

Atlas Mountains
I—in Morocco (modern Atlas Mountains); II—Ahaggar Mountains (classical Atlas Mountains); III—on Sicily (Etna); IV—on Crete (Ida); V—in Peloponnesos; VI—in Phrygia (Ida); VII—in the Caucasus (Elbrus); VIII—in Arabia (Jebel Atala); IX—in Ethiopia. The large dotted triangles under α and ß are regions of the so-called western (true) and eastern (Indo-Lemurian?) Atlantis, after J. Karst. The shaded region at the British Isles is land area which sank during the Flandrian and Lyonese transgressions

Thoth, an ancient Egyptian deity. This statuette is in the collection of the State Hermitage, Leningrad

from Crete, which had been carrying on a lively trade with Egypt as far back as the time of the first dynasties of the Ancient Kingdom (3000-2500 B.C.) (180/176). On Egyptian frescoes (146/33) the inhabitants of Keftiu (Crete) were portrayed as people with a red skin (hanebu).

If we go so far as to speak of sea voyages by the Egyptians themselves, we can of course question the viewpoint that the rock drawings in the Sahara (144/131) or at Tabarca, Tunisia (72/41) portray Egyptian ships; let us, furthermore, take note of the fact that the Mashwashi tribe of Tunisia was known to the Egyptians (146/32). As V. I. Avdiyev (180/185) points out, in the epoch of the Ancient Kingdom the Egyptians built ships and attached great importance to this industry. There are inscriptions telling of sea expeditions, for example, the inscription in the temple at Deir el-Bahri which says that the Queen Hatshepsut sent an expedition to the mysterious land of Punt somewhere on the shores of the Indian Ocean. Hennig (419/1,21) believes this expedition was sent in the year 1493-1492 B.C. G. Carter, the noted Egyptologist (266/177) wrote: "In our brief survey it is sufficient to mention that in the 15th century B.C. the islands of the Mediterranean were conquered by the Egyptians and called the 'Islands in the Middle of the Sea'." They were neither the islands in the Aegean Sea nor Minoan Crete, but of the Central or even Western Mediterranean. But a still larger sea expedition was, apparently, fitted out in a more remote period by Snofru, king of the IIIrd dynasty, who sent a fleet of 40 ships to the Lebanon (and also to Punt), as is borne out by the inscriptions on the Palermo Stone (146/24; 180/194).

The most ancient, purely mythological, data that may have a bearing on the Egyptians' knowledge of the legends of Atlantis and its destruction are linked up with the name of one of the most interesting and oldest deities of Western Egypt: *Thoth*. This god was regarded as the creator of sciences and art, the inventor of a written language and the patron of libraries, and is somehow linked up with the cult of the Moon. Moreover, his name is associated with the invention of scales, water clocks and the measure of length. He was patron of scientists and architects, being the only god of different peoples to play this role. The invention of alchemistry is also attributed to him.

An interesting point is that the ancient Mexicans had a divinity whose name was very similar. He was called Teot, Teut or Teute. He played the role of civiliser and, like the Hellenic Atlas, supported the sky (470/CXVI). The same concerns another divinity, *Quetzalcoatl*, civiliser of the Toltec-Aztecs. An idol of this god is extant. According to legend, Quetzalcoatl came from the east and also supported the sky. Possibly, the two divinities are identical. This problem requires careful and unbiased study. There are no grounds for Knorozov's (22/217) opinion that Quetzalcoatl is the deified king Tollan (Topiltzin Se Acatl).

The fact is that one of the steles indeed has a reference to Topiltzin Se Acatl Quetzalcoatl. But, as Knorozov himself (2740/22) writes: "Topiltzin had the title of Quetzalcoatl inasmuch as, apparently he was, at the same time, the high priest of the god Quetzalcoatl." Consequently, the god Quetzalcoatl and his high priest Topiltzin were not one and the same person. Topiltzin evidently reigned in about the years 923-946 A.D. He was, indeed, forced to flee to Yucatan (where Quetzalcoatl had the local name Cuculcan), but later he returned to Ascapotsalco, Mexico, where he died. As regards the god Quetzalcoatl, his cult existed long before the birth of Topiltzin; a temple to him was erected in Mitla, by the Toltec king Mitl, who reigned in about 770-829 A.D. (211/55, 200).

A fascinating study of the god Thoth was published in 1898 by the well-known Russian Egyptologist B.A. Turayev (403).

As sources for this study he used mainly the *Writings of the Pyramids* (inscriptions on pyramids of the Vth-VIth dynasty), the *Book of the Dead*, a collection of rituals for the dead (fully compiled only in the Sais epoch), and the *Writings of the Sarcophaguses* (VIth-VIIth dynasty). All these texts are written in the name of a deceased identified with one of the gods.

The ancient Hellenes identified Thoth with their Hermes and called him Hermes Trismegistos (thrice greatest) on the strength of epithets in ancient hieroglyphic inscriptions (403/164). Later antique authors, the Euhemerists and the Neo platonists, believed Thoth was an ancient king of Egypt. For example, the Egyptian priest and historian Manetho (4th-3rd century B.C.), who generally merits attention (180/137; 394), wrote of three kings of that name: Thoth I, Thoth II and his son Thath, whom the gods took to heaven. Thath is known as a divinity as well (266/195).

There is an interesting reference to a long and futile search for some IPWT of Thoth,* whose number was extremely important to Khufu (Cheops), first king of the IVth dynasty in the building of his pyramid (403/49).

The seat of the Thoth cult was at Ashmunein (Hermopolis), capital of Hare Nome in Upper Egypt. This nome was, in fact, independent at the close of the Old Kingdom and throughout the period of the Intermediate Kingdom. The position of Thoth in the pantheon of ancient Egyptian deities is not quite clear. The reason for this is, evidently, that the glorification of priests and the cult of Ra began as early as the period of the Vth dynasty (3rd millennium B.C.) (180/199). In ancient writings Thoth is described as an extremely powerful god and was referred to as "having existed from the very beginning", "unborn", "who created himself", "king of the ages" (403/164). He was a creator, who helped to break up the chaos (403/19). In some inscriptions he is mentioned side by side with the goddess Neith (*Book of the Dead*, chapters 114, 116 and 149). Later he is relegated to the octet of "deities of the 2nd rank", and according to various sources occupied different places in the genealogy of Egyptian deities (403/23, 27, 41).

There is good reason to believe that *although Thoth was an ancient deity he was introduced from some western land*. In all ancient hieroglyphic inscriptions he is linked up with the west, which was dedicated to him. In Chapter 161 of the *Book of the Dead* he plays the same role that the Hellenes ascribed to Atlas—he supports the vault of the heavens at its four corners. In the inscriptions of the pharaoh Userir-An, Thoth is called the "ruler of overseas lands". He is also called by the puzzling name of "providential guide of both lands" (east and west?) (403/54).

Usually he was portrayed with the head of an ibis, and most of his body—statues and also portrayals on sarcophaguses—was painted green.

The data on Thoth's birthplace are also interesting. In the inscription on the pyramid of the Pharaoh Pepi I (VIth dynasty) his name is mentioned in connection with the undeciphered name of a town, but, as B.A. Turayev (403/24) points out, this town was not Hermopolis, which is not mentioned in the *Writings of the Pyramids*. Thoth's birthplace is named in Chapter 24 of the *Book of the Dead* and in the hymn of the Pharaoh Ramses IV. It is the mysterious, undeciphered "lake of the flame of NSRSR", the "lake of two fires" (403/119-120). Many ancient writings refer to the "lake of Thoth" (403/34, 57). It should be borne in mind that *the ancient Egyptians had no direct knowledge of volcanic activity*. If we assume that people from volcanic localities came to Egypt in some remote age this might explain the vague references to volcanoes and why, as time went by, these references became incomprehensible and acquired the aura of fantasy.

---

* It has not been deciphered whether this is an object or a computation

Of the later writings that may be linked up with Thoth's birthplace, there are some that deal with a mysterious land called Siriat (57/102; 562). Joseph Flavius wrote that the sons of Seth, who lived in a happy land, possessed great knowledge, particularly of the elements of fire and water; they erected columns, one of brick and the other of stone, on which they made inscriptions about all their achievements. These columns were in the land of Siriat. In the *Chronicon*, Eusebius of Caesarea noted that Manetho, according to the latter's own words, drew the material for his history of the ancient dynasties of Egypt from inscriptions made by Thoth (Hermes) in the sacred language of hieroglyphs. These inscriptions were on columns that Thoth had built in Siriat (59). After the deluge they were translated and recorded in the books of Agathodemon, son of the second Hermes and father of Thath, and were hidden in secret hiding places in temples of Egypt.* Lore has preserved the tradition that Thoth had recorded extensive knowledge in 42 secret books called the *Souls of Ra*. These books were, apparently, in existence because they are mentioned in ancient inscriptions; moreover, there is testimony by later eye-witnesses, who claimed to have seen these books during religious processions. A still more curious note is to be found in the ancient Egyptian narrative *Satna*, which says that a book of Thoth was hidden in the sea and that anybody stealing it, as had once happened, would be severely punished (403/87).

All the books of Thoth, as all the books of the Egyptian priests, were probably destroyed on orders from the Roman emperor Diocletian.

There is a myth which says that Thoth saved other deities during a cosmic catastrophe on the Sun, which was "ill" after it had been "abused" by somebody (Chapter 123, *Book of the Dead*). Thoth's role of saviour is mentioned in chapters 17 and 97 of the *Book of the Dead* (403/42, 56, 58). Further, employing wings, Thoth carried the deities to the eastern side of the sky, "to the far side of Lake Ha" (403/31). Many researchers regard this myth as symbolising the daily movement of the Sun or even as a description of a solar eclipse, but the first assumption is contradicted by the statement that the Sun was "ill", and the second by the long and terrible struggle that took place at the time and by the disappearance of the Sun (Chapter 17, *Books of the Dead*).

If we sum up all that we have said about Thoth, we shall get the following somewhat fantastic picture (18/20). *Thoth came from a distant land, perhaps, that happy western land of Amenti, where the souls of the dead passed on to Aaru.*** In that land there was a town by a large lake or a sea, and in its vicinity were two active volcanoes.*

---

* Hennig (555/49) identifies Siriat with Madeira, while Dörpfeldt thinks it might even have been Malta or Pantelleria, but there are little grounds for both these assumptions.
** The Elysium of the Greeks.

Then some cosmic events took place in the land of Thoth's birth, and the Sun was eclipsed for a long span of time. Perhaps this eclipse was due to the eruption of a volcano. In any case, the gods were terrified. Thoth, who was the wisest among them, helped them to flee to the east across a large lake or sea. While they were on their way the Sun returned to its normal state. There is a possibility that this myth is an echo of the catastrophe that overwhelmed Atlantis.

Herodotus [II, 142-144] notes that according to what Egyptian priests had told him and his own observations (he saw 341 statues of high priests), the history of Egypt began 11,340 years before his visit to that country (this would correspond approximately to 11780 B.C.); prior to that the land was ruled by a dynasty of gods. However, O. Muck (80) thinks that Herodotus' calculation of the reign of each of the high priests is much too high. He feels it would be more correct to assume that there were four or five and not three generations per century. Thus, on the average, each high priest ruled for 20-25 years, which gives the total as 7,000-8,000 years. L. Zajdler (119/256) fundamentally agrees with Muck, but gives a lower average figure—17 years, which adds up to a total of 5,865 years.

The existence of the legendary dynasty of gods is confirmed by the Palermo Stone annals, which give the names of ten semi-divine kings; by the Turin Papyri, which state that this dynasty reigned 5,613 years before Menes united Egypt; and by the Egyptian historian Manetho, who dates it as 5,813 years before Menes. This gives us two dates when the reign of the demigod dynasty began: 10061 B.C. (according to Manetho) and about 9850 B.C. (according to the Turin Papyri). The latter date seems closer to the truth, *while the ten demigod pharaohs were the ten dynasties of Lower Egypt* which preceded the country's unification.

In the light of what Herodotus tells us, considerable interest attaches to what H. Alimen (182/134) writes about the prehistory of Egypt, namely: "All investigators agree that there is a gap between the end of the Paleolithic and beginning of the Neolithic in Egypt. It is quite possible that this developed Egyptian Neolithic partially originated outside Africa." Further Alimen notes that relics of the Badarian culture (5th millennium B.C.) include elements of foreign origin (182/141). It has been pointed out by J. de Morgan (333/117) that Egypt had no copper mines of her own and, consequently, the working of metal could not have originated there. Civilisation progressed remarkably in the Herzian epoch, which followed the Badarian period. The smelting and working of metal was developed, the working of stone reached an extremely high level of skill and a hieroglyphic type of writing, which has not yet been deciphered, was evolved. This culture arose in the Nile delta when the first brachycephalic tribes infiltrated into Egypt. A start was made in navigation on the Nile and in trade. Boomerangs, checkers and skittles were known. There are indications that the people were acquainted with iron and lead. This epoch has not been precisely dated (182/147-52).

Rock drawings on the road from Coptos (Gift) to the Red Sea portraying sea-going vessels with a high bow and stern show that foreign peoples invaded Egypt in the predynastic epoch. Drawings of these vessels have been discovered on a knife found at Jebel el-Arak. They are markedly different from the native ships (703).*

The apocryphal *Book of Enoch*, which is not recognised either by the Jewish or the Christian religions, likewise has references to some mysterious country far in the west, which might have been Atlantis. This book was probably written in the 2nd century B.C. The original is not extant, but a papyrus with a Greek translation of part of it has been found in Upper Egypt, and an Ethiopian translation exists in Ethiopia (606). Some investigators reasonably assume that the *Book of Enoch* was written much earlier than the other books of the Old Testament and was declared uncanonical as a consequence of major divergences from the official version; many parts of the *Genesis* are really plagiarisms of Babylonian myths (for example, the myth of the Deluge).

Generally speaking, Enoch is an extremely interesting personality of prehistoric Hebrew mythology. He was the fifth antedeluvian patriarch after Adam and was, allegedly, taken to heaven alive. He is associated with various mysterious occult sciences, including astrology and alchemistry. In *Chronicon*, Eusebius of Caesarea, one of the fathers of the Christian Church, says that according to the Babylonians Enoch invented astrology and that he was known to the Greeks as Atlas. For that reason Enoch is sometimes identified with Hermes Trismegistus.

Many passages in the *Book of Enoch* are interesting to atlantologists. Take the place where God shows Enoch a land in the west: "I was carried to the flame of the sunset, which consumes the setting of all suns, and to a fiery river, where fire flowed like water, draining into a great sea in the west. And I entered a great darkness where no flesh enters" [XVII, 4-6]. "And the Lord showed me a great mountain in the west. And in that mountain were deep and wide and slippery abysses; three of them were dark (rift valleys?—*N. Z.*) and one was light..." [XXII, 1]. "Over the light abyss there was a source of living water. And I went to another place, to the west, at the end of the world" [XXIII, 1]. "And I saw great and beautiful mountains that seemed to have been made of precious stones"** [XXIV, 1-6]. "And I saw valleys which were so deep and tortuous that none of them met" [XXIV, 2]. Further, Noah asks his grandfather Enoch: "What is happening in the land, what makes it labour and tremble so?" [LXV, 1-4]. From Enoch Noah learns of the impending Deluge, during which there were continuous earthquakes and "waters boiled" [LXXIX, 2-6]. This description does not tally with

---

* These vessels might have come from the valley of the Indus (Mohenjo-Daro, Harappa), a seat of prehistoric culture in India (642b).
** Perhaps glaciers?

the official Biblical version of the Deluge as given in *Genesis*. The mention of earthquakes preceding the Deluge is of particular interest. In our opinion, *the legend of the Deluge in the "Book of Enoch" might have been based on a western myth*, which the Hebrews could have learned from the Phoenicians, Philistines, Carthaginians or some other people. The Philistines, it will be remembered were the direct neighbours of the Hebrews and dominated them for some time. They were one of the "peoples of the sea". Biblical books state that they came from Crete (*Jeremiah* [47; 4]). Moreover, it is quite certain that the story of the voyage of the Carthaginian hero Hanno in the Atlantic, where for several days he sailed amid torrents of fire, was known at this period.

H. S. Bellamy (37/112-130) has made an attempt to find references to the destruction of Atlantis in Biblical texts, not in the narrations of the Deluge given in *Genesis* but in some of the prophets (Isaiah, Jeremiah, Ezekiel) and even in the latest of the holy books of the Christian Church—*The Apocalypse* or *The Revelation of John the Divine*. We cannot agree with all of Bellamy's conclusions, especially as they are interpreted from the standpoint of the cosmic ice theory, which will be dealt with in some detail in the concluding chapter.

Bellamy regards many of the texts in the above-mentioned Biblical sources as a rehash of earlier myths. Not all of the sources used by him are of equal value. For example, his references to Ezekiel are unconvincing, because they unquestionably concern the real Phoenician town of Tyre, then the centre of maritime trade. But his commentaries on the other texts merit close attention. Firstly, he quotes Jeremiah (died in Egypt in 570 B.C.),* who said he wrote a book on the calamities that would befall Babylon and that after it had been read the book should be thrown into the Euphrates [51; 60-63]. This, obviously, is a reference to some other, a more complete book written by the prophet which has not survived. Bellamy considers that a) this lost book was widely used by later Apocalyptist and b) that the prototype of the Babylon on which the prophet vented his spleen could not have been the real Babylon because in several passages the prophet's description does not conform to reality. Another indication that this was some other town or country is that the prophet said it stood by a great sea [51; 13] and described its destruction by the sea, by waves that rose out of the north and overflowed all the land [47; 2], saying that where the town had been nothing remained except the sea "with tumultuous waves" [51; 42]. Isaiah, too, speaks of a desert by the sea. If this had meant the sinking of the real Babylon, the sea would have come from the south and not from the north, and all the land, i.e., a large portion of the land surface, did not necessarily have to be flooded. The destruction of Babylon, let us note, was accompanied by the trembling of the earth [50; 44]. This

---

* Consequently, these texts were written before Plato lived.

is mentioned in yet another passage: "The land trembles and writhes in pain" [51; 29].

Bellamy analysed the texts of *The Revelation*, which were probably written between the 1st and 3rd century A.D. and draws the conclusion that where they speak of a symbolic Babylon destroyed for its sins, the texts, unlike other passages, were written in poor Greek and give the impression they are translations of excerpts from other sources. As in the *Book of Jeremiah*, the reference is to a Babylon "astride many seas" [17, 1]. The author of *The Revelation* symbolises this "Babylon" as a woman astride a crimson beast with seven heads and ten horns [17, 3-5]. In the following verses it is explained that the heads were the mountains of seven kingdoms, of which five perished, one still exists and another must appear [17, 9-11]. This passage rules out the usual interpretation that John the Divine meant Rome with its seven hills. As regards the ten horns, the author of *The Revelation* explains they are ten kingdoms which would in future appear for a short period [17; 12]. The interpretation given by the apostle himself is confused and nebulous. Bellamy underlines the similarity between this number of kingdoms and Plato's story of the ten kingdoms of Atlantis. The "Crimson beast", which St. John does not explain, most likely symbolises the crimson sea at sunset (the Atlantic), which antique authors frequently called the Great Sea of the West. This symbolic Babylon would be burned down to ashes [18, 8] and the smoke would be seen eternally [14; 8-19, 19,3] from a great distance [18, 9, 10, 15]. The destruction of this land is, for some reason, witnessed only by sailors, who watched in terror from a distance [18, 15-19]. It is doubtful if this meant Rome, which is situated far from the sea.

As regards this entire interpretation it should be noted that *at the time "The Revelation" was written Plato's legend of Atlantis was well known and his works enjoyed the profound respect of the apologists of Christianity*. It is, therefore, quite possible that John the Divine (or whoever it was that wrote *The Revelation*) used Plato's story for his mystic picture of the destruction of a symbolic Babylon. Furthermore, he might have known other sources as well.

Let us now turn to the question of the war between the Atlanteans and the pre-Hellenes. Attempts have been made to identify this war with some historical wars. B. L. Bogayevsky (13) offered the theory that the Atlanteans were defeated by a Cretan-Aegean people and that Atlantis perished in the Early Neolithic. In support of this theory one can only refer to the curious circumstance that the earliest settlements on Crete* (dated about 6700 B.C. [365/58]) were situated far from the coast possibly because the Cretans expected or feared an invasion from the sea. The impression is that the Cretans sought to

---

* The fact that Crete can be reached only by sea makes the problem of the earliest settlements on that island extremely fascinating. It implies that navigation had reached a high level of development at the time the first people made that island their home

settle in remote, well-hidden caves (365/244). But this, too, is far removed from a war between the Cretans and the Atlanteans.

The attention of atlantologists has been attracted by a disk made of baked clay which was found in 1908 in a palace in Phestos (190). Well-known to archaeologists, it is one of the outstanding relics discovered on Crete and dates back to the Middle Minoan IIIb period (about 1600 B.C.). Made by hand, it is covered on either side with hieroglyph-type symbols. The inscription runs spirally from end to centre, and each symbol was made with a special stamp. Apparently it represents one of many copies of some text.

The symbols have no bearing on Minoan writing. It has been established that the clay itself is not of Cretan origin either. The people portrayed on it wear the headdress of warriors of "peoples of the sea," who 400 years later came from the west, from the Atlantic, and invaded Egypt. This most likely favours the assumption that the disk is of western origin. J. D. S. Pendlebury (365/191) was extremely sceptical about the possibility of reading the text. He wrote that it would be best to pass over in silence the attempts that have been made to read this text. However, some time ago Marcel Homet (159/278-296) tried to decipher part of the text and came to the conclusion that the form of the inscription (spiral) and the text itself are linked up with religious, astrological and historical notions. He believes that some of the "phrases" refer to a calamity accompanied by the drowning of people in the sea. He feels there is some connection between this text and the Atlantis legend.

Let us now turn to some of the problems connected with the destruction of the pre-Hellenic kingdom. Many investigators, particularly Greek scholars, for example, P. Negris (80) and A. G. Galanopoulos (61, 62), have tried to find substantiation for this part of the legend in the assumption that the destruction of the pre-Hellenic kingdom is a rebound of some geological calamity in the region of the Aegean Sea. Generally speaking, it has been established that a large land mass known to geologists as *Aegeida*, subsided to form the present Aegean Sea. From the geological standpoint Aegeida sank quite recently, in the Pleistocene, in an interval between the glaciation periods, due probably to some elemental disaster. However, it is doubtful that intelligent man was already in existence and there are, therefore, no special grounds for considering that echoes of such a remote event could have reached our times. On the other hand, there are data enabling us to presume that the subsidence in this region continued into the period of recorded history. But, as we shall show, it is doubtful if this subsidence affected Attica, where Plato located the pre-Hellenic kingdom. Besides, it does not fit even chronologically into the date given by Plato.

Although Plato himself wrote that the pre-Hellenic host perished in an abyss and not from a deluge, some of his other data, which he gives in describing the pre-Hellenic kingdom, seem to indicate that whatever happened was accompanied by a deluge. That explains why some atlantologists linked the destruction of the pre-Hellenic kingdom up with deluge myths which were current among the early Greeks. There were as many as three such myths. The earliest is, apparently, about a deluge in the reign of King Beotius Ogyges. There are grounds for assuming (135/36) that this myth might have been linked up with a local flood in the Copais valley. However, many antique authors assert that this flood was universal and give some interesting details about it. For instance, according to the legend, passed on in different variants by Philochorus and Eusebius of Caesarea, after the flood Attica was uninhabited for a period of from 190 to 270 years. Marcus Terentius Varro, the Roman scholar, wrote that during this flood the colour, size and shape of the planet Venus changed, and night reigned continuously for nine months and that the volcanoes of the Aegean Sea were active throughout this period (37/72, 153).

The second—Deucalion—deluge is the most popular in Greek mythology. Galanopoulos (61, 62) ties the Atlantis legend up with this deluge, presuming that Atlantis was identical with Thera (Santorin Island) in the Aegean, where a devastating eruption occurred in about the year 1500 B.C. To lend his theory weight, Galanopoulos, like many other atlantologists, makes the assertion that Solon was wrongly informed by the Egyptian priests: the calamity occurred not 9,000 but only 900 years before his journey to Egypt. He locates the Pillars of Hercules in Peloponnesus, on one of the southern peninsulas. Thus, like many atlantologists before him, Galanopoulos links Atlantis up with Crete and the Minoan kingdom. As regards the Deucalion deluge, it is unlikely that it occurred in the Minoan period. Moreover, the myth about the Deucalion deluge quite obviously bears traces of having been borrowed from a Sumerian-Babylonian legend, which might have been brought to Greece by the Phoenicians. Thus, Galanopoulos' attempt to resolve the Atlantis problem by creating another Pseudo-Atlantis variant cannot be regarded as having been successful.

The third deluge in Greek mythology is associated with Dardanus and may be, in contrast to the first two, identified with real events. The Roman poet Virgil wrote that Dardanus was the grandson of Atlas and came to Asia Minor from Hesperia, a land in the extreme west (620/256, 416). At first he settled on the Island of Samothrace but a mighty flood forced him to flee to the continent. There, at the foot of Mount Ida he founded the mythical town of Dardania, which vanished from the face of the earth in deep antiquity. A very curious circumstance is that according to mythology, the rulers of Troy were descended from Dardanus. We know this from Homer's *Iliad. There is an interesting connection between the mysterious Hesperia and Troy.*

V. G. Childe (428/166) dates the earliest settlements on the site of Troy (known as Troy I and Troy II) as 2750-2500 B.C. Consequently, if there is any truth in the Dardanus myth, Dardania was founded much earlier than the above date. Diodorus [III; 52] mentions Hesperia as lying west of Lake Triton, near the ocean, not far from Ethiopia.* It was a large, fertile, verdant island with numerous flocks of sheep and goats, but its inhabitants did not till the soil. The Amazons came from this island. During an earthquake, Lake Triton, which was separated from the ocean by a narrow isthmus, was flooded and ceased to exist. The island of Hesperia probably disappeared as well. In any case, it would be hard to identify it with any of the islands existing today off the northwestern coast of Africa (for example, the Canary Islands or Madeira).

As regards the flood from which Dardan fled, Diodorus [V; 47] wrote that it was caused by the waters of the Black Sea pouring into the Mediterranean at the Cyanean Islands (at the entrance of the Bosphorus), when first the Bosphorus and then the Hellespont (Dardanelles) were formed. The sea, Diodorus tells us, flooded part of the coast of Asia Minor and the lowland on Samothrace. Consequently, this flood was caused by tectonic movements in the south of the Black Sea and in the north of the Aegean Sea.

Geological data confirm the authenticity of this legend. For this we must turn to the history of the Black Sea in the Quaternary period, which has been extensively studied (340). In early Euxine times, at the very beginning of the Quaternary period, the Black Sea was much smaller than it is today and received the waters of the Caspian which was on a higher level. Part of the water in the Black Sea drained into the Sea of Marmora. Because of the relatively high water-level in the Black and Caspian seas and the absence of direct communication with the Mediterranean (in those days the Dardanelles was a river and not a strait) the salt content in these seas was much smaller than it is today (442/100). A. D. Arkhangelsky and N. M. Strakhov (183) note that in the course of the Quaternary period the Black Sea had an outlet to the Mediterranean twice and to the Caspian three times. This was due to the tectonic movements in the region of the Bosphorus and in the northern part of the Aegean Sea. These tectonic movements evidently reached their peak about 5,000 years ago. This was the conclusion drawn by N. M. Strakhov (392), who studied sedimentation in the Black Sea. A. D. Arkhangelsky considers that the second, more modern break-through to the Mediterranean via the Dardanelles took place approximately 4,000 years ago. Thus, two investigators date these movements between 4000 and 2000 B.C., giving us the mean 3000 B.C. Academician D. I. Shcherbakov (442/101) feels that Diodorus Siculus might have meant this breakthrough when he related the legend about the Dardanian deluge.

In our opinion (123) this subsidence may be tied up with some of the adventures of the *Argosy*. The point is that it destroyed the shallow waters and reefs which made navigation dangerous at the

---

* The Ethiopia of the antique authors has nothing in common with modern Ethiopia. It simply meant a land inhabited by dark-skinned people.

entrance to the Bosphorus. These dangerous places and the powerful currents from the Black Sea to the Sea of Marmora gave rise to the legend that no ship could safely negotiate the strait and the Symplegades rocks. L. A. Yelnitsky (248/12) likewise believes there was a strong current. Inasmuch as the Argonauts sailed through the Bosphorus when the Symplegades rocks were a danger spot, *the "Argosy" adventure dates back to somewhere on the borderline between the fourth and third millennium B.C.*

Odysseus, evidently, accomplished his voyages in the period between the Trojan War (according to Greek legends—in the 12th century B.C.) and the adventures of the Argonauts. Like the Argonauts he might have been one of the "peoples of the sea", who extended their domains in the 4th-3rd millennium B.C. from west to east along the route Tartessos-Balearic Islands-Malta-Crete-Archipelago Islands-Troy. This was probably the route of the Argonauts, Dardanus, Odysseus and many other known and unknown mythical heroes of remote antiquity (123).

Chapter Six

ESOTERIC LEGENDS ABOUT ATLANTIS

In the books of the occultists references to the existence and destruction of Atlantis began to appear in about the year 1800. Earlier, among the alchemists of the Renaissance, there was a legend that alchemy, astrology and magic were born in the mysterious temples of Atlantis, where man first began to look for ways of turning common metals into gold and silver (334/13). In the second half of the 19th century, the Atlantis legend began to play a substantial role in the teachings of the theosophists, anthroposophists and all other occultists. J. Bramwell (49) notes the unity of the concepts of most varieties of modern occultism. The explanation, he says, is that all the data of the occultists evidently spring from one and the same source—ancient Indian books which the uninitiated cannot understand and are, allegedly, kept in secret underground temples in India. Actually the sources are the works of some prominent occultists— H. P. Blavatska (151), M. Manzi (78), W. Scott-Elliot (99), W. P. Phelon (85) and R. Steiner (103) to mention a few.

A prominent role in creating the occultist legend of Atlantis was played by Helena Petrovna Blavatska (nee Hahn—1831-1891). A Russian by birth, she spent almost her entire life abroad, travelling extensively in India. In 1875 she founded the Theosophical Society, whose work, as later investigations revealed, consisted of trickery. In 1888 she published her major work *The Secret Doctrine* (in three volumes: *Cosmogony, Anthropogenesis* and *Esoterism*), which was translated into many languages. In this work she developed the occultist legend of Atlantis with references to the *Book of Tiang*, of which only a limited number of copies are supposed to exist, and are, to all intents and purposes, unobtainable. One of these copies is supposed to be in some monastery in Tibet, and another in the Vatican; the latter copy is closely guarded. Blavatska claimed she read this book by clairvoyancy and other occult methods. But, properly speaking, it has no direct references to the destruction of Atlantis as such.

The anthroposophists (103) refer to the *Chronicle of Akasha*, supposed to be a record of a mystical legend of historical knowledge. They claim that our language can give only a remote idea of this chronicle. Actually, it has nothing in common with what we usually associate with the word chronicle. According to occultist doctrine, everything taking place in the world is recorded on surrounding objects in the same way as light, acting on film, forms a hidden image until the film is developed. The imprints of events form strata on objects, and with the aid of clairvoyance, accessible only to a few, to the "initiated", the occultists of the higher echelons are able to "see" pictures of the past and sort out their content. The Atlantis legend is only part of this "chronicle".

The fullest occultist legend about Atlantis was published in 1896 by Scott-Elliot (99) and Manzi (78). The former would have us accept his facts as genuine, claiming they came from the archives of the ancient occultist White Fraternity (85). But from the outset it must be noted *that Scott-Elliot's book, accepted as a bible by occultists, is a historical Utopian work teeming with details that are much too suspicious to be regarded as a serious narration of such an ancient chronicle as the history of Atlantis*. The work is founded on Scott-Elliot's acceptance of the idea that a civilisation far in advance of the end of the 19th century existed on Atlantis many millennia ago. Apparently *many modern "theories" of the existence of a superior civilisation in antiquity are in one way or another connected with or induced by a knowledge of the occultist legend about Atlantis*.

According to Scott-Elliot the first cataclysm occurred 800,000 years ago. The second geological catastrophe, which was not as destructive as the first, overtook Atlantis about 200,000 years ago. Atlantis was divided into two islands: *Ruta* and *Daitya*. According to Indian mythology, the daityas were evil spirits. Consequently, Daitya may be regarded as a "land of evil spirits". In the case of Ruta, the situation is somewhat more complex. In 1874, Louis Jacolliot (162/13) wrote that according to some Hindu myths there was once a huge continent to the south and east of India. It was inhabited by a people called Rutas. This word could be translated roughly as "warriors" or "conquerors". Jacolliot regarded Indonesia and Polynesia as the remains of that mythical continent. But this is by no means Atlantis, as described by Scott-Elliot.

Further, Scott-Elliot says the most devastating cataclysm occurred 80,000 years ago. Atlantis continued to exist as a relatively small island, Poseidonis, which was all that remained of Ruta. This was the Atlantis meant by Plato. As for Daitya, only a tiny islet remained. From that time the continents began to acquire their present contours. The Sahara was the floor of an ocean. The latter assertion underlines the absurdity of occultist geology, because the Sahara was never the floor of a sea in the Quaternary or even an earlier period (144/188). Lastly, in the year 9564 B.C. there took place the last, fourth cataclysm. Atlantis sank to the bottom of the ocean, and the land mass and the seas acquired almost their present boundaries. Manzi (78) gives the history of Atlantis in the same spirit.

The theosophists base their date of the destruction of Atlantis on a fantastic translation of part of the Madrid Mayan manuscript, also known as the Troano Code, which was published by A. Le Plongeon (165) in 1895. Le Plongeon describes a continent known as Moo and says it was destroyed 8,060 years before the Code was written. This arbitrary translation is not accepted by experts (Le Plongeon treated the text as though it were a rebus).

With the aid of a computer, Soviet scientists have translated the Troano manuscript, which proved to be a manual of ritualistic and astrological instruction for the different days of the year and was used by the Mayan priests as a sort of ritualistic calendar. For some reason the theosophists claimed the Code was drawn up in 1504 B.C. and thus obtained their date: 8060+1504=9564. Some atlantologists, while accepting the general tenor and date of the Le Plongeon translation, believed the Code was drawn up in 8498—8060=438 B.C., when the Old Empire flourished. They used the first date of the Mayan calendar, 8498 B.C., as their point of departure.

In a pamphlet (14) on occultism, V. V. Bogachev repeatedly pointed out that the maps furnished by Scott-Elliot were a far cry from the geological maps of the epoch described by him and that *the occultist legend abounds in geological errors and absurdities.*

The following table of the duration of the geological periods, compiled by H. P. Blavatska (151/750), shows how far removed the geology of the occultists is from science:

Geological epochs	Duration in millions of years*	
	According to Blavatska	According to scientific data
Archean + Cambrian + Silurian	171 20	over 1,000
Devonian + Carboniferous + Permian	103.04	175
Triassic + Jurassic + Cretaceous	36.80	155
Eocene + Miocene + Pliocene (Tertiary period)	7.36	68 5
Quaternary	1.60	1.0-1 5

* See Table 4 in the Appendix

In the history of his occultist Atlantis Scott-Elliot gives numerous details of its settlement by a succession of peoples. The occultist concept of these peoples differs greatly from the concept accepted by science. An example are the Akkadians, who, according to modern science, were a Semitic people. The reason that occultists draw a line of distinction between the Akkadians and the Semites is that when the "occultist Bible" was written science knew very little about the Sumerians, who preceded the Akkadians in Babylon. Generally speaking, *the occultist teaching of the peoples of Atlantis, their origin and migration has little in common with really scientific notions.* For example, they believe that intelligent man was already in existence several million years ago. At present the age of intelligent man (the Cro-Magnon race) has been established as 50,000 years at the most (265). As regards man's more ancient ancestors, the Paleoanthropes, the age of the Pithecanthropus is now estimated as 500,000-1,000,000 years, of the Sinanthropus as 400,000-500,000 years, and of the Atlanthropus as 200,000-300,000 years. These are the most ancient Paleoanthropes (380).

According to Scott-Elliot, the Atlantean capital in the period of the Mayan Old Empire was the City of a Hundred Gates situated 15°N, 40°W. As a matter of fact, bathymetric investigations in this region of the Atlantic have yielded nothing that even remotely resembles the main Atlantean kingdom as described by Plato. There is no hint of the huge mountains forming arcs round it on the north, west and south. Only the North Atlantic Ridge stretches far to the west of this region.

There is no doubt at all that the name itself and much of the description of the City of a Hundred Gates was borrowed from a description of ancient Babylon, which, according to legend, had a hundred gates, and its population was as large as that of the Atlantean capital of the occultists.

The legend of an extraordinary civilisation in Atlantis is intrinsically a part of the esoteric legend of that lost continent. In their narrations, the occultists speak of various new, allegedly unknown forms of power which the Atlanteans had discovered and used for technical purposes. A close analysis of all these "new" forms of power shows that they are a grotesque hybrid between the notions of a "living force", rejected by science long ago, and notions of atomic energy and so on. In this field R. Steiner (died in 1925), founder of anthroposophy, exerted himself more than anybody else. In the spirit of his day and correspondingly modernising the obsolete fantasy of the theosophers, he declared that Atlantean physics differed from modern physics (103). The implication, evidently, is that in those days the laws of nature were different from what they are today! To build up his occultist teaching he introduced elements which he borrowed from the scientific achievements of the 1920s, refurbished them to suit his purpose and gave them out as occultist revelations. That explains why such abstruse terms as "living force", "embryonic force of things," "growth force", "living force of seeds" and so forth are to be found in the works of occultists of various trends. In some cases the authors of these fantastic "forces" have only a vague idea of what they are talking about. *Scott-Elliot was obviously influenced by some of the fantastic novels of the end of the 19th century, whose authors invented new forces of nature.*

Scott-Elliot wrote that towards the end of the Atlantean Golden Age the emphasis was on jet aircraft, which replaced marine navigation for military purposes. At first glance, this seems to be a daring prevision. The first project for a jet engine was developed by the celebrated Russian revolutionary N. I. Kibalchich, who was executed in 1881. For decades his drawings collected dust in the secret archives of the tsarist political police and became known only in Soviet times. But inasmuch as Kibalchich gave a copy of his drawings to his defence counsel V. N. Gerard, some knowledge about them might have reached Scott-Elliot, most likely through Blavatska, founder of theosophy. In addition to this project, the use of jet propulsion was suggested by a number of inventors at the end of the 19th century and, for that reason, at the time Scott-Elliot wrote his book (1896) this principle could no longer be regarded as an absolute novelty.

Those who uphold the idea that the Atlantean civilisation had on a high standard of development interpret the numerous references to fire-breathing, roaring, flying dragons and serpents known to the Greeks, Germans, Slavs, Chinese, Indians and other peoples as dim recollections of Atlantean jet ships and punitive and tribute-collecting expeditions. The ancient Greek myth about the great enchantress Medea, who fled to Athens in a serpent-drawn chariot, is likewise linked up with these notions. Medea is said to have flown in a jet-propelled apparatus burning petrol as fuel (petrol was called "oil of Medea").

A. Braghin (48/214) has reported that the archaeological finds near San Salvador, Central America, include a clay cup (or plate). On it are portrayed a group of palms with people flying over them in machines emitting smoke and flames. Another report, this time from E. Georg (155/281) states that among the drawings in the famous cave temples of Ellora, India, there are some of flying ships. Georg considers that these drawings depict the battle mentioned in the Sanskrit epic *Ramayana*. A. Gorbovsky (239) followed this up by quoting a number of texts which describe mysterious weapons whose action resembles that of atomic weapons, flying apparatuses, and battles in which these weapons and apparatuses were used. Such texts are to be found in the *Mahabharata, Ramayana* and *Samarangana Sutradhara*. However, this requires more precise verification.

Mention must also be made of the occultist legend (439/300) that when Atlantis sank some of the Atlanteans saved themselves by fleeing to America and Africa in flying machines, and that others went to a number of planets in space rockets. This and other esoteric myths were used by Alexei Tolstoi for some of the chapters in his fantastic novel *Aelita*.

Some atlantologists who subscribe to the belief that the Atlantean civilisation was highly developed link that civilisation up with the myth of the ancient Egyptian divinity Thoth. They assume that Thoth came to Egypt from submerged Atlantis, where he had been a high-ranking scholar-priest. Before he died he was said to have desired to pass on his vast knowledge to mankind, which was still in a state of savagery, and set forth this knowledge in so-called *Emerald Tables*, a legendary text of unestablished origin reported by Medieval alchemists. These *Tables* were written in symbolic and highly figurative language.

Supporters of the theory of a highly developed Atlantean civilisation believe that Thoth and the higher caste of Atlanteans knew of many concepts which have been evolved by modern civilisation, namely, the unity and indestructibility of matter and energy, the identity of structure between the macrocosmos and the microcosmos, and so forth. This interpretation, given in a French magazine, is so interesting that it would be worth while citing it (455).

(I) "That which is below like that which is above, and that which is above like that which is below exist to perform miracles of one and the same thing." This is a brief exposition of the idea of the unity and structure similarity of the microcosmos ("that which is below") and the macrocosmos ("that which is above").

(II) "And in the same way as all objects came from one and the same thing and by the concept of one, all of them sprang from this matter through its application." This is an exact reproduction of modern views on the unity of matter and elementary particles, of which all matter consists. The first part of this phrase enlarges upon the idea of the development of all dead and living nature; the growth of crystals, the division of cells and so forth may serve as examples.

(III) "It is the father of all perfection in the Universe. His power is boundless on earth." This is a figurative allusion to the mighty forces concealed in primary matter.

(IV) "Separate the earth from fire, the fine from the crude, carefully, with great skill. This matter rises from the earth to the sky and at once again descends back to the earth. It collects the strength of both upper and lower things. And you will win the glory of the world, and all darkness will move away from you." This is the most interesting part of the *Emerald Tables* telling of the principles of mastering the inner energy of matter. First there is a reference to the necessity of separating inner energy ("fire") from the material substratum ("earth"), the bearer of this energy, which is linked up with the fine structure of matter, with elementary particles ("the fine from the crude"). This is an extremely dangerous process ("carefully") and requires great knowledge and special apparatus ("with great skill"). The released energy consists of a torrent of particles ("rises from the earth") and is connected with similar energy coming from outer space, cosmic radiation ("again descends back to the earth"). The link with cosmic energy and the unity of the processes on earth and in the Universe are implied by the phrase: "Collects the strength of both the upper and the lower things." Control over this process would be the greatest boon for mankind, because it would deliver it from want, misfortune and darkness.

(V) "This is the mightiest of all forces, it traps all that is elusive and penetrates into all that is impenetrable because that is how the world is created." This figuratively re-emphasises the primary nature of the inner forces of matter, which are the mightiest forces of nature and the source of all forms of energy in both the tiniest particles ("elusive") and in huge masses of matter ("impenetrable"); the Universe is arranged on the basis of this community and unity.

N. A. Morozov (334) notes that this is a unique alchemical document and regards it not as an alchemical treatise but as a philosophical poem. He holds that the *Tables* were written in the late Middle Ages. But this standpoint does not dovetail with the following:

1) the *Tables* are completely devoid of the usual medieval alchemical terms and views. There is no mention of the philosopher's stone or of mercury, sulphur and other attributes of the alchemists. The whole document is drawn up in a style that is quite unusual for medieval alchemical treatises.

2) The broad philosophical concept (even without the above interpretation) given in the *Tables* has nothing in common with the usual medieval discourses of the alchemists or even with the views of antique philosophers which were used as the foundation for alchemistry.

To return to the question of the highly developed Atlantean civilisation. If it was really highly developed, it is strange that it perished without leaving any material relics. The usual answer given by supporters of the theory that Atlantis had a sophisticated civilisation is that the ruling castes lived in isolation in order to appear as descendants of the gods in the eyes of the masses, whom they kept at a low cultural level. All scientific and technical knowledge, as well as all practical know-how, was in the hands of a numerically tiny caste. Moreover, nobody outside the ruling caste was permitted to do any work connected with the production of intricate machinery. Reluctant to educate the people and giving them only the rudimentary knowledge necessary for a primitive way of life, the ruling caste took with it all the higher knowledge when it perished. The attempts of the surviving Atlanteans to pass on at least the general principles of higher knowledge were doomed to failure because in those days the intellectual level of the masses was much too low to allow them to understand what they were told.

Some of the above is logical and *it is highly probable that material relics testifying to the existence of a superior civilisation will be found*. Lately, supporters of the theory that in the distant past there was a superior civilisation (irrespective of Atlantis) have offered a series of facts and documents to back up their theory. However, *an attentive examination of these "facts" shows that they are either obvious fabrications or newspaper canards, or that the documents have been misinterpreted (191). For that reason all references to such finds and documents have no scientific value.*

Some interest is evoked by relics portraying animals that had become extinct before the era of recorded history began. In Chapter Two we mentioned portrayals of extinct animals found in South America. The finds in Europe include a Scythian gold clasp with a portrayal of the sabre-tooth tiger (*Machaerodus cultridens*) (728/155). This animal disappeared from most of the world by the middle of the Quaternary period, but some specimens were still to be found in western Europe at the close of the Ice Age. No remains of the sabre-tooth tiger dating from the post-glacial period have been discovered. Y. Orlov (353) reported that a portrayal of a large-horned deer (*Megaceros euryceros*) was found on gold plates in a 5th century B.C. Scythian burial near Maikop, Soviet Union.

This animal is regarded as having became extinct during the post-glacial period and pictures of it have been found only in Aurignac cave-drawings made 20,000-30,000 years ago. The explanation is perhaps that in some areas these animals survived for a longer time than had at first been believed. The same concerns other animals, and their portrayals cannot serve as indisputable proof of a relic's exceptional antiquity.

When we analyse the esoteric legend about Atlantis as a whole, we cannot help but agree with J. Bramwell (49) that a great deal in it smacks of an acquaintanceship with I. Donnelly's book (56), which was published some fifteen years before Scott-Elliot's work. Much has simply been borrowed not only from that book but also from Bulwer-Lytton's (1803-1873) Utopian novels.

W. E. Coleman (102/57) has carefully analysed the occultist legend of Atlantis and shown what its real sources were. He demonstrated that Blavatska and her followers used Horace Wilson's translation of *Vishnupurana*, Alexander Winchell's *World Life* or *Comparative Geology*, Donnelly's work and other contemporary scientific and occult works. Blavatska interpreted and revised these works to suit her purpose (to substantiate theosophy), displaying outstanding literary talent and erudition, which she applied tendentiously. The so-called *Book of Tiang* is a rehash of the *Hymn of Creation* from the *Rig-Veda*. Furthermore, Coleman found the explanation for the word *Tiang*. Unfortunately his work was never published. All the material collected by him was destroyed during the great earthquake in San Francisco (102/58).

The fact that Scott-Elliot's work is most likely pure fantasy may be judged from his attempt to give it some semblance of a scientific treatise by filling it with pseudo-scientific chronology, and misrepresented geological and historical data of the level of the cheap editions of the close of the 19th century. That is why today much in his account seems absurd or only evokes a smile. Inasmuch as this pseudo-scientific approach completely exposes the occultists, they are now rejecting many of the pseudo-scientific elements they had formerly used, finally degenerating into mysticism and into verbosity that only they can comprehend, and regarding Atlantis only as a mythical symbol for the initiated, as a happy island for the gullible.

This makes it clear that *the esoteric Atlantis legend of the occultists is a product of their idle fantasy and has nothing to do with reality. All the concepts in it are based on pseudo-scientific or invented data and should be regarded as nothing more than a modern pseudo-myth.*

We should like to mention yet another fabrication, the article by Paul Schliemann, grandson of the famous German archaeologist Heinrich Schliemann (1822-1890), who discovered the ruins of Troy. This article was published in October 1912 by the *New York American* under the intriguing heading *How I Found Lost Atlantis* (106). Initially it made an impression, but was soon rightly assessed as a typical piece of sensationalism which could not be taken seriously. In scientific circles it was regarded as mystification founded on second-rate material (39/152). This account with its abundance of mysterious events, enigmatic documents that were never published again, and unexpected happy finds is written in the spirit of cheap thrillers. This view is confirmed in a letter by Professor I. M. Lourier of the State Hermitage* in reply to a query sent by me. Professor Lourier rejects Paul Schliemann's references to papyri at the State Hermitage.**

E. V. Andreyeva's (10/15) opinion that this article consists of nothing but pure inventions by an imaginative American journalist is supported by S. Hutin (161/175), who declares that no such person as Schliemann's grandson ever existed.

In spite of everything, present-day theosophists make much of this fabrication. Generally speaking, *it is high time to strike the Paul Schliemann "document" off the list of works meriting the attention of scientific atlantology* (120).

In the not too distant past there have been cases of resourceful adventurists reporting the discovery in the Atlantic of mysterious islands which they claimed were the lost Atlantis. A case in point was the report of the English skipper D. A. Robson (561, 572, 573) that in 1881 he discovered a new island west of Madeira and gave its exact location as 25°N 28°40′ W.

In 1943 the *Egyptian Mail* printed an article by H. B. Nichols reporting that a certain Mott had established the existence of Atlan-

---

* Letter from the State Hermitage, Leningrad, No. 1175, July 20, 1954.
** A detailed account of Paul Schliemann's article is given by E. V. Andreyeva (10/39-46).

tis at Toro* on the route to Nassau, Bahama Islands, and that he had founded an "Atlantis empire" with its flag (golden sunset on a blue background), issued triangular postage stamps and invited tourists to visit his "empire". After making a fortune the adventurist disappeared (107).

Probably ranking among such fantastic reports is the communication that a tiny, wooded island had been discovered in 1956 some 400 kilometres off the eastern coast of North America. While seamen were delivering their report and a warship was preparing to plant the US flag on it, the island sank to the bottom of the ocean (10, 109).

---

* A submarine mountain of this name is known east of the Bermudas.

NATURE AND ORIGIN OF OCEANS

Chapter Seven

BASIC GEOPHYSICAL AND GEOLOGICAL NOTIONS

The problem of Atlantis is intricate and many-faceted, but revolves round the question whether there ever was such a continent in the Atlantic, what caused its destruction and when it sank. Consequently, first and foremost, we must examine the data of modern geology and also of geophysics, sciences so closely inter-related that the term *geonomy* (V. V. Belousov) has been suggested to cover the entire range of the study of the Earth. It must be noted, however, that in most cases representatives of these sciences, like those of linguistics, history, ethnography and even archaeology are inclined to be sceptical about the Atlantis problem. They have dealt very briefly with the main, geological part of the problem, at best confining themselves to the most elementary data (22, 102). Yet, to understand the Atlantis problem properly one must have fairly extensive geological and geophysical knowledge, otherwise much will be missed. Both the atlantologist and the critic of atlantology must be well informed on questions such as the nature and the structure of the Earth's crust in the regions where Atlantis is supposed to have sunk, the age and features of the rocks on the ocean floor and of the submarine mountain ranges, their nature and history, and so forth. This knowledge cannot be obtained without at least examining the basic geophysical and geological notions, which are dealt with in this chapter. Moreover, in view of the different and frequently contradictory standpoints, we must also know the main trends of scientific thinking in geology and geophysics, for this will enable us critically to compare the different standpoints.

The point of departure of every concept of the geological history of the Earth is the notion of the Earth's origin as a planet. However, it is not our purpose to review and criticise cosmogonic hypotheses of the origin of the solar system.

We shall only mention that the different variants of the primary "hot" origin of the planets no longer satisfy science, especially as Soviet and foreign scientists have proved that no planet could have been formed out of white-hot masses detached from the Sun (292).

To have an idea of the many processes of the structure and history of the Earth, it is extremely important to understand the mechanical properties of the Earth's matter. They may be studied by the results of investigations of tides caused by the attraction of the Moon and the Sun and by the periodic small displacement of the poles. It has been established that the Earth is an extremely hard, resilient body with some viscosity. The Earth's modulus of hardness is equal to 1.5×10^{12} dyne/cm² as against 0.8-0.9×10^{12} dyne/cm² of the best grades of steel. In other words, *as a whole the Earth is much harder than steel*. Similarly, the Earth's viscosity is also very high—approximately 10^{19} poises (for tar it is about 10^{10} poises, and for glacial ice 1.2×10^{14} poises) (313/5-6). Consequently, *under rapid and abrupt loads the Earth will behave like an extremely hard body. On the other hand, its viscosity may be brought to light only under extremely prolonged and gradual loads.*

As a planet its cardinal feature is that it has a series of envelopes—the *geosphere*, of which the *atmosphere* is the external envelope. The natural waters on the Earth's surface form the aqueous envelope, the *hydrosphere*, which embraces all the seas and oceans. The hard part of the Earth is divided into two main portions: the external, thin *crust* (lithosphere) or layer A, and the inner, thick envelope, the *mantle* (or the sum total of the layers B, C and D). Still deeper is the Earth's *core* (layer E).

Our knowledge of the composition of the upper part of the lithosphere comes from a direct study of the rocks forming it. As regards the deeper layers, the data on their thickness and properties were obtained by studying the *velocity of seismic waves during earthquakes and man-made explosions*. Depending on their nature and on the nature of the rocks through which they pass, these waves travel at different speeds. Basically, seismic waves consist of two groups: *longitudinal* (P) and *transversal* (S). A feature of the latter is that they subside in a liquid medium (283/24-26).

Seismic investigations of the Earth's inner structure have shown that between the crust and the mantle there is a fairly sharply defined boundary called the *Mohorovicic discontinuity* (after Adrija Mohorovicic, the Yugoslav geologist who discovered it), below which the diffusion velocity of the longitudinal waves increases sharply to $V_p \geq 8.00$ km/sec. This surface is located differently in the various parts of the crust, but it is never lower than 70-80 kilometres. The upper part of the mantle, or layer B, runs to a depth of about 200-400 kilometres, below which begins layer C, whose features are a rapid increase in the diffusion velocity of seismic waves and in electric conductivity. It goes down to a depth of about 900 kilometres and is the centre of the deepest seismic foci; layer D extends to a depth of 2,900 kilometres. At this depth the diffusion velocity of the longitudinal waves drops unevenly and sharply and the transversal waves are completely dampened. This is the boundary of the Earth's core (layer E), which, judging by seismic data, is in a liquid state. Scientists are now once again returning to the notion that the core consists of liquid iron (313/32).

Gravimetrical data, i.e., data on the changes of the force of gravity in various places of the Earth's surface, make it possible to specify the thickness of the crust. Although the force of gravity is, on the average, more or less constant throughout the globe, there are some changes which depend upon the nature and thickness of the rocks. Depending on how adjoining masses of rock influence the force of gravity, the instrument readings show deviations from the conventional mean value, and this leads to the concept of so-called *anomalous forces of gravity*, which may be either positive or negative. These forces of gravity (free-air effect) are numerical values that have been found directly. But usually an amendment is introduced to exclude the influence of mountain masses (*Bouguer reduction* or, simply, *Bouguer anomaly*). The greater the mountain mass, the larger is the amendment, and for that reason beneath mountain ranges the Bouguer anomaly is usually negative; it shows the actual deficiency of the mass below sea level, while experimental numerical data give a positive value. Gravitational anomalies are expressed in units of acceleration: 1 milligal=0.001 m/sec^2 (283/9-10; 320/59). On continents the anomalies of the force of gravity change insignificantly (308). Negative anomalies predominate in folded zones. Positive anomalies occur most frequently in oceanic regions. Continental anomalies reach —500 milligals, and in deep-water depressions they exceed +400 milligals. But even in some continental areas we frequently observe small negative anomalies, and sometimes even positive anomalies of up to +100 milligals (283).

The crust's upper sedimentary granite layer, because of the predominance of silica and aluminium in it, is called *sial* (Si+Al). The name was suggested by the Austrian geologist Eduard Süess. Farther down the rock deposits have a smaller silica content but are richer in magnesium and iron. This layer is called *sima* (Si+Mg). The content of silica (SiO_2), anhydrite and silicic acid is the determining factor for classifying typical rocks in accordance with their composition. Those with the highest silica content are called acid rocks, those with a lesser content are called intermediate rocks, and those with the least content of silica are called basic and ultra-basic rocks (see Table 1 in the Addenda). Rock fusibility depends on acidity. For example, granite melts at a temperature of 750-850°C, while ultra-basic rock can be melted only at a temperature of 1,400-1,500°C.

The following petrographical data is necessary to understand the role played by various rocks, whose names will occur below. *Basalt*: a dark igneous rock characterised by its mineral content—feldspar (or leucite or nepheline), augite, magnetite and, sometimes, olivine. Where it is predominantly vitreous it is called *tachylyte* or basaltic glass. If the components are clearly distinguishable, but olivine and the vitreous base are almost completely absent, it is called *dolerite*. Where feldspar, leucite and nepheline occur together, the rock is called *basanite*. Such rock has a low content of augite and olivine. On the other hand, olivine may occur in considerable quantities in diabases, which consist chiefly of feldspar and augite with an admixture of magnetite. In diabases the olivine is usually hydrated into *serpentine*. Olivine is also the main component of basic *periodotites*, which may also include pyroxene and horneblende.

Trachytes and phonolites are also classified as igneous rocks. *Trachytes* are light in colour and consist of feldspar, horneblende, augite and, frequently, even quartz. Also in the same classification are *rhyolites* and *obsidian*, the latter being a vitreous rock. Consequently, these are mainly acid rocks. *Phonolites*, which are a nepheline *syenite*, consist principally of a mixture of feldspar and nepheline or leucite usually with other minerals. Lighter coloured phonolites, which have a richer feldspar content, are closer to trachytes, while the darker varieties in which nepheline and horneblende predominate are closer to basalts. *Andesites* are intermediate rocks between trachytes and basalts, and occur in many varieties. Geologically late andesites are more subsilicic and have a richer iron content.

Atlantis lies at a considerable depth in the ocean, and seismic reconnaissance is the only means by which we can obtain an approximate idea of the nature of the rocks beneath the ocean and of their depth in the region where Atlantis sank.

However, seismic waves travel at about the same velocity in many different types of rocks. The following is a list of major rocks with roughly the same wave diffusion velocities; longitudinal waves are convenient because they show a wide numerical difference for the different rocks.

1. $V_p = 1.5$-2.00 km/sec: unconsolidated sediments and sedimentary rocks, tuff.

2. $V_p = 2.2$-3.0 km/sec: consolidated sedimentary rocks (clay, some varieties of sandstone, gypsum, and so forth), pumice.

3. $V_p = 3.2$-4.5 km/sec: consolidated sedimentary rock (chalk, sandstone), metamorphosed rock (gneiss, some varieties of shale), some varieties of less consolidated rock (tuff, breccia).

4. $V_p = 4.5$-6.0 km/sec: granite, syenite, seprentinite, limestone, shale, dolomite and some varieties of marble.

5. $V_p = 6.5 \pm 0.5$ km/sec: basalt, gabbro and some varieties of dolomite and marble.

Velocities differ substantially in rocks of the same type but of different origin. Where pressure is higher, velocities increase, at first sharply and then at a slower rate. Recent investigations by F. Birch (465), who studied changes in the diffusion velocity of longitudinal and transversal waves depending on rock density, composition and pressure, have yielded some interesting results.*

It was found that *in sial subjected to pressures of over 1,000 kg/cm^2*

---

* See Table 3 in the Appendix

the diffusion velocities (6.2-6.5 km/sec) correspond to those found in basalts (gabbro) subjected to atmospheric pressure. In other words, the impression is that granites turn into basalts, which, actually, does not happen.

Asada Toshi (792), who has compared laboratory and field observations, convincingly shows *where the pressure is high 90 per cent of the rocks in which longitudinal waves reach a velocity of 5.9-6.3 km/sec are almost certainly granites.* Moreover, Soviet scientists (721) have demonstrated that where they are subjected to high pressures some metamorphic rocks, chlorite schist, for example reveal velocities close to those and typical of ultrabasic rocks: up to 7.52 km/sec at 4,000 kg/cm^2 as against, for instance, 7.70 km/sec for peridotite subjected to the same pressure.

A temperature rise evidently does not very considerably reduce the seismic wave diffusion velocity under high pressures. I. A. Rezanov (375, 376, 649a), for instance, believes that the difference does not exceed 0.1-0.2 km/sec even at a depth of about 35 kilometres.

He reasonably assumes that *the Earth's crust may consist solely of granitoids throughout,* while the so-called "basalt" layer should be considered as consisting of gabbro and metamorphic rock. *Only layers with a diffusion velocity of not less than 6.8-7.0 km/sec should be classified as gabbro proper (consolidated abyssal basalt).* Thus, present-day notions about the nature and composition of crustal and subcrustal rocks have to be radically revised.

Modern geophysical research has lead to the important conclusion that *the Earth's crust on the continents and on the ocean floor differs essentially as regards thickness and the distribution of rocks.* Acid and intermediate rocks, chiefly, diabases, tholeites and plateau-

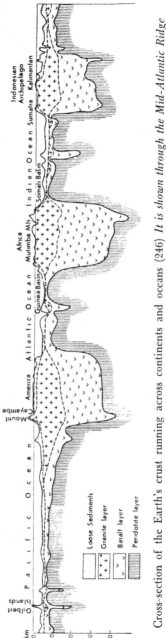

Cross-section of the Earth's crust running across continents and oceans (246) *It is shown through the Mid-Atlantic Ridge*

basalt, are the most typical for continents. In the case of oceanic volcanic islands and outpourings on the ocean floor the typical rocks are olivine basalts—oceanites. In the shape of thick effusions, ultrabasic rocks occur rarely on the surface of the Earth and have not been discovered on the floor of oceans.

The *continental crust* is complex and extremely thick (75-80 kilometres), particularly in regions with young mountain systems and where the "roots" reach down to a great depth beneath huge mountain ranges. Investigations by Soviet geophysicists (196/16) have shown that this increase in thickness evidently takes place at the expense not of the "granite" but of the "basalt" layer (also see 448/68). The crust thins out to 15-40 kilometres beneath immobile flatland.

The existence of a third type of the Earth's crust—the very unique *mid-oceanic ridges*—is now recognised (813/17). A whole chapter (Nine) is devoted to these ridges because they play a vital role in our arguments proving the existence of Atlantis.

The *oceanic crust* has a simpler structure and is much thinner than the continental crust. Underlying the thin layer of sediments (average—1 kilometre) are thin (up to 5 kilometres) layers of "basalt" rock (in the deepest places), while in shallower areas these layers are up to 10 kilometres thick. However, beneath islands and submarine ranges, the Earth's crust may be up to 15-20 kilometres thick.

There are grounds for assuming that *basalt is the universal rock of the Earth's crust underlying oceans and continents.* The basalt nature of most modern volcanic magmas favours this assumption. V. V. Belousov (196/7), for example, draws attention to the homogeneous composition of basalt of different ages and regions, and also to the predominant volume of basalt extrusions.

In the case of the mantle, we can only guess its nature on the basis of seismic soundings, and there are various theories on this point.

We tend to agree with V. A. Magnitsky (313/24) that the most acceptable surmise is that the composition of the mantle is eclogitic. For its chemical composition, eclogite hardly differs at all from basalt. If it is melted, it will, when cooled under a lower pressure, harden into basalt or gabbro. But when basalt cools under high pressures it will turn into eclogite. V. V. Belousov (196), G. C. Kennedy (268) and J. F. Lovering (599) consider that the eclogite hypothesis best satisfies the mantle's physical data.

It is extremely important to know the origin of granite if we are to understand the genesis of oceans (which is closely linked up with the history of the appearance and destruction of Atlantis). There are two theories on this subject. One is that granite is extruded continuously from the depths of the Earth, i.e., it is juvenile. The second is that it is a secondary product of the metamorphosis of the most ancient sedimentary rocks. In this case, the Earth's reserves of granite are not inexhaustible. If we accept the theory that granite is of metamorphic origin it means that any oceanic island situated far from a continent may be regarded as the remains of a submerged or shattered continent. On the other hand, the assumption that granite is of purely juvenile origin implies that it may appear anywhere, at any time and in any quantity. Scientists who believe that no continents existed in place of the oceans in antiquity willingly accept the hypothesis that granite is of juvenile origin.

Let us note that even the *crystallisation of basalts with a larger acid content than that of the mantle's supposed matter does not yield any considerable quantity of granite*. F. Y. Levinson-Lessing and V. N. Lodochnikov (294) have shown by experiment that the crystallisation of basalt produces 80 per cent gabbro, 10 per cent diorite, 5 per cent quartz diorite and only 5 per cent syenite, the basic variety of granite.* This has been confirmed by field observations of the distribution of granite. A. C. Waters (408/741) points out that where tholeiitic basalts were differentiated in North America they did not yield even andesite. But insofar as andesites exist and are closely associated with tholeiitic basalts, it follows that they were formed by the blending of basalts with more acid rocks.

The difficulties encountered in the granite problem may, we believe, be best overcome by accepting *the hypothesis that granites form as a result of the metamorphosis of ancient sedimentary rocks* (185, 285). This hypothesis also copes with the origin of the puzzling predominance of radioelements in granites (320/66; 414; 422).

A. Cailleux (483) offers interesting computations, showing that an average of about 13 cubic kilometres of solid materials is deposited in the oceans annually and this should have led, if we begin our count from the Cambrian period, to the formation of at least an 18-kilometre-thick layer of sediments. This is considerably thicker than the total thickness of oceanic sediments (0-2 kilometres) and the underlying crust (4-5 kilometres). The only explanation for this discrepancy is that a substantial portion of the sediments are metamorphosed into granite.

N. P. Vasilkovsky (813/38) belives that no more than 30 per cent of the granite layer consists of magmatic (juvenile) granite. The remainder of the granitoids are the product of the metamorphisation of sedimentary rocks.

The theory of the juvenile and increasing delivery of granite has been supported by E. N. Lyustikh and A. Y. Saltykovsky (310). Rejecting the possibility of basalts assimilating ancient granite layers, they also rejected the possibility of granites originating from sedimentary rocks formed through the erosion of ancient more basic rocks. However, when all their arguments are carefully weighed it will be found that they are not very convincing. The primary rocks of the Earth's outer surface, which are undoubtedly subjected to all

---

* It seems that nobody has obtained any tangible quantities of rhyolite experimentally through the crystallisation of basalts. Their occurrence among igneous, more basic rock is not an indication that rhyolites form as a result of differentiation.

sorts of erosion, were the products of the primary gravitational differentiation of the planet's dust material. Compared with the average composition of meteorite matter, it must have had a larger content of silica and other, lighter components. In the course of the thousands of millions of years of the Earth's prehistory (the Earth is considered to be at least 5,000 million years old) these primary rocks were completely eroded and reworked. A. P. Vinogradov (320; 2nd ed./49) writes that the *mean composition of sedimentary rocks conforms to a mean composition of a mixture consisting of two parts granite and one part basalt.* From this it follows that the primary matter was much more basic than modern granite, but that it was more acid than not only modern basalts but even andesites (see also 393a).

In line with the theories of Academician V. I. Vernadsky (320; 2nd ed./109), we consider that *granites are essentially a product of the transformation of former biospheres.* Academician Vernadsky (216) drew attention to the circumstance that in the Pacific the ooze is much richer in radioelements than granite or any other rock. We believe it is highly probable that *at the dawn of the Earth's history, when the most primitive life first appeared there might have been organisms that selectively absorbed radioelements and accumulated them in the most ancient sedimentary rock from which granites emerged by metamorphosis and refusion.*

On the possibility of living organisms selectively absorbing radioelements, a noteworthy hypothesis, suggested by A. E. Kriss (280), is that purple anaerobic sulphur bacteria owe their vital energy to the radioelements absorbed by them. There are many facts testifying to the selective, intensive absorption of radioelements by living organisms (279, 371, 409). Lastly, the fact that there is increased radioactivity in the borehole waters accompanying oil is well known.

M. S. Tochilin (400/30) draws attention to the circumstance that there was unquestionably very little oxygen in the Earth's atmosphere in the past and that an important role was played by the acid products of volcanic eruptions. In accordance with this, we assume that in the very earliest periods of the life of the Earth, when it was covered with shallow seas and had no oxygen in its atmosphere, the acid gases (sulphurous and carbonic acid gases, hydrogen chloride, and so forth) liberated from the depths dissolved in these seas and reacted with primary rocks to form water-soluble haloid and bicarbonate salts and colloid silicic acid. Then followed the appearance of the first microorganisms—anaerobes—which were incapable of photosynthesis. These organisms obtained their vital energy from the radioelements selectively absorbed by them. When they died, their remains, which sank to the bottom of the seas, had a high content of radioelements. Some organisms used colloid silicic acid for their shells as well. This, we believe, led to the formation of the most ancient sedimentary rocks with their high content of silica and radioelements. Subsequent metamorphosis of these rocks, causing them to melt and crystallise, yielded granites. Arguments approximating ours were advanced some years ago by G. C. Kennedy (268). A year after this book's Russian edition, the same views were propounded by V. A. Raznitsin (747), particularly where he speaks of the history of ancient sedimentary rocks. The discovery of oil at depths of many kilometres, where it comes from layers directly overlying granites or, as it is surmised, even from cracks in these granites, provides indirect confirmation of our hypothesis. An example is the Cambrian oil discovered in Siberia.

Let us now examine marine sediments, from which the main mass of sedimentary rocks subsequently took shape. By their origin these sediments may be divided into two large groups: sediments whose genesis is in one way or another linked up with land rock erosion (*terrigenous deposits*), and sediments formed by the vital activity of extinct or still existing marine organisms (*biogenous deposits*).

The *littoral zone*, i.e., the *beaches* and the *shelf*, (depth 0-200 metres) as well as the continental slope (and floor) are inhabited by *benthos*, and the mass of ocean waters is inhabited by plankton; and *pelagic organisms* live in the open ocean, far from shores. It is now customary to subdivide marine sediments according to their location: a) neritic (for the continental shelf), b) bathyal (for the continental slope), and c) abyssal (for the bed of the ocean). Attempts to compile a uniform classification of marine sediments to include their morphological and genetic features have not met with success and we shall therefore use W. Murrey's descriptive classification (269/155-181; 326).

I. PELAGIC DEPOSITS

A. *Pelagic abyssal deposits* occur in the deepest parts (abyssal zones) of oceans.

1. *Red Clay*. A brown clayey ooze, which occurs at depths beginning with 4,800 metres. It contains up to 57 per cent silicon dioxide and very little calcium carbonate, perhaps because it is leached out in deep waters. Red clay is linked up with deep-water ferromanganese nodules, which sometimes form round the remains of organisms.

2. *Radiolarian ooze*. A feature of this ooze is the presence of fragments of siliceous radiolaria. It has almost the same composition as red ooze.

B. *Pelagic epilophic deposits* occur along elevations and are the unchanged remains of dead organisms.

a) calcareous:

3. *Globigerina ooze* is composed of planktonic rhizopods—globigerina (species of foraminifera). It occurs at a depth of up to 6,000 metres. If calcium carbonate is removed from globigerina ooze with acid, the residue will resemble red clay.

4. *Pteropod ooze* is a calcareous ooze, 30 per cent of which consists of pelagic mollusk shells. It occurs in the tropics, mainly in the shallow water round islands to a depth of 3,000 metres.

b) siliceous:

5. *Diatomaceous ooze*, a product of the vital activity of planktonic diatoms. It occurs at depths from 1,000 to 5,700 metres.

II. TERRIGENOUS DEPOSITS

C. *Semipelagic deposits.*

6. *Blue mud*, occurs in shallow waters and continental slopes at depths from 200 to 5,200 metres. It forms under conditions of resurrection (due to oxygen shortage) and hence its colour.

7. *Green mud*, consists primarily of glauconite and occurs at a depth of from 200 to 1,000 metres.

8. *Lime mud*. These deposits are of varied origin.

D. *Littoral deposits*, occur in shallow zones off the coasts of continents and islands, usually no deeper than 200 metres.

9. Stones, pebbles, gravel, sand. Their composition varies and depends on the rocks composing the adjoining land surface. If their origin is due to the destruction of continental rock, their composition uzually includes a large percentage of quartz. Around coral islands, they are fragments of dead corals, and around volcanic islands they are the products of volcanic activity.

Sand and limestone found on the sea bed or on oceanic islands situated far from continents are important to the problem of Atlantis. Quartz sand is frequently an indication that it formed as a result of the destruction of granites on what was once land. Round volcanic islands we find different sands, for example, basalt sand, while round coral islands they are coral-limestone sands. There have been cases of sand being found in abyssal oceanic soil far from continental shelves and slopes. The size of the particles rules out the possibility that it is ooze brought by ocean currents or dust borne by winds. There are various theories about the origin of such sand (see Chapter Nine).

The discovery of remains of coral and limestone of coral origin is frequently a sign that there was shallow water in the locality, because reef- and island-building corals (of the *Madreporaria* order) live at depths of not more than 50 metres and at a temperature of 18-30°C. However, cases are known of some species living as far north as the 69th parallel at a depth of 350-500 metres and at a temperature of 6-7°C (431/44). Moreover, there are a number of species with eight horns (*Octocorallia*) and six horns (*Hexacorallia*), which inhabit sub-Arctic and even Arctic waters. Some of these cold-water corals of the *Madreporaria* order live at depths of even 2,200 metres (345). Hence, the presence of corals does not always mean there had been a subsidence—it is necessary to identify the species.

The subsidence of the Earth's crust, so important for an understanding of what caused Atlantis to sink, is most likely linked up with the thermal processes in the bosom of the Earth (this will be dealt with in some detail below). Consequently, to understand the processes causing tectonic movements we must know what gives rise to the heat in the Earth and the indices characterising terrestrial heat: the temperature of the heat flow and the geothermal gradient. V. A. Magnitsky (313/11-12) points out that it was believed the sources of the Earth's internal heat were: 1) the residue of the primary heat trapped from the Sun—the theory of the Earth's hot origin; 2) the differentiation of matter; 3) the energy of the Earth's rotation; and 4) the energy from the disintegration of radioactive elements. *The radioactive decay of uranium, thorium and potassium is now regarded as one of the main sources of the continuous regeneration of the Earth's internal heat.*

At first glance, it seems there should be larger concentrations of the heavier radioelements in the deeper layers. However, basalt, a widespread rock, has one-sixth of the radioactivity of the much lighter granite; while the radioactivity of heavy ultrabasic rock, of which, it is believed, the deeper layers of the mantle are composed, is only one-tenth of that of granite. If we proceed from the assumption that the Earth's primary matter was similar to that of meteorites, we shall find that the difference is even greater. Moreover, the higher radioelement content in granites plus their fusibility must have led to the predominance of granite magma in the products of modern volcanic eruptions as well. However, *most modern volcanoes discharge lava of a basic or intermediate composition (basalt, andesite). None of the theories of the juvenile origin of granite gives a more or less intelligent explanation of the prevalence of radioelements in granite or of the predominantly basalt-andesite nature of modern volcanic magma.* This gives the impression that the granite magma reserves have generally been always limited.

Is the Earth growing colder or hotter? This question is of considerable interest for an understanding of history. Some scientists believe that at the present stage of geological history the Earth is in a state of heat equilibrium (187). E. A. Lyubimova (305, 306) thinks that the heat-generating processes could not melt the Earth at the early stages of its existence, except the outer jacket of the iron core. Below a depth of 500 kilometres there must be almost adiabatic conditions, and the interior of the Earth must therefore be growing hotter. The outer portions, above 500 kilometres, must have started to cool 1,000-2,000 million years ago. With the passage of time the fusion centres moved deep into the Earth. On the basis of computations, Lyubimova considers that the Earth is gradually growing hotter.

It is worth noting that *modern methods of investigation have not shown positively that there is a continuous layer of molten magma either in the Earth's crust or in the upper strata of the mantle.** The undisputed existence of molten magma, proved by volcanic activity as well as by observations (for example, in the zone of Klyuchevskaya in Kamchatka), is now explained by the presence of individual local centres that neither interlock nor form a continuous stratum. Such centres do not exist permanently and may disappear or reappear. Their origin has not been lucidly explained. On the other hand, there have been cases when a number of volcanoes in the Andes, situated hundreds of kilometres apart, have been active at one and the same time. The origin and occurrence of local volcanic activity is still one of the most perplexing problems of geology. V. I. Baranov and A. S. Serdyukova (187) write: "For their content of radioactive elements, the products of volcanic activity are similar to usual rocks, and volcanic gases do not contain an increased quantity of helium. This indicates that the formation of molten lava is not due to an anomalously high radioactivity in volcanic rocks." Perhaps the sources of heat are processes other than the energy of radioactive disintegration, for example, as suggested by P. P. Izotov, the heat from tidal friction.

Some role in the appearance of centres of molten magma is, possibly, played by the difference in the heat conductivity of various rocks, even of those that have a relatively small content of radioelements, such as is to be found in basic and ultrabasic rocks. This conclusion is offered by A. A. Smyslov (390), whose computations have shown the possibility of centres of molten magma appearing at various depths from the Earth's surface, depending upon the nature and thickness of the rocks over the centre. An extremely important conclusion is that sedimentary rocks play a very prominent role. Because of their poor heat conductivity they act as a kind of screen that holds up the heat from the deeper strata.

These considerations are extremely interesting in that they help us to understand *the possibility of molten magma centres appearing in oceanic regions where a thick deposit of sedimentary rock accumulates on the floor of the ocean.*

On the other hand, Lyubimova (305) may be right in assuming that a more or less fully molten stratum really exists in the upper part of the Earth's shell at a depth between 100 and 700 kilometres. V. V. Belousov (196/18) is inclined to think this stratum is somewhat higher. He writes: "The surmise that this stratum of possible melting has a bearing on the stratum of low seismic wave diffusion velocities, situated at a depth of 100-250 kilometres, is extremely plausible."

We can now turn to the question of the *heat flow*, i.e., the total quantity of heat coming from the depths of the Earth to the surface, and of the *geothermal gradient*, i.e., the changes of temperature with

---

* The centrifugal effect caused by the Earth's rotation perhaps plays some role in the appearance and disappearance of volcanic centres. The theory is that from time to time this effect forces liquid magma up from the deeper strata through cracks and fissures.

depth. Both these indices bear a relation to the Atlantis problem because they can, for example, be tied up with the probability of the ocean floor melting, which must accompany the sinking of a land mass, a problem we shall discuss in some detail in the next chapter.

The heat flow is expressed by $K \times 10^{-6}$ cal/cm² sec, where $K = 0.1$ — —8.0. The highest numerical value of the heat flow is to be found in oceanic regions, particularly in some submarine mountain systems: the Mid-Atlantic Ridge (where Atlantis is believed to be located) and the East Pacific Ridge on which the Easter Island stands (205; 673/213).

As regards the geothermal gradient, it is the lowest on continents (80-150 m/degree) and the highest in oceanic regions (10-40 m/degree) (390). Moreover, between the Cocos Islands and Christmas Island in the Indian Ocean the geothermal gradient was found to be equal to 4 m/degree near the volcanoes and solfataras (257/15). Thus, *in some oceanic areas, despite intensive cooling by the water more heat is discharged than in continental regions.* The reason for this is not clear. Let us only note that for their thermal properties unconsolidated marine sediments are closer to water than to the solid phase (643).

H. H. Hess (422) suggested that *the serpentinisation of olivine basalts might be one of the reasons for the rise of the temperature of the floor of oceanic regions.* The formation of serpentine from olivine is a reversible reaction that proceeds approximately as follows:

$$\text{olivine} + \text{water} \leftrightarrows \text{serpentine} + 100 \text{ cal/gr (558)}.$$

If water flowed gradually from the depths of the Earth, the portion of the shell above 500° isotherm would have been subjected to a left to right reaction and serpentinisation would have made the temperature to rise.

What causes tectonic movements? The main forces influencing the Earth and giving rise to major changes in its structure and surface are: 1) centripetal force, i.e., the force of gravity; 2) centrifugal force set in motion by the Earth's rotation; and 3) the forces of thermal compression and expansion. Scientists have linked one or several of these forces up with the origin of tectonic movements.

First, a few words about the theories connecting tectonic movements with the Earth's rotation as a planet.

It is believed that a study of the processes involved in the Earth's rotation can help us to understand some features of the Earth's crust, namely, the predominance of continental masses in the Northern Hemisphere, and of oceanic masses in the Southern Hemisphere, the S-shaped curve of many planetary details, the location of the largest mountain systems, and so forth.

Back in 1912, A. Veronnet and then P. Appel believed that the force of gravity between the Earth and the Moon had to set up meridional tension in the Earth's crust, and maintained that precessions and tides caused tectonic movements. The parallels where most tectonic movements take place have been named *critical parallels* on the suggestion of the Soviet astronomer N. I. Idelson. This idea was substantiated mathematically by M. V. Stovas in 1951. But in addition to critical parallels, *critical meridians* were also noted on the Earth's ellipsoid, as was proved by G.N. Katterfeld (227/120; 303). The critical parallels are ±35°, ±62° and ±71°, while the critical meridians 60°E 120°W and 150°E 30°W.

A more detailed *hypothesis of critical parallels and meridians* and what follows from it are expounded in *The Face of the Earth* by G. N. Katterfeld (267). For our part let us note that this hypothesis quite adequately explains some morphological features of our planet as a rotating body. But it speaks rather of the direction than of the causes of tectonic movements.

A theory explaining a number of points and features of the Earth's geological history has been suggested by G. D. Khizanashvili (423). On the basis of the undisputed fact that the rotation axis must coincide with the axis of the maximum moment of inertia, he points out that a movement of mass on the Earth's surface or in the crust is bound to change the position of the axis of the moment of inertia.

Consequently, the Khizanashvili hypothesis postulates the sliding of the crust, as an independent body, on the surface of the mantle. He plausibly assumes that because of the difference in the radii of the axes of the terrestrial ellipsoid (difference 21.5 kilometres), any change in the position of the poles would substantially change the level of the World Ocean. The maximum changes must take place on the 40th-45th parallels. There would be regressions in the regions to which the poles would approach, and transgressions in the regions from which they move away. He emphasises that for this to happen it would be sufficient for the poles to migrate only a few degrees.

Generally speaking, although the Khizanashvili hypothesis is attractive because of its simplicity, it contains many shortcomings.

Another thing that draws attention to Khizanashvili's views is that they take into account the possibility of the lithosphere and hydrosphere moving independently of the movements taking place in the mantle. On this point, Magnitsky (313/37) writes: "If we accept that the crust as a whole moves, we can easily imagine that various deformations and cleavages, accompanied by relative horizontal shift of its parts, might have occurred in it."

An interesting hypothesis was advanced some years ago by the Rumanian scientist M. Arkhanguelski (757), who noted that the changes which might be caused in the density of oceanic waters by the melting of glaciers would sharply change the ocean level. For instance, if at the poles the sea water density rises from 1.025 to 1.027 the World Ocean level would drop six kilometres at the equator and rise 12 kilometres at the poles. If this computation is correct, it would signify that sea water density is a major factor in the appearance and disappearance of transgressions.

All suggested and universally accepted hypotheses explaining the possible causes of tectogenesis and tectonic movements generally and those linked up with the self-development of the Earth's matter without involving cosmic and astronomical factors may be reduced to the following main principles: *differentiation of matter, isostasy, convection, contraction* and *expansion*.

1. *Gravitative differentiation* is the rising to the surface of the lighter and the sinking of the heavier (by specific weight) components of the primary substratum, which, in the process, separates according to chemical composition. *Crystallisation differentiation,* i.e., the separation of the different minerals in magma as it cools, is closely linked up with gravitative differentiation. As far as we can judge, both types of differentiation coexist in the majority of cases.

Concerning crystallisation differentiation C. E. Wegmann (214) writes: "Basic minerals sink in the form of crystal showers and form basic and ultrabasic rocks; acid components accumulate beneath the roof. Inasmuch as it is accepted that a large portion of the magma rose in the shape of liquid melts, the decrystallised phases must again melt. This makes it not quite clear how the main masses, which have accumulated deep in the Earth, penetrate or are squeezed through the stratum of acid products of differentiation formed beneath the roof. At any rate, though this point is occasionally mooted it is never elucidated. These reservoirs of magma are mostly regarded as being juvenile. Thus, they must have taken shape in the pre-geological period of the Earth's history. However, geophysics has not yet proved their existence. Although the Earth has grown older, such subcrustal lakes of magma, if they have ever existed, must have survived here and there." Katterfeld (267/23) holds that "the very idea of a geochemical differentiation of our planet's matter in a liquid state is wrong".

2. *Isostasy* is the dependence between the thickness of the sial and the height of the Earth's surface. The thicker the slabs of sial, the higher is its surface and the deeper its foundation. Slabs of sial are like icebergs floating in the sea, i.e., the lighter slabs of sial float on the denser simatic substratum. The concept of isostasy was later applied to any type of rock in the Earth's crust.

3. *Convection* is linked up with the theory that in the Earth's shell there are convection currents which raise the hotter matter of the inner strata to the surface.

4. *Contraction* is the formation of folds on the Earth's surface as a result of a reduction of its radius by compression. Folds form like the wrinkles on the skin of a drying apple. Lately, alternative theories that the Earth is *expanding* have been advanced. Thermal forces are at the root in both cases.

On the basis of what we know of the Earth's crust and of most of the mantle, neither gravitative differentiation nor isostasy is possible. R. Malaise (605) logically points out that if our geophysical data are correct no convectional or isostatic movements can take place in the mantle because the enormous internal friction in such dense and hard strata would immediately kill such movements.

As regards isostasy as such, a close analysis of all available data shows that *it could take place (not completely, even at that) only if it covered the entire crust or very large sections of it*. E. N. Lyustikh (308) points out that all considerable deviations from isostasy, now known in many areas, have been caused by tectonic movements. *In themselves isostatic forces do not cause but stem from tectonic movements*: they either limit their amplitude or fix the level where these movements stop. Elsewhere E. N. Lyustikh (309) says R. Perrin showed that isostatic floating of sial in the sima is not possible for the simple reason that sial melts at a lower temperature than the sima (see also 323, 685).

S. A. Yevteyev and G. I. Lazukov (247a) point out that the uplift of land after the melting of large masses of glaciers is by no means the result of isostasy (glacier isostasy) but is due to purely tectonic processes. The Earth's crust is so hard and rigid that its thickness will not undergo any essential change even if it is burdened with an ice sheet several kilometres thick. We feel that heat from above and below is the most probable factor changing the height of land after the ice sheet melts, and that in the long run this is what expands rocks and causes uplifts of the Earth's surface.

Criticising the convection theories, Magnitsky writes (313/36): "Had there been a system of convection currents beneath the crust the thermal flow over the ascending currents would have been greater than over the descending parts of the currents; thus the entire surface of the Earth would have been covered with a system of cells with increased and reduced thermal flows in conformity to the size and distribution of the convection currents. However, present data give no indication of such a distribution of the thermal flow from the depths of the Earth." And further: "*Lastly, the very foundation of the hypothesis—the existence of convections—is absolutely vague: how does it tie up with the shell's enormous module of hardness, with its clear-cut division into several strata?*" (My italics—*N.Z.*) E. A. Lyubimova (600) likewise dismisses the convection theory.

E. N. Lyustikh (744) has written a series of papers subjecting this hypothesis to sharp and deserved criticism. He rejects the assumption that the mid-oceanic ridges (for details see Chapter Nine) coincide with the lines tracing a rising convection current, and that island areas and land mountain ranges coincide with the lines of the maximum vertical velocity of the descending current. This hypothesis, evolved by R. S. Dietz, is not borne out by either geothermal or gravimetrical data. It is contradictory and does not tie up with facts. The arguments of its other proponents (B. W. Gindler, S. K. Rucorn, J. Wilson, to mention a few) are founded on an artificial dovetailing of data. *All existing theories about convection in the mantle stem from erroneous premises, and so far there is little scientific foundation for this problem.* Besides, H. Jeffreys (570a) points out that a study of astronomical data concerning the Earth and its relation to other planets and to the Moon brings one to the conclusion that no convection is possible in the mantle.

Available data on the mantle structure shows that it is heterogeneous and, possibly, of a block composition (754). An indispensable condition for the existence of convection currents is that the mantle must be homogeneous. No confirmation of the convection hypothesis is to be found in the latest critical works either (see discussion in *Geophysical Journal of the Royal Astronomical Society*, Vol. 14, Nos. 1-4, 1967).

V. A. Magnitsky (313, 34) writes that the contraction theory does not explain the origin of the two types of crust and does not conform to the notion that the Earth has a hard shell. The process of the destruction of continents and the formation of oceans is not explained either. This theory sprang from the notion, rejected by modern science, that the Earth was once a mass of molten matter. If the Earth had indeed passed through a stage of melting, its hardening should have proceeded not from top to bottom but from bottom to top, because the heavier, refractory rocks would have sunk to the bottom.

However, the contraction theory still has many supporters because better than any other theory it explains the origin of the mighty forces that can compress the Earth's crust. Its proponents include W. N. Bucher (210), A. J. Eardley (264) and K. K. Landes (585). Both Elsasser and J. H. F. Umbgrove maintain that at the present level of our knowledge we cannot object to the theory that the Earth is shrinking. What causes this contraction and in what zones it is taking place is quite another matter (210). Concerning the contraction theory, the Canadian geophysicist G. Wilson (217) writes we can picture to ourselves that the central regions of the Earth are heated and expand, and that the external regions may either cool or become hot, but all the same the surface of the Earth will shrink because of the ejection of volcanic material. Thus, he says, we assume that regardless of whether the Earth cools or not, it shrinks as a result of volcanic activity.

The theory that the Earth is *expanding* has lately become increasingly popular.

It has been suggested by scientists both in the USSR and abroad. Some postulate a slight expansion (G. Wilson, van Deeke, M. Ewing), others believe that the Earth is expanding rapidly (V. B. Neiman, R. Fisher, B. C. Heezen, L. Edyed). Proponents of the latter idea suggest, for example, that initially the Earth's radius was only half or even one-third of the present radius, while its density was 35 g/cm^3! They reject the theory that continents or oceans are growing (341; 418; 447; 552). The theory of the expansion of the Earth is discussed at length by V. B. Neiman (341).

Y. M. Sheinmann (433a) analyses this theory and points out that while it explains some of the features of the Earth's structure it raises many other questions which it cannot answer. Besides, astronomical data on the slowing effect of tides on the speed of the Earth's rotation leads to the antipodal conclusion that the Earth is shrinking at a rate of about 4.5 centimetres per century (N. N. Pariisky). Some of the shortcomings of this theory, namely, that to expand the Earth must receive matter from outer space, are pointed out by one of its supporters, V. B. Neiman (341/66). A. E. Beck (458) demonstrates that throughout the Earth's geological history its radius could not have increased more than 100 kilometres. An increase of 1,000 kilometres or more could have been possible if the density of the primary Earth was constant and even or if the density grew with a decrease in depth (i.e., the reverse of what we have in reality) and if, in the past, the moment of inertia was 30-50 times smaller; all this is physically impossible. The most serious analysis of this theory is offered by Y. A. Trapeznikov (400a).

However, the idea of the Earth expanding (within reasonable limits) cannot be ruled out altogether as absurd, especially if we approach this theory from the standpoint of a hot interior of the Earth. On this point V. V. Belousov (196/12) writes: "The latter [abyssal fractures] might be linked up with the expansion of the Earth's interior under the influence of radioactive heating and the expansion and fracturing of the upper layers caused by this heating." *Contraction and expansion most likely play an equal role in the life of the Earth*, but it is hard to say which of these processes predominate today or which predominated in the past.

Our knowledge of geological history shows that an equal role was played in the formation of the surface of the Earth's crust by vertical uplifts, covering hundreds of metres and kilometres, and by horizontal displacement caused by faulting and folding. These displacements and thrusts spread over a distance of as much as tens of kilometres, but never thousands of kilometres as is maintained by the proponents of the drift of continents and the expanding earth theories (this question is discussed in the next chapter).

The *constriction hypothesis*, a variant of the contraction theory, first suggested more than a quarter of a century ago by N. Odhner (625-628), the Swedish biogeographer, has been particularly popular among atlantologists in the past decade. It was applied to the problem of Atlantis by R. Malaise (605). In its day it gave a simple and satisfactory explanation of many phenomena, and tribute has been paid to it by the author of the present book (130).

Its substance may be summed up as follows. According to Odhner and Malaise many tectonic movements are caused by thermal expansion and contraction chiefly in the Earth's crust, which is the most far removed from conditions of thermal equilibrium and, therefore, depends upon the temperature conditions in the atmosphere, hydrosphere and in the crust. The strata of the Earth's crust may thus be likened to a vault bearing the load of the tensions created by the thermal expansion or compression of the rocks of which it is composed.

Academician V. I. Vernadsky (215) analysed the problem of the cooling of the Earth and suggested that the hydrosphere plays a large part in this process. He wrote: "Beneath the depths of the ocean's hydrosphere the region of cooling penetrates still deeper in layers of the Earth's crust, layers which lie at a mean depth of more than ten kilometres from the land surface; granite and the basic masses of rock underlying the floor of the World Ocean are cooled in the hydrosphere." Taking into consideration the fact that, on the one hand, the water temperature in the deepest parts of the World Ocean is low (about 1-2° today and possibly 6-8° higher in the Tertiary period) and, on the other, that there is a fairly steep geothermal gradient beneath the floor of the ocean, one cannot but agree that *beneath the oceans and at the edge of the continents the crust is subjected to the highest mechanical tensions of thermal origin*. As is pointed out by D. G. Panov, a mass of *new* facts, which this hypothesis cannot explain, have been accumulated since its publication.

The diverse ways of development of individual parts of the Earth's crust have created two basic elements of structure: platform and folded regions. A feature of the platform regions is that they are divided into two tiers: the lower, folded foundation, and the upper, sedimentary cover. The ancient, pre-Cambrian foundation of the platforms frequently crops out directly to the surface. Such regions are called *shields*, for example, the Baltic and the Canadian shields. There are younger platforms with a Paleozoic or Mesozoic foundation.

After a platform's folded foundation takes shape it becomes less mobile, i.e., more stable. As a consequence, a platform region reacts to mountain-building processes with chiefly slowly developing oscillatory (*epeirogenic*) movements of the Earth's crust. In periods of uplift the sea retreats (*regression*), while in periods when the ocean advances shallow seas form (*transgression*). The alternation of periods of regression and transgression on the surface of the folded foundation leads to the accumulation of a cover of sedimentary rock. Traces of these processes are frequently found in the remains of ancient coastal lines (*terraces*) as well. The subsequent tectonic development of a platform witnesses its splitting and fracturing into an intricate system of uplifted and lowered blocks. The depressions that form as a result of subsidences are usually called *grabens*, and the blocks lifted above the surrounding regions are called *horsts*. Grabens and horsts are usually accompanied by deep and narrow valleys lying along abyssal faults, and these are commonly called *rift valleys*.* Moreover, faults cause vast and, frequently, very thick cover outflows mainly of basic rocks which lead to the formation of *plateaus*.

---

* These are valleys of tectonic origin formed along fractures and limited by faults. A feature of a rift valley are rectilinear fault slopes which give it the form of a deep ravine with a narrow floor and high, steep sides.—*Ed*.

Folded zones (orogenic zones or *geosynclinal regions)* are built up differently than plateaus. A feature of their structure is the occurrence of various, including igneous, rocks compressed in the folds. These rock layers are extremely thick—10 kilometres and more. In addition, shallow-water and also deeper-water sediments, which sometimes alternate, occur amid the sedimentary rocks. It is believed that the development of folded zones is linked up with particularly mobile regions of the crust called geosynclinal regions. The uplifted folds accompanying geosynclines are called *anticlines*.

Geosynclinal regions are active zones of the Earth's crust with the most active tectonic movements. The development of a geosynclinal zone may be divided into several phases, the first of which is a geosynclinal sea. This sea has a mixed relief with shallow and deep areas, many volcanic islands and a thick layer of marine sediments. Moreover, there are lines of abyssal fractures, which are frequently the epicentres of earthquakes, while magma, a sign of great volcanic activity, issues from the lines themselves. Then follows a period of folding, which turns the region into a folded zone, and further uplifts result in the building up of mountain systems. The *Caledonian, Hercynian (Variscean), Mesozoic* and *Cenozoic (Alpine)* are distinguished as periods when individual geosynclinal regions turned into folded zones. There have probably been other more ancient orogenic cycles in the Earth's geological history (see Table 4 in the Addenda).

Subsequently, the young folded zones were welded firmly together to form young platforms, in which further structural changes involving uplifts and subsidences took place.

There are many theories regarding the sequence of the development of the Earth's crust. Some geologists consider geological processes as being irreversible and that the Earth has already passed through the stage of the replacement of geosynclinal regions by platform zones. Others, on the contrary, believe it is quite possible that the trend towards the formation of geosynclinal zones may recur. Still others, N. I. Nikolayev (348) for one, agree with the irreversibility theory but maintain that there were the following consecutive stages in the development of the Earth's crust: pre-geosynclinal, geosynclinal, platform and post-platform. The last stage was predominant in the Cenozoic, and its subsequent development is expressed by the term *neotectonic*. This development was marked by extensive uplifts and subsidences accompanied by a diversity of neotectonic movements. An example of these movements is the geologically recent uplift (by 400 metres) of Novaya Zemlya or the Himalayas (337/264).

V. V. Belousov (196, 197) has suggested that *in the history of the Earth there were two great stages of tectogenesis—an ancient granite and a young basalt stage—which followed one another consecutively*. During the first stage the crust received acid (granite) material, a feature of geosynclinal-platform development.

The basalt stage included the following phenomena:
a) tectonic activation with the formation of vast grabens, depressions and tall plateaus; b) mass outpouring of plateau basalt; c) *basaltisation* of the Earth's crust as a whole; d) *oceanisation*—formation of inland seas and oceans through the destruction of the granite crust and its replacement with a basalt crust.

"If we study the phenomena we have enumerated," V. V. Belousov writes, "we shall see that a *basalt deluge* occurred in a number of places at different times. But there do not seem to be any indications that this deluge occurred on a substantial scale earlier than the end of the Paleozoic or the beginning of the Mesozoic, a period marked by the appearance of oceans, the first outflows of trap on platforms and the formation of characteristic depressions in the Trans-Baikal area and in Mongolia. This process undoubtedly gained momentum in the Mesozoic, the Paleogene and, in particular, the Neogene, when there were outbursts of post-platform activity leading to the formation of inland seas and large grabens and to a considerable extension and deepening of oceans. The 'basalt' thus started later than the granite stage, but inasmuch as in many places the granite stage was protracted, both stages overlapped." The next chapter deals with oceanisation in greater detail.

Chapter Eight

MODERN VIEWS OF THE ORIGIN OF OCEANS

The problem of Atlantis as a geographical entity is closely linked up with the problem of the origin of oceans, with a study of the nature of oceans and of the causes that led to their formation. The sinking of Atlantis may be regarded as a case of the depth of the ocean changing through the subsidence of land. It will, therefore, be in order first to examine present-day views of the nature and origin of oceans.

All the theories and hypotheses on this subject may be divided into two large groups. The first regards oceans as primary, primordial, extensive and invariably deep regions of the Earth's surface. The hypotheses developing this idea are known under the heading of the permanency of oceans. Proponents of the opposing hypotheses regard oceans as relatively young formations that supplanted ancient continents and shallow seas. Academician D. I. Shcherbakov (442/81) writes: "Scientists believe that in remote times continents were larger. They occupied the area of the present Atlantic and Indian depressions. The modern continents were small components of these continents. The southern continent, Gondwana Land, embraced the Indian and part of the Atlantic Ocean, as well as Brazil, Africa, the Indian peninsula and Australia. There were similarly huge continents in the Northern Hemisphere—the North Atlantic and the

Paleozoic continents. Then these continents split and parts of them sank in the ocean." This theory was founded on data provided by historical geology and paleonthology.

Below we shall try to prove that these theories best of all satisfy actual data. But, as a preliminary step, we must analyse opposing views.

In the past few decades a concept that oceans are permanent in the absolute sense has become widespread among geologists and oceanologists in foreign countries. This school of thought was elaborated chiefly by American scientists (415/32). A century ago, in 1864, the American geologist James Dwight Dana (494) advanced the proposition that an "ocean has always been an ocean". The basic principles behind the absolute understanding of the permanency of oceans were formulated by B. Willis (702): the great oceanic basins are a permanent feature of the Earth's surface and they existed in their present sites with insignificant changes of outline since the time water first appeared. Supporters of this hypothesis naturally rule out the possibility of Atlantis having existed, for this runs counter to the very foundation of their hypothesis.

Most Soviet geographers, geologists and geotectonicists negatively assess the extreme view of the absolute permanency of oceans. "This hypothesis is anti-historical, denies all development of the Earth's crust and relief, and as far as we are concerned it is totally alien and unacceptable. No Russian geologist supports this metaphysical hypothesis," wrote A. N. Mazarovich (314/93), who, earlier, had declared: "The theory of the permanency of oceans is purely static, thoroughly anti-dialectical and does not conform to modern facts" (p. 61). A very brief and clear-cut assessment of this hypothesis is given by K. K. Markov (319/270), who writes: "The face of the Earth took shape in the course of continuous development. There have never been everlasting features." The permanency hypothesis is negatively commented upon by many foreign geologists as well. This negative view was expressed most forcibly by the noted English geologist G. M. Lees in two of his papers (296, 593).

Now a few words about what is meant by the youth of oceans. First and foremost, attention must be drawn to the very concept of ocean. Usually it embraces two basic features: size and depth, i.e., a considerable area which is not bounded by land masses and has sufficiently vast, deep-water basins. Neither the supporters nor the opponents of the permanency theory object to the view that in remote times the oceans might have been much bigger than they are today, but they differ in opinion as regards the period in which deep-water regions were formed. The former consider that these basins are extremely old and that if not all then at least some had never changed their sites. The latter hold that the floor of oceans became deep at a later period, that the primary oceans were shallow and their configuration differed substantially from present-day oceans.

On the question of the age of oceans L. A. Zenkevich (258/385) writes that if we accept the age of, for example, the Pacific as 2,000 million years, a rate of sedimentation of 5 mm per millennium would have resulted in a bottom deposit of at least 10 kilometres thick. Actually, according to seismic measurements, the thickness of this deposit does not exceed 600-1,000 metres. Even if we accept E. L. Hamilton's (544) considerations about the possibility of sediments having been "compressed" (the formation of a stratum of about 1,000 metres thick as a result of the consolidation of a clayey mud layer of 2,500 to 5,000 metres), we shall still encounter many incongruities. L. A. Zenkevich, who supports the permanency of oceans theory, rejects all arguments that clash with it, refuses to consider them and believes that the changes in the density and properties of sediments were brought about by temperature and pressure fluctuations.* However, it should be noted that the Hamilton data used by him concern clayey abyssal muds. As regards lime muds, which are very widespread in oceans and were widespread in past geological epochs as well, a layer 300 metres thick, as computed by Hamilton, is equal to only 327 metres of primary lime mud (544).

A. Poldervaart (370), who accepts the proposition that the rate of sediment accumulation has not changed to any marked degree in the course of the Earth's geological history and that it does not differ from the modern rate, assesses the age of oceans within their present limits and depths as approximately 150-300 million years (average—200 million years, i.e., dating from the Mesozoic). Almost the same age is given by J. Wolbach and A. Holmes (434), who maintain that this was the time needed by the oceans to achieve their modern salinity, i.e., 100-300 million years. F. P. Shepard (673/195), for his part, draws attention to a circumstance which he regards as enigmatic, namely, that the fossils taken from the ocean floor and some submarine mountains do not date beyond the Cretaceous. This, he concludes, is proof that oceans are probably not very old. Academician D. I. Shcherbakov (442/83) writes: "The most ancient strata of the ocean floor date back to the early Cretaceous (100 million years ago). There evidently were seas and oceans before that but in their configuration they differed substantially from modern seas and oceans." But even the age 100 million years is plausibly disputed by G. D. Afanasyev (186/8). On the basis of his amendments to Poldervaart's computations he draws the conclusion that within their modern boundaries the oceans cannot be more than 50 million years old, i.e., the World Ocean took shape in the Tertiary period.

An attempt to establish the date of deep-water depressions and troughs was made by studying specific abyssal fauna, on the assumption that these depressions and troughs were of the greatest anti-

---

* See Note No. 1 (Appendix 2).

quity. L. A. Zenkevich and Y. A. Birstein (259) feel that the fauna groups of the abyssal depths should be regarded as relics that moved from shallow water to abyssal regions geologically a very long time ago. Usually this contention is supported by the fact of the discovery of *Neopilina galatheae*, which came from shallow water of the Lower Paleozoic.*

Some American commentators (614, 631), who cannot be suspected of adherence to the youth of oceans theory, recently criticised the views propounded by Zenkevich and Birstein, giving as their opinion that abyssal fauna are of geologically recent origin. Some time ago it was found that *Neopilina galatheae* also occur in shallow waters on the continental slope. R. Fisher and H. H. Hess (631), on the other hand, believe that oceanic troughs took shape not earlier than in the Tertiary period. The same concerns a number of other oceanic structures.

Most of the works on problems of marine geology and oceanology are now published by proponents of the theory that oceans and continents are permanent. Small wonder that works airing opposing trends are virtually swamped by the supporters of the permanency theory. Moreover, there have been cases (682) of journals in the USA and other countries refusing to accept papers criticising the prevailing views. There have also been cases of data given by leading proponents of the predominating trend failing the test of reality (252, 272).

The following views and hypotheses have been used with varying success to substantiate the permanence of oceans and continents:

1) the concept of a continuing gravitational differentiation of matter in the Earth's crust and the hypothesis that granites are of purely juvenile origin and that they issue uninterruptedly in considerable quantities from the depths of the Earth;

2) the theory that platforms are growing at the expense of oceans, i.e., that land is encroaching on the sea, a theory closely allied with the preceding proposition;

3) the concept that there is a deep-going, fundamental distinction between the oceanic and continental parts of the Earth's crust;

4) the theory that the Pacific Ocean formed in deep antiquity;

5) data on the radioactivity of rocks and on the role played by the latter in the Earth's thermal regime;

6) the hypothesis that the Earth is expanding;

7) the hypothesis of so-called turbidity (or suspension) currents to explain the origin of submarine canyons and the finding of terrigenous material on the ocean floor at great distances from land, and a number of other phenomena. Some of these problems have been dealt with in the preceding chapter, others will be examined here or below.

---

* See Note No. 2 (Appendix 2).

First and foremost, we must mention the views of the supporters of the expanding continents theory. They believe that continental-type areas of the crust grow in the course of geological time at the expense of the area of oceans. It is considered that the eternal existence and permanence of the Earth's crust within the limits of oceans is quite inevitable. If this is true, the existence of Atlantis at some remote period is completely ruled out.

In the USSR hypotheses that continents are expanding have been presented in different variants by G. N. Katterfeld (267), P. N. Kropotkin (281, 282), E. N. Lyustikh (307), V. A. Magnitsky (312), V. I. Popov (320; 2nd ed./519) and O. K. Leontyev (813). The most detailed hypothesis has been evolved by P. N. Kropotkin, who bases himself on the assumption that throughout the geological history of the Earth there were primary oceans whose rigidly defined areas never changed—oceanic platforms called thalassocrats by foreign authors. A. D. Arkhangelsky was the first to mark them on a tectonic chart of the Earth, but he accepted a more substantiated depth for them—5,000 metres. Below are some figures on the depth of oceans and the correlation between them (mainly after 391).

Ocean	% of marginal seas	Mean depth in m (without seas)	% of depth 3,000 to 6,000 m	% of depth > 5,000 m
Arctic	61.5	2,179	13.5	—
Atlantic	11.7	3,925	72.1	27.4
Indian	2.0	3,963	81.5	23.3
Pacific	8.0	4,282	80.3	30.9
World Ocean	9.7	3,795	—	24.5

Thus, *the oceanic platforms occupy not more than one-fourth of the surface of the World Ocean floor.*

Disputing Kropotkin's arguments, D. G. Panov (356/17) writes: "1) there are no grounds for the assumption that the 'oceanic platforms' were covered with waters of the ocean from the earliest periods of geological history; 2) like other regions of pre-Cambrian folding —stable blocks and platforms—they could react to mountain-building movements of a later period primarily with splits and vertical movements; 3) the absence of a sharply differentiated relief within the boundaries of the 'oceanic platforms' cannot serve as proof that they have never been subjected to folding deformations in the course of geological history."

Moreover, it seems somewhat strange that such thin layers of the Earth's crust could have survived unchanged in their primary state —the oceanic platforms are much thinner than continental platforms; and the latter platforms have also been subjected to splits and other changes in the course of geological history.

As W. N. Berry and A. J. Boncot (804) point out, the evidence that in Paleozoic platforms the geosynclines were located not along the rims of the platforms but within them does not confirm the theory that continents are growing. The data on the distribution of Paleozoic rocks likewise does not clash with the Earth's crust oceanisation hypothesis.

The next group of hypothesis is based on views about the partial permanency of oceans. Supporters of these views consider that the Pacific is the oldest ocean and, therefore, differs substantially from the Atlantic, Indian and Arctic oceans. From their standpoint the existence of Atlantis as an ancient geological object is not improbable. The most typical of this standpoint are the views of H. Stille (679, 680), who advanced the concept of a "proto-ocean" (the Pacific) and "neo-oceans" (other oceans). A. N. Mazarovich (314) likewise classified oceans under the headings of old and new. To corroborate this division, F. Press (254) offered the information that the nature of the upper mantle beneath the Atlantic and Indian oceans essentially differs from that of the mantle underlying the Pacific. However, this information requires further confirmation.

M. V. Muratov (336) analyses possible variants of an explanation for the unique morphology of the bed of the Atlantic and Indian oceans and draws what he believes to be the only acceptable conclusion, namely that this uniqueness is due to the fusion of material of the continental crust in the region of the beds of these oceans.*
"Incredible as this hypothesis may sound, there are arguments allowing us to consider it worthy of attention," he writes.

A popular hypothesis linked up with concepts about the antiquity and immutability of oceans is that of the *drift of continents*, which has been worked out in great detail by A. Wegener (213). It belongs to the hypotheses of *mobility*, i.e., concepts that crust tectonics are linked up not so much with vertical as with large-scale horizontal movements of great areas of the crust, including entire continents.

The Wegener hypothesis is founded on an assumed isostatic natation of platforms of granite continents on a basalt substratum. Wegener believes that initially there was a single granite continent —Pangaea. In the Mesozoic and the Cenozoic it split up and its pieces—separate continents—began drifting apart. Wegener considers that the reason for this drift was the breakaway of the Moon from the Earth in the region of the Pacific.** According to the Wegener hypothesis there is no place at all for Atlantis; the Mid-Atlantic Ridge is regarded as having been built by submarine lava discharged

---

* See Table 2 (Appendix 1)
** See G N Katterfeld (267/37, 72-73) on the physical and geological untenability of the theory that the Moon had torn away from the Earth in the region the Pacific

from fissures formed by the drift of America from Europe and Africa. However, when O. Muck (80/229) made a model in which the continents were joined into a single Pangaea he found that between the shores of North America and Europe there was a free region which made contact between continents far from complete. He considers that this was the site of Atlantis. A noteworthy point in this connection is that in 1877, thirty-five years before Wegener, E. V. Bykhanov published what is now an extremely rare book—*Astronomical Prejudices and Materials for a New Theory of the Formation of the Planetary System*—in which he develops views very similar to those of Wegener. Incidentally, he believed that the Atlantis continent did not sink but that it moved westward and exists to this day under the name of America.

The Wegener hypothesis was enthusiastically adopted by biogeographers, because, from their standpoint, it explained many facts concerning the distribution of flora and fauna (see, for example, 224). However, many Soviet geologists and geotectonicists appraise the hypothesis negatively.

For instance, Academician D. I. Shcherbakov (442/87) writes: "At the same time, there are a number of facts contradicting this hypothesis. If the granite continents moved along the basalt floor of the ocean they would have caused colossal deformations in it, but no sign of such deformations has been found. Besides, if the ocean floor had been subjected to deformations a new crust would have formed in some places. However, with the exception of a few islands, virtually the only seismically active part of the ocean is the mid-oceanic ridge. According to the theory of the horizontal migration of continents, a huge part of the Earth's crust must move as a single, integral mass. But when such a movement occurs the rift valley encircling any continent must broaden out at the rear extremity of the moving mass and close at its front extremity. No proof of such interaction has been produced."

V. A. Magnitsky (313/36) adds the following arguments against the theory of mobility: "Usually very little is said about why the continental-type crust took shape as a single spot amid the mass of oceanic-type crust. Similarly no explanation is offered as to why this spot existed as an integral whole in the course of 3,000 million years and then, in the course of the past 200 million years, it suddenly split and its parts were dispersed about the Earth's surface leaving oceans between them."

The very foundation of the Wegener hypothesis is undermined by the fact that the structure of zones may be traced from continents to oceans. Furthermore, as Academician A. N. Shatsky notes, it is contradicted by the occurrence of deep-focus earthquakes. Besides, a closer examination shows that there is only a seeming coincidence of the outlines of continents and that they diverge greatly when the outline of the shelf and the continental slope is taken into account.

Lately, the Wegener hypothesis has been criticised by biogeographers as well. This criticism is reviewed by S. V. Maximova (317).

Other prominent Soviet scientists who have spoken against the Wegener theory include Academician L. S. Berg (201), Professor K. K. Markov (319) and Academician A. N. Shatsky (430). Opposition to the hypothesis also came from the participants in a discussion organised in American journals (318). At the international colloquium held some years ago in France, V. S. Heezen (551) read a paper in which he showed that the *data on the topography and structure of the ocean floor clash with the theory of the migration of continents.*

In a criticism of the mobility theory Y. M. Sheinmann (754) wrote that until fresh convincing proof can be produced it is pointless for the proponents and opponents of mobility to argue. *The data that have so far been offered in favour of mobility are untenable and cannot serve as proof.* The mobility theory is not all-embracing, and it clashes with many theories. Mobility explains only side issues, fails to explain many unresolved problems of geology and causes enormous difficulties in answering a number of questions in other spheres of science. A. E. Sheidegger (660a) has likewise demonstrated that the works of the supporters of the migration theory contain erroneous primary data and errors in interpretation. In his opinion mountains were formed as a result of contraction.

In recent years, in connection with investigations into *paleomagnetism*, the theory of the drift of continents has begun to reappear in a new form. It turns out that the data of European and American authors always differ by several degrees. This difference is used in an effort to substantiate the drift of continents (284; 427/60-61).

A. Cox and R. Doell (491) assembled all the known material on paleomagnetic research and drew the conclusion that the Earth's magnetic field changed unevenly in the course of geological history (also see 442/35). An argument put forward by them in another paper (504) is of particular interest. They contend that although the magnetic field underwent repeated changes in the period from the Oligocene to the Early Pleistocene, the poles have hardly changed their location to this day. This rules out the possibility of considerable migrations of continents since the beginning of the Oligocene.

Interesting investigations have been conducted by F. G. Stehli (678), who shows that in the Permian the boundaries of the distribution of fauna ran parallel with the equator; this contradicts the assumption that the location of the geographical poles changed. J. F. Gellert believes that the same boundaries existed in the Paleogene (533).

After studying sediments in the north of Alaska (807), Ch. Smiley comes to the conclusion that the existence of a latitudinal climate in the Mesozoic comes into conflict with the pole migration, drift of continents and other theories of this kind.

There are a number of plausible objections to utilising data on paleomagnetism as a key criterion of the geological history of the Earth. First and foremost, we do not know if the magnetic and the geographical poles coincided in all geological periods. Even today the magnetic poles are situated at a considerable distance (20°) from the geographical poles and change their location, sometimes quite substantially, in the course of short spans of time. In recent years it has been found that there is a connection between the Earth's magnetic field and the surrounding radiation belts of charged particles, on the one hand, and the liquid core of the Earth, on the other. It is reasonable to suppose that the changes in these two fields could bring about considerable changes in the location of the magnetic poles.

Thus, as far as we can judge, *the paleomagnetic data available today are not enough to make broad generalisations or to shed more light on the Earth's geological history.*

To a certain extent Wegener's views may be linked up with a number of theories whose authors attach prime importance to the development of convection currents in the Earth's shell. The subsequent drift of the continents brought about the distribution of continental masses. According to these hypotheses, the lighter sial masses (which probably issued uninterruptedly as a result of gravitative differentiation) were evacuated to the surface in the process of the development of convection currents in the Earth's shell.

At the same time, the theory of the initial molten state of the Earth is accepted unconditionally and, directly or indirectly, the existence of vast layers of molten or semi-liquid, flowing magma is implied (356; 358; 502). These hypotheses do not take the existence at some remote period of Atlantis in account. This stems of itself from the notion of the immutability and antiquity of oceans, which also accompanies theories rejecting all possibility of continents having existed in place of modern oceans.

The theory of convection currents is one of the most popular today and is widely propagated, particularly by American researchers. However, it has many weak points, which we have indicated in the preceding chapter.

The theory that the Earth is expanding has gained currency in recent years. Scientists applying it to the problem of the origin of oceans have to contend with formidable difficulties, which force them to postulate the great and independent antiquity of deep-water basins. For that reason *those who support the ocean permanency theory eagerly accept the theory of an expanding Earth.* It is, therefore, hardly possible to expect them to adopt a positive approach to the Atlantis problem.

Properly speaking, *this theory explains only the origin of some structural features and not the appearance of oceans.* While coping satisfactorily with the origin of linear rents, fissures and faults on a planetary scale, it hardly explains the origin of the great fragmentation of the mid-oceanic ridges, one of which is linked up by us with the history of Atlantis, or the rounded shapes of most of the oceanic basins, shapes that do not fit into the geometry of linear rents, fissures and faults. This typical shape of oceanic basins is much better explained by the notion of the fusion of the Earth's crust in its thinnest places, beneath the floor of shallow seas and great strata of sediments.

This is not difficult to show, even with very simple models of tinctured paraffin or a mixture of paraffin and wax, where the lower layer consists of paraffin with a higher melting temperature (it can easily be coloured blue) and the upper layer of (yellow) paraffin with a lower melting temperature; the shallow places are burdened with a layer of sediments consisting of suitably sifted powders of other substances. When a model of a section of the Earth's crust made of paraffin with a low melting temperature is placed on high-melting-temperature paraffin kept at melting point, "windows" imitating basins will begin to appear; the mixed "magma" is coloured green. On such a model it is possible to study the behaviour of the "roots" of mountains subjected to subcrustal erosion and to trace the appearance of "island arcs". With the help of simple devices it is not difficult to imitate some tectonic movements caused by compression or expansion, folding and so forth. To reduce the plasticity of the paraffin it must be mixed with light and heavy sifted powders of suitable substances.

Inasmuch as even an expanding Earth does not save the ocean permanency theory, its proponents bring in cosmic factors, in particular, the assumption that the Earth had been hit by gigantic meteorites or asteroids. They hold that most of the ancient abyssal areas of the oceans are the sites of such collisions (466: 500; 545). Generally speaking, the idea that cosmic bodies, including hypothetical satellites, had played an active part in the Earth's geological history, that they had crashed down on Earth from time to time, is not new, having a history of more than half a century of its own (37; 138; 160; 461; 497; 536).

At the other end of the scale are theories that the modern oceans are young. In one way or another, this view is upheld (as we have already pointed out) by many Soviet scientists (G. A. Afanasyev, V. V. Belousov, M. V. Muratov, D. G. Panov, V. V. Tikhomirov, Y. M. Sheinmann and others) and some foreign researchers (R. W. van Bemmelen, J. Gilluly, G. and G. Termier, H. Stille). In principle, this group of hypotheses does not rule out the possibility of Atlantis having existed, even at a very late stage of the geological history of oceans.

D. G. Panov (356, 357, 358, 360) was one of the first to suggest a hypothesis founded on the view of the unity of the structure of the Earth's crust on continents and in oceans. The contrasts in the geological structure of continents and oceans steadily increased with the development of the Earth. The changes in the relief and structure were particularly marked in the Mesozoic, and resulted in the formation of the present oceanic basins. A further expansion and deepening of the oceans took place during a fresh recurrence of tectonic movements (neotectonics) in the Cenozoic.

The idea of the youth of modern oceans is also developed by V. V. Belousov (195), who writes: "Present-day continents are fragments of large ancient continents, and their angular boundaries conform more to this viewpoint than to the assumption that continents were built up as a result of the accumulation of sial issuing from the depths of the Earth. Is it too much to think of the melting of the granite stratum by the molten basic magma rising to the surface? This idea has been suggested by geologists and, from the standpoint of petrologists, it is evidently not fantastic."

Comparable views have been presented by many foreign scientists. J. Gilluly (234), for instance, believes that there might have been a thinning down of the sial stratum as a result of subcrustal erosion. R. W. van Bemmelen (197) comes round to the conclusion that the Earth's crust undergoes changes as it subsides, that it undergoes a process of "oceanisation". The basic force behind this oceanisation is the enrichment of the Earth's crust with basalt lava. As may be seen from the above, van Bemmelen's views harmonise with those held by many Soviet scientists.

Some interest is attracted by the considerations suggested by M. V. Stovas (751), who believes that in *the equatorial zone the sea is advancing and land subsiding*. The tendency of the land to subside began as far back as the Miocene and the Pliocene, and in places this is linked up with great fracture zones.

In conclusion of an earlier and repeatedly quoted paper, V. V. Belousov (195) writes: "Lately we have been getting facts pointing to the 'oceanic' nature of the floor of so-called inland seas. Through geological investigations it has been definitely established that in its deepest places, for instance, the Caribbean Sea and the Gulf of Mexico, the Earth's crust is devoid of a granite stratum. The same may be said quite confidently about the Mediterranean and the Black Sea. Could the interpretation of these data be that inland seas were the primary stage of the formation of oceanic basins?"

This forecast was strikingly confirmed by the results of seismic investigations not only in the Mediterranean (518), Caribbean (354, 445) and Black (238, 342) seas but also in an inland body of water like the Caspian (226). This is obviously a boost for the notion of the youth of oceans developed by Belousov. Thus, available data show that the Earth's crust had undergone a process of oceanisation, i.e., an evolution of the following pattern: epicontinental sea → inland or marginal sea → deep-water basin. In the deepest parts of the above-mentioned seas there is no granite stratum at all, but in some cases the thickness of the Earth's crust conforms to earlier continental conditions, preserving a depth of 20 kilometres in the Black and Caspian seas and a much smaller depth in the Mediterranean.

V. V. Tikhomirov (399) points out that the Red Sea, situated in the graben of an ancient platform and formed probably at the close of the Mesozoic, is an interesting example of basification (i.e, the replacement of acid rock, by basic). A sial stratum equal in thickness to the sial of the adjoining platforms could be expected under this sea. However, seismic investigations showed that in the region of the graben itself the sea floor is typically oceanic and that there is no sial in it. There is, consequently, no doubt that the former quite thick sial stratum was almost completely eroded and assimilated along the line of the cleavage (width—60 kilometres). Moreover, I. P. Kosminskaya (364/170) has demonstrated that on continents, too, sedimentary rock lies directly on a "basalt" foundation in old and stable downwarps.

P. H. Kuenen holds that the reality of the oceanisation process must be recognised on the strength of data concerning the geology of the Maritime Alps and the structure of the Ligurian Sea floor. It will be recalled that extinct species of coral of local origin, whose age has been determined as roughly 32,000 years, have been brought to the surface in this sea from a depth of 2,400 metres. Consequently, Kuenen says, one can question the arguments of the ocean permanency supporters that the geophysical properties of the oceanic crust differ from those of the continental crust. Besides, it will be noted that in this region major subsidences (of more than 2,000 metres) occurred in the epoch of man.

According to data obtained by Soviet geophysicists, the crust in the central and northern regions of the Sea of Okhotsk is of the continental type. It is 20-25 kilometres thick and consists mainly of granite. In the abyssal southern trough the crust is of the oceanic type and about 13 kilometres thick. In addition there are no essential differences between the Baltic Sea floor and the adjoining land areas, of which it is a sunken part. The implication here is that in this area oceanisation is only in its infantile stage (the age of the sea is only several tens of millennia) and is being held up by the tectonic uplift of nearby Scandinavia.

R. W. Girdler points out that the geophysical investigations conducted recently not only in the Red Sea but also in the gulfs of Aden and California have shown that an oceanic type crust is in the process of formation in these areas. Incidentally, Soviet scientists have established that in some regions (notably, the Ukrainian shield in the region of Ovruch) the typical continental platform is only five kilometres thick, and below it lies a basalt stratum.

It seems to us that the forecasts of no other hypothesis have been so convincingly confirmed as those of the oceanisation of the Earth's crust.

After investigating the structure of the Atlantic floor, this had to be admitted by even such loyal adherents of the permanency theory as J. and M. Ewing (518/303). They wrote: There is increasing evidence that only broad deep-sea basins have a simple structural configuration: sediments→ oceanic layers → mantle; in the intermediate regions the structure departs toward the continental type, possibly as the result of the intrusions, differentiation, change of the state or of the combination of this process in the Earth's crust and upper mantle. To this we can add: and as the result of oceanisation and the replacement and assimilation of acid continental rocks by more basic rocks.

In conclusion, it would be useful to sum up the geological and paleogeographical data in favour of the youth of modern oceans as cited by V. V. Belousov (196):

1) the "superposed" nature of the Atlantic and Indian oceans and the fragmented shape of the adjoining continents;

2) indications that in place of the present-day oceans there were land areas, which were the sources of clastic material, namely: a) clear-cut signs of the presence in remote times of continental sediments of the Karroo Basin beyond the boundaries of the present-day African continent; b) the transportation of granite boulders to Africa by Upper Paleozoic glaciers from the direction of the Indian Ocean; c) the transportation of clastic products to the Congo Basin from land which in the Mesozoic existed to the west of Africa; d) the removal of Cambrian and Silurian sediments from high land to the northwest of the Scandinavian peninsula; e) paleogeographical data on the existence in the Paleozoic of high land to the east of the Appalachians, where an ocean now stretches;

3) the dispersion of Gondwana flora in the Upper Paleozoic, which testifies to better land communication between South America, Africa, India, Australia and the Antarctic than in subsequent periods;

4) indisputable geological data on the subsident nature of the inland and marginal seas in the east of the Asian continent;

5) ditto concerning the formation of the Northern Atlantic in the Tertiary and Quaternary periods;

6) indisputable paleogeographical data on the existence of areas of high land in place of the present Mediterranean and Caribbean seas, as well as the existence of land areas and shallow seas in place of the Black Sea and the southern part of the Caspian; in all these areas the Earth's crust has an oceanic type structure;

7) the presence in the Pacific and the Atlantic of guyots overlain by shallow-water sediments dating, at the latest, from the Upper Cretaceous, and also data obtained from drilling in atolls which show that there had been a subsidence of land areas in the course of the Tertiary period;

8) coastal flexures,* which are particularly well defined along the

---

* Sharp bends in the layers of the Earth's crust with a stepped stratification of these layers caused by tectonic deformation. Continental flexures, the surface of whose bend coincides with the continental slope, form at the boundary between continents and oceans —*Ed*.

shore of the Atlantic (Greenland, North America, Africa). These flexures are an indication that the downwarp of oceanic depressions is of recent tectonic origin.

However, the youth theory is confronted with many difficulties as well, and has been comprehensively criticised from the standpoint of the ocean permanency theory by A. V. Zhivago and G. B. Udintsev (253). First and foremost, they questioned the existence of a relic subaerial relief on the floor of oceans. Submarine canyons* are one of the major oceanic features which they completely or partially reject as being of subaerial origin. Moreover, they reject the possibility that large continents had once existed in place of the submarine elevations in the World Ocean.

However, the absence of submarine terraces, valleys, hills and other typical attributes of an eroded landscape cannot be accepted as final proof that a given section of the sea floor could not have been subaerial in the recent geological past. We shall try to show that even an extremely rugged volcanic relief may be linked up with the existence of land in the past. We shall deal with this in detail in connection with the problem of Atlantis.

Sunken land areas can have a practically unchanged, inherited subaerial relief only if their subsidence was an orderly process. If it proceeded in slow stages there would be more or less sharply defined consequences of marine abrasion: flat-topped hills, terraces and so forth.

If the subsidence was of the nature of a destructive cataclysm accompanied by splitting, lava and other flows, the formation of volcanic cones, faults, out-thrusted blocks and cliffs, and so forth, the initial subaerial relief might be changed beyond recognition. This type of subsidence would give the sea floor the appearance of an extraordinarily fragmented, young volcanic relief (example—the destruction of Atlantis). Moreover, it is one thing when part of the ancient continental platform subsides as a result of fragmentation, and another when the region of subsidence embraces a geologically youthful land area as, possibly, had been the case with Atlantis.

The most complete case of a reworked relief would be its flooding and levelling by discharges of lava and other products of volcanic activity. An extreme case of this process would be the total assimilation of the former relief and the rocks of which it consists, and the melting and reworking of the latter into more basic material. In the last analysis this can lead to the formation of a completely different relief—a more or less level surface composed of volcanic rock, with separate volcanic cones, small hilly elevations, swells and so forth.**

A careful analysis of different views has brought the author of this work to the conclusion that *the only acceptable theory is that*

---

* This difficult problem is examined in the next chapter.
** See Note 3 (Appendix 2).

of the oceanisation of continents accompanied by the fusion of the floor and the subsequent replacement of acid by more basic rocks (suggested by V. V. Belousov and M. V. Muratov). This process continues to take place in marginal and inland seas. Its details, like those of the origin of the Earth's interior heat, are not very clear. A. A. Smyslov assumed that some role is, perhaps, played by the accumulation of thick layers of sedimentary rock.

V. V. Tikhomirov (399) considers that it is sufficient for a sial stratum even as thick as 20 kilometres to sink in the sea to a depth of about four kilometres for an energetic process of basification to begin. In the course of a geologically short span of time this process can obliterate all signs of the existence of a granite layer.

E. N. Lyustikh (309) came out with what seemed at first glance to be serious objections to the hypothesis suggested by V. V. Belousov and M. V. Muratov. These objections were based primarily on the somewhat tendentious view that oceanisation had always taken place where the Earth's crust is about 35 kilometres thick, i.e., only in the vicinity of great mountain systems. On plains, far from mountains, the crust is usually only 20 kilometres thick. But if the oceanisation process had embraced even great mountain ranges with a thickness of 50 kilometres and more, the crust in these places would have been reduced not to five kilometres, as E. N. Lyustikh suggests, but to 15-20 kilometres. An example of this are the island arcs in the Pacific which are now submerged mountain systems.

The oceanisation process takes place principally in primary shallow seas with a relatively thin sial stratum but an extremely thick layer of sedimentary rock. This makes it clear that not so much magma is required for the assimilation of granites by basalts as Lyustikh suggests. In fact, for the assimilation of granites into andesites (for example, along the margin of the Pacific and along the island arcs) only an equal quantity (in weight) of basalt is needed (see Table 2, Appendix 1).

There are weighty grounds for assuming that in cases of highly developed assimilation (for example, to the stage of tholeiites) the Earth's crust was initially composed of a thin layer of granitoids and a considerably thicker (for tholeiites—ten-fold in weight) layer of basalts. This approximate ratio is retained in sectors of the crust which have not yet been subjected to complete assimilation and is to be observed in some regions of the Pacific Ocean (for example, east of the Hawaiian Islands).

Lyustikh's further arguments stem from notions about the predominantly juvenile origin of granites through gravitative differentiation; quite understandably he draws the conclusion that crustal material could not melt in the substratum. Moreover, he rejects the suggestion that the granite materials melted and withdrew under the surrounded continents, maintaining that this contradicts the principles of mechanics. The sial level on continents is higher than beneath oceans. Therefore, in accordance with the law of intercommunicating vessels, sial must flow from continents to oceans and not vice versa (sic!).

These poorly founded views spring mainly from a complete disregard of the possible origin of granite through metamorphism from sedimentary rocks. If there is a thick layer of consolidated sedimentary rocks on the floor of an ocean or sea, it will, sooner or later, be subjected to metamorphism, which will lead to the formation of granites or granitoids. In this case the law of intercommunicating vessels leads to conclusions which come into conflict with Lyustikh's statements. Under conditions of equilibrium the presence of two coexisting liquids of different density (heavy basalt and lighter granite) will lead to the lighter liquid occupying a higher position in one of the limbs of the intercommunicating vessels. Where conditions are suitable, this light magma will begin to flow to the surface, the equilibrium will be destroyed, and the place of this magma will be taken by heavier magma flowing from the depths. Consequently, the light (granite) masses will withdraw to a higher place, i.e., in the direction of a continent. This withdrawal will be expedited by the pressure of the column of water on the floor of an ocean or sea. This process does not break any laws of physics or mechanics.

Similarly flimsy objections were raised by Lyustikh against the possibility of granites being absorbed by basalt magma. This process is not difficult to picture under conditions of sumbarine discharges of basalt lava through fissures in the primary granite floor. If the granite vault was rigidly joined to the continent in at least one place and then partially, under water, was covered with heavier basalt magma issuing from side fissures, conditions under which this heavier magma would at once harden in the upper stratum continguous to water would be created, depending upon the thickness of the granite layer, the basalt magma covering it and the water, and also on the flow velocity of the magma. The proximity of such an effective cooling agent as water makes the magma underlying the hardened stratum still more viscous and less mobile, bringing down its temperature. For that reason the granite vault, which is not a very good conductor of heat, cannot completely melt and rise to the surface of the now hardened basalt magma. It remains beneath this hardened layer of basalt and, gradually melting, mixes with the basalt, producing mixed rocks. This process can repeat itself over and over again and, in the end, lead to the complete replacement of granites. On the other hand, it may so happen that the quantity and temperature of the magma flowing from the depths of the Earth are not enough to completely melt and assimilate all the granite material. In that case, if there is a considerable quantity of granite it may remain unchanged beneath the layer of basalt magma hardened by water or, if there is not very much granite, it may take the shape of separate inclusions in basalt lava as, for example, in the case of the lava on Ascension Island.

There is good reason to assume that the later stages of alpine tectonic movements witnessed the exhaustion of granite material, of the products of the reworking of the most ancient sedimentary rocks. In our view it is improbable that there were considerable fresh deliveries of acid rock in the later periods of mountain-building at the expense of the differentiation of basic magma and the substance of the Earth's mantle.

G. L. Afanasyev (186/14) holds an analogous view. He writes: "For my part, I shall note the circumstance, which is now becoming ever more clear, that there probably were phenomena of magmatism on the boundary between the Mesozoic and the Cenozoic. Subalkaline and alkaline complexes of basic rocks—basaltoids and nepheline and feldspathoid rocks associated with them—formed in this period in many regions of the globe, both oceanic and continental."

H. Stille's (440) important observation of the successive decrease of the occurrence of granite intrusions has a direct bearing on the above views. Thus, granites of Variscian age are fairly widespread. In some folded regions one also finds Mesozoic granites. On the other hand, Lower Tertiary granites are relatively rare, while granites of Upper Tertiary age are exceptionally rare. It follows, therefore, as V. V. Belousov emphasises, *that at the later stages of geological history geobuilding material passes to more basic rock—andesite (where there is a link with the assimilation of granites) and, particularly, various types of basalt.* Basalts become the basic geobuilding material where neotectonic processes manifest themselves.

In conclusion, this is what V. V. Belousov writes about the nature and origin of oceans (196/22): "As we have shown earlier, the formation of oceans dates back to the beginning of the Mesozoic. Since then they have become larger and deeper. Various sections of the World Ocean are evidently at different stages of development. The North Atlantic is very young. It subsided quite recently, in the Neogene. It is not very deep, and although the crust underlying it no longer has a granite layer it is still fairly thick...

"The South Atlantic and the Indian Ocean are, apparently, older. Here the basins were formed by the subsidence of large blocks separated from each other by grabens such as are at present developed in East Africa and indicate the further direction of the spread of the ocean. These oceans are deeper than the North Atlantic and the crust underlying them has a typically oceanic structure.

"The Pacific is, as a whole, probably still older, although perhaps it became deeper more rapidly due to the particularly active fracturing of the shell. It is deeper than any other ocean.

"As an ocean grows deeper it witnesses changes in the composition of the outflowing basalt lava, which becomes more and more basic. Indeed, in the North Atlantic plateau basalts alternate practically evenly with tholeiitic basalts. Plateau basalts predominate in the Indian Ocean, while the most basic varieties of basalts such as oceanites occur in the Pacific. This allows us to assume that increasingly deeper strata of the shell formed of the more basic material, which chemically, however, remains within the basalt group, are mobilised in the process of oceanisation."

According to data of the Institute of the Physics of the Earth (of the Academy of Sciences of the USSR), reported by S. M. Zverev, a detailed seismic investigation of the Western Pacific has brought to light that below the Mohorovicic discontinuity *the structure of the upper layers of the mantle is as heterogeneous as that of the Earth's crust of the continents.* Two structural tiers have been found. Each consists of separate blocks. I. A. Rezanov writes: *"Does not this interesting fact prove that a continent, which later subsided, existed in this area of the ocean in the recent geological past? New data strongly reinforce the position of investigators who uphold the theory about the relative youth of oceanic hollows and the appearance of oceans in place of continents"* (821).

We have dwelt at length on the problem of oceans because it is the key to the whole problem of Atlantis. The first question asked is whether Atlantis might have existed as a land mass in view of the fact that where it was supposed to have been located there is now an ocean several kilometres deep. The answer to this can only be given by our knowledge of the nature and origin of oceans.

From what we know we can draw the general conclusion that *the outline and depth of the modern ocean are not ancient and immutable. They have changed and will change, and these changes range beyond the limits of the continental shelf. The outlines and depths of oceans are inconstant in time. In the present geological epoch—the Cenozoic—there is a clear-cut tendency of the oceans to expand and grow deeper, which is direct evidence of the process of oceanisation.* The author of the present work believes that *the maximum development of oceanic regimes with the final formation of deep-water basins was probably witnessed in the second half of the Tertiary and the Quaternary periods and that this process is still continuing.*

THE PACIFIC OCEAN AND ATLANTOLOGY

The problem of the Pacific Ocean merits a detailed review not only because this ocean is given an important role in many theories about the origin of oceans, as we have already pointed out, but also because of its interest to atlantology, whose second field of study after Atlantis is the former existence of land—archipelagoes of large islands or even continents*—in some part of the Pacific.

As distinct from Atlantis, regarding which we have a written legend but have not yet found relics of material culture, remains of vanished civilisations have been discovered in the region of the Pacific but written records of these civilisations have not survived (attempts to read the Kohua-Rongo-Rongo records on Easter Island

---

* See Table 5 (Appendix 1)

have not led to any indication of that island's history). These civilisations existed on the fringe of the ocean. First and foremost, mention must be made of the ancient civilisation of Easter Island and also of the lost legendary Davis Islands. The latter islands were discovered at the close of the 17th century in the region of Easter Island (27°S 105°W), but the next expedition failed to find them. Although Thor Heyerdahl's brilliant investigations have brought closer the solution of the riddle of Easter Island, we feel there are still many gaps in the history of the settlement of that island. If, indeed, larger land areas once existed in this part of the Pacific we would be justified in naming them *East Pacifis*.

The remains of a vanished and still more enigmatic civilisation, about which no trustworthy legends or traditions have been preserved, have been found in the region of the Caroline Islands. With this civilisation we link up the problem of *West Pacifis*.

Lastly, closer to the central part of the ocean, there may also have been a large land area consisting, most probably, of big islands. The present-day Hawaiian Islands (*Hawaiis*) are part of this archipelago. All these places are studied by atlantologists not without purpose—they are linked up with vast, submerged, geologically young mountain systems, which shall be dealt with in some detail in the next chapter. We shall only make the reservation that the problem of the lost continents and islands of the Pacific is much more complex than the problem of Atlantis. Here we shall review in the most general outline only one aspect of the geological part of the problem dealing with the nature and origin of the Pacific Ocean.

The marginal seas of the Pacific emerged in the geologically very recent past. In some of them—the Sea of Okhotsk and beneath the Japanese Islands—there is still a thin continental crust. According to Japanese sources the final separation of these islands as well as of Sakhalin from the continent took place only about 12,000 years ago. As early as 18,000-20,000 years ago there existed favourable conditions for the migration of plants, animals and human beings to the islands from the north and from the south.

Guyots, flat-topped submarine mountains first discovered by H. H. Hess, are an interesting feature of the Pacific and have a direct bearing on the young movements of its floor. Although they were subsequently discovered in other oceans as well, they do not occur in such large numbers as in the Pacific. In this connection, V. V. Belousov (195) writes: "Although the guyots probably owe their flat tops to erosion, they are an indication that the floor had subsided and the ocean had become deeper. In the central Pacific the guyots are at present situated at a depth of about 1,500 metres, which is roughly equal to the thickness of the coral structures. The guyots situated deeper may be classed as more ancient and as having begun their subsidence earlier."

Some attention must be paid to a hypothesis, suggested as early as 1934 by C. Johns (295), according to which the drop in the level of

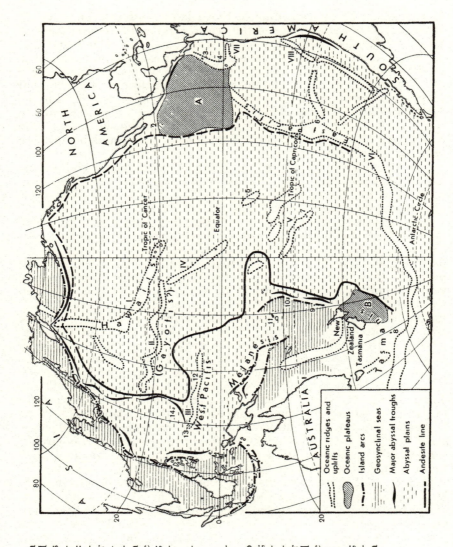

Map of the Pacific Ocean showing the principal ridges and plateaus as well as surmised lost continents. *Oceanic ridges:* I—Hawaiian; II—Mid-Pacific (Marcus-Nekker Mountains), III—Caroline; IV—Fanning; V—Ridges and plateaus in the southern part of the ocean, VI—East Pacific; VII—Carnegie; VIII—Naska.

Oceanic plateaus A—Albatross; B—New Zealand

Islands and Archipelagoes 1—Hawaiian Islands; 2—Revilla Gigedo Islands and Partida Island; 3—Cocos Island; 4—Galapagos Islands; 5—Marquesas Islands; 6—Easter Island; 7—Rapa Island (Rapaiti), 8—Macquarie Island, 9—Kermadec Islands, 10—Tonga Islands, 11—Fiji Islands; 12—Ponape Island; 13—Yap Island; 14—Guam Island

the World Ocean, assumed to be linked up with the existence of submarine canyons (see next chapter), is due to the subsidence of the Pacific floor and then to the outpouring of huge quantities of lava, as a consequence of which the general level of the ocean rose again.

Following up the Johns hypothesis, G. W. Lindberg (295/180) pinpoints the riddle of the bipolar distribution of marine mammals. During the period of glaciation, the northern, cold-loving fauna of the Atlantic moved south, but in the Pacific, for some reason, they moved northward, as though fleeing before a thermal barrier. Moreover, there is the puzzle of the occurrence of tropical coral fauna, requiring a mean annual water temperature of 19°, not only in Nomi Bay, near Tokyo, Japan, but also as far north as Penzha Bay in the Sea of Okhotsk. Inasmuch as any unilateral warping of the equator must be ruled out, Lindberg assumed that this rise of the water temperature was caused by the discharge of huge quantities of lava on the bed of the Pacific Ocean. G. D. Khizanashvili (424), on the other hand, believes that the northward migration of cold-loving fauna in the Pacific and their simultaneous southward migration in the Atlantic during the initial phase of the Pleistocene might have been due to a change in the ocean level in various latitudes as a result of a migration of the poles.

On the basis of present-day knowledge, it is considered as established that the Pacific floor has roughly the following structure: 0.3 ± 0.1 km—upper layer of sediments with a longitudinal wave diffusion velocity of 2 km/sec; a layer 1.0 ± 0.5 kilometres thick consisting of rocks with a wave velocity of 5 km/sec; a layer of 5.0 ± 1.0 kilometres with a wave velocity of about 6.8 km/sec; and a layer with a velocity of 8.2 km/sec.

Evidence that a sial crust had existed is to be found in various parts of the ocean, even in its central part. It is believed that the present boundary of the Pacific basin proper follows what is conditionally known as the *andesite line*. Andesite, a volcanic rock of sial origin, occurs between the continents and this line (407). Beyond the andesite line, within the boundary of the ocean, is a region of basalt volcanic rocks. Japanese scientists have found that west of the andesite line the Earth's crust is of the continental type. According to them, the basalt of the western part of the ocean is something like 10 million years old, while in the eastern part it is much younger—about 3 million years!

On the basis of the doubtful assumption that andesites originated primarily as the result of the crystallisational differentiation of basalts, G. A. MacDonald (602) suggests that there are two types of andesites—continental and oceanic. He maintains that almost all the andesites in the Pacific originated as a result of differentiation. In our opinion that is not enough proof for this assertion. The data given by D. S. Carder (484) at the World Oceanological Congress in New York in 1959 indirectly confirm the possibility of the Pacific andesites being of non-oceanic origin. He reported that in the

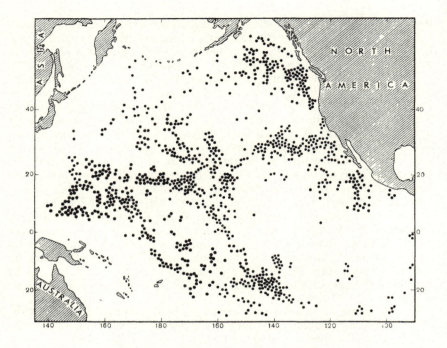

Distribution of submarine plateaus, guyots and submarine mountains rising to a height of over 900 metres above the surrounding Pacific floor (673, 192). Mountains are designated by heavy dots, and plateaus by clusters of light dots

Western Pacific (i.e., up to the andesite line) the Mohorovicic discontinuity lies at a depth of 15-18 kilometres, which differs essentially from the depth of the surface of the purely oceanic crust (5 kilometres for the centre of the Pacific). Beneath the islands of Guam and New Britain the crust structure is close to the continental type. R. W. Raitt (379) notes that there is a layer of sial nearly one kilometre thick in the east, in some regions between the Hawaiian Islands and North America. *Another interesting point is the existence of the small and absolutely isolated granite island of Partida* (19°N 112°W) west of the Revilla Gigedo Islands (323). In 1929 R. Shteinman logically concluded that this indicated the existence of a continent in the Pacific in the geological past.

R. A. Daly (247) and J. Gilluly (234) point out that clearly sial rocks have been found on many islands in the Pacific (Table 1, Appendix 1): even rhyolite on Easter Island; andesites on the Marquesas Islands; andesites on the Galapagos Islands; granite and schist on the Fiji Islands; granite inclusions and rhyolite on the Tonga Islands; granite on the Kermadec Islands; andesites on Chatham, Bounty and Oakland islands; and andesites and schist on Truk, Yap and

Man islands of the Caroline group.* Reasonably enough, the supporters of the ocean permanency theory fall back on the crystallisational differentiation of basalts to explain these facts.

It has now been established that beneath North Australia the Earth's crust is 40 kilometres thick, in the eastern part of the Coral Sea it is 20 kilometres thick, in the Fiji-Tonga-Samoa area it is 22-28 kilometres thick, while at the Tonga Islands it reaches a thickness of 36 kilometres! It is thinner, about 15 kilometres, in the region between the New Hebrides and the Fiji Islands and also between the Kermadec Islands and New Caledonia (814, 819).

Also interesting were the results of a study of the force of gravity in the Pacific. J.H.F. Umbgrove (407) declares that a positive anomaly of gravity, typical of the ocean floor, runs all the way from San Francisco to Guam via Hawaii. At Guam, however, there is a fairly strong negative anomaly. Gravimetrical measurements likewise confirm the sial nature of Yap Island.

At one time, the view that the Pacific was once a land mass—*Pacifis*—was quite widespread among geologists and paleontologists. This view sprang from investigations of the flora and fauna in the Pacific itself and on the continents framing it. The data provided by these investigations were, unfortunately, forgotten and ignored, being supplanted by the views linked up in one way or another with the ocean permanency theory.

The most ardent supporters of the Pacifis theory in pre-revolutionary and post-revolutionary Russia include I. D. Lukashevich and M. A. Menzbir (141, 143, 325). Lukashevich went so far as to compile a series of maps of Pacifis with all its changes up to its disappearance. Menzbir (325/76) wrote: "Objective scientific data tells us that the Pacific Ocean is not as ancient as one might think. Its tropical part evidently took shape not earlier than during the Miocene. But even later, much later, when man not only appeared but reached a certain level of culture, numerous islands, large and small, rose from its bosom." Let us bear in mind that Menzbir wrote these prophetic words more than 40 years ago.

Another point of which note must be taken is that the Pacifis theory has its supporters to this day both in the Soviet Union and abroad; its supporters abroad include H. Hallier (543), J. W. Gregory (539) and, quite recently H. I. Jensen (569a). The latter notes the presence of Mesozoic coal on New Caledonia. The Bulgarian geologist Mikhailovich (332) recently reverted to this theory. R. M. Demenitskaya (249/19) wrote, after analysing modern data on the structure of the Earth's shell beneath continents and oceans:

"Indeed, if the continent, replaced by the Atlantic Ocean, sank in the Mesozoic and the thickness of the crust diminished as a result of 'dissolution' processes, which we cannot as yet fathom, we do

---

* Some years ago Soviet geologists discovered granite on the volcanic Kuril Islands.

not have impressive facts to show that there could not have been analogous processes in the region of the Earth's surface presently occupied by the Pacific Ocean" (also see 730/89, 101).

The discovery of galaxias, a fresh-water fish, in New Zealand in 1764 favours the view that at one time there was a vast continent in the Pacific Ocean, particularly in its southern part. This fish occurs in the Southern Hemisphere between the 30th and 60th southern parallels in fresh waters of continents and some islands. Salt water is fatal to it and therefore its migration by sea must be ruled out. There have been many other puzzling cases of the occurrence of some fauna which cannot be explained without the theory that instead of the present ocean there once were vast tracts of land (241/92; 721).

There is a host of facts in favour of the surmise that a huge land area once existed in the Southwestern Pacific. J. Gilluly (234) notes: "But the clear geologic evidence from the southwest Pacific that the sial plates of Fiji, New Caledonia, and a host of other islands in the area between Fiji, New Zealand and Australia were formerly larger—though much of this area now lies at oceanic depths—seems to demand that at least some sial is also present in the deep ocean floor. True, much of this area lies under at least four kilometres of water, but the problem of its depression is still comparable to that involved in the uplift of the Tibetan Plateau. Granitic rocks in the Macquarie Island glacial drift may have come from a small mass, but it was doubtless nearby and hence now at great depth beyond the fault scarp bounding the island...."

In a paper published some years ago the Australian geologist R. W. Fairbridge (527) pointed out that the southwestern Pacific could be subdivided into two large continental provinces—Tasmanis and Melanesis. No Paleozoic-Paleogene marine or continental sediments are known in the Melanesian province. The elevations in this province probably represent a new crust formed by Tertiary and Quaternary eruptions. An andesite line runs along the eastern boundary of this province. The western edge of the Tonga Trough, across which the andesite line passes, is regarded by Fairbridge as the edge of a submerged continent, and the crust of the entire province as the result of basification. Melanesis was an integral continent long before the mid-Tertiary and parts of it submerged as a result of a very recent, young subsidence. As regards Tasmanis the possibility of its having existed is linked up with the riddle of the origin of the aborigenes of Tasmania, who could have reached the island only by land. Consequently, intelligent man was already in existence when there was a land link betweenTasmania and Australia.

Seismic investigations of the Tonga Trough (378) have shown that there the Earth's crust consists of four layers, of which the second from the top (subsediment layer) is three kilometres thick and longitudinal waves travel through it at a velocity of 5.2 km/sec, i.e., it cannot consist of "basalt" material. The surface of the Mohorovicic discontinuity lies, as on continents, at a depth of 20 kilometres. These are features that generally distinguish abyssal troughs from fault troughs (for example, the fault trough of the Red Sea), where the sial layer is completely assimilated. Here the process begins as a result of the youth of such troughs.

The vast *submarine* Caroline Plateau, over which are islands of the same name, is situated north of New Guinea. *This region is the home of the enigmatic Megalithic culture, about whose origin and people we have no trustworthy data to go by.* The fantastic legends of the natives of these islands are likewise extremely fragmentary. *The cradle of this culture was on Ponape* with its remains of a huge, mysterious port carved into basalt cliffs (Nanmatal, sometimes called the Venice of the Pacific). Unfortunately, this exceptionally interesting region of Western Pacifis is virtually quite inaccessible to archaeological and oceanological investigation because the Caroline Islands have been turned by the USA into a naval and air base and proclaimed a restricted area. The same situation obtained under the Japanese.

But in the central Pacific there is a region differing essentially from the surrounding area. This is the submarine Hawaii Ridge, which runs far to the north up to the Komandorskiye Islands. A colossal mountain system, it is a broad arched uplift (width—up to 1,100 kilometres) rising to a height of nearly 1,000 metres, along which are ranges of mountains. The summits of these mountains jut out of the ocean in the shape of the Hawaiian Islands. The northern part of these summits are levelled out and covered with accumulations of rounded pebbles (583). Proponents of the ocean permanency theory maintain that the pebbles were brought by drift ice. But what is the explanation for the flat summits if we exclude sea abrasion? Pebbles have been found much farther south. Pointing this out, G. V. Kort (275) offers the conjecture that during the Pleistocene drift ice reached as far south as 10th and not the 30th parallel. We feel there are little grounds for this assertion. If the pebbles are of glacial origin they must consist mainly of sial rock from the western part of North America and Alaska, where great glaciers descended to the sea during the Pleistocene.

The Hawaiian Islands are the only place in the central Pacific with active volcanoes; their magma is tholeiitic. But andesites also occur on these islands (234, 602). R. S. Dietz and H. W. Menard (499) have reported the discovery of submarine terraces on the base of the islands and considered that they had once been a shelf. The terraces were discovered at a depth of 350-370 metres; the submerged shoreline is 550 metres below the present water level. In some places evidence of the submerged shelf was found as deep as 700 metres. On the basis of a comparison of island and continental lava, R. Furon surmises that the *Hawaiian Islands were once part of a Pacific continent* (364a/54, 101). We believe that *in the not very distant past the submarine Hawaiian Ridge was a large land area—Hawaiis; perhaps the sinking of its remains was witnessed by man*—let us recall the

Polynesian legend of a happy motherland named Hawaiki about whose location there are the most diverse guesses. Moreover, we believe that *at one time Hawaiis may have been a chain of islands or even a large land mass across which man* (possibly Mesolithic and Neolithic pre-Ainu and Mongoloid tribes) *migrated* from Asia to America and to the south of the Hawaiian Islands—to Polynesia.

Drawing conclusions from the investigations conducted during the 34th cruise of the Soviet expedition ship *Vityaz*, V. G. Kort (275) writes: "Several formerly unknown submarine mountains of volcanic origin have been discovered; they were islands that had submerged. The discovery of these mountains supplements former notions of the occurrence of volcanism in the Pacific Ocean and confirms that there were island bridges linking up the continents lying along the periphery of the ocean."

A series of latitudinal fractures of various thickness stretch in the Eastern Pacific in a westerly direction from America. They are stepped faults fringed by a mountain range along the ledge and extending westward for many hundreds and even thousands of kilometres. These fractures are (from north to south): Mendozino, Pioneer and Murrey (from the shores of California, USA), Molokai and Clarion (from the shores of Mexico), Clipperton (from the shores of Central America) and, possibly, Galapagos, Marquis and Sala y Gomez (from the shores of South America).

According to recent investigations conducted by American scientists, the Mendozino scarp running almost along the 40th parallel from California to 160°W is a submarine range measuring 10-15 kilometres in width with its crest at a depth of 2,000 metres. In the south it reaches a depth of 4,400 metres and in the north 3,200 metres. Rounded basalt boulders and pebbles have been found on it. According to the investigators this indicates that at one time the range was a chain of islands. The fault bordering the range in the north is geologically very young and is the epicentre of earthquakes.

The Andes-Cordillera system runs along the entire Pacific seaboard of the two Americas. V. V. Belousov (192) thinks its structure gives us grounds for believing that its eastern half is a folded zone with the western part lying beneath the waters of the ocean. He (194/510) considers that the submarine Albatross Plateau (adjoining the region of the Cocos and Galapagos islands) and other elevations, one of which is Easter Island, were part of this mountainous country.

He does not rule out the possibility of these islands once having had links with some submerged land masses. Regarding the crust structure of this region, J. Oliver, M. Ewing and F. Press (352) write: Gutenberg drew the conclusion that the points close to (and east of) the highland correspond to the continental crust 20-30 kilometres thick. There are some doubts about the reliability of this method, but the conclusions are evidently correct. Daly points to the typically continental rocks of Easter Island and assumes that the plateau is a large but relatively thin layer of continental rock. Available data confirm this, but they are not sufficiently convincing.

A granite layer has been discovered beneath the submarine Cocos and Carnegie ranges and the Galapagos Islands! These mountains run east of the East Pacific Range, on which Easter Island stands (813/258). An interesting legend has been recorded by the Heyerdahl expedition (812). According to this legend, in a fit of anger a giant named Uvoke caused the subsidence of a large continent, the remnant of which is Easter Island. Hence the island's strange name: Te-Pito-Te-Chanua, meaning Centre of the Earth.

G. P. Woolard (706) points out that in the deeper part of the ocean east of Easter Island the Earth's crust is only four kilometres thick, of which a layer of crystalline rock has a thickness of two kilometres, while in the region of the submarine Naska Range, situated to the north-east and stretching from the Mid-East Pacific Ridge in the direction of Peru, it is 15 kilometres thick. West of Ecuador there is another system of submarine mountains—the Carnegie Range, which stretches in the direction of the Galapagos Islands and is separated from the continent by a narrow trough.

It may be firmly assumed that *Easter Island is genetically linked up with submerged land which sank and underwent considerable reworking as a result of a catastrophe; we call this land East Pacifis.* The criticised views of J. Macmillan Brown that an archipelago that was genetically and ethnically linked up with Easter Island might have existed in the recent past is thus unexpectedly given some confirmation.

The extremely interesting paper read by Cronwell (254) at the 10th World Pacific Congress *on the discovery of coal on Rapa Island* (Rapaiti, south-west of Mangareva Island) *provides irrefutable testimony of the fact that there was a continent in that part of the ocean.* The flora on the island likewise dates back to remote antiquity. On the basis of these discoveries, which, incidentally, passed unnoticed, Cronwell assumed *the existence of a vast submerged land area in and south of the region of Polynesia.*

Let us now make a few generalisations. R. Rewelle (647) points out that the Pacific witnessed intensive geologic activity during the latter history of the Earth. Investigations on Bikini and Eniwetok atolls showed that they took shape as atolls on the volcanic base in the Tertiary period. The origin of the fossils raised from the Mid-Pacific Ridge proved to be of Oligocene shallow water. Even proponents of the antiquity of the Pacific like H. W. Menard and E. L. Hamilton (411) had to admit at the 10th World Pacific Congress that the present submarine mountain systems had once been islands, became shallow banks and then sank deeper. The most ancient finds are Cretaceous reef corals.

Ehara Shingo (508), who has studied the tectonic history of Japan, believes that the tectonic movements in the Pacific started during the Lower Miocene. We are of the opinion that in the Atlantic Ocean, as well, tectonic activity dates from the same period.

A study of the tectonic and geologic conditions of the Pacific expanses has brought D. G. Panov (363) round to the conclusion that in the light of modern data the Pacific is geologically young and that large areas in it had subsided in the course of neotectonic movements. "Most of the Pacific floor," he writes, "is an activated platform far removed from an immutable or 'pregeosynclinal' state, which is frequently ascribed to it. Like the other oceans, the Pacific is young although it retains features inherited from past evolution."

Obviously, *the notion that the Pacific dates back to great antiquity will have to be deposited in the archives of geological hypotheses.* We fully subscribe to the words of V. V. Belousov (194/511): "It may thus be asserted that very recently, partially even in the age of man, the Pacific Ocean grew considerably at the expense of great chunks of continents which, together with their young ranges of mountains, were inundated by it. The summits of these mountains are to be seen in the island garlands of East Asia."

Chapter Nine

SOME FEATURES OF OCEANS

Over the past decades oceanological investigations have led to discoveries that come into conflict with the ocean permanency theory. They include the finding of submarine valleys and canyons, flat-topped submarine mountains (guyots), submerged rock benches, deep-water sand of a clearly local terrigenous origin, remains of shallow-water flora and fauna (and even fresh-water fauna) beyond the limits of the shelf and slope of continents, as well as enormous submerged mountain systems (mid-oceanic ranges with an extremely complex, rugged relief).

It is very important to bear these facts in mind when we deal with the problem of Atlantis, because in many cases they provide unquestionable testimony either of the youth of the oceans themselves, of great subsidences or of the onetime existence of large land areas that had been in subaerial conditions for a prolonged period.

All these facts belie the ocean permanency theory, basically undermining its very foundation, namely, the view that the ocean floor is immutable. New, ancillary hypotheses, some of a semi-fantastic nature like the hypothesis of turbidity currents, have been advanced to save the mainstays of the permanency theory; factors like submarine erosion and bed currents are considerably overrated. Much of this chapter is devoted to a critical analysis of these hypotheses and views.

It goes without saying that these questions, particularly those of mid-oceanic mountain ranges, are of great importance to the Atlantis problem, because we link up the onetime existence of Atlantis with one of these ranges (the Mid-Atlantic). We must, therefore, very thoroughly scrutinise the nature, causes and time of the appearance of these ranges.

Moreover, there are grounds for believing that the sinking of Atlantis was only one of the stages of great tectonic subsidences characterising the process of oceanisation, which took place simultaneously in many parts of the globe. This brings us to the hypothesis of a global transgression during the Quaternary period, considerations about which shall be given at the end of this chapter.

A. SUBMARINE VALLEYS AND CANYONS

Let us start with an analysis of the not very clear problems of *submarine valleys and canyons*. V. N. Saks (385) notes that many hundreds of these valleys and canyons have been discovered along the shores of both Americas, the shores of Europe and Africa, in the Mediterranean Sea and the Indian Ocean, along the eastern seaboard of Asia and near many oceanic islands. Thus, submarine valleys and canyons occur throughout the world. Moreover, it has been found that there are numerous small valleys on the continental shelf. During the past decade canyons running parallel to the shores of continents have been discovered on the ocean floor.

As D. G. Panov (362) points out, there is now some uncertainty regarding the very terminology and its interpretation. Some investigators draw a distinction between submarine valleys, submarine fjords and submarine canyons, others do not recognise this distinction.

Submarine canyon is the name given to submarine valleys that have the same cross-section and bed as land canyons.

Properly speaking *submarine valleys* are unquestionably underwater continuations of river valleys now in existence or which had existed.

Submarine fjords are a feature of the shelf of some sections of continents and of individual polar islands. They have a typical trough-like cross-section and frequently carry moraine.

Submarine valleys may be divided into three types (362). The first two types are submarine valleys proper, which may be either inherited or of modern origin. Modern submarine valleys are linked up with the creep of unconsolidated sediments down shelves: inherited valleys are chiefly inherited and date from the period of glaciation, when they were carved into hard rock: they are also to be found in off-shore shallow water and on the surface of shelves. The third type consists of submarine canyons, among which canyons of the continental slope (as well as at the continuation of submarine valleys of the shelf) are distinguished from canyons on the floor of ocean basins.

A number of hypotheses has been offered to explain the origin of these valleys and canyons. These may be divided into two large groups: those upholding the subaerial origin of valleys and those ascribing the appearance of submarine valleys and canyons to purely oceanic factors.

The marked resemblance of submarine valleys and canyons to similar forms of relief on land makes the subaerial origin theory most acceptable; such is the opinion of many prominent scientists. Academician L. S. Berg (198/305) writes: "Thus, together with the American professor, F. P. Shepard, and with G. W. Lindberg we are convinced that submarine valleys are subaerial formations, the result of the inundation of usual, land river valleys." J. Bourcart of France (209, 283) expresses his views more categorically: "The theory that canyons are the result of erosion provides the only satisfactory explanation of the facts known to us." However, ocean-bed canyons were later discovered running parallel to the continental slope. Their relation to existing or formerly existing rivers has not yet been established.

Similar formidable difficulties arise when we attempt to find the causes that led to the inundation of valleys. Here we must assume that the considerable changes in the level of the World Ocean were much greater than the eustatic changes caused by glaciation, or recognise the similarly considerable changes in the balance between land and sea as a result of the sinking of the ocean floor. Neither of these hypotheses is acceptable from the viewpoint of the permanency theory.

The contradictions between the theory of the subaerial origin of submarine valleys and canyons and the views held by many American oceanologists and geologists, have induced a group of American investigators (514) to put forward a number of objections and adopt hypotheses postulating that these forms of relief originated as a result of submarine erosion, particularly by currents carrying huge masses of fine mud and sand (so-called turbidity currents, with which we shall deal at some length). Pressured by the objections of the supporters of the submarine erosion theory, E. P. Shepard, who had explained away many of these objections, was ultimately compelled to depart from his initial views.

The only hypothesis that successfully copes with the numerous difficulties is that advanced by G. D. Khizanashvili (423/127). He writes: *"The dynamics of the axis of rotation and the water level of oceans bring the level vacillation into line with the immutability of the quantity of water in oceans.* There is only one explanation to all the enumerated phenomena: a different mutual position of the ocean bed and the water level, i.e., *a different depth of the ocean with a different position of the axis of rotation.* Essentially, the riddle of the submarine valleys would alone be enough to make this assumption inevitable."

In our view, D. G. Panov (362; 730/191-194) comes closest of all to resolving the problem of submarine valleys and canyons. He links their origin up with tectonic processes in continents—the continental shelf—and on the ocean floor, or with neotectonic movements on the floor of the World Ocean. In some cases the Earth's crust was simply warped along the border zone of the continent—the ocean—with the resultant formation of a continental flexure, whose development caused the surface of the continental shelf and slope to sink.

Other cases witnessed the formation of tectonic ruptures and fractures, which determined the location and occurrence of submarine canyons on the continental slope. As regards canyons on the ocean floor, their origin depends on the formation of ruptures in the Earth's crust. Some of these fissures were the source of basalt eruptions, while various forms of volcanic relief formed along others.

Lastly, in more rare cases, fissures were formed without any displacement in the plane of the rupture, and these gave shape to submarine canyons. *"The sinking and extension of ocean and sea basins are the only satisfactory explanation of the world-wide occurrence of submarine canyons and of the diversity of their types,"* D. G. Panov writes in conclusion (my italics—*N.Z.*). On the basis of their investigations of the rocks into which canyons have been carved, F. P. Shepard and K. O. Emery (668) opine that submarine valleys and canyons could have been formed only during the Cenozoic, the Pleistocene, to be more exact. Thus, the endemic fauna of the islands off California indicate that their subsidence occurred during the early Anthropogen. Investigations of the submarine canyon of the Congo River show that it took shape very recently in terms of geologic time. Using the land canyon data accumulated by F. E. Matthes, Shepard reckoned that submarine canyons are likewise of subaerial origin and gave their age as less than 100,000 years, possibly even as little as 10,000 years.

Investigations conducted some time ago by American scientists yielded testimony that the submarine valleys along the shore of New England were formed in the epoch preceding the last glaciation and that they were not connected with the drop of the ocean water level during glaciation.

Recognition of tectonic movements as being the agents forming submarine valleys and canyons takes the sting out of the arguments about their subaerial or submarine origin, because different types of canyons can take shape both subaerially and under water. However, this gives the supporters of the ocean permanency theory grounds for maintaining that the occurrence of submarine canyons is not proof of the youth of oceans. A. V. Zhivago and G. B. Udintsev (253/27) write: "In the light of the new views about the nature of submarine valleys, their existence is by no means an indication of a considerable amplitude of ocean-level fluctuation. These valleys, springing as they do from tectonic activity, experienced the influence of subaerial processes only along their upper portions." The prime weakness of this argument is that on land as well many river valleys and canyons owe their origin to tectonic activity. In spite of their arguments, both Zhivago and Udintsev have to agree that many submarine canyons were at one time subaerial. Another point is that it is difficult to draw a borderline between former subaerial and proper oceanic parts of a canyon (if the latter exist at all).

This, too, is admitted by Zhivago and Udintsev: "Although the division of submarine canyons into separate parts, linked up primarily with erosion and with the scouring and accumulating activity of suspension streams, can be traced in general outline, detailed and comprehensive investigations, including the collection of samples of basic rock and bed sediments, are required before these boundaries can be determined accurately." This concept overrates the role of turbidity (mud) streams, which are the favourite brainchild of American oceanologists.

B. GUYOTS

Let us now turn to the question of flat-topped mountains, commonly called guyots. A. V. Zhivago and G. B. Udintsev (253/27) write: "Flat-topped submarine mountains or guyots were also regarded as proof of broad regional subsidences of the Earth's crust in the region of oceans. However, investigations over the past few years have shown that flat-topped guyots, which are eroded surfaces, lie at the most diverse levels. Mountains did not sink simultaneously or at the same rate; this was a purely local phenomenon. Consequently, these facts, too, cannot be regarded as proof of the youth of oceans." Yet it is a fact that guyots did sink to considerable depths. It is quite another matter how this fact is interpreted. As we have pointed out earlier, *we have no grounds whatever for asserting that the sinking of guyots was an unhurried, smooth process whose rate was the same everywhere.* On the contrary, the occurrence of faults, cracks and so on in the affected regions proves that this process developed chaotically. The nature of the subsidence was the same throughout the region under consideration, but in each separate locality its rate could have been different. The height of the individual mountains—future guyots—in relation to the sea level or the surrounding locality was likewise dissimilar. The reference to the great thickness of the coral structure, as the above authors further point out, is likewise not proof in favour of the relative antiquity of the ocean around them. So far we have detailed data only for two coral islands—Bikini and Eniwetok atolls—where boring has brought volcanic rock to light.*

C. DEEP-WATER SAND AND TURBIDITY CURRENTS

Terrigenous material—relatively large particles of sand, which could not have been transported either by the wind or the usual sea currents—have been found in cores taken from the bed of oceans by oceanographic expeditions. This *deep-water sand* has been discovered in many places and at different depths, particularly in the Atlantic

---

* See Note No. 4 (Appendix 2).

and Indian oceans. Remains of land plants have been found in some of the cores.

Sediments consisting of particles of terrigenous origin, occurring on the ocean floor far from shores and the continental shelf, could have been carried there either by the wind or ocean currents. But in both cases these are extremely small particles called *aleurite* (measuring 0.01-0.10 mm) and *pelite* (measuring a maximum of 0.01 mm). Larger particles, measuring up to 1.00 mm are usually called *sand*, and still larger particles are called *gravel*.

Although the wind can transport continental dust over great distances seaward (for example, Sahara dust has been found in marine sediments many hundreds of miles from the shore), this dust only leads to the formation of aleurite and pelite. Off-shore swells can disturb floor sand, but, as observations have shown, this material moves very slowly. Only the fine sludge, raised from the floor, takes a long time to settle and may be carried over long distances. Ocean waves in stormy weather are the only agents that can raise sand and even larger particles from depths of several tens of metres. But even in this case, it is highly improbable that sand can be transported very far from the shore. It should be noted that off-shore flotation processes can result in the foam formed by the surf carrying sand particles measuring 0.1-0.5 mm and even larger than 3 mm over quite long distances from the shore but not for hundreds of kilometres.

As regards the ability of ocean currents to transport large terrigenous particles, the Gulf Stream, the most powerful of ocean currents with its velocity of 2.5 m/sec off Florida where it edges along the ocean, can roll pebbles of the size of a pigeon egg along the bed of the ocean. But where it enters the open ocean its velocity drops to 20 cm/sec and this enables it to transport only fine sand (up to 2 mm). In the open ocean its velocity is less than 1 km/hour. At this velocity it can carry only the finest particles of silt. Under these conditions the Gulf Stream crosses the North Atlantic Ridge and approaches the shores of Europe. Consequently, *this is sufficient testimony that the fairly large particles of sand found in these places could not have been transported either by the wind or the Gulf Stream*. Incidentally, it may be mentioned that according to data accumulated by V. P. Zenkovich particles with a diameter larger than 1-2 mm are moved only by the action of waves, and those with a smaller diameter (0.05 mm) only by the action of currents. Particles with an intermediate diameter (sand) drift under the combined action of both these factors.

The conclusion suggests itself that the deep-water sand located at great distances from modern land was deposited there as a result of the sinking of some nearby land in the past. But this conclusion does not suit the supporters of the ocean permanency theory. They maintain that this sand was brought by *turbidity currents* (233) to which they attribute quite incredible powers such as the carving out of submarine canyons in all sorts of rock, including granite, the transportation of suspensions of mud, sand and even pebbles over distances of thousands of kilometres from the shore, the building up of mountains of a height of several kilometres, the ability to cross elevations likewise of a height of several kilometres, and so on and so forth. Today this is one of the most fashionable hypotheses among oceanologists and marine geologists. Attempts to apply it in all cases, attempts which are far from being always successful and frequently beneath objective criticism, are to be found frequently in most present works, particularly of the American school. *This hypothesis is now the main foundation for the ocean permanency theory; it is an obstruction to an objective understanding of the nature and history of oceans and is clearly a conservative factor retarding science.* We must, therefore, closely examine it, especially as it has never been subjected to serious criticism.

First and foremost, it must be stated that the exponents of this theory usually tie up data obtained both from direct observations in shallow (fresh-water) lakes and bays and from laboratory investigations imitating the conditions obtaining in oceans but, as a rule, ignoring the fact that in the ocean the processes take place in more dense salt water and, what is most important, at depths of many hundreds of metres and even kilometres, i.e., under a pressure of many hundreds of atmospheres. The turbidity currents from low pressure regions move to extremely high pressure regions.

It is not known how a turbidity current behaves in reality. No laboratory installations can reproduce the real conditions of the movement of these currents in the depths of the ocean and no theoretical computations can take all these features into account. The papers that have been published so far cover only the data on the silting up of harbours but are unconvincing if one wants a more or less accurate picture of what really takes place on the ocean floor. The latest paper published by L. V. Poborchaya (368) likewise suffers from its uncritical approach to the theory of turbidity currents and to experiments imitating the movement of these currents at great depths.

The supporters of this theory name three basic causes giving rise to these currents: 1) river currents, 2) underwater landslides, and 3) earthquakes (368). Let us once more take a closer look at the terminology itself. At the very outset we must precisely distinguish individual mud currents from so-called "classical" turbidity currents of the American school of thought. The only place where such "currents" can exist is at the continuation of river valleys. The streams of mud springing from gravitational causes (landslides) or earthquakes are sporadic, casual suspension flows but by no means currents. It would be absurd to reject such flows.*

---

* Unfortunately we do not have objective data on the distance that can be covered by landslides or on their dependence on the thickness of the sediment layer and the angle of inclination

Back in 1936 R. A. Daly (493) suggested the existence of floor currents that carry substantial quantities of silt, sand and even large particles. Water containing mineral matter in the shape of suspensions is denser than clear water. The turbidity current must therefore flow beneath the clear water. Daly assumed that large quantities of silt must have been disturbed by storm waves in the glacial periods of the Pleistocene, when the sea level had been somewhat lower. R. C. Sprigg postulated that even river water carrying silt is denser than sea water and that, therefore, it sinks after it discharges into the sea.

Criticising the turbidity currents theory, K. K. Landes (585) writes that no currents of this kind have been found in the ocean despite the fact that some large rivers carry sediments to the head of submarine canyons with a steeper floor gradient than, for example, the artificial fresh-water Lake Mead in the USA. Phenomena similar to turbidity currents have been discovered there as in some Swiss lakes. Moreover, large rivers like the Congo, which flow to the sea, carry their sediments with fresh water until, due to a slackening of the velocity, these sediments begin to sink to the bottom through the underlying calm salt water. No turbidity currents have been discovered there. *The available data of observations of turbidity currents unquestionably concern individual, sporadic flows as well as ordinary landslides. Besides, landslides are not constantly functioning currents*, as the theory's supporters would have us believe. *Nobody has ever observed constant turbidity currents (specifically currents like the existing constant normal surface sea currents). The entire body of proof that has been offered concerns individual, shortlived flows.* Even the rupture of submarine cables—14 times in the course of the past 25 years (550)—in the Magdalena River canyon, Colombia, indicates that underwater landslides frequently occur there by virtue of purely local conditions. The same concerns the mud flow observed by the French oceanologist J. Y. Cousteau during a descent in a bathyscaphe off Toulon.

In the course of several years the proponents of the turbidity current theory maintained that the rupture of a cable after an earthquake in the region of the Grand Newfoundland Bank in 1929 was caused by a turbidity current moving at a very high velocity (444). We feel it is about time this myth was exploded. Soon after that earthquake the geologist A. Keith and the seismologist E. A. Hodgson, both of Canada, investigated the rupture spot and came to the conclusion that the break occurred along the fissures in the Earth's crust in Cabot Strait and was due to purely seismic causes (673/106). The Swedish scientist B. Küllenberg (582) studied this phenomenon and found that the picture of the destruction provides no evidence of turbidity currents or of consistently increasing destruction. According to F. P. Shepard (673/30), K. Terzaghi (whom Shepard regards as an outstanding authority on hydromechanics) thinks that a temporary dilution of the sediments moving wave-like down the slope after the earthquake made the cable sink deep into the liquescent layer of sediments, twisting and stretching it until it snapped. This explanation completely rules out interference by turbidity currents or even high-speed flows. The resistance of the water, Shepard says, is evidently another factor making high velocities improbable.

It is our opinion that *if turbidity currents were constant, uninterruptedly functioning factors playing such an important role and serving as the cause of the rupture of inter-continental cables, a cable link between continents would hardly have been possible because these currents would be continuously tearing all telegraph cables, something we do not in fact observe.*

P. H. Kuenen (581) endeavoured to use the turbidity current theory to explain the formation of submarine canyons, rejecting the hypothesis of the subaerial origin of these canyons. As proof he offered a series of laboratory experiments on plaster of Paris models of the sea floor and shore. The positive results of these experiments were transferred to the conditions under which submarine canyons form in the ocean. However, what was an easy and quick success on models made of soft material like plaster of Paris and on laboratory-scale "canyons" becomes extremely doubtful when transferred to rock such as granite and to distances of many kilometres. Shepard feels that *it is useless to enlist the assistance of turbidity currents because no proof has been produced of their ability to erode hard rock such as granite.* To this it may be added that even for rock of medium hardness it is necessary to assume the long existence of continuously functioning turbidity currents, while in the case of rocks such as granite the action of such currents must be computed in terms of many millennia. However, as we have already pointed out, no permanently functioning turbidity current is known. Any statement that in the Pleistocene such currents were usual but that in our age they have ceased, remains nothing more than an unproved conjecture. Besides, even if such currents had indeed existed as constant and continuously active factors and were able to carve submarine canyons in rock, these canyons would, instead of their clearly defined V- or box-shape, have been much more flatter and would not have had sharp angles. A flattened shape is typical of submarine valleys, which are unquestionably continuations of land river valleys. The reason that the canyons would have had a flattened shape is that moving in underwater conditions and encountering the resistance of the water layers in front of them, the mass of turbid water would have flowed not as a narrow current, as a land river, but along a broad fanwise front. This fanwise shape is typical of deltas at the mouth of submarine canyons, where sediments are carried and precipitated.

The most comprehensive criticism of the turbidity current theory has been offered by Dr. Hans Pettersson, one of the leading modern oceanologists and the head of the Swedish oceanographic expedition on the *Albatross*. On the basis of his own investigations and the work of the expedition he draws the following conclusion (633/149): "So far they [turbidity currents] have not been directly observed in the open ocean, and their importance in eroding the compact material in submarine canyons is doubtful since the water they carry is already overloaded with sediment. This view is shared by Shepard, the American authority on submarine canyons. Attempts to set up artificial turbidity currents along submarine canyons through explosions have so far failed. Recent observations carried out in moderate depths in Swedish fjords, where great quantities of sediment were dumped, failed to give any evidence for turbidity currents of any notable velocity." E. C. Buffington (477) reports that the latest attempts to set up artificial turbidity currents in La Jolla Canyon (California) have likewise failed. He noted that none of the seven induced landslides gave rise to such currents. All the phenomena attributed to turbidity currents may be explained by the activity of low-density and low-velocity flows. What induces the turbidity currents described by American authors remains unknown.

Many of the scientists who have studied the problem of submarine canyons have convincingly proved the complete untenability of the theory that these canyons were formed by underwater erosion set off by so-called turbidity currents [L. S. Berg (198), J. Bourcart (209), G. W. Lindberg (295/102), F. Machatschek (323), M. V. Muratov (336/64), A. E. Scheidegger (660), F. P. Shepard (669, 670, 671, 673) and others].

Another problem which the turbidity current theory is supposed to solve is that of deep-sea sand. The proponents of this theory claim that the discovery of this sand is further proof of the reality of these currents. They base themselves on the assumption that the sand might have been transported by turbidity currents over distances of many hundreds and even thousands of kilometres from the shores of continents. D. B. Ericson, M. Ewing and B. C. Heezen (514) devoted a thick volume to a substantiation of such views. Their main argument is founded on a review of a study of a series of deep-water cores taken chiefly at the foot of the continental slope near the underwater canyon of the Hudson River. It was found that in some cores from the abyssal plain, at a depth of more than 4,000 metres, the lower layer of typical deep-sea sediments (red clay) was covered with a thick layer of terrigenous sand. There is no doubt that the sand layer, which is of relatively recent origin, was brought to the abyssal plateau along the channel of the submarine canyon. This is proved by the absence of sand in the upper layers of the neighbouring cores taken from outside the limits of the canyon. This brought the above-mentioned authors round to the surmise that the sand was transported by turbidity currents. In other works (444, 515) the advocates of this theory cite some other cases; they draw attention to the regular bedding (according to particle size) of the deposited sand as proof in favour of their theory.

In reality things are much more simple. Observations have shown that until a certain time sediments of the most diverse origin can lie undisturbed even on fairly steep inclines. For example, in some regions of the North Pacific D. Moore (252/138) discovered undisturbed sediments on inclines of as steep as 15°. To appreciate the significance of this figure let us point out that down to a depth of 1,830 metres the incline of the continental slope is: 5°20′ in the Pacific, 3°05′ in the Atlantic and 2°55′ in the Indian Ocean, thus averaging 3°34′ in the World Ocean as a whole. The mean composition of the sediments is accepted as 60 per cent ooze, 25 per cent sand, 10 per cent gravel, 5 per cent test, and so on (673/129).

Some time ago D. Moore (617) published more detailed results of his observations and laboratory investigations of submarine landslides and their connection with turbidity currents. On the overwhelming majority of submarine slopes the sediments were found to be stable; in deep-water regions landslides are an extraordinarily rare phenomenon. Sediments were found to be unstable only on the slopes of river deltas, the sides of submarine canyons and other analogous places of the shelf and slopes. The sphere of activity of turbidity currents, which are undoubtedly a derivative of landslides, is restricted only to off-shore and shallow-water provinces of oceans. All sediments and forms of floor topography, attributed to the action of turbidity currents, are actually the product of landslides.

On the question of the causes of landslides we can state the following. *When earthquakes occur the sediments lying undisturbed run in a lava-like flow down the continental slope, particularly if this slope is sufficiently steep. This movement of sediments is facilitated by tremors, especially those directed down the slope. Where the slope is very steep, and the displaced layers of sediments are sufficiently thick, a large number of tremors along the direction of the slope can move these sediments over a considerable distance, sometimes as far as the edge of the abyssal plain.* At great depths the movement of sediments is caused not by turbidity currents but by the sequence and direction of tremors during earthquakes (633/143).

On this score Dr. Hans Pettersson (633/76) writes: "While leaving open the question of the predominance of turbidity currents in special provinces of the sea, the only correct assertion seems to be that the theory, according to which they are the predominant cause of bottom currents at great depths in the ocean, does not get confirmation from our present-day knowledge of deep-sea sediments. There are no grounds for stating that all cases of the vast flat floor at great depths are the work of turbidity currents. Accordingly, *it would be useless to collect and study bed cores of sediments because there would be the suspicion that these layers had been shuffled by turbidity currents*" (My italics—*N. Z.*).

Recently F. F. Osborn (629) pointed out that in the light of present-day knowledge it would hardly be possible to produce facts to confirm that turbidity currents can transport coarse detritus. E. C. Bullard (478) is frankly sceptical about turbidity currents being a means of transporting detritus, considering that today the turbidity current theory presents a sorry spectacle. Analysing the potentialities of turbidity currents from the standpoint of the turbulent current theory, Bullard comes to the conclusion that their movement over long distances even across a flat floor is unlikely. On the basis of his analysis of observations of the distribution of sediments allegedly transported by turbidity currents, he offers a number of other considerations rejecting the turbidity current theory.

If we study the statistics of Lamont Observatory, USA, concerning the composition of deep-sea cores and the content of sand in them, we shall find that different investigators offer different conclusions. Thus, according to staff members of the above-mentioned observatory (444), of the total of 500 cores taken in the North Atlantic, 230 (i.e., about 42 per cent) contain layers of sand or aleurite formed by turbidity currents. This implies that these currents embrace almost half the North Atlantic. However, interpreting the same data, F. P. Shepard (673/180) says that only 134 of the 550 cores (i.e., only about 25 per cent) had layers of sand, and from this he draws the antipodal conclusion that most of the North Atlantic floor is not embraced by turbidity currents. A glance at a chart showing the location of the stations (see 444, Fig. 1, or 417, chart 28) makes their scantiness in the region of the Mid-Atlantic Ridge conspicuous. The conclusions of the exponents of this theory have not been confirmed in the Indian Ocean either (579).

The most objective approach to the turbidity current theory has been adopted by Professor M. V. Klenova, the eminent Soviet oceanologist (273/183). She writes: "It seems to be necessary to make a special study of the question of suspension—'turbidity'—currents because some American investigators attribute to them an obviously exaggerated role in the process of the formation of marine sediments. Cores taken from great depths in the southern part of the North America Basin have likewise failed to substantiate the view that sandy interlayers occur in abyssal plains" (also see 579). However, O. K. Leontyev (813/228) considers that "there is no reason to question the reliability of the data obtained by the Lamont Observatory expedition".

Even some Soviet oceanologists, who support the turbidity current theory, are compelled to admit the immoderation of the attraction for this theory. For example, G. B. Udintsev (404/49) writes: "In the Pacific turbidity currents could play a substantial role in levelling the relief only in the eastern part of the ocean, where the zone of the continental slope directly abuts the ocean bed. In the other parts of the ocean, where the zone of the continental slope is separated from the floor by troughs, which are traps for suspension currents, it is doubtful if the latter play any role in levelling the floor topography."

J. K. Righby and H. L. Burckle (652) maintain that some clearly terrigenous materials, found near the southern spurs of the North

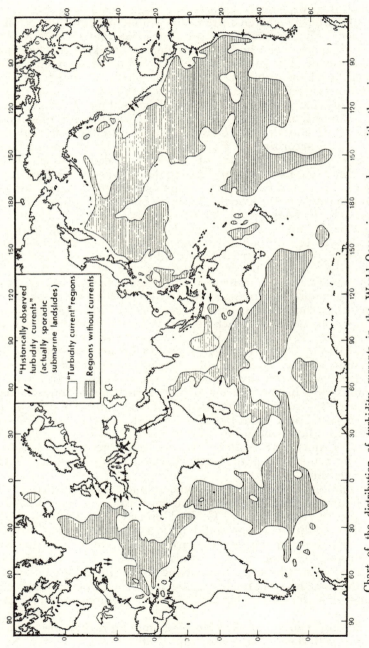

Chart of the distribution of turbidity currents in the World Ocean in accordance with the views of the supporters of the turbidity current theory (509)

Atlantic Ridge were brought there by turbidity currents from the African continent.* But in order to do this the currents would have had to accomplish fantastic work—carry these materials in compact form over a distance of more than 900 kilometres and ascend the slopes to a height of about one and a half kilometres, because between the shore of the continent and the station, at a depth of 3,577 metres, where terrigenous materials were discovered, there is a trough 4,967 metres deep!

Similarly incredible are the assertions of H. W. Menard (612), who seriously reported to the International Symposium in France that turbidity currents could travel a distance of 2,000 kilometres along the bed of the ocean. What a fabulous task has to be accomplished by these currents to carry a suspension of large particles of sand and clay in face of the resistance of a water column pressured by many hundreds of atmospheres!

The height of an uncritical attitude to turbidity currents is the case cited by A. V. Zhivago (252/138) concerning a paper read at the International Oceanographic Congress in New York in 1959: "In many cases the interpretation of individual forms of floor topography as being linked up with turbidity currents is unrealistic. Thus, at the seminar on 'The Form and Structure of Ocean Basins', an American scientist cited a tall and narrow range rising more than two kilometres from the bed as an example of the activity of turbidity currents. This range, according to the speaker, was built up by turbidity currents flowing in one and the same direction over a long period."

N. S. Zolotnitsky (730) says bottom turbidity currents can be started only rarely at the mouth of rivers by water with clastic suspension. The currents so started are small and slow.

The immoderation of the enthusiasm for the turbidity current theory has become obvious even to the fathers of that theory and lately the province embraced by these currents has been greatly reduced on charts.

All the anomalies in the origin of deep-sea sand and in its distribution according to grain size over distances even relatively close to the edges of continents can be quite easily explained without the help of turbidity currents. The turbidity current theory cannot explain the occurrence of deep-water sand in such places of the ocean where the floor topography makes inconceivable even the surmise that there are turbidity currents. That is probably why the advocates of this theory obscure their investigations in the vicinity of oceanic ridges (for example the Mid-Atlantic), where no landslides from the shores of continents can penetrate. One gets the impression that these investigators deliberately ignore the provinces where the factual data

---

* This and other similar considerations are cited without a critical assessment in a paper by L. V. Poborchaya (368), thus clearly giving the uninformed reader a one-sided orientation.

cannot serve their theory. The biased nature of the researches of the supporters of this theory has been noted by H. Pettersson (633, 148) and K. K. Landes (585).

The problem of turbidity currents and deep-sea sand has been closely reviewed at a meeting of the Geological Association held in Wiesbaden on March 15-18, 1957 (568). Observations have shown that, *as a rule, in the Atlantic and Indian oceans sand layers occur near the slopes of large submarine mountain systems: the Mid-Atlantic and the Mid-Indian ridges. Many authorities consider that in remote times these ridges towered above sea-level and were eroded; the products of erosion moved down the slopes of these ranges to the ocean floor.* The view that submarine ranges are the sources of materials for deep-sea sand is shared by leading oceanologists (Drigalski, O. Mellis, J. Jarke).

D. BOTTOM CURRENTS AND SUBMARINE EROSION

When it was found that the turbidity current theory could not explain many facts or sustain the ocean permanency theory, the latest data on *bottom currents* were called to the rescue.

Modern instrument investigations of ocean currents have made it possible to establish that high-velocity currents do indeed develop in the depths of the open ocean. However, the velocities of true bottom currents are such (253) that only tiny particles can be moved. These currents are able to influence only the uppermost sediment layers because the underlying layers are kept compact by the pressure of the overlying water column. The latest investigations (544) have shown that this compactness can be very considerable. On the other hand, in the case of submarine ranges local bottom currents can be effective as agents washing away sediments. However, some imaginative oceanologists are beginning to attribute to bottom currents, as to turbidity currents, the ability to transport large quantities of sediments over great distances and to raise sediments bedded at great depths. The assertion of the Lamont Observatory staff that most of the sediment cores investigated by them were hopelessly shuffled cannot be accepted as gospel (273, 517, 579). The explanation is that for their stations they selected localities where landslides are most frequent.

According to available data (813/51), sand erosion (particle size— 0.1-1.0 mm) begins at a current velocity of 18-65 cm/sec, while mass transportation takes place at a velocity of only 15-24 cm/sec. For gravel and pebbles the critical velocity is several times higher. It is now believed that the action of powerful currents like the Gulf Stream and Kuroshio can be detected even at depths of 2,400 metres (signs of ripples?).

Mention must be made of the experiments of N. Oulianoff (630), who reported that the bottom currents observed by him could not transport the suspended terrigenous particles found in sediments. As regards the ripples attributed to bottom currents, at great depths these ripples are induced by the vibration of the Earth's crust linked up with seismic and volcanic activity; this has been proved by Oulianoff by experiments with sea floor models.

Thick layers of sedimentary materials have been discovered on the floor of the open ocean. Inasmuch as it cannot be assumed that these layers had been transported from the direction of land areas by almighty turbidity currents or by bottom currents, the proponents of the ocean permanency theory explain that they are the products of *underwater erosion*. Attempts are made to use this unclear and inadequately studied process to explain the occurrence of considerable layers of sedimentary materials on the slopes and in the vicinity of submarine mountain ranges. The past subaerial existence of these ranges should be recognised, and this would fundamentally undermine the very theory that oceans are permanent.

On land the erosion of rock is called forth by mechanical or chemical factors. The principal factors giving rise to erosion on land are: temperature changes and the mechanical action of wind and water, with temperature changes playing the main role in the initial stages. Purely chemical factors as well as the solvent action of water are, with the exception of special regions, co-subordinate. Under water most of the powerful eroding factors lose much of their strength, while aeolian erosion plays no part at all. Moreover, the temperature of the various ocean layers does not have such large annual and daily amplitudes as on land. The existence of mechanical erosion by underwater currents cannot be denied (219, 236, 272), but it is a far cry from the powerful erosion caused by water streams on land. Dissolution and chemical erosion possibly play a larger role than on land, but they are extremely slow processes. S.K.E. Wakeel and J. P. Riley (697) are inclined to believe that the origin of none of the argillaceous (non-calcareous) sediments is linked up with the underwater "weathering" of volcanic rock. Argillaceous sediments are of continental origin. Hence, it must be appreciated *that under water the erosion of rock proceeds at an incomparably slower rate than on land.* This also explains the "fresh" appearance of many samples of rock taken from the ocean floor as well as the "virginal" character of the ocean bed topography so seldom to be found on land.

E. MID-OCEANIC MOUNTAIN RIDGES

During the past decade oceanographic expeditions have established the existence in all oceans of formations whose nature and origin have yet to be fully elucidated. These are so-called *mid-oceanic mountain ridges*, which are enormous submarine mountain systems with a unique and frequently extremely rugged topography.

B. C. Heezen (418) regards them as the third major type of topography of the Earth's surface, equal in importance to sialic continents and the basalt bed of oceans. In the Atlantic Ocean there is the giant mountain system known as the Mid-Atlantic Ridge. In the north it gives way to the Reykjanes Ridge, which runs across Iceland and ends in a spur, called Mohns, in the Arctic Ocean. In the Southern Hemisphere this mountain system skirts round South Africa and links up with a smaller but also vast mountain system in the Indian Ocean—the Mid-Indian Ridge. One gets the impression that this double Atlantic-Indian mid-oceanic ridge is the natural frontier of the continental massifs of Europe and Africa in the west and the south (for details see Chapter Thirteen).

There are similar ridges in other oceans: the Lomonosov and Mendeleyev ridges in the Arctic Ocean and the Mid-Pacific, Hawaiian, Carolina and East Pacific ridges in the Pacific. Easter, Naska and Carnegie islands, the Albatross Plateau and other elevations are summits of the East Pacific Ridge. This submarine mountain system evidently somewhat resembles the Mid-Atlantic Ridge and, as V. V. Belousov (168) logically assumes, represents the submerged western fringe of the great Cordillera-Andes system.

H. H. Hess (422) notes the following facts, which were observed during a study of mid-oceanic ridges:

1. Almost all of them are linked up with basalt volcanism.
2. Peridotite xenoliths are the only foreign rocks brought to the surface by volcanoes in the oceanic ridges.* Peridotite issues are known at two points in the Mid-Atlantic Ridge.
3. Small linear ranges running parallel to the main axis of the oceanic ridges are almost always non-existent.** The presence of such small ranges could have been expected if they consisted of folded rock. Steep fault scarps, usually running at a sharp angle to the axis of the main ridge, have been discovered on some of the small ranges. In some cases they were found to possess a fairly high degree of seismicity.
4. *In oceanic ridges there usually are indications that at one time they were much higher with regard to sea level* (my italics—N. Z.). These indications include eroded surfaces of the flattened tops of the ridges, the terraces on their slopes, and guyots (flat-topped seamounts).
5. *Most of the rocks of which are composed the islands towering over the ridges* (in cases where their age can be established) *date from the Quaternary and some from the Tertiary. Pre-Tertiary rocks are not encountered there* (my italics—N. Z.).

Further, Hess cites three variants of the theory explaining the origin of mid-oceanic ridges. The first assumes that they owe their

---

* Evacuations of sialic materials are known on some ranges.
** As M V. Klenova points out, this does not conform to reality. Recent investigations have brought to light small ranges running parallel to the main mid-oceanic ridges.

origin to the eruption of basalt lava along fissures in the Earth's crust. The materials accumulate in a lens-shape pile which causes the crust to bend. Small depressions may form on the floor along the edge of the ridge. The sinking of the ridge is a slow process, which leads to the formation of banks and atolls. The Hawaiian Ridge is a typical example.

The second variant assumes the outpouring of basalt magma on the surface with the partial encroachment of the peridotite substratum. A number of factors lead to rapid submergence. An example of this is the Mid-Atlantic Ridge. The third variant assumes the thickening and bending of the upper part of the basalt crust with the partial melting of the bent portion, which leads to andesite volcanism and diorite intrusions. Such a ridge may be the first, undeveloped stage of a normal island arc. The Walvis Ridge may be a typical example.

According to the first theory, Hess concludes, an oceanic ridge may be linked up with calm tectonic conditions or with rotational stresses and the formation of ruptures accompanied by movement along the strike; the second theory presupposes extension and the third—horizontal compression perpendicular to the ridge. All three are working theories.

The views expressed by V. V. Belousov (196/23) about the nature and origin of mid-oceanic ridges are extremely interesting. He writes:

"The Mid-Atlantic Ridge has been investigated more thoroughly than any other submarine system. Seismic soundings have shown that beneath the ridge is a considerably thick layer of basalt, which is wedged into the underlying substratum in the shape of a deep root (up to 30 kilometres thick). A study of the surface of the ridge has brought to light the fact that a fault trough runs along its crest. This is, undoubtedly, an indication that the rocks were stretched when the ridge rose. On the other hand, the sinking of the Mohorovicic discontinuity beneath the ridge shows that the latter corresponds to the zone of the uplift of basalts melted at a great depth and to the zone of the evacuation of additional heat from below, and together this led to a deeper bedding of the border between eclogite and basalt. There is thus an unquestionable link between the ridge and the abyssal fracture. The Mid-Atlantic Ridge passes across Iceland where an Upper Pliocene fault trough lies along its length. This gives us grounds for assuming that the entire ridge is a very young formation.

"The Mid-Indian Ridge branches out at the Chagos Island. One branch runs directly northward with the basalt Deccan Plateau situated on it. The other branch with a belt of earthquake epicentres turns to the northwest and runs to the Red Sea. It must be assumed that like the Mid-Atlantic Ridge, the Mid-Indian Ridge is situated on a fracture along which molten basalt rose to the surface. This fracture is the zone where molten basalt influences the Earth's crust most intensively. The testimony for this is provided by the structure of the Red Sea, where along the ridge the continental crust is already partially destroyed and basalted and where a fault trough has taken shape. Its relation to the submarine ridge is the same as that of the Iceland fault trough to the Mid-Atlantic Ridge."

G. T. Wilson (217) writes the following about mid-oceanic mountains: Ten years ago Gutenberg and Richter published charts from which it could be seen that most of the known submarine ridges are centres of shallow earthquakes. In 1956, on the basis of a comparison of bathymetric and seismic data, Ewing and Heezen (523) first came forward with the assumption that the mid-oceanic ridges are a continuous system ringing the Earth. This system extends from north to south along the floor of the Atlantic Ocean. Then it turns and passes between Africa and the Antarctic along the centre of the Indian Ocean, where it branches out and reaches the northern shores of Asia. The main ridge continues running south past Australia and New Zealand, crosses the Pacific Ocean and reaches Easter Island. From there its least known branches stretch to South America and also to the Hawaiian Ridge and farther, probably up to Kamchatka and the western Pacific. Another branch, perhaps, forms the Lomonosov Ridge, discovered by Soviet scientists, and crosses the Arctic Ocean. The undeveloped ridges in this area and the low volcanic activity are testimony that the present situation there had taken shape very long ago and, perhaps, embraced a large portion of the Earth's history.

One cannot agree with all of Wilson's statements. First and foremost, it is doubtful if there is an unbroken global mid-oceanic ridge. Further, one cannot agree that the ranges are undeveloped and that there is low volcanic activity. The conclusion that this ridge is of great antiquity is no longer supported even by the authors of this concept. Wilson now considers that the ocean basins began their development from the mid-oceanic ridges, gradually separating the continents.

Lately, as we have already mentioned,* the problem of the mid-oceanic ridges is linked up with the theory that the Earth is expanding. The principal exponents of this idea are B. C. Heezen (418) and M. Ewing (525). Postulating the existence of a single global mid-oceanic ridge, they advance the following propositions:

1. The ridge is continuous and may be found along a length of 40,000 miles (or over 72,000 kilometres); a fault of a planetary order, it passes across all the oceans in the world. It divides the oceans through which it passes, the exception being the southeast Pacific. In some places its branches link up with continental masses, and the extensions of these branches are to be found on continents.

2. A feature of the ridge is the existence of a deep rift valley or fracture 20 to 80 miles (33-143 kilometres) wide and 0.5 to

---

* See Chapters Seven and Eight

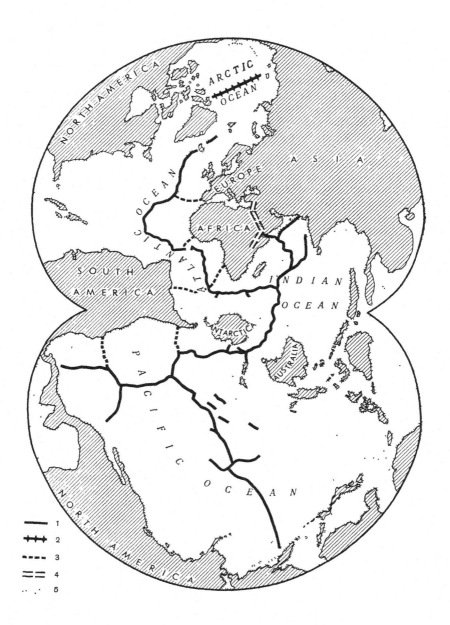

Mid-oceanic ridges and chart of mid-oceanic fractures in the Earth's crust (217; somewhat modified) 1—mid-oceanic ridges of basalt origin; 2—mid-oceanic ridges of continental origin; 3—latitudinal oceanic ridges linking up mid-oceanic ridges with continents, 4—East African fault trough, 5—depth. less than 2.750 metres

1.5 miles (900-2,700 metres) deep. This feature is most apparent in the Mid-Atlantic and the Mid-Indian ridges, but is not discernible in the ridges of the Pacific Ocean. The rift valleys display an analogy and link with some major continental fractures (for example, the East African fault trough).

3. Along the ridge, coinciding with the rift valley, is a seismic belt with shallow (30-70 kilometres) earthquake hypocentres. In places, along the system of rift valleys, this belt stretches onto continents.

4. As distinct from land mountain systems, the chain of submarine mountains comprising the ridge consists of a thin upper layer with a longitudinal wave diffusion velocity of 4.5-5.0 km/sec, and a deeper mass 30-40 kilometres thick, where the velocity rises to 7.3 km/sec.

5. Geologically the global mid-oceanic ridge is a relatively young and constantly changing formation, which is proved not only by the topography but also by the absolute age of the rocks forming the ridge; at the most these rocks date from the close of the Tertiary period. According to Heezen and Ewing, the expanding Earth theory best of all explains the origin of the ridge. G. T. Wilson points out that the increase of 1,100 miles (about 2,000 kilometres) in the Earth's circumference in the course of 3,250 million years would have increased its surface by exactly the area occupied by the surface of the ridge.

So far this original hypothesis has very few supporting facts. First of all, the continuity of the ridge has not been proved. On this score Academician D. I. Shcherbakov (442/95) writes: "American scientists are endeavouring to introduce the idea of a single submarine chain of mountains linking up all currently known submarine ridges into a single system and attempting to find rift valleys in their centre. That is hardly correct." The authors of the hypothesis themselves admit that rift valleys are not found everywhere. Even in the Mid-Atlantic Ridge, which has been investigated more than any other, such a large section as the Reykjanes Ridge has neither a rift valley nor earthquake hypocentres. Neither is there any regularity in the division of oceans into two halves by the ridges. On the contrary, *most marked is the propensity of the ridges to run parallel to the shelf of the adjoining continent. Moreover, there is an unquestionable link with the continent by means of spurs and an identity of the morphostructure of fractures; consequently, many mid-oceanic ridges have a genetic link with continents and are by no means inherent exclusively in oceans. The presence of deep roots beneath some of the mid-oceanic ridges likewise corresponds sooner to a continental rather than to an oceanic structure.*

It is not so simple as it seems to apply the expanding Earth theory to the problem of the origin of mid-oceanic ridges. If we picture the Earth's crust fracturing from internal expansion, the resultant fracture would be in the nature of a deep canyon (of the type of some deep-sea canyons that usually run parallel to the shelf of continents), because if this fracture was the source of magma it would build up a cupola-like elevation and a low and broad ridge. The entire area would have the appearance of a swelling. On the other hand, it is difficult to credit the formation of tall ridges with a well-defined disjunction having deep "roots" to solely the expansion of the Earth. The East-African fault trough is likewise no exception if we regard it as a whole and do not seek an external resemblance to rift valleys. The mechanism of the formation of deep "roots" is better explained by the processes of bipartite stresses (i.e., fold formation) than by fractures and faults. We must take into account the fact that in the case of the Mid-Atlantic Ridge it has been proved beyond dispute that when it was formed it bore the impact of a lateral stress (Saint Paul's Rocks and other places), which hardly dovetails with expansion processes—lateral stresses are inherent in compression processes, when the edges of fractures are not widened but compressed. Therefore, we consider that *in some cases the formation of mid-oceanic ridges is linked up with compression processes as well.*

It seems most probable to us that *the mid-oceanic ridges are not a single system.* True, all of them are situated in oceanic regions but that cannot be accepted as proof of their identical origin. From that angle the opinion of H. H. Hess (558), who suggests that there are at least two types of mid-oceanic ridges, is closer to reality: "old" ridges (submerged to a depth of 1,000-2,000 metres) with guyots and atolls, and "young" ranges as yet not possessing these landmarks but having high-temperature heat flows. G. G. Shorr and R. W. Raitt (673) likewise feel that there are two types of mid-oceanic ridges. One of them is the Mid-Atlantic Ridge with its extremely rugged topography and deep roots. The second type comprises some of the submarine ranges in the Pacific representing arched uplifts. The structure of the arched ranges differs from both that of the continental and oceanic crust, although it is closer to the latter. In many places their crust is almost normal for the oceanic type of cover but it is underlaid by a subcrustal layer with a longitudinal wave diffusion velocity that is unusually low for the ocean floor; these rocks, it should be pointed out, are situated much higher than the surrounding ocean bed.

There are grounds for presuming that the *Lomonosov and Mendeleyev ridges, which are composed of sedimentary and metamorphosed rock, took shape as the continuation of continental folded and faulted structures.** These are yet another type of mid-oceanic ridge that does not fit into the notions of M. Ewing and B. C. Heezen. We feel that *initially folding processes might likewise have played a role in the building up of some of the mid-oceanic ridges and that not all the valleys running parallel to them are true rift valleys.*

---

* For a detailed description of these ridges see Chapter Sixteen.

On the basis of everything known about the mid-oceanic ridges it seems that they must be divided into three categories.*

1. Ridges of fold-block origin with deep roots. They were formed with the participation of sedimentary and metamorphosed rocks and have a direct genetic link with ancient continental mountain systems. Part of the oceanic regions between these ridges and the continents still bear some evidence of their continental origin. Examples: the Lomonosov and Mendeleyev ridges.

To this type of range we must attribute the West Australian Range in the Indian Ocean, whose structure is close to that of the continent. The submarine Cocos and Carnegie ranges, which branch out in the direction of the American continent from the East Pacific submarine range, as well as the Walvis Ridge in the South Atlantic are probably of this type too.

2. Ridges of a complex fold-fault origin with developed volcanism and great, deep roots. Folding linked up with lateral compression evidently predominated at the first stages of the formation of these ridges. These processes gave way to faults, fissures and sinking, which were accompanied by volcanic activity. *These ridges likewise have a genetic link, most frequently a unilateral one, with the adjoining continent.*** *They are a fringe wall, as it were, connected with the continent by lateral spurs, which sometimes extend into the structure of the continent.* The oceanic regions between these ridges and the continents have been subjected to considerable oceanisation. In the past these ridges were "basalt continents" that had passed through the stage of upthrust above ocean level: today they are in the stage of subsidence. Examples: the Mid-Atlantic and Mid-Indian ridges.

3. Ridges of an arch origin (oceanic walls). They have neither roots nor a direct genetic link with adjoining continents. They are a kind of growth within the limits of the oceanic crust proper and, possibly, they are undeveloped basalt continents that perhaps have not passed through the stage of upthrust above ocean level (like the Mid-Pacific Ridge) or have gone through that stage with little change (like the Hawaiian Ridge).

The intermediate link between the two latter types is the East Pacific Ridge on which is situated Easter Island. It is broader and somewhat lower than the Mid-Atlantic Ridge. According to H. W. Menard (612a), as distinct from the extremely rugged Mid-Atlantic Ridge, the crest of the East Pacific Ridge has a very gentle topography. However, the Soviet expedition on the ship *Ob* (253/27) found the topography in the region of Easter Island extraordinarily faulted. The question of the bathymetry of the East Pacific Ridge

---

* Also see (730/202-205).
** These connecting links of the Mid-Atlantic Ridge are the Walvis, Sierra-Leone, and Azores-Gibraltar ridges ; the Naska, Cocos, Carnegie and other ranges are links of the East Pacific Ridge

remains to be elucidated—there is very little factual data. Let us note that north of this ridge lies the vast Albatross Plateau.

H. W. Menard thinks there might be direct contact between the ridge and the North American continent in the region of California; perhaps its extension is somewhere on the continent proper. Its structure resembles that of arched ridges (the theory is that it does not have roots) but, evidently, it is closely linked up with the structure of the adjoining continents, particularly with lateral branches of mountain ranges (612a).

From the above it follows that there are mid-oceanic ridges that occupy an intermediate position between these three types. *It is still premature to regard the mid-oceanic ridges as a genetically single morphostructural planetary detail.* The same concerns the universality of rift valleys. Not all of them are really rift valleys; some are ravines created by two or more parallel folds. The epicentres of earthquakes do not always coincide with these valleys, and the valleys themselves do not always have indications of intensive volcanic activity (see Chapter Thirteen). More painstaking and unbiased observations are necessary here because the location of epicentres may not emerge beyond the limits of the most massive part of a mountain chain and, in this respect, it may not be an exception.* The profile similarity between the East African fault trough, the Mid-Atlantic Ridge, the Arctic Plateau and the Southwestern Pacific Ridge, cited by B. C. Heezen (418), is insufficient to prove the complete genetic similarity of all these mountain systems—they differ substantially from each other. Some of these profiles indicate a fault structure, others a purely volcanic or, perhaps, folded structure. The presence of a deep valley is by no means evidence of its fault origin. B. L. Afanasyev (719), for instance, takes the Central Asian rift valley as an example to prove convincingly that these valleys are arches that had caved in. Rift valleys and vaults are products of the general compression of the Earth's crust. This question is still not clear and requires careful study, primarily of the continuity of rift valleys. A number of profiles in different oceans cannot "lay down the law".

Of great interest to the problem of Atlantis is the possibility that the mid-oceanic ridges had been subaerial; this idea has been advanced by H. H. Hess (422). A. V. Zhivago and G. B. Udintsev (253/28) have come to a similar conclusion: "Here it must be noted that the narrow, elongated submarine ranges cannot, of course, be regarded as submerged continents or parts of such continents, although *in the past the summits of these ranges were evidently in a*

---

* Our view has been confirmed by a study of the location of earthquake epicentres given in a chart of a book by B. C. Heezen, M. Tharp and M Ewing (417, Diagram 29), where of a total of over 90 epicentres in the region of the Mid-Atlantic Ridge between 17° and 50°N only less than 20 are directly in the rift valley; the rest are on the crests or on the slopes.

subaerial position; this fits in excellently with paleozoological and paleobotanical data (my italics—*N. Z.*). Quite recently many of these ranges were bridges linking up continents and were the route for the migration of fauna and flora." However, it should be noted that *firstly, the area occupied by the mid-oceanic ridges is not smaller than the area of the present continents* (according to Heezen [418] it is equal to that of all the continents), *and, secondly, the land area when the ranges were subaerial could have been thousands of kilometres long and many hundreds of kilometres wide, representing fairly large land masses.*

On the question of mid-oceanic ridges V. E. Hain (415/5-7) writes: "*The rugged topography of the slopes of the submarine ranges was evidently formed under subaerial conditions, by river erosion* (my italics—*N.Z.*). This is indicated by the finding of fresh-water fauna on the slopes of the Mid-Atlantic Ridge. It must be pointed out that even today some sections of the ridge jut out above the surface of the ocean in the shape of islands.... *It is quite possible that there were many more such sections in the relatively recent past*" (my italics—*N. Z.*).

In passing let us take note of the view of Academician D. I. Shcherbakov (442/88): "In ocean rift valleys earthquakes usually take place at a relatively small depth—about 30 kilometres below the Earth's surface. No earthquake epicentre deeper than 70 kilometres has been registered there. Deep earthquakes with epicentres situated 700 kilometres below the surface occur almost exclusively in the region of high-seismic submarine depressions and the chain of islands girdling the Pacific Ocean. This indicates that the mid-oceanic rift belongs to the category of other structures. The small depth of the seismic activity in it shows that there the Earth's crust is thin and weak." Consequently, *the origin of the mid-oceanic ridges is linked up with tectonic movements in the Earth's crust and in the subcrustal layer, and not with deep faults in the mantle.*

We assume that the *basalt nature of a considerable portion of the mid-oceanic ridges is an indication sooner of their youth rather than of their antiquity.* Besides, the very properties of basalt as a geobuilding material brings us to the conclusion that the above-water structures made of it are shortlived. Attention must be drawn to these properties.

Firstly, it is necessary to mention the equilibrium in the basalt-eclogite system and the attendant consequences. Pointing to the low bedding of the Mohorovicic discontinuity on the borderline between eclogite and usual basalt, V. V. Belousov (196/7) writes: "The volume of material increases by approximately 15 per cent and the basalt roof rises. When the temperature falls or the pressure rises, part of the basalt in the base of the crust will pass into eclogite, which must cause an uplift of the Mohorovicic discontinuity, a diminution of the volume and a bend of the roof of the basalt."

The properties of the eclogite-basalt system thus bring us to the conclusion that the emergence of purely basalt structures is necessarily followed by their subsequent subsidence. This conclusion may also be drawn from other, simpler considerations. We may legitimately assume that in the temperatures and pressures under which basalt does not pass into eclogite it is not such an exception as water; hard basalt must, therefore, sink in liquid basalt.

Let us now picture the following. As a result of various causes, a basalt structure has emerged which has basalt "roots", for example, a mid-oceanic ridge. Under the influence of a series of factors (of which the fall of the melting point of basalt due to pressure is of no little importance) pockets of liquid, molten basalt begin to form beneath hardened basalt structures. Further, stresses arise which reach a magnitude where cracks form through which basalt magma issues, for example through cracks at the foot of a mid-oceanic ridge. In this case the great density of the molten basalt diminishes sharply. The hard basalt structure begins to sag and sink, squeezing more and more molten basalt magma through the crack.

Consequently, *sooner or later the basalt structures in oceans must sink.* This is confirmed by the basalt foundation of the Hawaiian Islands and by guyots and volcanic islands, particularly in the Pacific Ocean.

The currently fashionable expanding Earth and convection currents theories are used to explain the nature and origin of mid-oceanic ridges. M. H. P. Bott (764) believes that the mid-oceanic ridges are young structures; Darwin Ridge (Mid-Pacific Ridge), he says, emerged in the Mesozoic, and the Mid-Atlantic and East Pacific ridges in the Tertiary. It would seem that these uplifts should have a negative gravity anomaly of over 200 milligals, but in fact this is not observed. Recent geological, geophysical and geochemical data force us to consider that the de-densification of the mantle due to partial melting at depths of 100-150 kilometres is the basic factor behind the uplift of the mid-oceanic ridges.

O. K. Leontyev (741; afterword in 119; 756) echoes these and similar views about the antiquity of oceanic abyssal plains and about the expansion of continents at the expense of the ocean floor and the differentiation of mantle material (this obviously explains his negative attitude to Atlantis and the fact that on almost every point he shares the views of the American school). He believes that these ridges owe their origin not to crustal processes but to more general causes. He sees evidence of this in the extension of oceanic ridges onto continents (British Colombia, California, East Africa). J. L. Worzel (789) considers that the drift of continents and the convection currents theories cannot explain the structure of oceanic basins and ridges. He links their formation up with stresses in the Earth's crust.

Interesting considerations have been offered by Y. M. Sheinmann (753). In addition to known features of the mid-oceanic ridges, he speaks of one which he noticed, namely, the considerable increase of the heat flow beneath the crust. This is evidence of the degeneration of a mid-oceanic ridge, an example being the East Pacific Ridge. Sheinmann believes that the Mid-Atlantic Ridge cannot be older than the Alpine folded zone.

F. THEORY OF THE ANTHROPOGEN GLOBAL TRANSGRESSION

For a number of years R. W. Fairbridge (526) has been working on the idea of a global eustatic oscillation of the ocean level and of the synchronic nature of many off-shore terraces in various parts of different oceans. He believes there is a sort of cyclic recurrence linked up with the alternating advance of glaciation and interglaciation, namely: a long cycle of glaciation lasting approximately 85,000 years with a terrace amplitude of 50-100 metres, and a short cycle of interglaciation lasting some 25,000 years with an amplitude of 10-25 metres. Fairbridge sees these long oscillations as being due not only to climatic factors but also to tectonic movements accompanying the subsidence of the semi-continental crust and the deepening of the marginal seas. This is a global process. Glaciation and interglaciation are dealt with in detail in Chapter Sixteen.*

It must be noted that the presence of terrace remains located higher than the present ocean level may perhaps be explained by tectonic uplifts of off-shore localities (regressions) which faded out slowly by the close of the Pliocene. Moreover, as K. K. Markov (319/142) writes, "the observed deformed position of ancient shore lines is a consequence of secondary movements of the Earth's crust under whose influence the initial horizontal surface was turned into a more or less complex and irregular surface."

If to the fact of the existence of synchronised terraces and guyots we add facts linked up with the formation in the Anthropogen of many submarine valleys and canyons of indisputable subaerial origin, the conclusion that there was a *great transgression in the Anthropogen* suggests itself. It was caused by extremely powerful tectonic movements that embraced not only the ocean bed but also shelves and some coastal regions that previously had been subaerial parts of continents.

The surmise that there was a global transgression in the Anthropogen was advanced by many investigators, foremost among whom were G. W. Lindberg, R. Malaise and F. P. Shepard. Similar conclusions were drawn independent of them by the author of the present book. This surmise was advanced to explain facts which later were given a totally different explanation from the standpoint of the ocean permanency theory.

Subsequently, pressured by supporters of that theory, Shepard repudiated many of his initial views.

---

* Concerning synchronised terraces also see J. H F. Umbgrove (693/144) and G. D. Khizanashvili (423/52-56, 67-73).

The great Anthropogen transgression theory was developed most comprehensively by Lindberg (295/141). He came to the conclusion that the ocean level oscillated namely in the Anthropogen, but that the amplitude of this oscillation did not exceed 400 metres. This oscillation was expressed in the alternation of three phases of regression and three phases of transgression; today we are witnessing the last phase of a transgression. In the Anthropogen the transgression proceeded at a catastrophically rapid rate.

As regards the possible maximum fall of the World Ocean level as a result of eustatic oscillations called forth by glaciation, we suggest the following considerations. Between the islands of Bali and Lombok in Indonesia there is a strait which is 15 miles wide and 341 metres deep at its lowest point. This strait forms a kind of boundary (Wallace's line) between two zoogeographical regions that differ sharply from each other, as was noted by Wallace as far back as 1892. The implication is that in the glacial period the World Ocean level could not have dropped lower than 300 metres, otherwise the rivers on those islands would have merged into a single river system and had identical fauna (241/93).

A shortcoming of Lindberg's viewpoint is the assumption that in connection with glaciation the amplitude of fall and rise was very small. The presence of deep marginal seas formed by subsidences does not tie up with this assumption. *The great Anthropogen transgression was of a tectonic nature.* It will be recalled that Academician D. V. Nalivkin considered that when the Japan Sea was formed at the close of the Pleistocene (338) the ocean level might have dropped by 3,000-3,500 metres, which was undoubtedly of the nature of a catastrophe.

J. Gilluly likewise writes that many former continental regions sank relatively recently by at least 3,000 metres, which is a feature particularly of the Atlantic seaboard. In the Atlantic the zone of the replacement and subcrustal erosion of sial is broad, in the Pacific it is narrow (234).

There is another noteworthy circumstance, namely that throughout the world the great Anthropogen transgression might have been accompanied by extremely violent volcanic eruptions. Interlayers of volcanic ash embracing huge areas have been found in all oceans. It has not been established whether this ash originated from land or underwater eruptions. In the case of the Atlantic Ocean this widespread occurrence of volcanic ash was found by Soviet oceanographic expeditions (272). The same has been noted in the Pacific Ocean by J. L. Worzel (708). There ash is widespread as well, and it has been established that it was deposited in the course of only a few years (452; 524). Volcanic ash has been found in bed sediments of the Indian Ocean, too.

The question arises of the water replenishment source of the World Ocean in the event of a deep subsidence transgression. G. W. Lindberg (295/159) offers an interesting computation showing that huge hidden potentialities of increasing the quantity of water in the World Ocean lie in volcanic eruptions and magma effusions. For example, if the intensity of volcanic activity were to rise a hundred-fold as compared with the contemporary level, the emission of vapour over a period of a thousand years could raise the World Ocean level by 100 metres. This does not include magma water.

In this connection the spotlight falls on V. V. Belousov's (195) considerations regarding the changes in the World Ocean level and the necessity of recognising the additional delivery of water to the ocean from erupted magma. He points out that erupted magma, particularly basalt magma, which has a 4 per cent water content, is unquestionably a source of additional water.

R. Rewelle (648) likewise opines that, generally speaking, ocean water is a secondary phenomenon and that it does not owe its origin to condensation of primary water from the atmosphere in remote antiquity. It has been "squeezed out" of the depths of the Earth. It has been coming from that source throughout the Earth's history (also see 320; 2nd ed./108). These views fit in well with the theory of the youth of oceans.

The great Anthropogen transgression is treated from a somewhat different angle by R. Malaise (76), who draws upon the already mentioned Odhner constriction hypothesis and applies the theory of this transgression to the history of the sinking of Atlantis. He declares that inasmuch as at the close of the Pliocene the cooling process embraced both Hemispheres, transgression was global. The almost intact channels of the now submerged canyons are testimony and a yardstick of the catastrophic velocity of that transgression. "There is no doubt whatever," Malaise writes, "that this transgression was a catastrophe for all living nature. It is the author's opinion that no better borderline can be found between the Tertiary and Quaternary periods than that catastrophe."

In our opinion the subsidence of the ocean floor began as a result of the thinning out of the Earth's crust beneath ocean basins induced by the melting of their beds in the Tertiary period and that that led to a drop of the ocean level. This was accompanied by an outburst of mountain-building, also in the centre and along the edges of ocean basins, and by giant ruptures and faults with immense effusions of lava under water. At the time many of the mid-oceanic mountain systems protruded above ocean level. The contrast between continents and oceans reached its maximum. This situation obtained at the close of the Miocene and, particularly, in the Pliocene (323/638). H. T. Stearns (677) points out that the uplift of continents indubitably dates back to the end of the Pliocene. He holds the view that the simultaneous uplift of the Mid-Atlantic Ridge (as well as other mid-oceanic ridges) raised the ocean level by at least 170 metres and, perhaps, as much as 365 metres. He links the existence of the highest marine terraces with this uplift.

Then followed the reverse process that witnessed the upthrust of the ocean floor and the subsidence of the edges of continents. All these processes proceeded sporadically, the processes along the edges of the continents lagging behind those on the ocean bed. This gave rise to powerful stresses on the ocean floor-continent borderline, leading to a subsidence and even to the break-away of parts of continents adjoining the edges of oceanic depressions. Sharply defined fault lines appeared running parallel to the continents and the mid-oceanic ridges, leading to the disengagement of sections of the ocean floor encompassed by such lines. These marginal ruptures and subsidences evidently occurred simultaneously, setting off a global tectonic transgression, which, possibly, has not yet ended.

The great Anthropogen transgression could be excellently explained by the hypothesis offered by G. D. Khizanashvili (423). A rise of the ocean level of at least 1,500 metres in the region where it is assumed Atlantis sank would be understandable. The considerable shift of the Earth's geographical poles, postulated by the hypothesis, must have been accompanied by tectonic movements and volcanic activity caused by the sliding of the Earth's crust as a whole. Such processes should have embraced the globe. However, there is still very little evidence to back up the Khizanashvili hypothesis. Besides, this concept treats the transgression and the tectonic movements and the volcanic activity accompanying it as the consequence of the sliding of the entire Earth's crust. If that is the case, what caused this slide? The causes adduced by the author of the hypothesis are actually the consequences of the slide.

ATLANTIC

Chapter Ten

THE ATLANTIC OCEAN

In size the Atlantic is second only to the Pacific, and without its enclosed and marginal seas it has an area of 82,424,000 square kilometres (its entire area is equal to 93,363,000 square kilometres) with a depth (excluding seas) averaging 3,925 metres (391). In the north it abuts upon the Arctic Ocean without any sharply defined boundary. To a certain extent the Arctic Ocean may be regarded as a direct extension of the Atlantic, this being proved by the penetration of Atlantic waters far into the Arctic Ocean and also by many morphological and geological conditions that these oceans have in common. Therefore, when we study the history of the Atlantic, particularly its northern part, we cannot ignore the history of the Arctic Ocean.

Historically and geologically the Atlantic is divided into three zones:

1. The northern part, known as *Scandicus**, begins south of the so-called Atlantic Sill, a submarine elevation between Greenland, Iceland and Scotland which serves as the boundary between Scandicus and the Arctic Ocean. It ends at the line linking the Hebrides up with the eastern tip of Labrador.

2. The central part, or *Poseidonis*, occupies the rest of the Atlantic in the Northern Hemisphere along a line linking Cape Verde in Africa with Cape Calcanjar in South America.

3. The South Atlantic—Archhelenic.

A. OCEANIC ISLANDS

There are few islands in the purely oceanic part of the Atlantic. Of the greatest interest to us are: *Iceland*, which, as we shall show, is genetically linked up with the lost Atlantis, and *Makaronesia* (the Azores, Madeira, Canary and Cape Verde islands).

---

* This name is most frequently used for the marine depressions in the Norwegian and Greenland seas —*Ed*

Iceland, which is composed of Upper Tertiary basalt, is the central part of the *Thule Basalt Plateau;* basalt is also widespread in the adjoining oceanic and continental regions. Today the island is a horst of a once vast area of basalt eruptions. F. Machatschek (323) writes: "This is, evidently, also the remains of a land mass of unknown dimensions, but which was even larger in the Miocene, where the accumulation of volcanic products began in the Lower Tertiary on the unexposed foundation."

The elevation occupied by Iceland is cut up by fault scarps and intricate fault troughs, the largest of which, the *Central Iceland Fault Trough*, is the centre of present-day earthquakes and volcanic activity (442/90). This trough is much younger than the North Atlantic Ridge (600,000 years). It is therefore *questionable if it has a genetic link with the ridge's* Median Valley (656a). Besides, the submarine Reykjanes Ridge, of which Iceland is a direct extension, does not have a median valley either (see Chapter Twelve). More ancient meridional fractures predominate in the north. The most ancient parts of the island are its northwestern and eastern regions, which consist of a Tertiary basalt plateau with substrata of brown coal and lignite containing remains of plants. This basalt must be regarded as dating from the Lower and Upper Miocene. The Quaternary basalts, chiefly in the central part of the island, coincided in time with the intensive development of the sheet glaciation of the Pleistocene (256/205). An interesting point is that acid lava like rhyolites has been found in Iceland; some of the mountains almost entirely consist of rhyolites. However, as S. Thorarinsson (446, 688) reports, they occupy an area equal to only about one per cent of that of the island. There were about twelve eruptions of rhyolite lava during the past 10,000 years. This, it seems to us, indicates that Iceland is located on part of what had once been a continental platform, the rocks of which were subsequently almost completely assimilated by basalts, the remains being left in the shape of rhyolite magma.

The fact that the assimilation process has gone very far is shown by data on the structure of the Earth's crust in Iceland given by M. Bath (457). The crust is 27.8 kilometres thick, i.e., of the same thickness as the crust of the continents, but its composition is more of the oceanic type. The upper layer, which is 2.1 kilometres thick and has a longitudinal wave diffusion velocity of 3.7 km/sec, is regarded by Bath as a layer of lava and volcanic tuff. The second, about 16 kilometres thick and having a longitudinal wave diffusion velocity of 6.7 km/sec, is regarded as a basalt layer. The third layer, whose nature has not been accurately determined, is 10 kilometres thick and has a longitudinal wave diffusion velocity of about 7.4 km/sec. Precisely this is the real basalt layer.

According to S. Thorarinsson (791) the structure of the Earth's crust in the region of the Central Iceland Fault Trough is as follows: upper layer is a layer of a sedimentary rocks and plateau-basalt (thickness—about three kilometres); longitudinal wave diffusion velocity in the basalt—4.2-5.1 km/sec, which is not very high for basalts; a layer with a maximum thickness of 16 kilometres and a velocity of 6.3 km/sec (true basalt!); a layer whose thickness has not been established but which has a velocity of about 7.4 km/sec. It is noted that the North Atlantic Ridge does not have a layer with a wave diffusion velocity of 6.3 km/sec. This velocity can also indicate granitoids (792). G. P. I. Walker (787) believes that petrological evidence indicates that *the island stands on a shattered microcontinent* (remains of a continental block).

Some data on the Quaternary history of Iceland is given us by D. G. Panov (355) on the basis of investigations conducted by Kjartirsson. Great vertical tectonic movements took place on the island in late glacial and post-glacial times. It has been established that during the last glaciation there was no ice sheet on the eastern shore of Iceland. Powerful volcanic activity has been in progress in Iceland since the Tertiary period.

There are grounds for assuming that territorially Iceland was much larger in the not very distant geological past. Machatschek (323/599) writes: "Thus, when the Pleistocene glaciation began, Iceland was a large land mass with a different contour; however, the occurrence of relic plants and animals shows that the ice sheet did not cover the entire area."

V. M. Litvin (298) reports that V-shaped submarine valleys with morphological indications of their erosion origin have been discovered on the shelf of the island. He thinks that the subsidence took place on the eve of or during the early Quaternary period but does not substantiate this conclusion in detail.

Two greatly fractured terraces divided by a steep ledge have been discovered on the submarine slopes of Iceland at depths of 500 and 800 metres (262/12). Deeper still (1,700 metres) there are terraces and a stepped ascent to the submarine Reykjanes Ridge in the southwestern part of the island (733).

South of Iceland and west of the Hebrides is the tiny rocky island of *Rockall* (57°36′N 13°42′W) towering in solitude over a vast bank. It is a little over 20 metres above sea level and has a circumference of only 90 metres. Nearby, protruding from the sea are the *Hasselwood Rocks* and 1.25 miles (or about 2.3 kilometres) to the east are the *Helena Reefs*. For several miles the tiny island is encircled by shallow water (depth—70-200 metres). These places are hazardous to shipping, particularly in stormy weather; the little island itself is difficult of access. It has been visited only four times—in 1811, 1862, 1921 and 1955—and was officially annexed by Britain only on the last visit (529).

Rockall Island is composed of granite, whose high sodium content distinguishes it from ordinary granite. Named rockallite this rock is a heterogeneous mixture of quartz, feldspar and a rare mineral called egyrin, which consists of zirconium silicate and sodium with an admixture of considerable quantities of rare soils. Greenland is the only other place where this mineral is known.

The erratic behaviour of the compass needle indicates that Rockall Island is strongly magnetic. Samples of basalt have been brought to the surface from the sea bed round the island (529, 657).

A few words must be said about the islands of the Central and South Atlantic, of which St. Paul's Rocks, Ascension, Tristan da Cunha, Gough and Bouvet are situated on the giant Mid-Atlantic Ridge.

St. Paul's Rocks (1°29′N 29°15′W) have a total area of only 0.3 square kilometre and are part of the so-called *Dassy region* situated between this island and Fernando de Noronha. This highly active seismic and volcanic region occupies an area of about 700,000 square kilometres and more than 90 powerful seaquakes have been registered in it (212/221, 222, 230). It will be recalled that of the 94 underwater eruptions in the 18th-20th centuries, 21 were in this zone. We believe that the enigmatic island mentioned by the 4th century Roman poet Rufus Festus Avienus (181) lies in this zone: "And farther out in the sea is an island with lush grass; it is dedicated to Saturn. The forces of nature on it are so unbridled that if a ship draws near to it the sea round the island becomes ruffled, the island itself trembles, the open sea heaves and shudders, while the rest of the sea remains as calm as a pond" (419/1,64). This wonderfully describes a seaquake with accompanying underwater volcanic eruptions. It seems to us that reports of such an island might have been brought by Cretans, who probably sailed in these latitudes.

Two new islands appeared near St. Paul's Rocks in 1932 and vanished shortly afterwards. The rocks were intensely shaled peridotite and basalt with veins of serpentine and mylonised dunite.

W. G. Melson (782) gives us some of the latest data about the composition of St. Paul's Rocks. They are composed mainly of peridotites with a high content of magnesium and very little silica and alkali. However, nearly 30 per cent of the surface of the southeastern islet consists of rocks that substantially differ from peridotites and have a large content of sodium, potassium, aluminium, calcium and iron, and very little magnesium. Like the peridotites, these rocks have been metamorphosed—according to radio-isotope dating—not earlier than 500 million years ago and not later than 50 million years ago. There is evidence of the great antiquity of some of the peridotite dikes (750)—roughly 4,500 million years, but this age, greater than any known, evokes doubt and must be checked. On this point Leontyev (813/225) writes: "This date is by no means identical with the age of the mountains themselves, but it may be regarded as evidence that St. Paul's Rocks are either an erratic mass or a stock of the ultrabasic rocks forming the mantle."

Fernando de Noronha (3°50′S 32°52′W) is a small island with an area of 22 square kilometres towering up to 100 metres above sea level. This island and the rocks in its vicinity are composed of alkaline basalts and trachytes; phonolites also occur (450). About 150 kilometres from this island, near the coast of Brazil, lies Rocas Atoll (3°52′S 33°49′W) with its dangerous coral reefs. Standing five or six metres above sea level, this atoll measures 3.5×2.5 kilometres.

The Island of Trinidad (20°15′S 29°30′W) is a picturesque rock situated 1,200 kilometres from the coast of Brazil. East of it are the three barren, steep and inaccessible *Martin Vaz Islands*.

Ascension Island (7°55′S 14°33′W) has an area of 88 square kilometres. Geologically a young extinct volcano, it is almost entirely made up of lava flows composed of basalt and trachydolerite. Andesites, gabbro, peridotite, obsidian and even rhyolite occur (188). The base of the volcano may be traced by outcrops of granite and gneiss debris and the inclusion of granite in the basalt streams and trachyte domes (256/215). In our opinion this island provides an excellent example of the absorption of the sialic base by basalt magma. It should be borne in mind that it is situated on the Mid-Atlantic Ridge.

St. Helena (15°54′-16°1′S 5°38′-5°47′W) is perhaps the largest island (123 square kilometres) in the South Atlantic. It is the rim of a solitary volcano with its highest point reaching 700 metres above sea level. It is older than Ascension Island and has already been considerably eroded. Outcrops of trachytes and phonolites occur in its southern part. The underwater pedestal has a diameter of about 130 kilometres. The composition of the primary magma of this volcano, which is probably of pre-Tertiary age, is close to that of Gomera Island of the Canary group (209). At one time it had a dense forest blanket.

Tristan da Cunha (37-38°S 12°W) is a group of three islands: two small and a large island with a total territory of 116 square kilometres. The large island was believed to be an extinct volcano which ceased to be active many thousand years ago. But on October 11, 1961 it suddenly came to life and the entire population had to be temporarily evacuated. The highest point of the volcano is 2,300 metres above sea level.

The island is composed of basalt, trachyte and phonolite, but andesite, granite and gneiss also occur (666). This indicates a link with a granite pedestal. It is noteworthy that the climate is even (20° in summer and 14° in winter) and there is endemic arboreal vegetation—the tree *Phylica nitida*, which grows to a height of nearly six metres.

Gough Island (40°20′S 9°55′W), which has an area of 73 square kilometres, is situated about 400 kilometres south of Tristan da Cunha. It stands on a pedestal about 600 square kilometres in size and is an undulating plateau with steep slopes and narrow valleys. Composed of Late Tertiary basalt (594) it is about 600 metres above sea level. Essexite, sodalite and phonolite (188) are encountered. The highest point is Peak Edinburgh (910 metres). Brought into being by the activity of ancient volcanoes, this island was once covered with glaciers, possibly when it was part of South Atlantis. Trees of the species *Phylica* and *Sophora tetraptera* are a characteristic element of the island's vegetation; these species also occur on Reunion Island, New Zealand, Chile and some Pacific islands (563).

Bouvet Island (54°46′S 3°24′E), a volcano rising to an elevation of 936 metres, has an area of 44 square kilometres. It is covered with glaciers and is extremely hard of access. Rhyolite is encountered.

B. CURRENTS AND WINDS OF THE NORTH ATLANTIC

Let us now examine the currents of the North Atlantic, particularly the *Gulf Stream*, which tremendously influences the climate of all Atlantic countries (207/56-59; 260/236-38; 346/42-49; 438/312).

In the tropical latitudes of the Atlantic, the northeasterly and southeasterly trade winds give rise to currents, which as they draw closer to the equator, grow in intensity and turn more and more to the east. Merging, they form the Equatorial Current, whose northern and southern parts are, for the sake of convenience, called the *North* and *South Equatorial currents*. At their source a precise boundary between these two currents may be discerned only from May or June to November, when the extremely shallow *Equatorial Countercurrent* appears in the zone of the weakest winds, between 3° and 10°N. This countercurrent runs eastward and ultimately reaches the Gulf of Guinea.

The North Equatorial Current, started by the northeasterly trade wind, begins at Cape Verde and initially heads westward; near the Antilles it gradually veers to the west-north-west and passes between 8° and 20°N at a velocity not exceeding 37 kilometres a day. The South Equatorial Current, which owes its origin to the southeasterly trade wind, rises almost at the coast of Africa in a belt situated at about the 10th parallel. It is much stronger and more stable than the northern current because the southeasterly trade is a swifter blowing wind than its northeasterly counterpart. At the Brazilian coast, near 5°S, it forks out into two branches. The southern branch races to the southwest and is called the *Brazil Current*, and the northern, more powerful branch, runs along the coast of Guiana as the *Guiana Current* with a velocity of 55-111 kilometres a day. Farther west this current merges with the northern branch of the North Equatorial Current and enters the Caribbean Sea as the *Caribbean Current*. Moving at a velocity of 65-93 kilometres a day, this merged current heads for the coast of Honduras and Yukatan and from there enters the Gulf of Mexico via the Gulf of Yukatan. In the Gulf of Mexico its main masses turn eastward in the direction of Cuba and, passing between Cuba and Florida as the *Florida Current*, it returns to the Atlantic.

The Florida Current flows north of the Gulf of Florida to the region of Cape Hatteras, where it veers away from the American

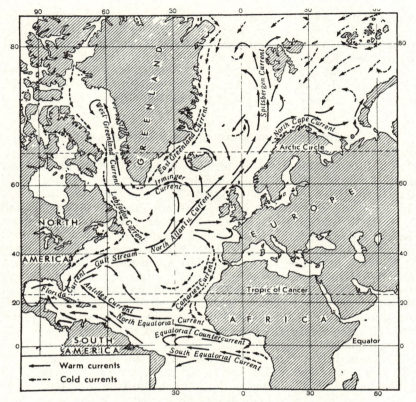

Chart of currents in the North Atlantic (346/42)

shore. In the Gulf of Florida the axial part of this current reaches a velocity of 148 (and sometimes as much as 240) kilometres a day, transporting about 90 cubic kilometres of water an hour. The current reaches a depth of 700 metres. It is about 75 kilometres wide and the temperature of its upper layer (150 metres) is above 20°.

The second branch of the North Equatorial Current is called the *Antilles Current* where it flows along the Antilles and the Bahamas; its speed is 19-37 kilometres a day and, beginning at the coast of Puerto Rico, it transports about 163 cubic kilometres of water an hour and reaches a depth of 800 metres.

The Florida and Antilles currents merge where they enter the ocean and form the Gulf Stream, the great current of the North Atlantic. This combined current begins at Cape Hatteras and flows northward at a velocity of 130 kilometres a day in its axial part and transports about 192 cubic kilometres of water an hour; in its marginal parts its speed is half that of the centre. Starting with 600-700 metres its depth diminishes to 180 metres as it moves farther north. East of the Grand Newfoundland Bank is the so-called *Gulf Stream delta*, where the current forks out into several branches. South of Nova Scotia the speed of the Gulf Stream drops to 70 kilometres a day. South and southeast of the fringe of the Grand Newfoundland Bank, it meets the cold Labrador Current flowing southward and hugging the North American coast almost all the way to Cape Hatteras. Whirlpools are observed on the boundary between the warm and the cold currents.

The *North Atlantic Current* begins in the region of the Grand Newfoundland Bank. Its northernmost branch, the small Irminger Current, flows to the western coast of Greenland and moves along it almost up to the 66th parallel as the *West Greenland Current*. This current melts the ice transported from the Arctic by the *East Greenland Current* beyond Cape Farewell in Greenland. North of the 66th parallel this current, now cooled, possibly turns and links up with the Labrador Current.

Another, much smaller branch, flows in the direction of Iceland, usually reaching its southwestern coast and somewhat softening its climate.

The third and main branch of the North Atlantic Current moves directly eastward, forking out into two branches at approximately 45°N 40°W. The southern branch turns to the southeast, washing the shores of southwestern Europe and Africa; cooling and becoming the cold *Canaries Current,* it flows farther south, ultimately mingling with the North Equatorial Current. Near the Azores the Canaries Current flows from northwest to southeast, and off Portugal it runs from north to south, spreading to the Strait of Gibraltar, where part of it enters the Mediterranean Sea. Most of this current flows far from the coast, between Gibraltar and Cape Verde, and only a small branch moves along the African coast up to Gambia. This current is one of the reasons for the droughty climate on the adjoining parts of the continent and on the Makaronesian islands. It begins to grow warmer only at the 40th parallel.

The northern part of the North Atlantic Current, whose velocity is increased by the prevailing southwesterly winds, crosses the Atlantic at a speed averaging 22 kilometres a day. This branch washes the coast of western and northwestern Europe from the Bay of Biscay to the North Sea and makes the climate of these regions warmer. The main mass of water flows to the Norwegian Sea north of Ireland and Scotland, from where part of it turns west of the Faeroes in the direction of Iceland. North of Iceland this branch turns eastward and links up with the southeastern branch of the East Greenland Current. Only two per cent of the Gulf Stream passes between Iceland and the Faeroes, 94 per cent flowing between the Faeroes and the Shetland Islands and four per cent running between the Shetland Islands and Scandinavia. The quantity of water transported by it varies, more than doubling in some years and falling to one-sixth of normal in other years (316).

In the higher latitudes the main mass of the Gulf Stream waters move along the coast of Norway in the direction of Novaya Zemlya, gradually sinking beneath the waters of the Arctic Ocean. From North Cape part of the warm water moves towards Spitsbergen, making the climate milder and keeping the western coast of this archipelago almost completely free of ice.

Data accumulated over the past 50 years indicate that between the Faeroes and Scotland the current flows at a rate of 18 cubic kilometres per hour (316). At the Lofoten Islands near the coast of Norway it slows down to almost four cubic kilometres per hour, nonetheless greatly influencing the climate. Thus, at the Shetland Islands (60th parallel), the mean temperature of the water should normally have been 2°C, but in fact it is 10°C, while at the coast of Norway (65th parallel) the difference is even more striking: instead of being zero it is 8°C. The following indicative computation of the heat balance of two seas—the Arctic Ocean and the Black Sea—has been made by V. V. Shuleikin (441/75). The figures give cal/cm^2:

		Arctic Ocean	Black Sea
1	Heat radiation of the sun and sky	33,700	82,000
2	From the warm current of the Atlantic	38,000	—
3	From the air-water heat exchange	—	11,000
4	From the waters of rivers	4,100	—
5	From the formation of ice	11,200	—
	Total	87,000	93,000

Thus, *with the total values being relatively close to each other the heat radiation deficiency is covered by the Gulf Stream.* That is exactly what Shuleikin says: "In the Arctic Ocean the heat equilibrium is restored thanks to the intervention of the warm current from the Atlantic."

Of the currents of the South Atlantic, interest is attracted by the cold current flowing from the shores of Antarctica. In the eastern part of the South Atlantic the cold Antarctic current is held up by the submarine South Atlantic and Walvis ridges.

Near the Romanche Trench part of the cold waters break through to the shores of Africa. In the western Atlantic the Antarctic deepwater current splits into two branches at the Romanche Trench. The longer, northwestern branch loses itself almost at the Bermuda Islands. Cold water with a temperature of about 1°C is traced along the western slope of the Mid-Atlantic Ridge nearly up to the 24th parallel (530; 633).

To conclude our description of the currents and winds of the North Atlantic it must be pointed out that between the 3rd and 10th parallel there is a calm zone, which is, however, subject to tornadoes, while north of this zone is the realm of the northeasterly trade winds. In the region of the trade winds storms are less frequent than elsewhere in the Atlantic. North of the equator the region of the trade winds lies some 400 kilometres away from the seaboard. On the other hand, variable winds, mostly westerlies, blow between the 30th and 40th parallels: southwesterly in summer and northwesterly in winter.

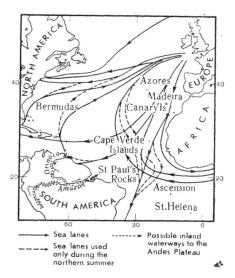

Routes used by sailing vessels in the North Atlantic (661)

Sailing boats took some 40 days (in exceptional cases—15-25 days) to cross the Atlantic. Storms made it possible to shorten the crossing (419/1,166). J. Cortesao (488) maintains that for sailing vessels the voyage across the Atlantic was much simpler and less dangerous than coasting along the western shores of Africa. In our day as well successful attempts have been made to cross the Atlantic in both directions in extremely primitive vessels. *Evidently, the equatorial region was for ancient mariners the most convenient place for crossing the Atlantic in either direction.* It is not that this is the narrowest part of the ocean but that *this is where the Equatorial Countercurrent passes in the shape of a narrow and long ring in the direction from the mouth of the Amazon.* Although this is not a fast current (mean velocity—0.5-0.7 kilometre per hour), it provides a fairly simple but long route to Africa, making it necessary for ancient mariners to sail from the mouth of the Amazon to the northeast, to a region situated roughly 40°W and 6-8°N. Provided use was made of the northeasterly trade wind it was, as we have pointed out, fairly easy to sail to the shores of America.

C. THE SARGASSO SEA AND THE SPAWNING OF EELS

A unique feature of the North Atlantic is the existence of a body of water known as the *Sargasso Sea* (164, 398). This great tract of ocean is densely overgrown with weeds called *Sargassum bacciferum.* These weeds occur in other parts of the World Ocean (the near

West Indies, for example), but nowhere do they grow in such profusion as in the Sargasso Sea.

There must have been greater accumulations of these weeds in the Atlantic in remote antiquity. Pseudo-Aristotle reported that there were sandbanks, oozy shallows and accumulations of weeds beyond the Pillars of Hercules. Pseudo-Scylax (360 B.C.) wrote that oozy shallows and weeds prevented ships from sailing farther than Cerna. The philosopher Theophrastus (390-305 B.C.), regarded as the father of botany, says in his *History of Plants* [IV, VI, III], that, according to hearsay, there was a great accumulation of weeds west of the Pillars of Hercules.

The most characteristic region of the Sargasso Sea is situated between 20-40°N and 35-60°W, stretching 5,000 kilometres from west to east and 2,000 kilometres from north to south. The northeasterly trade wind blows in this region. The absence of storms earned the Sargasso Sea the name Ladies' Sea as far back as the Middle Ages. The water temperature is 17-23° in winter and 23-27° in summer.

An interesting point is that the Sargasso weeds are not related to the West Indies weeds. Also puzzling is the circumstance that *neither the flora nor the fauna of the Sargasso Sea has any biological link with West Indies forms*, which would have been natural in view of the territorial proximity and present-day direction of the currents. On the contrary, *the fauna of this sea is closer to that of the Mediterranean, while some deep-water species of Sargasso plankton belong to the species currently inhabiting the surface of the Norwegian Sea. We feel that this latter fact is testimony in favour of the onetime above-water existence of the North Atlantic Ridge (i.e., of Atlantis) with a cold current beginning north of the Shetland Islands flowing past its eastern shore. When the ridge sank the cold-water plankton, which had until then lived at the surface, moved to a deeper part of the ocean together with the cold waters.* L. V. Worthington and W. S. Metcalf (707) point out that *today waters from the Norwegian Sea are traced only along the eastern but not the western slopes of the North Atlantic Ridge.* To this day the ridge is, consequently, a sufficiently formidable barrier to the deep-lying cold waters of the Norwegian Sea, preventing them from reaching the Sargasso Sea.

The spawning of European eels (*Anguilla anguilla*) is one of the riddles of the North Atlantic, because like their American kin (*Anguilla rostrata*) they lay their eggs in the Sargasso Sea (278). The spawning centre lies at an equal distance in the southeast of the Bermuda Islands and in the northeast of the Bahamas, in the deepest and saltiest part of the North Atlantic (between 22-30°N and 48-62°W). The spawning season begins in early spring and ends in mid-summer. With the aid of the Gulf Stream the eel larvae swim to the shores of Europe, taking from two and a half to three years to accomplish the journey. P. Y. Schmidt (436) has suggested that during the glacial period, as a result of the flooding of the entire northern part of the Atlantic with cold water, the Gulf Stream flowed in a different direction; it was a circular current moving not to the north but along Portugal and Africa, from north to south. He believes that in those days the European eel spawned at the Canary Islands, while the American eel at the Bahamas. But S. V. Kokhnenko (278/27) reasonably points out that eels require a region with maximum favourable conditions for spawning and not simply a permanent spawning place of their parents.

An attempt to solve both these riddles was made by L. Germaine (156), who suggested the hypothesis that the Sargasso Sea overlies a former land area that had subsided beneath the ocean waves as far back as the Miocene and that the present-day fauna and flora of that sea are the "surfaced" population of the littoral and upper levels of the sublittoral of that land area. This hypothesis best explains both riddles, but it clashes with the fact that the Sargasso Sea overlies the deepest parts of the Atlantic Ocean, and there is no testimony to show that land existed there even in the Tertiary period.

However, all these difficulties can be surmounted if we assume the existence of Atlantis east of the present Sargasso Sea, in the region of the North Atlantic Ridge. If that assumption is accepted we should find the location of the currents to be quite different, and the Eastern Sargasso Sea would be in the region between this ridge and the Cape Verde Islands. This sea disappeared after the sinking of Atlantis and its population was carried by the North Equatorial Current to the Western Sargasso Sea, which exists to this day. In our opinion this explanation best of all resolves both riddles of the Sargasso Sea.

D. DISTRIBUTION OF FORAMINIFERA

A knowledge of the distribution of plankton rhizopods of foraminifera (383) is of great assistance in establishing the history of the Atlantic, particularly in the stages linked up with glacial periods.

There have been numerous varieties of foraminifera. Two globorotalia—*Globorotalia menardii* and *Globorotalia truncatulinoides*—are currently the most widespread in all oceans. While the former is primarily warmth-loving, the latter can live in both warm and cold waters. *Globorotalia menardii* is regarded as the older of the two varieties. The cold- and warmth-loving varieties of *Globorotalia truncatulinoides* are distinguished by the coiling of the test spirals. The coiling of the cold-loving variety is dextral, while that of the warmth-loving variety is sinistral. Investigations conducted by D. B. Ericson, M. Ewing, G. Wollin and B. C. Heezen (517) have confirmed the observations of G. Schott, who found that the distribution of *Globorotalia menardii* can serve as a good indicator of the climate, showing whether it is cold or warm. Where the climate is cold this foraminifera disappears. *Today* Globorotalia menardii are

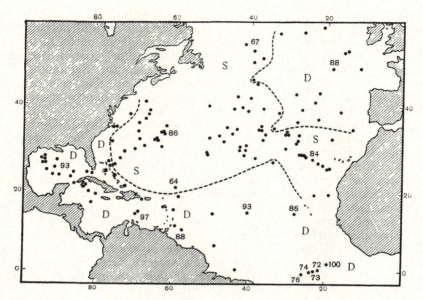

Distribution of dextral and sinistral foraminifera in the North Atlantic (516)
S—sinistral; D—dextral; the figures at S and D show the percentage of
a given variety

not to be found north of the line running through the Azores and the Canary Islands. *They are extremely sparse in the Sargasso Sea.* The latter circumstance is very puzzling because the waters of that sea are warmer than of the ocean surrounding it. Consequently, temperature conditions are by no means the reason for the absence of *Globorotalia menardii* in the Sargasso Sea (517/261). We consider that *this riddle can also be explained by the onetime existence of an Eastern Sargasso Sea east of Atlantis. After Atlantis sank, although* Sargassum bacciferum *were moved to the west, part of their plankton remained south of the Azores-Canary Island line.* That was why the cold Canaries Current (which is not so cold as to destroy these foraminifera), which exists to this day, did not hinder their continued existence in their former home.

Much more baffling is the distribution in the North Atlantic of both dextral and sinistral varieties of *Globorotalia truncatulinoides* at present and in the past (according to studies of cores). The investigations of D. B. Ericson and G. Wollin (516) have shown that currently there are two or three large provinces inhabited by different foraminifera. The northeastern quadrant is inhabited by cold-loving dextral foraminifera. The central zone, stretching from northwestern Africa to North America, is inhabited by sinistral foraminifera. The equatorial Atlantic is inhabited by dextral foraminifera.

One gets the impression that sinistral foraminifera had broken through to the east and wrecked the initially large area of dextral foraminifera.

The distribution of dextral and sinistral foraminifera was found to be different in deep-water cores. At one time, *more than 10,000 years ago, the currently central province of sinistral foraminifera east of the North Atlantic Ridge was non-existent—at that time this province was occupied by dextral foraminifera*, whose existence there is computed in tens of thousands of years.

Some 2,000 years ago dextral foraminifera were predominant in the south equatorial province as well, where they continue to exist to this day. Moreover, on the basis of their study of the distribution of cold- and warmth-loving foraminifera, Ericson, Ewing, Wollin and Heezen (444, 517) have proved that a rapid rise of the temperature of the surface waters of the North Atlantic took place 10,000 years ago. C. Emiliani believes that this temperature rise occurred 13,000 years ago. Generally speaking, his dating differs from the dating of staff members of the Lamont Observatory (510-513; 655).

Also noteworthy is the following statement by Ewing and Heezen (523/527): "Over wide geographical areas *Globorotalia truncatulinoides* shows striking changes from dextral to sinistral direction of coiling, accomplished in periods of time reckoned at less than a century." Consequently, the replacement of one form by the other was of a catastrophic nature, and supporters of the ocean permanency theory are helpless when it comes to explaining what caused this replacement.

One gets a satisfactory explanation only if one assumes *that at one time there was a barrier, which meridionally divided the Atlantic Ocean and gave cold-loving foraminifera the possibility of penetrating far to the south, to the equator. When this land barrier disappeared the region of the cold-loving foraminifera diminished, while the warmth-loving variety spread eastward, forming a single central province. The sinking of the barrier was unquestionably a catastrophe.* All other explanations, including the verbose explanation offered by Ericson and Wollin about the biological variability of foraminifera and so forth, do not hold water.

E. DIATOMS AND PTEROPODS

R. W. Kolbe (577, 578) published the results of his investigations of diatoms or algae, whose silicified remains were discovered in some cores taken in the tropical Atlantic by the Swedish oceanographical expedition on board the *Albatross*. In the process of its vital activity, the diatom absorbs carbon dioxide through photosynthesis and is, therefore, in need of light. It lives in the upper layers of both salt and fresh water; the fresh-water varieties differ from those inhabiting salt water. Kolbe studied diatoms from the following stations:

Station No.	North latitude	West longitude	Depth (metres)	Distance (kilometres)	
				from Africa	from America
234	5°45′	21°43′	3,577	930	1,960
235	3°12′	20°25′		990	1,900
238	0°7′	18°42′	7,315	1,050	1,990

The core at Station No. 238 was obtained from the Romanche Trench. All cores showed the presence of diatoms, but the most interesting proved to be a core from Station No. 234 obtained from an elevation that may be regarded as the eastern island of a onetime subaerial equatorial archipelago. It is interesting because the lower layer consists entirely of fresh-water diatoms (18 species). Kolbe cautiously assumed that although the core gave the impression it was taken from the floor of a onetime fresh-water lake, the fresh-water diatoms are most likely from the Niger or the Congo and were transported by the Guinea Current to the place where they were found. Very logically, however, R. Malaise (75) takes issue with this argument, stating that in any case the fresh-water diatoms would have been mixed with marine species as had been observed in some other cores. Malaise justifiably maintains that the *core was taken from a onetime fresh-water lake situated on a submerged island.* Kolbe himself (578, 652) subsequently had to agree with Malaise.

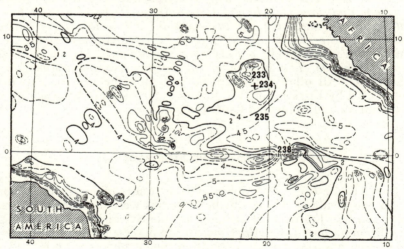

Chart of the equatorial Atlantic, where fresh-water diatoms have been discovered (75)
The cross indicates the location of Station No. 234; the figures in heavy type give the location of other stations. The depth is in kilometres

There is another riddle of the North Atlantic which attracts attention: *pteropodean ooze, which usually gravitates towards islands, was discovered not only on the Azores Plateau but also east of the Madeira Islands and even close to the more southerly parts of the North Atlantic Ridge (212), where islands are non-existent today and were non-existent in post-Columbus times.* Fairly large areas with pteropodean ooze sediments are known in the region of the South Atlantic Ridge. They are perhaps linked up with the onetime existence of a South Atlantis.

Chapter Eleven

MAKARONESIA

Makaronesia is accepted as the collective name of five groups of North Atlantic islands situated closer to the southwestern coast of Europe and the northwestern shore of Africa than to America and possessing some common biogeographical features: 1) the Azores with their cliffs and the Formigas reefs; 2) the Madeiras with Porto Santo Island and the uninhabited Desertas islets; 3) the Canary Islands; 4) the uninhabited Salvages Islands north of the Canary Islands—they comprise islets and groups of small rocks; 5) the Cape Verde Islands.

All these islands have a Mediterranean climate. The temperature is even throughout the day and year. H. Schenk (225/119) gives us the following climatic data:

	Cape Verde	Canaries	Madeira	Azores
North latitude	14°54'	28°25'	35°28'	37°45'
Mean annual temperature	24.5°	20.8°	18.4°	17.3°
Mean annual precipitation, mm	323	335	683	715

Frosts are unknown on these islands, but snow that quickly melts sometimes falls on the peaks of the mountains. These are the Fortunate Isles of antiquity.

They form the *Makaronesian* or *Atlantic floristic region*, whose flora may be regarded as a pre-glacial relic. This flora had at one time been widespread. It will be recalled that evergreen forests gravitated towards the Atlantic and from there they migrated eastward; deciduous forests are widespread in the west. The remains of Tertiary flora on all the Makaronesian islands and even in Iceland and on Spitsbergen show its identity on this huge territory, which is testimony that this was once an unbroken region. On this score E. V. Wulf (225/131) writes: "The unique nature of the Makaronesian flora and its high paleoendemism are testimony of the longstanding isolation of these islands from continents, but this is not proof that they had always been isolated from the continents." Moreover, it is our opinion that there are full grounds for assuming that each of the Makaronesian archipelagoes was separated from the continents at a different time. This becomes especially clear when we compare the Makaronesian flora with the flora of some of the islands in the South Atlantic.

Nearly a hundred years ago J. D. Hooker (223/23) noted the following features when he studied the flora of the Atlantic islands:

1) The flora of these islands is closely linked up with continental flora from which it originates. In the case of the Azores, although they are closer to America than, for instance, the Madeira Islands, they have fewer American species, and only a very small number of American species have been found on St. Helena Island. 2) The island flora is typical of a more moderate climate than continental flora. 3) It has many features distinguishing it from continental flora. 4) Annual endemic plants are very rare.

B. Kubart considered that the oldest flora is on St. Helena Island and the youngest on the Azores; this is confirmed by data on the number of endemic species. The relation between species of arboreal and herbaceous vegetation is extremely important for an estimate of when the islands separated. Here, as K. K. Markov (320; 2nd ed./229) declares, the point is that generally until the Lower Pliocene grasses did not participate in the formation of vegetative landscapes. For example, in England, the percentage of arboreal species, which was 97 in the Eocene, dropped to 51 in the Lower Pliocene and to 22 in the Lower Anthropogen, and is only 17 today. In the Makaronesian islands E. W. Sinnott likewise noted that the percentage of grass is higher where separation from the continents took place later.

If the data on the endemicism of flora are complemented with data on the endemicism of fauna (18/57; 720), we shall get the following figures for the Atlantic islands:

Islands	% of endemics		% of herbaceous plants
	flora	fauna	
Tristan da Cunha	—	23	—
St Helena	85	up to 50	37
Canary Islands	48	—	68
Cape Verde Islands	36	4	—
Madeira	20	3	—
Azores	8	0	88

This table indicates that *the Azores are the youngest of the Makaronesian islands and that in the Atlantic the sinking of land proceeded from south to north.* Consequently, the *South Atlantic is the oldest subsidence region.* This is confirmed by currently known facts from geological history and also by the seismicity in the South Atlantic, where it is considerably weaker than in the North Atlantic (244).

Makaronesian fauna has been studied by L. Germaine (63, 64, 65), who found it extremely homogeneous and of continental origin. Three factors predominate in the zoological history of these islands. They are: 1) the continental, desert nature of the land fauna and its homogeneity; 2) the conformity of this fauna to that of Southern Europe and North Africa but not to tropical America; 3) the exceptional poverty of potamic fauna. The latter circumstance rules out all considerations about the American origin of the island fauna, while the other two facts indicate the predominant conformity to the Old World. The faunistic coincidence is particularly striking for the European Miocene. Germaine supposes that the Makaronesian fauna is inherited and is a survival of the European Miocene fauna. A. Chopard (212), who has noted the kinship of the flora and fauna of the Azores to European Miocene species, likewise feels that this flora is an indication that the islands had at one time been linked up with Europe.

Germaine notes that the Makaronesian archipelagoes provided refuge to some species of animals inhabiting the Antilles and Central America. It is noteworthy that 15 species of marine mollusks occur only along the coast of Portugal, at the Antilles and in Central America. The discovery of remains of one and the same species of land snail in the Quaternary sediments of North Africa and the Canary Islands has led Germaine round to the conclusion that these islands were separated from the continent in a fairly late epoch. "These islands," he writes, "are an extension of the African mountains, from which they were separated in recent times, possibly at the beginning of the present geological epoch." There are grounds for surmising that the Canary Islands broke away from the other Makaronesian islands long before they separated from Africa.

Opinion is divided about the geological nature of the Makaronesian archipelagoes and about the time they were formed. R. F. Scharff (95) believes that in the Miocene the Azores and the Madeira Islands were still linked up with Portugal, and that the South Atlantic continent stretched to Morocco and the Canary Islands. The Azores and the Madeira Islands broke away in the Pliocene and both parts of the Atlantic—the North and the South—linked up, but the destruction of the remaining portion of land and the links with the continents surrounding the ocean continued for a long time. Even in the early glacial epoch the Atlantic islands were part of the continent. C. F. Dollfus (86/79) writes that the separation of the Canary Islands occurred after the Miocene. L. Gentil (534) regards the Canary Islands as an extension of the Grand Atlas and considers that separation began at the close of the Pliocene and that, possibly, there were links with the continent as late as the mid-Anthropogen. He dates the separation of the Madeira and Canary Islands from the Tortonian age of the Lower Miocene, noting, however, that the Tortonian and even the later, Plaisancian layer on the shore of Morocco, underwent destruction. In other words, powerful movements of the Earth's crust took place in this region in post-Tertiary times and the straits between the Canary Islands and Africa grew deeper.

Some years ago R. Kreici-Graf (580) published an extensive paper on the geological history of Makaronesia. He dealt with the problem of vertical movements in this region of the Atlantic and linked the existence of the Makaronesian islands up with the subsidence of the perimeter of the Iberian Peninsula. Until the Miocene inclusively, the rocks in this region accumulated in folds, which extended into the region of the modern continental shelf as well. Round the ancient cores of the islands there are Cenozoic formations, chiefly limestones. In the region of Makaronesia there were repeated tectonic movements, the most important of which were: 1) in the Upper Cretaceous or Paleogene, when they resulted in sediments crumpled into folds and elevations to a height of 2,000-3,000 metres; 2) in the Miocene when uplifts reached a height of 200-400 metres; and 3) in post-Tertiary times, as testified by the broken bedding of Miocene rocks and their position at various levels. Volcanic processes were similarly important; in some places the accumulations of volcanic materials reached a thickness of 2,000-3,000 metres. According to J. Bourcart, the tectonic movements on the Canary Islands are interpreted as alternating uplifts and subsidences, while subsidences are more characteristic of all the rest of the Makaronesian islands. Limestones older than Miocene age have not been found on the overwhelming majority of these islands (p. 116).

Kreici-Graf maintains that no remains of the pre-volcanic (continental) pedestal have been found on the Makaronesian islands (with the exception of Maio and the Cape Verde Islands) and that all the old observations on this score were erroneous (p. 77). This conclusion stemmed from Kreici-Graf's conviction that acid rocks are the result of differentiation and not of metamorphism. He, therefore, attached no importance to the finding of acid rock samples and omits mention of them. Moreover, he does not mention the investigations of H. Hausen (547), who found acid lava on the Canary Islands, despite the fact that the results of these investigations were published several years before his (Kreici-Graf's) own work and must have been known to him (he refers to a number of Hausen's works where no mention is made of acid lavas). This selectivity of facts raises doubts about the objectivity and correctness of his conclusions in spite of his having put together a great deal of interesting information.

In a recently published small but comprehensive monograph dealing with the volcanism of the Makaronesian islands (779), Machado points out that although the lava of these islands is usually attributed to the so-called "Atlantic petrographic province", a substantial difference is observed between the lava of individual archipelagoes. While the presence of more basic basalt and more acid andesite lavas is typical of the Azores, the Madeiras may be termed as being intermediate, and the lava of the Cape Verde Islands and, in particular, of the Canaries, is very close to the continental type. All the lava have a similarly high sodium content as the igneous rock of southwest Portugal. Machado, who has closely studied the entire Atlantic petrographic province, reasonably assumes that there is a great deal of data to indicate the probable existence of submerged remains of the sialic crust (which, I should like to add, continues to be assimilated by basalt). It will be recalled that the rocks comprising the tiny Rockall Island likewise have a high sodium content. This little island is undoubtedly a remnant of the typical sialic crust even though there is igneous basalt around it.

Let us now deal with some of the island groups separately.

The *Azores*. These are mountainous islands with deep valleys and an abundance of ravines. A feature of their landscape is that there are numerous round or oval craters (calderas), most of which are filled with water. The peaks on the islands tower to an altitude of 1,000 metres or a little higher, and only Pico Island has a mountain rising to 2,320 metres. These are volcanic islands and all are seismically active. Particularly violent earthquakes and eruptions took place in 1522, 1691, 1720, 1808 and 1811. Changes in the relief of the islands have been recorded by man. For example, Fogo Bay on São Miguel Island took the place of a giant crater in 1563. A new islet, Sabrina, which was destroyed by ocean waves several years later, appeared near São Miguel Island in 1811. And recently, in 1957, a new islet—Kapelinis—appeared near Fayal Island, subsequently becoming part of it.

Pre-Miocene volcanic formations are known only on Santa Maria Island and the Formigas Rocks. These are basanites, which have been subjected to destruction down to a depth of more than 150 metres (as has been shown by boring). The basanites contain beds of basalt and red scoria conglomerates. There are post-Miocene trachytes, essexites and basalts on other islands. Kreici-Graf makes passing mention of andesites as well, indicating that the outcrop sequence of igneous rock is as follows: basalts → trachytes and andesites → olivine basalts (580/160). The lava on the different islands is very similar and of a clearly alkaline nature. This also concerns the basalts (256/209). Basalt lava and scoria are interbedded with limestones only on the western side of Santa Maria Island, on an abrasion plateau standing 80 metres above sea level. Among these

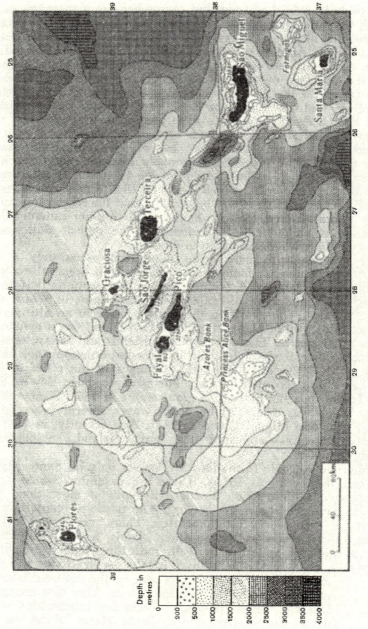

Bathymetric chart of the submarine Azores Plateau with the Azores Islands
The figures at the islands give the height of mountains in metres

rocks there occur mid-Miocene shallow-water fossils and Upper Miocene foraminifera remains. Similar limestones have been discovered on the shelf of the Formigas Rocks as well.

V. H. Fonjaz (529a) reports that the islands of Corvo, Flores (!), Santa Maria and Graciosa are non-seismic. Andesite-basalt is the predominant type of lava flow, while on some islands it consists of trachytes. In our view the presence of andesite volcanism is extremely noteworthy because it is an indication of assimilation processes in the submerged continental mass.

Accumulations of large fragments of granite, gneiss and various sedimentary rock have long been known on the southwestern shore of Santa Maria Island and on the eastern coast of Terceira Island. It is believed that these fragments were transported to the islands by drift ice during the last glaciation (323). In our opinion, this location of the rock fragments is testimony that *during the Pleistocene there was a cold current between Terceira and Santa Maria.* As far back as 1860 G. Hartung (84/63), who found erratic boulders, noted that they were situated very close to the modern shoreline. Consequently, *the foundation of the islands rose some 100-200 metres when glaciation came to an end.* However, it is believed that at present the Azores are a region of considerable age-old subsidences—up to 5.3 mm per year (328) and that since the end of glaciation there has been a subsidence of at least 40 metres.

It is known that there have been frequent uplifts of the Earth's crust after glaciation. If in the Pleistocene the islands were larger and taller than they are today, the post-glacial uplifts may have been linked up with local glaciers. This thesis could be backed up by the discovery of traces of ancient glaciation on the summits of the Azores. However, F. Machado (private report) maintains that *no traces of ancient glaciation have been discovered on the Azores.* Today snow is to be seen for a few weeks in winter only on the peak of Pico Island, where the snow line does not drop below 1,500 metres. Inasmuch as on all the other islands the peaks are below this height they are free of snow. Corvo and Flores are evidently the only islands with traces of ancient glaciation. This assumption is based on the intensive and unusual erosion of some of the valleys on these islands. If this erosion is of glacial origin, Flores and Corvo—summits of the present submarine North Atlantic Ridge—were tall and covered with glaciers in the Pleistocene. These glaciers might have been the sources of local erratic materials. The glaciation on Corvo and Flores islands might be an indirect indication of the once subaerial existence of the North Atlantic Ridge, in any case of the sector adjoining the Azores submarine plateau. However, Kreici-Graf, who does not believe that there were considerable subsidences in the region of the Azores, considers that the valleys on Flores and Corvo were carved out not by ice but by water. This selectivity is strange, to say the least, because nothing of the kind is to be found on the other islands.

An explanation of the absence of glaciation traces on the Azores may be that in the Pleistocene these islands were 500 metres above their present level and their peaks could, therefore, not have served as a place for the formation of permanent glaciers. If we accept this theory we have to revise the concept of the possibility of the submarine Azores Plateau having been upthrust very high in the epoch of its subaerial existence. On the other hand, if the foundation of the islands sank two or more kilometres at the beginning of the Holocene, the end moraines of the glaciers must now be situated at a considerable depth. Moreover, signs of glaciation may have been completely covered by products of Holocene volcanic eruptions. This problem remains to be studied.

Kreici-Graf (580) considers that post-Pliocene volcanic activity was predominant on the Azores and that the appearance of ash cones is linked up with this activity. In his opinion, the maximum uplift took place in sectors where young active volcanoes are non-existent, this being proved by the sinking of Tertiary limestones in the direction of such volcanoes. The morphology of the islands is determined by the duration of post-volcanic erosion. Subsequent general levelling of the surface was interrupted only by the latest volcanic activity. In the Upper Cretaceous or Paleogene marine sediments, compressed into steep folds (!), were raised to a height of at least 2,000 metres, and there was an uplift of another 200 metres in the Miocene; but in post-Tertiary times, Kreici-Graf says, there was a further uplift, this being confirmed, allegedly, by the broken bedding of the Miocene rocks and by their distribution at different levels. We know very little about the geological history of the Azores and cannot conjure up a complete picture.

Very curious stories are linked up with some of the Azores. Most of these stories concern Corvo Island, including the finding of Carthaginian coins (554) and the statue of a horseman pointing to the west (46; 419/I). With regard to other islands there also are legends about the finding of enigmatic inscriptions on gravestones and even of sunken towns (48/43; 137; 149; 161/76).

Madeira (256/209) is a volcanic ridge 70 kilometres long and 20 kilometres wide. Modern volcanic activity is absent. Mid-Miocene limestones with fossils occur; remains of Tertiary plants have been found. The island appeared on a longitudinal tectonic fissure of possibly Miocene age. Madeira was evidently known to the Cretans, Phoenicians and Carthaginians.

The *Cape Verde Islands* were uninhabited when they were discovered by Europeans. They found many trees, fresh water and salt on one of these islands.

Madeira Islands

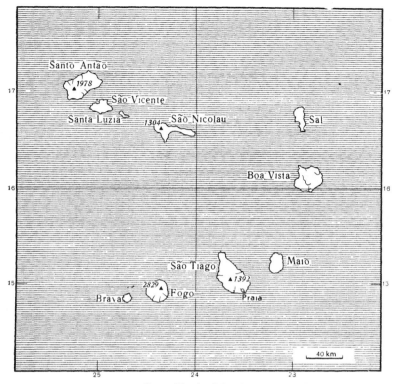

Cape Verde Islands

A. Chevalier (486) reported that he found dolmens and rock inscriptions in the Berber language. G. R. Crone (419), however, doubts the existence of the dolmens and considers that the rock inscriptions were made at the close of the 15th century by Berber slaves brought to the islands by the Portuguese. There is a legend, according to which, seven enigmatic statues were found on the islands (161/75).*

Although these islands are of volcanic origin, they are evidently situated on a continental foundation. They consist of volcanic rocks, beneath which are continental crystalline rocks. Upper Cretaceous, on Maio (580), and Eocene sediments (209) have been brought to light. According to C. Burri (479), the rocks of which these islands are composed are generally characterised by a high content of silica; a similarity is observed even with the rocks in Rhine province, Germany.

---

* For other legends see (34).

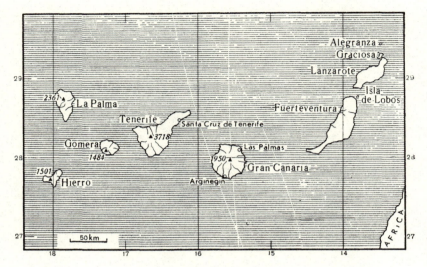

Canary Islands

The islands had a high precipitation during the glacial epoch but today they have a droughty climate and many plants and animals of that period are now extinct. Plants of the species *Cyphia* and *Nidorella* abound on the islands. They are not to be found in Europe and on other Makaronesian archipelagoes, but are typical for South Africa, a fact which indicates that the islands were at one time linked up with that continent (225/121). There is evidence that some of the fauna are of American origin. Generally speaking, the islands have been inadequately investigated.

The *Canary Islands* are usually divided into two groups: the eastern or *Purple Islands*, which include Fuerteventura and Lanzarote, and the western or *Fortunate Isles*, which embrace all the others. The Fortunate Isles are integral or destroyed cones of volcanoes, while the Purple Islands are more reminiscent of the nearest continent. The entire archipelago is a single mass rising from the depths of the ocean. J. Bourcart (209/263) has established the presence of rhyolites amid Miocene and Pliocene sediments. H. Hausen (547) has confirmed the occurrence of sial rocks but regards them as being unexpected. Giving the results of the Finnish geological expedition of 1947-51, he points out that typically continental acid lava was ejected on Tenerife throughout its history. Similar lava has also been found on Gran Canaria. This is an exception in the Mid-Atlantic petrographic province, which is characterised by basalt lavas.

Petrographic, geological and paleogeographical data indicate that the Canary Islands have a close genetic tie with Africa. *They are a fragment of a small continental block that was shattered and subsided in the geologically recent past, most likely in the Anthropogen.*

Moreover, these islands have been repeatedly subjected to processes of subsidence and uplift, with the former being predominant.

Nonetheless, on the basis of a number of facts, one of which is that there are Miocene terraces rising to a height of 800 metres, A. Bleton (762) suggests that the Canary Islands are most likely of submarine volcanic origin. It must be noted that subsidences are still taking place in the Moroccan Atlas Mountains, while in the Canary Islands area, which is more mobile, this process took place alternately in two directions. However, the latest report from P. Rothe (801) that on Fuerteventura Island the Paleozoic rocks are shot with igneous rock allows us to draw the conclusion that the *Canary Islands are part of a continent.*

In deep antiquity the Canary Islands were probably the prototype of Homer's and Hesiod's Fortunate Isles. Unquestionably, they were known to the Cretans, Phoenicians, Carthaginians, Etruscans and Arabs (419/I, 62-72; II, 427-84, III, 165-75, 238-56; 231).

THE RIDDLE OF THE GUANCHES

The Canaries were the only islands of Makaronesia where Europeans discovered an autochthonous population of extremely ancient origin. Many atlantologists link these islands up with the location of Atlantis. The information about the natives of the Canary Islands and their culture given below is drawn mainly from a short paper by A. Bajocco, the Italian paleoethnologist of the Canary Islands, written specially for this book and supplemented by us from other sources, chiefly from the work of Bory de St. Vincent (47; also 231; 467).

Prior to the arrival of Europeans the Canaries were fairly densely populated: there were more than 20,000 inhabitants. The most densely populated were Tenerife and Gran Canaria. The conquest of the islands by the Spaniards was started in 1402, and all the small islands were conquered by 1405. Tenerife and Gran Canaria, which had the largest population, were subdued at the close of the 15th century. The aboriginal population was almost completely exterminated in the desperate and unequal struggle (they had neither metal weapons nor firearms) against the invaders. And 150 years later there was not a single pure-blooded aborigine left on the islands.

The aborigines of the Canary Islands are usually called *Guanches*, which is not quite correct. The word *guanch*, probably of Berber origin, means native or son. Consequently, it did not signify the name of a people. The Spaniards first came into contact with typical Guanches on Tenerife who called themselves Guanchtinerf or "native of Tenerife".

Paleoanthropological investigations, conducted principally by R. Verneau (695), led to the conclusion that the population of the Canary Islands was autochthonously heterogeneous and that, in fact, the islands were settled by four different ethnic groups. This was established by Verneau on the basis of his analysis of skeletons, particularly the remains of skulls.

The most noteworthy type showed a likeness to Cro-magnon man, the ancient representative of intelligent man inhabiting Europe during the Upper Paleolith. Verneau called this type Guanche proper. North Africa, too, was peopled by the Cro-Magnon race. Later Verneau's opinion about the likeness of the Gaunches to Cro-Magnon man was backed up by Falkenburger (86/113). It should be noted that Cro-Magnon man appeared in Europe not later than 30,000 years ago. He represented a Europoid race.

The Cro-Magnons of the Canary Islands—the Guanches proper—were tall (over 180 cm) *dolichosephali*. Giants, over two metres tall, are mentioned in the legends and records of the Spanish chroniclers (47/68). They had broad faces with a triangular chin, large and deep eye sockets and sharply-defined eyebrows. Many of them were blue-eyed blonds and some were even red-haired. All the chroniclers agree that the Guanches were a very handsome and attractive people. The women of Gran Canaria were noted for their beauty. The Guanches loved music, songs and dances; their dances were very successful in Europe. The Cro-Magnon-Guanches comprised the bulk of population of Tenerife and Gran Canaria islands.

The second ethnical group, called Semitic by Verneau, was largely a mixture of various kindred ethnical groups, which present-day anthropologists term as Mediterranean peoples. They were moderate *dolichocephali* and not as tall as the Cro-Magnon-Guanches. They had a long, oval face with a thin nose and black hair. The Semitic group inhabited part of Gran Canaria, and Hierro, and some were to be found on Tenerife. Gomera Island was inhabited by short-statured Berbers.

The third group comprised *brachycephali* with a short and thick body. They had broad faces, with a large and flat nose. Arguments rage over the origin of this group, and some scholars think they are Mongoloids (85). The fourth group has not been identified, but it was probably a mixture of various ethnic groups, including Negroids.

Although some words of the language of the Canary aborigines have survived, it is not possible to establish its grammar. Initially the language was evidently of Berber origin, and Arab elements were later added to it.

This hypothesis, however, is refuted by the latest investigations. For example, Y. N. Zavadovsky (811/7), a leading Soviet expert on the Berber language, cites the opinion of prominent French experts to the effect that the language spoken by the Guanches is not of Berber origin, that it is an absolutely isolated language. This is indirectly supported by the theory of the extremely ancient origin of the Guanches, whose ancestors reached the Canary Islands by an overland route (see end of the section on the Guanches). The dialects of the different islands developed in isolation, and language intercourse was sometimes difficult. It is interesting to note that a language of whistles, i.e., conversation by means of whistling and not words, exists on Gomera Island to this day.

The Spanish chroniclers tell us that the aborigines did not have a written language. J. de Viera y Clavijo (47/54) is the only one to point out that on La Palma a cave of one of the chiefs had many hieroglyphic inscriptions, particularly on a rock shaped like a gravestone. Rock inscriptions, which may be divided into three types, have been found on all the Canary Islands. The first consists of petroglyphs such as are to be found throughout Europe. Dating from prehistoric times they are, apparently, not a proper written language but symbolic signs for magical or religious purposes. The second are regular hieroglyphs, which it is now believed have a direct link with the hieroglyphic writing of Crete. This type of written language was widespread on the westernmost islands—La Palma and, particularly, Ferro. The certain disorder in the arrangement of the signs led some investigators to the assumption that they were nothing more than copied texts for magical purposes; the content of the texts for the copyists remained unknown. Other investigators consider them genuine inscriptions. The third type consists of a usual written language, whose symbols are partially of Paleonumidian and partially of unknown origin. Moreover, wholly Paleonumidian inscriptions, which probably originated from the Carthaginian alphabet, have been discovered. The latter two types were widespread on the eastern islands. None of the inscriptions discovered on the Canary Islands has been deciphered.

Prior to the coming of Europeans metal was unknown on the Canary Islands (none of these islands have metal-ore deposits); the culture was Neolithic. Implements and weapons were made of stone or wood; wood was made extremely hard by a special process of impregnation and working. Pottery was very widespread on all the islands. In many ways it is reminiscent of the ancient stage of Cretan pottery. On Gran Canaria the pottery was carefully made and finished and is said to bear a likeness to even Cypriot pottery. A unique pottery style, which had no analogy anywhere else, existed on La Palma. Statuettes of people and animals, resembling the European Upper Paleolithic and Neolithic statuettes, have been found on Gran Canaria. *Pintaderas*—a stamp of stone or other material for placing colour patterns on the human body for magical or religious purposes—were widely used on some of the islands. They resemble similar objects that were in use throughout prehistoric Europe and also in America.

The main occupations of the islanders were farming and the breeding of goats, sheep and pigs. Their food consisted mainly of grain and other plants with the addition of animal products. Food consisting principally of meat (mutton) and milk predominated only on La Palma; no fish was eaten (467). Fishing was popular chiefly on Gran Canaria. Fish were caught with nets in coastal waters. There was no sea-fishing; the islanders had neither boats nor rafts. Prior to the coming of Europeans wine and fermentation products were unknown. The only beverages were water and milk. Fire was obtained by rubbing sticks together.

There were different types of dwellings. On Tenerife, for example, the population lived in caves. On Hierro and La Palma they lived in huts, and on Gran Canaria in stone houses. Gran Canaria was the only island with small towns, the largest of which, Arginegin (462), consisted of 400 houses. Stone dwellings were also built on Fuerteventura and Lanzarote.

Temples, as we understand them, were non-existent. G. Boccaccio (467/XVI) tells us that when the Portuguese visited Gran Canaria in 1341 they saw a building in which was a stone statue of a naked man covered with an apron of palm leaves and holding a sphere in his hand. In this building there were no drawings, ornamentation or inscriptions. It is understood that this statue was taken to Lisbon, but nothing is known of what happened to it after that. On Fuerteventura the Ephacenes sect had sacrificial altars of a megalithic type with fences round them. Megalithic-type structures are generally known on the Canary Islands.

The Canarians buried their dead differently on the different islands. Most of the burials were in caves (Tenerife, Gomera, La Palma, Hierro). On Gran Canaria they built pyramids of large stones put together without mortar, and sometimes conical mounds or even towers resembling the megalithic towerlike nuraghes on Sardinia or the chullpas of pre-Inca Peru. On Fuerteventura and Lanzarote the dead were buried in megalithic-type stone tombs. The nobility (chiefs and priests) usually buried their dead after they were embalmed by a caste of embalmers who employed various methods identical to those employed in ancient Egypt. Mummies were wrapped in animal skins, which were carefully sewn up. This method of burial was recently discovered by the Italian paleoethnologist F. Mori (618, 619) at Fezzan, Libya, as well; it was the burial of the mummy of a two-year-old child of Negroid origin, which was likewise sewn up in a skin. This burial has been dated by radiocarbon as about 3400 B.C., i.e., pre-dynasty times in Egypt. On the basis of this find A. Bajocco drew the conclusion that Fezzan and the Sahara were where the Canary Islands population initially came from. There are grounds for believing that on the islands embalming had been practised for many centuries. For example, it has been established by radiocarbon that one of the burials on Tenerife dates from only the 8th or 9th century A.D. On the other hand, some of the mummies that have been found are undoubtedly of very great antiquity (47/61). Each of the burial caves on Tenerife had several hundred mummies, while in some there were nearly a thousand. The entrances to the caves were bricked up.

The forms of marriage that existed on the islands give an indication of the level of culture. Monogamy predominated, but polygamy was practiced on Hierro (apparently as a result of Arab influence). Elements of the matriarchal system, including polyandry, existed on Fuerteventura, Lanzarote and Gomera.

The islanders were ruled by local chiefs. On Tenerife there were nine dwarf "kingdoms", whose chiefs were frequently at war with each other. There was a priest caste, which was particularly well organised on Gran Canaria, where it was headed by two high priests. An institution of virgin nuns, very similar to the institution of priestesses in Babylon and to the organisation of "virgins of the sun" of Inca Peru, also existed (47/96; 231).

The most baffling riddle of the Canary Islands is the origin of the autochthonous population. The aborigines were not acquainted with even the most primitive forms of navigation; they had neither boats nor rafts. This is indicated by all the chroniclers. However, Leonardo Torriani, a 16th century chronicler, maintained that in his time the Canarians had vessels built of local dragonwood. But, as Bajocco points out, when this question was studied by specialists it was found that Torriani's assertions did not hold true for more ancient times (before the arrival of Europeans).

Various reasons, including some of a religious nature, such as a taboo on sailing (231), were advanced to explain this riddle, but none could satisfactorily explain everything, especially as the Spanish chroniclers recorded practically nothing about the myths, legends or religion of the Canarians.

All this had brought many atlantologists round to the view that the Guanches were, perhaps, descendants of the Atlanteans, and that the Canary Islands are the last remains of Atlantis. The Soviet historian B. L. Bogayevsky (13) was an ardent supporter of this theory. He wrote: "It is most probable that parts of the African continent broke away in the early Neolithic, giving rise to quite large islands. A new island, consequently, lay in the 'Atlantic' in front of the 'Pillars of Hercules'. This island, whose size popular fantasy could always exaggerate was, possibly, the Atlantis of Plato."

Paleoethnical investigations show without a doubt that there was once a link between the aborigines of the Canary Islands and North America. The only problem to be solved is how the ancient Cro-Magnons went there from Africa. The sea route must evidently be ruled out. The only acceptable assumption is that in the epoch of Cro-Magnon settlement (i.e., 20,000-30,000 years ago) the Canary Islands had a land bridge with the continent. Later the settlement of the islands by other ethnic groups might have taken place via a sea route. Many variants of this thesis may be offered. It is quite possible that the Cretans played an important role in the settlement of the western Canaries. Later as A. Gaudio (231) assumes, there might have been a forcible settlement of the islands by Phoenicians or Carthaginians, and the peoples ousted by them were continentals, who had no knowledge of navigation. The aborigines of Tenerife had some legends about the arrival of part of the island's population from the east (231). The problem of the settlement of the Canary Islands is a very intricate one and much remains to be explained.

Chapter Twelve

TOPOGRAPHY OF THE ATLANTIC FLOOR

The first general data about the floor relief of the Atlantic Ocean were obtained some hundred years ago by the *Porcupine* (1869-77), *Challenger* (1872-76) and *Gazelle*, (1875-77) expeditions, but a serious study of Atlantic topography was started only with the introduction into practice of depth soundings with automatically recording echo sounders.

The first major oceanographic expedition which investigated the Atlantic Ocean with echo soundings was the 1925-27 German expedition on the ship *Meteor* that took more than 67,000 measurements. The data obtained by this expedition, particularly in the South Atlantic, have not lost their importance to this day.

Large-scale investigations of the Atlantic floor relief were started after the Second World War, particularly during the past decade. The largest volume of investigations in the North Atlantic has been accomplished by the Lamont Observatory, USA, whose ships—the *Atlantis, Caryn* and *Vema*—took measurements of the floor depth over a distance of more than 300,000 miles in the period from 1946 to 1956. A Swedish round-the-world expedition on the ship *Albatross* operated in the North and Equatorial Atlantic in 1947. Investigations on a smaller scale were conducted by Danish and German expeditions on the ships *Dana, Hauss* and *Anton Dorn* (1955-58). Soviet scientists joined in the investigations of the North Atlantic floor in 1956. The most interesting of these investigations were conducted in 1957-58 by the expedition ship *Mikhail Lomonosov* under the International Geophysical Year Programme. These investigations are being continued to this day on other vessels.*

Before we go on to a study of Atlantic topography we must mention *Floors of the Oceans* by B. C. Heezen, M. Tharp and M. Ewing (417). Translated into the Russian with a foreword by G. B. Udintsev, it deals with the North Atlantic between the 17th and 50th parallels. But even within these limits the floor is inadequately described. This book is nothing more than a summary of the work of the US Lamont Observatory. The investigations of scientists of other countries are mentioned selectively and very superficially. The extensive Soviet oceanographic investigations under the International Geophysical Year are left out completely.

The authors deal mainly with the morphology of the western part of the North Atlantic (the shelf and continental slope of the USA

---

* An outline survey of the history of investigations in the Atlantic is given in a paper by A. V. Ilyin (262).

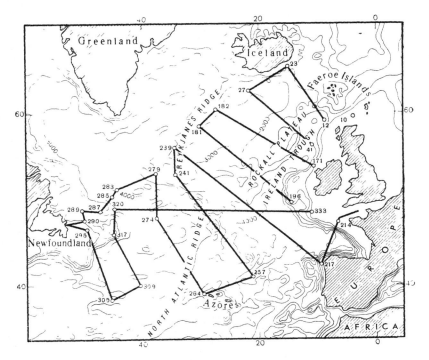

Chart of measurements taken by the *Mikhail Lomonosov* in the North Atlantic (262/119)

and the Bermuda Rise) and, partially, the North Atlantic Ridge. With regard to these regions the book offers valuable factual material, and those interested in the western part of the North Atlantic, which bears no direct relation to the Atlantis problem, are referred to it.

A fairly comprehensive review of recent works dealing with the Mid-Atlantic Ridge has been written by X. Le Pichon (177).

The Atlantic has fewer deeps than the Pacific (209). Depths of from 0 to 2,000 metres occupy 27 per cent of the Atlantic and only 10.5 per cent of the Pacific. On the other hand, depths of from 2,000 to 4,000 metres are to be found in 47.3 per cent of the Atlantic and 65 per cent of the Pacific. Deeper sections occupy approximately the same area in both oceans.

In the Atlantic Ocean there are depressions, the Mid-Atlantic system of mountains, a submarine continental slope, island arcs with accompanying marginal trenches, and ancient submerged structures. The depressions are divided into two categories: a) ancient (Paleozoic and Mesozoic) and b) young (of Tertiary-Quaternary age). The ancient depressions contain uplifts with volcanic structures

(Bermuda Rise, Cape Verde Islands). Ancient submerged structures are somewhat displaced with regard to their extensions to the continent (734).

Modern investigations have brought to light at least 25 deep trenches in the Pacific and only four in the Atlantic (just one in the Indian Ocean) with the following maximum depths (405):

Trench	Latitude	Longitude	Depth (metres)
Puerto Rico	19°38′N	66°00′— —68°30′W	8,385 ± 30
South Sandwich	55°07.3′S	22°46 5′W	8,264 ± 100
Romanche	0°13′S	18°26′W	7,728 ± 15
Caiman (together with Bartlet and Oriente)	19°10′N	79°53′W	7,057

The maximum depths of the Atlantic are in these trenches.

A feature of the Atlantic is the frequent occurrence of terraces (733). They are particularly in evidence in the northern part of the North Atlantic, where they are encountered at various levels: 200, 500 metres and deeper. The most widespread are terraces at a depth of 470-520 metres, which M. V. Klenova synchronises with terraces at a depth of 180-200 metres in the Barents Sea and at a depth of 300 metres in the Greenland Sea. She points out that a terraced structure is to be found at greater depths as well. She considers that terraces lying at a depth of 1,700 metres are the most typical in the North Atlantic Ridge.

If all the water of the Atlantic were to be drained away, the first thing that would strike the eye would be a mammoth mountain system running S-wise from the Arctic Circle to the Antarctic. This system, usually called the *Mid-Atlantic Ridge* (sometimes, quite unhappily, the Atlantic Wall) is situated meridionally and resembles the giant Cordillera-Andes mountain system.

X. Le Pichon (777) singles out the region between 52°N and 30°S as the most typical for the Mid-Atlantic Ridge; regions farther south have distinguishing features of their own. Soviet scientists (733; 734) approach this problem somewhat differently. They feel that *in the Mid-Atlantic system not only the submeridional northern and southern regions but also the extremely unique equatorial latitudinal zone should be singled out.* In the northern and southern regions an axial position is occupied by an infantile ridge with ancient ridges and flanks along its margin. Besides, the entire Mid-Atlantic Ridge is divided by transversal faulting. The most ancient of the sub-latitudinal structures are precisely what caused the ridge to bend and acquire its S shape.

In its equatorial part the Mid-Atlantic Ridge rapidly flattens out and even breaks off here and there. This makes it possible to distinguish two parts: the *North Atlantic Ridge* in the Northern Hemisphere, and the *South Atlantic Ridge* in the Southern Hemisphere. The width of the ridge is from 500 to 1,400 kilometres, and its depth of subsidence averages 2,740 metres. Its mean height above the surrounding deeps is 1,830 metres, but there are many sections towering to a height of 3,500-4,000 metres. This mountain system has an extraordinarily intricate topography and actually consists of three parallel ranges in the South Atlantic and two in the North Atlantic. Moreover, there are latitudinal spurs, some of which reach the continents. V. M. Lavrov (737) reports that on the basis of data obtained in 1963 by an expedition on the *Mikhail Lomonosov* it has been established that the latitudinal equatorial part of the Mid-Atlantic Ridge (east of 23°W) differs in structure from the northern and southern branches of this mountain system and that it must be regarded as an independent region—the Equatorial Atlantic Ridge.

B. C. Heezen (551) writes that the Mid-Atlantic Ridge occupies roughly one-third of the ocean floor, keeping fairly exactly to the middle. A cross-section would show an intermittent but fairly even height reduction from the centre in both directions. Approximately in the centre of the ridge there are very considerable depressions of the rift valley type and beyond them, on either side of the ridge, lies a highly faulted plateau. Moreover, on the ridge itself there are numerous volcanic cones. Some are under water, and others jut out on the surface in the form of individual islands or even archipelagoes. Such cones are also to be found on the spurs of this ridge. The tallest sections of the ridge have an extremely dissected topography and on some of the slopes there is a host of terraces and regular valleys, which make the ridge resemble some parts of the Alps or other intricately dissected mountainous areas on land. On the basis of a study of the structure of the Earth's crust beneath the ridge, the borderline between it and the purely oceanic crust is now regarded as passing through isobath 3,500 metres (759). According to magnetic measurements, the eastern boundary of the ridge runs exactly along the isobath 3,660 metres, while the western boundary is 300 kilometres to the east of it. One is struck by the *asymmetry of the ridge*: in the west the boundary is 200 metres farther away from the ridge axis than the eastern boundary (800).

The major morphological elements of the Atlantic floor are*:

North America Basin (417). The northern part of this basin, known as the *Sohm Abyssal Plain* is T-shaped and has a maximum depth of nearly 5.5 kilometres. Southwest of this plain is the vast *Bermuda Rise* separated from the shelf of the eastern coast of the USA by

---

* The depths are given in the Soviet *Marine Atlas (Morskoi atlas)*. Vol. 2, *Atlas of the World (Atlas mira)*, and in *Floors of the Oceans* by B C Heezen, M. Tharp and M. Ewing (417).

the *Hatteras Plain*, which in the south communicates with the abyssal *Nares Plain*; the latter has a maximum depth of 6,491 metres. In the southwestern part of the North America Basin is a trough which reaches down to 6,960 metres at its deepest point, and near the Island of Puerto Rico is a deep trench of the same name (417).

European-African Basin. This basin has a very rugged topography and embraces a large number of irregularly-shaped abyssal plains of various length. For example, west of the Iberian Peninsula lies the abyssal *Iberian Plain*, which in the north communicates with the *Biscay Plain*; farther south is the small *Tagus Plain* with depths of nearly 5 kilometres. There are similar depths (4-5 kilometres) in all the other northern abyssal plains. The abyssal plains off Africa are larger. The most noteworthy of these is the Madeira Plain, which communicates with Monaco Trench lying west of the Canaries and has a maximum depth of 6,492 metres. Furthermore, mention must be made of the abyssal Cape Verde Plain lying west of the islands of the same name (maximum depth—7,010 metres). The maximum depths of the troughs in the centre of the basin are 6,067 and 6,470 metres. Two terraces are clearly defined on the smooth floor of the North African Basin—at depths of 5,380-5,580 and 5,600-5,680 metres. Towering over these terraces are seamounts standing about 1,000 metres above the ocean floor, and small hills not more than 200 metres high (733). Near the equator the North Atlantic Ridge is bisected by the very deep Romanche Trench. In the vicinity of the equator the most outstanding is the Guinea Basin, where the average depth is more than 5,000 metres (maximum depth— 6,363 metres).

South of the equator the Mid-Atlantic Ridge resumes its meridional direction; arranged symmetrically to it are a number of basins, including two pairs: the Brazil Basin in the west and the Angola Basin in the east, the Argentine Basin in the west and the Cape Basin in the east. The Brazil Basin is intricately shaped with depths of more than 5,000 metres predominating; its maximum depth is 6,537 metres. The shape of the Angola Basin is less faulted with depths of over 5,000 metres predominating; its deepest point is only 5,734 metres. The Argentine Basin is shaped more like an ellipse; its deepest point—6,202 metres—is in its southern part. Cape Basin, the smallest of the four, is separated from the Angola Basin by the submarine Walvis Ridge, which links the South Atlantic Ridge up with Africa. In the Cape Basin there are several seamounts running parallel to the Walvis Ridge. The deepest point in the Cape Basin is 5,373 metres.

South of 45° the morphology of the submarine topography of the southernmost part of the Atlantic changes considerably. The Mid-Atlantic Ridge abruptly changes its direction from meridional to latitudinal. Its direct extension, the African-Antarctic Ridge, runs eastward to the Indian Ocean. This ridge separates Cape Basin from the African-Antarctic Basin which abuts the Antarctic. West of the Mid-Atlantic Ridge a section of the submarine South Antilles Ridge separates the Argentine Basin from the more southerly marine expanses linked up with the structures of the Western Antarctic.

A chain of submarine mountains between Greenland and Europe, passing across Iceland and the Faeroes, is the natural dividing line between the Atlantic and the Arctic. This chain is called the *Atlantic Sill*. In its turn it is subdivided into the Greenland-Iceland Sill (which crosses the Denmark Strait) and the Iceland-Faeroes Rise, while between the Faeroes and the Shetland Islands there is the Wyville-Thompson Ridge. The latter two are sometimes regarded as one sill—the Iceland-Shetland, which is frequently and incorrectly called the Wyville-Thompson Ridge.

The *Greenland-Iceland Sill* is a latitudinal elevation with isobaths of 300-400 metres. It is divided by a narrow trough where the shallowest point is 591 metres. The sides of the sill descend steeply towards both the Atlantic Ocean and the Greenland Sea. Its surface is slightly dissected and there is a number of sandbanks (242, 299, 344). K. N. Nesis (344/898) believes that the depression dividing the sill is a tectonic fault.

The *Iceland-Shetland Sill* has been investigated by Soviet expeditions on the *Mikhail Lomonosov*, *Rossiya*, *Sevastopol* and *Ekvator* (218, 243). This is a latitudinal sill. Its western part, the *Iceland-Faeroe Rise*, is a more or less triangular elevation, with its foundation at the shelf of Iceland and its summit at the Faeroes. It is widest (129-147 kilometres) in its centre and narrowest (only 27-37 kilometres) near the Faeroes. Its boundary is well-contoured by the 500-metre isobath. The centre is slightly elevated (to a depth of 350-400 metres from the surface). On it are the Rosengarten and several other banks lying at a depth of 160-285 metres. Most of the banks are situated between 63-64°N 10-12°W. The surface of the rise is even with several hills. South of the centre of the rise is a large plateau with depths of 420-450 metres and an undulating floor. A prominence 80-100 metres high and nearly 27 kilometres long of clearly abrasion origin has been discovered in the centre of the rise. Saddles separate the rise from the shelves adjoining the islands. At a depth of 500-600 metres there are protrusions and depressions 30-40 metres deep; N. A. Grabovsky believes they are submerged river valleys; they might be of tectonic origin.

Interesting results have been received by a Soviet expedition on the *Ekvator* (243) during an investigation of the *Wyville-Thompson Ridge*; it proved to be only a large bank limited on the west and east by deep-water depressions with depths of 1,000 metres. The ridge itself is characterised by the 500-metre isobath, and the minimum depth above it is 412 metres. Its floor is fairly even.

M. V. Klenova and V. M. Lavrov (272) draw attention to the existence in the northeastern part of the North Atlantic of a submerged mountainous zone, the *Faeroe Upland*, which embraces the

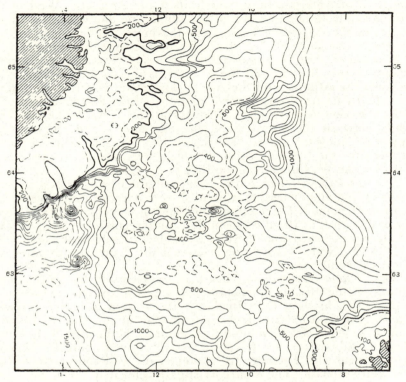

Iceland-Faeroe Rise (218). Isobaths in metres

great Rockall Plateau and a strip of shallow-water banks of volcanic origin (Faeroe, Bill Bailley's, Outer Bailley, Rosemary and so on) situated on a single pedestal south of the Faeroes. The shallowest of these banks is Faeroe, where the minimum subsidence is 87 metres.

The *Faeroe Upland* (272) has asymmetrical sides: the eastern are precipitous and the western are gently sloping. Terraces are to be found at depths of 465-500 and 680-700 metres. A range with much steeper sides than the central massif is traced west of this upland.

The mountain ranges surrounding the upland are considerably eroded and run in a northeasterly direction. Their extension may be traced to the slopes and shelf of the Hebrides and farther. By the general character of the topography it may be considered as a product of Caledonian folding. The surface of the centre of the Faeroe Upland is flat and bounded by steep ledges. This upland descends by stages to the Iceland Basin stretching westward up to the Reykjanes Ridge. The floor of the basin is flat with depths ranging from 2,000 to 4,000 metres. Terraces are to be found on the slopes at depths of 510-530 and 1,500 metres.

Between the slopes of the British shelf and the initial, northern part of the Mid-Atlantic Ridge lies the shallow-water *Rockall Plateau*. In its centre there is a bank with a shoal where the minimum depth is 180-200 metres. According to latest data obtained by Soviet expeditions (243/261) the Rockall Plateau is separated from the British Isles by the broad Ireland Trench, which is predominantly 2,000 metres deep. This trench has even, slighty dissected slopes and reaches a depth of about 2,500 metres. On the plateau are two small mountain ranges (average width—not more than 150 kilometres) divided by a flat submarine valley; in relation to the valley these ranges rise to a height ranging from 500 to 1,500 metres. On the western range there are many V-shaped submarine valleys from 1.1 to 1.5 kilometres wide and 60-70 metres deep. Small absolutely level plateaus are to be found on both ranges. Between the rugged surfaces of the upland and its gently sloping and even sides there is a series of terraces 300-400 metres wide. Altogether six terraces have been located at a depth of 950-1,000 metres.

In the southwest a large submarine elevation called *Porcupine Bank* (464, 542) is an extension of the continental shelf of Ireland. This elevation is somewhat smaller than the Rockall Plateau but it does not have a rocky island. Porcupine Bank proper (minimum depth—154 metres) is situated west of Ireland (464, 542).

M. V. Klenova and V. M. Lavrov (272) note a parallelism of some elements of the topography of the floor and shelf at the British Isles. The Hebrides, the Orkneys and the Shetland Islands, as well as the Caledonian Basin of Scotland, stretch in the same, northeasterly direction. *The direction of the North-Atlantic Ridge and of the Reykjanes Ridge is noteworthy; they skirt round, as it were, a stable and deeply-submerged massif.*

The *European Basin* proper (sometimes called the West European Basin) has the following geomorphological regions: 1) an abyssal plain (4,800-5,200 metres) situated at the foot of the European continental slope; 2) the Ireland Trench, which is an extension of the abyssal plain between Ireland and the Rockall Plateau; 3) submeridional elevations in the central part of the basin—two mountain ranges with a subsidence depth of 3,700 metres among depths of 5,000 metres; 4) a hilly plain (with elements of mid-mountain topography and volcanic structures) with a total depth of 4,000-5,000 metres. Moreover, there are individual elevations rising to a height of 1,000 metres and more above the floor. This region adjoins the Mid-Atlantic Ridge (286).

As M. V. Klenova and V. M. Lavrov report (272) the floor topography of the European Basin is extremely varied. The maximum depths are near the shores of the Iberian Peninsula. Three giant benches (evidently of fault origin) 300-400 metres high and more than 200 kilometres wide are a leading morphological feature of this basin. On the lowest bench is the Bay of Biscay Plain and part of the floor of a basin situated northwest of Spain. The uppermost

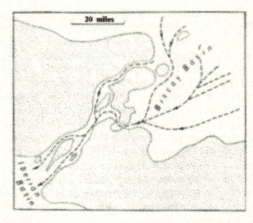

Submarine Iberian Canyon (588)

bench, despite being levelled out, carries elevations, the largest of which (110 kilometres) are shaped as cuestas* and tower 900 metres above the foothills (262).

Between the southwestern tips of Ireland and Britany the continental shelf along the edges of St. George Strait and the English Channel has long and narrow crests stretching from the northeast to the southwest from Labadie-Cockburn Bank across the Grand and Little Plaice banks to Chapelle Bank. The largest crest is about 300 kilometres long and from 10 to 18 kilometres wide; the depth over it is not more than 50-100 metres. The sides at the terminal of this crest (48°30′N 10°30′W) are extremely steep (212/252; 464; 542).

A very interesting discovery was made by an English oceanological expedition on the ship *Discovery-2* in the region of the abyssal Biscay and Iberian plains. A. Laughton (588) reports that in the Biscay Plain there are several V-shaped sources of a long submarine canyon that has all the elements of the bed of a former river: tributaries, islands, a delta with an island, and so forth. The sources merge into a single channel cutting through the mountain sill and emerging in the flat abyssal Iberian Basin, which lies 180 metres below the Biscay Plain. There are clear-cut levees along the banks of these channels. This canyon, which may be legitimately called Iberian Canyon, is about 90 kilometres long and 1.8 to 7.2 kilometres wide. It has a flat box-shaped bed. Cores showed that the lower layers contained quartz sand, evidently of ancient origin. Being a supporter of the turbidity currents theory, Laughton believes that this obviously river canyon was carved out by such currents. We feel that *it would be closer to reality to see in the submarine Iberian canyon traces of a mighty river whose tributaries were the Seine, the Loire, the Garonne and other rivers.* Some geologists (for example, Ewbery) are convinced that this river (the Paleo-Seine) existed in the Tertiary period.

In the next work (796) it is pointed out there is a series of terraces on the walls of the channel cut through the sill between the

---

* Cuesta is the name usually given to an elevation with one face steep and the opposite gently sloping parallel with the dip of the strata It is typical of the topography of many foothill folded regions.—*Ed.*

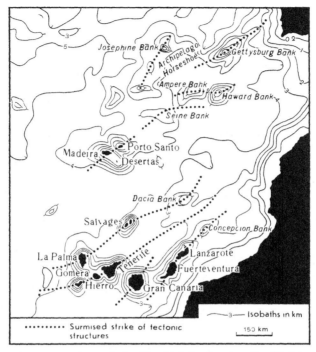

Bathymetric chart of the North Atlantic near the Madeira and Canary Islands with shallow-water banks (209)

two abyssal plains. The channel itself is cut to a depth of 182 metres. There are clearly defined terraces at depths of 4,958-5,005 metres. The terraces excellently *correlate with seismic and acoustic soundings—this being evidence that their origin is due to erosion.* At a depth of 364 metres below the floor level there is a solid foundation. The sediments dredged from the slopes of the channel were not older than the Miocene.

Interesting features of the floor topography west of the Strait of Gibraltar are described by P. N. Yerofeyev (346/89-90). The foundation of the floor topography is an almost latitudinal hollow separating the continental banks of Europe and Africa. Eastward the hollow passes into the Mediterranean, where its depth reaches 1,840 metres. Its terminal in the Atlantic is fringed on the north, west and south by a system of shallow banks rising some five kilometres from the depths of the ocean and spreading from the shores of Portugal to the Canary Islands. The pedestal of the Madeira Islands is probably also genetically linked up with this system. These submarine mountains form a loop embracing the western end of the hollow. Many of the banks have been known for a long time, and some were probably known in remote antiquity when they were shallower. The data on their minimum depth of subsidence are somewhat contradictory (84/44; 580/104; 661/117): Ampère Bank (35°07′N 12°52′W)=60 metres; 110 metres; (50-151 metres); Gettysburg Bank (36°30′N 11°37′W)=55 metres; (42 metres); Dacia Bank (31°10′N 13°40′W)=91 metres; (86 metres); Josephine Bank (36°38′N 14°17′W)=150 metres; (151 metres); Conception Bank (30°N 13°W)=161 metres; (161 metres); Coral Patch Bank (34°57′N 11°57′W)=795 metres; (660 metres); Seine Seamount (33°54′N 14°27′W)=146 metres; (148 metres).*

These banks may be subdivided into three groups. The southernmost lies on the pedestal of the Canary Islands (Dacia, Conception). East of the Madeira Islands is the Seine Seamount. The numerous other banks are situated north of the Madeira Islands, forming a *submarine archipelago* called *Horseshoe*, approximately 500-600 kilometres west of the Strait of Gibraltar (417).

Between the northern part of the Horseshoe Archipelago (with Josephine Bank) and Cape São Vincente lies Gettysburg (Gorringe) Bank, which, discovered in 1876, is situated 200 kilometres away from Portugal. It was described some years ago by the Soviet oceanologist P. N. Yerofeyev (250a; 346/90). Its summit, which is about 40 metres from the water surface, is divided by a saddle of more than 800 metres in depth. A deeper saddle separates the bank from a submarine range of mountains stretching to the northeast and linking up with the continent south of Lisbon. Both summits of the bank are framed by terraces sloping to the northeast; that is why on the northeastern slope the ancient shore line is 400 metres lower. East of the southern tip of Horseshoe is Ampère Bank, while still farther east is the deeper-lying Coral Patch Bank. This entire group of submarine mountains is genetically inter-related. The southern mountains are volcanic cones, while the northern are of tectonic origin. This is undoubtedly a region of geologically very recent subsidences and it has not been thoroughly studied. Small wonder that some time ago 270 kilometres north of the Madeira Islands, on the southwestern tip of Horseshoe (35°52′N 16°31′W) an English expedition (590) discovered a new submarine mountain with some curious features at a depth of 1,247 metres. Shortly before this discovery was made, an American expedition found yet another submarine mountain of this archipelago 90 kilometres to the northeast.

Let us now deal at greater length with the North Atlantic Ridge, which is of the greatest interest to atlantologists. The most closely studied section of this ridge lies between the 17th and the 54th parallels, where it is from 800 to 1,400 kilometres wide (607).

Reykjanes Ridge, which is an extension, as it were, of the southwestern tip of Iceland, is usually regarded as the northern end of the North Atlantic Ridge. This ridge was studied in fairly great detail by a German oceanographical expedition in 1957-58, which

---

* The figures in brackets are from a map of the Atlantic published in the USA in 1956 under the editorship of J. C. La Gorce

made echo soundings of more than 50 profiles from the southwestern tip of Iceland down to 57°N, mainly between 64 and 60°N. The results of these investigations were given in the works of G. Dietrich (498) and J. Ulrich (692).

Reykjanes Ridge runs for approximately 1,200 kilometres in a northeasterly direction—southwest from the tip of Iceland and down to 55°N. Farther south it turns into the North Atlantic Ridge. In its northern part it is about 200 kilometres wide, narrowing down to 60 kilometres in the south. Where it approaches the shelf of Iceland its width likewise diminishes, and in the region of the crest itself it is only 20 kilometres wide. This ridge, much narrower than the North Atlantic Ridge, is not traced on Iceland itself and is, evidently, an independent province of the North Atlantic Ridge, or even an independent range of mountains.

Its crest lies at a relatively small depth—about 200 metres—near the shelf and at less than 1,000 metres elsewhere. The ridge itself towers above the surrounding ocean floor to a height of from 700-900 metres in the centre to 1,600 metres at its southern extremity; near the shelf it is only 100-300 metres high.

The crest is alpine with sharp peaks and deep troughs or V-shaped valleys. It is generally very rugged and resembles a horst in the north, which gradually disappears in the south, where it gives way to sharp-tipped forms. Volcanic cones have also been discovered on the ridge. Although the sides of the ridge are generally steep they are less rugged than the crest.

J. Bourcart (209) points out that south of the Reykjanes Ridge there are folds oriented perpendicularly to it. These are the Mont-Minia Mountains. Furthermore, he notes that a large elevation begins at about 51°N; this is the Telegraph Plateau. South of the plateau are the Faraday Hills, an elevation with volcanoes likewise situated crosswise to the ridge. With regard to these elevations he writes: "If we recognise the Minia 'mountains' and the Faraday Hills as being a Caledonian folding, the Telegraph Plateau is, evidently, a shield or ancient arch that bears a close resemblance to Greenland (with a different strike) and, like the latter, it is surrounded by folded chains. However, some scientists regard this plateau as the missing section of the Hercynian chain between Nova Scotia and Europe."

On the subject of the Telegraph Plateau F. Machatschek (323/584) writes: "Part of the North Atlantic situated north of the North America and West European basins and formerly known as the Telegraph Plateau is indeed a region with a very complex structure with differences of up to 2,000-3,000 metres in depth over a distance of 20-30 kilometres, to which broad shelves abut on either side."

Professor G. Dietrich (private communication) points out that on the basis of echo soundings the Reykjanes Ridge should be regarded as part of the North Atlantic Ridge. If a depression really exists in the southern part of this ridge, it is only a detail of a single mountain system. Available data obtained through echo soundings do not indicate the presence of a deep depression which would have made it possible to regard the Reykjanes Ridge as an independent mountain system. This is also the view of Soviet oceanologists. However, in this region there is a ravine nearly 5,000 metres deep.*

The latest bathymetric investigations showed that between Canada and Greenland there is a median ridge. It has been named the Median Labrador Ridge. Rising near Baffin Bay (64°N) it makes a detour round Greenland in the south and, evidently, fuses with the North Atlantic Ridge in the vicinity of 53°N. But inasmuch as neither earthquake epicentres nor magnetic anomalies are linked up with this ridge, *it seems more probable to us that it has a genetic link with Reykjanes Ridge. Can it be an extension of the latter ridge?* Like other median ridges it skirts round a continental massif. Its crest is covered with a layer of sediments 1,000 metres thick, and the ridge itself is characterised by a longitudinal wave diffusion velocity of 5.5 km/sec. According to Soviet scientists beneath this ridge the Earth's crust is only 10 kilometres thick! This requires further verification (504c; 818, 823). The contours of some elevations resemble those of cuestas with steep southern sides. The slopes themselves are terraced and have a hilly relief.

The northern part of the North Atlantic Ridge (from the Azores to where it links up with Reykjanes Ridge) has been investigated by a Soviet oceanographic expedition on the *Mikhail Lomonosov* (262). North of the Azores the ridge runs in a northeasterly direction, but in the region 50°N 30°W it turns abruptly and runs in a northwesterly direction all the way to the southern tip of Reykjanes Ridge. A section more than 1,500 kilometres long has been studied. In this area the ridge topography is rugged, with large amplitudes of height and extremely steep sides. The alpine type of topography predominates. A feature of the depressions or troughs separating the highlands and mountains is the V-shaped cross-section. The beds of many of them are even or quite flat, while the sides are steep. It seems to us that the assumption that *this kind of trough valleys might have been formed by glaciers if in the glacial period the range was subaerial* merits some attention. A more detailed investigation to check this assumption would be extremely desirable.

G. L. Johnson (805) tells us of the recent discovery near 56°N of a fracture in the shape of a transversal depression lying at a depth of more than 1,000 metres. There is no magnetic anomaly.

In the northern part of the North Atlantic Ridge the depressions and other negative forms of the topography have a considerably thicker layer of sediments than the positive forms. One of the features of the morphology of most of the uplifts within the studied section of the ridge is the absence of small, secondary dissections on the sides. This may be explained by two different assumptions.

---

* Some considerations favouring the possible existence of a depression are given on p 361.

According to one, this is, as we believe, the result of the activity of glaciers during the subaerial existence of the ridge; this feature is not to be found in the considerably more southerly sections of the North Atlantic Ridge. On the other hand, A. V. Ilyin (262) feels that *"this may be explained as proof of the relative youth of the topography"* (my italics—N. Z.). At the same time, on the sides of individual eminences, at the most diverse depths, there are narrow horizontal steps or terraces. This feature is to be found along almost the entire length of the ridge. The topography of the sides in the investigated area northwest of the Azores is characterised by an alternation of gently sloping sections and large mountain masses and elevations with a mostly levelled floor (the action of glaciers?). There is very little difference between the two sides of the ridge.

On the slope of the ridge north of the Azores is Chaucer Bank (roughly 42°N 30°W) in which there are depressions with terraced sides. On them are denuded wings of layers inclining from different directions: there is denser rock in the core. These structures, with contours resembling calderas, are 20-30 kilometres wide. South of the 44th parallel on longitude 30°W there is (against a general background of depths of 3,335-3,440 metres) a plateau with depths of 2,155-2,360 metres (i.e., a height of about 1,000 metres) with a relatively smooth surface—which is unusual for this region of the ridge (733).

Ilyin (262 129) hazards the guess that there is a submarine range linking up the submarine Azores range in the north with the North Atlantic Ridge. He writes: "In outline this ridge is a semi-arc with a radius of about 600 kilometres. It adjoins the pedestal of the Azores in the south and the eastern slope of the North Atlantic Ridge in the northwest. New submarine mountains, which possibly indicate the existence of an unbroken submarine range, were discovered during the fourth cruise of the *Mikhail Lomonosov*." Between this range and the crest of the North Atlantic Ridge there is a huge region with a levelled floor and depths of down to 3,928 metres in the east and nearly 3,300 metres in the west.

Curious features of the floor topography northeast of the Azores (36-48°N) were discovered some time ago (740; 765). Part of the structure runs parallel to the structure of the Azores Plateau. The most noteworthy point is the 200-mile long King Trough, hemmed in by mountain ranges with Anti-Altair Seamount among them. The southeastern extremity of the trough is cut by a broad wall extending over a distance of about 500 miles from the northeast to the southwest. Palmer Ridge stretches in a northwesterly direction and is asymmetrical due to several horizontal terraces. This ridge is composed of metamorphic and igneous rocks (serpentinite, amphibolite, gabbro) and is covered with loose Tertiary sediments.

The North Atlantic Ridge is adjoined by the large submarine Azores Plateau, which is wider in its northern part. This plateau lies east of the ridge, and only two islands of the Azores Archipe-

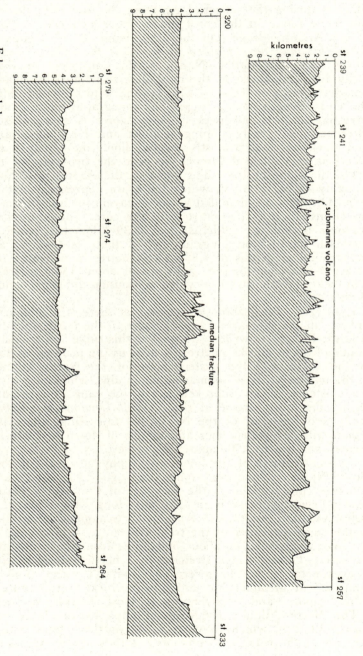

Echo-sounded section across a northern region of the North Atlantic Ridge between stations 239-257, 320-333 and 264-279 (262/126, 130) See chart on p. 217

lago—Flores and Corvu—are situated on the North Atlantic Ridge proper, on a section sometimes called Dolphin Ridge. The other Azores are on the eastern spurs of the plateau.

The *Azores Plateau** is a huge elevation with an area of some 135,000 square kilometres rising with steep sides from depths of about 4,000 metres. It may be considered that the plateau proper begins at a scarp with a relative height of 3,100 metres. On the north and south it is bounded by steep fault scarps with a dip of nearly 15° and a relative height not exceeding 1,000 metres. The southern slope is an intermediate terrace zone of a submarine plateau between the North Atlantic Ridge and the North African Basin. This plateau begins at the 37th parallel where the depth of the first scarp is 3,300 metres. The relatively fault-free northern half of the plateau is separated from the southern half by a clear-cut trough with a slightly concave bed. This trough is more than 50 kilometres wide and its relative depth is about 500 metres. It may possibly be a transversal fault filled with marine sediments and volcanic material. The southern half of the plateau has three cone-shaped summits towering to a relative height of about 2,500 metres. The two extreme summits bear the absolute markings 1,150 (considerably faulted) and 1,040 metres and are situated in a latitudinal direction on a common elevated base between the 32nd and the 34th parallels. South of the 33rd parallel, beyond a scarp with a depth of 100 metres, begins the even slope of the floor of the North African Basin (242).

The Azores Plateau ends with a series of ranges standing in several rows and stretching from the North Atlantic Ridge. In the main part of the plateau they run absolutely parallel to each other in a southeasterly direction and then fan out to the east, east-southeast, southeast and south-southeast. Eighteen main axes of these ranges with a mean distance of about 24 kilometres between them may be made out (487, 709).

The following details about the topography of the Azores Plateau are given in the works of G. Wust (709) and H. Cloos (487). On the southwest it is bounded by slopes rising to a height of about 1,100 metres and has a series of ranges on which are some of the Azores. Two submarine ranges extend from the pedestal of São Miguel Island. They link up not with Terceira but with the pedestals of São Jorge and Pico islands, forming a submarine extension of these elongated islands and surrounding together with them and with São Miguel Island a long depression stretching from east-southeast to west-northwest. In the west-northwesterly direction the depth of this depression is fairly even (from 1,200-1,500 to 1,500-2,000 metres), but in the east-southeasterly direction it dips quite steeply to a depth of more than 3,000 metres, forming an irregular bowl with Swallow Trough (3,509 metres), which is, evidently, a

---

* See Fig. on p. 206.

fault trough. There are deep depressions in the São Jorge and Pico ranges. Some 10-15 miles south of the Pico Range the depths diminish to 1,500 and even to 1,000 metres. This is a steep range, which has been given the name Altair Mountains. Cupola-shaped submarine elevations have been discovered in other places of the Azores Plateau. The Terceira Mountains stretch from the edge of Terceira Island, while northwest of Graciosa Island there have been discovered two parallel cupola'd uplifts—named the Graciosa Range. The deep depression between Graciosa and São Jorge resembles a crater. A similar parallelism has been discovered in the elevations linked up with the Azores (230 metres) and the Princess Alice banks (37°58′N 29°18′W; 440 metres).

Eight ranges and eight depressions can be distinguished in the central and eastern parts of the Azores Plateau. The Flores Range is part of the North Atlantic Ridge.

So-called oceanic wells—round or oval depressions with a diameter of 10-30 kilometres and a depth of about 1,000 metres—comprise one of the features of the Azores Plateau topography. It is thought that they were formed as a result of large-scale subsidences along fault scarps followed by uplifts; the latter were accompanied by the emergence of submarine volcanoes which subsequently became guyots (769). D. C. Krause (735) mentions considerable subsidences, saying: *"Errosion terraces lying at a depth of 1,000 metres are evidence that a change of height had taken place at one time"* (my italics—N. Z.). This concerns the Azores Plateau proper as well as the adjoining region of the North Atlantic Ridge.

F. Machado (604) has come to the conclusion that the depressions in the Azores Plateau are of tectonic origin: they are 20-30 kilometres wide. Along them are rift valleys interrupted by islands and banks. Three rift zones are distinguished. Two of them intersect at a sharp angle at São Miguel Island.

I. Tolstoi (690) believes that the mountain ranges of the Azores Plateau are very likely a manifestation of the trans-Atlantic elevation. From its point of departure at the Grand Newfoundland Bank this elevation crosses the North Atlantic Ridge at the Azores and runs to the shores of Spain and Africa across the Gettysburg and Josephine banks. Approximately the same view is held by some Portuguese investigators (448/314; 613).

D. C. Krause (775) is likewise coming round to a similar view. He points to the existence of two tectonic zones: an eastern and a western. The eastern zone begins at São Miguel Island and consists of a number of mountain ranges, valleys and fault scarps, which are associated with magnetic anomalies, some of them pronounced. In this area the Santa Maria Ridge, which contains some volcanoes, forms the tip of the Azores Plateau. In the west it wedges into the Median Valley of the North Atlantic Ridge, disappearing in its axis. A flat-bottomed trough, which is deeper in its southern portion, is situated south of this ridge at longitude 26°W. Farther south this trough is fringed by a narrow ridge (15 kilometres wide and 1,000 metres high); in the south this ridge is steeper than in the north. It skirts round the Azores Plateau in the east from longitude 25.5°W. Still farther south, the ocean floor stretching eastward consists of ranges of low mountains and troughs oriented east to west and dissected by transversal structures. A magnetic anomaly reaching 400 gammas is linked up with this ridge. Another flat-bottomed trough runs along the edge of an asymmetrical ridge east of longitude 26°W. This ridge gradually disappears near longitude 30°W.

The western tectonic zone runs for 1,750 kilometres to the west of the Azores Plateau, between the 38th and the 32nd parallels, along the southern side of the abyssal Sohm Plain up to longitude 51°W. It is about 100 kilometres wide. The topography consists of a small ridge along the axis of the basin. There are large seamounts in this zone.

So far the most extensive data about the Azores Plateau have been gathered by the expeditions on the Monacoan ship *Le Rossignol* and the German ship *Altair*. New features of the floor between Flores and Fayal islands were brought to light during the fifth cruise of the Soviet ship *Mikhail Lomonosov*. New submarine mountains (236) with subsidence depths of 929, 821, 674 and 520 metres were discovered along the 30th meridian. The guyot (former island) with the smallest subsidence (188 metres) is situated 38°57′N 29°51′W and has been named after the ship *Mikhail Lomonosov*. At a depth of 400 metres it is fringed by a terrace. Traces of recent volcanic activity have been found on this seamount and it must, therefore, be regarded as a submarine volcano in the heart of the Azores Plateau (242).

Abundant and extremely interesting topographical data are given in the latest charts, for example, on the physiographical chart of the North Atlantic compiled by B.C. Heezen and M. Tharp (417). We find that south of the Azores there is a second mountain system running parallel to the islands. In the preliminary communication (549) on the discovery of this system it is regarded as a broad mountain range or plateau extending to the southeast from the North Atlantic Ridge, beginning at about 37°N 32°W and ending at 30°N 28°W. On this elevation there are tall peaks, now guyots, with a relatively shallow subsidence of the summits: *Atlantis Bank* (Seamount) (34°N 30°15′W)=267 metres; it is situated 185 kilometres away from the main chain of the North Atlantic Ridge; *Plato Bank* (Mountain)=377 metres; *Cruiser Bank* (Seamount)=294 metres; and the end mountain—*Great Meteor Tablemount* (30°N 28°30′W), whose tip is 270 metres below water (323/582) but marked on the Heezen-Tharp map (417) as lying at a depth of 450 metres. One gets the impression that if the ocean level were to drop by only 500 metres, we would have another archipelago resembling the Azores.

The most detailed description of the topography of a relatively small part of the North Atlantic Ridge has been given by I. Tolstoi

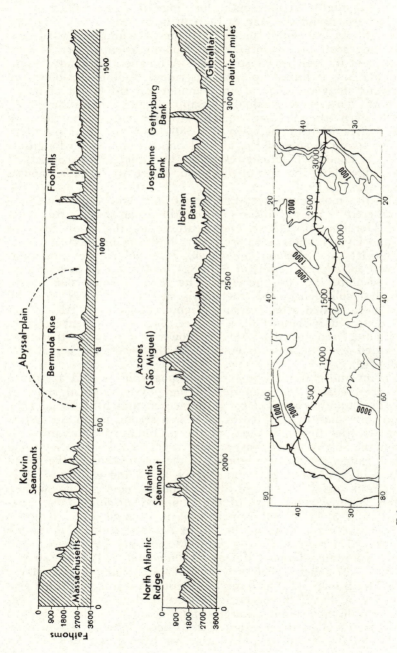

Echo-sounded trans-Atlantic section across the North Atlantic along the Massachusetts-Gibraltar line (509/1061). Vertical magnification=40:1

and M. Ewing (689). Their investigations were centred chiefly on a section of the ridge between 30-34°N 40-43°W. These investigations of the floor region genetically linked up with the ridge were divided into three distinct morphological zones: 1) the main chain with isobaths below 2,700 metres; 2) the terrace zone with isobaths 2,700-4,600 metres; and 3) the foothills with isobaths 4,600-5,300 metres. Farther stretches an abyssal plain with depths of more than 5,300 metres.*

Heezen, Tharp and Ewing (417/117-24) suggested a somewhat different morphological classification of the North Atlantic Ridge, dividing it into two main provinces: the province of the crest and the province of the sides. In addition, they subdivided the province of the crest into a rift valley, rift mountains and a high fractured plateau. The latter is characterised by depths ranging from 2,760 to 3,496 metres. The province of the sides is likewise subdivided into three provinces: upper (3,036-4,332 metres), middle (4,040-4,600 metres) and lower (4,324-5,152 metres) stages. However, this is by no means a convenient classification for understanding the causes of the emergence of this topography and suffers from a certain arbitrariness of selection because by affiliating the topography to one or another part of the new classification we cannot get an idea of the depth of subsidence or other features. We shall therefore refrain from using it.

It should be noted that scientists of the American school and their supporters do their best to ignore the existence of terraces, particularly stepped terraces, in the ridge. These *terraces are direct evidence of the prolonged subsidence of the ridge, a subsidence that took place sporadically.* This clashes with the convection currents theory, according to which convection currents rise in the region of the ridge, which is regarded as a crustal rupture. Mountain ranges, it is held, rise with these currents. That is why M. Ewing and his associates (417/121) object to the application of the term "terrace" to all the slopes of the ridge. They write that this term, as used by Tolstoi, does not correspond to the term "steps" as used by them. Tolstoi defined his terraces as continuous series of flat platforms, each of which is from one to 50 miles wide. They occur in a zone of 200-300 miles. The topography form, according to this definition, is called an intermontane basin, after a suggestion by Heezen and others. The location of intermontane level basins is shown in a chart. These basins, it is said, are to be found only to the southwest of the Azores. Consequently, Ewing does not deny the existence of terraces as described by Tolstoi, but limits the region where they occur. Future unbiased investigations will show how true this is. But in the meantime some supporters of the American school's views

---

* Echo-sounded sections of the North Atlantic Ridge at 29-43°N. 31-38°W are given in *The Floors of the Oceans* by B C. Heezen, M. Tharp and M Ewing (417), Figs. 36-42.

on terraces go farther than their teachers. Juggling with figures and selecting their data, they maintain that the existence of steps in the ridge is an illusion. This concerns even steps as understood by M. Ewing, and not only terraces! (731).

To this we shall add that contrary to A. V. Ilyin's (756a) assertions, *absolute symmetry is by no means observed along the entire length of both sides of the North Atlantic Ridge.* On the contrary, the western slopes are narrow in some places, and the eastern slopes in others. Asymmetry is particularly striking in the Azores Plateau, which is genetically part of the ridge: a chart clearly shows that on the west the ridge is much narrower than on the east, and if the plateau itself is added to this, the difference will be much more marked.

Recent investigations (806) have likewise *cut the ground from under the hypothesis that the anomaly is situated symmetrically relative to the median line of the ridge.*

The extensive investigations of the ridge morphology by M. and J. Ewing and M. Talwani (525a) lose much of their value because they do not give the locations of the stations. Instead, the authors give the distance in miles along the course of their ship, and this entails special computations on a chart and, besides, the routes were selected quite casually.

North of the Azores the ridge stretches from northwest to southeast, and south of the islands—from northeast to southwest.

Topographical data indicate that the perpendicular areas of the ridge have shifted. Initially the ridge stretched linearly, but along some of its sectors it subsequently was dissected by displacements running across its axis (785). M. V. Klenova and V. M. Lavrov (734) note the existence of great transversal fractures: North Atlantic (52-53°N) and the Azores (37-39°N). There is a large number of major fractures in other regions, particularly in the southern portion of the ridge. One of them is described below.

Somewhat north of the 30th parallel, the North Atlantic Ridge is dissected by the 60-mile long Atlantis fracture zone (770). St. Paul's Seamount is situated at the beginning of this zone. In the region of the zone, west and east of the ridge, there are narrow mountain ranges and depressions. This region of the ridge has the character of a fault trough (deepest point—5,124 metres—in the west), which stretches from the 41st to the 43rd parallel. Its floor proved to be irregular, being divided into two hollows more than 4,760 metres deep. Between them is a chain of mountains with their summits 4,026 metres below water. There are no terraces on the sides. We have named it the *Poseidon Fault Trough.*

In the investigated region (between the 30th and 34th parallels), the *Main Chain,* which is more than 275 kilometres wide, consists of a series of parallel ranges separated from each other by narrow valleys. Some of these ranges rise from a depth of less than 1,500 metres. Note has been made of the asymmetry of the sides—the

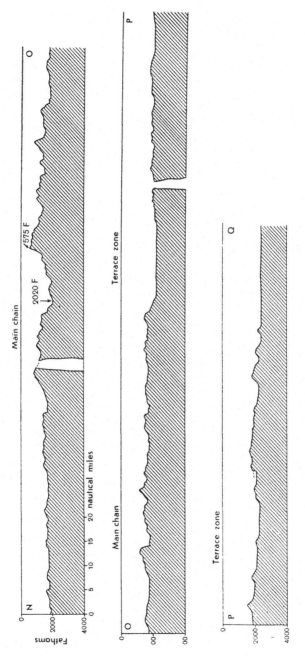

Echo-sounded section of the floor in the region of the North Atlantic Ridge (690). Vertical magnification = 33:1
1 fathom = 1.83 metres

eastern sides are usually steeper than the western. Formations resembling terraces were discovered only on the external edges in the shape of flat-bottomed valleys in the intermediate region between the Main Chain and the Terrace Zone.

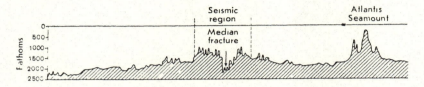

Echo-sounded section of the North Atlantic Ridge with the Median Valley along the 30th parallel (509, 1088) Vertical magnification = 40 1

An interesting feature of the Main Chain is that the narrow crest, which is a little more than 100 kilometres wide, has a remarkable depression—the *Median Valley* (or Median Fault), which cuts the Main Chain along almost its entire length in the direction of the ridge (417; 442/88; 509/1065; 560). Today it is considered that this depression is a rift valley. According to Heezen, Tharp and Ewing, the solitary rift valley was well-defined in 20 of the 26 studied profiles of the North Atlantic Ridge (between the 18th and the 49th parallel): in five cases concerning the southernmost of the investigated sections of the ridge there were even two and three rift valleys.*

The Median Valley has a V-shaped transverse cross-section which makes it look like a narrow canyon. Its mean bed width is from 10 to 40 kilometres and at the summits of both adjoining chains it is from 30 to 60 kilometres wide. The bed of the Median Valley is uneven with high prominences. Its depth is 2,750-4,575 metres, averaging between 3,700 and 3,900 metres. In some places it is even lower than the surface of the floor of the basins abutting the range on either side. The minimum depths over the western and eastern chains of the range are about 1,500 and 1,300 metres respectively, and that of the valley is more than 2,000 metres, here and there going down to 3,900 metres. The dip of the sides is 10-12° (263; 417). This valley has indeed the appearance of a devil's ravine that had never seen the light of day.

A. V. Ilyin (263) draws attention to the difference between the rift valley of the North Atlantic Ridge and an abyssal trench. The bed of the latter is flat while that of the rift valley is faulted. "Although by its linear dimensions the rift valley is comparable with abyssal trenches, the nature of its faulting is in many ways different," Ilyin concludes.

* Echo-sounded profiles (altogether 26) of the North Atlantic Ridge with data on the position of the rift valley are given in (417, Fig. 45) as well as in Chart No 23 in *Floors of the Oceans* by B C Heezen, M Tharp and M. Ewing.

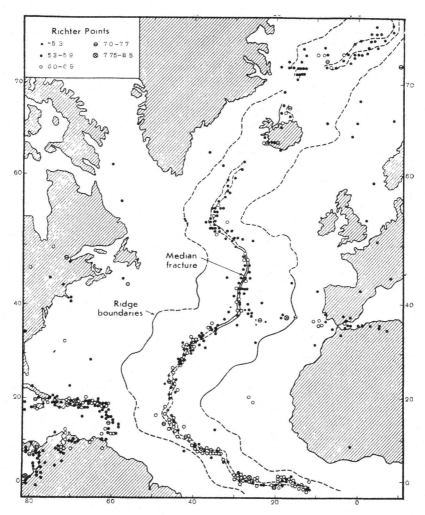

1910-1956 earthquake epicentres in the North Atlantic (509/1087)

According to American investigators (417, 509) the Median Valley has yet another feature: it is a narrow belt of many earthquake epicentres; another such belt, running in the east, stretches across the Azores in the direction of the Iberian Peninsula.* It is believed that in this second belt there is an Azores-Gibraltar Ridge with the same topography and structure as the North Atlantic Ridge and where a

---

* The disastrous Lisbon earthquake of 1755 may have been linked up with this belt

rift valley is also assumed to exist (417). There is a third zone linked up with the Equatorial Atlantic, where earthquakes are more frequent, but it, too, adjoins the North Atlantic Ridge (Dassy Zone, see Chapter Ten). According to L. A. Misharina, in the Atlantic earthquake epicentres lie at depths not exceeding 45 kilometres. In the region of the ridge, they are usually at a depth of 33 kilometres (784).

Most of the epicentres of the earthquakes taking place in the Median Valley and along the North Atlantic Ridge generally have hypocentres at a depth of 30-70 kilometres; consequently, they are not below the uppermost part of the subcrustal layer and are by no means associated with the processes deep in the mantle.

Another point that must be noted is that a considerable positive magnetic anomaly is associated with the Median Valley, while a negative magnetic anomaly of about 300-500 gammas (417/128; 448/97) is in the chains of mountains adjoining it on the west and east. This anomaly has been best of all studied at around the 25th parallel, where its value is somewhat above 250 gammas. But so far the largest value has been found near 48.5°N (somewhat above 500 gammas).* There are grounds for assuming that this anomaly is linked up not with the topography or structure of the locality but with the properties of the subcrustal material in this spot.

Flores and Corvu islands lie west of the Median Valley. A series of parallel broken off hollows and ranges with volcanoes have been discovered in this region. In the central part is a high magnetic anomaly (over 1,500 gammas). On either side this zone is fringed by depressions (735).

The most detailed data on one of the sections of the Median Valley is given in a work by M. N. Hill (560). *The investigated section is not an unbroken valley and it ends in the south near 46°40′N* (it has not been established how far it stretches northward). This section is situated approximately between longitude 27° and 27°30′W. It is at least 140 kilometres long and the floor depth ranges from 2,300 to 4,000 metres. The floor is uneven and faulted. Something in the nature of a channel has also been observed. However, its origin is not linked up with landslides; the great depths along the "channel" rule out this possibility. In our opinion *it is a former river or stream channel when the ridge was subaerial.* The floor is about 9 kilometres wide. The valley's sides are very steep, rising to 1,600-2,100 metres below the ocean surface and forming two parallel mountain chains with a distance of some 18 kilometres between their summits. *A transversal valley stretching westward has been discovered at roughly 47°40′N.* It is not yet known if it runs across the entire ridge. In the investigated sector there are neither magnetic anomalies nor traces of volcanic activity. On the whole, the data

---

* An anomaly with a value of 800 gammas has recently been brought to light.

offered by Hill substantially differ from those reported by Heezen and Ewing.

A section of the Median Valley between the 22nd and the 23rd parallel and near longitude 45°W has been cursorily dealt with in a recent work (737). In this section the floor lies at a depth of 3,800-4,100 metres and is fringed by mountains rising to 1,900-2,650 metres below the ocean surface; one of the peaks is 1,170 metres below the ocean surface. The floor of this section is uneven, growing shallower to the north where it ends at a sill 3,150 metres deep. Two egg-shaped depressions have been discovered west of the crest: a northern, 4,350 metres deep and measuring 6×10 kilometres, and a southern depression, 4,020 metres deep and measuring 6×12 kilometres.

Further investigations, the results of which are given by B. D. Loncarevic (794), covered the region west of the Median Valley. This region near the valley itself is only 20 miles wide and its depth averages 2,220 metres; at least 15 peaks have been discovered in it. The most noteworthy of these is Peak Confederation, which is located at 45°20′N 28°10′W. The edge of this mountainous region runs along isobath 2,590 metres. West of it the nature of the ridge undergoes an essential change and the author writes: "*The province adjacent to the Rift Mountains was named High Fractured Plateau by Heezen. The existing detailed surveys near 45°N do not justify this name.*" This province may be described as a sedimentary basin with well-defined, elongated mountains running across it. The principal feature of this province is a submarine range 20 miles long and several miles wide. One of its peaks has been named Bald Mountain. It has an unusually level surface and is situated near 45°12′N 28°54′W. The mountain ranges in this province have a northern orientation with a slight deviation to the west, as distinct from other mountain chains running parallel with the Median Valley.

A paper devoted to the Median Valley in the sector 46-46°10′N 28-28°30′W was published some time ago by British and Canadian scientists (778). According to this paper the valley floor is rugged and narrow. In the north the valley ends in two volcanoes which erupt through the surface of the slopes. Altogether three pairs of volcanoes have been discovered in the region of the valley. With the exception of this locality, the valley floor dips from south to north from a depth of 3,100 metres to a depth of 3,570 metres over a distance of about 50 miles. In the south the valley evidently narrows down. There is evidence of another valley running parallel west of the above valley. It is deepest (3,566 metres) at 45°42′N 27°46′W. On either side of it are ridges with sharp peaks. The mean magnitude of the free anomaly of the force of gravity is about 40 milligals in air and 200-220 milligals in the Bouguer reduction. This is not the same valley as described above.

Soviet oceanological expeditions have established that the Median Valley extends northward, but there are as yet no data to show that it is unbroken in this sector. Along the 50th parallel it was crossed only twice by the *Mikhail Lomonosov*. At this point the ridge is about 185 kilometres wide; there is a rift valley. But no rift was found in the Reykjanes Ridge.

In 1957-58 a German oceanological expedition (498; 692) reported that although it crossed the Reykjanes Ridge 40 times in a zone stretching from the tip of Iceland to the 56th parallel, it did not find a rift valley; two such valleys (if they are rift valleys!) were discovered only at the extremity of the ridge; one is narrower along the middle of the crest, while the second, which is wider, lies east of the first. G. Dietrich (498) links up the absence of earthquake epicentres with the absence of a rift valley.

The above data clashes with the Heezen-Tharp-Ewing (417) conjecture that there must be a rift valley along the entire length of the North Atlantic Ridge. On this score A. V. Zhivago (252) writes: "These and some other materials cited by Dietrich in his paper (at the International Oceanological Congress in Washington in 1959— *N.Z.*) makes one doubt the accuracy of the data obtained by the Lamont Observatory, although on the whole their significance to the investigations of the Atlantic floor remains great." The Median Valley is, evidently, not everywhere clear-cut; in some cases the "rift valley" does not differ from many other valleys situated within the limits of the ridge, and in other cases there is, instead, a series of smaller valleys. *There are, therefore, full grounds for assuming that the Median Valley is not a continuous fault*, and it is by no means, as Heezen and Ewing maintain, part of what in their enthusiasm they term the World Fault running across all the oceans of the Earth, although similar morphological structures have been observed in other oceans.*

Our views on this subject found confirmation at the Second International Oceanographic Congress in Moscow. Summing up the papers read at that congress, A. V. Zhivago (726) noted that despite the Ewing-Heezen assumptions, it has now been established that instead of being a continuous fault the rift (median) valley is a complex system of elongated depressions, each of which may even possibly be of a different age.

Very interesting data is cited by F. G. Fuglister (530/4), who writes that *in the region of the Median Valley the temperature is much higher and the water much salter* than outside it. This is particularly striking at Station No. 56 (36°18′N 33°49′W) where the expedition ship *Chain* obtained cores from a depth of 2,896 metres. The same picture was evidently found at 32°14′N 35°50′W. The higher water temperature may be explained, as observations have shown, by the fact that there are larger and warmer currents near some of the mid-oceanic mountain ranges, but it is hard to

---

* Doubts as to whether the valley cutting the ridge is really a rift valley forces us to favour the term Median Valley

explain the somewhat higher salinity because this is a phenomenon found only in the Median Valley and is not to be observed on either side of the ridge, where the salinity and the temperature are lower. This rules out the theory that salter surface layers had subsided to the floor of the ocean. The higher salinity could stem from the additional delivery of salt by volcanic activity. But, as we have already pointed out, volcanic activity has not been found throughout the Median Valley. This question awaits extensive investigations. It is our guess that perhaps *not very long ago, when the ridge was still subaerial but already in the process of subsidence, sea water penetrated into the Median Valley and later its salinity increased as a result of evaporation* (as in the case of the Kara Bogaz Gol Bay and the Caspian Sea). When the ridge finally sank, the narrowness of the valley and the great height of its sides isolated it sufficiently to preserve the high salt content of the water. With the aid of radiocarbon dating it has been established that the abyssal waters in some parts of the ocean near the North Atlantic Ridge (58-53°N 32-21°W) are 1,600-1,750 years old (434). *Taking the unique conditions of the Median Valley into account, its subsidence could have taken place several thousand years ago.*

As regards the warm current, the data on it, expressed in terms of $K \cdot 10^{-6}$ cal/cm^2 sec are as follows: for the Median Valley $K = 6.0$-7.0; for the ridge itself $K = 1.5$-3.4 and for the abyssal plains on either side of the ridge $K = 1.2$-1.4 (417; 645; 716).

The Median Valley is an exceptionally interesting place of the Earth's crust and its study has only been begun. Some years ago it was investigated from a bathyscaphe by the noted French oceanologist J. Y. Cousteau, who took some thought-provoking photographs of its sides, but regrettably they have not yet been published. These photographs were made at a depth of 3,000 metres (private communication).

The *Terrace Zone,* situated on either side of the Main Chain, is 370-555 kilometres wide and forms an integral whole with the Main Chain. It consists of terraces separated by a series of ledges; some known prominences are on the external side of this zone. Most of the terraces are at the following depths: 2,688, 3,011, 3,202, 3,294, 3,385, 3,568, 3,751, 3,843, 3,934 and 4,017 metres; of these, the most frequent are 2,686, 3,385, 3,751 and 4,017 metres. They are evidently terraces of the main subsidences (689).

The lowest terrace is at 4,574 metres. The internal eastern edge of this terrace is marked by the broad summit of a small elevation, which is itself separated internally by a series of narrow ranges rising from a depth of 3,843 metres. The next terrace adjoining it, at a depth of 4,017-4,154 metres, is about 46 kilometres wide and is noteworthy for its amazing smoothness. Similar terraces on all the profiles between 35 and 30°N are approximately on one and the same depth. *The striking evenness of these terraces (4,000-4,200 metres) and the identity of the depths of subsidence, in our opinion, bring one round to the idea that they might have been the surface of a shelf when the ridge was still in a subaerial position.*

The 111-185-kilometre-wide zone between isobaths 4,017-2,688 metres situated on either side of the ridge is characterised by a series of flat terraces and by identical depths for hundreds of miles on either side of the ridge. A terrace lying at a depth of 3,477 metres was traced for more than 166 kilometres along the main direction of the ridge. The terrace at 3,751 metres can be traced for nearly 148 kilometres, while the terrace at 3,843 metres probably stretches for about 185 kilometres farther to the west. It is quite possible that these terraces form a series of horizontal surfaces outlining the external edge of the highest parts of the North Atlantic Ridge.

In our opinion, a plausible explanation of *this entire picture*, about which I. Tolstoi writes: "... we do not know the processes that created the terraces and this strange type of surface," *is that the shelf and the littoral plain that had surrounded the North Atlantic Ridge when it was subaerial had subsided by stages, leaving behind benches.*

The *Foothill Zone* between the western abyssal plain and the Terrace Zone bears no resemblance to either the Main Chain or the Terrace Zone, being an independent morphological unit. In this zone there are summits, many of which reach a height of over 900 metres. Along the entire boundary between the Foothills and the Terrace Zone there is an unbroken mountain range lying in many places at a depth of less than 3,700 metres below the water surface. There is a depression on its western side and another on its eastern side. The western depression is deeper, in some places reaching a depth of 5,500 metres, while the deepest point in the eastern depression is 4,600-4,700 metres. The floor of the depressions is flat. In our view *the edgemost range of the Foothills might have been something in the nature of a barrier reef during the subaerial state of the North Atlantic Ridge.*

South of the 12th parallel the depth fluctuates within the considerable range of over 1,000 metres. There the ridge acquires a more latitudinal direction and is accompanied by parallel chains and spurs that create a very intricate picture. The northern side of the ridge is twice as long as the southern side and rises in steep ledges at an angle of more than 20° to a relative height of up to 1,000 metres. Although the southern side is likewise extensively faulted, its ledges are flatter (the dip is only 6°) and more clear-cut and have a relative depth of up to 2,000 metres (242).

N. A. Grabovsky, R. H. Greku and A. P. Metalnikov (242) give some interesting details that have been brought to light along the 30th meridian. Two rift valleys with an absolute bed depth of 3,500 metres and a mean width of 30-35 kilometres have been discovered at the end of the North Atlantic Ridge between St. Paul's Rocks and the Romanche Trench. Two other faults have been found on the northeastern side of the ridge, but as distinct from the axial valleys they have a flat floor lying at a depth of about 4,500 metres.

In the region of the Equatorial Atlantic Ridge the topography is extremely rugged, and only recently it became possible (and only in general outline at that) to establish its key features. A series of so-called fracture zones have been brought to light (533a; 533b; 737; 770). Most of these zones run in a near-latitudinal direction. In some cases they follow one another somewhat away from the ridge's main direction.

The Equatorial Atlantic Ridge proper has a latitudinal strike and it is sharply asymmetrical and narrow (not more than 100 kilometres). Its crest comprises two chains lying 2,000-3,000 metres below the ocean surface and divided by a narrow median valley which is about 15 kilometres wide; the floor of this valley drops to a depth of 4,270-4,730 metres; the western, shallower part, has a flat floor, while the topography of the floor of the eastern part is badly faulted. A third chain of mountains, which has the Romanche Trench between it and the second chain, stretches from 21° to 16°30′W.

And now some details about the topography. The Barracuda Fault lies at the western boundary. The Vema fracture zone, situated at 7-11°N 35-45°W, consists of a series of transversal ridges and depressions, the largest of which is the Vema Trough (maximum depth—5,189 metres). With a width varying from eight to 20 kilometres, it extends for more than 900 kilometres and has an outlet in the direction of Guiana.

Its sides tower about 3,000 metres above the floor, and a sill separates it into a western and eastern part. West of 25°W is a system of parallel depressions running in a latitudinal direction and adjoining the

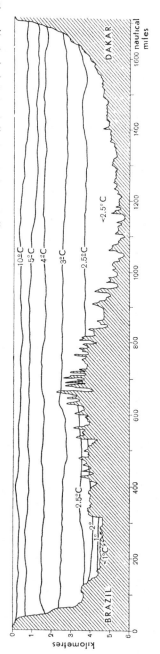

Echo-sounded section of the floor and water isotherms in the Central Atlantic from Brazil to Dakar, Africa (509/1082). Vertical magnification = 1000·1. The cold bottom Antarctic current is shown on the left

Vema Trough. The southern slope of the trough is a huge hilly plateau lying at a depth of 3,400-4,000 metres with rounded peaks rising to 1,000 metres and higher; some of these peaks are active volcanoes. At 1°30′S this plateau is split by a narrow (1.5-4.5 kilometres) ravine with an even floor and depths of 5,500-5,770 metres. Facing the northern crest is a depression (depth—up to 5,400 metres; length—about 800 kilometres; width—85-100 kilometres) with a seismically active floor. This depression ends at a ledge 300-400 metres high, which separates it from the abyssal Sierra Leone Plain. Earthquake epicentres are linked up with this ledge, while the abyssal plain is seismically quiescent.

In the south, east of the Romanche fracture zone and running parallel to it, is the Chain fracture zone, which has been traced for a distance of nearly 180 miles. While the former zone is situated approximately at the equator (between longitudes 10° and 20°W), the latter is located between longitudes 15° and 20°W. This zone is extensively faulted, with parallel valleys and mountain ranges. The maximum depth (5,470 metres) was found at 15°5′W.

Near the equator the North Atlantic Ridge acquires a direction close to latitudinal and breaks off at a deep depression in the ocean floor known as the Romanche Trench. H. Pettersson (633/141-142) notes that this is an extremely interesting region of the Atlantic, being a vast transversal subsidence of the ridge at its very extremity, at a point where it turns east and is narrowest and sharpest. This subsidence reaches a depth of more than 7,000 metres, while some 10 miles southeast of it the ridge rises to a height of about 2,600 metres below the ocean level. The difference in levels corresponds to the gradient 25:100.

V. M. Lavrov (739) gives us the following data about the Romanche Trench. It consists of two elongated basins running latitudinally for a distance of 400 kilometres. Its width between the crests adjoining it does not exceed 55 kilometres. According to American investigators it is deepest (7,856 metres) at 0°16′S 18°35′W. These dimensions, Lavrov points out, are typical of so-called greenstone sags. Indeed, outcrops of such rocks have been found on the North Atlantic Ridge (731). The two basins are interconnected by a V-shaped ravine 5,900 metres deep. The median Romanche Ridge with its even contour and relative height of 550-1,170 metres above the floor has been traced in the centre of the furrow along its long axis. An interesting point is that a similar ridge was discovered in the Puerto Rico Trough. This, as Lavrov notes, is evidence of definite *morphological similarity between the Romanche Trench and the troughs in the island arcs.* As in the Puerto Rico Trough, the ravines located north and south of the median ridge lie at different levels. Their width does not exceed 1.5 kilometres. The floor is quite flat, but in some places it undulates. The Romanche Median Ridge is likewise undulating, with the mountains reaching a height of several hundred metres. This ridge is possibly composed of sedimentary rocks.

It will be recalled that abyssal troughs are as a rule situated close to either continents or island arcs. The Romanche Trench is the only exception: in our opinion this is testimony in favour of the theory that alongside the trough there was land which had subsequently subsided; in other words, *this unique feature in the location of the Romanche Trench in the heart of the Equatorial Atlantic is indirect proof that this part of the North Atlantic Ridge had a subaerial existence.*

Another fracture zone, named Guinea, was discovered some time ago; data about it were published by D. C. Krause (579a). Stretching for a distance of about 850 kilometres from the Sierra Leone shelf between 8° and 9°N, it consists of a series of ridges and troughs with high magnetic anomalies. In the west it evidently links up with the Vema fracture zone. There is good reason to believe that the Guinea fracture zone is part of a vast trans-Atlantic rupture running from Guadalupe Island (in the Antilles) in the west to at least 59°W, and that it includes the Barracuda fracture in the west and the Vema, Chain and Romanche fracture zones in the centre.

Farther south, the Mid-Atlantic Ridge, now the South Atlantic Ridge, turns in a meridional direction with a subsidence depth of less than 2,500 metres. We shall not deal with the South Atlantic Ridge or the South Atlantic as a whole because they have no relation to the problem of Atlantis.

The Bermuda Rise, which has been investigated in fairly great detail by US and Soviet oceanologists (273; 417) is a unique morphological feature of the North Atlantic floor. But since it has no relation to Atlantis, we shall not stop to describe it either.

Some 260 kilometres northeast of the Bermuda Islands, at the pedestal of these islands, is the small submarine Muir Archipelago lying at a depth of 1,350-2,200 metres; it is probably of tectonic origin (417).

Another submarine archipelago, an arc of submarine mountains, lies between the Bermuda Islands and New England (623). It stretches for a distance of about 1,600 kilometres from the northwest to the southeast of the George Bank shelf (near the Gulf of Maine). Tentatively this archipelago may be divided into three large groups: a western archipelago of small mountains (eight mountains) lying at a great depth (some 3,700 metres) across the continental slope; the central Kelvin archipelago (three mountains—subsidence depth= 1,450-1,650 metres) consisting of guyots with terraces and known through past investigations (417); and an eastern archipelago consisting of the largest submarine mountains (eight mountains at a depth of 325-880 metres from the surface), the edgemost of which stands on the northeastern outskirt of the Bermuda Rise.

East of this archipelago is the *Corner Elevation* (417) situated south of the Grand Newfoundland Bank; the submarine mountains of this archipelago have a subsidence depth of nearly 2,800 metres.

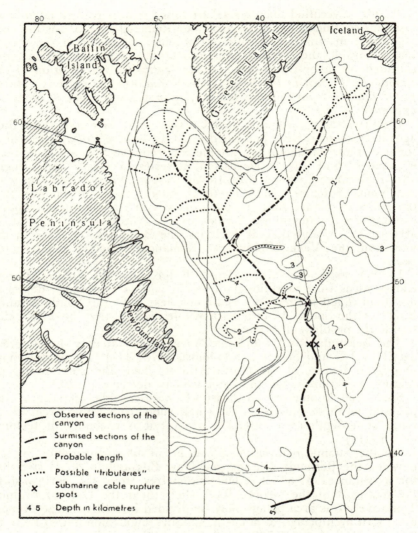

North Atlantic submarine canyon (509/1066)

Possibly, these mountains are an extension of the Bermuda-New England arc and that here we have a tectonic structure linking the North American continent with the North Atlantic Ridge.

The Grand Newfoundland Bank was unquestionably a subaerial region during the last glaciation. From west to east it stretches for about 400 kilometres and from north to south for more than 500 kilometres. In shape it is almost a regular square with depths of less than 100 metres. There is a trough only near Newfoundland, and it is scarcely 200 metres (262).

A direct extension of the Grand Newfoundland Bank, *Flemish Cap* shaol with its depths of about 200 metres is separated from the former by a submarine strait nearly 1,200 metres deep. South of Flemish Cap and southeast of Newfoundland as its submarine extension, as it were, is the *Southeastern Newfoundland Ridge*. With a subsidence depth of from 2,700 to 4,000 metres, this ridge is 110-180 kilometres wide (417). *The link elements of the second tectonic structure extending all the way to the North Atlantic Ridge* may be beneath the sediments somewhere in these regions. Some geologists regard Flemish Cap as a remnant of the Appalachian mountain system.

A striking feature of the North Atlantic floor in these regions is the great *Mid-Ocean Canyon*, which was discovered some years ago (521; 417). It has no direct relation to the canyons of the shelf or to the submarine river valleys, but runs across the very floor of the ocean nearer to the continental slope. It has been studied over a distance of 2,200 kilometres and is believed to be something like 4,500 kilometres long. It has been traced from the 52nd down to the 38th parallel. Its eastern side is about 95 kilometres from the lower edge of the North Atlantic Ridge. This side is lower than the rocky western side and consists of sedimentary rocks. The walls of this canyon are steep and the bed is flat; on the whole it is box-shaped with the slope angle ranging from 21° to absolute verticality. Its depth is from 185 metres at the 52nd parallel (the total depth at this spot is 4,500 metres) to 18 metres at the 38th parallel. Its width is from 5.5 to 9.5 kilometres. This canyon, which follows a tortuous path, forms a narrow (5.5 kilometres at its widest point) crevice in the submarine Newfoundland Ridge.

R. Malaise (76) considers that the Mid-Ocean Canyon is of subaerial origin, and is inclined to think it was the channel of a Pliocene river with its source far in the north. He sharply objects to attempts at explaining its origin as being due to the action of turbidity currents. However, as G. Dietrich reports (498), careful echo sounding has failed to bring to light the system of canyons which Heezen believed existed south of the Davis and Denmark straits. Other facts seeming to favour the subaerial origin of the Mid-Ocean Canyon are the presence of meanders, sand on the canyon bed, and the change from a deep and narrow canyon to a broad valley, as well as the fact that it is not a concentration point of earthquake epicentres, which would have been the case if the canyon, as a deep fault, would have been of purely tectonic origin. F. P. Shepard (672) advanced the view that a considerable role might have been played by turbidity currents in shaping the Mid-Ocean Canyon. We consider that here a big role was played by tectonic factors; turbidity currents have nothing at all to do with it. The possibility that the canyon might at one time have been subjected to the action of subaerial factors should not be ruled out.*

Generally speaking, we consider that *the theory about the purely tectonic origin of the North Atlantic canyon leads to the assumption that its emergence is linked up with the subsidence of the ridge and, perhaps, with the simultaneous formation of the "rift" valley of the North Atlantic Ridge*; the fact that the western side of the canyon is higher than the eastern side by approximately 20-25 metres serves as indirect confirmation of this assumption (417).

A submarine canyon, more than 600 kilometres long, was discovered in the northwestern part of the abyssal Sohm Plain (417). It runs past the mountains of the submarine Kelvin Archipelago, which gives us the right to call it *Kelvin Canyon*. This canyon likewise runs parallel to the shelf and the continental slope. Possibly it is an extension of the Mid-Ocean Canyon and that the missing part is buried under sediments.

Some time ago Heezen and his associates reported the discovery of yet another submarine canyon—the Equatorial Canyon (553), which runs across an abyssal plain parallel to the North Atlantic Ridge and the continental slope of Brazil in the region of Fortaleza for a distance of more than 600 kilometres. This canyon is from two to nine kilometres wide and about 185 metres deep. It has steep sides, and the discovery of sand and gravel on the bed was seized upon by the authors to attribute its origin to turbidity currents (sic!).

MYTHICAL ISLANDS OF THE NORTH ATLANTIC AS A PROBLEM OF ATLANTOLOGY

To this day the Atlantic, particularly its northern part, witnesses considerable tectonic movements. Cases of new islands appearing and disappearing have been registered in recorded history. For example, such cases occurred near Iceland in 1240, 1422, 1783 (419/II/201) and quite recently, in 1963; in the region of the Azores —in 1811, 1867 and 1957; and near St. Paul's Rocks—in 1932 (10/109-110).

In the preceding chapters we mentioned interesting facts about very recent subsidences. Let us recall the fresh shells on the Rockall Plateau, the absence of a sufficiently thick layer of sediments in the Median Valley of the North Atlantic Ridge, the probable changes in the depths of some banks compared with ancient data, the disappearance of shallow water over the Milne and Echo banks (272) and so forth. If to these facts we add the information reported on 14th-16th-century charts and portolanos, which doggedly indicate enig-

---

* The opinion about the former subaerial position of this canyon as part of the Tertiary Paleo-Hudson has the support of G. W. Lindberg, who believes that in its upper reaches the Paleo-Hudson communicated with some rivers flowing from the European continent (721).

matic islands (particularly north of the Madeiras), that subsequently could not be identified, as well as the many legends about mythical islands in the Atlantic, we involuntarily find ourselves desiring to compare all this with the contemporary data of oceanology and marine geology. An interesting point is whether the present-day banks, shoals and submarine plateaus are not some of the islands mentioned in legends. This idea has been advanced by the American geographer W. H. Babcock (149/25) with regard to the banks situated west of the Strait of Gibraltar. He writes: "All considered, it seems far from impossible that some of these banks may have been visible and even habitable at some time when men had attained a moderate degree of civilisation. But they would not be of any vast extent." He expressed this view in connection with the Atlantis problem.

Some geologists have likewise accepted the possibility that the Atlantic was the scene of catastrophic changes in the geological past and that catastrophes are not ruled out at present, in recorded time. For example, the French geologist P. Termier (177) wrote: "While the continental shores of this ocean now seem to be immobile, the floor of the Atlantic is in motion throughout the eastern zone for a distance of about 3,000 kilometres, embracing Iceland, the Azores, the Madeiras, the Canaries and the Cape Verde Islands. Today this is an unstable zone of the Earth's surface, and the most fearful cataclysms may take place in this zone at any minute." Termier's view is shared by the noted Soviet tectonist D. I. Mushketov (337/454).

After closely studying the materials at our disposal, we consider that the following regions had evidently subsided recently and that some mythical islands could be associated with them:

1) The Iceland-Faeroes Rise and the Faeroe Plateau with their banks; 2) Reykjanes Ridge; 3) Rockall Plateau with its bank and small island; 4) Porcupine Plateau with its bank; 5) the series of banks between Cornwall and Brittany; 6) the submarine plateau west of Galicia, Spain; 7) the large group of prominences and banks between Portugal and the Madeiras west of the Strait of Gibraltar, primarily the submarine Horseshoe Archipelago; 8) the banks and shoals of the North Sea. In all these places we do not exclude the possibility of islands having existed even in the period of recorded history; some of them might have been inhabited.

A critical study of the data given in 14th-16th-century portolanos and charts made it possible to identify many of the islands indicated in them with currently existing islands. But the location of some of the legendary islands mentioned by antique and medieval authors has not been established, and most investigators are inclined to treat them as being completely mythical. They are:

a) antique islands: Thule, Cassiterides (Tin), Abalus (Amber), Ogygia, Scheria and Tartessos. As we have pointed out in Chapter Four the latter three islands are linked up with the Atlantis problem;

b) medieval islands: Antilia (149/144-163; 419/IV/274-79), Brazil (149/50-67; 419/IV/305-14; 321-25); Bouss (149/175-78), Virgin (419/IV/30S-09), Green (149/94-113), Ys, Lyoness, Mayda (149/81-93), St. Brendan's (149/34-49) and Seven Cities (149/68-80; 419/IV/271-94; 282-84).

There are many hypotheses about Thule Island. It was discovered and briefly described by the 4th-century B.C. Greek navigator and geographer Pytheas of Massilia (Marseilles). He reported that it was situated some six day's journey by sea (1,200 kilometres) to the north of Britain and one day's journey (about 200 kilometres) from the Arctic Ocean. About Pytheas' travels and about Thule Island we only have fragmentary accounts by later authors: Strabo [1,69; II, 114-15; IV, 201], Placidus [III, 17] and Pliny [IV, 40]. In their originals the works of Pytheas have not survived to our day. Strabo doubts the authenticity of the information reported by Pytheas, referring to the fact that he had not found any mention of Thule Island by any other author and that nobody had been able to locate that island. This is very reminiscent of the history of the Atlantis problem! Strabo doubted if so close to the zone of ice edible fruit was grown, millet (oats, according to K. Mullenhoff) sown, livestock bred and a beverage made from bee's honey. However, R. Hennig (419/1, 179) convincingly proves that the information given by Pytheas had always been truthful; he was very observant and his geographical descriptions were accurate—he can be regarded as a scientist in the loftiest meaning of the word, who accomplished a feat meriting respect.

According to Pytheas the inhabitants of Thule were a civilised people who used the plough and had some knowledge of astronomy; it is worth noting that they threshed grain in "large houses" (roofed threshing-floors).

The problem of the location of Thule cannot be regarded as having been settled, because Pytheas pointed out that in the summer the night was only two or three hours long on Thule. It should, therefore, be located between the 61st and 63rd parallel. Some scholars believe that Pytheas' description fits the north of Iceland, but grain does not grow (and has never been grown) there and it has never had bees, and, generally speaking, we have no proof that Iceland was inhabited in Pytheas' day. Hennig (419/1,188) feels that an identification of Thule with Iceland belongs to the category of now rare historical errors. Personally, he is inclined to side with Fridtjof Nansen, who believed that Thule is Norway in the region of Trondheim. But the warm climate described by Pytheas does not fit that part of Norway, particularly as Pytheas travelled during the period of the so-called climatic catastrophe (207/277), when in Western Europe the climate was much colder than it is today. In our opinion the only explanation is that Thule was located in the mainstream of a great marine current, which was somewhat warmer than the present-day Gulf Stream. This version becomes plausible (see Chapter

Sixteen) only if the route of the northeastern branch of the Gulf Stream was barred by some large land area, which deflected the current more to the north than to the east. Therefore, almost the entire mass of the Gulf Stream flowed in a more compact stream than today to the northeast, west of the British Isles, in a direction between Iceland and Norway. It is our view that Thule Island, which subsequently sank in the sea, was situated somewhere in the region of the Faeroe Plateau.

The earliest Irish seafarers reported a strange land called Bouss, which sank beneath the ocean waves (also see 529/13). The land or island of Bouss continued to be marked on very late maps. On a map issued in 1578 it is located at 57.5°N, while a detailed map showing this island was published as late as 1673.

Southwest of Iceland, according to a Catalonian map compiled in 1480, lies Green Island. An inscription to a map compiled by Ries in 1508, in which it is stated that "an island burned up" in 1456 between Iceland and Greenland, possibly refers to Green Island (419/II/201). Like Bouss, this island is sooner linked up with the volcanic activity of the submarine Reykjanes Ridge.

The tiny island of Rockall, about which little is known, was about the only island that played no special role in most of the investigations into the location of the mythical islands of the Atlantic. Scholars like Babcock (149) and Hennig (419) do not mention it at all, and only T. J. Westrop (519/13) devotes part of his work to it. An Anglo-Saxon map dating from the year 998 shows what islands were located west of Scotland. A mythical island called Daculi was known to be situated northwest of Ireland. Although a Portuguese map issued in 1550 names "Rochol" island, the earliest mention of Rockall, giving its exact location, dates from as late as 1606.

There is much more information about the mythical islands located directly to the west of Ireland on the submarine Porcupine Plateau. Most of them are regarded as mirages. The Anglo-Saxon map of 998 gives this region as the location of a large island. Subsequently there appeared the island of Brazil (O'Brazil—Fortunate Isle), which should not be confused with the mythical Virgin Island, which likewise was said to have been situated west of Ireland. Hennig (419/IV/310) regards the myth about the Virgin Island as an echo of the legend about Ogygia Island with its goddess Calypso. The Island of Brazil was marked on all the charts and portolanos compiled between 1325 and 1571. Some of these charts and portolanos had three islands with one and the same name: west and southwest of Ireland and on the Cadiz parallel. In connection with these legends exceptional interest centres on the report that some 250 miles west of Ireland a fishing trawler raised from the floor of the sea (evidently, in the region of a bank) a pot made of grey clay with a Latin inscription roughly scratched on it (146).

Brazil Island remained on maps for a very long time. A map

published in 1553 gave its position as 53°N. Even the Pardy map of 1830 indicates a Brazil "Rock" at 51°10′N.

The island of Mayda (Asmayda, sometimes called Man) was located south or southwest of Ireland by medieval cartographers. It is to be found in much later maps as well. On the Pardy map it is situated south of the Brazil Rock, while on a map published in New York in 1814 its location is given as 46°N 20°W.

There is incontestable evidence of considerable subsidences of land west and southwest of Britain and Brittany. V. G. Childe (428, 22) writes of the great transgression of the sea in 1900-1800 B.C., which was called forth by massive subsidences of the shore not only of the British Isles but also of Denmark and Sweden. The time of that transgression approximately coincides with the last break-through of the Gulf Stream into the Kara Sea; this has been computed by M. M. Yermolayev (25). At the same period there was seismic and volcanic activity in the eastern Mediterranean.

The entire area west and southwest of the British Isles, particularly of Cornwall, continues to be a region of transgression. A slow subsidence is taking place to this day in England and Wales at a velocity of not less than 1-2 mm a year (327). On the sea floor near the Scilly Isles O.G.S. Crawford found the remains of stone structures and artifacts made of flint. A legend about the lost island of Ys and of another island, called Lyoness (49/183), is associated with these subsidence regions. Lyoness was located between the tip of Cornwall and the Scilly Isles. It had a large town, and when the island sank there was only one survivor, a man named Trévillion, who swam to the shore on a horse. The Bretons have a similar legend —about the island of Ys, which was, according to one legend, supposed to have been situated somewhere above the present Trespass Bay and, according to another, at Doirnenier Bay (161/101). Inasmuch as the island was sinking, King Gradlon (or Grallon) erected a high wall around it and built sluice gates. But one stormy night, his dissolute daughter Dagout, during one of her adventures, accidentally opened one of the sluice gates and the water rushed in and flooded the town. Gradlon saved himself, like Trévillion, by swimming to the continent on a horse. The two legends are very similar and probably recount one and the same event.

To this day in many places along the coast of England and Cornwall there are remains of flooded forests and habitations, and human skulls are found. It is presumed that the shore of Norfolk subsided some 2,500 years ago, while that of Devonshire as long ago as 3,500 years. Other data lead to a figure giving the date as 4,000±1,000 years ago (644; 650/322-23).

Rufus Festus Avienus, the Roman poet (181/83-134), mentions a mountainous land called Estrimnides with a ridge of high mountains forming a cape in the west. This ridge faced the south where lay a gulf with large islands rich in tin, lead and other metals. From there it was a two days' journey (about 400 kilometres) to Ireland.

Estrimnides is usually identified with Brittany, but the presence of large islands and the ridge facing south instead of west does not fit Brittany. However, to this day, as in antiquity, an island lying west of Cape Finisterre is called Ouessant.

Between the Iberian Peninsula and Britain, probably closer to the former, there were the mysterious *Tin Islands* or the Cassiterides of the ancients, which for many centuries had been the source of tin for the whole of Western Europe and other areas. Hennig (419/I/199) says that at present there are sufficient data to maintain that in antiquity Europe was completely independent of Asia in the supply of tin. Strabo [111, 5, §11] tells us that the Cassiterides were a group of ten islands in the open sea north of Artabros Habour (now La Coruña, northwest Spain). Some were desert islands, others were inhabited. Ore was obtained from shallow mines and exchanged for copper articles, ceramics and salt. The inhabitants were livestock breeders. Pliny [IV, 34; XXIV, 47, 156] likewise writes that the Cassiterides were 60 miles (about 90 kilometres) west of the northwestern extremity of Spain. The same location is given by Ptolemy. Consequently, these islands cannot be the Scillies. Elsewhere Pliny [VII, 56] writes that the first man to learn about them was Midacrites, whom some scholars identify with Melkarth, the Phoenician god of trade and navigation, and others with the Phrygian King Midas, who, according to Hellanicus, lived in about the year 979 B.C. Trade with the Cassiterides was conducted by Tartessians (419/I) and Cretans. Then the latter were ousted by the Phoenicians, who initially traded through Tartessos and then, like the Carthaginians, independently. The Romans learned of the Cassiterides very late: they were visited, Strabo [111, 5, §11] tells us, by Publius Crassus in about the year 96 B.C. (419/I/290). Later, mention of the Cassiterides gradually disappears from literature. Hennig (419/I/124) believes that these islands should be identified with the British Isles, unfoundedly completely ignoring the testimony of Strabo and Pliny [as well as of Ptolemy!] on the grounds that this testimony is unreliable. For our part, we are inclined to regard as more reasonable the conclusion of J. O. Thomson (146/91) that none of the present groups of islands corresponds to the description of the ancient authors, either for their number or other features. We believe that these islands, having been located in a region of tectonic subsidences, no longer exist. They probably sank in the early centuries of the present era. But their location remains unclear. Agreeing with E. Le Danois, S. Hutin (161/99) thinks that they might have been located near the Great and Little Salt banks south of Ireland and west of Cape Finisterre, somewhere between 48°-49°N 8-10°W with bedding depths of about 65 metres in the case of the first and about 20 metres in the case of the second.

Atlantologists are particularly interested in the region of shallow-water banks and submarine mountains west of the Strait of Gibraltar, whose concentration is dealt with by A. Laughton (588). In this connection let us recall that southwestern Spain and the adjoining part of the Atlantic Ocean is a region of age-old subsidences and tectonic movements generally. This area, as we have already stated, embraces the earthquake epicentre zone running from the North Atlantic Ridge in the direction of the Iberian Peninsula. A. Rey Pastor (649) points out that both the estuary of the Guadalquivir River and the lower reaches of the Guadiana River are tectonically mobile regions. It must be assumed that the region to the west and southwest, now covered by an ocean, is likewise tectonically mobile.

In *De mirabilibus auscultationibus* [136] Pseudo-Aristotle wrote that with a fair wind behind them Phoenicians sailing from Gadir *discovered, after a four days' voyage (i.e., after covering some 700-800 kilometres), a shoal, which dried up at low water (i.e., at low tide)*. These shoals were densely covered with weeds and were inhabited by tunny, whose flesh was of exceptionally high quality. These shoals are non-existent today. Moreover, as A. Brehm points out in his *Life of Animals* (Vol. VIII), after the disastrous Lisbon earthquake of 1755 the subsidence of the sea floor wrought such substantial changes in the shelf that the tunny abandoned their old spawning ground.

Hennig (419/III/280) notes that for some reason all medieval portolanos and all the maps compiled in 1350-1430 give the location of mythical islands almost exclusively to the north of the Madeiras. An analysis of these maps shows that in most cases and for many reasons these islands cannot be identified with the Azores. The Soligo map of 1485 (419/IV/81) indicates two islands (!) in the region of the submarine Horseshoe Archipelago and also some unidentified spots (islands?!) near the present Gettysburg Bank. If we heed the directions of antique authors (see Chapter Four) about the location of islands like Erytheia (west of Portugal) or Tartessos, it is quite probable that these islands might have been located in the present submarine Horseshoe Archipelago and then sank beneath the ocean level. One of these sunken islands might have been Scheria of the Phaecacians described by Homer in the *Odyssey* and which, like Tartessos, was probably visited by Cretans.

Of the mythical islands of the North Atlantic, marked on ancient maps as situated far in the west, note must be made first and foremost of *Antilia*. It seems that the inscription on the Pizigano map of 1367 is no longer regarded as the first mention of Antilia (419/I/465). Authentic mention of this island first appeared on maps in 1424. There is evidence that a Portuguese ship visited this island in 1430 (149/72). Antilia is frequently described as a large island situated between 37° and 40°N (1508 map).

On the Piri Reis map of 1513 it is located near the equator. Piri Reis wrote that it was uninhabited and had many animals and birds. We cannot agree with Hennig (419/IV/294) that the Antilia of Piri Reis may be identified with the islands discovered by Columbus; on a Piri Reis map a Turkish admiral separately points out the shore of Antilia discovered in 1492 (the year of Columbus' voyage). During his voyages Columbus never reached the equator.

Antilia is very frequently confused with the legendary *Island of the Seven Cities*. It is interesting to note that Martin Behaim, the German navigator and geographer (149/144), says that Antilia was visited by a Spanish ship in 1414. If Hennig is right in dating the appearance of Antilia on maps not earlier than 1424, the reference then can only be to the Island of the Seven Cities.

The legendary island (or islands) of *St. Brendan*, named in honour of the Irish abbot who died in 577, is shown on many ancient maps. The name most probably comes from a Christianised version of the ancient Irish saga about the travels of Moeldune. The greatly distorted and embellished story about this voyager deals perhaps not with some presently lost islands but with a visit to existing islands and even the shore of North America. St. Brendan's Island is located west of the Canaries in such a late document as a map published in 1598. It is similarly located on a map dated 1275 (149/89).

It seems to us that the Island of the Seven Cities has some relation to sections of the North Atlantic Ridge where pteropods are being brought to light, while Antilia was one of the islands of the submarine Equatorial Archipelago (for example, where fresh-water diatoms were discovered), although atlantologists usually link it up with more southerly parts of the North Atlantic Ridge proper.

Of the other regions of recent considerable subsidences note must be made of the southern part of the North Sea (212), which was dry land during the glacial period. The shallowest part of that sea, the Dogger Bank, was undoubtedly land not very long ago, this being proved by the finding of various artifacts and even human remains. Its average depth does not exceed 20 metres. According to F. Netolizki (82), when Atlantis was in the process of subsidence this bank was 60 metres above the present sea level, i.e., it was a low-lying island. Netolizki reaches this conclusion on the basis of a rate of subsidence of about 5 metres per millennium. The size of Heligoland diminished substantially during the period of recorded history. Near that island J. Spanuth (100) found the remains of an ancient settlement on the sea floor. He identifies this settlement as the capital of Atlantis! Evidently, as Hennig (419/I/193) supposes, *Abalus*, the Amber island of antique authors, was situated in the region of the North Sea, perhaps west of Schleswig-Holstein. He reasonably says that geological data rule out identifying Abalus with Heligoland, and comes to the conclusion that Abalus is non-existent today.

Strabo [VII, 2, 1] writes that the Cimbri, a Germanic tribe, were forced to leave their homeland by floods and destructive irregular tides, in whose existence, he, Strabo, did not believe. Possibly these irregular (non-periodic) tides were tsunamis caused by tectonic subsidences and that they flooded the homeland of the Cimbri. Strabo tells us that in defending themselves against these terrible tides the Cimbri even fought them in the open sea with weapons. Quoting

Ephorus, a Greek historian who wrote in about 340 B.C., he says that the Celts, too, were compelled to leave their homeland because their settlements were flooded. These floods started a wave of migration, which ended with the invasion of Italy by the Cimbri and the Teutons in the 2nd century B.C. In Italy they were crushed by the Romans.

Radiocarbon dating (620a) along the southern shore of the North Sea made it possible to establish the date of three main transgressions of this sea in the Holocene: the first was in 8000-7650 B.C., the second in 5500-2500 B.C. (climatic optimum) and the third began in about the year 300 B.C. and has not yet ended. The subsidence of Thule Island as well as the destruction of the homeland of the Cimbri and the Celts are possibly linked up with the maximum reached by the latter transgression.

All available data point to the fact that *tectonic movements substantially influenced the destiny of the peoples living along the Atlantic*.

It is our opinion that *we have every reason for assuming the possibility that in the North Atlantic individual islands and banks had subsided in the period of recorded history and that these subsidences were cataclysms. This explains the failure to identify some of the mythical islands mentioned in folk legends and by antique authors; some of these islands might have been inhabited.*

Chapter Thirteen

NORTH ATLANTIC FLOOR

In order to understand the geological history of the Atlantic we must have data on the nature of its floor and bottom sediments. Regrettably very little has been done in the way of investigating the rocks and bottom sediments in the area of the surmised subsidence of Atlantis. To date no oceanographic expedition has set itself questions linked up with the problem of Atlantis. This also concerns seismic and gravimetric investigations of the thickness of the Earth's crust.

A. SEISMIC AND GRAVIMETRIC INVESTIGATIONS

H. M. Field (528) believed that in the Atlantic the Earth's crust comprised sunken ancient sediments. B. Gutenberg (244/337) likewise assumed that this may be a region with a thin continental crust and that granite may be absent. S. I. Bubnov (208/162) accepted the existence of a thin sialic layer.

Some years ago E. A. Savarensky, O. N. Solovyova and A. P. Lazareva (373), who studied group velocities of Rayleigh waves for a number of earthquakes in the Atlantic, came to the conclusion that in the North Atlantic the Earth's crust is sooner single-layered with a thickness averaging about 25-30 kilometres.

M. Ewing (525a) points out that according to available data the layer of sediments is from 2,000 to 3,000 metres thick in the North American, Argentine and other basins of the Atlantic, and less than 50-100 metres in the Pacific and the Indian Ocean. The reason for this great disparity still remains to be elucidated. It seems to us that the reason lies in the different levels of oceanisation: a much larger area of continental land was eroded and swallowed by the Atlantic Ocean than by the other oceans; besides this took place much later than in other regions of the World Ocean.

Before proceeding with a description of the results of seismic investigations of the thickness and nature of the rock layers on the Atlantic floor, we must take into account the latest data obtained by F. Birch (465; also see Chapter Seven) on the substantial rise of the velocity of longitudinal waves when pressure is increased. In the light of this data, former conclusions regarding the nature of rocks corresponding to various velocities must be radically revised, and, in the context of many of these data, a close examination may show that the theory about their granite or basalt nature is untenable.

For our purposes the western North Atlantic is much less interesting than the eastern part, and we shall therefore not go beyond briefly mentioning it.* The Bermuda Rise and the Caribbean Sea are of some interest.

The Bermuda Islands are a region of considerable subsidences, which exceed the magnitude of the eustatic fluctuations of the ocean level during the glacial period. Weathered volcanic rocks, brought to the surface by boring, showed that these islands subsided at least 290 metres (209/259). In the Pleistocene there was volcanic activity and the shore line changed at least four times (273/149; 622). Investigations of the thickness of the Earth's crust at the eastern edge of the Bermuda Rise, at a depth of 2,220 metres, revealed that there the sedimentary rock layer (with a wave diffusion velocity of 4.04 km/sec) is 2.68 kilometres deep. Underlying it is a layer with a wave diffusion velocity of 5.36 km/sec (518). J. L. Worzel and M. Talwani (709) found that at the seamounts near the Bermuda Islands the surface of the Mohorovicic discontinuity passes at a depth of 20 kilometres, but in the adjoining regions of the ocean its depth is only about 10 kilometres.

Seismic investigations of the Caribbean Sea (518, 717) have shown that in it oceanic type sections of the Earth's crust alternate with continental type sections. Interesting results have been obtained by M. Talwani, G. H. Sutton and J. L. Worzel (683); they found that beneath Puerto Rico Island the Earth's crust is about 30 kilometres thick, but lower, in the Puerto Rico Trough, it proved to be unexpectedly very thick; there the surface of the Mohorovicic dis-

---

* For details about the western North Atlantic see 273 and 518/300.

continuity passes at a depth of 20 kilometres; moreover, they discovered five layers of sediments and rock with longitudinal wave diffusion velocities of 1.54, 2.1, 3.8, 5.6 and 7.0 km/sec.

Back in 1926, after comparing the structure of the Virgin Islands and the Greater Antilles (Cuba and, in particular, Puerto Rico), Meyerhof (323/504) pointed out that they are the eroded remains of a once monolithic but now faulted land mass, whose platform is an extension of the Pliocene surface of Puerto Rico Island. This brought him round to the conclusion that the abyssal fault trough at this island took shape before the Pliocene. There is a very interesting communication that the remains of fossil mammals on the islands of Anguilla and St. Martin are an indication of these islands' recent link with South America.

R. C. Mitchell (616), who studied the lithology and sediment formation in the region of the Antilles and the Caribbean Sea, believes that *the ablation region supplying material for the formation of rocks was somewhere in the eastern part of the Caribbean. The present islands in that region were evidently once arranged round a sunken continent, which emerged in the Mesozoic, or in the Triassic at the earliest.* J. Butterlin (480, 481) likewise holds that continental conditions might have existed in this area.

If it is taken into consideration that andesites, which can be regarded as the product of granite assimilation by basalts, are the typical igneous rock of the Antilles, and also the fact that rocks with a wave diffusion velocity corresponding sooner to granites (354; 445) have been discovered on the elevations and pedestals of the islands, we shall find that here we have a fine example of the incipient absorption of sial by sima, with the assimilation of granites by basalts and their conversion into andesites. The lowest layer, where the diffusion velocity is slower than in the mantle material, evidently consists of mixed material.

The largest number of stations in the region of the North Atlantic Ridge was probed by J. I. and M. Ewing (518/305-309; 560). They postulate the olivine-basalt nature of the ridge, taking as their point of departure general considerations on the link of oceanic volcanic activity with outpourings of basaltic lavas. On this basis they identify the upper layer of the ridge, where the mean longitudinal wave diffusion velocity is only 5.15 km/sec, with basalt (sic!) rocks. The deeper layer has a velocity of 7,21 km/sec, but here and there the velocity drops to 6.2-6.3 km/sec, while in the adjoining abyssal areas there are places where the velocity rises to about 8.0 km/sec. If we take into account the latest works of F. Birch[*] (465), we shall find that at the pressures to which the ridge, lying at a depth of several kilometres, is exposed not all of the Ewings' interpretations conform to reality. *For the upper layer, which is 1-5 kilometres thick, the prevailing wave diffusion velocity of 5.15 km/sec is much too*

---

[*] See Chapter Seven.

low to indicate the presence of basalt or even granite; it sooner corresponds to compact sedimentary rock of the schist or limestone type; it may be volcanic tuff but data on their velocities are not available and, besides, these porous rocks could have been formed only subaerially. We feel that *if the upper layer of the North Atlantic Ridge is composed of consolidated and metamorphosed sedimentary rocks of the limestone or marble type (as well as of volcanic tuff), the surface of the ridge, when it was subaerial, must have been greatly eroded and that it must have had sharply pronounced small and large forms of topography with considerable amplitudes making it resemble broken terrain of the karst type.* It seems to us that the observed topography of the North Atlantic Ridge fits this description.

There can be no serpentinites here either, because for them the velocity is much too low (at the ridge's depth of subsidence the velocity must be above 6.0 km/sec). The deeper layer, which in some places of the ridge has a velocity of 6.2-6.3 km/sec, cannot consist of basalt-gabbro, which at this depth would have had a velocity of at least 7.0 km/sec. The observed velocities fit either granite or serpentinites. The velocity of only the lowest layer (7.2 km/sec) fits gabbro (basalt).

The data given by M. N. Hill (560) for the eastern sides at 46.5°N 27°W speak in favour of the non-basaltic nature of the upper layers of rocks of the North Atlantic Ridge. In these places the unconsolidated sediments are only 130 metres thick. Underlying them is a layer of rock, 1-2 kilometres thick with a longitudinal wave diffusion velocity of only 3.6 km/sec. These are probably consolidated sedimentary rocks. They are underlied by rocks whose wave diffusion velocity (up to 6.4 km/sec) fits serpentinites or granites. But in adjoining areas this layer has a much lower velocity—only 5.7 km/sec—and its lower boundary has not been established. It is difficult to judge the nature of this layer; it may be composed of gneiss, which at these depths may have a velocity of somewhat less than 6.0 km/sec.

The discovery of layers of heavy clay in the southern part of the ridge (759) is evidence in favour of the above considerations.

In an earlier work J. and M. Ewing (518) used notions about isostatic equilibrium for their assumption that material with a wave diffusion velocity of 7.3 km/sec forms "roots" about 25-30 kilometres deep beneath the ridge. But in a later work (776), in which they sought proof for the convection currents theory, they rejected the "root" surmise and maintained that this region continues deep into the mantle for a distance of 400-800 kilometres. Yet a study of earthquakes on the ridge makes it clear that their epicentres lie at a depth of only 30-40 kilometres! It is also strange that this "knife" in the mantle covers only a narrow zone: the MedianValley ± the ridge crest, on the sides of which the crest is said to be purely oceanic and the velocity at the Mohorovicic discontinuity surface, we are told, rises to the normal 8.0-8.5 km/sec. As regards the crustal structure beneath the ridge slopes, the sedimentary rocks overlie a stratum 0-5 kilometres thick showing a velocity of 3.0-5.8 km/sec. The authors believe that this stratum is composed of "modified" (weathered?) basalt. The amplitude of this stratum is much too high for an accurate identification of its nature, but it is most probably metamorphosed sedimentary rock. Below it is a layer with a velocity of 6.8-7.6 km/sec; in some places it has the shape of a wedge. Apparently, this is real basalt. The general aim of the work is to prove the absence of the Mohorovicic discontinuity beneath the ridge (which rose from the mantle by convection currents!)

On the basis of Table 5, which gives the longitudinal wave velocities in the ridge, one does indeed find that the Mohorovicic discontinuity crops out only in a few cases and the data fluctuate within fairly wide limits. It seems to us that *observations have been inadequate for any hasty conclusions.*

It should be noted that seismic observations of earthquakes and not of weak artificial explosions reveal anomalous curves running across the western side of the North Atlantic Ridge and southern Greenland. These curves do not dovetail with any theoretical curve for the horizontally-stratified structure of the Earth's crust (784).

Gravimetrical investigations yield a somewhat different picture. F. A. Veining-Meinez (694) found that the Azores Plateau has a positive gravity anomaly of +200-300 milligals; in the adjoining basins the anomaly rises to +413-424 milligals (283/38,56). The ridge itself is characterised by weak positive anomalies within the limit of +30-50 and even 0 milligal. Beneath the Median Valley the anomaly becomes negative, reaching —3 and even —20 milligals (417/128; 716). Gravimetrical data have given A. G. Gainanov and P. A. Stroyev (793) grounds for assuming that beneath mid-oceanic ridges the thickness of the Earth's crust increases to 12-25 kilometres, that *"seismic observations, as in the case of those conducted in the North Atlantic Ridge, give a smaller figure for the thickness of the Earth's crust than gravimetrical observations* (my italics.—N.Z). This difference is probably due to a change in the density of the matter in the upper mantle beneath the Mid-Atlantic Ridge, or, let us add, to a systematic error in the measurements, especially as seismic measurements may err ±1.5 kilometres, as the authors themselves point out.

Although available data are insufficient for a final judgement, *the values of the anomalies sooner approach the specifications known for some continental but not oceanic regions.*

Recently there has been increasing support for this surmise. In the chapter "Some Features of Oceans" we have, for example, mentioned the views of J. W. Kerr (795), who believes continental remnants underlie the median ridges. B. D. Loncarevic's (794) report of the *discovery of granites and metamorphic rocks near the Median Valley* likewise brings one round to this surmise. Somewhat different results are given in his latest paper, namely, that according to F. Aumento *the longitudinal wave diffusion in the upper layers of the ridge (5.0-5.8 km/sec) is equal to that of basalts*: the 12 basalt samples obtained from the ridge had a density of 2.58-2.95 g/cm^3, and laboratory tests showed a velocity of 4.82-5.88 km/sec (average —5. 18 km/sec), which when the pressure was increased rose correspondingly to 5.34 and 6.30 km/sec. However, *these results differ sharply from the data obtained by all other investigators* (see Table 3 in the *Appendices*) *and therefore require weighty confirmation.*

The Ewings regard the Reykjanes Ridge as an extension of the North Atlantic Ridge because their observations have shown the structure of the Earth's crust beneath both ridges to be similar. Beneath the North Atlantic Ridge the thickness of the sediments fluctuates from 0.1 to 0.8 kilometre, but beneath Reykjanes Ridge it is more uniform: 0.4-0.8 kilometre. The "granite" or "pseudogranite" layer (longitudinal wave diffusion velocity of 5.60-5.83 km/sec) is 3-4 kilometres thick beneath Reykjanes Ridge. Beneath it is rock with a longitudinal wave diffusion velocity of 7.24-7.63 m/sec.

The Ewings (518/303) give the following mean data for the eastern Atlantic Ocean (east of the Mid-Atlantic Ridge), which is not as deep as the western part of the ocean.

With an average depth of about 4.5 kilometres this part of the ocean has a sediment layer of a little over one kilometre thick, and beneath it is a "basalt" oceanic crust nearly five kilometres thick, in which the longitudinal wave diffusion velocity averages 6.52 km/sec. Underlying this crust is a substratum where the mean wave velocity does not correspond to that of pure mantle matter because it is substantially lower—7.81 km/sec. We feel that the Ewings do not have sufficient data to substantiate the above mean figures. For example, the regions close to the shores of Europe, particularly in the north, are obviously of a continental nature. The observations conducted by M. N. Hill (425) show that there is a thick layer of sediments (1.9-3 kilometres) lying on a "granite" layer 2.7-3.4 kilometres thick in the eastern North Atlantic (53°50′N 18°40′W) approximately 1,000 kilometres west of Ireland and somewhat west of the Porcupine Bank. Beneath it is a "basalt" layer with a longitudinal wave diffusion velocity of 6.3 km/sec. On this question N. M. Hill and A. Laughton (426) write that the fluctuating thickness of the sediments and the broken topography of some sectors of the floor of the eastern Atlantic show that *in typically abyssal regions there were mountain-building processes on the same scale as on the continent. Possibly in these sectors there are not only volcanic but also folded submarine mountains* (my italics—*N.Z.*). Somewhat above this they note: Further experiments must be conducted in order to decide if here we have a submerged continental region or a region that is intermediate between continents and the deep ocean.

A study of the structure of the Earth's crust in the region of Cruiser Seamount by J. L. Worzel and M. Talwani (709) has shown that in this region there is a gravitational anomaly and that the Mohorovicic discontinuity surface lies at a depth of more than 20 kilometres, while in the adjoining parts of the ocean floor it is to be found at a depth of 10 kilometres.

While reporting the discovery of this new seamount, which is part of the Horseshoe Archipelago, Laughton, Hill and Allan (590) point out that for the upper 450 metres the wave velocity is about 2 km/sec, down to a depth of 2,200 metres it rises to 3.7 km/sec, and deeper it grows to 5.3 km/sec. This velocity does not fit basalts: in our opinion, the structure of the Earth's crust in this region is closer to that of the continent.

During the Swedish oceanographic expedition on the ship *Albatross*, F. Weibull (699), who was a member of that expedition, obtained seismograms of one of the sections of the floor between the Madeiras and the North Atlantic Ridge, according to which this region has an extremely thick layer of sediments—nearly 3,538 metres. If we assume that these sediments are of purely abyssal origin, we shall find that to take shape they would have required about 500 million years, a period of time, as H. Pettersson states, which does not command trust. Although Weibull's data have been contested by representatives of the American school, they are evidently trustworthy, especially as Hill and his associates (425; 426) have shown that in the eastern North Atlantic there are sediment layers up to 2,960 metres thick. Moreover, according to data obtained by H. Berckhemer (204), the thickness of the sedimentary rock layer, determined through a study of seismic waves from earthquakes that occurred in the region of the North Atlantic Ridge (epicentre at 30°N 42.5°W) along the section between the epicentre and Lisbon (so-called Route V), averages 1.2 kilometres, while in other places it drops to 0.5 kilometre (according to data obtained by Soviet scientists, the thickness of the sediments in the Madeira region averages 1.4 kilometres). And Berckhemer makes an interesting admission: *"The great thickness of the sediments discovered along Route V possibly indicates the presence in this region of erosion products from the Mid-Atlantic Ridge"* (my italics—*N. Z.*). Coming, as it does, from a staff member of the Lamont Observatory this is a very valuable remark. (See Table 5, Appendix I).

British scientists investigated the region between Madeira and the Cape Verde Islands (Canary Basin), with the centre at 29°15'N 25°5'W and found that the Mohorovicic discontinuity surface lies at a depth of 13.2 kilometres. Over it is a rock layer 5.2 kilometres thick with a wave velocity of about 6.3-6.8 km/sec. Still higher is a stratum two kilometres thick with a wave velocity of 4.1-4.5 km/sec, and overlying it is a thick layer of sedimentary rock.

It will thus be seen that an essential difference is coming to light between the western and eastern Atlantic, this being particularly true of its northern half. B. Gutenberg (244) notes that *the Mediterranean zone of earthquakes links up with the epicentre zone of the North Atlantic Ridge but does not cross it and does not link up with the Antilles region, which belongs to the Pacific seismic zone.* In this connection let us recall that there is an essential difference in the nature of the lava discharged by the volcanoes of these two zones—in the Atlantic zone it is basaltic lava, while in the Pacific zone (including the Antilles) it is andesite lava. Small wonder, therefore, that when J. P. Rothe (656) studied seismic activity in the Atlantic, particularly in the South Atlantic, he came to the conclusion that the Mid-Atlantic Ridge is the natural boundary, as it were, between the eastern part of the ocean floor, supposedly composed primarily of sialic rock (which later was proved to be incorrect), and the western part, composed mainly of simatic rock.

In most cases even adherents of the limited ocean permanency theory have to recognise the appreciable difference in the nature of the floor of the North Atlantic west and east of the North Atlantic Ridge. For example, I. Y. Furman (28) writes: "While maintaining the view that the main elements of oceanic basins are constant and stable, it must be considered that in the Atlantic Ocean such a stable downwarp was the western, relatively submarine ridge, while the eastern downwarp underwent substantial changes."

According to contemporary geophysical data, the structure of the Earth's crust beneath the abyssal basins in the eastern Atlantic does not, evidently, differ from the crust structure in the western Atlantic. But there is a noteworthy difference in the case of the shallower parts, a difference that is particularly striking in the northern half; *in the eastern half of the North Atlantic the floor is more continental than in the western half.* In our opinion *there are many facts to show that the eastern half is of younger origin. From this angle, Rothe's view of the role of the Mid-Atlantic Ridge as a natural barrier between the two halves retains its validity, although today it must be given a somewhat different content, i.e., it must be regarded as the boundary of the eastern (Eurasian-African) continental massif.*

B. STUDIES OF BEDROCK SAMPLES

Let us now examine the fragmentary data at our disposal on the actual composition of the bedrock of the Atlantic floor, particularly the region of the North Atlantic Ridge interesting us most. Apparently the earliest find was made in 1885 when the expedition on the ship *Talisman* obtained bedrock samples containing trilobites from a depth of 4,225 metres at 42°21′N 17°12′W [as well as at 42°19′N 21°17′W and 44°20′N 17°12′W, according to other sources (517/232), but all in the region of the abyssal Iberian Basin]. In that same year, 1885, Edwards assumed that the trilobites were transported by drift ice. R. Furon (531), however, linked this find up with the existence of the Mid-Atlantic Ridge as far back as the early Paleozoic, considering that floating ice could not sail so far south—they would have been obstructed by the Gulf Stream. D. B. Ericson, M. Ewing, G. Wollin and B. C. Heezen (517/232) support the view about the erratic nature of the finds, pointing out that material of clearly glacial origin had been found at 46°55′N 18°35′W, i.e., somewhat to the north of the spot where the *Talisman* expedition obtained its samples. In our opinion, *all these finds are effectively explained by the existence of Atlantis, when a powerful cold current carrying drift ice with erratic boulders over a relatively long distance to the south flowed past its eastern edge.* Naturally, if we accept the view about the unchangeableness of the Gulf Stream and the non-subaerial origin of the North Atlantic Ridge, this opinion will seem to be unfounded.

Also interesting was the finding in 1898 (according to some sources, in 1858, a date which is more probable) of a piece of fresh-looking vitreous lava (*tachylyte*). It was found during an attempt to raise a sundered section of a trans-Atlantic cable north of the Azores in the region of the North Atlantic Ridge (47°N 29°40′W) from a depth of 3,100 metres. This find remained shelved until 1913, when P. Termier (26; 115) drew attention to it. Studying similar lava from the Island of Martinique, which brought to light the marked difference between lava that solidifies slowly in the air and lava that solidifies quickly in water, he drew the conclusion that lava yielding tachylyte could have formed only in the absence of spressure and not under water. He estimated the age of the found tachylyte as approximately 15,000 years because, in his view, older tachylyte would have crystallised. On the find itself, Termier (177/132) writes: "One inevitably arrives at the conclusion that the land area that was situated some 900 kilometres north of the Azores and, perhaps, embraced these islands, subsided into the sea in a period so relatively recent that geologists call it 'real'; indeed, for us, contemporaries, it is as though it happened yesterday."

The assertion of some critics (119/340) that this piece of tachylyte was transported (how? by whom?) from a volcano in the Azores does not hold water. Firstly, the spot where it was found is 900 kilometres away from the Azores, and it is incredible that it could have been transported such a long distance across rugged terrain. Secondly, the cable simply broke off a piece of the parent rock, thus accounting for its fresh appearance.

The views and conclusions of Termier, particularly in connection with his assumption of the reality of Plato's Atlantis, were sharply criticised by many scientists, especially by the American C. Schuchert (96; 97), who claimed there were many weak points in Termier's theory.

Some of Schuchert's objections (for example, about terraces) are not convincing, but his remarks that a vitreous structure takes shape sooner under the influence of pressure and that tachylyte could have formed on the ocean floor as well merit attention. In fact, rapid cooling frequently leads to the preservation of an amorphous, vitreous state. Properly speaking, the question of the origin of tachylyte remains unsettled. Similar types of volcanic rock fragments were later found on the crest of Reykjanes Ridge, where samples of volcanic tuff were brought to the surface in addition to volcanic glass and basalt.

V. M. Lavrov (286a) reports that samples of silica- and alumina-rich basalts have been obtained in the region of the active submarine Mikhail Lomonosov volcano between Fayal and Flores islands (about 39°N 29°50′W) from a depth of 430-750 metres. Still richer (up to 58 per cent silica) trachyandesite glass was obtained from a depth of 1,300 metres at Station No. 263 (38°55′N 28°34′W). Unquestionably, this is sial rock!

On the whole, according to published data, the samples obtained in the region of the North Atlantic Ridge were mainly specimens of olivine gabbro. It will be noted that experiments have shown that at a temperature of 500° and a pressure of not less than 10,000 atmospheres basaltic glass crystallises into gabbro (268). Basalt, serpentine and diabase have also been discovered. West of the range at a depth of 4,110 metres the samples consisted chiefly of serpentine; one of the samples was a piece of tremolite asbestos with nearly six-inch long fibres. With regard to this find M. Ewing (519/291) wrote: *such rock is generally considered typical of continents and not of the ocean bottom* (my italics—*N. Z.*). O. Mellis (610) informs us of an interesting find—pieces of gabbro weighing about 636 grams brought to the surface in a core 600 kilometres east of the Bermuda Islands (29°21′N 58°09′W) in the region of an abyssal plain lying at a depth of 5,450 metres. This spot is near a basin slope with a very strange geomorphological structure; the northern part of the basin has a very rugged and extraordinarily broken relief.

A number of the rock samples obtained near and from the slopes of the North Atlantic Ridge by the American expedition on the ship *Atlantis* were studied by J. Shand (666). They came from adjoining sectors situated between 30-34°N 40-45°W from depths ranging from 1,500 to 4,600 metres. Most of them are pieces of gabbro-basalt (with and without olivine) and serpentine.

Some of them attract notice. For example, the only sample of diabase was obtained at Station No. 20. But a more interesting find was that of a piece of weathered basalt at Station No. 8. It was brown in colour and greatly modified, chiefly at the expense of olivine. Hydrous ferric oxide and zeolites were discovered. "Stale" basalt was also obtained at Station No. 20; it had no olivine in it. There were greenish products of disintegration. All the serpentine specimens showed a high level of hydration and other changes. But in most cases the basalt looked exceedingly fresh. Shand considers that the basalt on the ridge has no mineralogical or other features to distinguish it from land basalt. On the other hand, with regard to the serpentines, he considers that they are older than the basalt. *It seems to us that the occurrence of weathered basalt favours the theory that the North Atlantic Ridge had a subaerial existence.*

Very interesting data were obtained as a result of the dredging of the ridge slopes in a sector at 22-23°N 44°30'-46°15'W (759). The drag brought not pelagic sediments but gravel, pebbles and sand of terrigenous origin, and it was established that these materials formed *in situ*. In addition to fresh basalt and diabase, the samples included greenstone rock and considerable quantities of weathered basalt. This basalt was greatly modified, cracked and laminated. It was not established if this "weathered" basalt originated in subaerial or submarine conditions; however, we feel that the cracks and the lamination indicate its subaerial origin, *especially as the finds included conglomerates and rounded basaltic rubble in parent rock, also containing shallow-water shells*. In view of the fact that the above samples came from different spots in the named locality from depths of more than 3,000 metres, *the conclusion must be drawn that the ridge underwent a considerable subsidence (of about 3,000 metres)*.

Further study of the samples, particularly of the greenstone rocks, made it evident that *the North Atlantic Ridge is formed not only of basalt but also of diabase and greenstone rocks* (781). An analysis yielded the following data:

Composition	Greenstone Rock %	Basalt %
SiO_2	49.7—50.8	49.1
Al_2O_3	15.3	15.3
$Fe_2O_3 + FeO$	7.2—9.3	10.9
MgO	8.9—9.3	8.0
CaO	6.4—7.3	10.6
Na_2O	2.9—4.5	2.9

Hence, it follows that greenstone rocks are somewhat less basic than basalt. On this point the authors write: "If greenstone rocks similar to those found on the 22nd parallel prove to be a quantitatively important component of the Mid-Atlantic Ridge, the interpretation of seismic, magnetic and gravimetric data relative to the ridge cannot be founded on a model presupposing the presence solely of fresh basalt rocks, serpentine and non-serpentinised ultrabasic rock in a simple pancake sequence of layers." The authors believe that greenstone rocks play the principal role in the ridge structure.

V. M. Lavrov (739) likewise reports interesting data. It was found that although clastic material consisting of minerals and ultra-basic rock debris and the products of their metamorphism (serpentines) predominates in the Romanche Trench, it is completely non-existent in the bottom sediments along the fringe of the trench. Moreover, it does not occur in the sediments of the adjoining basins and intermontane depressions.

Rounded granite and sedimentary rock boulders with characteristic scratches indicating their glacial origin have been found in some places along the eastern slope of the North Atlantic Ridge. These boulders were evidently transported by drift ice during the glacial period. *Let us draw attention to the striking fact that there have been no reports about erratic boulders having been found on the western slopes of the North Atlantic Ridge.*

In addition to erratic boulders, the finds include some solidified oozy "stones" that are much too soft and weak to withstand compression caused by the movement of glaciers or transportation by drift ice (520/618). They are probably of local origin.

Exceedingly interesting data on samples of rock obtained by a drag from the Median Valley north of the Azores (46.5°N 27°W) are reported by M. N. Hill (560). These were fragments of limestone and acid igneous rock. But contrary to expectations based on general assumptions of the nature of the ridge, not a single sample of basalt or other igneous rock was obtained. Coarse-grained fractions of some of the cores brought to the surface from the floor of the valley contained particles of gneiss, which gave grounds for assuming that these rocks are of British, Iceland and Greenland origin and that they were transported by drift ice. Indeed, the latitude where the investigated section of the Median Valley is located allows for the penetration of drift ice, but this can be hindered by the Gulf Stream. However, as Hill points out, photographs taken of the floor to elucidate this question showed the presence on the slopes of the valley of considerable quantities of angular rock fragments and debris which do not by any means look like products brought by drift ice. This, Hill writes, is testimony that *the studied samples are of local origin and have not been transported from elsewhere. This forces us to ponder the question whether the Median Valley is not really a rift valley. Is the rock of which the upper part of the ridge consists more acid than is now supposed? After all, as we have already stated, the longitudinal wave diffusion velocity in the upper layers of the North Atlantic Ridge likewise does not favour the theory that these layers are composed of basalts.*

On the other hand, J. Reitzell (645) has reported that yellow ooze and a large number of sizable fragments of volcanic glass were raised from the floor of a small valley 50 kilometres northeast of the Median Valley (51°18′N 29°35′W), where an abnormally high warm current was discovered. He thinks that these finds are traces of contemporary or Pleistocene volcanic activity.

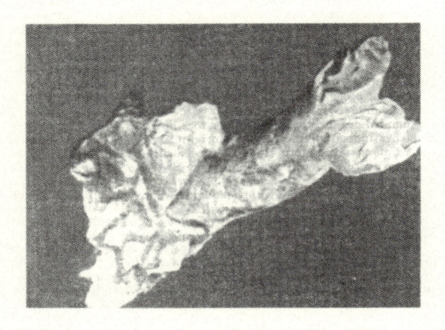
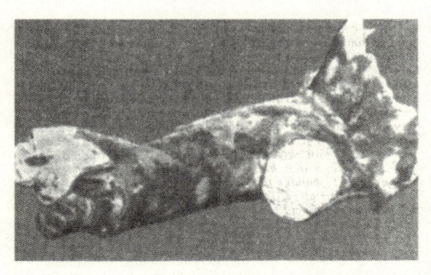

Coral fragments from the North Atlantic Ridge. Depth 2,500 metres.
Photographs by N. N. Yerofeyev and V. M. Lavrov (241/53)

Loncarevic (794) points out that according to Aumento, the rock samples from the Median Valley and from adjacent areas situated at 45°-45°30′N and 28°-28°30′W proved to be alkaline tholeitic basalts with a high alumina content. On the other hand, the basalts obtained farther west showed unexpected results. Loncarevic writes: *"On Bald Mountain, 35 miles west of the Median Valley repeated sampling located an unexpected occurrence of granitic and metamorphic rocks.* Similar rocks, dredged previously from the ocean floor, have always been interpreted as being ice-rafted. Bottom photographs of the seamount indicate a markedly different terrain; *the seamount itself has also a different orientation and shape from known volcanoes in the area.* Studies are in progress to account for the presence of these rocks, and for the unusual features of the seamount."

Some interest centres on rocks discovered on islands of the South Atlantic Ridge. T. F. W. Barth (188) states his considerations regarding the composition and evolution of the magma of this ridge. These considerations are based on a study of crystallisation differentiation and, mainly, on a comparison of selective analyses of basalt. Regrettably, he says nothing about the conditions under which the sial rocks (rhyolite, granite, andesite, gneiss) were found or about their origin. Such rocks were discovered on all the islands of the South Atlantic Ridge. It is also worth mentioning that quartz sand and other minerals of continental origin were obtained by the expedition on the ship *Gauss* (209/271) from the western slopes of the submarine Walvis Ridge, which links the South Atlantic Ridge up with the shores of Africa. *It is our opinion that the finding of quartz, granite and so forth on South Atlantic islands is testimony in favour of the assumption that sialic materials had participated in the build-up of the South Atlantic Ridge.*

S. K. Gipp (236) writes that samples of rock debris, gravel and soil (including *broken shells, which is an indication that there was shallow water*) were obtained in the region of the Mikhail Lomonosov Seamount from depths of 420-751 metres. Among the studied samples there were pieces of dark-grey vesicular basalt, which looked very fresh. Other finds included scoria, caked and mixed with foraminifera ooze. This too favours the view about very recent submarine volcanic activity and about the subsidence of seamounts.

A piece of strongly disintegrated coral of the *Oculinidae* genus, which was covered with a layer of black manganese oxide was raised by the German oceanological expedition on the ship *Altair* from a seamount of the same name (44°33′N 45°33′W) at a depth of 1,300 metres (496). J. G. Helmcke presumed that the presence of coral is an indication that this seamount was once subaerial. Similar samples were obtained in various spots on the North Atlantic Ridge; this is mentioned casually by M. Ewing (519/286). Farther north, at 56°16′N 33°25′W, the expedition on the ship *Mikhail Lomonosov*, using a steel cable, brought to the surface, together with bedrock, a piece of dead alcyonarian coral of the *Isis* genus from a depth of 2,500 metres. This piece was directly linked to the bedrock, thereby incontestably proving that it was not an accidental find. *"Insofar as corals grow only in shallow water, it may be assumed that the North Atlantic Ridge subsided from the water surface to a great depth"* (my italics—*N.Z.*), N. N. Gorsky concludes (241/53). *Consequently, in this area at least, the North Atlantic Ridge sank to a depth of about 2,000 metres. But these are warmth-loving corals, and this fact favours the assumption that at one time the Gulf Stream flowed farther west of its present route, evidently sweeping along the western slopes of the then subaerial North Atlantic Ridge.*

This view has received confirmation in the investigations of S. K. Gipp, who writes that during the 1958 cruise of the oceanographic ship *Sedov* an attempt was made to obtain soil samples from a newly-discovered bank on the western fringe of the North Atlantic Ridge. The shallowest part of this bank was found to be 900 metres from the water surface. The position of the stations were: 35°58-59′N 40°19-20′W. No sediments were found at a depth of 1,300 metres; the samples contained several coral fragments and corallites covered with a thin layer of ferro-manganese oxide. However, some lime mud and coral fragments were obtained from a depth of 1,775 metres. Gipp notes that *the investigated bank is a coral reef that subsided not very long ago;* the facts leading to this conclusion are the exceedingly broken rock topography and the absence on it of a more or less thick layer of sediments.

Similarly interesting results were obtained during an investigation conducted on Atlantis Seamount (549). Parts of its summit were found to be covered with rock debris and pebbles, while elsewhere there was rippled sand. Similar ripples have been observed on the slopes (due to seismic activity?) of this seamount, particularly at a depth of 732 metres (northern slope). About a ton of flat and round pteropodan calcarous formations of enigmatic origin, called "sea biscuits",* was obtained from the summit of the seamount. With the help of radiocarbon dating it has been established that this sample of sea biscuit was 12,000 years old. *"The state of the lithification of the limestone suggests that it may have been lithified under subaerial conditions and that the seamount may have been an island within the past 12,000 years,"* the authors of the investigation conclude (my italics.—*N.Z.*).

Interesting finds on Great Meteor Seamount (roughly 30°N 28°W), situated more to the southeast, are reported by R. M. Pratt (640). Rock fragments, debris and pebbles were raised from the sides of this seamount at a depth of 650-713 metres. Among these finds attention is attracted by *a large fragment of coral reef limestone* (60×54 cm). Moreover, *there were fragments of continental sialic rock,* including coarse-grained rose granite (containing orthoclase,

---

* "Sea biscuits" are dealt with in some detail in Chapter Two.

quartz, biotite and plagioclase); schist containing garnet, quartz and biotite; medium-grained diorite, as well as three-inch pebbles of solid quartz. The photographs illustrating the paper show that these fragments do not give the impression of being either rounded pebbles or boulders: they are sooner clastic products. Neither are there traces of glacial striation. Fine limestone sand and dead corals were all that were found on the summit of the seamount. Lime mud and round pebbles of volcanic rock were obtained from the slopes.

However, photographs of the southern slope, taken at a depth of 512 metres, show the occurrence of large quantities of poorly sorted and practically unrounded rock debris. The deeper layers consist of massive rocks with spots of white sand. Photographs taken at a depth of 1,280 metres show the occurrence of limestone similar to the fragment raised with a dredge and, possibly, consisting of reef limestone. Pratt believes that the discovered sialic materials are most probably of erratic origin. If that is true they could not have been brought by modern drift ice. Although there have been reports of drift ice south of the Azores, the data obtained by Pratt from the International Ice Patrol indicates that there are no grounds for trusting these reports and assuming that considerable quantities of erratic material had been transported to the region of the seamount by modern ice. Consequently, such transportation, if it had taken place at all, might have been accomplished during the Pleistocene. The present location of the Gulf Stream rules out the penetration of the region of Great Meteor Seamount by drift ice.

But even during the Pleistocene, if, as many American investigators are inclined to believe, the Gulf Stream followed the same route as it does today, the position with regard to the penetration of drift into this region of the Atlantic could hardly have been different. We consider that *the finding of erratic materials at the foot of Great Meteor Seamount is further proof that a powerful north-to-south cold current flowed along the eastern shores of the then subaerial North Atlantic Ridge (Atlantis).* Furthermore, the presence of reef limestone to a depth of over 1,000 metres indicates that the seamount subsided to a depth of more than 1,000 metres. This means that in the same way as Atlantis Seamount, Great Meteor Seamount was a subaerial mountain like the entire plateau on which it stands. In addition, the finding at the foot of Great Meteor Seamount of sialic materials similar in appearance and composition to the materials found in the Median Valley insistently suggests that the question of the actual origin of such materials should be seriously studied and that they might be local.

Of similar interest are the data reported by A. Laughton, M. N. Hill and T. D. Allan (590) about some recently discovered mountains in the Horseshoe Archipelago (34°52′N 16°31′W) situated 276 kilometres north of the Madeiras. Well-rounded basalt pebbles have been obtained from the top of one of these mountains. But *a well-rounded (non-glacial!) boulder consisting of microcline granite measuring* 10×8×6 cm was obtained some two kilometres from the top at a depth of 1,435 metres. Many of the boulders and pebbles were coated with a layer of manganese oxide about 2 mm thick, which corresponds to an age of about 4,000-14,000 years. It must be noted that sialic rock fragments were found on Seine Bank located farther south, as far back as 1901 by a German Antarctic expedition (323/593). Taking into consideration the data, given above, on the structure of the Earth's crust in the region of the submarine Horseshoe Archipelago, we are of the opinion that *the Horseshoe Archipelago is a region which had subsided quite recently and that its structure is close to the continental type.*

The opinion of many geologists that the Iceland-Faeroe Rise is of sialic origin and that it was once subaerial is confirmed by the results of investigations conducted by Soviet oceanologists (218), who studied rock samples taken from the surface of the rise. Gravel, pebbles, rock debris and boulders occur almost throughout the rise. Gravel was found at a depth of 735 metres, and boulders even as deep as 940 metres. The rock samples that were found were basalt, diabase, gneissose granite, sandstone and limestone. This is testimony of the fact that *there are sialic materials in the structure of the Iceland-Faeroe Rise.*

L. Bertois and A. Guilcher (463)* have reported the results of their investigations in the region of Porcupine Bank. The clastic material contained granite, syenite, quartzite, metamorphic schist, ancient limestone and other rock of continental origin. Tertiary basalt was also found. It has been established that *many of these fragments were not brought by drift ice but came from a glacier that once covered the bank: they were eroded not by water but by ice.*

Interesting data indirectly confirming the probability of the geologically recent subaerial existence of presently submerged land between the North Atlantic Ridge and the Iberian Peninsula were obtained as a result of a study of rock and soil samples from the deepest parts of the European Basin. For example, a dredge brought coarse sand and rock fragments up from the surface (depth—5,300 metres) of the plain at the westernmost tip of the Iberian Basin (41°15′N 14°30′W), and samples of metamorphic rock, lava and limestone from Galicia Bank (49°30′N 11°53′W) from a depth of 700 metres (715). A. Cailleux (482) writes that from a depth of 4,225 metres, 600 kilometres from the shores of Galicia (44°20′N 17°11′W), a drag brought many quartz and limestone pebbles, the latter predominating. The pebbles looked quite fresh. The distance from the continent is much too great to enable us to assume that their occurrence is due to a submarine landslide. We must also rule out any suggestion that they are of glacial origin, because the rocks of which

---

* Regrettably, we were unable to get a copy of an earlier work by Bertois devoted to a study of the rocks and sediments of the Atlantic continental plateau (L. Bertois, *Annales de l'Institute océanographique*, 23, 1-63, 1946).

the pebbles consist are not of the kind usually carried by drift ice. There can be no question of their volcanic origin. Cailleux, is, therefore, puzzled about their origin.

C. BOTTOM SOIL AND SEDIMENTS

We must first make a general assessment of the sedimentation processes on the North Atlantic Ridge. In this we shall draw mainly upon the work of X. Le Pichon (777). Investigations over the past few years have made it amply apparent that relative to the thickness of sediments there are two basic zones: the crests with the Median Valley and the sides of the ridge. Generally, between 30°N and 30°S the total quantity of sediments on the ridge is not large, its thickness not exceeding several hundred metres. If the crests are excluded, the difference between some of the abyssal plains and the ridge will be found to be not very sharp. On the ridge sediments accumulate mostly in the depressions between elevations, frequently forming pockets. *As a rule, the sediments are very mobile*, this being due to the high seismic activity in the ridge, to frequent earthquakes. Therefore, *it would be logical to expect to find considerable quantities of sediments in the adjoining abyssal plains, but that, according to American investigators, is not the case* (525b). While this is more or less true in the case of the western basins, the same cannot be said about the eastern basins. A much more interesting observation is the one that refutes the assumption that along the edges of the ridge there must be an abnormally large accumulation of sediments from higher portions of the ridge (525b). Le Pichon (777) says that *this insignificant quantity of sediments is an indication that it corresponds to only a short period of the Cenozoic*. Sediments of not more than 12 metres thick have been discovered only in the Median Valley. Le Pichon believes they represent only several hundred millennia. Generally, all the sediments on the ridge, he says, are either of Pleistocene age or contemporary.

In the light of the above, attention must be drawn to the following. It is not easy to obtain a core from the ridge peaks or even from its slopes. There is always the possibility that the selected spot has little or no sediments at all. Success is achieved only when the core tube strikes a pocket. For that reason, the references by some critics (756a) to the fact that cores of 3.5-5 metres have been obtained from the ridge proves nothing. The tubes might have struck a pocket or a formerly subaerial gulf. This may be expected in view of the extremely rugged shoreline of Atlantis (a mountainous country with an extensively broken topography). The above-mentioned sedimentation on the ridge likewise contradicts the further assertions of the critics (756c) that sediments accumulate on the ridge's flat sections as well. As we have already stated, this is prevented by the high seismic activity in the ridge. Below we shall show how untenable are the assertions (756d) that the sediments on the crest and the slopes are mostly of pelagic biogenous origin. Sediments of this kind are practically non-existent on the crest, while on the slopes they are principally of terrigenous origin. In the Median Valley as well the sediments are of the same origin (759). If there are any pelagic sediments on the ridge they will be found to be nearly contemporary. It should be borne in mind that *the overwhelming majority of sediments found in cores and reported to be of Tertiary age were from abyssal plains.*

And now a few words about whether the data on the mean velocity of sedimentation (mainly biogenous) are applicable to sediments obtained from the ridge. It seems to us that here we risk a huge margin of error, especially if we use mean data for the entire ocean and if we postulate the extrapolation of results obtained for new and latest sediments to the depths of the ages. Firstly, the very frequent earthquakes set off very frequent landslides and the mixing of sediments. Secondly, when the methods of absolute chronology are used for dating oceanic sediments they are not free of error. For instance, radiocarbon dating is applicable to an age not above several tens of thousands of years; further extrapolation on its basis is not reliable. Other methods are complex and likewise not free of gross error. Some cases are cited by Le Pichon (777).

One of the first serious attempts to obtain a cross-section of the sediments on the North Atlantic Ridge was made by C. S. Piggot (637; 638), who studied a series of 13 cores taken along the line Halifax-Falmouth. One of these cores was obtained near the summit of the North Atlantic Ridge, and the others from each of its sides. On the western side, about 30 kilometres from the summit, the sediments contained remains of warmth-loving foraminifera of the species now inhabiting the Gulf Stream. This indicates that here sedimentation was slow and more or less homogeneous. A completely different picture is given by the sediments from the eastern side of the ridge, likewise taken at a distance of about 30 kilometres from the summit. They contained thick layers of sand and gravel along with remains of cold-loving foraminifera. Here sedimentation obviously took place during a period when the climate was colder than today—in the period of the last glaciation. In this connection J. Bourcart (209/266) writes: "Evidently the cores did not reach the base of ancient Quaternary (Paleolithic) layers. The tube went through four thick layers of glacial (terrigenous sediments of icebergs) and inter-glacial sediments (globigerina ooze interspersed with substrata of volcanic ash). The upper glacier layer was covered with globigerina ooze. It should be noted that these layers are very thin along the American and European continental platforms, as well as on the ridges tremselves (for example, Core No. 8 was only 1.20 metres long). This thinness of the sediments is evidently due to erosion by fast-flowing currents, which could not have existed at the present water depth of 1,300 metres over the ridge; it is testimony of a great uplift of the ridge in the Quaternary period. One

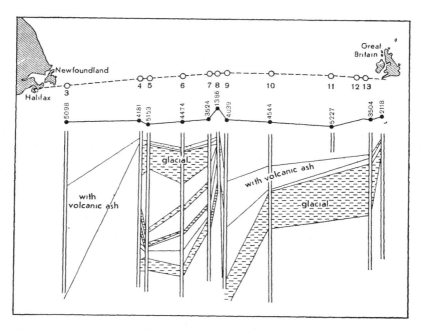

Core samples from the North Atlantic floor along the line Falmouth-Halifax (209).
White circles—station numbers; dots—depth in metres

must assume that *the ridge was above the water level during the glacial phases* (my italics—N.Z.). On the other hand, in the European-African Basin the sediment layer is so thick that instead of four glacial layers only one was discovered. *The polar currents, deflected by the Earth's rotation towards the Newfoundland Banks, ended in those days evidently more to the east, where they were stopped by the then subaerial Atlantic Ridge* (my italics—N.Z.). The penetration of *Cyprina islandica* into the Mediterranean Sea during the Sicilian epoch may serve as proof that these cold currents existed during the glacial epochs." In conclusion, quoting phytogeographical data (see Chapter Fourteen), Bourcart says: *"All this points to the uplift and subsequent subsidence of the Mid-Atlantic Ridge* (my italics—N.Z.). It goes without saying that here, as in the case of the troughs of the Sunda Archipelago, continental sediments from the summits of extremely steep crests could have been attracted into the adjoining deep depressions. But even if that were the case, *we have to recognise the fact that the Atlantic Ridge had to be above the water level."*

This view is shared by R. Malaise (76), who writes: "The present sedimentation in the area of the Gulf Stream is uniform and free from inorganic mud. The bottom streams are too slow to transport sand and mud for any distance, and such transportation can only be accomplished by surface currents carrying drift ice. *This difference in the sedimentation univocally indicates that the Gulf Stream was prevented from passing over the Mid-Atlantic Ridge, that must have reached above the surface of the sea* (my italics—*N. Z.*). During the entire Ice Age and for thousands of years after its end a cold marine current from the north passed along the eastern side of the ridge, and drift ice was brought by the same current as far south as the Azores. Erratic boulders are therefore found abundantly along the *eastern* shores of these islands, that were part of the Mid-Atlantic Ridge, but erratic blocks are entirely wanting on their western side." In this connection it will be recalled that the same difference was found in soil cores taken much farther south from both sides of the ridge.

J. R. Conolly and M. Ewing (767) report the interesting observation that glacial material is almost completely non-existent in North Atlantic sediments for the interval 11,800-15,820 years ago. Deeper layers contain alternating but nonetheless *considerable quantities* of this material up to the 30th parallel.

In the light of the above, interest centres on the data reported by N. M. Vikhrenko and V. K. Nikolayeva (219) on the nature of suspension in the waters above the North Atlantic Ridge. *In the stream of the North Atlantic current crossing the ridge the water is very clear.* Above the ridge proper the quantity of suspension increases with depth, but it is generally not very large. A small increase in suspension is observed over the western slopes of the ridge (but not along the eastern slopes!). In autumn the quantity of suspension over the ridge increases and most of it moves closer to the main chain of mountains. The largest quantity is observed in the region of the Azores. There is a small quantity of volcanic glass, but it is not found everywhere. M. V. Klenova, V. M. Lavrov and V. K. Nikolayeva (274) inform us that on both sides of the North Atlantic Ridge suspension distribution changes uniformly with depth. The increase in the quantity of suspension over the ridge itself, particularly with depth, is due to the stirring of the sediments on the slopes. Present hydrological conditions over the ridge differ essentially from the conditions that obtained on both sides of the ridge in the geologically very recent past. These data uphold the view expressed by Malaise.

Some fragmentary data on soil cores taken on the North Atlantic Ridge are given in the early works of M. Ewing (519; 520). *The sediments in the cores were not the usual abyssal sediments; they were the products of chemical changes and mechanical working of the rocks forming the North Atlantic Ridge. We believe that this is indirect testimony of the subaerial erosion of these rocks. The same concerns the Azores Plateau,* where fragments of rock and clay were obtained from a ravine on the northern slopes at a depth of 3,111 metres. But this was not abyssal clay and it contained many

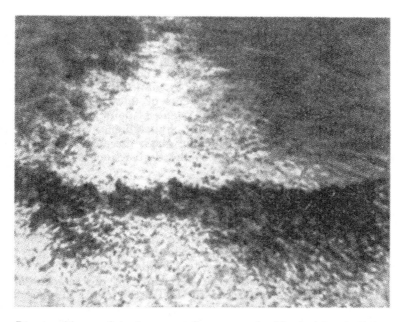

Direct evidence of terrigenous sediments on the North Atlantic Ridge. The dark transversal band consists of gravel and sand which, as a result of a landslide, overlay strata of white abyssal globigerina ooze.
Photographs after Elmendorf and Heezen (509/1074)

angular fragments. M. V. Klenova and N. L. Zenkevich (273/146) write that a piece of soaked, solid, uninundated (!) clayey limestone was brought to the surface at Station No. 403 in the region of the Azores Plateau.

Although the information at our disposal is scanty it nevertheless gives us the following picture of the distribution of sediments in the region of the North Atlantic Ridge. *There are practically no sediments on the Main Chain, but on the terraces the layer of sediments was found to be more than 300 metres thick* (690). However, investigations conducted by American scientists (732) in recent years have shown that while the crest of the ridge is almost bare of sediments, the layer of sediments in the depressions is about 100-200 metres thick, or somewhat thinner than indicated in earlier works. It should be noted that these data concern the more southerly parts of the ridge—the Equatorial and South Atlantic Ridge. As A. V. Ilyin (263) points out, *the floor of the Median Valley is almost completely free of modern open sea sediments. He presumes that this favours the assumption that the rift valley is of recent origin and that it is still in the process of formation, i.e., in the stage of development.* During its relatively short span of existence the rift valley has not become filled with modern sediments.

According to M. and J. Ewing and M. Talwani (525a), the sediment layer is generally thin on the North Atlantic Ridge. Most of the crest is devoid of sediments, while on the sides the sediments are mostly in pockets, where the layer is from 50 to 600 metres thick (the latter figure is for the equatorial part). The finding of considerable layers of sediments in these pockets is, naturally, explained by the action of omnipotent turbidity currents of unestablished nature. In another work (773), the American scientists point out that the sand on the ridge contains olivine, augite, hypersthene, enstatite, amphibole, quartz, plagioclase and volcanic glass; the authors believe that these minerals owe their origin to the destruction of olivinic theoleite.

In one of their latest works J. and M. Ewing (803) summarise their observations as follows: The inconsiderable layer of sediments in the axial region of the ridge grows thicker in the direction of the sides, and there is a sharp increase *at a distance of approximately 100-400 kilometres from the axis. This ledge, they believe, appeared in all regions of the ridge about 10 million years ago, when the period of quiescence gave way to tectonic activity.*

The following view about the sediments on the terraces of the North Atlantic Ridge is offered by I. Tolstoi (690): "Unquestionably, these terraces are or have been regions of intensive sedimentation." At the same time, *the adjoining Foothill Zone has a much thinner layer of sediments, while in the Median Valley there are practically no sediments at all.* This sounds strange if we recognise the existence of landslides and the formation of sediments by submarine erosion.

The layer of sediments on the platform of the Azores pedestal is much thicker than in any other region of the North Atlantic Ridge. Why is precisely the Azores Plateau so rich in sediments if these sediments are the result solely of underwater landslides and erosion? To precipitate landslides there must be a rich reserve of sediments on the slopes. The small quantity of sediments in the Median Valley is a sign that the submarine erosion on the ridge is not as intensive as many scientists are inclined to believe. Interesting in this connection is an early statement by M. Ewing (519/288): "Our hypothesis was that the long, level terraces, with sediments ranging up to 3,000 feet in depth, were submerged shore lines. If so, the steep cliffs rising from them should have boulders at their bases as do wave-cut cliffs on our shorelines today. It is, of course, extremely radical speculation to identify these level stretches more than two miles below the sea surface as former beaches. Such a theory would require the obvious but almost incredible conclusion that the land here has subsided two miles or else the sea has risen by that amount."

Ten years later the same view was advanced by F. Shepard (673/167), who wrote: "On the sides of the ridge there are terrace-like features with flat floors. At first it was thought that these might represent wave-cut terraces cut into a submerging mountain chain, but it was soon found that the terraces are underlain by thick masses of sediment, so that they are now interpreted as deposits formed by turbidity currents(!!!) in basins blocked by ridges, just as sediments form in the artificial lakes behind dams until the basins are filled up to the level of the dam spillway." In that case why did the almighty turbidity currents hesitate to fill the Median Valley to the brim? We feel it would be simpler and closer to the truth to assume that *the thick layers of sediments on the terraces of the North Atlantic Ridge are the result of the onetime subaerial position of the ridge, when it was partially eroded by atmospheric agents. Subsequently, where the ridge sank, the sediments were displaced and they settled on the terraces that were formed by submarine landslides and bottom currents on the ridge.* Neither turbidity currents nor submarine erosion have anything to do with this.

Some years ago the American oceanologists of the Lamont Observatory published a summary of works (517) on the study of the microfauna, lithology, granulometry and chemical composition of the bottom sediments in the North Atlantic. In many of the cores the sediments were found to have been shuffled as a result of landslides. In our opinion this is due to the not quite happy choice of sites for stations. Of the 2,000 samples at the Lamont Observatory only a very small number is from the North Atlantic Ridge, the Azores Plateau and the eastern North Atlantic. This selection of materials, confined chiefly to regions of the continental slope and the adjoining abyssal western North Atlantic is evidently the result of a desire to circumstantiate the turbidity currents theory because these are regions where landslides are most frequent.

Generally, as J. F. Hubert (565a) says, the features of the deep-sea sands and aleurite in the North Atlantic indicate that they took shape not from turbidity currents but as a result of bottom currents transporting sludge and suspension.

A series of works dealing with North Atlantic sediments appeared later. In a summary of these works Le Pichon (777) says that *pre-Pleistocene sediments were found in only 33 of the 300 studied cores. All the pre-Pleistocene cores were from abyssal plains between the 23rd and the 33rd parallels.* One of the cores contained Cretaceous sediments. A core from the base of Plato Seamount (33°05′N 29°18′W), at the very edge of an abyssal plain, proved to be the only one with Eocene sediments; these were mixed with sediments of Miocene age. The Eocene sediments were evidently eroded (how? by what?) when the Miocene sediments were deposited.

As regards the cores from the ridge itself, the most interesting were from a region 22-23°N 44°30′-46°W (759). It was found that in the Median Valley, where the sediment layer is only a few tens of metres thick it *consists not of white lime mud but of brown mud with an abundance of local sand-covered rock fragments. These sediments cannot be called "pelagic"*, as some critics (765d) insist.

In each of the depressions west of the Median Valley, where the sediment layer reaches a thickness of 80-230 metres, it was found that the sediments consisted of products of the destruction of local rocks. Heavy brown clay alternated with layers of deep-sea foraminifera sand (evidently, the result of the erosion of ancient compact mud?). A feature of all the cores is the absence of large quantities of standard abyssal light-coloured foraminifera mud: the upper layers in the cores consisted of brownish mud, chiefly of terrigenous origin.

We feel there are no grounds for Leontyev's (813/228) assertion that the presence of relic subaerial (terrigenous!) sediments on the ridge is geologically unfounded.

Considerable interest is attracted by investigations of the bottom soil in the Equatorial Atlantic, particularly in the vicinity of the Romanche Trench. The German expeditions on the ships *Gazelle* and *Gauss* operating along the edge of the North Atlantic Ridge near the Romanche Trench obtained cores containing sand of clearly terrigenous origin; it comprised minerals of granite, gneiss and crystalline schist (290). One of these cores (length—46 cm) consisted of: a) red clay—13 cm; b) brown clay with substrata of sand—12 cm; c) sand-free grey clay with light and dark stripes—7.7 cm; d) clay—11 cm; e) globigerina ooze—1.8 cm (bottom layer). Layer "b" contained minerals forming hypersthenic gneiss—continental rock. No matter how the presence of these sands near the abyssal Romanche Trench is explained—washing down from the sides of the ridge by underwater currents or as the result of landslides—*the sialic nature of part of the sediments typical of continental shoals is extremely noteworthy*.

The investigations conducted by the Swedish oceanographic expedition on the ship *Albatross* has supplemented and corroborated the data obtained by earlier expeditions in the region of the Romanche Trench (633/95). Different types of abyssal sand were found at a distance of about 2,800 kilometres farther to the west, north of the equator. A 9-metre soil core, whose upper part consisted of fairly homogeneous red ooze, was obtained here at a depth of about 4,400 metres. Layers of sand of continental origin were seen in the lower part of the core. An unexpected find in a still lower layer consisted of vegetation remains: twigs, nuts, and fragments of the bark of dicotyledonous shrubs. Lastly, the bottom layer was found to include remains of shallow-water benthonic foraminifera that live at depths ranging from 100 to 200 metres. H. Pettersson (633/97) writes that these remains were found approximately half-way between Guiana and the North Atlantic Ridge (7°29′N 45°10′W); this is more than 900 kilometres from the mouth of the Amazon, and this distance, despite the speed of that river, rules out all possibility of these remains being of river origin.

However, F. M. Locher (597), who shares the views of the American school of oceanographers, assumed that both the sand and the vegetable remains were transported by the Amazon. On the whole, his data sooner concerns not the sample mentioned above but samples obtained from the floor of the Equatorial Atlantic. Besides, these cores had a much thinner layer of sand, which was not so abundant or coarse. Moreover, *a mineralogical and petrological analysis of the materials from these cores showed an extremely striking difference compared with the materials found in the estuary of the Amazon, which casts doubt on the premise that these cores likewise originated from the Amazon.* The omnipotent turbidity currents were, therefore, called to the rescue and the hypothesis was advanced that these currents might have transported the materials in question somewhere from the shores of South America.

All the above-mentioned facts led Hans Pettersson (633/97) to the conclusion that a *"large island harbouring vegetation and with a fairly extensive shelf crowned the Mid-Atlantic Ridge north-northwest of St. Paul's Rocks and became submerged during a catastrophe of seismic-volcanic character a few hundred thousand years ago"* (my italics—*N.Z.*). If this is considered to be impossible, Pettersson says, it must be remembered that the present-day surface currents in that region flow from southeast to northwest, i.e., opposite to the direction in which the transportation of sand, foraminifera and vegetable remains may be assumed. F. M. Locher and F. B. Phleger avoid this difficulty with the aid of the all-powerful turbidity currents. But, as Pettersson shows, the floor topography in this region does not favour turbidity currents even if such existed at all.

As regards the sediments in the Romanche Trench, the cores showed that besides the usual pelagic material, the upper layers contain a large quantity of terrigenous material—fragments and products of mechanical crushing of ridge rock, or products of the metamorphism of these rocks. In some cases this material is interbedded in Tertiary carbonaceous deposits. The cores contained all types of sediments—from sand to clay mud—which were characterised by the occurrence of clastic, carbonaceous and silica-carbonaceous facies. Modern sediments are represented by serpentine deposits with rock fragments. The heavy sand was found to include amphibole, olivine, epidote and sphene (588a, 739).

V. M. Lavrov (737) likewise reports that on the Equatorial Atlantic Ridge the sediments consist of black clayey mud containing some two per cent organic hydrocarbon. Sediments of this kind occur in the Guinea Basin and nowhere else in the Atlantic. The reason for this is not known.

Let us now deal with sediments from the north and east of the North Atlantic Ridge, which neither belong to it nor have a direct link with its location. First and foremost, mention must be made of the surface sediments of the Iceland-Faeroe Rise. J. Jarke (569) tells us that fine-grained sand of clearly terrigenous origin has been discovered on the Atlantic side of the rise at depths beginning with

1,620 metres. He believes that marine currents washed this sand off submerged land which in its subaerial state had occupied the area now embraced by the rise.

More detailed data are given by Soviet oceanologists (218). A large part of the rise is overlain with muddy sand. Shallow-water shells occur almost everywhere; the largest concentration of these shells is to be found at depths of less than 400 metres. Particles of basalt, andesite (!) and diabase have been discovered in the sand. In the southwestern part of the rise the sand contains a lot of quartz. Volcanic rock is encountered mostly in sectors abutting on Iceland, where basalt sand predominates in the shoals; on the other hand, in the vicinity of the Faeroes there is quartz sand as well. *All this favours the theory that the Iceland-Faeroe Rise was once a subaerial region.*

According to the reports of the 1896 expedition on the ship *Granuisle* (529/79), a drag operating near the tiny Rockall Island at a depth of about 200 metres brought to the surface fine sand and many intact shallow-water shells of off-shore species that had evidently disappeared from this area long ago. From this Spotswood-Green drew the conclusion that the *Rockall Bank subsided not very long ago* (to a depth of not less than 200 metres, we would add) and that the former theories about the possibility of these shells having been brought by fishermen as bait cannot be accepted. This being testified to by the quantity of the shells and by their nature and condition.

With regard to the sediments on Porcupine Bank L. Berthois and A. Guilcher (463) write that there is fine sand at a depth of about 200 metres in its centre. Deeper-lying sand with an admixture of gravel was discovered north of the bank between the 200- and 400-metre isobaths. In the southern part of the bank there is finer sand.

Great interest is attracted by the report that layers of volcanic ash have been found in cores. M. N. Bramlette and W. H. Bradly (469) reported that *substrata of volcanic ash was discovered in the upper layers of the cores obtained by C. S. Piggot*; they had been deposited *10,000-12,000 years ago* (computed on the basis of their radioactivity). This indicates that in those years the North Atlantic was the scene of powerful volcanic eruptions, a hypothesis recently reconfirmed by investigations conducted by Soviet oceanologists as reported by M. V. Klenova and V. M. Lavrov (272): "A preliminary examination of soil cores showed that an appreciable change of facies in time is taking place in the upper layers (1-25 cm). The topmost layer, consisting of sandy brown mud or mud enriched by foraminifera is being replaced by coarse-grained sediments with gravel and pebble. The coarse-grain level is particularly in evidence on the slopes and surfaces of banks and on submarine plateaus. For example, on the slopes of the Grand Newfoundland Bank the underlying layer containing gravel and pebbles extends to the south

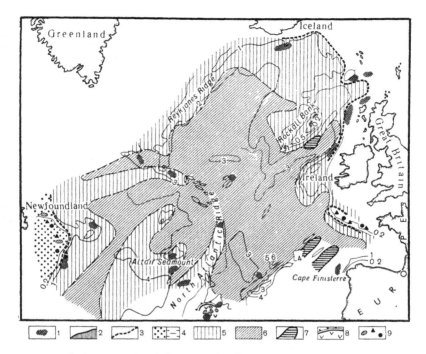

Facies of the upper level (1=25 cm) of bottom sediments in the North Atlantic (272/42)

1—outcrops of basic rock; 2—ancient clay; 3—boundary of clastic facies; 4—clastic facies, sand and sandy mud; 5—carbonaceous (calcerous) clastic facies; 6—carbonaceous (calcerous) facies; 7—argillaceous facies; 8—volcanogenous facies; 9—coarse clastic facies. The depths are given in kilometres

to a depth of more than 3,000 metres. It thins out on the plain of the North America Basin. A similar level was discovered by P. N. Yerofeyev on the slope of Gorringe Bank and on the submarine pedestal of the Cape Verde Islands.

"Extensive areas are occupied by volcanogenous facies on the 25-85 cm level. They adjoin volcanic cones in the European Basin and the Atlantic Ridge. If, according to Schott, the rate of sedimentation for carbonaceous sediments in the Atlantic Ocean is equal to 1.2 cm per 1,000 years, and for debris (blue mud) it is 1.78 cm, we shall find that the deposition of volcanic sediments, i.e., the activity of submarine volcanoes, dates back to 10,000-15,000 years or the end of the last Ice Age."

To this we must add that in our opinion the origin of volcanic ash depends not so much on underwater as on subaerial eruptions of the explosive type, as is believed by Bourcart. In any case, the coincidence of the dates obtained by different methods is extremely noteworthy.

The bottom soil of the northeastern North Atlantic has been

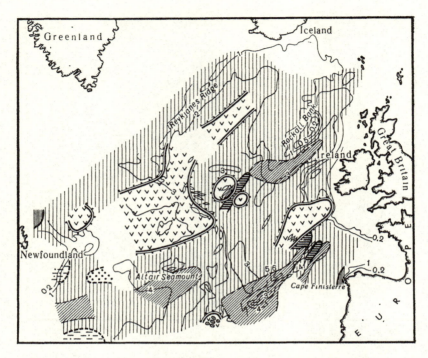

Facies of the underlying level (25-85 cm) of bottom sediments in the North Atlantic (272/42). For symbols see p. 285

probably studied more systematically, thanks to the work of the 1957-58 Soviet expedition on the ship *Mikhail Lomonosov*. V. M. Lavrov (286) writes that the expedition established the existence of several geomorphological provinces with a similar stratification of bottom sediments. Everywhere the lithological boundary between the carbonaceous layer and the Pleistocene sediments is clearly demarcated. Lavrov gives us the following data on individual geomorphological provinces in the European Basin.

Abyssal plain. The feature here is the presence of clastic material and substrata of sorted sand alternating with deposits of ooze and clayey mud. This clastic is overlain by two carbonaceous levels with foraminifera on top. In none of the cores was the sorted sand on the surface. This shows that such sand no longer forms. Possibly it dates back to the Würm Glaciation. In some places the cores showed solid white chalk (of the drawing type) underlying the clastic deposits at the bottom.

Ireland Trench. Here the post-glacial sediments are much thicker than in abyssal zones. Landslide deposits occur.

Submeridional central plateaus. White chalk is observed on the surface in many places. The most highly lithified chalk was found on the western slope of the Reykjanes Ridge as well as on the elevations of the Faeroe Plateau.

Hilly Plain. Here clastic-carbonaceous, carbonaceous and volcanogeneous sediments lie on solid chalk-like rocks. The presence of these sediments is typical for this province, which borders on the North Atlantic Ridge. Volcanogeneous sediments are found only in layers between ancient and modern chalk deposits. On the surface of the floor such deposits are known only in the region of the Azores near Fayal Island, where in 1957-58 there was a disastrous volcanic eruption and a new island appeared.

Other places besides the European Basin, where volcanogeneous facies have been found in North Atlantic bottom Pleistocene sediments, are: the floor of the Denmark Strait, in the Iceland Basin, on the continental slopes of Canada and Europe in the region of 50°N, on the southern half of the North Atlantic Ridge and in the northeastern part of the North America Basin. We believe that this distribution of the maximum volcanogeneous sediments is linked up with the intensive volcanic activity in the North Atlantic Ridge, Reykjanes Ridge and Iceland. As regards chalk deposits, whose age has, regrettably, not been determined because cores have not penetrated the entire Pleistocene layer, they are most likely of interglacial age.

Chapter Fourteen

GEOLOGICAL HISTORY OF THE ATLANTIC OCEAN

A. VIEWS ON THE GENERAL GEOLOGICAL HISTORY OF THE OCEAN

No single, unanimously accepted view exists on the geological history of the Atlantic Ocean. There are several reasons for this, the main one being our inadequate knowledge of the geology of oceans in general.

This explains why various views emerge on the origin, structure and history of the Atlantic Ocean, despite the fact that it has been investigated more thoroughly than any other ocean (314/103; 364/126-34). The following views are current today.

1. The Atlantic is permanent and has been in existence from the earliest periods of the history of the Earth. This view is expounded to this day by the exponents of the ocean permanency theory. The objections to it are the same as to the permanence of oceans generally. Besides, in the case of the Atlantic, attention can be drawn additionally to: a) the subsidence of folded systems of continents beneath the ocean level on either side of the ocean; b) paleobotanical and paleozoological data about the exchange of flora and fauna between both sides of the ocean; c) the extremely rugged and relatively young topography of the Mid-Atlantic Ridge; d) the preponderantly Neogene age of the sediments on the ocean floor; e) the existence of submarine

canyons of subaerial origin, limestone in shallow-water regions and abyssal terrigenous sand far from the shelf and slopes of the ocean (also see 337).

2. A compromise view is held by B. C. Heezen and some other scientists, who had formerly been ardent supporters of the ocean permanency theory. They seek to apply the earth expansion hypothesis to the history of the Atlantic Ocean. Some of these scientists continue to regard the abyssal plains as being ancient and recognise the Mid-Atlantic Ridge as being young; others speak vaguely about the possibility of the entire ocean being of youthful origin.

3. The Atlantic Ocean is a widened fissure that took shape after America "drifted" away from Europe and Africa (the hypothesis of A. Wegener and other mobilists). Properly speaking, there is little difference between the views of the exponents of the expanding earth theory and those of the mobilists.

4. The Atlantic is a recent geosyncline and the Mid-Atlantic Ridge is its central geoanticline that is in the stage of uplift. This view, springing from the theory that the continents are growing at the expense of oceans through a transition from geosynclinal to platform stages does not dovetail with all that we now know about the Atlantic Ocean.

5. In its geological past the Atlantic was mainly a land area which broke up and sank. This, A. N. Mazarovich (314) points out, is close to the truth although it does not characterise the tectonic structure that took shape after destruction. He writes: *"The nature of the Atlantic floor suggests that it is a mountainous country that was flooded as a result of major subsidences"* (my italics.—N. Z.). Mazarovich says that the Atlantic Ocean is a modern geosyncline of the oceanic type that is sinking instead of being in the stage of uplift. A. D. Arkhangelsky (184) expounds almost the same viewpoint but maintains that the structure and age of individual parts of the ocean are different. He, too, recognises that the ocean formed as a result of the sinking of folded and platform structures. Some time ago Y. M. Sheinmann (433) drew attention to the youth of the Atlantic Ocean and to the destruction of continental massifs through subsidence. He is of the opinion that the ocean is a young geosynclinal region.

N. M. Strakhov (393/154) pointed out three circumstances testifying to the fact that there were continents where the Atlantic now exists. The first is that on none of the continents fringing the ocean does the geological structure end at the present-day shores; they bear clear-cut traces of their extension on the ocean floor. The second is that the structure of the continents on either side of the ocean has many points of identity. There apparently was some kind of communication between the now separated continental massifs, and the floor of the modern ocean has probably buried these bridges. The third circumstance is that the so-called continental islands of the Atlantic and of the adjoining part of the Arctic (Canary Islands, the Antilles, Cape Verde Islands, Spitsbergen, Franz Josef Land) lie on the extensions of continental mountain ranges. Strakhov considers that structural units of continents must exist on the Atlantic floor as well. G. M. Lees (593) believes that continental structures continue into the Atlantic for a distance that has not yet been established.

The folded zone of the Mediterranean Sea ends in an arc probably west of the Strait of Gibraltar and does not extend westward. The western Mediterranean is a young oval stoping formed at the close of the Tertiary period and fitting into the periphery of the Alpine uplift. The view that the Alpine folded chain of the Mediterranean extends across the Atlantic is thus now considered as having been rejected (192).

Regrettably, in recent years all these considerations have been forgotten or ignored under the influence of the latest fashionable scientific trends in geology, particularly those energetically developed by American scientists. Only some foreign scientists have not buried in oblivion the vast experience of historical geology. For example, J. Gilluly (234/26) writes: "Along many coasts of the Atlantic type a former land surface extends seaward beneath coastal sediments for an unknown distance.... In many parts of the Atlantic coast we have comparable evidence of a geologically young change of former land to submarine. On the east coast of Greenland a flexure in the pre-basaltic surface carries a former extension of the island below the sea for a strike length of several hundred miles. Sedimentary features of Karroo sediments in South Africa seem to have a source in what is now the South Atlantic.... The list of former continental areas now drowned off structurally quiescent coasts could be very greatly extended."

In view of the fact that the Atlantic Ocean has been inadequately studied, no single and generally recognised view exists as to the time of its emergence or as to its geological history. E. Hennig believes that the ocean existed as far back as the Lower Cretaceous. H. Stille is of the opinion that the Atlantic reached approximately its present dimensions already in early Tertiary times (202/311). J. M. Gregory (538) assumes that a sea basin that could be called the Atlantic Ocean was non-existent throughout the Paleozoic and the Mesozoic. In the south the Gondwana continent was a bridge between Brazil and Africa until the close of the Cretaceous period. In the north the Atlantic Ocean took shape only in the Jurassic period as Tethys, a gulf of the latitudinal World Ocean.

The history of the Atlantic Ocean is dealt with in a monograph by H. Ihering (567), who writes that at the close of the Cretaceous period the Atlantic Ocean consisted of two basins: Tethys, the northern basin, and Nereis, the southern basin. Tethys was linked up with the Indian Ocean in the east and with the Pacific in the west; it was a latitudinal body of water running round the entire globe. Central America was non-existent. In the north was a continent embracing Labrador, Greenland, Iceland, Spitsbergen and part of continental Europe. It could be called Hyperborea. A tropical continent

—Archhelenis—separated Tethys from the southern latitudinal Nereis Sea. In the west the latter sea was bounded by South America and in the north and east by the shores of Archhelenis, which, however, was not an unbroken continent; it consisted of three parts. In the south an integral continent embraced part of South America, Antarctica and South Africa. The disintegration of Archhelenis began during the Upper Cretaceous from north and spread southwards. This barrier was completely destroyed in the Miocene, and Tethys linked up with Nereis, laying the beginning for the formation of the Atlantic Ocean. The disintegration of the northern continent began as early as the Tertiary period, after which the modern distribution of land and sea gradually took shape. In the Pliocene North America linked up with South America, separating Tethys from the Pacific; the Gulf Stream appeared, the cold Labrador Current was ousted and in the north the climate became milder.

During the Pleistocene the cold Antarctic waters penetrated to the north, as a result of which the annual isotherm dropped by 10°, and only 23 out of 45 species of mollusks survived. The final link-up of separate parts of South America as well as of the formerly divided parts of North America gave these continents their modern outline. This description very briefly touches on the Tertiary and the Quaternary, periods that interest us most.

Similar views on the history of the Atlantic are advanced by E. Le Danois (591) in a work devoted to the life and history of the Atlantic Ocean. He considered that the northern continents, the Canadian and the Northern (Hyperborea), were linked up by a polar bridge across Iceland; another, northern, bridge passed across the Telegraph Plateau and the Wyville-Thompson Ridge. The third bridge was Proto-Atlantis stretching between Spain and the Antilles, and the fourth, the Equatorial bridge, linked up the tips of Brazil and West Africa. Le Danois' Atlantis bridge ran from southern Spain across Gibraltar and part of Morocco, took in the Canaries and the Cape Verde Islands, crossed the ocean and reached the modern Antilles. Le Danois dates these bridges back to the Hercynian orogenesis. They existed as late as the Tertiary period, during which they gradually disintegrated. The final subsidence of that part of the bridge, which Le Danois calls Atlantis, took place in the Miocene, i.e., about 10,000,000-20,000,000 years ago. The concept about intercontinental bridges in the Atlantic is upheld by V. E. Khain (415/24) as well. He believes that the ocean existed in the Paleozoic but that in the north and at the equator there were intercontinental bridges. He sees a remainder of the North Atlantic bridge in the Archean gneiss of northwest Scotland and the Hebrides, regarding them as the Eris platform, the eastern outskirts of the once vast ancient continent of Lawrencia (North Proto-Atlantis).

G. W. Lindberg (721) is of the opinion that the subsidence of the North Atlantic land area to a depth of 4,000-5,000 metres took place at the end of the Tertiary period. He connects it with the probable existence of the vast Paleo-Hudson river system, which included the rivers of Western Europe and North America and had its source near Iceland. The submarine North Atlantic canyon is part of the ancient Paleo-Hudson channel.

Y. M. Sheinmann (755) observes that in addition to lengthwise dislocations, there are transversal faults in the tectonic topography of the Atlantic floor. These include the younger transversal rift-like depressions in the Mid-Atlantic Ridge, as well as wall-like uplifts (one of which passes across Iceland, another across St. Paul's Rocks, and yet another runs from Brazil to Walvis Ridge). The age of these uplifts has not been determined. M. M. Ivanov found that the magnetic fields in the Atlantic fall into two types. In the North and South Atlantic they come close to the continent type. *In the median zone from the West Indies and Guiana to the Iberian Peninsula and North Africa the magnetic fields are similar to those observed in the Alpine zone of Eurasia.* This similarity with continental structures and magnetic fields is evidence that an identical relationship exists in oceans as well. In other words, *there is good reason to return to the hypothesis postulating the extension of the Alpine folded zone to the Atlantic floor as well.* But there are no grounds for considering that the folded structures that have taken final shape on the continent are buried here. In this region the emergence of submarine basins and the formation of the ocean dates from the first half of the Mesozoic, i.e., the period when the Alpine geosynclines were only looming. It is difficult to say what they looked like in view of the overlying ocean-forming process. M. M. Ivanov believes that *the Mid-Atlantic Ridge does not influence the nature of the magnetic field.* Relict structures do not manifest themselves in the floor morphology. *On the basis of what we now know we have to reject the idea that the Mid-Atlantic Ridge is an ancient scar marking where continents ruptured and drifted apart. It is much younger.*

The transversal wall-like uplifts are evidently similar in nature. A striking feature is that the Iceland uplift embraces the locality of a continental belt that was in existence quite recently (in the Paleogene). The same may be assumed with regard to other transversal uplifts. They are probably much older; this is borne out by data available to historical geology.

J. T. Wilson (788) approaches the history of the Atlantic from a totally different angle. Being a supporter of the drift of continents theory, he believes that the Atlantic was opened twice: in the period from the Lower Pre-Cambrian to the Mid-Ordovician in the form of a meridional zone, and from the beginning of the Cretaceous, but no longer along the old Paleozoic line. From the Upper Ordovician to the Carbon the ocean was closed.

It seems to us that the Atlantic Ocean embraces structures of various ages, which developed differently in the north and the south. Its pre-Mesozoic platforms broke up and subsided. In the Cenozoic the processes of subsidence and expansion became still more intensive and were accompanied by great outpourings of basalt. The most recent investigations of the Atlantic floor have definitely established the youth of many of its parts—submarine volcanic activity, and seismicity, particularly in the region of the Mid-Atlantic Ridge; this is attended by the appearance of fissures, the sinking of terraces and other indications of large-scale tectonic movements. We believe that *the Atlantic is a very young ocean and that its final formation, when it acquired almost its present shape, took place geologically very recently, within the memory of man.* Academician D. I. Shcherbakov (442/83) points out that current investigations of rocks from the ocean floor have led scientists of Columbia University, USA, to the conclusion that the absence of samples dating back to more than 100 million years is evidence that the basin of the Atlantic Ocean began to form only in the Mesozoic.

B. ORIGIN OF THE MID-ATLANTIC RIDGE

Before we launch on a more detailed study of the geological history of individual regions of the Atlantic Ocean, we must review the history of the views about the origin of the Mid-Atlantic Ridge, which runs along the entire length of the ocean and is of vital importance to the Atlantis problem.

There are many theories about the origin of this ridge, but so far no single view has been found to be universally acceptable. Back in 1900 Haug contended that it was a median anticline rising in a geosynclinal region. In 1910 F. B. Taylor believed that it was a horst. In 1924 A. Wegener advanced the theory that it was the floor of a fissure which widened before the separation and movement of the continents fringing it. Essentially the same view was propounded by G. A. F. Molengraaf in 1928. That same year L. Kober came forward with the view that the ridge is a recently submerged region of Alpine orogenesis. In 1930, using as his argument the data on the ultrabasic nature of St. Paul's Rocks and the obvious indication that there were great pressures when the peridotite of these rocks underwent metamorphosis, H. S. Washington offered the view that at the time of its formation the ridge was subjected to great lateral pressure. From this he drew a conclusion in favour of the conflicting "torsion" of the two Hemispheres theory and considered that this theory explained not only the predominant direction of the ridge but also its bend at the equator; these considerations merit attention (also see 267). In 1936 F. Kossmat said that the ridge emerged as a result of compression following the subsidence of oceanic depressions in the Cretaceous and Tertiary periods; this compression lifted the ridge above the surrounding terrain. In 1940 W. N. Bucher drew attention to the similarity of the continental and oceanic structures, particularly of the South Atlantic and the regions surrounding it. In 1947 A. D. Arkhangelsky maintained that the ridge was a folded uplift amid a developing geosyncline. In 1947 J. H. F. Umbgrove noted the symmetry

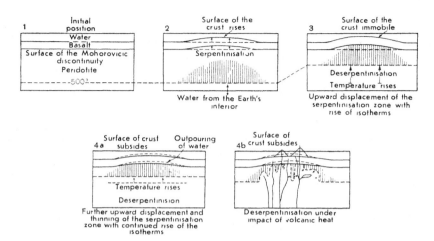

Chart of the development of serpentinisation and deserpentinisation in the Mid-Atlantic Ridge (421)

between the distribution of basins and ridges in the South Atlantic and on the African continent. In 1960 S. Bubnov likewise found a similarity between the structures of the Atlantic and Africa.

Let us now examine newer and more interesting considerations, which in our opinion merit a detailed study. We feel that the considerations put forward by H. H. Hess are particularly interesting. In his first paper (422) he suggests the following theory about the formation of the Mid-Atlantic Ridge: "It involves brecciation of the peridotite substratum by great masses of basalt magma perhaps over an upward convection current in the mantle. Some blocks of peridotite, engulfed in basalt, may be present at the surface, as perhaps is the case in St. Paul's Rocks. The somewhat lower density of this column as compared to the columns on either side of it permits its surface to rise well above the ocean floor. During the time when some molten basalt was present and the temperature of the column as a whole was higher and hence less dense, *the ridge might have stood high above the sea level* (my italics.—*N. Z.*). An upward convection current beneath it would also tend to lift the ridge, and cessation of the current to let it subside." Although this concept is developed from the standpoint of the ocean permanency theory and the hypothesis on convection currents, it recognises that at one time the Mid-Atlantic Ridge stood above sea level and that it subsequently subsided rapidly.

In another paper Hess (421/419) develops his serpentinisation theory, applying it to the Mid-Atlantic Ridge. He writes: "Until recently most geologists would have supposed that the Mid-Atlantic Ridge was either a folded mountain system with consequent thickening of the crust above the Mohorovicic discontinuity or alternatively that it was a thick section of volcanic material lying on normal oceanic crust or intruded into it. Now it seems more likely that it represents a welt of serpentine. Serpentinised peridotite was dredged from large fault scarps on the ridge by Ewing *et al*. The flanks of the ridge once stood much higher than today as indicated by paired terraces along its east and west slopes. Presumably some deserpentinisation has occurred since maximum serpentinisation. The problem of why serpentinisation was concentrated in the Atlantic along a median line can perhaps be explained in several ways."

The constriction (628) theory gives the following view on the emergence of the Mid-Atlantic Ridge. Prolonged heating of the ocean during the Cretaceous and Tertiary periods led to a thinning out of the Earth's crust beneath the ocean through subcrustal erosion. Naturally, this process was most intensive in the central parts of the ocean, where the crust is generally thinner and the depth and quantity of sediments the greatest. At the same time, due to the expansion of the ocean floor called forth by the heating of the waters, the floor bulged, i.e., it formed an arch. This moved the sediments to the deeper parts along the edges of continents, while a meridional fissure appeared along the median line where the Earth's crust is thinnest and least strong. Under the impact of lateral pressure on either side of the expanding layers of the Earth's crust there appeared two parallel folded ridges, while the initial fissure between them, sufficiently wide from the very outset, formed the beginnings of the future Median Valley. At the close of the Pliocene and during the Anthropogen, when the ocean waters began to cool and the floor started contracting and growing deeper with the formation of an arch, stretching gave rise to another fissure along the line of the Median Valley, the subsequent subsidence of the entire ridge narrowed the Median Valley, giving it its present-day shape. During the Anthropogen, the spasmodic cooling of the waters and floor of the ocean, in connection with periodic glaciation, led to the formation of paired terraces marking the subsidence on either side of the ridge.

As we have pointed out in Chapter Nine, B. C. Heezen (418) and M. Ewing (525) used the expanding Earth theory to explain the origin of mid-oceanic ridges, and found that there was a striking similarity between the Mid-Atlantic Ridge and the East-African faults (also see 442/90). M. Ewing links the origin of the ridge up with convection currents in the Earth's mantle.

We have repeatedly pointed out[*] that the existence of convection currents is extremely doubtful and does not tie up with many geophysical data. We do not know exactly how the thickness of the different rock layers of the Earth's crust is distributed beneath the fault troughs of East Africa and the Median Valley of the Mid-Atlantic Ridge. V. A. Magnitsky (313/48) points out that beneath

---

[*] See chapters Seven and Eight.

the East-African fault troughs the thickest strata are negative anomalies (in these areas the Earth's crust is likewise the thickest); these strata are located beneath rift valleys and not the adjoining parts of the continent. But the Median Valley may not be a rift valley along its entire length. Part of it might have been formed as a result of folding. This requires further investigation, including seismic and gravimetrical measurements. On the basis of the results of the oceanographical expedition on the ship *Albatross*, F. F. Koszy and M. Burri (579) see a considerable *analogy between the North Atlantic Ridge and the Lebanon Mountains,* particularly the southern part of the latter near Kimmerdgien. Moreover, they find that both ridges follow the same direction.

On the basis of concepts about the behaviour of the eclogite $\rightleftarrows$ basalt system, L. U. De Sitter (674) offers the following explanation of the origin of the Mid-Atlantic Ridge. He says that the ridge is situated in a field of stretching directions which cause a general reduction of pressure with a partial transition of the eclogite to a less dense phase (basalt) beneath the ridge, thereby giving rise to a compensating uplift. This takes place at a depth of about 30 kilometres, where the mean longitudinal wave diffusion velocity is 7.4 km/sec. In the Tertiary basalts of the axial zone of the range this process was attended by the formation of a rift. These basalts are about 30 million years old.

Le Pichon (777) stresses that *the ridge's geological history is complex and dissimilar in all its parts. The evidence of differences in geomorphology, magnetic anomalies and sedimentation clearly prove that there are two distinct provinces: a northern province and another province south of 30°S. Sedimentation was much more prolonged in the south than in the north* (see also p. 203). He writes: "This ridge probably acquired its modern shape mainly at the close of the Mesozoic, but in the early Miocene (early Pliocene in the North Atlantic) the crust north of 30°S was fissured, and massive outpourings of lava destroyed the sediment cover. The Walvis and Rio Grande ridges were formed in the epoch, at the close of which the rift area was the only active zone; as a matter of fact it is quite possible that the rift formed much later, perhaps in the Pleistocene, as in Iceland." He adds that the adjoining abyssal plains are not older than 70 million years, while the fracture zones have been quiescent during the past 50 million years. We feel there are little grounds for this conclusion because the ridge zone continues to be seismically and volcanically active to this day. For more details on the age of the ridge rocks see p. 296.

A. E. Scheidegger (660a) believes that the rift valley of the Mid-Atlantic Ridge was formed as a result of tension caused by common compression through the constriction of the Earth's crust, and that the expanding Earth theory need therefore not be accepted.

We have mentioned that many scientists regard the Reykjanes Ridge as the northernmost section of the Mid-Atlantic Ridge.

A. V. Ilyin (261), however, regards Reykjanes as a much older ridge, pointing out that its situation and a number of other features are essentially different from those of the Mid-Atlantic Ridge. This section of the Reykjanes Ridge uplift belongs to the ancient Atlantic platform called Eris or Proto-Atlantis, in which it might have been singled out by lines of deep fault troughs. At their northern tip the fault troughs determined the development of great volcanic activity which contributed to the origin of Iceland and, more to the north, of Jan Mayen Island. In this connection N. A. Grabovsky (243/96) writes: "The northeasterly orientation of the Reykjanes Ridge and of the submarine Rockall Plateau gives us grounds for assuming that *during the first phase of its development this ridge was linked up with Caledonian orogenesis*" (my italics.—*N. Z.*).

In the past many geologists dated the emergence of the Mid-Atlantic Ridge from Mesozoic times. In the case of the South Atlantic Ridge there are some grounds for this opinion. But the formation and subsequent subsidence of the Mid-Atlantic Ridge most probably proceeded gradually from south to north. We are inclined to believe that the argument in favour of the ridge's Mesozoic age is based on analogies and not on facts.

The answer to the question about the age of the North Atlantic Ridge is given, on the one hand, by the finding of Miocene limestone on the Azores Archipelago and, on the other, by a direct determination of the age of rock samples from the ridge. D. R. Carr and J. K. Kulp (485) examined a grey basalt rock obtained from a depth of 4,279 metres at 30°01′N 45°01′W. Its cross-section contained only 5 per cent olivine of a fresh appearance. Its age was found to be between 14,400,000 and 16,400,000 years, which corresponds at the earliest to the beginning of the Miocene and at the latest to its end. B.C. Heezen (418) writes about later investigations: ... "the large bazalt boulder recently brought to the surface also serves as evidence of the ridge's youth. Potassium-argon dating shows that *this rock crystallised from molten material a little less than 10 million years ago*" (my italics.—*N.Z.*).

Olivine basalt samples from the crest of the ridge (depth 1,400 metres) at 45°51′W were found to be from 8.5±1.5 million years to one million years old, while an old sample of tholeite basalt proved to be 18±6 million years old (777). Another basalt sample from the Median Valley at 45°N was found to be 29±4 million years old (778). V. V. Belousov (196/24) draws approximately the same conclusion: "The Mid-Atlantic Ridge runs across Iceland, where an Upper Pliocene fault trough lies along its length. This gives us grounds for thinking that the entire ridge is a very young formation." Thus, the *Mid-Atlantic Ridge formed in the period between the end of the Miocene and the Pliocene; its uplift evidently dates from the Pliocene. That is when Atlantis emerged.*

Unexpected data were quite recently obtained by a group of scientists (759) while investigating a section of the ridge between the 22nd and the 23rd parallels. It was found that there are sharp morphological and structural distinctions between the ridge and the sides. The crest runs linearly, is almost free of sediments (including the Median Valley) and has fresh rocks devoid of a manganese cover. On the other hand, the direction of the sides is not nearly so linear, the valleys contain thick layers of sediments, and the rocks show numerous clear-cut changes (weathering) and have a thick manganese cover. This led the scientists to the assumption that there is a considerable age difference between the crest and the sides. On the basis of the accepted sedimentation rate of 2.7 cm/1,000 years (517) they found that the sediments in the Median Valley (i.e., the very crest) were 100,000 years old and those on the sides at least 10 million years old. For a region with such a rugged relief, where landslides play a tremendous role and are often caused by seismic activity, these ages are highly improbable.

With similar timidity the scientists write about the reasons for this age difference: "The finding of metamorphosed basalt on the sides of the Median Valley critically substantiates the older hypotheses about the vertical movements along this zone." Although they mention the drift of continents as a possible alternative, they fail to see that it would be simpler to attribute the discrepancy between the structure of the crest and the sides to a onetime subaerial position of the ridge. If this is accepted everything will fit into place and this incredible age difference will not be required (see p. 280).

It is reported that American oceanologists are coming to the conclusion that the age of individual parts of the North Atlantic Ridge differs depending on their distance from the Median Valley. Thus, the centre of the valley is only 13,000 years old, while the rocks 6.5 kilometres to the east are dated as being 290,000 years old, 16 kilometres away they are dated as being 740,000 years old, and 60 kilometres away—as 8 million years old. Although these data require further and repeated checking, *the extreme youth (Holocene age) of the Median Valley itself is noteworthy.*

With regard to the South Atlantic Ridge there is much that remains to be cleared up. There are grounds for assuming that it did not form and subside in the same way as the northern ridge. Bathymetric data indicate that it is a much larger mountain system than its northern extension. Its upthrust probably started earlier and in it folding processes predominated over faulting. This is testified by three great parallel chains of mountains; the northern ridge has two chains. Morever, there are similarly weighty grounds for assuming that sialic materials might have played a substantial role in the formation of the ridge. This is borne out by the finding of such materials on all the South Atlantic islands situated on the ridge. Sialic rocks were also brought to the surface from Walvis Ridge, the eastern spur (209). The shallowest spot (only 936 metres) is evidently over this spur at 25°27'S and 6°8'E (212). An interesting point is that the natives of Southwest Africa, whose shores are reached by

Walvis Ridge, have vague legends about a continent that once existed to the west of their countries and sank beneath the ocean waves (653/81).

All these facts as well as the large areas covered by pteropod ooze near the South Atlantic Ridge suggest that there was a land area—South Atlantis—in this region. Also important are the phytogeographical data reported by J. Bourcart (209/289). The only tree of the Antarctic islands, *Phylica nitida*, is to be found in the area from Tristan da Cunha in the Atlantic to Amsterdam Island in the Indian Ocean. All these and intermediate islands (Bouvet, Marion, Crozet) are situated on a single submarine chain of mountains, now known as the Atlantic-Indian Rise. Moreover the occurrence on them of wingless insects and land crustacea has compelled some zoologists to speak of the unity of the fauna of these islands. Indirect evidence of the once subaerial position of the Mid-Atlantic Ridge as a whole is the migration of stormy petrels from the North to the South Atlantic, to the Tristan da Cunha Islands, where they build their nests. To reach these nesting grounds they have to fly a distance of at least 10,000 kilometres. At one time this route evidently followed the line of the ridge when it was subaerial.

Consequently, we can assume that *not very long ago a large section of the South Atlantic and Mid-Indian ridges as well as the intermediate Atlantic-Indian Rise, which links them into a single mountain system, were considerably above sea level and constituted a subaerial land mass*. We are inclined to believe that this land mass existed as early as the Tertiary and, perhaps, partially during the Anthropogen as well.

C. GEOLOGICAL HISTORY OF SCANDICUS

Most of the northern part of the Atlantic was once the Eris platform. In the west it was bounded by the Caledonian structures of North America and in the east by the similar structures of Scandinavia and Great Britain. For a long span of time the Eris platform was occupied by a vast North Atlantic continent (Proto-Atlantis). A more or less faulted mountainous mass of land, this continent existed as late as the Devonian and the Carboniferous periods. But some parts of it began to sink during the Permian period, and the complete break up of Proto-Atlantis proceeded apace in the Eocene, which witnessed the discharge of enormous quantities of basalts over a huge area (Thule Basalt Plateau), which embraced Iceland. Today in place of the demolished and submerged continent there is a marine basin with depths of several kilometres, characterised by intensive volcanic and seismic activity. The floor topography contains traces of young subsidences, as we have already pointed out.

Interesting considerations regarding the geological history of the northernmost parts of Scandicus, in connection with the problem of the amphiboreal distribution of marine animals, are offered by

K. N. Nesis (344). He writes: "The high endemism level of the abyssal fauna of the Norwegian and Greenland seas and the occurrence among them of a number of endemic genera are an indication that these seas were once isolated from the Atlantic in the course of a fairly long period, possibly for at least several million years. On the other hand, the obvious genetic bond of their fauna with that of the Atlantic is evidence that at one time (evidently not later than the middle of the Tertiary period), these seas were linked up with the Atlantic Ocean. The emergence of the Atlantic Sill as an integral system must therefore be dated from the middle or second half of the Tertiary period, i.e., the Eocene-Miocene. This fits in well with geological data. On the shores of Greenland washed by the waters of the Denmark Strait, in Iceland and on the Faeroes geological maps show only erupted rocks of Tertiary and Quaternary age. According to H. Holtedahl (564), this area underwent a period of mountain-building during the Cenozoic. During the Eocene or at the beginning of the Oligocene mountain ranges were formed oriented in a northwesterly direction, and a great plateau appeared in the region of Iceland. In the Miocene, after a period of relative calm, a mountain-building process began which is continuing to this day: this gave rise to mountain ranges running from north to east (Mohns Ridge—Iceland), accompanied by the appearance of huge fissures and the sinking of individual sections of the Iceland Plateau. This process evidently involved the further deepening of the Scandicus Basin."

Nesis follows this up with a review of the further history of the Atlantic threshold. He considers that the island pedestal of Greenland did not subside during the Pliocene, and that the shelf of this island was much shallower than today. The whole of the Greenland-Iceland Sill was situated within the 200-metre isobath (modern shelf). During the period of maximum glaciation, the Denmark Strait was completely ice-bound. In the post-glacial period the depth of this strait was about what it is today.

As regards the Iceland-Faeroe Rise, back in 1904 F. Nansen wrote that its surface is an abraded plateau whose abrasion started when the shoreline was 500 metres below its present level. In his opinion, denudation took place in post-Pliocene times. A similar view is held by M. V. Klenova (269/443). The investigations conducted by Soviet oceanological expeditions over the past few years have in the main confirmed Nansen's theory. For example, in connection with the discovery of an obviously abraded scarp in the central part of the rise Soviet oceanologists (218/112) write: "On the basis of this one may assume that the elevation in the central part of the rise was once above water and that some of the hills on the surface of the sill are, consequently, abrasion relics." Then they go on to say: "During the glacial period, when the sea level was low, the sill hindered the penetration of Atlantic waters into the polar basin. Possibly there was an ice barrier of the type of the present Antarctic barrier in the Ross and Weddell seas and, consequently, in addition to having been subjected to marine abrasion the surface of the sill was processed by glacial denudation agents." However, as we shall show below, the solely eustatic drop of the ocean level as a result of glaciation was insufficient to bring the sill above the water level. Commenting on the river valleys observed in the region of the Iceland-Faeroe Rise, N. A. Grabovsky (243/92) writes: "There are grounds for surmising that these are erosion forms of Pleistocene glaciation origin."

Referring to the theory that during the inter-glacial epochs the North Atlantic Current had broad access to the Arctic, Nesis (344) considers that in those epochs the Wyville-Thompson Ridge could not have been subaerial. But even in the glacial epochs it must have been covered by water to some extent and some part of the warm Atlantic waters must have penetrated into the Arctic, otherwise a stable anticyclone would have reigned there and glaciers could not have developed. However, this is a not very convincing argument. The waters of the Atlantic could have penetrated into the Arctic by other routes (see Chapter Sixteen). Moreover, no proof has been produced of the existence of a stable anticyclone.

We shall now attempt to present a picture that one gets if it is assumed that stepped tectonic (and not eustatic) subsidences took place in the region of the Atlantic Sill. The fact that such subsidences had taken place is proved by the existence of submarine terraces at different levels.

I. At the level of the modern 1,000-metre or higher isobath the entire Atlantic Sill would become subaerial with a height of at least 500 metres above the ocean level. The Wyville-Thompson Ridge would be an island separated by straits from the modern Faeroes and the Shetland Islands. These islands would then be parts of two great land masses separated by the Ireland Strait, which, in its turn, would communicate with the Norwegian Sea through straits on either side of Wyville-Thompson island. Large masses of land in place of the Atlantic Sill, the Faeroes and the Rockall plateaus, and the subaerial Reykjanes and North Atlantic ridges, formed an integral whole and completely cut the Gulf Stream off from the Arctic. The straits were filled with pack ice, and the land lay under a thick blanket of ice. This signified maximum glaciation.

II. With the ocean level at the modern 500-metre isobath the Denmark Strait would be a narrow canal allowing a fraction of the Gulf Stream to penetrate into the Greenland Sea. However, this penetration would be hindered by the chain of islands between Newfoundland and the North Atlantic Ridge, which would still be subaerial. The Iceland-Faeroe Rise, like Wyville-Thompson island, would be somewhat smaller but would continue to exist subaerially. The Faeroe and Rockall plateaus would still prevent the Gulf Stream from flowing in an easterly direction.

III. At the present 400-metre isobath the ocean level would considerably widen the Denmark Strait. The Iceland-Faeroe Rise would still link up the islands, but Wyville-Thompson island would be submerged, a fact which would not, however, influence the direction of the Gulf Stream.

IV. At the present 300-metre isobath the ocean level would appreciably widen the Denmark Strait. Both halves of the Greenland-Iceland Sill would be subjected to intensive shallow-water abrasion. There would be an archipelago in the strait itself. The Iceland-Faeroe Rise would be an island, part of which might be subjected to powerful wave abrasion. The entire subaerial part of the Atlantic Sill would be covered with ice. But the warm waters of the Gulf Stream would penetrate into the Iceland Sea. The subaerial Reykjanes Ridge would, possibly, separate the Gulf Stream into two branches. The eastern branch would, evidently, be smaller because of the certain resistance of the subaerial islands in the region of Mount Minia and the northern tip of the North Atlantic Ridge. The subaerial Faeroe and Rockall plateaus would still have a sheet of ice, although the former would probably have become an archipelago.

V. At the level of the present 200-metre isobath the ocean would correspond to its level during the Ice Age, which is the level of the contemporary shelf. The Denmark Strait would be fairly wide but it would still have tiny islands. The Iceland-Faeroe Rise would continue to exist in the shape of a small island or an archipelago of small islands. There would still be an island on part of the Faeroe and Rockall plateaus. The subsidences in the region of the Reykjanes and North Atlantic ridges would have allowed the Gulf Stream to flow in a fairly powerful current into the Arctic via the Iceland Sea and the straits at the sill; but during the Ice Age this did not happen.

Consequently, *during the Ice Age the Atlantic Sill was on a much higher hypsometric level than the presumed eustatic drop of the ocean level, and its subsidence was unquestionably a purely tectonic process that ended geologically very late.* Modern bathymetric data leave no grounds for the assumption that during the Ice Age the emergence of the Atlantic Sill above sea level was due solely to eustatic fluctuations.

According to Soviet scientists the magnitude of the geothermal gradient on the Wyville-Thompson Ridge is typical for continents. On the basis of the vast material at his disposal, V. M. Litvin (797) logically surmises that *in the Tertiary period the entire sector of the ocean between Greenland, Jan Mayen Island, Scotland and Iceland was a huge basaltic plateau.*

The geological position of the Rockall Plateau, which is most likely a submerged relic platform, is interesting. The submarine terraces on its sides were undoubtedly formed by abrasion when the ocean was below its present-day level. The flat tops of its mountains likewise point to its subsidence. A. V. Ilyin (261) believes that these tops were formed by abrasion in the process of subsidence. The hills observed on the plateau may be denudation relics, while the submarine valleys known in this area have a typically erosion profile. The existence of these valleys is possibly linked up with glaciation. In this connection N. A. Grabovsky (243/94-95) writes: "The emergence of terraces and flat plateaus is associated with the abrasive activity of waves when the plateau was on a much higher hypsometric level. The flat topography of the upper part of the plateau, the gently sloping floor and the small difference in the height of individual forms *are evidence that the topography underwent prolonged levelling under subaerial conditions* (my italics.—*N. Z.*). Structurally, the orientation of the Rockall Plateau coincides with that of the folded Caledonian structures of northwestern England and of Norway, which, in the opinion of E. D. Pavlovsky, were predetermined by more ancient deep-seated faults." From this it may be inferred that *the highest part of the Rockall Plateau took shape and developed in subaerial conditions*. The presence of granite on Rockall Island is, in our opinion, evidence in favour of the view that *the Rockall Plateau is a product of the assimilation of ancient Tertiary granites by outpourings of basalt* (we have mentioned that basalts have also been discovered round the island). On this point I. Fisher (529/81) writes: "Rockall had begun to emerge from scientific mystery, as the last sea-eroded relic of a mountainous island belonging, not to Britain in the morphological sense, but to the ancient barrier-lands between the Atlantic and the Arctic Ocean." A. V. Ilyin (262) believes that the most likely assumption is that there is a connection between the Rockall Plateau and the abyssal faults that broke up the ancient Eris platform. He dates the formation of these faults from pre-Tertiary times. A revival of tectonic movements, accompanied by the appearance of faults and increased volcanic activity, took place in the Tertiary period, which witnessed the formation of the Faeroes and the submarine volcanoes, in whose place there now are the Faeroe, Rosemary and other banks. A large region in the northern part of the Atlantic, embracing the area interesting us, subsequently subsided. The topography, which initially developed under subaerial conditions, was changed by marine abrasion during the process of subsidence and then by the accumulation of sediments. We thus believe that *there are grounds for regarding the Rockall Plateau as a remnant of a huge (sialic) continent that today lies at the bottom of the ocean.*

Identical results were obtained by Soviet oceanological expeditions with regard to Porcupine Bank (262), which is incontestably a westward continuation of the continental mass of the British Isles.

Through a study of the migration of flora and fauna it has now been established that the final separation of Britain from France took place about 7,000 years ago, and that Ireland separated much earlier.

Summing up the results of the Soviet oceanological expeditions in 1957-59, M. V. Klenova (271) writes: "By the nature of the floor surface in the North Atlantic one can easily distinguish more ancient elements of the topography, elements linked up with Caledonian folding in Europe, and younger, including volcanic, forms."

Among the large shoals in the northernmost part of the Atlantic some interest is drawn by the Grand Newfoundland Bank. A. V. Ilyin (262/122) writes: "The location of the Grand Newfoundland Bank above the 100-metre isobath gives us reason to assume that *during the Ice Age it was a huge island with the modern Newfoundland Island as its highest point* (my italics.—N.Z.). Newfoundland Island may have been separated from the large eastern island by a shallow strait."

D. GEOLOGICAL HISTORY OF POSEIDONIS

A. N. Mazarovich (314) points out that the history of the Central North Atlantic is much more complex, and that many of the known facts are contradictory. The mountain-building movements during the Upper Paleozoic led to the formation of a young platform. It resembled the West-European platform created by Hercynian folding. The existence of this platform may be traced to the Upper Triassic, when subsidence resumed and the sea gradually spread towards America. The resultant basin was linked up with the latitudinal Tethys Ocean via the Iberian Peninsula; traces of the existence of Tethys may be seen in Central America.

Subsidences involving vast land areas began in the Upper Cretaceous, and a sea appeared along the shore of North America; the sea spread to the west and east of Greenland as well. It may be said that the expansion and deepening of the northern part of the ocean developed from the close of the Triassic to the end of the Upper Cretaceous.

In the Cenozoic there were further major subsidences and the Atlantic folded system sank beneath the ocean level; its remnants are the Azores. According to Mazarovich the Mid-Atlantic Ridge subsided during the Eocene, but its last remnants sank within man's memory. Our views about the latest history of Poseidonis in connection with the history of Atlantis and new data are given in the next chapter.

According to British scientists (765), some 60 million years ago, Palmer Ridge north of the Azores was part of the North Atlantic Ridge, although at the time the former ridge, as such, was non-existent. Between 60 and 20 million years ago, this foundation of the future ridge was covered with Eocene-Oligocene pelagic sediments. Following this, when serpentinisation set in, King Trough and Palmer Ridge were formed. The precipitation of younger sediments began later near the crest.

Of the regional features of Poseidonis, the Azores Plateau is the most interesting for our problem. On the basis of experiments with

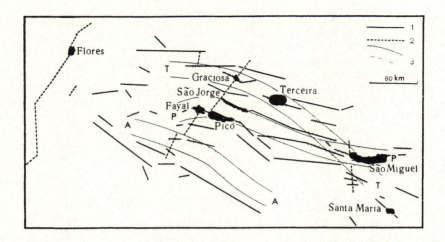

Main axis of the submarine ridges and tectonic structures of the Azores Plateau (487; 604)
1—axes direction of the latitudinal ridges (after Wüst), 2—axis direction of the Mid-Atlantic Ridge and the parallel meridional ridges (after Wust); 3—strike of rift structures (after Machado). A—Azores banks rift, P—Pico rift, T—Terceira rift

a clay model, H. Cloos (487) showed that the topography of the Azores Plateau was formed by faults in the Earth's crust running parallel to the longest section of the dome (northwest to southeast), with accompanying outpourings of magma. Somewhat earlier J. Agostinho (449) offered the view that the cardinal morphological features of the Azores Plateau are linked up with faults and attendant volcanoes running from the northwest to the southeast. His explanation of the appearance of this prominence is that it is situated on the intersection of two tectonic movements: the almost north to south movement, which is typical of the Mid-Atlantic Ridge, and the almost west to east movement formed of a consecutive line of plateaus and banks: Grand Newfoundland-Flemish Cap-Milne-Altair-Azores Plateau-Josephine and Gettysburg banks.

Investigations conducted by Portuguese scientists (448; 314; 613) some years ago indicate that the folded system of the Azores runs parallel to the folds of the Iberian Peninsula and of northwest Africa, and also to the sunken part of the Earth's crust between these two land areas and the islands themselves. Tangential stresses are observed in the Earth's crust running opposite to each other, from the southeast and from the northwest. If that is true it is quite possible that there is a genetic connection between the Azores and the adjoining sections of the continent.

I. Tolstoi (690) writes that if the Azores Plateau owes its present state to the superposition of two separate structural-tectonic processes, then the mechanism of the formation of many ranges in this plateau, as suggested by H. Cloos, must be revised. The structure of some of the Azores differs from that of the North Atlantic Ridge; it probably does indeed stem from the combined effect of at least two major structural disturbances.

Further, Tolstoi points out that there is a rough and inadequately established synchronisation between the periods of peak volcanic activity both in Iceland and on the Azores. L. Hawkis (548) believed that in Iceland the greatest outpourings of basalt might have taken place in pre-Miocene times. J. Agostinho (449) assumed that there was pre-Miocene volcanic activity on the Azores as well. Synchroneity is observed also in post-Miocene times and much later, in the Anthropogen.

For our part we shall note that in these regions of the North Atlantic, including the Canaries, there is some synchroneity in the major earthquakes of our historical period as well. For instance, in 1755 there was the devastating Lisbon earthquake, whose epicentre was evidently in the elevations between the Azores and the Iberian Peninsula, while in 1783 there was a similarly destructive earthquake and volcanic eruption in Iceland. Somewhat earlier, in 1730, a fissure with enormous outpourings of lava appeared on Lanzarote (Canary Islands). There was a violent earthquake on the Azores in 1720. In the period from 1720 to 1783 the North Atlantic was thus the scene of intensive seismic and volcanic activity (18/68).

P. N. Yerofeyev's (250a) studies of the geology of the banks west of the Strait of Gibraltar brought him to the conclusion that some of them (the Gorringe-Gettysburg bank, for instance) are a tectonic block, the subsidence of whose northeastern extremity in the Anthropogen led to the formation of a bend, which separated them from the continent. Their genetic link with the Iberian Peninsula is also indicated by the presence of serpentinite identical with the serpentinite of the Sierra Ronda on the continent.

Interesting views are offered by A. V. Ilyin (261/129) on the range of submarine mountains lying north of the Azores Plateau and, evidently, genetically associated with it: "If it is assumed that this submarine range is part of the North Atlantic Ridge, *the existence of the abyssal region between them may be explained by the sinking of a huge mountain range to a depth of about 2,000 metres*" (my italics—*N. Z.*). In this connection let us recall the finding of a dead coral at a depth of 2,500 metres (mentioned in the preceding chapter). Further, in his analysis of the floor structure in the European basin Ilyin writes: "*The discovery on the basin floor of forms resembling cuestas allows us to guess the existence of a relic land topography that sank as a result of vertical tectonic movements. The flat-topped submarine mountains lying at a depth of several hundred metres and situated south of the Azores are further evidence of the possible subsidence of considerable sections of the floor*" (my italics —*N.Z.*).

In the case of the Equatorial Atlantic Ridge, V. M. Lavrov (737) considers it is a marginal bend similar to continental tectonic structures; this is borne out by bottom sediment columns. The topography of the Mohorovicic discontinuity surface is reminiscent of a geosynclinal section, the evidence for this being the absence of magnetic anomalies. The marginal bend along the northern front of the ridge formed in the Cenozoic. Tectonic bending continued during the Anthropogen. All this is evidence of the ridge's geological youth; from the very beginning it had a latitudinal structure, inherited from the transversal Pernambuco structure, which emerged during the Lower Turonian (Cretaceous period).

In another work V. M. Lavrov (739) offers some new considerations regarding the Romanche Trench. He considers that it is part of an abyssal fracture zone, and that it is older than the newly-formed structures of the Equatorial Atlantic Ridge. After this ridge was formed, Turonian bending continued. The compression phase led to the appearance of the Romanche wall.

E. GEOLOGICAL HISTORY OF ARCHHELENIS

The southern part of the Atlantic Ocean is bounded by two pre-Cambrian platforms: the Brazilian and the African, which in remote times were, evidently, the single continent of *Gondwana* (364/139; 608; 641). The existence of this hypothetical continent in the Paleozoic and the Mesozoic was assumed by many geologists on the basis of paleobotanical and paleozoological data. Gondwana comprised South Africa, part of South America, India and, possibly, Australia and Antarctica; in those times Antarctica was not covered with ice, although extensive glaciation is known to have affected the Southern Hemisphere in the Permian period.

In the past few decades, due to the predominance of the ocean permanency theory (the existence of Gondwana clashes with this theory), the problem of Gondwana was repeatedly subjected to a critical revision. C. Mayr (608) argues that between Africa and South America there may have been a land link at least 180 million years ago but not earlier than 130 million years ago.

Gondwana's disintegration began in the Triassic period, this being attended by great outpourings of basalt, particularly in South America. Deep subsidences took place at the Albian stage and continued in the course of the entire Cretaceous. Laramide folding, which apparently led to the emergence of the South Atlantic Ridge, developed when the subsidences ceased. However, in the South Atlantic Laramide folding did not create a platform structure, while the mountain systems formed by it sank during the Cenozoic. The abyssal basins of the South Atlantic are likewise the result of very young subsidences.*

---

* For details about Gondwana see (237a) and also (821).

A detailed study of the geological structures (820) east of Brazil and southwest of Africa confirm the assumption that they are of common origin. Gondwana deposits have recently been discovered in the Antarctic, too. Cross-sections of the Gondwana layers on either side of the South Atlantic correlate excellently. The source of clastic—Parana tillites (Brazil)—lies in the east within the boundaries of the ocean. As regards South African tillites, it has been established that they were ice-rafted from the west, from the direction of the ocean. The Brazilian tillites have been found to contain quartzites not indigenous to the country. However, there are similar quartzites in South Africa. These and other data lead us to the conclusion that *the South Atlantic was non-existent until the mid-Mesozoic.* The break-up of Gondwana began later than was formerly believed, namely during the Early Cretaceous and was accompanied by powerful basaltic volcanism.

Furthermore, there is evidence that a land bridge existed between the South Atlantic Ridge and Africa. N. Odhner (624), who studied mollusks in southwest Africa, wrote: "There are other faunistic facts supporting the surmise that land areas stretched from north to south, and that possibly today part of this land is the South Atlantic Sill [Ridge] and another part—the banks of southwest Africa."

Lemuria, once a bridge between India and Madagascar, is regarded as a remnant of Gondwana in the Indian Ocean. The mid-oceanic ridge, now linked with the rift valleys of Africa and Arabia, appeared later. The remains of Lemuria and of the ridge evidently subsided during the Anthropogen, within the memory of man. Evidence is to be found in legends of the Tamils, a South Indian tribe which traces its ancestry from the Dravidians, the most ancient inhabitants of India. According to these legends, recorded in the 13th century, Tamil culture originated in a mythical southern continent. This continent, with its capital South Madura, sank in the ocean 10,000 years before these legends were transferred to writing.

The discovery of a "microcontinent" in the region of Seychelles Bank (495a; 780) came as a complete surprise to many oceanologists, who had rejected the idea of a Gondwana-Lemuria: a granite layer nearly 15 kilometres thick was discovered within a radius of 250 kilometres, and in this layer the Mohorovicic discontinuity surface lies, as on continents, at a depth of roughly 30 kilometres. Outcrops of granite occur on the Seychelles Islands as well. We are certain that similar microcontinents will be discovered elsewhere if, of course, instead of concocting fashionable hypotheses, efforts are made to find them. According to latest geophysical measurements, *the structure of the submarine West Australian range is typical of the continental crust. Fragments of continental rocks have been discovered on the southern slopes of the range.* The surface of the Mohorovicic discontinuity lies here at a depth of 20 km.

S. N. Bubnov (208/162) draws attention to the substantial difference between the structure of the South and the North Atlantic. He considers that the South Atlantic structure only slightly deviates from the continental block type, greatly resembling Central and South Africa. "In the southern part of the Atlantic, between Africa and South America," Bubnov writes, "there is an identical structure in the shape of a system of fields; in the west and east, the central sill in the south of the Atlantic Ocean is adjoined by broad basin-like depressions, between which lie narrow secondary sills forming a juncture between the median sill of the Atlantic and the loftily uplifted blocks of the African and American coasts." We have practically no trustworthy data on the structure of the South Atlantic floor and it is, therefore, hard to say if Bubnov is right.

In our opinion *there is a certain symmetry in the structure of the South and North Atlantic floors with the sole difference that the morphological elements of symmetry of the South Atlantic are in the west of the South Atlantic Ridge and not in the east as in the case of the North Atlantic Ridge.* This is possibly the result of the different directions followed by the tectonic movements in the Southern and Northern Hemispheres. Moreover, some of the morphological elements of symmetry are more strikingly expressed than others. For instance, the bench near Brazil on which is situated the island of Fernando de Noronha is not as well pronounced as an analogous bench at the Cape Verde Islands. The extremely interesting and almost unexplored Rio Grande Rise is somewhat reminiscent of the Azores Plateau, but there is a more distinct link with the continent; on the other hand, the link with the South Atlantic Ridge is cut short by a depression. A noteworthy point is that a gravitational anomaly of 150 milligals is connected with the Rio Grande Rise, while in the surrounding area the anomalies are twice as large. This shows that the Earth's crust beneath this rise is extremely thick (730/62). This region is evidently a semi-destroyed, submerged region, but it is a more ancient and thicker tectonic structure than in the north and connects South America with South Africa through the Rio Grande Rise and Walvis Ridge.

Another point of interest is that some years ago American scientists investigated the sedimentary rock layer in the adjoining Argentine Basin and found that in some places it was more than 2,500 metres thick. Underlying it were four kilometres of rocks with a longitudinal wave diffusion velocity of 4-5 km/sec, and below them a 7.5-kilometre thick layer of rocks with a longitudinal wave diffusion velocity of 6.4-6.5 km/sec (525a).

ATLANTIS AS A REALITY

Chapter Fifteen

ATLANTIS AS A BIOGEOGRAPHICAL AND GEOLOGICAL REALITY

A. GEOLOGICAL ATLANTIS

The possibility that there once were so-called bridges between continents was raised in the 1850s in order to explain the distribution of some plants and animals. This idea was advanced by many biogeographers and geologists. Back in the 1850s E. Forbes assumed that in the Ice Age Ireland extended far to the west and that that land area sank in geologically recent times. This hypothesis does not disagree with modern data on the existence of the shallow Porcupine and Rockall plateaus with their glacier-delivered rocks.

As early as 1897 E. Hull was one of the first geologists to use the existence of Atlantis to explain the onset of the Ice Age in Europe as a result of a deflection of the Gulf Stream; we shall analyse this question in the next chapter. Some years later J. Klein hazarded the supposition that there once was a large continent which stretched from Newfoundland to the Cape Verde Islands. In 1902 R. F. Scharff wrote that he believed the Azores and Madeira Islands were linked with the Iberian Peninsula in the Miocene. The separation took place in the Pliocene, but the destruction of the remnants of the link continued for a long time afterwards. The problem of a Miocene Atlantis is important and will be reviewed below with due consideration for data provided by paleobotany and paleozoology.

Some biogeographers have used the hypothesis about the existence of land in part of the Atlantic (geological Atlantis) in order to explain the connection between the flora and fauna on either side of the ocean. Considerations of this kind were suggested during the first decades of the present century by L. Germaine and E. Le Danois. Germaine (64), for instance, believed that Proto-Atlantis embraced all the Makaronesian archipelagoes as well as Portugal and Morocco. This continent, he said, existed as late as the Early Tertiary, when it included part of America. Central America, the Antilles and the Bermuda Islands separated from it in the Miocene. Prior to the Tertiary period the Mediterranean Sea was inhabited exclusively by warmth-loving tropical fauna. Cold-loving species first appeared in it at the beginning of the Miocene and then again in the Pliocene. A belt of shallow seas existed between Proto-Atlantis and West Africa at the close of the Miocene or the beginning of the Pliocene. A strait giving Arctic waters access to the Mediterranean Sea might have been located along the Rockall-Portugal line. However, Germaine regarded only the Canary Islands as the heart of antique Atlantis, flatly rejecting the Azores as a possible alternative.

Meanwhile, Le Danois (591) believed that Proto-Atlantis included the western and central parts of the Iberian Peninsula, Morocco, Mauritania, the continental plateau west of the Strait of Gibraltar, linking up Cape Saint Vincent with Madeira, and the pedestals of the Canary and the Cape Verde Islands. In the west Proto-Atlantis stretched all the way to the Island of Puerto Rico and included part of the Antilles. This continent was formed by Hercynian folding. The North Atlantic Ridge was non-existent at the time. Proto-Atlantis existed in the shape of a "bridge" until the Miocene, but its continental remnants are extant to this day. The mountain systems formed by this Hercynian folding were the Spanish Mezeta, Sierra Nevada and the Riff Mountains in Morocco. Alpine orogenesis gave shape to the Atlas Range, while the Bethyco-Riff mountain system was separated in the north by the North Bethys and in the south by the South Bethys straits, which formed the bridge between the Atlantic and the Mediterranean. Le Danois believed that this large island was the main kingdom of Plato's Atlantis. Subsequently, somewhere around the year 6000 B.C. there were considerable tectonic movements in this area; these movements drained the ancient straits but formed the Strait of Gibraltar. To the west and the east of the new straits part of the land sank to the bottom of the ocean. Some of the Atlanteans saved themselves on the Canary Islands and formed the nucleus of the Guanches, the autochthonous population of these islands.

It seems to us that this late dating of the draining of the northern and southern straits and of the appearance of the Strait of Gibraltar is improbable. However, it must be said that, properly speaking, opinion is divided regarding the history of the latter strait. Some geologists think that in the Anthropogen it was repeatedly drained.

Many Soviet geologists and biogeographers likewise accept the theory that there might once have been land in the North Atlantic. N. M. Strakhov (393/262), for instance, believes that in Upper Miocene times communication was established between North America and Europe and that there was a migration of Probiscidea, Carnivora and Rhinocerotidea to America and of Equidea to Eurasia. These links and migrations narrowed down at the close of the Upper Miocene and the beginning of the Pliocene but did not cease altogether. In the Miocene warmth-loving fauna were forced to the south, and towards the end of the Pliocene, when the weather became colder, the flora changed approximately to the forms we know today.

Regarding the last stages of the geological history of the North Atlantic, Academician L. S. Berg (203) wrote: "According to generally accepted views, at the end of the Pliocene and the beginning of the Quaternary period a narrow strip of land running across Britain, the Faeroes and Iceland gave Europe access to Greenland. It would be sufficient for the modern level of the ocean to drop 500 metres for this communication to be restored. *This bridge was possibly destroyed when the Atlantic Ridge finally sank, i.e., relatively recently*" (my italics.—*N.Z.*).

Contemporary bathymetric data indicate the practical non-existence on the Atlantic floor of great submerged latitudinal mountain chains which might be regarded as the remnants of large intercontinental bridges. To one extent or another most of the latitudinal chains are linked up with the Mid-Atlantic Ridge. Some investigators have advanced the idea that *the exchange of flora and fauna might have taken place across the Mid-Atlantic Ridge.** An exchange of this kind excellently explains cases of bipolar distribution of flora and fauna.

The important role of the Mid-Atlantic Ridge in the bipolar spread of flora and fauna has been stressed by Academician L. S. Berg (201), who recognised that the Mid-Atlantic Ridge is a vast mountain system that sank in the ocean. He writes: "It is not known when this ridge sank in the sea. Possibly, as Kober thinks, in the Mesozoic. At least part of it subsided recently. The submarine canyons are evidence that in the region of the Atlantic there recently were transgressions that left land areas at a depth of at least 1,000 metres below sea level.

"The recent, Quaternary, existence of the Atlantic Ridge explains many features of the geographical distribution of plants and land animals as a bipolar distribution."

Academician Berg concludes: "There are all sorts of considerations regarding the biogeography of the Atlantic countries, but sight must not be lost of the sinking of the Atlantic Ridge, part of which subsided in Quaternary times. *The exchange of flora and fauna took place here not across some hypothetical bridges but across the spurs of the Atlantic Ridge or the chains of islands that stretched from the Atlantic Ridge to the east or west towards the continents*" (my italics.—*N.Z.*). We feel that Academician Berg's opinion merits attention.

B. PALEOBOTANICAL DATA

The paleobotanical data enlisted to show the onetime existence of Atlantis were first critically analysed by V. V. Bogachov (14), who may rightfully be regarded as the founder of Soviet scientific atlan-

---

* See E. Du Rietz (505) for the role played by mountain ranges generally in the bipolar distribution of flora.

tology. His works have not lost their importance despite the fact that they were published half a century ago.

"Back in 1845, a study of fossil Miocene flora of Switzerland, Bavaria, Austria-Hungary, Germany and France," Bogachov writes, "and a comparison between them and their counterparts in North America compelled F. Unger (117) to assume that in the Miocene Europe and North America communicated across the present Atlantic Ocean, either via an unbroken land belt or a chain of large islands...

"Oswald Heer undertook to develop this idea (1855-59). His popular book *Urwelt der Schweiz* (the first edition was published in 1864) gave broad currency to his intelligent proofs and won many supporters for the idea of a Miocene Atlantic.... It seemed that the existence of Atlantis in the Miocene had been firmly established, but soon this was contested by Asa Gray and J. Oliver.

"... Oliver and Gray suggest that the exchange of flora between America and Europe took place not across the Atlantic but via Beringides, because, given all other equal conditions, this route has the advantage that it requires the least vertical displacements in the Earth's crust.

"During the Miocene Iceland was part of a great North Atlantic land area, which had luxurious arboreal vegetation (deposits of brown coal with remains of bald cypresses—*Toxodium distichum*); subsidences accompanied by huge volcanic eruptions began at the close of the Miocene. Basalt lava blanketed the layers containing vegetation remains. In the Pliocene part of Iceland lay submerged in the ocean. A slight uplift raised the deposited marine sands above sea level. Volcanic activity has not died down to this day.

"Strata containing Miocene plants overlaid by basalt lava are also observed on the Faeroes and in North Ireland; these strata were likewise part of a large North Atlantic land area. The remains of a mighty river system running from the north are seen on the Iberian Peninsula, and from this it must be inferred that in the north, i.e., in the region of Britain, the North Sea and part of the Atlantic Ocean there was a large land area that collected the waters for this river system" (Paleo-Seine).

Bogachov continues: "The plants that predominated numerically and flourished most luxuriantly in Europe during the Miocene are now to be found only in North America; besides, the most important of these grow in the eastern part of that continent, i.e., closest to the Atlantic Ocean. This American nature of our vegetation was imparted by some evergreen oaks, maples, plane trees, *Liquidambar*, Sequoia, *Taxodium* (bald cypress) and other species. True, there were, in addition, some typical representatives of Japanese flora, partly flora of the Canary Islands, and some Australian species (about which it must be noted that they are the last remains of pre-Eocene flora). Towards the end of the Miocene the Australian species died out, the American began to move into the background, and the Mediterranean-European and Asia Minor species became predominant."

The objections raised by Asa Grey and J. Oliver to Heer's views may be reduced to three arguments: first, the determination of plants by Unger and Heer is not quite reliable because it is based almost exclusively on a study of leaves; second, representatives of European Miocene flora grow to this day in Asia, particularly in Japan and are to be found also on the western coast of North America; third, the similarity between the European and American species might be due to convergence, i.e., independent emergence of similar species where suitable conditions obtained.

However, W. Studt and E. Irmscher (223/316) justifiably consider that the existence of a narrow bridge in the region of the Bering Strait is not enough to explain the common features of North American and Eurasian flora. Their explanation for this similarity is that North America must have had direct communication with Europe and that there this flora spread right up to East Asia, where it survived, while in Europe it was destroyed by glaciation.

E. V. Wulf (224) writes of the interesting studies of the paleogeography of the tulip tree (*Liridodendron tulipifera*) conducted by K. K. Shaparenko. Today this tree grows in the southern Atlantic states of the USA between the 30th and the 45th parallels. In addition, there is a variety of this tree in China, known as *Liridodendron chinensis*. The tulip tree flourished in North America during the Upper Cretaceous but it disappeared towards the close of the Cretaceous and made no appearance in the course of the Tertiary period as well. On the other hand, it was observed in Europe. The variety *Liridodendron Procaccini* grew in Britain and Iceland during the Eocene, and in the Miocene it spread rapidly in Eurasia, reaching the Pacific shore. During the Pliocene this variety of the tulip tree was confined to two separate areas, one of which was in Southeast Asia and the other in the southern part of Western Europe. The last remains of that tree were found in layers dating from the beginning of the Anthropogen; in Europe this tree later disappeared completely. On the other hand, the same European variety, *Liridodendron Procaccini*, appeared in North America at the beginning of the Anthropogen after a long period of absence, covering the entire Tertiary period, and was the ancestor of the modern American tulip tree.

This is extremely mysterious, Wulf writes, because the possibility of seeds being brought by birds must be ruled out—neither birds nor animals eat tulip tree seeds. They could not have been air-borne either, because they are not adapted for such transportation. True, they can remain in sea water for long periods and there is the possibility that they were transported by sea currents. But in this case it has to be assumed that the currents flowed in a different direction than today.

At present evidence is steadily piling up that land communication between Europe and North America existed very recently, during the Ice Age, and that it lay across the northern regions of the Atlantic Ocean. E. Dahl (492) writes that representatives of Arctic flora of the western shore of the ocean have been repeatedly found in Europe and, conversely, representatives of European flora are known in America. A study of the Alpine flora of Scandinavia revealed the absence of species that might have originated from the Alps, the Urals or the south and east Scandinavia. All such typical species are plants that moved to these countries after the Ice Age. On the other hand, western plants of Trans-Atlantic origin are represented by more than 25 species, including mosses and lichens. One cannot imagine, Dahl writes, that after the Ice Age western species of plants could move to Scandinavia from the south; the reason for this is that they are non-existent in the Alps. All the species of the Alps are either of northern or eastern origin. Western Arctic (American) elements of flora are known not only in Scandinavia but also on the British Isles. On the other hand, small areas of European Arctic flora are known on the eastern coast of North America. Many of the biogeographers referred to by Dahl are of the opinion that *the community of Arctic flora in Greenland, Iceland, Scotland and Scandinavia make it possible to speak of the existence in geologically recent times of a direct land communication between all these countries, and it is highly improbable that this was a post-Ice Age communication.* However, it is not known when this communication existed. On the other hand, the fact that there are Trans-Atlantic species of flora in Scandinavia is an indication that during glaciation ice did not cover the whole of Scandinavia. Dahl found two small coastal provinces in southwest Norway that were apparently free of ice and afforded a refuge for Trans-Atlantic Arctic flora. Similar data is available with regard to eastern Iceland.

C. PALEOFAUNISTIC DATA

Extensive paleofaunistic data in favour of geological Atlantic are given in the monographs of T. Arldt (451), H. Ihering (567) and other biogeographers. A brief summary is to be found in a work by J. Imbelloni and A. Vivante (69/73-85).

On this subject V. V. Bogachov (14) writes: "O. Heer noted the similarity of the Miocene insects and land snails of Western Europe with those of Central America. Another factor indicating the one-time existence of Atlantis is the similarity and the occurrence of quite a few identical species of Miocene corals in Central America and Europe. It is well-known that corals settle only along coasts, never descending deeper than 40 metres. The remnants of this strip, which linked continents, might have survived for a long time 'in the shape of islands." The same opinion was offered later, in

1925, by H. Gerth (323), who studied the distribution of coral reefs in the Atlantic (the Bermuda Islands, Central America, the southern coast of Brazil, Cape Verde, the Gulf of Guinea). He said that *very recently there must have been a group of islands stretching across the entire ocean. Thanks to them and with the assistance of sea currents coral polypi might have spread along the following route: West Indies-Fernando de Noronha-St. Paul's Rocks and farther across unknown (now submarine) islands in the direction of West Africa.*

V. V. Bogachov ends his comments on Miocene Atlantis with the following critical remarks: W. Cobelt has proved that on the Madeira Islands and the Azores the flora and fauna include many locally-evolved, endemic species, in other words, that these islands had separated from the continent long ago. The only American animals on these islands are developed flying species. The land mollusks are unique, but are kin of the European Miocene mollusks. This is evidence that the islands separated from Europe during the Miocene, but it is hard to establish when they were linked with America.

"The North American animals (particularly land mollusks) differ sharply from their European brethren, and the only animals common to both areas are Miocene types. Hence the conclusion that the land communication between Europe and North America was cut off during the early Pliocene at the latest. However, even in Pliocene times North America continued losing considerable land areas, which sank in the Atlantic Ocean."

New factual data have forced scientists repeatedly to return to the idea of bridges across the Atlantic, because without them much could not be explained. Let us examine some of these facts. As far back as 1904-1910 the Argentinian scientist F. Amegino (69/80) showed that the migration of some Argentinian mammals could be explained solely by accepting the theory that there was a bridge between Guadalupe in the Antilles and Senegal in Africa, a bridge that must have existed in the Miocene. According to T. Arldt (69/83; 451/1, 107), the mastodon, an animal of European origin, migrated to America on two occasions. A paleomastodon of the *Tetrabelodon* species inhabited America already in the mid-Tertiary period. The real mastodon appeared in America only in the Pliocene, but became extinct apparently soon after the end of the Ice Age. It is usually assumed that the mastodon migrated from Asia across land in the region of the Bering Strait. However, as K. N. Nesis (344) points out, in the Pliocene the Bering Strait was already open and a powerful current flowed through it into the Arctic. In our opinion, therefore, *there could not have been a second migration of the mastodon to America from Asia. This animal reached America not by an eastern but by a western route.*

Matters are even more complicated in the case of the horse and its ancestor, the *Hipparion*. While protohipposes were widespread in North America during the Upper Miocene, the *Hipparion* and the *Hyppodactilus*, according to Arldt (451/1, 108), appeared in the Old World only during the Lower Pliocene. The data concerning the occurrence of the forerunners of horses in the Lower Pliocene are generally vague not only with regard to America but with regard to East Asia and India as well. However, there are many arguments in favour of the North American origin of the Hipparion.

In order to explain the migration of the Hipparion from Florida, USA, to Europe, L. Joleaud (69/80; 571), writing in 1922, again returns to the idea of a bridge between Morocco and the Antilles. He proposed the same theory to explain the migration of some species of pigs (*Hystracidae*) from South America to Africa. In the opposite direction, he says, there was a migration of the African antilope (*Hippotraginidae*)—to the pastures of North America. He assumed that there was a bridge during the Sarmatian and Pontian stages of the Upper Miocene and the Astian stage of the Pliocene. However, it is currently felt that Joleaud's theories have not been adequately proved (323).

Another interesting fact is that today the manatee (*Manatus*) occurs not only in the Senegal and other African rivers but also in the Amazon (69/84). Its ancient ancestors have been found in Pliocene strata in South Carolina, USA, in Miocene strata in Argentina, in Eocene strata in Egypt and in Oligocene strata in Europe. Representatives of this species have also been discovered on St. Helena Island (567/161).

Some time ago P. Paulian (632) drew attention to isolated areas of monk seals, of which the *Monachus monachus* inhabits the Mediterranean and the Canary Islands, and the *Monachus tropicalis* inhabits the Antilles. However, he considers the theory that the Mediterranean is the original homeland of these seals as being beneath criticism on the grounds that no land exists between the Old and the New World, and therefore seeks an explanation in polyphyletism (the appearance of one and the same species in different places). But possibly these seals inhabited Atlantis and are the marine animals dedicated to the kings of Atlantis as described in a legend recorded by the antique author Aelian.

One of R. Malaise's (166/62) early works describes a species of saw-insect (*Pseudomonophadnus*) that occurs both in Tierra del Fuego and Europe, as well as a Holarctic species, *Pristofona*, that was discovered in South Brazil. He believes that these insects migrated along the Mid-Atlantic Ridge at the end of the Pleistocene. In his next work (74/129, 208) he speaks of the butterfly *Leptida sinapis* as a possible example of migration across Atlantis. It occurs not only in its homeland, the paleo-Arctic, but also in the neotropical region of South America, and it is not to be found in Africa.

G. Klingel reports that some species of butterflies periodically fly from Delaware to the east, in the Atlantic, where they pass the Bermuda Islands and perish in huge numbers farther eastward, in the ocean, as though looking for land that was once there.

G. W. Lindberg (721) drew attention to the amphiatlantic distribution of fresh-water fish (carp, grayling, pike), which cannot live in salt water, considering this evidence of the existence at the end of the Tertiary period of land with a single river network in place of the North Atlantic.

D. SOVIET SCIENTISTS ON THE REALITY OF ATLANTIS

D. I. Mushketov (337/117) was perhaps the first Soviet geologist to state unequivocally, more than 20 years ago, that he firmly believed that Atlantis once really existed: "Thus, the entire Atlantic Ocean is an element of very recent subsidence and caving. This idea, known from very ancient times, is expressed in the famous myth about the destruction of Atlantis that has been geologically explained by Termier" (137).

Another noted Soviet geologist, A. N. Mazarovich (314/105), writes: "Also noteworthy is the ancient Greek legend about the lost kingdom of Atlantis that was situated somewhere to the west of the Strait of Gibraltar. Most probably this marked the final sinking of what perhaps was a large land area built by Upper Cretaceous folding."

This was also the view of the well-known Soviet marine geologist Professor M. V. Klenova (269/411): "A huge continental block lies at the bottom of the ocean in the region of the Canary Islands, the Azores and the Cape Verde Islands. It is regarded as the Atlantis about whose destruction we know from ancient Greek sources."

Academician Vladimir Obruchev, the world-famous Soviet geologist and geographer, whole-heartedly supported the theory that Atlantis really existed. In 1947 (349/278), analysing the possibility of geological catastrophes, he wrote: *"The legend is plausible because in the eastern Atlantic all the islands are volcanic, while some geological and zoological data indicate that there was a large land area between Europe and America"* (my italics.—N. Z.).

Some years later, in 1954, Academician Obruchev again returned to the Atlantis problem in his paper *The Riddle of the Siberian Polar Region* [we quote after E. V. Andreyeva (19/120-21)]. He wrote: "The subsidence of a considerable land area some 10,000-12,000 years ago (i.e., in the 8th-10th millennia of our era) can no longer surprise geologists and geographers or awaken distrust and unbelief among them. For that reason *from the geological point of view the legend about Atlantis, about the destruction of a large kingdom inhabited by a civilised and warlike people is by no means incredible, impossible or inadmissible. The sinking of Atlantis was perhaps not as sudden and rapid as related by the Greek philosopher Plato in the ancient Greek legend; it might have taken several weeks or even months, or years, which is quite possible from the viewpoint of neotectonics, while its consequences in the form of shrinking and dying glaciation in the Northern Hemipshere is quite admissible, natural and inevitable* (my italics.—*N. Z.*). Present-day glaciation of the Southern Hemisphere does not contradict the assumption that in the Northern Hemisphere glaciation was cut short when the warm waters of the Gulf Stream gained access to the Arctic Ocean through the sinking of Atlantis."

An unfinished paper dealing with Atlantis was found among the papers left by Academician Obruchev when he died. In this paper (24a) he links the destruction of Atlantis up with the rise of the ocean level caused by the melting of Ice Age glaciers and snow. The Easter Island problem was also regarded by him in the light of the probability of the ocean level rising as a result of the melting of Ice Age glaciers.

In a book devoted to the origin of continents and oceans, D. G. Panov (364/174) writes: "With halts and delays the destruction and subsidence of remnants of land masses, where now there are submarine ranges and uplifts, proceeded throughout the entire Quaternary period. *Atlantis sank beneath the ocean waves, Lemuria disappeared in the Indian Ocean, and the land area in Polynesia and Melanesia* descended deep into the Pacific Ocean" (my italics.—*N. Z.*).

In conclusion, here are the words of I .Y. Furman (29), a Soviet atlantologist and geologist: "The most important thing is to give up any sweeping rejection of the very possibility of a continent or large archipelago having existed in the central part of the Atlantic or the possibility of a major seat of ancient civilisation having appeared in that area."

E. GEOLOGICAL HISTORY OF ATLANTIS

In our review of the possible geological history of Atlantis we shall not use the known paleogeographical patterns drawn up by T. Arldt (451) or H. Ihering (567), because in respect of oceans all these patterns are extremely hypothetical, being founded on insufficient data; besides they have now become obsolete.

First and foremost, we shall note that in our opinion *a more or less large land area could be linked up only with the North Atlantic Ridge. One derives this conclusion after studying the topography of the North Atlantic floor and the data on the structure of the Earth's crust beneath it.*

Let us first decide if we can regard Atlantis as a continent. If we approach this problem from the standpoint of the usual concept of a continent as an ancient sialic block we cannot, of course, call Atlantis a continent. We believe that *Atlantis was a large young land area without an analogy in the past and essentially differing from ancient continents. We have every right to call it a "basalt continent"* and there are many reasons for considering it one of the *youngest and short-lived continents on our planet. The basalt nature of Atlantis was what predetermined its short subaerial existence.*

The basalt nature of the base of the North Atlantic Ridge is evidence that this mammoth mountain system and the land masses that once adjoined it were formed by young neotectonic processes and that when these processes began there was no longer a sufficient quantity of sialic material, which had been remelted and assimilated by basalt. Therefore, when we speak of the history of Atlantis we can only go back as far as the Miocene-Pliocene.

Atlantis had its largest land mass in the Pliocene. It was probably a large peninsula of the Northern Continent (*Hyperborea*), which included Greenland, Iceland and, perhaps, some parts of North America; at some time it possibly embraced a small part of Europe. Generally speaking, in Pliocene Atlantis, as distinct from Miocene Atlantis, the land areas adjoining the North Atlantic Ridge were arranged differently—the larger masses were in the north; in Miocene Atlantis the larger land areas were probably in the south. Already then there were considerable water expanses between Atlantis and the neighbouring continents. Throughout the history of Atlantis these expanses were inconstant due to the unremitting tectonic movements. While Miocene Atlantis still had a direct link, in the centre and in the south, with Europe, Africa and America, Pliocene and then Anthropogen Atlantis had a link chiefly in the north. Semi-inland seas formed to the east of Atlantis and the general temperature drop that began at the close of the Pliocene brought cold-loving fauna into those seas. In Villafranc times this fauna began to penetrate southwards, reaching as far as the Mediterranean Sea. Indicative of this period is the cold-loving mollusk *Cyprina islandica* discovered in the sediments of the Calabrian terraces in the Mediterranean. However, as L. S. Berg (202/140) points out, the occurrence of this mollusk is by no means evidence of the penetration of Arctic waters. This is a typical boreal and not Arctic mollusk and it perished on the shores of Greenland from cold when these shores began to be washed by Arctic waters. It is to be found to this day in the more southerly latitudes of the Atlantic, for example, at Cadiz. It cannot, therefore, be regarded as having originated in the Arctic; its home was in the Iceland Sea.

During the Anthropogen, Atlantis sank gradually. Its paleogeography throughout the Anthropogen is given in the greatest detail by R. Malaise in the monograph entitled *Atlantis as a Geological Probability* (74) and in a paper (76); our description is based on these works. We have supplemented Malaise's theories with our own considerations founded on latest data—after all many years have passed since Malaise first published his works.

Northern, cold-loving fauna continued to penetrate into and flourish in the Mediterranean Sea during the Sicilian transgression in that area. For example, in that period the mollusk *Cyprina islandica* reached as far as the islands of Kos and Rodhos in the Aegean Sea.

In those times Atlantis occupied the entire Azores Plateau and the North Atlantic Ridge. The bridge in the north—Hyperborea (Greenland-Iceland-Faeroe Islands)—was still in existence. Possibly there was a narrow strait between Scotland and the Faeroes. Atlantis was thus an extremely long peninsula with a very irregular outline, along whose eastern edge a powerful cold current flowed mainly towards the Bay of Biscay. From there it turned towards the Iberian Basin and then towards the southeast, where it rushed into the Mediterranean via the Strait of Gibraltar. According to Malaise, this was the Mindelian Glaciation.

The picture reversed during the Mindelian-Riss interglacial interval, which corresponds to the Tyrrhenian transgression in the Mediterranean. Fauna now inhabiting the region of Senegal, Guinea, the Cape Verde Islands and the Canaries, moved into the Mediterranean Sea, where it is no longer to be found. The size of Atlantis somewhat diminished at the expense of the bridge to Africa (between the mountain ranges of Atlantis and the Canary or Cape Verde islands) and also of some northern regions. But, probably on the base of the modern submarine Horseshoe Archipelago and east of it, there appeared several large islands which gave direct communication between Atlantis and Europe. That explains why the warm Equatorial Current, pushing the cold current towards the southeastern shores of Atlantis and finding its passage to the western Atlantic blocked, broke through into the Mediterranean in a powerful stream, bringing with it tropical and subtropical fauna. Part of this fauna continued to inhabit this sea during the Riss-Wurm interglacial interval, but in Riss times moderate climate forms began to appear near the African coast.

The size of Atlantis drastically diminished towards the close of the last glaciation. The bridge in the north, between Greenland and Europe, was broken in several places. Throughout its length, from the tip of Iceland to the Cape Verde Islands latitude, the North Atlantic Ridge was still subaerial, although in many places it was very narrow and dismembered by transversal faults. From time to time that allowed the Gulf Stream to flow in fairly wide streams towards the Arctic Ocean through the gaps between Greenland and Iceland and between Iceland and the Faeroes, although Atlantis still prevented it from reaching the shores of Europe. Besides, even in the Arctic the Gulf Stream flowed at relatively short intervals in the interglacial periods. A cold current continued to flow along the eastern shores of Atlantis, coming from the north and transporting drift ice and boulders from Iceland, the subaerial Faeroes, Rockall and Porcupine mountains and from the glaciers on the North Atlantic Ridge itself. This drift ice moved to the eastern islands of the present Azores Archipelago as well as to the more southerly islands of the eastern North Atlantic; in that period the Azores Plateau was partially still a subaerial region.

According to Malaise, Atlantis existed in the form of a relatively

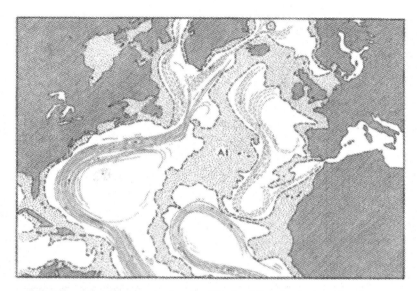

Atlantis and sea currents in the North Atlantic during the Sicilian Transgression, after Malaise (74/133)
The dotted lines indicate cold currents
At—Atlantis

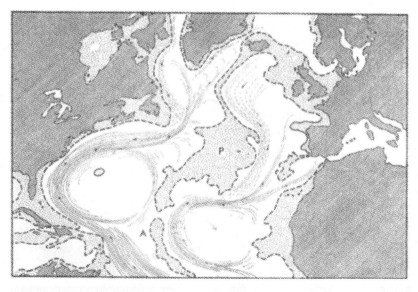

Atlantis and sea currents in the North Atlantic at the beginning of the Mindelian Interglaciation, after Malaise (74/147)
A—Antillia; P—Poseidonis

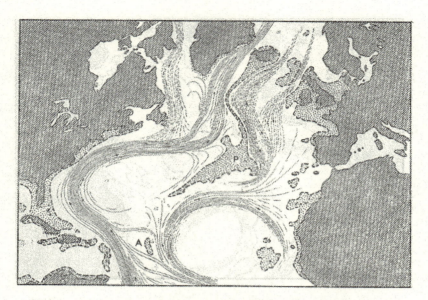

Atlantis and sea currents in the North Atlantic during the Würm
Glaciation peak, after Malaise (74/148)
A—Antillia; P—Poseidonis

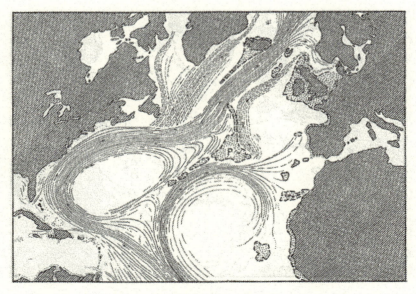

Atlantis and sea currents in the North Atlantic during the climatic
optimum, after Malaise (74/150)
P—Poseidonis

small island (usually called Poseidonis) also in post-glacial times, including the European Bronze Age (4000-1500 B.C.), which corresponds to the end of the climatic optimum in Europe. During that period the axis of the Gulf Stream passed between Iceland and the Faeroe Islands—giving Iceland a warmer climate than today—but one of its branches penetrated as far as the western shores of Sweden, where it came up against an obstacle between Iceland and the Faeroe Islands (Thule Island?). Rockall and Porcupine were partially subaerial plateaus. On the other hand, a cold current, originating at the shores of Denmark, skirted round the British Isles via the Irish Strait, and flowed to the eastern shores of Poseidonis. Malaise dates the final subsidence of Poseidonis as 1200 B.C., linking this date up with the invasion by the "peoples of the sea" in the region of the Mediterranean (see Chapter Seventeen).

F. ATLANTIS AND MAN

If Atlantis existed and occupied the area we believe it did, it would be logical to assume that it was inhabited not only by animals but also by man. It is interesting that the Plato legend speaks of the independent emergence of man in Atlantis. However, the inclusion of Atlantis among the possible areas where intelligent man developed is still in the sphere of hypotheses that are inacceptable to anthropologists, although the location and other features of Atlantis might have been favourable. Atlantis had a multitude of isolated valleys where anthropoids might have lived in isolation from predators. After all the ancestors of man had very little natural means of defence and attack and could survive in the struggle against nature and predators only by inventing their first weapons—sticks and stones—and then fire. The frequent volcanic eruptions in Atlantis very early acquainted its inhabitants with fire, while earthquakes forced them to keep moving and changing their way of life. Moreover, there was an abundance of excellent material for the making of implements—obsidian and other vitreous volcanic rocks (18/100).

Interesting observations regarding the conditions facilitating the humanisation of apes were suggested by Academician P. P. Sushkin (396). He considered that man's ancestor, who evolved from tree-climbing forms, was an inhabitant of rocky places and an open landscape. The change of settlement from rain forests to mountainous regions was not voluntary but the result of tectonic uplifts that changed the locality into mountainous terrain. The conditions of life deteriorated, and man's ancestor had to include in his diet meat from other animals. Meanwhile, life in a moderate climate led to the invention of fire.

The presence of considerable magnetic anomalies in the region of the North Atlantic Ridge (448/97) is of particular interest in the light of the hypothesis offered by Y. G. Reshetov (646). According to this hypothesis, man's evolution is closely bound up with regions of geophysical anomalies (gravitational and magnetic), which, in their turn, have a direct bearing on the biological processes taking place in the cells of a living organism under the influence of electrical and magnetic fields. Reshetov believes that the critical 35th parallel is the zone of such geographical anomalies, and that all the greatest civilisations of antiquity developed in that region. This zone also lies across the North Atlantic Ridge somewhat south of the Azores, while running diametrically along it is a region of folds and faults, accompanied by gravitational and magnetic anomalies.

It is worth quoting a serious investigator like J. De Morgan (333), who in principle did not reject the possibility of Atlantis having existed and the role played by it in the distribution not only of animals but also of man. He dealt with this problem in two works. He wrote (p. 19): "The Mediterranean Sea was undoubtedly broken up by land areas and the New World probably communicated with Europe across Atlantis or some other continent. There are in the world many regions whose zoological kinship with other regions forces us to think that between them there were continents which disappeared recently." And in conclusion (pp. 280-81): "As regards North America it possibly communicated with Europe across Atlantis or some other continent via Novaya Zemlya and Iceland, which have remained above sea level, as their highest points. But apparently this assumption has no serious grounds although the post-Tertiary geographical distribution of seas seems to confirm it. However that may be, even and if *in fact there was a single seat of the emergence of Paleolithic Industry, a seat that was perhaps located on a lost continent* (my italics.—N. Z.), the spread of this industry was not a matter of a single day and, consequently, synchronism cannot be accepted for any type of this industry encountered in all other regions." These words, it will be noted, were written in 1921, when there was very little data to indicate that Atlantis once existed.

The following chronology of various cultures during the Upper Paleolithic in Western Europe (632a) is now accepted as the most likely.

Gravettian—35,000-30,000 years ago;
Perigordian—33,500 years ago;
Aurignacian—32,000-29,000 years ago;
Proto-Magdalenian—24,000-20,000 years ago;
Solutrean—22,000-20,000 years ago;
Magdalenian—15,000-10,000 years ago.

Gravettian culture was in existence as late as 17,500 years ago. People of the first two cultures might have co-existed with Neanderthal man, who was already dying out by then. The dates were determined by the radiocarbon method.

Let us now look into the theories of some atlantologists. L. Spence (101) believed there were three waves of migration from Atlantis:

people of the Aurignacian culture (Cro-Magnons)—about 25,000 years ago; people of the Magdalenian culture—about 16,000 years ago; and people of the Azilian-Tardenoisian culture—about 10,000 years ago.* G. Poisson (86), too, tied up the problem of the spread of Cro-Magnon man with Atlantis and pointed, on the one hand, to a work by H. Cotteville-Giraudet on the similarity between Cro-Magnon man and some Indian tribes of North America and, on the other, to a work by Falkenburger about the same similarity of the Guanches of the Canary Islands.

Generally speaking, the region where Cro-Magnon man first appeared and the route travelled by him to Europe have not been satisfactorily established. In Europe we find him already as an anthropologically fully shaped type of *homo sapiens*. The Magdalenians evidently differed somewhat from Cro-Magnon man. Their culture has not been encountered either in Africa or in the Mediterranean area (182). In Europe they migrated from south to north, and they lived in the north until almost 7000 B.C. (675). The Magdalenian culture appeared abruptly and, as de Morgan (333) points out, Magdalenian art disappeared for reasons we do not know. De Morgan said: "Had Magdalenian art not disappeared, mankind would probably have developed much faster and the magnificent age of Pericles might have started several millennia sooner." Some time ago H. Delaporte drew attention to the riddles surrounding the origin of Aurignacian culture as well. He (496a) points out that the origin of this culture is likewise nebulous.

The easy sea communication between the remnants of Atlantis and Northern Europe, R. Malaise (74/211) declared, was due to the existence of Atlantis as late as the Bronze Age and also to the warm and cold currents on either side of it. Further he refers to a work by G. Halldin, who believed that the rock drawings on the southern coast of Sweden are of rafts with a superstructure. In the bow of the rafts there is the figure of an animal (totem or deity). These drawings have now been found to date from the very beginning of the European Bronze Age, and some of them are probably even older. They are evidence that Sweden was visited by foreign seafarers, who came not in sailing vessels or boats but on rafts, whose construction is unusual for Europe. Malaise finds that the design of these rafts bears a great resemblance to that of ancient Peruvian rafts, similar to Thor Heyerdahl's famous raft *Kon-Tiki*. On rafts like these, as Heyerdahl's (416) experience shows, it is quite possible to make a long sea voyage. Malaise thinks that the seafarers using these rafts brought bronze and other metals, which they exchanged for fur and amber.

Interesting considerations in favour of the probability of ancient contacts between the inhabitants of eastern Canada and north-western Russia are offered by F. Ridley (651). He points to the startl-

---

* See Table 7 (Appendix 1).

ing resemblance between the pottery of the aborigines of Canada, living on the shore of Lake Ontario, and similar articles found in Karelia, on the shores of the White Sea and in the mouth of the Pechora and Ob rivers (Gorbunovskaya culture), samples of which he saw in the State Museum of History in Moscow. The Gorbunovskaya culture, on the Ob river, is stratigraphically the most ancient; the museum's experts have dated it as 3000-2000 B.C.; the other cultures are somewhat younger, dating from 2000 B.C. In North America an analogous culture is dated between 2400 B.C. and 400 A. D. However, the Asian ceramic cultures, including the Baikal and Lena River cultures, have little in common with these cultures. On the basis of these facts Ridley drew the conclusion that there might have been contact between North America and Europe during the Neolithic. That epoch corresponds to the end of the climatic optimum. If it is assumed, as Malaise did, that remnants of Atlantis existed until the middle of the 2nd millennium B.C., the enigmatic resemblance of cultures territorially so wide apart will be easily explained.

Malaise's belief that the last remnants of Atlantis sank very late evidently merit the closest attention. In this connection let us recall the final replacement of some species of foraminifera by others, when about 2,000 years ago their modern areas of occurrence took shape in the eastern North Atlantic, while in the more southerly parts of the ocean the cold-loving species have been completely ousted by warmth-loving forms (516). *If we accept these theories it will not be difficult to explain some vague and evasive passages in the myths and legends recorded by ancient authors. For example, it would make clear the strange words applied to the ocean by Homer —"reverse flowing"—and his understanding of oceans as "rivers circling the Earth". It would explain the geography of Odysseus's travels, and the mystery of Ogygia and Scheria, and show why Odysseus left Ogygia on a raft and not in a boat. The reports of Marcellus, Pseudo-Plutarch and others acquire reality. The number of facts in favour of this hypothesis is overwhelming.*

Chapter Sixteen

ATLANTIS, THE ARCTIC AND THE ICE AGE

A. CAUSES AND TIME OF GLACIATION IN THE ANTHROPOGEN

Important developments are taking place in the geological history of the Earth during the current, Quaternary period: a great glaciation enveloped a huge area of the Earth, particularly in the Northern Hemisphere; and in this period man appeared. This induced Academician A. P. Pavlov, the noted geologist, to suggest the name *Anthropogen* for the Quaternary period. In view of the fact that the Ice Age began in the Pliocene and is a major factor for both geo-

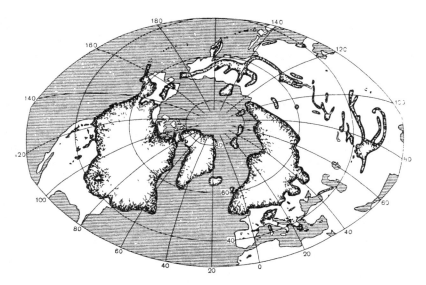

Maximum Pleistocene glaciation in the Northern Hemisphere (431)

logical periods, S. A. Kovalevsky suggested uniting them under one name—*Krionogen*. The transfer of the lower boundary of the Anthropogen to cover part of the Upper Pliocene, the so-called *Villafranc*, was recommended in 1948 at the 18th International Geological Congress.

In its turn, the Anthropogen is subdivided into several stages. In connection with the addition of Villafranc, the most ancient stages of the Anthropogen, which are characterised by a much warmer climate than today, substantially differ from the Ice Age, i.e., the *Pleistocene* proper. The Anthropogen ended in post-glacial times, in the Holocene, which began 10,000-12,000 years ago and persists to this day.

There are two variants of Anthropogen chronology: the "long chronology" covering about 1,000,000-1,800,000 years, and the "short chronology" which accords the Pleistocene a period of only 250,000-350,000 years. The explanation for this is that radio-isotope methods of specifying the absolute chronology for the interval 50,000-2,000,000 years (429; 434) began to be developed only in recent years. Radiocarbon dating has fully justified itself for periods of up to 50,000-60,000 years (413). Some of the popular and latest variants of Anthropogen dating are given in Table 6 (Appendix 1). The column headed *Pacific Ocean* gives the results of our calculations, for which we accepted (for Holocene dating) a mean sedimentation velocity of approximately 4 cm/1,000 years.

The Ice Age is studied best of all in Europe and North America.

Clear-cut indications of considerable glaciation are also known in other continents, particularly in South America. But in South America and Australia glaciers were less widespread.

In Europe the centre of the ice sheet was in Fennoscandia. Back in 1912 G. De Geer (582) established the absolute chronology of all phases of the gradual retreat and delay of the Fennoscandia glacier and the date of its final continuous retreat (8515 B.C.), which was later confirmed by radiocarbon dating.

At present it is generally accepted that there were several glaciations during the Anthropogen and that in the intervals there were warm interglacial periods of various duration. But far from all scientists recognise this viewpoint. They consider that there was only one glaciation and that in the interglacial periods the glacier did not disappear completely, that it only retreated to the north (the monoglaciation school). But recent data shows that in the interglacial periods the ice sheet melted completely even in Scandinavia.

C. Emiliani (510-513a), who agrees with the "short chronology", assumes that the duration of individual glaciations did not exceed 25,000-35,000 years and that the minimum temperatures were observed 20,000, 60,000, 110,000 and 150,000 years ago, and the maximum temperatures 180,000, 230,000 and 285,000 years ago.

Inasmuch as to this day no universally accepted terminology exists for the alternation of glaciation and interglaciation and each country uses its own terminology, we gave preference to the Alpine terminology of A. Penck and E. Brückner. They established four main glaciations in the Alps: *Gunz* (earliest), *Mindelian*, *Riss* and *Würm* (which ended recently). These names derive from the localities where the end moraines of the glaciers of these epochs were discovered.

Today there are grounds for stating that in Europe and North America glaciation was almost simultaneous (720); naturally, each region had its own local features. But for a number of reasons in North America the delays in melting were more frequent and sometimes there were periods when instead of retreating the ice sheet advanced; moreover, it melted completely somewhat later than in Europe (434).

Opinion is divided as to what glaciation was more intense and more prolonged. At present, many scientists are inclined to believe that the Würm Glaciation was the greatest (541), but this theory is contested. However, all scientists share the view that the Holocene began about 10,000-12,000 years ago. This dovetails with repeated radiocarbon dating.

On the basis of a study of the levels of littoral Anthropogen terraces in different parts of the World Ocean and taking into account the absolute chronology of Emiliani (511, 512, 513) and other scientists, R. W. Fairbridge (526) drew a somewhat different conclusion on the time and amplitude of the ocean level's eustatic fluctuations, linking them up with glaciation and interglaciation periods:

Glaciation (G) and Interglaciation (I), in brackets for North America	Absolute chronology in years B C	Eustatic fluctuations of the ocean level in m	Mediterranean terraces
Holocene (I)	0-8,000	+3	(Flanders?)
Würm (Wisconsin) (G)	maximum—23,000	—100	
Eemian (Sangamon) (I)	68-108,000	+3 —18	Monastery
Riss (Illinois) (G)	maximum—128,000	—55	
Hoxen (Yarmouth) (I)	148-203,000	+30 —55	Tyrrhenian I and II
Mindelian (Kansas) (G)	maximum—218,000	—5	
Cromer (Aftonian) (I)	248-318,000	+80 —100	Sicilean
Gunz (Nebraska) (G)	maximum—348,000	—55	
Villafranc (I)	no exact data	+130 —200	(Calabrian?)
Danube (G)	insufficient data	?	?

However, P. Wolstedt, the noted authority on the history of the last glaciation, believes that submarine terraces were formed as a result of uplifts in continental regions because, in his opinion, during the Pleistocene the ocean level was much the same as it is today. Since the Antarctic glaciers were formed much earlier than the last glaciation, the ocean level could not have dropped. If the Antarctic and Greenland glaciers were to melt, Wolstedt points out, the ocean level would rise 80 metres. Shepard, on the other hand, contends that the ocean level rose more than 100 metres, reaching its maximum 20,000-60,000 years ago at a rate of eight metres per thousand years. According to K. K. Markov and M. A. Suyetova (745), the melting of the Antarctic glaciers would raise the ocean level 59 metres; they believe that during maximum glaciation the ocean was 110 metres below its present level, but that during the warmest interglaciation it rose 10 metres above the modern level.

In the southern glaciation-unaffected latitudes of the Northern Hemisphere, the glaciation periods are established on the basis of drops of the snow-line level in the mountains. There the *pluvial* and *arid* periods correspond to the glaciation and interglaciation periods respectively. The alternation of such periods has been most thoroughly studied in Africa. In the pluvial epochs even large deserts like the Sahara were excellently watered and had mighty rivers, great lakes, luxuriant verdure and a large animal population. But even in the arid periods the Sahara was more a savannah than a desert.

Atmospheric circulation and the distribution of precipitation show that during the glacial periods the maximum rainfall was in the equatorial-tropical belt and in the regions adjoining the edges of the glaciers (207; 434).

According to latest data, during the maximum of the last glaciation the temperature drop in the low-lying equatorial regions reached 3° and in the mountains it was equal to —5°; between the 35th and

40th parallels it was equal to 6-9°; and between the 50th and 55th parallels it dropped as much as 10-13.5°. Therefore, in that period, the northern boundary of the subtropics was at 30-38° instead of the present-day 40-55°.

The data on the area and quantity of ice during the latest glaciations have been revised. In the light of our knowledge of the melting of ice on surviving glaciers, it must be assumed that after the Great Ice Age the ocean level rose approximately 180 metres (442/72). But that is the level of the modern shelf (200 metres). Consequently, during glaciation the shelves were dry land and the area of the continents was larger than today.

Much has been written on the reasons giving rise to the glaciation periods and there are numerous views and theories on this subject, and many of them give different interpretations of one and the same factor (431; 434). Some scientists altogether reject the existence of glaciation periods, but it must be said that such scientists are very few.

All the surmises on the emergence of glaciation periods may be summed up as follows (431/215):

a) Cosmic Causes:

1. absorption of solar radiation by inter-stellar matter;
2. primary changes in solar radiation;
3. changes in elements of the Earth's orbit;
4. the fall of ice satellites on the Earth (160).

b) Terrestrial Causes:

5. displacement of the poles and drift of continents;
6. changes in the nature of the Earth's surface—distribution of land and sea, height of land, presence of mountains;
7. composition of the atmosphere—cloudiness, carbon dioxide content and volcanic dust;
8. changes in ocean salinity;
9. intra-terrestrial processes—radioactivity, cooling.

Analysed more closely some of these causes have been found to be ineffective or improbable (causes 1, 4, 5, 8 and 9) (431/215, 225, 231, 244, 246).

The hypothesis linking up glaciation either with changes in solar radiation or with the periodicity of the elements of the Earth's orbit are most favoured by climatologists.

H. C. Willet (701) points out that if the intensity of solar radiation diminished the temperature drop would, first and foremost, affect the tropics and reduce the meridional gradient of temperatures. There would, therefore, be a change in the general content of moisture in the atmosphere as a consequence of an abatement in general circulation, and a reduction of cyclonicity and of the total precipitation at all parallels. Thus conditions unfavourable to glaciation would have been created.

The authors of another group of hypotheses take into account the influence of the periodic (434/143) changes of some parameters of the Earth as a planet. These primarily include: 1) changes in the ecliptic angle (angle of the Earth's axis); 2) changes in the eccentricity (elongation) of the Earth's orbit; 3) changes in the time of the equinoxes (precession). These authors believe that inasmuch as all three parameters change simultaneously, climatic changes may be expressed by a summary curve.

Changes in the angle of the Earth's axis have a period of duration of about 40,000 years and take place within the limit of 24°36′ and 21°58′. At present the angle is 23°27′30″. In addition, solar radiation changes average 4 per cent per degree of axis angle, particularly in polar regions. This is the most important of all the above factors. The eccentricity of the Earth's orbit is now equal to 1/60 and changes approximately every 90,000 years, while the precession of the equinox has a period of about 21,000 years. These two factors play a much lesser role in the processes changing the solar radiation reaching the Earth.

From the mathematical standpoint the most detailed theory of the dependence of the Earth's climate on the periodic changes of the Earth's parameters as a planet was evolved by the Yugoslav scientist M. Milankowitsch (329), who graphically depicted computed values for the past 600,000-1,000,000 years. Later W. Soergel remade Milankowitsch's radiation curve into a "glaciation curve". However, the Milankowitsch-Soergel computations and arguments evoked reasonable objections. Following in the footsteps of Milankowitsch, D. Bačak (320/158, 2nd ed.) made an attempt to specify his results and provide them with confirmation. However, Bačak's assumptions were not convincing. Subsequently, other attempts were made to apply Milankowitsch's theory, whose attraction lies in its simplicity.

H. C. Willet (701; 434/79) notes that the Milankowitsch-Soergel theory clashes with many factual data obtained in recent years and confirmed by absolute chronology methods, particularly for the late and post-glacial period. Moreover, van Woerkom (434/179), who recomputed the Milankowitsch curve according to more recent, specified data, writes: "Our conclusion must be that the changes in insolation, caused by changes in the Earth's orbit and in its axis of rotation, are insufficient to explain the periods of glaciation."

M. Schwarzbach (431/243), a recognised authority on historical climatology, writes: "Consequently, we must adopt a sceptical approach to the climatic explanation of the radiation curve. The foundation of this astronomical hypothesis proves to be quite unreliable" (also see 320/153).

The influence of factors like cloudiness, and changes in the content of volcanic ash and carbon dioxide in the atmosphere merit close attention. Thus, the solar constant can change substantially as a result of the absorption of radiation by water vapour and dust. Even in ordinary circumstances its value, depending on local conditions, may be halved or reduced even further (320/141). Inasmuch as the albedo of clouds is equal to 80-100 per cent, and the Earth's mean albedo as a planet is only 45 per cent, the Earth, if it were completely enveloped by clouds (like Venus), would receive half of its present dose of solar energy. The Earth's cloudiness is accepted as equal to about 50 per cent (320; 168, 2nd ed.; 434/109-13).

The "carbon dioxide theory" was suggested by S. Arrenius in 1909. His argument was that being transparent for visible light, carbon dioxide (like water vapour) absorbs great quantities of infrared rays reflected by the Earth's surface and thus prevents heat from escaping into outer space. This creates what is known as the hothouse effect. J. London (598) considers that if the present carbon dioxide content were halved it would reduce the Earth's surface temperature by 3.3°. Conversely, the doubling of this content would raise the temperature by 3.6°. However, according to E. Philippi (434/228), high carbon dioxide solubility in water would cause its increased absorption by the waters of the ocean and this would bring the atmosphere's gas content to a balanced amount (also see 366; 434/108).

Any reduction of the intensity of solar radiation as a result of the presence of volcanic ash in the atmosphere is due, as C. E. P. Brookes (207/246) points out, to the scattering and reflection of radiation and not to its absorption. It may drop, apparently, as much as 15-20 per cent. If such losses were to take place over a long period, the Earth's mean temperature could fall by 5.6°, which would be quite enough to set off glaciation. Observations conducted in the 19th and the 20th century showed that solitary volcanic eruptions of the explosive type never caused an appreciable temperature drop.

Some theories link glaciation up with mountain-building processes. On this score, Brookes (207/246) writes: The most probable causes of glaciation in general were uplifts and orogenesis, the inaccessibility of high-latitude basins to warm ocean currents and, possibly, the presence of considerable quantities of volcanic ash in the atmosphere. All these factors were on hand at the beginning of the Quaternary period. A reduction of the CO_2 content in the atmosphere might have been an additional factor. However, with the exception of volcanic ash, all these factors are stable and do not change so quickly as to cause a consistent alternation of glacial and interglacial epochs.

The theories that mountain-building processes influence glaciation are rejected by Academician L. S. Berg (200). It is, however, hard to agree with his arguments and conclusions because they are founded principally on an interpretation of an individual case—the bi-polar distribution of marine mammals. His criticism hardly touches purely geological processes that might have forced the Earth's temperature to drop. The latter view is enunciated by I. D. Lukashevich (304), who believes that during the transgression epochs the land temperature rose by 1-2°, while in the shallow seas that formed at the expense of land great masses of ocean water were heated. On the other hand, during regressions the land area increased and was quickly cooled. However, the temperature of the surface waters of the ocean did not drop at once. On the contrary, it even rose during a certain period at the expense of the warm water draining from the drying seas. According to Lukashevich, the regression periods were characterised by a pronounced contrast between land and sea temperatures, and this led to glaciation.

At this point we must mention the recent sensational hypothesis on the causes of glaciation put forward by M. Ewing and W. L. Donn (446; 522).

According to this hypothesis, during the Cretaceous and Tertiary periods the North Pole was in the northern Pacific and then shifted eastward. At the end of the Tertiary period the poles moved to their present position.

The conditions favouring glaciation ceased as soon as the glacier spread to the Arctic Ocean. There was an exchange of waters between the Arctic and the Atlantic oceans and the transition to interglaciation began.

Ewing and Donn believe that present-day Arctic temperatures are the maximum for interglaciation and that the next glaciation may be expected in the course of several thousand years!

But even a cursory examination of this hypothesis brings one to the conclusion that it poorly ties up with facts. For instance, present-day temperatures of the Arctic are by no means optimal. The optimum was reached, probably, about 5,000-7,000 years ago, when trees still grew within the Arctic circle. Yet no glaciation followed.

This semi-fantastic hypothesis has been extensively criticised by R. Malaise (76) and N. Odhner (168), who pointed out that the key was not in the "pumping" of moisture from the ocean but in tectonic movements (also see 323).

M. Schwarzbach (663), a leading authority on the problem of glacial periods, raises the following objections to the Ewing-Donn hypothesis: 1) the phases of glaciation are arbitrarily simplified and condensed in time; 2) no explanation is offered as to why the melting of the Canadian and Scandinavian glaciers, which began when ice covered the Arctic Ocean, did not spread to Greenland; 3) the distribution of cyclones and the weaker glaciation of Siberia as compared with that of Canada are unsatisfactorily explained; 4) the significance of the Iceland-Faeroe Rise in the division of the polar and Atlantic water masses is unfoundedly exaggerated; 5) pre-Tertiary glaciation is not taken into account.

To this it may be added that even present-day supporters of the theory about the movement of the poles admit that there is nothing in paleomagnetic data to show that in the Anthropogen there were changes in the situation of the poles that could dovetail with the Ewing-Donn hypothesis (284/10; 427/53). Academician D. I. Shcherbakov (442/85) writes: "... in the recent geological epochs (Quaternary period, the Neogene and the Upper Paleogene) the position of the ancient magnetic poles approximately coincided with that of the modern geographical pole." I. I. Shell (667), R. W. Buechley (476), P. Colinvaux (735) and Dzerdzeyevsky (809) have likewise criticised the Ewing-Donn hypothesis.

In passing, it may be noted that glaciation has been explained by G. D. Khizanashvili (423/61-67) from the standpoint of his own hypothesis, i.e., as being the result of short migrations of the poles.

Some years ago the Yugoslav scientist T. Segota (664, 665) advanced some interesting ideas about what caused the glacial periods. He considers that the factors giving rise to these periods include high latitudes, the uplift of mountains and geographical isolation from the central, warm parts of the ocean. Depending on the distribution of land and sea there are two types of glaciation: continental (glaciation of a continent surrounded by a cooled sea), this being typical of the Antarctic, and honeycomb (separate ice-bound sections of land round a frozen sea), which is typical of the Arctic. Glaciation began in the Antarctic. Segota dates its emergence from the Upper Pliocene. As a result of this glaciation there was a general cooling of the Earth's atmosphere and a drop of the ocean level, which, in its turn, led to glaciation in the region of the North Pole. This was facilitated by the uplift of land in the high latitudes of the Northern Hemisphere (and, in our opinion, of Atlantis). Subsequently, glaciations underwent pulsation, which, however, in Segota's view, did not depend on any extra-glaciation factors but was the result of the very mechanism of glaciation as being linked up with the temperature and humidity in the glaciation and adjoining regions. Glaciers grow when the temperature is relatively low and there is considerable humidity in the air and, on the contrary, they begin to degenerate and decrease when the temperature in their own and adjoining regions drops sharply and the air is dry. Consequently, according to Segota, glaciation diminishes not only when the temperature rises but also when it falls drastically, for then the nourishment of glaciers is cut short.

Segota (664) believes that the glaciation of the Antarctic began 4,330,000 years ago and achieved its maximum roughly 874,000 years ago (Danube glaciation in Europe).

What then are the most probable causes of glaciation? Schwarzbach (431/248-49) holds that climate is influenced by two main factors: changes in solar radiation and changes in the appearance of the Earth (i.e., in the distribution of land and sea and in elevation —*N.Z.*). "... But these factors, acting at different times, did not lead to glaciation." We know very little about the changes in solar radiation. *But if we discard the notion that there is a compulsory community of reasons giving rise to glaciation at different geological epochs, it seems to us that it would be most plausible to look for these reasons in purely terrestrial factors.* C.E.P. Brookes (207/256) writes: "Summing up, we find that for the occurrence of the Ice Age as a whole, the 'geographical' theory seems to be the only adequate one, with possibly some help from CO_2."

This is the viewpoint of Russian climatologists. For instance, in 1881, A. I. Voyeikov (220) wrote: "We may have a Greenland temperature such as obtained during the Miocene, and glaciers may appear in Brazil without any change in the mass of present currents and without any change in the mean air temperature. All that is required for this is a change in physical geography that would alter the direction of currents." Academician P. P. Lazarev (287/208) pointed out: "A reshuffle of the distribution of land and continents, and of land and sea would make the climate warm where it is now cold, because the ocean currents flowing from the equator and failing to reach these countries today might have done so in past geological epochs."

P. Belliar (760) likewise believes that *glaciation sprang from the distribution of land and oceans. Astronomical and climatic theories can explain only secondary fluctuations.*

Brookes (207/63) likewise assigns a big climate-making role to warm ocean currents: "Thus we see that during warm periods all the circumstances worked together to maintain the temperature of warm ocean currents in the high latitudes. Since these warm currents were also accompanied by warm winds, it will be seen that with large, open oceans and low, level continents the extension of warm temperate oceanic climates into the immediate neighbourhood of the poles does not involve any insuperable difficulty." The movement of air masses also considerably influenced the climate. Brookes attributes quite a substantial role to tall mountain ranges as barriers to winds.

B. ATLANTIS, THE GULF STREAM AND THE ICE AGE

Atlantis, a mountainous, meridionally oriented country, which undoubtedly stretched for many hundreds of kilometres in the Atlantic Ocean, could not, in our opinion, have failed to exert a tremendous influence on the climate of the continents adjoining the Atlantic, particularly of Europe. It is easy to appreciate that Atlantis prevented the warm Gulf Stream from penetrating to the north and, particularly, to the east. Possibly, a large Bermuda Island, on the one hand, also situated in the north, and then the continental Grand Newfoundland Bank together with Flemish Cap (an island or a peninsula of *Grand Newfoundland*, to use our own paleogeographical terminology), on the other, deflected the Gulf Stream from the shores of North America as well. The tall and steep mountain ranges of Atlantis held up part of the warm, moisture-laden Atlantic winds. The air masses moving along the western side of the North Atlantic Ridge and gradually cooling left their moisture on the glaciers of Atlantis, Greenland, Labrador, Iceland and other northern islands. Cold and dry masses of air moved to the south and east from the glaciers of Scandinavia and North Atlantis. At various periods of the geological past warm currents broke through to the north in mighty streams along the western coast of Atlantis, thawing great land areas, the North Atlantic islands and even the Arctic. This, in our view, is what the climate of the North Atlantic was like when Atlantis was subaerial (18/88).

It may be surmised that mid-oceanic ridges rose in the Miocene and the Pliocene and formed large land areas in the South Atlantic, the Indian Ocean and the Pacific. As a consequence, there appeared in the Southern Hemisphere latitudinal ranges (the existence of which is confirmed by modern bathymetric data), which cut the Antarctic off from the warm equatorial currents. If we accept this theory we shall then easily explain the Ice Age in the Southern Hemisphere and the glaciation in the Antarctic.

Brookes (207/18) points out that the theory that glaciation started when the Gulf Stream was shut out of the water circulation system of the North Atlantic had been advanced a very long time ago. He reviews the following possibilities:

1. The existence of a strait between North and South America. Here he reasonably adduces that the opening or closure of the Panama isthmus would not have influenced the Gulf Stream.

2. An eastward movement of the South American coast. But the subsidence or uplift of the sea bed by 300 metres would not have changed the quantity of water flowing into the Gulf Stream. However, a 2° displacement of the Brazil coast to the north could have reduced the influx of warm water by 40 per cent.

3. An increase in the velocity of the northeasterly trade wind. This increase would have moved the current to the south, but the mechanism that could produce such an effect is quite inexplicable.

4. As a fourth possibility, Brookes considers the probable existence of an Antilles continent, but says nothing more about such a variant. Understandably, *apprehensions about mentioning Atlantis have completely excluded the most probable of all variants, one which Brookes did not consider, namely, the subaerial existence of the North Atlantic Ridge.*

Yet from time to time the idea that Atlantis and the Gulf Stream were instrumental in giving rise to glaciation in the Northern Hemisphere is entertained by some scientists. Evidently, it was first mentioned by E. Hull (in 1897). In Russian literature this idea was quite independently elaborated on by P. N. Chirvinsky (148) in 1913: "The Gulf Stream, which was non-existent until Atlantis sank, began moving northward huge quantities of warm water, which evaporated easily and condensed into snow on the cooled continents." But Chirvinsky's theory that glaciation was caused by the

Gulf Stream cannot be accepted because large land areas are needed for a long-lived ice sheet. The existence of both the Gulf Stream and of cooled but smaller land areas (for example, Greenland) is certainly not giving rise to an Ice Age.

Writing of the influence of the land area on the process of glaciation, Brookes (207/18) says that when the land area increases the winter cooling effect springing from its size at first increases, reaching its maximum when a round island's radius is equal roughly to 10° latitude. When the island's radius amplifies further, the general effect continues to mount but its mean value begins to diminish. Cooling allows the snow blanket to spread much farther south than in cases where cold winds are held up by a latitudinal mountain range.

Brookes notes that the critical diameter of an ice sheet for 75°N is about 1,040 kilometres. If the diameter is smaller winds blow without hindrance, but a diameter of 1,600 kilometres and over allows a glacial anticyclone to become established. Naturally, the critical diameter will be larger in the lower latitudes, but a powerful reverse influence is exerted by mountain ranges and plateaus (the computation was given for a level surface); the exact laws governing these conditions have not been ascertained. If we apply these considerations to the northern part of Atlantis we shall find that in the north it must have been fairly wide, which, in fact, it probably was not, judging by bathymetric data. But in the early Anthropogen to the north of it there was, evidently, a vast land area (Hyperborea), which, in addition to Greenland and Iceland, included the presently submerged Atlantic Sill, the Reykjanes Ridge and the submarine Rockall and Faeroe plateaus. Since the water expanse between this land area and Atlantis was not large, the glaciers from that land embraced this water expanse and probably extended onto Atlantis.

F. B. Phleger (635), who accepted the theory that in the Pleistocene the Atlantic coastline was stable and the Gulf Stream acquired its modern direction, was compelled to assume that in that age the warm waters from the tropics circulated as though in an "extensible stepped pipe", i.e., in the direction of the high latitudes the breadth of the warm currents rapidly diminished. He attributes this phenomenon to the formation of a massive barrier of Arctic waters, which drove the warm current to the centre of the Atlantic. To back up this theory, Phleger mentions the finding of glacial pebbles and boulders as far as 40°N, i.e., the iceberg limits of that period.[*] On the basis of all these considerations Phleger draws the conclusion that cold Arctic waters flowed south of this latitude and that pack ice reached the 40th parallel. He writes: "It is doubtful whether the northern

---

[*] The occurrence of small pebbles in the sediment cores studied by H C Stetson and referred to by Phleger might have been transported by the glaciers and rivers of Atlantis The question of their origin can only be settled by a careful petrographic analysis Besides, erratic materials have been found much farther south of the Phleger limit.

edge of the Gulf Stream system reached a latitude much higher than that of Cape Hatteras on the North American continent" (roughly 35°N).

We are not inclined to accept the notion that during the Ice Age (without the existence of land in the North Atlantic) the Gulf Stream was a much smaller current and that it did not flow far in the Atlantic. This notion was called to life in order to sustain the ocean permanency theory. As we know, the Gulf Stream rises in the equatorial and tropical regions of the Atlantic and owes its origin to the northeasterly trade wind. However, there are no grounds for considering that during the Ice Age the temperature of the Earth's equatorial and tropical regions fell so low as to affect the velocity of the trade winds which drive warm waters. There is nothing in paleofloristic or paleofaunistic data to indicate a considerable temperature drop in the equatorial and tropical regions during the Ice Age. *In order to reduce the spread of the Gulf Stream to any appreciable extent there had to be a marked change in the power and velocity of the trade wind.* In its turn, this would have caused the temperature of the equatorial and tropical regions to fall drastically and greatly change atmospheric circulation.

During the Ice Age the temperature dropped chiefly in the high latitudes, calling forth a sharp latitudinal temperature decline and, conversely, a more powerful atmospheric circulation. Under these conditions, if we accept the existence of the present shoreline or even take into account the drainage of the shelves (i.e., a lower ocean level), we shall find we have no grounds for believing that the Gulf Stream could have been compressed into a narrow stream between two broad and powerful cold currents: the Coriolis force, in any case, would have held it close to the shores of continents. There is no doubt that the Gulf Stream delta would also have continued to exist in some form and it would by no means have spread like an "extensible stepped pipe". But even if the Gulf Stream, being saltier and therefore more dense, had flowed below a cold current desalinated by drift ice and therefore of a lesser density (like the Atlantic waters in the Arctic), it would have continued to carry warmth-loving plankton, which in reality never occurred as is shown by the history of the cold-loving and warmth-loving foraminifera and other organisms inhabiting the eastern North Atlantic. Similarly improbable is the notion that pack ice might have spread across the entire North Atlantic down to approximately the 40th parallel, *with the Gulf Stream in existence and in the absence of a land area*, which could fuse such colossal icefields. However, everything fits when we assume the subaerial existence of the North Atlantic Ridge. In the light of this assumption it is possible to explain facts like the drift-ice transportation of erratic boulders to the eastern side of the ridge down to the 30th parallel, the absence of such boulders on the western slopes, the occurrence of reef corals at the western slopes, and so forth.

The theory attributing to Atlantis the key role in the appearance and disappearance of glaciers in the Northern Hemisphere was propounded by the Soviet atlantologist E. F. Hagemeister (30). She wrote: "There was, evidently, some obstacle preventing the southern current from reaching the polar regions. This obstacle could only have been a land area in the Atlantic.... The Ice Age set in.... Thousands of years went by. Atlantis slowly began to subside. Inch by inch its northern and southern tips sank in the water. Eventually, only its central part remained above water. This was the Atlantis of Plato, and it is mentioned by even more antique authors. Moreover, legends about it have remained among almost all the ancient peoples of both the western and the eastern coast of the Atlantic.... When Atlantis finally sank, the warm equatorial current moved in a broad stream northwards, carrying warmth to the ice-bound shores of Europe. The climate rapidly grew warmer, and the ice melted or retreated to the north. The Ice Age ended. Our theory is backed up by the circumstance that in time the destruction of Atlantis coincides with the end of the Ice Age...."

In an afterword to Hagemeister's work, Academician V. A. Obruchev said the following about her theory: "The new data on the depths in the North Atlantic confirm that they are of relative recent origin and that their age roughly coincides with the time of the destruction of Atlantis as stated in ancient legends. Furthermore, it is interesting to compare the time of Atlantis' sinking and the end of the Ice Age in the Northern Hemisphere—both these events took place 10,000-12,000 years ago. This gives us grounds for thinking that *Atlantis was the barrier that prevented the warm Gulf Stream from reaching the north, the Arctic Ocean. The appearance of this barrier early in the Quaternary period gave rise to glaciation round the North Pole. The sinking of Atlantis reopened the road for the Gulf Stream*, (my italics—*N.Z.*) and in the north its warm waters gradually ended the glaciation round the North Pole, while round the South Pole glaciation exists to this day." Academician Obruchev reiterated this point of view in a letter to the author of this work on December 27, 1955: "This island lay in the path of the warm Gulf Stream where it flowed from the Caribbean Sea to the North Pole, and its destruction cleared this road, allowing the warm current to reach the Arctic Sea and reduce its glaciation to its present state; on the other hand, the continent occupying the South Pole has a thick cover of snow and ice to this day" (18/92).

Opponents of atlantology (756) argue that, firstly, there were several glaciations and that they alternated with warm interglaciations, while the subsidence of Atlantis was a single, swift process, and, secondly, the post-glacial transgression was not a sudden catastrophe. We feel that arguments of this kind are far-fetched. We by no means rule out the significance of other factors influencing the appearance and disappearance of glaciers (for example, the periodicity of solar activity, and so on). However, we believe that changes in the distribution of warm sea currents play the key role in the emergence of various climate conditions. After glaciation there were sharp climatic fluctuations and this called forth the so-called "little ice age" or "climatic upheavals". On the other hand, no further outburst of glaciation has taken place inasmuch as the distribution of the warm sea currents have remained unchanged. Further, although Plato speaks of "one disastrous night and day", the subsidence of Atlantis was a drawn-out process. But from the geological standpoint it may be called swift. Warm interglaciations were caused not only by changes in the land-sea relationship but also by fluctuations of solar activity, and other climatic factors. The subsidence of the long meridional ridge continued throughout the Pleistocene, and this gave rise to the most unexpected changes in the flow direction of warm currents—drawing closer to the continents and then moving away from them, the remnants of the ridge playing the role of traffic regulator.

As regards the post-glacial transgression, cause and effect are deliberately confused. While the subsidence might have been a short-lived catastrophe, the melting of huge quantities of ice cannot be represented as a lightning process: unquestionably, it took many long years. Moreover, time (centuries on end) was needed to warm the oceans, which had been cooled by water from the melted glaciers.

Foreign scientists give preference to the idea that only the Atlantic Sill was above sea level. But it must be stated beforehand that this concept does not explain many factors (for example, the cold and warm currents on either side of the North Atlantic Ridge).

H. J. E. Peak and H. J. Fleare (207/68) believe that glaciation was caused by the uplift and sinking of land stretching from Labrador across Greenland, Iceland and Scotland. They point out that when this bridge was continuous there was little or possibly no ice at all in the northern half of the Atlantic Ocean. Much later glaciation periods correspond to lesser uplifts, i.e., to the time when the bridge was not continuous and large quantities of ice appeared in the sea. The interglacial periods coincided with the submersion of the bridge, when land sank below its modern level.

Peak and Fleare are of the opinion that a great deal of ice accumulated in the Arctic basin, which was closed at the time, and that its level was, therefore, higher than that of the other oceans. When from this basin the water broke through into the Atlantic, it brought with it Arctic fauna to the middle latitudes.* Thus, on the coast of Sicily, which is 91 metres above the present sea level, there are remnants of fauna now inhabiting only the most northerly regions of Europe.

The theories offered by H. E. Forrest (60) on the existence of a North Atlantean continent and of Atlantean Alps are a development of these views. He considered that this continent occupied the

---

* Not Arctic but boreal! See Chapter Thirteen.

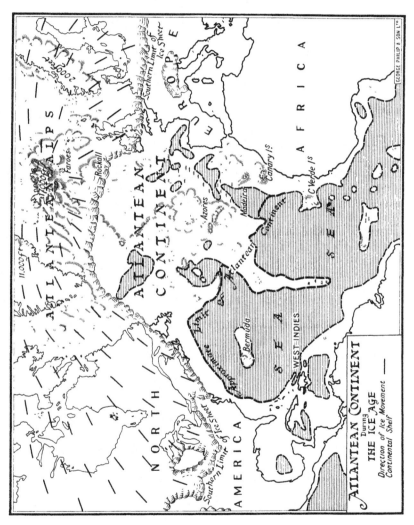

Map of the Atlantean continent, after Forrest (60)

entire north of the Atlantic and stretched all the way to the Azores. Forrest's Atlantis was thus a vast peninsula joining Europe to North America. He sited the Atlantean Alps in Iceland, assuming that they were some 3,000 metres above sea level. He used the latter assumption to explain the amplitude of subsidence, and he computed their location in the direction of the furrows left by glaciers when they moved from the common centre. Thus, in contrast to the usual views, Forrest considered that the centre of glaciation was not in Scandinavia but in Iceland. On the basis of data on the glaciation of Britain he distinguished three glaciation periods. Inasmuch as after the third period the British Isles were no longer covered with ice, Forrest's conclusion from this was that the Atlantean continent had subsided.

As is pointed out by G. Poisson (86/70-72), the Forrest Glaciation should not be identified with the usual Penck-Broeckner system. Poisson offers his own variant. The North Atlantic bridge was not very prominent at the close of the Pliocene and the beginning of the Pleistocene. Then, after the Gunz Interglaciation, this bridge acquired the shape of Forrest's continent, in which Iceland was the Atlantean Alps and the centre of glaciation, from where glaciers spread to the east, south and west. This corresponds to the Mindelian Glaciation. After that there was the next glaciation, which took place under the same conditions as the preceding glaciations, but was more intensive, possibly due to the subsidence of the Atlantean Alps. This was the Riss Glaciation. Lastly, the bridge broke up into several parts, Scandinavia and Canada got their own centres of glaciation, and the British Isles were free of ice. This was the Würm epoch.

The principal objection to the Forrest-Poisson theory is that nothing confirms the existence of tall Atlantean Alps in Iceland.

C. GEOMORPHOLOGY AND GEOLOGICAL HISTORY OF THE ARCTIC

The glaciation of the Northern Hemisphere is, as may be judged, directly bound up with the history of the North Atlantic and Atlantis. In its turn, the history of the North Atlantic is closely bound up with that of the Arctic, the refrigerator of the Northern Hemisphere as it is sometimes called, all the more so that the Arctic Ocean is a direct continuation of the Atlantic. Understandably, the climate of the Arctic largely depended on the onetime existence of both Atlantis and Hyperborea. The history of the Arctic and that of the North Atlantic are inter-related and, therefore, it is absolutely necessary to look into some aspects of the geomorphology and geological history of the Arctic, because this study can produce some confirmation that Atlantis really existed.

The geomorphology of the Arctic has been inadequately studied and a universally recognised terminology for the different elements of its topography has not been established. Every author uses his own terminology for new topography elements discovered by him. In this book we have borrowed terminology from works by Soviet and American authors (289; 297; 300; 397; 501; 723; 748; 783).

There are two adjoining seas between Greenland, Iceland and Scandinavia. These are the *Greenland* and *Norwegian* seas, which are genetically bound up rather with the Atlantic Ocean. The basins of these seas are hollows more than 3,000 metres deep and separated by a submarine ridge. Both basins have a broken floor topography, and the maximum depths are: 4,864 metres in the Greenland Sea, and 4,487 metres in the Norwegian Sea. J. B. Rigg (654) informs us that the oceanographic expedition on the *Northern Princess* discovered *an ancient submerged shoreline in the Barents, Greenland and Norwegian seas at a depth of 200-400 metres*. This depth is clear evidence of tectonic rather than eustatic subsidence.

Between Spitsbergen and Greenland is the *Nansen Sill*, which is roughly 90 kilometres wide and reaches down to depths of 1,280-1,400 metres. Its surface is slightly undulating. *The general smoothness of the topography suggests that this is an ancient submerged structure.* R. S. Dietz and G. Shumwey (501) believe that *both the topography and the length of this sill are evidence of its continental nature.* Soviet oceanologists have found that it is not an unbroken mountain chain; it has transversal depressions, the deepest of which (over 3,000 metres) is the Lena Trough.

A long submarine range extends from Iceland deep into the Arctic Ocean. Some scientists regard it as an extension of the *Mid-Atlantic Ridge* in the Arctic and call it the *Mid-Arctic Ridge*. The Iceland-Jan Mayen Ridge, on whose extremity is situated the volcanic Jan Mayen Island with the extinct Beerenberg Volcano (2,274 metres), stretches from Iceland along the continental slope of eastern Greenland. Farther, running obliquely across the ocean, is *Mohns Ridge*; this is a series of parallel crests standing 600-1,500 metres below the ocean surface and separated from each other by deep hollows. There are some seamounts with a subsidence depth of 550-850 metres. Lastly, the continental slope of western Spitsbergen is hugged by the Knipovich Ridge. All these ridges consist of accumulations of individual and groups of mountains with truncated (eroded?) or concave (volcanoes?) summits. Foothill terraces, typical of the Mid-Atlantic Ridge, are non-existent.

In the region of Jan Mayen Island and west of it is a rupture in the median ridge, which here represents a left-hand displacement. This is where most of the earthquake epicentres are concentrated. Analogous to the Atlantic Sill, in the region of Jan Mayen Island, on either side of the Mid-Arctic Ridge there are wall-shaped chains of mountains with levelled summits and steep sides—*Mohns Ridge*.

Farther, beyond the Nansen Sill, are two basins: the western, *Amundsen Basin*, and the eastern, *Nansen Basin*. These are flat basins, which have hardly been investigated, with depths of at least 4,000 metres. They are separated by the Gakkel (or Otto Schmidt)

Ridge and adjoined by a region of Arctic seamounts. Along the ridge axis is a series of rift valleys 20-40 kilometres wide and aggregating more than 1,000 kilometres lengthwise. The amplitude of the topography height is more than 4,000 metres. The ridge fades out in the direction of the Laptev Sea. Numerous conical seamounts, possibly of volcanic origin, rising from depths of about 4,200 metres, have been discovered in this area.

The asymmetry of some of the mountains rising to a height averaging 1,000 metres above the ocean floor brings us round to the assumption that tectonic subsidences had taken place here. B. C. Heezen and M. Ewing perceive a connection between this region and the polar extension of the North Atlantic Ridge. The cross-section offered by Heezen (418/63, Fig. 7, Cross-section 3) as proof of the extension of the World Mid-Oceanic Ridge to the Arctic Basin, likewise concerns this region of Arctic seamounts and not the Lomonosov and Mendeleyev ridges of the Arctic Ocean. Today Heezen wisely no longer includes either the Lomonosov or the Mendeleyev Ridge in his hypothetical world ridge.

Lomonosov Ridge, the first median ridge of the Arctic Ocean, is situated between the Novosibirsk Islands and Ellesmere Island in the Canadian Arctic archipelago over a distance of 1,800 kilometres across the entire Arctic Ocean. It towers 3,000-4,000 metres above the floor of the adjoining basins. The shallowest of the known depths—936 metres—was discovered by a Soviet expedition in 1954. The depths above this ridge evidently range from 900 to 1,450 metres, the maximum not exceeding 1,650 metres. In some places *the peaks of Lomonosov Ridge (width—up to 26 kilometres) are flat terraces which may be regarded as having been formed by the abrasive activity of ocean waves*. The sides of the ridge are somewhat convex at the top. The ridge's asymmetry (the northern slope is not as steep as the southern), the convexity of the sides and the simple topography indicate a folded structure; there are a number of fault scarps with wide benches. Rock debris, pebbles, gravel and sand have been found on the ridge. Y. Y. Gakkel does not think they are of glacial origin; only part of them were brought by icefloes, but the majority are of local alluvial and deluvial origin (229).

Mendeleyev Ridge (according to American authors this is the Central Arctic Ridge or Alpha Ridge, named after the submarine which explored this region) is the second median ridge of the Arctic Ocean. It runs almost parallel with Lomonosov Ridge, beginning north of Wrangel Island and running up to the islands of Ellesmere and Axel Heiberg. It was discovered in 1954 by the Soviet North Pole-4 Drifting Station. Its width is from 200 to 900 kilometres, and its average height above the floor of the adjoining basins is 900 metres; the shallowest spot known so far is 1,246 metres deep. The central part of this range is a plateau about 100 kilometres wide, with an average submersion depth of about 2,300 metres ; it towers 2,000 metres above the floor of the adjoining basins. *Individual peaks of the Mendeleyev Ridge with a submersion depth of 1,250-1,340 metres have proved to be guyots; they give the impression that they were formed by wave erosion.* The gentle topography of the hills and the feeble seismicity suggest that the ridge is not young.

Y. Y. Gakkel (230) writes the following about this ridge: "By its fairly intricate structure this extensive system (or, at least that part of it that abuts on the Siberian shelf) belongs to block mountains with radial-concentric zonation of large blocks. One of the centres of these tectonic deformations is situated at 77°30′N 171°15′W. In the structure of the Mendeleyev Ridge there evidently are Upper Paleozoic limestones and sandstones. As regards the soil on the Mendeleyev Ridge and the formation of its topography, an essential role was probably played by glaciers." He feels that the abundance of boulders, rock debris and pebbles, particularly on the southern slopes, is due to the reworking of local rocks and not to transportation by drift ice.

Many Soviet scientists (723) believe that the Lomonosov and Mendeleyev ridges have no analogies in any other ocean. This is emphasised by the uniqueness of the Arctic Ocean, which in many ways differs from all the other oceans. This is evidently due to its youth.

Both ridges are very similar isostasically but differ from each other by the magnetic properties of the rocks of which they are composed and by their topography. They are not seismic and have no direct indication of modern volcanic activity or other features of mid-oceanic ridges.

The *Makarov Basin* (or the *Central Arctic Basin* as it is called by American authors) is wedged between the Lomonosov and Mendeleyev ridges from the south. This is a small abyssal amorphous basin with depths of more than 3,900 metres and it probably has a thick layer of sediments.

The *Beaufort* or *Canadian Basin* is the largest abyssal basin of the Arctic Ocean. It stretches from the Mendeleyev Ridge to the Alaska shelf and has depths of about 3,850 metres.

Soviet geophysicists (724), who studied the floor structure in the Arctic Ocean, arrived at the following conclusions. In some areas the sediment layer is nearly 3,000 metres thick. In the western part of the ocean the Mohorovicic discontinuity surface lies at a depth of 4-8 kilometres, and many places are devoid of a granite layer. Near the Pacific Ocean the discontinuity surface goes down to 10 kilometres, and *beneath the Lomonosov and Mendeleyv ridges it drops to a depth of 15-20 kilometres. The crustal structure in the northern region is not everywhere typically oceanic, the latter being found only in individual scattered areas encircled by an intermediate type crust.* We feel that this is evidence of the extreme geological youth of the Arctic Ocean, a region where, in effect, oceanisation has only just begun.

Let us now deal with the geological history of the Arctic. According to V. P. Saks, N. A. Belov and N. P. Lapina (386), the Lomonosov

Ridge is of Mesozoic origin and was not subjected to Alpine orogenesis. The Western Arctic is a geosyncline, and the Eastern Arctic is a pre-Cambrian platform (Hyperborean shield). The deep hollow in the western part took shape at the close of the Mesozoic. At the beginning of the Tertiary period the marginal seas of the Arctic dried up and the water basin was limited only to the abyssal hollow. Up until the mid-Tertiary period a strait that connected the Arctic Basin with the seas in the south of Eurasia and with the Atlantic Ocean passed across the Kara and Greenland seas. Thanks to this strait the polar regions had a mild climate and arcto-Tertiary flora.

According to a reconstruction by V. P. Saks and his associates, land predominated in the Tertiary period and there were few water expanses. The present-day ratio of land and sea and of warm and cold currents in the Arctic is more beneficial than the above reconstruction, but it is a very far cry from a moderate (to say nothing of a subtropical) climate (18/94). In this connection, it will be recalled that according to C. E. P. Brookes (207/185) the distribution of land and sea north of the 40th parallel was an extremely important climatic factor for the Northern Hemisphere; the emergence of centres of cold, which is inevitable when the land area is sufficiently large, depends on precisely the land-sea ratio.

Y. M. Pushcharovsky (372) has come to the conclusion that the Arctic Ocean is a young formation that appeared on continental-type structures. He finds proof for this theory in the structural geology of the region, the length of the shelf, the small dimensions of the abyssal plains and so on. D. G. Panov (359) considers that during the Anthropogen, following the epoch of considerable outpourings of basalt in the Tertiary period, the Arctic became a region of great subsidences and the formation of transgressional seas.

We believe that the theory advanced by K. N. Nesis (344) in connection with the origin of amphiboreal species of marine mammals is more substantiated than that of V. P. Saks and his associates. The settlement of the North Atlantic by Pacific species proceeded through the Arctic along the shores of North America. The Bering Strait formed in the Eocene when the climate in the Arctic was still very warm. But the Eocene species differed radically from modern species. At the end of the Pliocene the Bering Strait was reopened once again. It was wider than today and had a depth of 150-300 metres. That was when amphiboreal species that reached as far as Iceland and the British Isles penetrated into the North Atlantic via the Arctic Ocean.

Migration proceeded along the Arctic shores of North America (but not along the shores of Siberia due to the subaerial situation of the Lomonosov Ridge!), which were washed by a powerful Pacific current. During the Upper Pliocene, therefore, the Arctic Ocean was not the body of cold water we know today. The Greenland-Canadian Sill had already subsided and the then warm Labrador Current flowed unhindered to the shores of Newfoundland and New England. When the Ice Age set in the Bering Strait was a land area that shut out the warm Pacific Current. The sea level dropped sharply, mainly as a result of tectonic movement. For example, in the Barents Sea it fell 200 metres, at the shores of Norway and Iceland 270 metres, and in the Arctic Basin as much as 500-700 metres. The shelves were covered with ice, and the glaciers along the shores of Newfoundland and Labrador descended directly to the sea.

During the Pleistocene the shelf along the coast of the USSR (over a distance of 500-1,700 kilometres) lay beneath a sheet of ice (783). On Franz Josef Land the ice sheet began to diminish rapidly about 16,000 years ago, following which islands appeared. This is proved by the discovery of terraces 55-520 metres above the modern sea level (725). According to the latest data obtained by Soviet scientists (817) the Mid-Arctic Ridge took shape at the boundary between the Neogene and the Anthropogen. This is borne out by considerable geological, geomorphological and paleogeographical evidence. For example, the volcanite of the ridge is genetically identical with the Late post-Neogene basalts of the Central Fault Trough of Iceland. *The finding of ancient rocks on the submarine Iceland-Jan-Mayen-Mona Ridge shows that in this area the ancient Caledonian mountain chain was destroyed and the modern Mid-Arctic Ridge appeared in its stead.*

Radioactive dating has yielded very interesting data on the Ice Age in the Arctic and on the penetration of later Atlantic waters into the Kara Sea. M. M. Yermolayev (250) gives us the following information: "The modern hydrological regime of our Arctic shelf seas, whose distinguishing feature is an intricate structure of the water mass that contains three different hydrochemical complexes, *took shape some 3,000-5,000 years ago. About 10,000-12,000 years prior to this the Gulf Stream penetrated into these seas* (my italics.—*N.Z.*), when the hydrological regime resembled the modern variant but the upper layers of water had a somewhat lower content of manganese." N. N. Lapina (291), who studied soil cores, reports that all the sediments are terrigenous and that the maximum glaciation in this area ended 100,000-105,000 years ago, when the shore-line in the Greenland Sea was at a depth of about 700 metres, in the Barents and Kara seas at a depth of 400-500 metres, in the Laptev Sea at a depth of 300-400 metres and in the East Siberian and Chukotsk seas at a depth of 100-200 metres. The warm interglacial period lasted about 40,000 years, the Zyryansk Glaciation 32,000-35,000 years, the Karga Interglaciation about 12,000 years and the Sartan Glaciation 9,200-10,300 years. Modern interglaciation in the Arctic's Pacific region began 9,000 years ago and in its Atlantic region 11,000 years ago. It must be noted that the Arctic chronology of glaciation after Saks and Lapina (291; 386) substantially differs from the European and American; this is due not only to the specific nature of the Arctic but also to the fact that the absolute chronology was evidently determined not by the radiocarbon method but by the method of the mean velocities of sedimentation in oceans.

Soviet scientists (815) believe that the *Arctic Basin took shape on the borderline between the Pliocene and the Anthropogen.* The period of even 25 million years for the beginning of the formation of abyssal plains is, in their opinion, much too high.

D. ARCTIC CLIMATE

The geological history of the Earth shows that in the region of the poles glaciation is not a normal feature. Today, as K. K. Markov (320/247-249) points out, *the climate in the Arctic is characterised by sharp and abnormal super-cooling and continentality created by the ice cover on the sea and the ice blankets on land.* Since ice and snow reflect more than 80 per cent of the solar energy reaching them, that is what gives rise to super-cooling in the Arctic. In fact, in the period from May to August there is enough direct and diffused light, for example, along the Spitsbergen parallel, to sustain as much organic matter as there is along the Central Europe parallel. In the recent geological past, when there was no ice in the Arctic, the climate there was moderately warm and relatively even, with clear-cut maritime conditions.

Speaking of the Arctic climate in the recent geological past, V. N. Saks (384) points out that in the pre-Ice Age, i.e., at the end of the Tertiary and the beginning of the Quaternary, there already was drift ice in the Arctic seas, the islands had glaciers, and the deciduous forests had been ousted by conifers. Throughout the Anthropogen the alternating closing and opening of the Bering Strait had little influence on the climate of the adjoining regions of Siberia. Of greater importance was the non-existence, at the beginning of the Anthropogen, of the Aleutian Islands, because this gave the warm Kuroshio Current access to the Bering Sea, and the warm Aleutian low was displaced to the north.

We feel we can picture the following individual elements of the changes in the distribution of land and sea in the North Atlantic and the Atlantic regions of the Arctic that might have had an essential influence on the climate in the Arctic (and in the extreme north of the Atlantic):

1. Changes in the configuration of Novaya Zemlya and Franz Josef Land and in the width and depth of the straits between the Barents and the Kara seas; 2. the existence of land in part of the Barents Sea; 3. the uplift of the Nansen Ridge; 4. the uplift of the Greenland-Iceland Sill and the closure of the Denmark Strait; 5. the uplift of the Reykjanes Ridge; 6. the uplift of the Iceland-Faeroe Rise; 7. the uplift of the Wyville-Thompson Ridge; 8. the closure of the straits between Greenland, Baffin Island and Labrador; 9. the uplift of the Grand Newfoundland Bank and Flemish Cap; 10. the existence of Atlantis (uplift of the North Atlantic Ridge) and the subaerial state of the entire Rockall Plateau.

Of these combinations, only the combinations 4+6+7 fully isolated the Arctic from the warm waters of the Atlantic. All other variants do not rule out the possibility of the warm Atlantic waters penetrating deep into the Arctic. Even variant 2 or 3 or 2+3 do not exclude this possibility, although the penetration would have proceeded farther east.

We consider that *the variants under which the Gulf Stream could collect into a powerful compact torrent are of considerable interest. First and foremost, these variants require the existence of Atlantis, which would have acted as a barrier to the present-day fanning out of the Gulf Stream at the approaches to the shores of Europe.* The "warmest" variant would have been possible under combinations 10+8+6+5+2 or 10+9+8+4. Under these variants the Gulf Stream, a massive torrent, would have reached the North Pole and, provided it encountered the Lomonosov Ridge in an abovewater state, it would have turned in several branches towards the Kara and the Laptev seas. In that case the climate of Taimyr Peninsula would have been much warmer than today, but in the polar regions of North America it would still have been cold.

Indeed, well-preserved remains of forest vegetation of undoubtedly post-glaciation age have been found in the extreme north of Siberia, far within the Arctic Circle. Extremely significant is the discovery of the remains of trees that grew in the Taimyr Peninsula between the 72nd and 76th parallels. Such finds are not rare in that area: the most northerly, reported by L. D. Miroshnikov (331), was discovered at 76°33′N. Regrettably, we could not find works in which these important discoveries were dated by the radiocarbon method.

Incidentally, in Siberia mammoths lived 44,000-33,000 years ago, yet the remains of a mammoth discovered in the Taimyr Peninsula was found to be only 11,450 years old (all ages were determined by radiocarbon dating).

In our opinion, *in the extreme north of Siberia, within the Arctic Circle, the climate could have been warm provided a powerful Atlantic current, flowing into the Arctic basin, encountered a barrier in the shape of subaerial Arctic median ridges which forced it to turn towards the shores of the Taimyr Peninsula.* The warm Atlantic current could have reached so far north if the Gulf Stream was collected into a compact torrent and did not fan out, as it does today, at the shores of Northwestern Europe. This was most probably the case if, firstly, the Gulf Stream flowed into the Arctic through the Denmark Strait (in which case the Iceland-Faeroe Rise was subaerial) and, secondly, if remnants of Atlantis and a subaerial Rockall Plateau prevented it from flowing to the shores of Europe.

Consequently, *the finding of trees within the Arctic Circle may be interpreted as indirect proof of the existence of Atlantis in the epoch of the so-called climatic optimum* (5th-3rd millennium B.C.), which was assumed by R. Malaise (74/155) on the basis of other considerations. The great length of this period sooner favours the assumption that the climatic optimum was due to purely terrestrial, geographical reasons rather than to changes in solar activity.

In this connection it may be mentioned that American scientists, who recently investigated the Mendeleyev Ridge (between 84°-85°N and 168°-169°W), discovered sediments with remains of moderate climate foraminifera *(Globorotalia crassiformes* and others).

E. THE LOMONOSOV AND MENDELEYEV RIDGES AND THE PROBLEM OF ARCTIS

The possibility that *the Lomonosov and Mendeleyev ridges were subaerial in the relatively recent geological past* is accepted by many Soviet and some American scientists. A. F. Treshnikov (401), for instance, considers that the Lomonosov Ridge might have been partially subaerial during the Sartan Glaciation (18th-7th millennium B.C.). Elsewhere (402) he writes: "It is not to be ruled out that some of the peaks or summits of the Lomonosov Ridge might be close to the ocean surface or even above the water level"; in other words, he considers that there might be islands that have not yet been discovered. Y. Y. Gakkel (227/129) shares this view, writing: "... consequently, in periods when direct communication between the Arctic Basin and the Atlantic was broken, not only the Nansen Ridge and the continental shoal but part, if not the whole, of the Lomonosov Ridge was subaerial." Concerning the onetime subaerial location of the Mendeleyev Ridge, Y. Y. Gakkel (230) writes: "The age of the upper layer of sediments is determined as 9,300±180 years. This age corresponds to the beginning of the post-glacial period. Consequently, *this mountain system, like the Lomonosov Ridge, was above sea level in the Quaternary period*" (my italics.—*N. Z.*).

Faunistic data favour the onetime subaerial situation of both these ridges. The difference between the marine fauna of the western and eastern parts of the Arctic Basin was noted by G. P. Gorbunov in the 1940s. Later this was confirmed by E. F. Guryanova in connection with the Lomonosov Ridge. On this subject K. N. Nesis (343) wrote: "According to E. F. Guryanova it (the Lomonosov Ridge) stood above sea level in the Quaternary period. She has established that in the Ice Age there were in the Arctic two centres of the formation of marine high-polar Amphipoda: the Kara and Chukotsk-American centres. Today species of the Kara centre spread eastward only up to the northwestern part of the East Siberian Sea, while species of the Chukotsk-American centre reach only the northeastern part of that sea. Apparently the barrier in the region of the East Siberian Sea, the Novosibirsk Islands and Wrangel Island, i.e., in the region of the Lomonosov Ridge, existed over a fairly long period and disappeared quite recently, in any case, during the post-Littorina epoch." The Littorina epoch corresponds to the climatic optimum and ended only about the year 2500 B.C. Y. Y. Gakkel (227/87), in his turn, notes: "A long time ago attention was drawn to the fact that the walruses inhabiting its waters have split into two alien herds. Evidently this disunion exists from the time when the Lomonosov Ridge was above sea level."

The hypothesis that these two ridges are sunken ancient mountainous countries and not young structures still in the stage of uplift is confirmed by data obtained by an American submarine expedition (501). Flat weathered summits at depths of not less than 1,300 metres are an indication that the Mendeleyev Ridge was once subaerial. The same concerns the Lomonosov Ridge, about which Dietz and Shumwey write: The summits of the ridge were eroded in more ancient times by the action of waves when the sea level was approximately 1,400 metres lower than today (501/1326). Hence, *in the recent geological past the Lomonosov and Mendeleyev ridges* subsided at least 1,400 metres.

There are grounds for believing in the onetime existence of Arctis, the younger sister of the legendary Atlantis. *In the period of the climatic optimum and, perhaps, somewhat later Arctis might have been the bridge across which man migrated from Asia to America.* In other words, the Bering Strait might not have been the only bridge for migration to that continent from Asia. In connection with the possibility of the submerged Lomonosov and Mendeleyev ridges having been the land of Arctis, D. G. Panov raises the problem of the settlement of Eskimos. The most ancient cultures of the American Arctic are the most northerly and the closest to the approaches of the ridges to the shores of America. Take the most ancient—the Independence culture. Radiocarbon dated as having existed around 2000 B.C., it had its seat on Peary Land (293). Moreover, all subsequent Eskimo settlement proceeded mainly from north to south. This is confirmed by archaeological finds and by historical data, for instance, the data on the colonisation of Greenland.

D. G. Panov also ties up the problem of Sannikov Land (135/135-182) with the former subaerial existence of the Lomonosov and Mendeleyev ridges. In his opinion, Sannikov Land might have been one of the submerged summits of these ridges. Gakkel (816) believed that Arctis existed even in the Late Tertiary (evidently in the Holocene).

Arctis is thus a problem of scientific atlantology and should be closely studied by atlantologists. It has only recently come into focus and it is very important to begin accumulating not only geological but also historical and ethnical material. It is quite possible that the epic tales of the peoples inhabiting the Arctic seaboard of both Asia and America, particularly the Eskimos, might contain some mention of Arctis.

F. SETTLEMENT OF AMERICA IN CONNECTION WITH GLACIATION AND ATLANTIS

The Ice Age in North America brings to the fore the problem of that continent's settlement by man. Inasmuch as the remains of neither the anthropoid nor the paleo-anthropoid have been found in America, it is believed that man migrated to America from other continents. Theoretically there could have been several variants of such migrations; of these the Asian (via the Bering Strait) is the most popular because of the similarity between the Amerindians and the Mongoloids of Asia and the seeming simplicity of that route. However, in closely analysing the real conditions that obtained in East Siberia and in Alaska during the Ice Age and the interglacial periods, L. A. Brennan, T. N. Lee, F. Rainey, P. Tolstoy, C. S. Chard and other American anthropologists now indicate the great hardships of that route, which became accessible only after the complete melting of the glaciers on either side of the straits.

Through radiocarbon dating it has been found that the most ancient camping sites of man in North America are more than 25,000 years old. At present we know of at least three such ancient sites: 1) near Louisville, Texas—earlier than 37000 B.C.; 2) on Santa Rosa Island, California—about 28000 B.C.; and 3) near Tule Springs, Nevada—over 28000 but not earlier than 33000 B.C. (471).

Even older camping sites, whose age lies outside the possibilities of radiocarbon dating, have been discovered on Santa Rosa Island (761). Another camping site more than 30,000 years old has recently been brought to light near Pueblo, Mexico. Stone implements roughly dated as 35,000-40,000 years old have been found in Illinois, USA.

I. K. Ivanova (799) reports that at the 7th INQA Congress the general opinion was that *man appeared in America 15,000-20,000 years ago*, i.e., at the beginning of the Holocene. E. A. Zamyslova (824), however, considers that man reached America much earlier. To back this up she draws attention to the discovery in Midland, Texas, of the bones of fossil man beneath layers of the Folsom type.

Opinion is divided about the duration of the Wisconsin Glaciation of North America.* According to the "short chronology" it began about 30,000 years ago, while the "long chronology" gives its beginning as 60,000-80,000 years ago. However, there are data to show that there was a short interglacial period about 20,000 years ago, and that a powerful glaciation (Farmdal) set in some 30,000 years ago.

In North America the Ice Age evidently had three centres: western (Rocky Mountains), eastern (in the region of Labrador) and between them the centre of the Keewatin Glacier. During the maximum glaciation all these three centres merged into a single glacier and the whole of North America, from ocean to ocean, was encased in ice. Obviously, under these conditions man could not have migrated from Asia across the Bering Strait. It also seems improbable that there was a long sea route on the western coast of America, where huge glaciers descended to the sea. Besides, as we know, Upper Paleolithic man knew nothing of navigation.

---

* See Tables 6 and 7 (Appendix 1)

Note must be taken of the fact that so far Paleolithic camping sites have not been found in Eastern Siberia. E. A. Abramova (718) reports that Mount Afontova (radiocarbon dated as only 20,000 years old) is the oldest known settlement in Siberia. But camping sites of even that age have not been discovered east of the Yenisei (i.e., Mount Afontova), including the Chukotka Peninsula, across which, according to the theory of the settlement of America from Asia, migration proceeded. Moreover, the oldest camping sites in the Bering Sea region were discovered not on the continent, but on the Aleutian Islands near Alaska; they have been dated as only 8,425 years old (465a). Consequently, all the dated camping sites belong to Holocene times, when man was already using primitive boats to sail along coasts.

It is doubtful if there was a large wave of migration to Alaska 10,000-14,000 years ago, when the climate was so cold that even the dwarf tundra birch died out. In Alaska tundra existed for a long time, the beginning of which lies beyond the possibilities of radiocarbon dating (487a).

It should be noted that the most ancient settlements of man in North America date from the time when Eurasia was inhabited mainly by Neanderthals, and intelligent man was only just appearing. However, we do not know who this ancient man of America was—a Neanderthal or an intelligent man. The majority of facts and opinions tend to favour *homo sapiens*, especially as neither the remains of Neanderthal man nor typical artifacts of his culture (Mousterian) have been discovered in America. Similarly, no traces of Neanderthal man have been found in East Asia. Consequently, the possibility of Neanderthal man having migrated from Asia to America must for the time being be ruled out.

The supporters of the Asian origin of the ancient Paleo-Indians have now propounded the theory of an interglacial corridor—a valley in the Rocky Mountains that was free of ice. However, there are some weighty arguments against this theory. First and foremost, we have no data to show either the length or the continuity of such a corridor, as well as of its direct contact with that part of Alaska that lay under an ice cap. Then the very nature of the supposed corridor—its narrowness, great length and extreme poverty of vegetation and consequently of food for man—would have made a journey along it extremely difficult and highly improbable. The valley grew wider and more negotiable only when the glacier began to retreat. This corridor, as Brennan (471/119) tells us, was still closed even during the latest advance of the glacier (Tazewell-Cary stage) about 18,000 years ago. Moreover, he considers that under any variants of the glaciation chronology, the inhabitants of the most ancient settlements did not have to pass through this corridor; this is indicated by their way of life, which shows that they were not a cold climate people, i.e., a people who came from the north. The mass migration of tribes across the corridor began only when glaciation ended, i.e., when the glacier began to melt rapidly (10,000 years ago).

The glaciation of Alberta Province, Canada, directly adjoining the Cordilleras in the East, was recently studied by C. P. Gravenor and L. A. Bayrock (537), who found that *during the last glaciation the ice sheet spread from the northwest, crossed the northern and central part of Alberta Province and linked up with the Cordillera glacier in the west.* The ice sheet retreated northward and northeastward. It crossed the central part of Alberta 31,000 years ago and left the south and centre of the province 11,000 years ago. These data do not support the theory that there was a corridor between the Cordilleras and the Keewatin glacier.

Anthropological and paleoanthropological data indicate that not only Paleo-Indians but also some of the present Amerindians have features distinguishing them from modern Mongoloids. It is quite possible that part of the ancient Paleo-Indians did not come from Asia. Yet any route other than the Bering Strait is considered improbable. During the Upper Paleolithic migration across the Pacific Ocean must be ruled out because this would have entailed at least a minimum knowledge of navigation or the existence of great island bridges across the ocean. Also suspect is the hypothesis that migration proceeded along the supposedly ice-free western seaboard of America, which is now submerged due to the eustatic rise of the ocean level (concerning the improbability of this route see 323/418). Much less probable is the fantastic idea that the Paleo-Indians migrated across the Antarctic. As regards the possibility that America was settled from the east across the Atlantic Ocean and Atlantis, the bias of Americanists towards any probability of the existence of Atlantis has left the study of this possibility to a few atlantologists. R. Malaise (76/217), for example, drew attention to the similarity between the flint implements of the Solutrean culture of Western Europe and analogous artifacts from the settlement in Sandia Cave, New Mexico, USA, radiocarbon dated as being about 17,000 years old. This similarity was noted in 1950 by K. MacGovan (603).

In its pure form the Solutrean culture covered a very small area: Western France and Northern Spain. *This painstaking technique of working stone,* as P. P. Yefimenko (251/366) writes, *appeared quite unexpectedly and then, for reasons still unfathomed, disappeared until the Late Neolithic.*

Malaise has suggested that *the Solutreans might have reached North America only via Atlantis,* which was still in existence during the Sandia culture epoch. The American archaeologist E. F. Greenman found Solutrean artifacts in Newfoundland and associated their origin with contact with Europe. L. A. Brennan (471/224), who studied the problem of the settlement of eastern North America, came to the conclusion that there was a genetic similarity between the Solutrean culture of Western Europe and the culture of the Paleolithic Llano people. However, he assumed that Paleo-Indians might have migrated to Europe and taken with them a more sophisticated method of working flint implements (p. 226). Yet *the migration of the Llano people* (or, on the contrary, of the Solutreans to America) could have taken place only if the North Atlantic Ridge was subaerial, i.e., only via Atlantis. Confronted with Malaise's investigations (75), Brennan timidly mentions this possibility but rejects it in the same breath (p. 232), evidently under the influence of the bias of the Americanists against the idea of Atlantis.

In a personal communication Brennan drew our attention to the fact that the largest concentration of ancient settlements with flint artifacts, made by the fluted points technique, is in the State of Alabama, USA, and that it would not have been difficult for the tribes of this culture to migrate from the Antilles via Florida. In his opinion the artifacts found at the Clovis site are probably of eastern and not of western origin.

It seems to us that *provided the equatorial archipelago of Atlantis was in existence, the most ancient migration of tribes from the Old to the New World might have taken place even as early as the Upper Paleolithic.** In this case this migration might have brought these tribes first to Guiana, Venezuela, the Antilles and Eastern Brazil. That, we feel, is where archaeologists must look for traces of the first settlers of the American continent. The northern route (via Poseidonis-Newfoundland) was much more difficult and became accessible only in the epoch close to the time when Atlantis finally sank. This was the route of the Late Mesolithic and Early Neolithic tribes.

The finding of relics of the so-called Sambaqui man is perhaps evidence in favour of our assumptions. Sambaquis (642a) are great heaps of "kitchen waste", primarily mollusk shells, which have been found in many places along the coast of Brazil. Similar piles of shells are known in Florida, Algeria, Portugal and Denmark. The Sambaquis are of different ages: the oldest have yielded human skulls of exceptional thickness—nearly 14 mm, which is four times as thick as the skull of *homo sapiens*. This is an indication of the antiquity of Sambaqui man.

According to A. Laming and J. Emperaire (584a) Sambaqui culture had two periods: an early period, which began before the 10th millennium B.C. and ended around 5500 B.C., and a late period dated from 4000 B.C. to the close of the 1st millennium B.C. A curious point is that shell piles in Portugal have been shown (by radiocarbon) as dating from 5400-3200 B.C.

Interesting investigations have also been conducted by M. F. Homet (159/94, 104), who discovered in unexplored regions of Brazil a remarkable rock drawing (Rock Pedra Pintada) and curious burials, in double urns, of Cro-Magnon people, whose skeletons were covered with red ochre.

---

* The *Popol Vuch* (sacred book) of the Guatemala Quechua, one of the Mayan tribes, says that the ancestors of the Quechua came from a land beyond the sea in the east, where they lived side by side with white and dark-skinned peoples (470/211, Chapter 3, part 3)

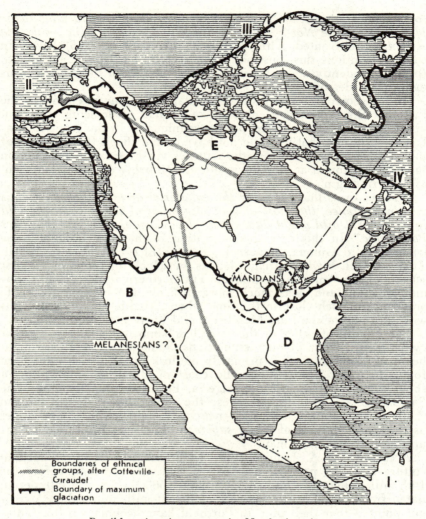

Possible migration routes in North America:
B—area of settlement by brachycephalic Amerindians, after Cotteville-Giraudet; D—area of settlement by dolichocephalic Amerindians, after Cotteville-Giraudet; E—area of settlement by Eskimos, after Cotteville-Giraudet; MANDANS—area of maximum settlement by Europeoid Amerindians ("white Indians").
MELANESIANS?—surmised area of maximum settlement by Melanesian ethnical groups, after Cotteville-Giraudet; I—possible migration route of dolichocephalic Upper Paleolithic Paleo-Indians in the epoch of maximum glaciation; II—main migration route of Mongoloid Mesolithic and Neolithic tribes in post-glacial times; III—possible migration routes of Eskimos via the Arctis during the climatic optimum epoch, after D. G. Panov; IV—possible routes of later migration by Mesolithic and Neolithic Europeoid tribes during the climatic optimum epoch (according to Malaise)

This custom, known in Neanderthal burials, was very widespread, particularly in Europe, as late as the Bronze Age. It should be noted that, as Homet points out, neither burials of this kind nor the presence of Cro-Magnon man were known in America. This question requires further careful study.

We should like to mention that J. J. Hester (772) is inclined to believe that ancient man settled chiefly in South rather than North America. The camping sites discovered in Venezuela are about 17,000 years old. The dating of extremely primitive stone implements by D. Ibarra Grasso (566) is suspect because it is based on the external appearance of these implements, a factor that does not guarantee their antiquity.

It is our opinion that *in the ancient settlement of America some role might have been played by Atlantis as a convenient intermediate bridge between the Old and the New World.* The future will show whether we are right.

Chapter Seventeen

LOCATION, CAUSES AND DATE OF THE DESTRUCTION OF ATLANTIS

A. PRINCIPAL VARIANTS OF THE LOCATION OF ATLANTIS

The paramount task of scientific atlantology is to establish the most probable location of Atlantis, which would conform to Plato's description of its topography and confirm or reject the date of this enigmatic continent's destruction as conveyed to us by legend. Naturally, in our study we rule out all the Pseudo-Atlantises, which were sited by their authors in places that had nothing in common with legend. Mentioning this, the American geographer W. H. Babcock (149/17) says: "The location of Atlantis, according to Plato, is fairly clear. It was in the ocean, 'then navigable', beyond the Pillars of Hercules; also beyond certain other islands, which served it as stepping stones to the continental man surrounding the Mediterranean. This effectually disposes of all pretensions in behalf of Crete or any other island or region of the inner sea."

The location must satisfy three main conditions. Firstly, it must be a region within the present Atlantic Ocean; the geomorphological and geological data must testify to the possible subaerial existence of now submerged land of considerable size. Secondly, this land must be situated west (or southwest or northwest) of the Strait of Gibraltar. And, thirdly, its topography (with due account of any islands that may exist there) must substantially conform to Plato's description.

At present there are four variants of Atlantis linked up with different submerged regions of the Atlantic; however, not all of these variants satisfy the above three conditions. F. Gidon (69/277-289) and then Ph. Russo (92) associate the Atlantis legend with the Flanders transgression, which they consider took place about 10,000-12,000 years ago and embraced many regions in Europe. In particular, they assume that the largest subsidence areas were round the British Isles and in the North Sea. Prior to this subsidence these islands and part of this sea were a single land area communicating with the continent via the then non-existent English Channel. A similar theory was suggested by C. Beaumont (150), who tied up the legend of the destruction of Atlantis with the Lyoness transgression in southwest Britain and believed that that part of Britain was the northern part of Atlantis.

The British variant has many weak points. It clashes with Plato's description, despite the fact that it is in the Atlantic Ocean: the location of the partially submerged continent is too far north, instead of being in the west; the flora and fauna are much poorer; the Kingdom of Eumelus (at Gadir) was by no means an "island's outskirt", and the entire topography does not correspond to Plato's description. This is a Pseudo-Atlantis.

The second variant is more acceptable, because it sites Atlantis in a region west of North Africa, at the Canary Islands. The main substantiation for this variant is the Guanches, the very ancient autochthonous population of these islands. Most of the supporters of the Canary variant are French atlantologists. Among Soviet atlantologists it is supported by B. L. Bogayevsky. Geologically, the Canary variant is founded on the assumption that the continental structure of northwestern Africa must extend deep into the Atlantic in the direction of the Canary and Cape Verde Islands, ending somewhere between these islands. That led some geologists to the belief that between the two archipelagoes there once was an arc that is now submerged and partially destroyed. However, geological investigations over the past few years have shown that such an ancient arc exists along the coast of the continent and not deep in the ocean. Moreover, a shortcoming of the Canary variant is that it limits the Atlantis subsidence area and hardly corresponds to Plato's description.

The third variant is of much greater interest. It directs the search for Atlantis to a gulf situated in the Atlantic between the southwestern part of the Iberian Peninsula and the western coast of Morocco. In this region there are many poorly explored shallow banks and entire submarine archipelagoes. H. Pettersson (84/44) believes that if the ocean level were to drop only by 200 metres (as was the case during the Ice Age) it would bare a large archipelago with an area of at least 350 square kilometres. M. V. Klenova considers this locality as very suitable for the location of the legendary Atlantis, especially if account is taken of the probable considerable rise of the ocean level not as a consequence of eustatic changes after glaciation but due to recent displacements of the poles, as is believed by G. D. Khizanashvili. The latter's computations indicate that in the region of the Strait of Gibraltar such a rise could reach about 1,500 metres.

Although at first glance this variant seems to fit in very well, it unfortunately does not conform to some of the conditions of Plato's Atlantis. Firstly, the bathymetry of the ocean floor in this region rules out the existence of land of the size mentioned by Plato for the principal kingdom of Atlantis. Then, even if the ocean level were to drop by 1,500 metres, this Atlantis would not have had tall and unbroken mountain chains running from the north, west and east. It seems to us that this location is suitable for the siting of the kingdom of the second Atlantean, Eumelus, which had communication with the rich southwestern region of Spain. It is quite possible that the region of these islands may have been the location of such legendary islands as Scheria, Erytheia and Tartessos (see Chapter Twelve).

Plato's description best of all fits in with the fourth, Azores variant, which links Atlantis up with the North Atlantic Ridge and its spurs. This variant is favoured by the bathymetry of the ocean floor and by the data on the late separation of the Azores from the continent.

The Jesuit monk Athanasius Kircher was the first to site Plato s Atlantis in the region of the Azores and even offered a rough map. In *Mundus subterraneus*, published in 1665, he writes of Atlantis as an island that had once existed. Bory de St. Vincent (47), a naturalist and geographer who lived in the reign of Napoleon, considered that all the Makaronesian islands were remnants of Atlantis and that the Guanches, the indigenous inhabitants of the Canary Islands, were the remnants of the Atlanteans. He situated Atlantis between the 12th and 41st parallels and compiled a chart giving a rough outline of some parts of its coast.

The author of this present book likewise tends to favour the Azores variant. The acceptability of this variant has also been proved by the Soviet atlantologist E. F. Hagemeister, who read a paper about this site at the Estonian Academy of Sciences on November 30, 1954.

B. OUR RECONSTRUCTION OF ATLANTIS

Any attempt at a paleogeographical reconstruction would be extremely interesting. On the whole, atlantologists have made quite many attempts, rough ones it is true, to give a picture of the contours of Atlantis. Regrettably, most of these attempts did not rest on sufficient bathymetric and geological data.

So far we have no possibility of marking on a map the contours of Atlantis even approximately as they existed in the epoch preceding the main subsidence. There are many reasons for this. One of the basic reasons, in addition to the undoubtedly rugged shoreline,

Reconstruction of Atlantis, after Bory de St Vincent (47)

is that we do not know how Atlantis sank and to what periods we have to attribute the terraced subsidences that have been brought to light: whether they are linked up with stoping or existed long before the land subsided. We are of the opinion that part of the stepped subsidences took place after the destruction of Atlantis.

If we proceed on the basis of bathymetric data our difficulty will lie in choosing the maximum isobath. If we accept the maximum depth where rocks bearing traces of weathering have been discovered (more than 3,000 metres), we shall find that Atlantis was a gigantic peninsula; that could be true of the end of the Pliocene. On the other hand, the discovery of terrigenous sediments in very deep parts of the ocean (for example, the Romanche Trench) makes the method founded solely on bathymetry unreliable. Also not very reliable are data on the abyssal finds of corals and the arguments that the intermontane spaces of the Atlantic lie at great depths.

In our reconstruction, the basic isobaths are not below 2,500 metres and not above 3,500 metres. These are approximately the upper and middle stages of the North Atlantic Ridge on a chart of physiographic provinces compiled by Heezen, Tharp and Ewing (417/Chart No. 20 in Appendix).

In our opinion during the Ice Age the territory of Atlantis embraced the North Atlantic Ridge up to the Romanche Trench including the Azores Plateau. The northern boundary of Atlantis presents a difficult problem; in the south the boundary was the Romanche Trench. The bathymetry of the ocean in the region of the juncture between the North Atlantic and the Reykjanes ridges is very important. The latter, explored by German expeditions up to the 57th parallel, is, in their opinion, a direct extension of the North Atlantic Ridge. A map published in 1956 by the American National Geographic Society (edited by J. C. La Gorce) shows abyssal hollows on either side of the ridge roughly at the 53rd parallel; there the ridge is exceedingly narrow. On the latest Soviet map (1 : 2,000,000), published in 1963 and edited by L. K. Zatonsky, this hollow is shown north of the Faraday Hills and cutting the ridge from north to south at a depth of 3,000-3,500 metres. We feel that *immense importance attaches to the question of the hollow separating the Reykjanes Ridge from the North Atlantic Ridge. Its existence leads one to the surmise that in this spot there might be a submarine canyon through which the river systems of America and Europe might have communicated as late as the end of the Miocene and in the Pliocene* (295a). *Secondly this hollow is indirect testimony in favour of the view that these ridges differ from each other*. Considerations about the distribution of ocean currents towards the close of the Ice Age bring us round to the conclusion that there was a strait separating Atlantis from Great Iceland.

Atlantis may be pictured as a meridionally situated continent sooner long than wide and consisting of three main parts: a wide northern island on the foundation of the Azores Plateau—*Poseidonis* or *Azoris*; and a long and narrow southern island—*Antillia* —and the *Equatorial Archipelago*, of which St. Paul's Rocks are a remnant. At the 31st parallel between Poseidonis and Antillia there was a narrow straits which we have named the *Poseidon Straits*. One or several narrow straits probably separated Antillia from the Equatorial Archipelago between the 5th and the 10th parallels.

Along the western fringe of these islands, running almost meridionally, there was a great mountain system—the North Atlantic Ridge. Submarine today, but in those days it had peaks rising to a height of two or three kilometres, or even higher. In the north of Poseidonis was the second mountain range of Atlantis. At present forming the Azores Islands this was the *Azores Ridge* and it was probably an integral mountain system. In the south of the Azores Plateau, running nearly parallel to the Azores Ridge, there was a chain consisting of several groups of mountains separated from each

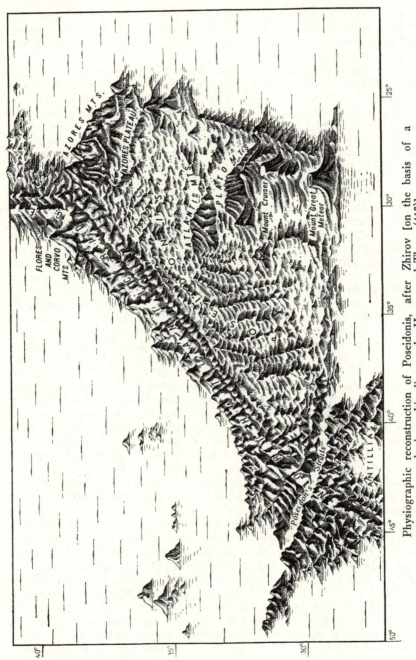

Physiographic reconstruction of Poseidonis, after Zhirov [on the basis of a physiographic diagram by Heezen and Tharp (417)]

other by saddles. The groups closest to the North Atlantic Ridge have been named *Atlantis Mountains* by us; the *Plato Mountains* form their southeastern extension—we have named these mountains partially in conformity with the Heezen-Tharp physiographical chart (417). The main kingdom of the Plato legend was evidently situated somewhere here, perhaps between the two latitudinal ranges, but sooner south of the Atlantis and Plato mountains.

A somewhat different view is offered by the noted Swedish atlantologist Dr. Réne Malaise. In a letter to the author of this work on May 19, 1968 he writes: "The Danish engineer M. Frandsen (153a) was looking at a depth-chart of the Azores and observed that at a depth of 600-700 fathoms above the surrounding sea-bottom there was an even plateau to the south of the islands. This plateau is sheltered from the north by the present Azores with their summits 4,000-5,000 metres higher than it, and to the west by the main range. To the southwest the plateau is limited by a somewhat lower mountain swell studded with high, flat-topped, now submarine seamounts. The most prominent of these seamounts have been named by American oceanographers Atlantis, Plato, Cruiser and Great Meteor. The horizontal plateau-land is clearly visible on Plate 22 [Heezen, Tharp and Ewing (417)] on the 'Transatlantic Topographic Profile I' (between the Atlantic Seamount and the Island of São Miguel). As an experiment, Frandsen made a sketch with the measurements of the Atlantis Plain given by Plato, viz., 400 by 600 kilometres (Frandsen counted a stadius = 200 metres) and on the same scale as the chart. It fitted very well to the submarine plateau-land of the chart. By studying the depth-curves he found the declination of the plateau to be on an average 1:900; the plateau consisted accordingly of a real plain of a size about 2/3 of present-day Finland. On his sketch he drew in the contours of the mentioned canals and the circular ditch and likewise the squared lots of 'ten stadia each way'. According to Plato the surrounding ditch had a length of ten thousand stadia ($\approx$2,000 kilometres [1,850 kilometres]) and the number of squared lots was 60,000. By measuring the ditch on his sketch Frandsen found it to be 2,040 kilometres and the number of lots to be 60,700, an acceptable difference. Having worked with irrigation in open and closed canals for thirty years he wanted to control the declination of the water-level in the canals if adequate. He found the fall of the water to be 1 : 300 and 1 : 600, which according to modern principles is acceptable, although barely for the last figure. The current in the canals was accordingly too slow to cause any difficulties of navigation for the row-galleys of the time."

However, according to O. K. Leontyev, who supports the ocean permanency and expanding continents theories, "from the standpoint of marine geology and geomorphology there are no grounds for surmising that Atlantis existed here". As one can see, Leontyev ignores all the facts clashing with the theories upheld by him: for

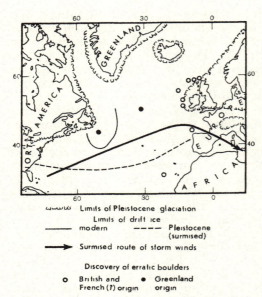

Ice and climatic conditions in the North Atlantic during the Pleistocene and today, according to the theory of the unchangeability of the Gulf Stream (704)

example, the basaltic and andesite volcanic activity on the Azores islands and plateau, the existence on the latter of cut terraces at a depth of 1,000 metres, and a series of other data given in the preceding chapters.

There are some grounds for believing that from the north and down to the 40th parallel Poseidonis was partially under glaciers. This surmise rests on the fact that boulders and sediments of glacial origin have been found approximately up to this latitude from the eastern side of the North Atlantic Ridge and the Azores. On the chart referred to by J. Wiseman and C. Ovey (704) some of these finds are attributed to the Greenland and British glaciers. However, the finding of a boulder east of the North Atlantic Ridge is strange to say the least. Wiseman and Ovey consider that it is of French origin, which we doubt very much. We consider it quite probable that when Atlantis existed some of its mountain peaks were covered with glaciers during the Ice Age, and that these glaciers could have served as the source of drift ice. We are quite positive that in the collection of samples taken from the eastern slope of the North Atlantic Ridge by the Lamont Observatory expedition there are glacier-eroded basalt rocks originating directly from the ridge itself. It is also quite possible that similar samples may be found in the collections of other oceanographic expeditions.

We have attempted to create a physiographic chart of Poseidonis (66) on the basis of the physiographic chart of the North Atlantic compiled by Heezen and Tharp (417). Regrettably, when we were making the reconstruction we could not avail ourselves of the latest data about the spurs of the North Atlantic Ridge that were discovered some years ago by various expeditions but not entered into the charts of the Atlantic floor.

In the north Poseidonis separated from the ice-bound island of Great Iceland, which in those times embraced the Reykjanes Ridge. This island appeared after the disintegration of the Atlantic Sill. On the other hand, the Rockall Plateau existed in that period in the shape of a huge ice-covered island or, much earlier, as a large peninsula that somewhere at the beginning of the Pleistocene united the entire subaerial Atlantic Sill, Greenland, Iceland and the Faeroes. We have some justification for naming this ice-covered land *Hyperborea*, in memory of the legendary Hyperborean people who lived far in the north.

The British Isles were an unbroken land mass, a peninsula extending from France; Porcupine Bank was a Peninsula linked to Ireland. Most of the North Sea was a land area where the highest point was the Dogger Plateau. The English Channel was a river.

In the west, Atlantis was washed by the semi-inland Bermuda Sea; in the north of this sea the Great Newfoundland island or peninsula with a chain of shoals and banks and a spur of Atlantis as well as an island archipelago north of the Bermudas served as a barrier to the massive northward penetration of the Proto-Gulf Stream. This was mainly a ring stream and it was much smaller than today because at least half of the Antilles Current was prevented from flowing westward by Antillia Island. Moreover, from time to time the Gulf Stream was supplanted by a powerful cold current flowing from the north and, possibly, partially through the straits between Newfoundland and Labrador. This cold current, whose existence is proved by paleobotanical data on the coastal vegetation of New England, evidently (in the shape of a submarine stream) penetrated even the Gulf of Mexico and the Caribbean Sea; this is also borne out by the fact that the Florida Peninsula appeared in the very recent geological past.

An analysis of cores from the floor of these basins has shown the presence of eleven layers of cold- and warmth-loving foraminifera (635). This, we feel, is evidence in favour of the surmise that there was tectonic instability in the region of Florida and Great Newfoundland (where violent earthquakes take place to this day, for example, the earthquake of 1929). The Caribbean Sea was probably much smaller in those days due to considerable and now submerged land areas, including the land area of the Antilles, that were a peninsula (264/391; 616). These subsidences occurred within man's memory, as testified by many legends current among the natives of the Antilles (17; 57).

The Bermuda Islands and the now submarine archipelagoes in their vicinity were fairly large islands. A branch of the Proto-Gulf Stream flowed past them, creating favourable conditions for the then most northerly development of corals. However, some scientists believe that a branch of the Proto-Gulf Stream penetrated as far north as the 55th parallel (where coral remains have also been discovered). This is probably connected with subsidences in the region of these islands.

East of Atlantis, between it and Europe, there were some semi-inland seas, whose number and configuration it is at present difficult to determine because, in our opinion, this part of the North Atlantic was subjected to intensive tectonic activity and frequent subsidences. The shallow Iceland Sea was possibly still in existence between Reykjanes Peninsula and Rockall Island. A small branch of the Gulf Stream, divided by the Reykjanes Peninsula, flowed through this sea along the eastern shores of Great Iceland to the Norwegian Sea. The narrow Irish Strait between Rockall Island and the British Peninsula, enabled the cold current from the Norwegian Sea to flow to the south. Part of the Gulf Stream that reached this sea transported icebergs and icefloes as the cold Irish Current, which farther became the Proto-Canary Current. The cold Irish Current flowed into the Biscay Sea, where icebergs abounded.

It must be pointed out that cold-loving Yoldia and high-Arctic mollusks have been found on the floor of the modern Bay of Biscay (269/373). *This can only be explained by the subaerial existence of the North Atlantic Ridge (i.e., Atlantis) with glaciers on it and on the more northerly islands (particularly Rockall Island).* It will be recalled that the English Channel was non-existent at the time.

The Biscay Sea was much smaller than the present-day gulf due to the existence of a vast mountainous land to the southwest of Britain and to the southeast of France (Estrimnides). Atlantis was closest to Europe at two points, where one can assume there was a chain of islands between it and Europe. The first, in the north, lay in the direction of Porcupine Peninsula, where near the mountain range there probably was a plateau similar to the Azores Plateau. The second, southern point, was between the present Azores Islands and Cape São Vincente in Portugal to the southwest of which stretched a large archipelago; numerous banks have taken the place of this archipelago. We have named it the *Erytheia Archipelago*. The chain of islands stretching from this archipelago to Atlantis ran along the now submerged Azores-Gibraltar Ridge. Some of the islands of this archipelago were fairly large and possibly existed until recorded times (Erytheia, Scheria, Tartessos).

The sea east of Atlantis was the source of the great cold Proto-Canary Current. However, its massive penetration towards the shores of Africa was hindered by the Erytheia Archipelago. Therefore, between Atlantis and Portugal the Proto-Canary Current turned into a ring stream and only part of it broke through to the shores of Atlantis, passing between the present-day islands of Terceira and Santa Maria. Gradually moving away from the shores of Atlantis, this part of the current flowed along the ocean surface almost up to the equator. A small cold branch passed between the islands of the Erytheia Archipelago. But the Proto-Canary Current, like the Canary Current today, never reached the shores of Africa, and the climate in the Sahara was, therefore, more humid. In those days the modern Canary and Cape Verde Islands were integral land areas with shallow straits separating them from the continent. A branch of the ring East Equatorial Current approached them, making the climate of northwestern Africa warmer and more humid.

At the equator there was the Equatorial Archipelago, whose islands approached quite close to the shores of both South America and Africa. This archipelago was probably a remnant of the intercontinental bridge of Miocene times. When it was in existence it was probably not very difficult for primitive man to travel between the Old and the New World. In this area the largest land mass was situated near St. Paul's Rocks. A somewhat smaller island was located to the northwest on the presently submerged Sierra Leone Ridge (where fresh-water diatoms have been found). The Romanche Trench is accepted as the southern boundary of Atlantis. Therefore, the southern extremity of Atlantis did not stretch across the equator. The warm current flowing through these regions (the East Equatorial Current) can hardly be called North Equatorial since it had its source north of the 10th parallel and flowed in a ring, washing the southeastern shore of Atlantis and the northern shores of the Equatorial Archipelago; the East Sargasso Sea was located in these places.

C. POSSIBILITY OF GEOLOGICAL CATASTROPHES AND ATLANTIS

The absence of cataclysmic (in the geological sense) catastrophes during the past 5,000 years has given rise to the view that ours is an epoch of tranquilly developing processes which do not change the long-established appearance of the Earth. On a geological scale this span of time comprises less than 0.5 per cent of the present geological period, the Anthropogen. On the basis of the data for such an infinitesimally short geological period it would be unfounded to consider that all major tectonic movements have stopped long ago. They are continuing before our very eyes: witness the devastating earthquakes in Chile and Iran. *There are still less grounds for extrapolating the modern tranquil state in the depths of the ages, through millennia and tens of millennia.* There is more than meets the eye in antique myths and in the writings of antique authors about the frequently repeating, considerable changes of the face of the Earth, about the appearance and disappearance of countries and seas. To the ancients this mobility of the Earth's crust did not seem as incredible as to us. *Our generations, i.e., the generations of mostly young nations, have forgotten the legends of the past or have lost their belief in them.* Academician D. V. Nalivkin (338) writes the following in a paper on geological catastrophes: "Observations of catastrophic phenomena are limited by a time span of not longer than 4,000-6,000 years. For geological processes this is a short period and it is quite possible that some of the most terrible catastrophes have not been recorded in the chronicles of mankind. We do not know what these catastrophes were like or how they influenced the accumulation of sediments, but we must take into account the possibility of their having taken place. We must not fit into modern standards all that has happened on the Earth throughout the billions of years of its existence." In another paper (339) Academician Nalivkin stated: "Generally speaking, the hypothesis that in many littoral regions the topography of the sea floor was formed subaerially has not yet become properly widespread. It is particularly strange to oceanographers, who have grown accustomed to a relatively stable shoreline. But we geologists, on the contrary, have grown accustomed to countless and frequently very rapid and substantial uplifts and subsidences both of continents and of the ocean level. As far as we are concerned, the subaerial creation of the littoral topography of the sea floor and its subsequent sinking to depths of 2,000-3,000 metres are a grandiose yet not unusual phenomenon." Further he analyses in detail such a cataclysmic catastrophe as the post-glacial (Holocene) formation of the Sea of Japan. It will be borne in mind that the final separation of the Japanese Islands took place in the Holocene, and that in the region of the Ligurian Sea land sank 2,000 metres about 32,000 years ago.

Although contemporary science has departed from the theory of catastrophism as it was propounded by C. Cuvier, it nonetheless does not deny that ours is part of the epoch of great movements of the Earth's crust. This is excellently put by G. W. Lindberg (295/121): "Lyell's uniformism theory, which refuted the Cuvier interpretation of catastrophes, was positive in its day but at present it is in this sense narrow and unsatisfactory. Its narrowness was first pointed out by Frederick Engels in *The Dialectics of Nature*."

Present-day geology attaches great significance to the latest movements in the Earth's crust, which in our day embrace neotectonic processes. For example, Academician V. A. Obruchev (350), who formulated the concept of neotectonics, said: "It may be asserted with full grounds that neotectonics adequately explain all the features of the modern land topography throughout the world." In an afterword to a paper by E. F. Hagemeister (30), he wrote: "Much has now changed in our approach to mountain-building processes. Scientists are attaching growing importance to vertical tectonics, including those taking place today. The recent disastrous earthquakes in Greece, Turkey and Indonesia [as well as in Chile and Iran—*N.Z.*] prove that there is continuing restlessness deep in the Earth, a restlessness that accounts for all neotectonic phenomena." Many other leading geologists share this view. For instance, V. V. Belousov (193) writes: "We must give up the idea that tectonic activity is dying down in the Earth." A. D. Arkhangelsky (184) believed that the present period is witnessing a revival of geosynclinal regimes with the tectonic subsidence of tall mountains created by Alpine orogenesis. He regarded the Tyrrhenian and Black seas as well as the marginal seas of the Pacific—the Sea of Ōkhotsk and the Sea of Japan—as young subsidences and pointed out (p. 312): "The latter half of the Tertiary and the Quaternary are characterised by an extraordinarily broad development of vertical tectonics of a block nature."B. L. Lichkov

(302) very convincingly proves that the present epoch (the Holocene) is part of the glacial period (Pleistocene) of tectonic changes and that vast alterations of the Earth's crust are taking place to this day. The noted geomorphologist F. Machatschek (323/635) writes: "Consequently, the modern geological period is not one of tectonic calm, of an absence of orogenic changes."

Facts indicating very late and considerable tectonic changes of the Earth's crust during the Pleistocene and later are cited by C. Cotton (489, 490). These include the uplift of the mountain ranges in New Guinea, New Zealand, America, the Himalayas, Central Asia and elsewhere. For instance, the maximum uplift of the Sierra Nevadas, USA, occurred only 235,000 years ago (also see 454). The central mountain range in New Guinea took shape only at the close of the Pleistocene; its present form was given it by intensive erosion in a tropical climate. Meanwhile, in Indonesia some of the islands are only several thousand years old.

The entire experience of man indicates that all known catastrophes, in one way or another caused by tectonic changes, were very short-lived, whether they were earthquakes, tsunamis or explosive volcanic eruptions.

As regards the subsidence of Atlantis, there is unquestioned proof that this took place rapidly. This proof is in the replacement of dextral by sinistral foraminifera following the sinking of the North Atlantic Ridge. As we have already pointed out, M. Ewing and B. C. Heezen (523/527) showed that this process took less than a century. Besides, it should be borne in mind that the replacement covered a huge area and that a lot of time was needed to settle this area with new species. We therefore consider that *basically the sinking of Atlantis was a catastrophe of very short duration* and that Plato was probably right in writing of "one disastrous night and day". Naturally, we also consider that this basic subsidence might definitely have been preceded by subsidences of a lesser scale.

Critics of atlantology (756/61) offer the far-fetched argument that if the Mid-Atlantic Ridge subsided it had to force the ocean level to drop by about seven metres. No traces of such a drop, they say, exists. Here it should be borne in mind that the South Atlantic Ridge, which at the time evidently included more than half of the entire Mid-Atlantic Ridge, sank many tens of millennia before the northern and equatorial sections. This is proved by an analysis of flora and fauna (see Chapter Ten) as well as by data cited by Le Pichon (777). According to our own computations the subsidence of the North Atlantic and Equatorial Atlantic ridges might have caused the ocean to drop not more than three metres. This is the magnitude of the Flandrian Transgression (see p. 329) if we consider that such a terrace really existed. But this is not all. The critics overlook the simple fact that the melting of glaciers forced a rise of the ocean level, which, as even the most modest computations show, might have easily compensated for the small drop caused by the sinking of the ridge.

Even if more detailed data is obtained in the future on the topography of the ocean floor where Atlantis sank, it will not be easy to recreate a picture of Atlantis, of its configuration and topography before it sank. It should also be noted that even if there will be the possibility of exploring the ocean floor with new types of bathyscaphes it will be very hard to find material remains of the Atlantean culture because of the lava streams, ash and volcanic tuff overlying them.

We do not think it unlikely that Atlantis was destroyed by a natural tectonic process which took place under somewhat unusual conditions. Being a "basalt continent", Atlantis emerged geologically very late. It was, therefore, doomed to subsidence due to the geobuilding properties of basalt rock. Possibly, some role was also played in this by serpentinisation and deserpentinisation, particularly during the final stages of its existence. Thus, *we believe that the sinking of Atlantis was inevitable because of its very nature*, and that the same fate overtook analogous mountain systems in other oceans.

Our critics (756/60) say we are not consistent, that, on the one hand, we do not reject the possibility of sialic materials participating in the creation of basalt continents and, on the other, we maintain that they are primarily basaltic. Moreover, we are misrepresented as having stated that Atlantis was a regular sialic continent. One critic (119/342) writes: "If it existed only 12,000 years ago, a continental crust would have been discovered where it sank." It is not known where he got this assertion, because nothing of the kind is to be found in our book. We shall leave it to his conscience and proceed with our argument. We do not deny that in remote antiquity there might have been ancient land in place of the North Atlantic Ridge, that later it was supplanted by a shallow sea and this was followed by the emergence of a ridge. But this does not imply that sialic rocks of an ancient continent have survived to this day. They were oceanised long ago, in the course of hundreds of millions of years. Their place was taken by new rocks formed of the metamorphosed sediments of the shallow sea. Possibly they are responsible for seismograms showing readings far different from what could be expected from basic rocks. These readings characterise the top rocks of the ridge (see Table 5). On the other hand, the underlying rocks fit in well with the indices for basalts. Basalts have also been found directly on the ridge. The inconsistency, which our critic speaks of, therefore exists only in his imagination.

Even more astonishing is the allegation (756/60) that we see a direct link between the Rockall and Porcupine plateaus and the North Atlantic Ridge. We know our subject well enough not to confuse the shelf of these plateaus with the North Atlantic Ridge. Our critic evidently gave our book only a cursory reading and treated it with preconceived prejudice, and that accounts for the somewhat tendentious evaluation.

Some years ago Kamilla Abaturova (114) suggested that the destruction of Atlantis might have been due to the expansion of the Earth.

Without taking the development of tectonic processes into account, many atlantologists have suggested their own and, for the most part, fantastic theories about the reasons of the destruction of Atlantis. Some of them looked for this reason in the depths of the Earth as, for example, L. Spence (101) or J. Churchward (153). Spence believed that Atlantis sank as a result of an explosion in a subterranean cavity; this hypothesis is not supported by any facts known to modern geophysics. Churchward's explanation for the destruction of his fantastic continent of Mu in the Pacific Ocean was that it was brought about by the explosion of an entire stratum (or belt) of subterranean cavities.

D. COSMIC THEORIES OF THE DESTRUCTION OF ATLANTIS

Very many atlantologists sought the cause of Atlantis' destruction in cosmic phenomena. For example, a theory that links the destruction of Atlantis up with a cosmic body—a comet, an asteroid or a large meteorite (119/282-302)—is very popular, particularly among astronomers. We must point out that *the Plato legend contains no indication and not even the vaguest hint that Atlantis perished as a result of a cosmic catastrophe.* Plato was not indifferent to events of this kind and if such an event caused the destruction of Atlantis or even accompanied it, he would have given it prominence. Generally speaking, *most cosmic theories either spring from an interpretation of myths territorially very remote from the scene or are the work of the authors' imagination.*

G. R. Carli (152), who in 1784 published a work tying up the destruction of Atlantis with the appearance of some comet, was probably the first to give rein to this group of theories.

Prominent among them is the *Welteislehre*, the theory of cosmic ice, suggested in 1912 by the Austrian engineer H. Hörbiger (138, 160). Following Hörbiger's death in 1931, his followers attempted to turn his theories into a kind of universal doctrine explaining the history of the solar system, the Earth and mankind. Moreover, this doctrine touches problems directly concerned with that of Atlantis, the Deluge and the glacial periods. Inasmuch as it clashes with conventional cosmogonic notions, and inasmuch as Hörbiger and his followers championed many clearly erroneous and purely fantastic propositions, it is usually ignored altogether by astronomers, physicists and geologists. However, some of the hypotheses advanced by Hörbiger have found confirmation during the past two or three decades. We feel that if the theory is shorn of its pseudo-scientific shell, many of its hypotheses will be found to be quite interesting (714).

Hörbiger drew attention to the Earth's wealth of water, to the fact that there is more water on it than on other planets, and connected this with the onetime existence of ice satellites. Professor B. Y. Levin (292), the noted Soviet cosmogonist, wrote: "Terrestrial atmosphere and the hydrosphere evidently originated not only through the sorption of gases by solid particles but also through the precipitation of ice bodies similar to the nuclei of comets." According to Hörbiger, the number of ice satellites that fell on Earth corresponds to the number of basic geological eras, i.e., besides the modern Quaternary Moon there were a primary, secondary and Tertiary Moon, which fell on the Earth.

Hörbiger did not specify when the Tertiary Moon fell on the Earth. It would seem most realistic to tie up this event with the start of glaciation in the Anthropogen, i.e., the Moon fell at the beginning of the Ice Age. However, on the basis of computations in line with the calendar on the "Gates of the Sun" in the Temple of Kalasasay at Tiahuanaco, Bolivia, Hörbiger's followers came to the conclusion that this Moon fell about 22,000 years ago, after which the Moonless period, mentioned in the myths of some peoples, lasted for 10,500 years, when the modern Moon appeared (460/183-189; 119/358).

The Hörbiger school links the destruction of Atlantis up with the appearance of the modern Moon, declaring that as it drew nearer it attracted water from the poles towards the equator. At their meeting point, the two waves, the northern and the southern, formed a wall several hundred metres high and inundated many countries lying along the shores of oceans. This gave rise to marginal and inland seas. In addition, the approach of the Earth's satellite caused volcanic magma to rise from the depths of the Earth and this sparked earthquakes and volcanic eruptions. Much of this took place in Atlantis, as a result of which it was destroyed (37; 138).

A similar hypothesis about the fall of two Earth satellites—ancient Lell, which disintegrated into Saturn-like rings in pre-Cenozoic times, and Perun, which fell at the close of the Cretaceous—has been suggested by L. E. Pukhlyakov (746). The impact of the latter body formed abyssal areas in the Western Pacific. This, he says, increased the Earth's rotation speed, changed the plane of rotation and displaced the poles in the Cenozoic. However, there is very little geological evidence in favour of hypotheses of this kind.

Prominent among the asteroid theories explaining the destruction of Atlantis is a fantastic one advanced by S. Bashinsky (11) in 1914. He considered that the catastrophe was called forth by the fall of a huge asteroid, which later formed the continent of Australia. The shock split the continent in the Atlantic, moving part of it westward to form modern America, which is the legendary Atlantis! The crack along the centre served as the foundation for the Mid-Atlantic Ridge. This theory has no geological facts whatever to support it.

Professor N. Bonev, the eminent Bulgarian astronomer (36, 37, 38, 39), suggested a theory that the destruction of Atlantis was caused by the fall or passage near the Earth of an asteroid of the size of Ceres, which perhaps even collided with the Earth somewhere near Atlantis.

Professor M. M. Kamienski (71, 163), member of the Polish Academy of Sciences and a leading authority on comets, studied Halley's comet over a period of many years and came to the conclusion that in the distant past it undoubtedly passed very near the surface of the Earth. The enormous difficulty of calculating the date when Halley's comet made contact with the Earth was surmounted only recently; as a result it was possible to specify the initially computed date 9564 B.C. as 9541 B.C. Of all the asteroid-comet theories, the one proposed by Professor M. M. Kamienski seems to us to be the most probable.

An exhaustive theory attributing Atlantis' destruction to a collision with a giant asteroid was worked out by the German atlantologist and engineer Otto Muck (80/249-300). His point of departure was that this asteroid might have been the Carolina meteorite, which was discovered in 1930 with the aid of aerial photography. W. F. Prouty (642) writes that craters are to be found over a huge area—some 83,000 square miles (about 215,000 square kilometres)—along the entire US Altantic seaboard from Florida to New Jersey. More than half of this area is densely dotted with these craters, of which there are at least 140,000! There are so many small ones that it is hardly possible to count them; Prouty thinks there must be more than half a million! In the opinion of F. A. Milton and W. Schriever (611) these craters were formed by meteorites of comet origin, which cut into the Earth at a sharp angle to the horizon, in a southeasterly direction. Some of them were tandem-meteorites and they exploded when they hit the Earth.

With the aid of a magnetometer investigators showed a high level of magnetism in 26 craters. J. H. Waldo (698) came to the conclusion that the craters were in fact made by meteorites and that the collision probably took place late in the Pleistocene. M. M. Kamienski and L. Zajdler are inclined to believe that they are traces of the collision between the Earth and Halley's comet.

Otto Muck argues that the main mass of a large meteorite fell in the Atlantic. Naming it Planetoid A, he believes that it had a diameter of about 10 kilometres, weighed some 200,000 million tons and moved at a velocity of 20 km/sec. According to his computations, the force with which the meteorite hit the Earth was equal to the monstrous explosion of 30,000 hydrogen bombs.* This explosion turned great quantities of water into vapour and started a gigantic tidal wave that brought about the Deluge. An analogous view is offered by Professor N. S. Vetchinkin (32/No.12).

---

* According to computations by the Polish astronomer J. Gadomski (119/279), half of Europe would be destroyed if the Earth were hit by an asteroid with a radius of 4,250 metres An asteroid with a radius of 8,500 metres would destroy half of Asia, while an asteroid with a radius of 17,000 metres would destroy half of the Earth's surface

All theories of this kind ignore the simple fact that *by hitting the Earth an asteroid or satellite of such vast dimensions as to cause a geological catastrophe would lead to such a rise of temperature as to turn considerable masses of the fallen body and the Earth to vapour; all life would have been destroyed on Earth, which, in fact, never happened.* Geology does not give us any indication of a general destruction of life on the Earth in any of the geological epochs. Taking the thickness and strength of the Earth's crust into account, it is highly improbable that smaller meteorites might have produced the required effect. Moreover, all these theories take no account of modern data on the thickness of the Earth's crust and of the properties of its mantle, and are based on antiquated assumptions that a thin crust overlies a molten mantle (128).

E. DATE OF THE SINKING OF ATLANTIS AND ANCIENT CALENDARS

The next problem is that of the date when Atlantis sank. Most of the scientists who approach the Atlantis problem seriously are always confused by the date given in Plato's legend: 9000 + the date of Solon's visit to Egypt (total—about 9600 B.C.), if it is accepted that the war between the pre-Hellenes and the Atlanteans and the destruction of Atlantis were close to each other in time. But, inasmuch as this date does not conform to the usual concepts, many atlantologists sought a way out of the difficulty by attributing to the Egyptians a lunar and not solar calendar with a lunar month as a year. The Spanish chronicler Pedro Sarmiento de Gamboa (69/36) was evidently the first to advance this idea. In a book published in Cuzco, Peru, in 1572 he maintained that 9,000 lunar years corresponded to only 869 solar years. He therefore dated the destruction of Atlantis as 1320 B.C. In 1675 the same view was advanced by Olaf Rudbeck of Sweden (90), who located his Pseudo-Atlantis in Sweden and considered that 8,000 lunar months equaled 666 lunar years, hence calculating that Atlantis perished in the year 1226 B.C.

This idea continues to attract atlantologists to this day. However, it clashes with everything that we know of the ancient Egyptian calendar. It was a calendar of an agricultural people, whose life was closely bound up with the phases of the Moon, with the flooding of the Nile. The ancient Egyptians, therefore, counted time by solar and not by lunar years, proceeding from the fact that the flooding of the Nile commences with the heliacal rising of the Dog Star (Sirius). Their year consisted of twelve 30-day months plus five additional non-working days. This is stated by Herodotus [11, 4] and in the Ebert papyrus (180/321). In its turn, *each month was divided either into three long decades or six short pentads (387/8). This division alone shows that the ancient Egyptian calendar had nothing in common with the lunar calendar.* In fact it was simpler and more harmonious than our modern calendar.

However, this did not prevent J. Spanuth (100/21-23) from referring to the lunar calendar in order to uphold his theory that Atlantis was located in Germany, near present-day Heligoland, where submerged ruins have been found. He substantiates this conjecture with the argument that to this day the Egyptians use a lunar calendar, citing as proof the memoirs of ex-King Farouk of Egypt, a very doubtful source, to say the least. Spanuth prefers to ignore the fact that the lunar calendar was introduced in Egypt after that country was conquered and forcibly converted to Islam. All the peoples professing that religion use the lunar calendar (387/89).

A. Paniagua, [we cite J. Imbelloni and A. Vivante (69/69)], went to the other extreme. He maintained that the dates given to Solon by the Egyptian priests were computed not by solar years but by Sothic cycles of 1,460 years each. The ancient Egyptian year was almost six hours shorter than the true year; every four years, therefore, the Dog Star was late by a day, so that the solstice returned to the true day once every 1,460 years, the lag amounting to one year. In other words, the "shifting" calendar cycle was equal to 1,461 years (387/9). If, as Paniagua does, we accept the Plato legend as equal to a Sothic cycle, we shall find that Atlantis was destroyed more than 13 million years ago, i.e., in the Tertiary period! It is, however, more than doubtful that the Egyptian priests had the geological knowledge of 19th and 20th century scientists.

Many atlantologists have drawn attention to the ancient calendar systems, finding in them a unity of origin and of initial dates, which are sometimes very close to the date of the destruction of Atlantis. For example, I. Donnelly (56/43, also see 37, 178) drew attention to the coincidence between the ancient Egyptian and Assyrian calendars. One of the dates of the Egyptian calendar giving the commencement of a Sothic cycle corresponds to the year 139 A.D. One of the cycles of the Assyrian calendar commenced in the year 712 B.C. The Assyrians had a lunar calendar which gave the cycle as equal to 22,325 lunar months or 1,805 years. Both calendars, however, had a common initial date, as may be seen from the following simple computation: a) Sothic cycle: $1,460—138=1,322$; $1,322+(7\times1,460)=11,542$; b) lunar cycle: $712+(6\times1,805)=11,542$. This computation was known to the ancient Babylonians. Thus, the initial date of both calendars is in the mid-twentieth millennium B.C.

The initial data of the Mayan calendar* is usually considered as the fourth millennium B.C. This initial date is interpreted differently by different authors: according to J.E.S. Thompson it is the year 3113 B.C.; according to H.J. Spinden it is 3373 B.C.; and according to I. G. Morley it is 3433 or 3440 B.C. (211). This has been

---

* The Mayan calendar is dealt with comprehensively by the Polish astronomer Dr. Ludwig Zajdler (119).

specified by radiocarbon dating at the temple in Tikal, Guatemala (658); it is now considered that Thompson's dating is most probable, but Spinden's dating may also prove to be right (due to the error allowance in the radiocarbon method). The Mayas, it must be noted, got their calendar from another people, the Olmecs, whose steles give more ancient dates than those of the Mayas. An interesting point is that according to the Mayan steles thirteen baktuns of 114,000 days each passed before the initial date of the so-called long calendar (290). One gets the impression that this latter date was the true initial date of the calendar. Inasmuch as the Mayan year was equal to 365.242 days (which is more accurate than our Gregorian calendar), 13 baktuns are equal approximately to 5,125 years. Thus, the legendary beginning of the Mayan-Olmec calendar dates from the middle of the ninth millennium B.C. The German astronomer R. Henseling (556; 557), who carefully studied the Mayan calendar, drew the conclusion that its initial date was the year 8498 B. C. However, it is hard to say if this is correct, because on the calendar stone at Tikal there is an even more ancient date: 12042 B. C. Y. V. Knorozov (22/218) points out that Stele No. 10 at Tikal gives a veritably astronomical date: 1,841,639,800 days (probably 13,000 baktuns). He believes that there were two "zero points" in the Mayan chronology: the first was 3113 B.C. after the Thompson correlation, and the second was 5041738 B.C. He considers that the first date can probably be compared with the birth of Christ, and the second with the creation of the world according to Christian chronology. The first date fits into the second. But it is not known what mythological or other events are referred to by the dates 3113, 8498 and 5041738 B.C.

The Aztecs evidently adopted the Toltec division of the mythological history of the world into four or five eras, which different sources characterise differently (211). The official Calendar Stone in Mexico speaks of five eras. The first, the era of the Four Ocelots, tells of the extermination of a tribe of giants by the ocelots, a species of wild cat. The second, the era of the Four Winds, ended with the turning of human beings into monkeys. The third, the era of the Four Rains, ended in a great conflagration. The fourth, the era of the Four Waters, ended with a world-wide flood and the turning of human beings into fishes. The present, fifth era, is to end with an earthquake. According to Ixtililxochitl, the first era (Sun of Waters) ended in a flood and the second (Sun of the Earth) in an earthquake; the world was inhabited by giants. During the third era (Sun of the Winds), violent hurricanes swept everything from the face of the earth. The fourth is the modern era. The most interesting chronology is offered by the Vatican Code A-3738, which gives the duration of the different eras. According to this Code, the first era lasted 4,008 years and ended in a flood. The second, 4,010 years long, was an era of hurricanes. The third era, after 4,801 years, ended in a fire, and the fourth era, which was 5,042 years long, was marked by terrible famine. The modern fifth era, according to some sources, began in the year 751 B.C. (495/42). Consequently, the four eras of the Vatican Code, totalled 17,861 years and the Deluge took place in 5,042+4,801+4,010—751=13102 B.C., while the era of fire (volcanic eruptions) ended in the year 8301 B.C. These dates are symptomatic; the latter date is close to the date given by Henseling.

Bellamy (37/107) compared the ancient calendars of the Hindus and the Mayas. But first, a few words must be said about Hindu mythological chronology. According to this chronology the Great Yuga or the Great Age comprises four eras linked up with the beginning and end of the world. Each age has a so-called Twilight, which procedes and accompanies an era proper and consists of one-tenth of the latter. The first era, the Krita Yuga, had a duration of 400+4,000+400=4,800 years; the second, Trita Yuga—300+3,000+300=3,600 years; the third, Dvapara Yuga—200+2,000+200=2,400 years, and the fourth, Kali Yuga—100+1,000+100=1,200 years. *The Great Yuga of mankind thus lasted 12,000 years, a figure that draws our attention.* But in addition to this chronology of mankind there was a chronology of gods; in each era a year was 360 times longer than the year in the chronology of man. Thus, the Great Age of Gods was 12,000×360=4,320,000 years in our reckoning. Hence the Brahma Day was equal to 4,320,000×2×1,000=8,640,000,000 years, while the Brahma Year runs into the astronomical figure of 8,640,000,000×360=3,110,400,000,000 years.

Bellamy accepted the initial date of the Kali Yuga as the year 3102 B.C. The Hindu solar-lunar calendar has a cycle of 2,850 years. He considered that the initial date of the Mayan calendar corresponded to the Spinden correlation—3373 B.C., and gave the duration of a heptad of baktuns as 2,760 years. We thus get the following: a) Hindu calendar—3,102+(3×2,850)=11652 B.C.; b) Mayan calendar—3373+(3×2,760)=11653 B.C. This produces dates that come very close to those of the Egyptian-Assyrian calendar. Both the Mayan and the Hindu mythological chronology operate with enormous cycles of time. Regrettably, we do not as yet have an exhaustive all-embracing work in which ancient calendars are compared.

Using Henseling's data, O. Muck (80/379-397) links up the initial data of the Mayan calendar with the destruction of Atlantis. His date, according to his reckoning, corresponds to the opposition of the Sun, Venus, the Moon and the Earth. Dr. Ludwig Zajdler (119/279) found errors in the Henseling-Muck computations; after they were rectified it was found that the initial date of the Mayan calendar is December 6, 8499 B.C.

The astronomer L. Filippov (58, 59), who is associated with the Algerian Observatory, scrutinised some ancient myths and legends. Thus in the Texts of the Pyramids (mentioned in Chapter Five), he found an indication that there was a land of volcanoes far in the sea. According to Manetho and his description of the Land of Siriat (also see 119/97-99), a catastrophe overcame that land during the period of the first Thoth. According to Hipparchus, the 2nd century B.C. Greek astronomer, a new cult of gods was introduced in Egypt during the movement of the spring equinox from one sign of the Zodiac to another. Insofar as Thoth had Cancer as his sign of the Zodiac, Filippov surmised that the date of Atlantis' destruction corresponds to the time when Thoth fled from the doomed Land of Siriat (Atlantis) and is linked up with his sign of the Zodiac. Specifying this, he considers that Atlantis perished in the year 7256 B.C., when the spring equinox was at Epsilon Cancer.

Also interesting are some of the considerations suggested by Dr. L. Zajdler (178/40-57); they are founded on a study of ancient calendars. All ancient calendars may be divided into two groups: one in which the hours of the day are of the same length, and the other, probably more ancient, in which the hours are dissimilar and depend whether they are day or night hours. Although the number of hours in some of the second group of calendars is identical, due to the changes in the duration of night and day at different times of the year, the length of day and night hours will be different during each season. The Egyptian and Mayan calendars belong to this group. This is not the only similarity between them. Although the Mayan year had 365 days, it was divided into 18 months of 20 days and there were five canicular days dedicated to religious holidays. These five additional days are a feature of both the Mayan and Egyptian calendars.

The Mayan calendar was more accurate than our modern calendar. Taking into account the possible accuracy of the measurements made by the Mayan-Olmec priests at their observatories, *astronomers have come to the conclusion that they are the world's oldest astronomers because at least 10,000 years of observation are required to obtain such measurements* (178; 556; 557).

The study of the data on the longest and shortest days in calendars with uneven hours likewise lead to interesting conclusions (178/49). For example, in the Mayan calendar the longest day had 13 hours and the shortest—11 hours. This corresponds to the tropical regions of the Earth. *In the Egyptian calendar the ratio between the longest and shortest day* (12 hours 55 minutes and 11 hours 05 minutes) *does not correspond to any locality in Egypt. Instead, it corresponds to localities 1,000 kilometres in the south.* These figures almost coincide with the figures in the Mayan calendar. Taking into account, moreover, the unevenness of the hours, which is a feature of both calendars, Dr. L. Zajdler has suggested the surmise that *both these calendars might have had one and the same source—the tropical regions of Atlantis.*

F. POSSIBILITY OF LATER DATES OF THE FINAL SUBSIDENCE OF ATLANTIS

Serious attention is attracted by the theory assuming that the last remnants of Atlantis sank very late and connecting this with the time of the military expansion of the so-called "peoples of the sea", who came to the Mediterranean area from the west, mainly by sea. In alliance with Libyan tribes, these peoples invaded Egypt as far back as the 13th century B.C. They were first engaged in battle by the pharaoh Merneptah (1251-1231 B.C.), who caused an inscription describing this to be made in the Karnak Temple. The coalition between the "peoples of the sea" and the Libyans was finally smashed by the pharaoh Ramses III (1204-1173 B.C.). The description of the battles and the victories of this pharaoh are to be found on the walls of the ruins of the large temple at Medinet-Habu near Thebes.

J. Imbelloni and A. Vivante (69/240) note that when Crantor, a disciple of Plato's, visited Egypt he was probably shown not the history of Atlantis but the wall inscriptions describing the battles of the Egyptian pharaohs against the "peoples of the sea". Besides, by that time the priests themselves might have lost all memory of the true substance of these inscriptions and their contents.

The decisive sea battle took place in 1195 B.C. Since the vessels of the invaders had only sails and those of the Egyptians could be impelled by oars, the dead calm that set in deprived the invading ships of their manoeuvrability and the invaders suffered a crushing defeat. A similarly overwhelming defeat was inflicted on them on land in a battle at the Libyan border, where more than 25,000 men were killed. The Egyptians, too, suffered enormous losses in these battles; the "peoples of the sea" drove them out of Palestine and Syria and deprived them of their communication with Crete.

The Egyptian inscriptions dating back to those times contain interesting information about a great catastrophe that occurred in the homeland of the "peoples of the sea". In one of the inscriptions at the Medinet-Habu Temple W. F. Edgerton (507) read that the land of the Libyans was enveloped by fire and that they had to fight their way eastward through a wall of flame. The same is reported about the homeland of the "peoples of the sea", "whose forests were a raging inferno and they had before them a sea of fire". These inscriptions state that the homeland of the "peoples of the sea", their islands were hit by violent earthquakes and all the towns were destroyed simultaneously. Those who endeavoured to leave the sinking islands by sea were driven back by a terrible storm (tsunami). To save themselves they fled to the east.

This gives great weight to R. Malaise's (74, 76) theory that the invasion of the Libyans and the "peoples of the sea" was linked up with a great geological catastrophe affecting the remnants of Atlantis and the Atlantic seaboard of Western Europe and Africa. The subsidence of the last large remnants of Atlantis, which were the highest points of the North Atlantic Ridge, finally changed the direction of the eastern branch of the Gulf Stream and, generally, of all the currents along the shores of Western Europe and Northwestern Africa. The Equatorial Current running towards the Strait of Gibraltar, veered to the west, and its place was taken by the present cold Canary Current. This caused the climate to acquire a more pronounced continental nature, reduced precipitation, and the Sahara finally became an arid desert. Droughts, famine, earthquakes and great outpourings of lava along the shore of Atlantis forced the peoples of the Atlantic seaboard of Western Europe and North Africa, as well as the survivors of the population of the southern parts of Atlantis and some northern countries, to flee eastward. This was what lay behind the invasion of the "peoples of the sea".

However, there are some grounds for believing that the last remnants of Atlantis in the extreme south of the North Atlantic were destroyed much later (18/50). Indirect testimony of this is found in the periplus of Hanno, which is a fragment from a description of the voyage made by Hanno, the Carthagenian navigator, who sailed down the shores of West Africa, south of the Strait of Gibraltar (249/43-50). The expedition was excellently organised and the fleet under Hanno's command was said to have carried nearly 30,000 colonists. R. Hennig (419/I/109) gives the date of this voyage as approximately the year 525 B.C. The periplus of Hanno was found in a 10th century Greek manuscript, which was published in 1533; it is the only known record of the voyage. It is believed that it was written by Hanno himself and was kept at the Temple of Baal in Carthage. The Greek translation known to us is full of errors, and the end of the manuscript has been lost. Hennig thinks that after Carthage was captured by the Romans the original was copied by the Greek historian Polybius.

Hanno's voyage lasted several months. At first, Arrian reports, Hanno sailed eastward (evidently going round West Africa) and then turned southward. After founding the southernmost colony—Cerne—he sailed from a gulf called Western Horn to the gulf called Southern Horn. During this part of the voyage Hanno and his men spent at least a week sailing back and forth along the shores of a country where a fearful eruption of lava was taking place. This is described as follows: "Hurriedly raising sail, we went past a sultry country where the air was fragrant. Great streams of fire flowed from it to the sea. The land was inaccessible because of the heat. For four days and nights we sailed within sight of this fire-enveloped land. In the middle was a fire that was taller than all the others. It looked as though it was touching the stars. In the daytime this proved to be a great mountain called Theon-Ohoma or the Chariot of the Gods. Three days later, sailing past the streams of fire, we reached the gulf called Southern Horn" (419/I/110).

Hennig thinks that the Chariot of the Gods is Mount Cameroon, which is known for its volcanic eruptions (the most recent of which took place in 1909, 1922 and 1925). But this hardly fits in with the description. According to Herodotus, a vessel of those days sailed 185-220 kilometres a day, *which means that Hanno sailed over a distance of 1,300-1,500 kilometres along the coast of a land witnessing powerful outpourings of lava.* This was by no means a usual even if violent volcanic eruption; it was sooner a cataclysm. Hanno evidently did not reach as far south as Hennig believes; besides, the region covered by lava from Mount Cameroon is not so great. *The Carthagenian navigator Hanno was perhaps a witness of the destruction of the southern remnants of Atlantis* (18/50); the periplus does not state on which side of his ship Hanno saw the burning land. We think this spot was situated south of the Cape Verde Islands (in the region of the former equatorial archipelago of Atlantis)*, where fresh-water diatoms were discovered not long ago on a seamount. This surmise is indirectly confirmed by Hanno's statement that some of the islands visited by him previously had the character of coral atolls on a submerged volcanic base (a lagoon with an island in the centre). In this area there are coral structures only near the Cape Verde Islands (212).

G. CHRONOLOGY OF EVENTS OF THE LAST GLACIATION AND THE HOLOCENE AND ESTABLISHMENT OF THE MOST PROBABLE DATE OF THE DESTRUCTION OF ATLANTIS

In conclusion it would be useful to compare a number of dates of various origin, which are directly or indirectly concerned with the history of Atlantis, and on that basis attempt to determine the most probable date of the destruction of Atlantis and also if it sank at once or gradually.** The dates given below are in years before our era (132).

I. ASTRONOMICAL DATES

1 Initial date of the Hindu calendar, after Bellamy (37/123)	11653
2 Initial date of the Egyptian and Assyrian calendars, after Donnelly (56/43)	11542
3. Spring equinox in the first sign of the Zodiac (Leo) at the Temple of Dender, Egypt, after Bellamy (37/113), approximately	11000
4. Collision of Halley's Comet with the Earth, after M. Kamienski (71, 575)	9541
5 Initial date of the Mayan-Olmec calendar, after Henseling-Zajdler (178, 557)	8498-8499

---

* Our theory about the possible destruction of the last remnants of Atlantis in the south of the North Atlantic (in connection with the periplus of Hanno) has been used for a thrilling story by A. I. Nemirovsky in *Beyond the Pillars of Melcartes*, Moscow, 1959.

** Climatic, archaeological and other data are given in Table 7 (Appendix 1)

6	Beginning of astronomical observations by the Central American peoples, after Henseling (557) and Zajdler (178) at least	8000
7	Arrival of the god Thoth in Egypt (spring equinox in the sign Cancer), after Filippov (58, 59)	7256
8	Taurus epoch, after Kamienski (574)	4500-2350

II GEOLOGICAL AND CLIMATIC DATES

9	Date of basaltic glass, after Termier (115) ..... about	13000 (?)
10	Beginning of the retreat of the ice sheet in Europe, after De Geer (532) . . about	13000
11	Belling Interglacial in Europe, after Barendsen, Deevey and Gralenski (456)	11250-10500
12	Subaerial location of the Atlantis Seamount, after Broecker and Kulp (474, 549) ...... about	10000
13	Great volcanic eruptions in the North Atlantic, after Bramlette and Bradley (469), and Klenova and Lavrov (272) . . . . about	10000
14	Alleroed Interglacial in Europe, after Barendsen, Deevey and Gralenski (456)	10000-8500
15	First considerable penetration of warm Atlantic waters into the Arctic, after Yermolayev (250)	10000-8000
16	Two Creeks Interglacial in North America (388), about	9500
17	Retreat of the Alpine, Schliren glacier, after Shnitnikov (437)	9400-9300
18	Last eruption of the Eifel volcano, after Straka (681)	9350
19	Rapid warming of the North Atlantic waters, after Emiliani (511) . . . . about	9000
20	Beginning of the continuous retreat of the glacier in Scandinavia, after De Geer (532)	8515
21	First change of the habitation of foraminifera in the eastern North Atlantic, after Ericson and Wollin (516) . . . . about	8000
22	Last climatic maximum in Europe, after Barendsen, Deevey and Gralenski (456)	5000-2500
23	Final break-through of warm Atlantic waters into the Kara Sea, after Yermolayev (250)	3000-1000
24	Climatic catastrophe in Europe, after Brookes (207)	500-150
25	Final consolidation of contemporary conditions in the North Atlantic, after Ericson and Wollin (516)	Beginning of our era

III HISTORICAL DATES

26	Paleolithic in South America (Wiscachini culture, of the Moustier type), after Ibarra Grasso (566) . about	50000 (?)
27	Oldest settlements of man in North America (471, 475, 592) . . . . more than	30000
28	Later Neanderthals (Moustier culture) in Western Europe, after Tavernier and Heinzelin (686) . before	32000
29	Cro-Magnon man (Aurignacian culture) in Western Europe (265, 686)	24500-11500
30	The Deluge, after the Vatican Code, about	13100 (?)
31	Dynasty of Gods in Egypt, after Herodotus .. about	12000 (?)
32	Magdalenian culture in Western Europe (265, 675, 686)	11000-7000
33	Masma culture in South America, after Ruzo (171) . . . . about	10000 (?)
34	Dynasty of Gods, after the Turin papyrus ... . about	9850 (?)

35.	Destruction of Atlantis, after Plato . before after Muck (80/381) and Zajdler (119/254) . . . before	9600 8570
36.	End of the era of volcanic eruptions, after the Vatican Code . . . . about	8300 (?)
37	Town-type settlement buried beneath a lava field at Pedregal, Mexico, after Bellamy (37/113) earliest about	8100 (?)
38	Beginning of the Neolithic on Crete, after Evans (365) . . about	8000 (?)
39	Buffalo rock-drawing culture in the Sahara (Tassili), after Lhote (595/26)	8000-6000
40	Azil-Tardenhauz culture in Western Europe (686)	7500-5500
41	Town-type settlement in Palestine (576) . . about	6840
42	Pile-dwellings (Neolithic) in Switzerland (265) . about	6750
43.	Beginning of the Neolithic on Crete, after Pendlebury (365) . . . . about	6700 (?)
44.	Turdetan chronicles, after Strabo . . before	6000
45	Oldest Megalithic culture on Malta (503)	6000-5000?
46.	Oldest "copper culture" (Chalcolithic) at Oconto, USA (471/262)	5500-5000
47	First pharaoh (Menes) of a united Egypt, after Manetho	4248 (?)
48.	Pre-dynastic Egypt (182)	4000-3500
49	Megaliths in Scandinavia, after Montelius (373/215)	4000-2000 (?)
50	Town-type settlement in Panama (Cocle culture), after Verril (696) . . . earlier than	3000 (?)
51.	Ancient Minoan Kingdom on Crete (428)	3000-2000 (?)
52	Ancient town on the site of Troy (Troy I-II), after Childe (428)	2750-2500 (?)
53.	Tomb of Zoser, IIIrd dynasty pharaoh of Egypt, builder of the first large pyramid (596). . . . about	2800
54	Destruction of Aldland in the Atlantic, after the Frisian chronicle *Oera Linda Boek* (119)	2193 (?)
55.	Middle Minoan Kingdom on Crete (428)	1850-1550 (?)
56.	Invasion of Egypt by the "peoples of the sea"	1300-1150 (?)
57.	Great eruptions of lava in the Central Atlantic, after Hanno	525 (?)

The dates that have not been specified by radiocarbon (the most objective method) are given with a question mark.

The above dates, in our opinion, indicate that *events of considerable importance took place between the 12th and 8th millennia B.C. in the history of the North Atlantic and of the peoples inhabiting its shores. These events were connected with a great volcanic and tectonic catastrophe and were mirrored in the memory of man. There are grounds for believing that they are directly linked up with the geological cataclysm that shook the Northern Atlantic, including Atlantis, which was first recorded by Plato. Moreover, this cataclysm evidently hit not only the Atlantic Ocean but also regions adjoining the Mediterranean and Caribbean seas and the inland seas of the North Atlantic.* Possibly there were similar catastrophes in the Indian and the Pacific oceans.

Many investigators point out that Plato's date of the destruction of Atlantis synchronises with many geological and other events. For example, Y. G. Reshetov (87) draws attention to the fact that this date harmonises with the eruption of Eifel and Puy de Dome, and

Surmised location of Atlantis between 25°N and 45°N

with the tectonic activity in the Balkan Peninsula, the Carpathians, the Caucasus and elsewhere. A. A. Gorbovsky (239, 240) likewise underscores this date. G. Arrenius (453) notes that the end of the last glaciation was accompanied by violent volcanic eruptions at Lake Laahern in Central Europe, in Iceland and the North Atlantic generally, in the Mediterranean, along the entire Andes Coast of Central and South America, in Patagonia and other areas. Was this outburst of tectonic activity of a word-wide scale? However, all these data are not enough to enable us to specify the date of the destruction of Atlantis. For the time being we have to assess it roughly and consider that *Atlantis was destroyed in about the year 9500±1500 B.C.; this date comes very close to the date given us by Plato.*

It seems to us that there are grounds for assuming that in the sinking of Atlantis there were two stages, the first between the 13th and 10th millennia B.C., and the second, the most considerable, between the 9th and 8th millennia B.C. Generally speaking, the main subsidence of Atlantis took at least 5,000 years, but the final subsidence was in the nature of a cataclysm. It is quite probable that the main subsidence left small remnants of the destroyed continent which, perhaps, finally sank in the north along the latitude of the Azores (to the north and south of them), in about the year 1300-1200 B.C. Evidently, the southernmost remnants, in the equatorial region, finally sank later, in the 6th century B.C. However, all these latest dates require further confirmation (132).

The following assessment of our conclusions regarding the history and geomorphology of Atlantis has been given by D. G. Panov (364a): "On the basis of a comparison of geological, archaeological, historical and ethnographic data N. F. Zhirov has come to the conclusion that Atlantis sank at the beginning of sub-Arctic times. This conclusion fits in very well with the data on Quaternary paleogeography."

CONCLUSION

In this book an attempt has been made to settle some of the basic problems of scientific atlantology. Moreover, the author set himself the task of proving that scientific atlantology has the right to exist and showing that it is by no means a scribble founded on haphazard conclusions, tendentious fabrications or "foreign anti-scientific idealistic trends". Accusations of this kind are frequently heard and seen in the press or at public debates from people most of whom are only very slightly acquainted with this complex problem from not very trustworthy works, in which the uncritical authors let themselves be carried away by their imaginations, or treat the subject with prejudice.

It seems to us that scientific atlantology is now freeing itself from pseudo-atlantological rubbish and that sufficient material has been accumulated to give it the status of a young scientific discipline. If the present book lays the beginning for introducing atlantology into the range of scientific disciplines, the author shall feel he has achieved one of his major objectives.

As the reader can judge for himself, we have tried to assemble the most trustworthy facts, as well as notions and theories providing testimony that Atlantis really existed. By generalising and critically analysing the assembled material we have made an attempt to answer questions that have been confronting atlantologists for more than 2,000 years, namely: Did Atlantis really exist in the place and at the time stated by Plato? Is the Atlantis legend an echo of reality or is it nothing more than a piece of brilliant fantasy?

The author believes that *today most of the scientific data indicate that Plato's Atlantis really existed*. True, there is much ground for argument about details regarding its location. Another question is whether the real Atlantis conformed to the embellished description given by Plato. The reply to this is that *after Plato's information about Atlantis is critically analysed and shorn of its exaggerations and propagandistic material there is nothing in it that can clash with the views of modern science*.

However, some specialists, not only linguists and literary critics (22; 22a) but also oceanographers and geographers who align themselves with the thalassocraton, drift of continents, convection currents, expanding Earth and other fashionable theories, flatly refuse to consider the onetime existence of Atlantis (119/336-343; 756; 813). Sad as it sounds, but a careful scrutiny of this criticism shows that it is conspicuously prejudiced and that it is not even free of errors. Regrettably, the debate that was started was cut short after an opponent of atlantology had his say. In the preceding chapters, as well as in some recent works (728; 729), we replied to some clearly tendentious and erroneous assertions by critics.

It would be useful to cite the evaluation of Plato's information about Atlantis given by V. A. Bryusov (32/9/28): "If we assure that Plato's description is a fabrication, we must then admit that he was a superhuman genius, who foretold scientific development for millennia ahead.... Is it not superfluous to say that with all our respect for the brilliance of the great Greek philosopher, such foresight is inconceivable, and we consider it more plausible that Plato had at his disposal materials (Egyptian) of great antiquity." Indeed, modern science is in possession of data to show that in the Atlantic Ocean there is the submarine North Atlantic Ridge that might have existed subaerially in times close to those mentioned in the Plato legend. Some areas of this land possibly existed until historical times. If that is true, the land in question might have been inhabited.

Another question that the reader of the present book may legitimately ask is: Apart from simple cognition, can atlantology yield anything of practical value? This question must be answered separately for each of the basic aspects of the problem. In the historical-ethnographical field, atlantology, like history, archaeology, anthropology and ethnography, with which it is closely allied, allows for a new approach to a number of cardinal problems of interest to these sciences. It must be noted that *solely the fact of establishing the reality of Atlantis (irrespective of the Plato legend) as a geological and geographical object of the time when intelligent man appeared (perhaps even later) would unquestionably cause a revolution in the present views about the development and settlement of mankind.* This would put the whole of ancient history in a new light and smash some traditional canons and dogmas. This is perhaps one of the reasons for the hypercriticism and prejudice with regard to the Atlantis problem.

In addition, atlantology is closely bound up with vital problems of oceanology and neotectonics; with the problem of the origin of oceans, the time of their formation and the possible existence of land areas in them; with the causes of glaciation; with the possibility of contemporary catastrophism. The establishment that Atlantis really existed as a huge mass of land would fundamentally undermine the ocean permanency theory. The negative attitude to Atlantis by oceanology and geology, as we have repeatedly indicated, stems from this theory.

If Atlantis really perished in the geologically not very distant past and the catastrophe was so all-embracing, we shall have to ponder over the question of what caused this catastrophe and whether anything of the kind will ever happen again. This holds true of the Ice Age as well. In a letter to the author of this book on December 27, 1955, Academician V. A. Obruchev, creator of neotectonics, wrote: "The elucidation of the former existence of the Atlantis Island and the significance of its destruction to the relaxation of glaciation in the North Pole is of great historical as well as practical (geological) value and it may be hoped that the Academy of Sciences will assist in settling this problem." These words, written by Academician Obruchev shortly before his demise, may serve as a fine scientific behest to Soviet geologists, historians and oceanologists. I regret to say that although fourteen years have passed since these words were written very little has been done. More than thirty years ago B. L. Bogayevsky (13/23) wrote: "It seems to me that it is high time to raise the Atlantis problem to the level of scientific interests and thereby remove it from the sphere of Devigne-like dilettante discussion and solutions arrived at by mystical manipulation in the manner of the occultists and theosophists." These words hold true today, because in the USSR the Atlantis problem has not yet gone beyond mass-circulation publications and magazines.*

Understandably, the final confirmation of the reality of Atlantis can only be given by further objective investigation, chiefly in the sphere of oceanology and marine geology. This will require work in the field and in the laboratory. The investigations in the laboratory will have to include the making of models of North Atlantic and Arctic ocean currents giving different variants of the above-water position of the submarine ridges. We feel that such models would best be made after the method suggested by Academician P. P. Lazarev (288/541). Oceanological expeditions must, first and foremost, complete a careful investigation of the bathymetry of the entire length of the North Atlantic Ridge, particularly in the equatorial region of the Atlantic Ocean and on the approaches to the Reykjanes Ridge, and finally establish the area and topography of the Azores Plateau, including the northern and southern submarine ridges running parallel to these islands.

Furthermore, it must be established if there are traces of glaciers on the ridge itself, on the Azores and in other submerged places of the North Atlantic. Lastly, the nature of the North Atlantic Ridge must be ascertained not on the basis of hypothetical surmises but by thorough seismic sounding, magnetic and gravimetric measurements and the collection of an adequate number of rock samples. The same concerns the Median Valley, which must be carefully explored

---

* See References.

throughout its length. The submarine Horseshoe Archipelago (Erytheia) must be similarly explored. All these investigations may be conducted without the sending of special expeditions, but simply by including them in the programme of conventional oceanographic expeditions operating in these regions. Regardless of the results, such investigations will undoubtedly add to our knowledge of the nature of oceans.

To date, the most serious Soviet and foreign works on scientific atlantology are largely the products of lone enthusiasts, who, understandably, could not fully and objectively cover the entire range of problems in this field. Willy-nilly, therefore, all works of this kind bear the tint of amateurism. This present work is no exception and the author begs the pardon of his readers and critics. He hopes that the next work on scientific atlantology will be the collective effort of scientists specialising in different disciplines.

APPENDIX 1

REFERENCE TABLES

Table 1

Mean Chemical Composition of Major Rocks (244, 465, 602)

(Average Values)

Rock	Density g/cm^3	Principal components, %			
		SiO_2	Al_2O_3	$Fe_3O_3 + FeO$	MgO
I Acid rocks:	2.6—2.7	65 and over	12.0—16.0	less than 1.5	less than 0.5
rhyolite		74.0—78.0	13.0—14.0	”	”
granite		70.0—74.0	12.0—15.0	”	”
gneiss		70.0—72.0	13.0—15.0	”	”
granodiorite		65.0—67.0	15.0—16.0	”	”
II. Intermediate rocks.	2.7—2.8	52.0—60.0	16.0—18.0	up to 14.0	2.0— 6.0
andesite, usual and hypersthenic		59.0—60.0	17.0—18.0	6.0— 8.0	2.5— 3.5
trachyandesite		58.0—59.0	17.0—18.0	7.0— 8.0	1.0— 2.0
augite-andesite		57.0—58.0	17.0—18.0	7.0— 7.0	2.0— 3.0
diorite		52.0—55.0	16.0—17.0	9.0—11.0	4.0— 6.0
III. Basic rocks:	2.8—3.1	46.0—53.0	12.0—17.0	8.0—14.0	5.0—17.0
diabase		50.0—53.0	14.0—16.0	10.0—12.0	5.0— 8.0
tholeiitic andesite		51.0—52.0	13.0—14.0	13.0—14.0	5.0— 6.0
tholeiite		50.0—51.0	13.0—16.0	4.0—10.0	4.0— 7.0
trachydolerite		49.0—50.0	16.0—17.0	10.0—11.0	4.0— 5.0
gavaite (andesite basalt)		48.0—49.0	15.0—16.0	11.0—12.0	4.0— 5.0

Rock	Density g/cm³	Principal components, %			
		SiO₂	Al₂O₃	Fe₃O₃+FeO	MgO
alkaline andesite		47.0—48.0	14.0—15.0	11.0—12.0	7.0— 8.0
basalt, gabbro, norite, eclogite		46.0—49.0	12.0—16.0	8.0—12.0	6.0—17.0
IV. Ultra-basic rocks:	3.1—3.3	37.0—45.0	0.1—6.0	over 7.0	over 20.0
peridotite		44.0—45.0	1.0—6.0	"	34.0—41.0
dunite		37.0—42.0	0.1—1.0	"	43.0—52.0

Formulas of Some Rock-Forming Minerals
(MgO > FeO)

1. Augite (pyroxene group) — mixture:
   $(MgO + FeO) \cdot CaO \cdot 2SiO_2 + (MgO + FeO) \, Al_2O_3 \cdot 2SiO_2$
2. Hypersthene (pyroxene group)
   $(MgO + FeO) \cdot SiO_2$
3. Leucite $K_2O \cdot Al_2O_3 \cdot 4SiO_2$
4. Nepheline $Na_2O \cdot Al_2O_3 \cdot 2SiO_2$
5. Olivine $2(MgO + FeO) \cdot SiO_2$
6. Feldspars:
   orthoclase and microline $K_2O \cdot Al_2O_3 \cdot 6SiO_2$
   albite $Na_2O \cdot Al_2O_3 \cdot 6SiO_2$
   anorthite $CaO \cdot Al_2O_3 \cdot 2SiO_2$
7. Hornblende (pyroxene group) — mixture:
   $3(MgO + FeO) \cdot CaO \cdot 4SiO_2 + 2(MgO + FeO) \cdot CaO \, Al_2O_3 \cdot 3SiO_2$
8. Serpentine $3(MgO + FeO) \cdot 2SiO_2 \cdot 2H_2O$

Table 2

Rough Assimilation Compositions
(granite with 72% silica + basalt with 40% silica)

Product of Assimilation	% of granite	% of basalt
Andesite	50	50
Trachyandesite	40	60
Diorite	25	75
Diabase	20	80
Tholeiite	10	90

Table 3

Longitudinal Wave Diffusion Velocities in Rocks at Pressures of up to 10,000 kg/cm² (465, 721, 722, 766)

(Average values; the figures in brackets give the minimum and maximum values)

Rock	Density, g/cm²	Longitudinal Wave Diffusion Velocity, km/sec		
		P = 1,000 bars	P = 4,000 bars	P = 10,000 bars
Limestone	2.62 (2.54—2.73)	5.59	5.86 (5.56—6.32)	6.64 (6.62—6.66)
Tuff	2.63 (2.59—2.67)	5.92 (5.60—6.27)	6.08 (5.80—6.37)	6.11 (5.93—6.28)
Granite	2.64 (2.58—2.68)	5.89 (5.18—6.20)	6.22 (5.70—6.51)	6.40 (6.25—6.61)
Sandstone	2.65 (2.54—2.74)	5.57 (5.54—6.20)	5.91 (5.63—6.43)	6.11 (5.85—6.66)
Quartzite	2.65	6.02 (5.87—6.18)	6.11 (6.00—6.22)	6.40 (6.26—6.46)
Serpentinite	2.68 (2.60—2.92)	6.31 (6.10—7.08)	6.53 (5.80—7.18)	6.66 (5.90—7.33)
Marble	2.70	6.61	6.72	6.76
Gneiss	2.71 (2.64—2.85)	5.89 (5.62—6.10)	6.13 (5.85—6.33)	6.40 (6.17—6.64)
Granodiorite	2.77 (2.70—2.80)	6.01 (5.54—6.20)	6.14 (5.97—6.63)	6.68 (6.56—6.71)
Schist	2.84 (2.73—3.11)	6.32 (5.54—6.88)	6.58 (5.89—7.38)	6.72 (6.06—7.53)
Dolomite	2.84	6.98	7.09	7.22
Diorite	2.88 (2.80—2.92)	6.30 (6.23—7.04)	6.89 (6.60—7.18)	> 6.71
Diabase	2.98 (2.92—3.02)	6.70 (6.50—6.81)	6.74 (6.57—6.85)	6.89 (6.63—6.98)
Gabbro	2.98 (2.87—3.09)	7.00 (6.76—7.05)	7.10 (6.80—7.13)	7.22 (6.80—7.24)
Chlorite Schist	3.03 (2.95—3.06)	7.25 (6.86—7.40)	7.35 (7.07—7.52)	—
Peridotite	3.20 (3.12—3.27)	7.68 (7.30—7.90)	7.88 (7.70—8.06)	> 8.03
Eclogite	3.38 (3.32—3.44)	7.45	7.71 (7.46—7.89)	7.83 (7.69—8.10)
Dunite	3.71 (3.24—3.74)	7.60	7.90 (7.27—8.14)	8.13 (7.36—8.25)

After I. A. Rezanov (376) the pressures indicated in the table correspond to the following depths:
    1,000 bars = 3.5 kilometres;
    4,000 bars = 14 kilometres,
    10,000 bars = 35 kilometres.
For the ocean: 100 bars = roughly 1 kilometre of depth

Table 4

Absolute Chronology of the Earth's Geological History
(186a, 221, 231) : '000,000 years

Orogenesis	Geological Era	Geological period	Absolute chronology		
			Beginning	End	Duration
	I. Pre-Geologic		5—7000?	3450	
Shamvayan*	II. Katarchean		3450	2650	800
Svenofennian*	III. Archean		2650	1850	800
Grenville*	IV. Proterozoic I (Algonkian)		1850	1150	700
Indian Ocean*	V. Proterozoic II (Riphean-blue)		1150	600	550
	VI. Paleozoic		600	225	375
Caledonian		1. Cambrian	600	500	100
		2. Silurian	500	400	100
		a) Ordovician	500	420	80
		b) Gotland	420	400	20
Hercynian (Variscian)		3. Devonian	400	320	80
		4. Carboniferous	320	270	50
		5. Permian	270	225	45
	VII. Mesozoic		225	70	155
Cimmerian		6. Triassic	225	185	40
		7. Jurassic (Lias + Dogger + Malm)	185	140	45
Laramide		8. Cretaceous: Lower (Neocomian + Albian + Aptian)	140	70	70
		Upper (Cenomanian + Turonian + Cognacian + Senonian + Danian)	140	100	40
	VIII. Cenozoic		100	70	30
Alpine			70	0	70
		9. Tertiary	70	1.5	68.5
		Paleogen:	70	25	45
		a) Paleocene	70	50	20
		b) Eocene	50	40	10
		c) Oligocene	40	25	15
		Neogen:	25	1.5	23.5
		d) Miocene	25	10	15
		e) Pliocene	10	1.5	8.5
		10. Anthropogen (Quaternary) (Villafranc + Pleistocene + Holocene)	1.5	0	1.5

* The date and chronology of pre-Cambrian mountain-building has not been finally established — **Ed.**

Table 5

Some Data on the Crustal Structure Under the North Atlantic
(425, 426, 518, 560, 739)

Station number	Location of Station	Station Coordinates and Seismic acoustic profiles		Mean depth, km	Sedimentary strata		Magmatic rocks	
		North latitude	West longitude		Thickness, km	Velocity, km/sec	Thickness, km	Velocity, km/sec
1	2	3	4	5	6	7	8	9

I. North Atlantic Ridge

Station number	Location of Station	North latitude	West longitude	Mean depth, km	Thickness, km	Velocity, km/sec	Thickness, km	Velocity, km/sec
D-13	On the east side of the ridge, south of Atlantis Seamount	32°50'—34°46'	34°46'—34°04'	1.28—3.66	0.39	1.71	31.12 deeper	5.01 7.21
D-14	West of the ridge, 370 miles from Station D-13	32°52'—41°04'	43°52'—41°35'	3.20	0.56	1.71	2.09 deeper	4.97 7.27
D-3	Near the crest, incline from west to east	30°27'	40°04'	2.74	0.22	1.72	3.33 deeper	5.38 7.42
D-4	East of the crest	30°31'	37°16'	3.21	0.31	1.72	1.16 deeper	4.55 6.26
A-152-18	On the western slope, of the Azores Plateau	34°74'	39°13'	3.34	0.22	1.70	?	5.23
A-152-17	Near the crest, north of the Azores Plateau	40°42'	27°51'	2.34	0.22	1.70	?	6.08
A-180-1	West of Flores, along the slope across the ridge to the south of the Azores Islands	38°45'—38°45'	39°25'—38°40'	5.12	0.56	1.70	2.71 2.51 deeper	5.45 6.84 8.10
A-180-2	Ditto, extension eastward	39°05'—39°10'	37°40'—36°35'	4.44	0.20	1.70	1.90 1.81 deeper	3.72 6.46 8.00

1	2	3	4	5	6	8	7	9
A-180-3	Ditto, farther east	38°50'—38°40'	35°40'—34°55'	3.91	0.36	1.80	2.79 deeper	4.31 7.91
A-180-4	West of Flores, along the slope across the ridge to the south of the Azores, farther east	38°40'—38°40'	34°55'—34°20'	3.90	?	?	2.72 deeper	4.04 7.30
A-180-5	On the Azores Plateau	38°05'—38°20'	31°45'—31°05'	1.72	0.58	1.80	1.77 deeper	4.86 7.24
A-180-6	Ditto, south of the islands	37°45'—37°40'	39°20'—28°55'	0.70	?	?	1.66 deeper	3.15 5.42
A-180-7	South of the Azores Plateau	35°35'—35°00'	26°00'—26°05'	4.02	0.09	1.80	5.25 deeper	4.47 6.21
B-10-3	West of the crest	33°06'—33°09'	43°34'—42°50'	3.50	—	—	0.65 deeper	3.57 6.35
B-10-4	Near the crest; 5.8 km to mantle	33°04'—33°08'	39°57'—39°47'	2.86	—	—	1.97	4.56
B-10-5	Over the Median Valley; 7.38 km to mantle	33°07'—32°54'	38°34'—38°10'	2.80	—	—	0.70 3.88 deeper	3.50 5.84 8.27
B-10-6	East of the crest; over 12 km to mantle	31°55'—31°40'	35°30'—35°05'	3.60	0.24	1.63	1.43 deeper	4.71 6.79
B-10-7	Ditto, more to the east; over 12 km to mantle	31°42'—31°48'	35°04'—34°32'	3.60	0.17	1.63	2.15 deeper	4.52 7.09
B-10-8	Ditto, more to the east; 9.33 km to mantle	31°53'—31°53'	32°59'—32°26'	4.30	0.15	1.67	2.52	4.83
B-10-9	West of Cruiser Seamount; 11.3 km to mantle	31°51'—31°51'	30°54'—31°23'	4.30	0.71	1.83	1.53 4.59 deeper	5.06 6.87 8.51

1	2	3	4	5	6	7	8	9
A-180-37 to A-180-41	West of Romanche Trench	01°05′—00°04′	20°53′—23°36′	3.68—4.20	—	—	1.46—2.12 deeper	4.59—4.94 6.67—7.19
A-180-40	Ditto; 9.4 km to mantle	00°12′—00°09′	22°24′—22°58′	3.89	—	—	1.46 4.05 deeper	4.59 6.43 8.03
A-180-42	Ditto, in southern latitudes; 8.28 km to mantle	00°04′—00°58′S	23°36′—24°07′	3.47	0.35	1.67	1.72 2.74 deeper	4.82 7.19 8.49
A-180-43 to 180-46	Ditto; in southern latitudes	00°08′—01°05′S	23°18′—26°28′	2.73—4.13	0.10—0.45	1.62—1.73	1.52—1.93 deeper	4.28—5.05 6.51—7.09

Stations A-180-47 and A-180-48 are 6.85 and 9.41 km respectively away from the mantle with velocities of 8.26 and 8.30 km/sec respectively

1	2	3	4	5	6	7	8	9
F-10	On the ridge proper	52°43′—52°44′	32°30′—33°42′	3.38 (2.94—3.84)	0.78	1.72	?	7.36
CR-42	On the eastern slope	46°43′	27°09′	1.84	—	—	0.6—1.1 deeper	3.8 5.7
DY-27	Ditto	46°23′	27°12′	1.54	0.13?	—	3.6 deeper	1.2 6.4
E-3	Reykjanes Ridge, west of the slope, 400 miles from Iceland	58°45′—59°14′	32°16′—31°38′	1.52	0 38	1.70	2.87 deeper	5.60 7.24
E-4	Ditto, 150 miles to the northwest	61°03′—61°30′	29°07′—28°28′	1.37	0.39	1.75	4.32 deeper	5.83 7.63

1	2	3	4	5	6	7	8	9
E-5	240 miles south of Iceland	60°14′—59°45′	22°54′—22°45′	2.38	0.19 0.82	1.72 1.94	2.84 deeper	5.71 7.17
		II. Norwegian and Greenland Seas						
F-9	Northeastern edge between Iceland and South Norway	67°32′—68°07′	00°21′—01°00′	3.37	0.14 0.76	1.70 1.83	2.76 deeper	5.36 8.04
F-7	250 miles southeast of Jan Mayen Island	69°38′—69°07′	02°28′E—03°45′E	3.18	0.43 0.63	1.80 2.00	3.01 deeper	5.37 6.94
F-6	Greenland Sea, 150 miles North of Jan Mayen Island	73°47′—73°28′	10°03′—08°37′	1.28— 3.05	0.49	1.72	3.04 deeper	5.06 7.38
F-5	Near the ridge slope, north east of Jan Mayen Island	71°36′—72°07′	05°36′—04°44′E	2.96	0.23 0.49 1.38	1.70 2.01 3.60	2.56 deeper	5.26 7.69
F-4	Continental edge southwest of Medvezhy Islands	73°23′—72°58′	09°27′—10°16′E	2.27	0.57 0.95	1.79 2.23	2.40 deeper	4.96 7.55
		III. Eastern North Atlantic						
E-6	Southwest of Rockall Bank	54°01′—54°34′	21°15′—21°23′	2.98	0.87 1.24	1.81 1.94	4.10 deeper	5.80 7.43
E-10	Between Rockall and Porcupine Banks, west of the British Isles	54°59′	14°06′	2.75	0.42 1.42 3.55	1.70 2.65 3.20	deeper	6.96
E-12	Between the Faeroes and Scotland	59°48′—59°56′	07°09′—06°29′	0.55	0.25 1.56	1.73 2.24	?	4.91
E-7	Western edge of the Iberian Basin, abyssal area	40°49′—40°18′	19°01′—18°54′	5.49	0.86	1.73	4.31 deeper	6.46 7.68

1	2	3	4	5	6	7	8	9
E-8	Iberian basin, 40 miles south of the plateau's north edge	41°10'—41°39'	16°01'—16°03'	4.85	0.88	1.74	3.81 deeper	6.78 7.77
E-9	West-European Basin west of the Bay of Biscay	45°52'—46°25'	15°23'—15°49'	4.39	0.89	1.72	3.62 deeper	6.26 7.65
D-12	Midway between Northeastern Spain and the south of Iceland	46°17'—46°50'	09°25'—10°17'	4.50	1.17 0.50	1.71 2.24	6.49 deeper	6.14 7.77
D-5	Abyssal region of the Canary Basin west of Madeira	31°55'	23°02'	5.17	1.10	1.71	4.61 deeper	6.49 8.04
D-6	100 miles to the east-northeast	32°49'—32°51'	18°58'—18°55'	3.45	1.50	1.69	?	6.64
H-9	Continental slope west of the British Isles	48°20'	11°20'	3.75	1.4	2.1	8.1 deeper	5.40 7.94
H-16	Farther west, in an abyssal plain	47°48'	17°20'	4.45	2.0— −2.8	2.1	4.2— −5.0 deeper	7.13 8.18
H-18	Northwest of station 16	48°52'	15°00'	4.75	1.1	2.1	?	5.80
H-10	Southeast of station 16	46°53'	15°45'	4.80	0.00— −1.3	2.1	?	6.56
H-17	West of station 18	48°21'	16°49'	4.60	0.7	2.1	3.4 deeper	6.30 7.80
H-11	Northwest of station 18	49°58'	18°33'	4.45	0.9	2.1	?	6.75
L-1	Western Iberian Basin	41°15'	14°30'	5.30	0.2	?	2.7 1.3 deeper	4.00 6.8 8.1
L-2	Halpsia Bank	49°30'	11°53'	0.7	thin		4.0 deeper	4.8 7.1

397

IV. Western North Atlantic

1	2	3	4	5	6	7	8	9
D-2	Abyssal terraces west of the median ridge	30°25'	47°39'	4.36	0.56	1.72	3.11 deeper	6.62 7.94
A-173-5	Northern slope of the Bermuda Plateau	32°46'—32°30'	64°31'—64°29'	2.22	2.68	4.04	?	5.36

Stations with the index H — after M. N. Hill and A. Laughton, indices CR and DY after M. N. Hill, index L — after data of the Discovery II expedition, indices D, E, F, A-152, and A-180-1 to A-180-7 — after J. T. and M. Ewing, indices A-180-37 to A-180-48 — after data by other scientists of the Lamont Observatory.

Table 6

Glaciation Chronology

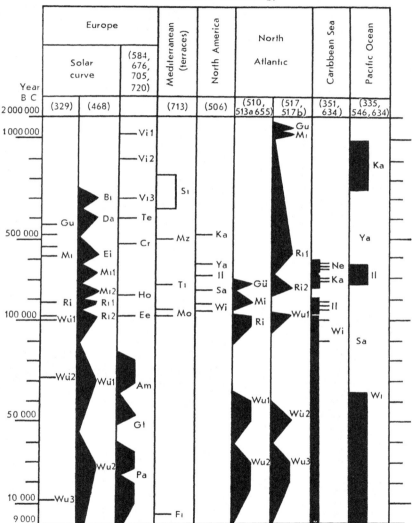

Am — Amersfoort Interglaciation, Bi — Biber Glaciation, Cr — Cromer Interglaciation; Da — Danubian Glaciation, Ee — Eemian Interglaciation, Ei — Eiburon Glaciation, Fl — Flandrian Terrace, Gt — Gottweig Interglaciation, Gu — Gunz Glaciation, Ho — Holstein Interglaciation, Il — Illinois Glaciation, Ka — Kansas Glaciation, Mi — Mindelian Glaciation, Mo — Monastirean Terrace, Mz — Millazzo Terrace, Ne — Nebraska Glaciation, Pa — Paudorf Interglaciation, Ri — Riss Glaciation; Sa — Sangamon Interglaciation, Si — Sicilian Terrace, Te — Tegelen Interglaciation; Ty — Tyrrhenian Terrace, F₁ — Villafranc, Wi — Wisconsin Glaciation, Wu — Würm Glaciation, Ya — Yarmouth Interglaciation

Table 7

Chronology of Late and Post-Glacial Times

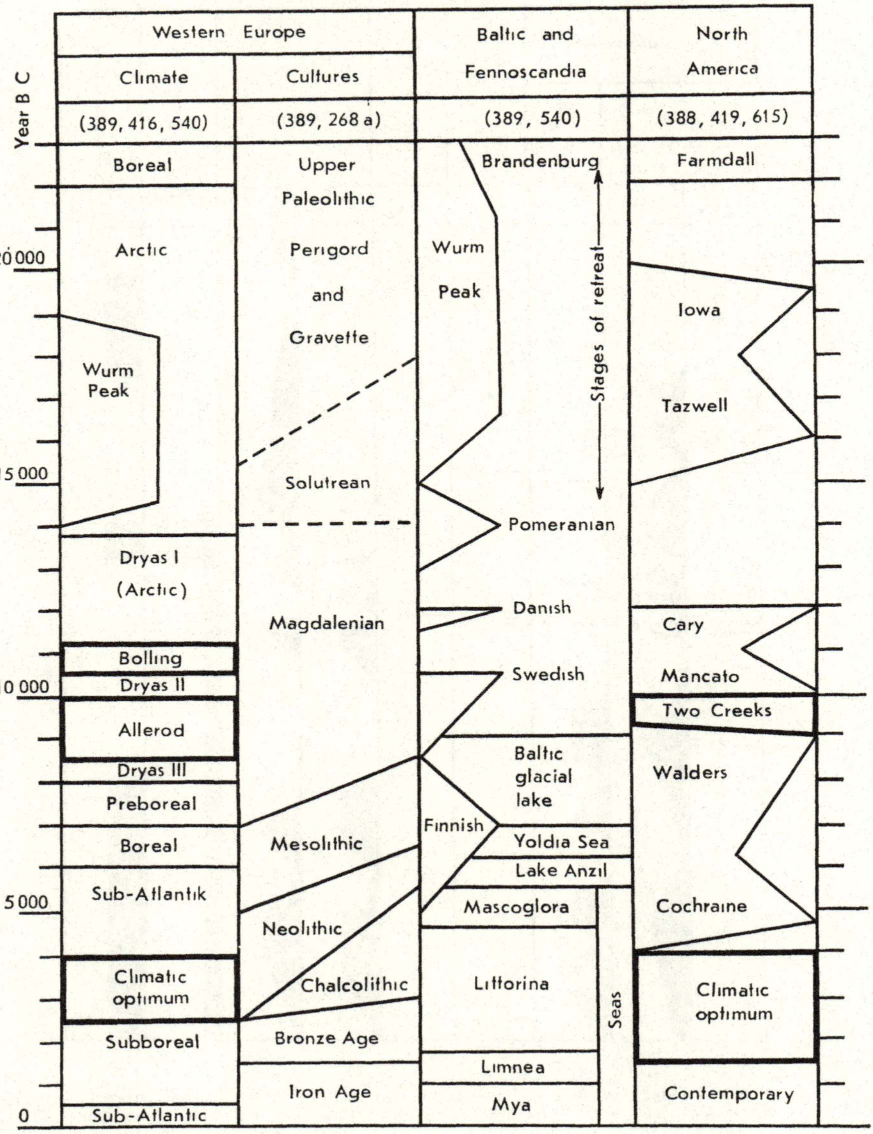
Western Europe
Climate
(389, 416, 540)
Cultures
(389, 268 a)
Baltic and Fennoscandia
(389, 540)
North America
(388, 419, 615)
Year B C
20 000
15 000
10 000
5 000
0
Boreal
Arctic
Wurm Peak
Dryas I (Arctic)
Bolling
Dryas II
Allerod
Dryas III
Preboreal
Boreal
Sub-Atlantik
Climatic optimum
Subboreal
Sub-Atlantic
Upper Paleolithic
Perigord and Gravette
Solutrean
Magdalenian
Mesolithic
Neolithic
Chalcolithic
Bronze Age
Iron Age
Brandenburg
Wurm Peak
Stages of retreat
Pomeranian
Danish
Swedish
Baltic glacial lake
Finnish
Yoldia Sea
Lake Anzil
Mascoglora
Littorina
Seas
Limnea
Mya
Farmdall
Iowa
Tazwell
Cary
Mancato
Two Creeks
Walders
Cochraine
Climatic optimum
Contemporary

APPENDIX 2

Note 1 (to p. 131). The data used by E. L. Hamilton to resolve the problem of the age of oceans cannot yield convincing results. Indeed, because of the uneven depth of the different parts of the ocean, sediments could not have consolidated uniformly in them. Moreover, the very fact of the consolidation of marine sediments cannot be used to determine the age of oceans because in only the latest stages of the development of oceans there have been large outpourings of basalt that buried the ocean-bed-changing sediments over large areas. In the course of geological history the velocity of sedimentation has steadily increased. It would be wrong, therefore, to compute the existence of oceans on the basis of some constant velocity of sedimentation.

Note 2 (to p. 132). Even if we allow for the possibility of the ancient existence of abyssal fauna in modern oceans, its preservation, in the light of the natural changes that the ocean floor underwent during the latest stages of geological history (Cenozoic-Anthropogen), must be completely ruled out. The volcanic eruptions, which covered enormous areas and were accompanied by the ejection of gases and toxic vapours, substantially changed the natural conditions in the abyssal regions of oceans and could not have favoured the preservation of ancient abyssal fauna. This fauna might sooner have survived in shallow regions, from where, as the oceans grew deeper and wider, they moved to greater depths.

Note 3 (to p. 142). The absence of a relic topography on the ocean floor cannot, as A. V. Zhivago and G. B. Udintsev believe, serve as proof of the antiquity of oceans. Most of the floor of the World Ocean underwent active changes during the Neogene-Anthropogen. It developed in two basic directions. Firstly, there were powerful volcanic outpourings over huge areas. Secondly, some parts of the ocean floor underwent uneven vertical movements, as a result of which great quantities of sediments accumulated in some areas, while other areas were denuded of sediments. This excluded the preservation of relic topography. These changes are young geologically and they make it exceedingly difficult to reproduce a picture of the former distribution of land in place of the present oceans.

Note 4 (to p. 160). The different depths of the guyots are linked up with the uneven and differentiated movement of the ocean floor. This only provides further proof that it is wrong to regard the ocean floor as ancient and unchanged areas of the Earth's crust, as primary platforms. Like all the other parts of the Earth's surface, the ocean floor had an intricate and diversified geological life and underwent many uneven vertical displacements.

REFERENCES

I. Bibliography, Reviews and Periodicals

1. d'Abartiague W. L. (1937), *Essai de bibliographie de l'Atlantide*, Bayonne.
2. Bettini L. (1963), "Bibliographie des etudes en langue italienne sur l'Atlantide", *Atlantis* (Genova), I, Nos. 1, 2.
3. Gattefossé J., Roux C. C. (1926), *Bibliographie de l'Atlantide et des questions connexes*, Lyon, 1700 References.
4. Gattefossé J. (1959), "Deux siecles de publications atlantologiques", *Atlantis* (Paris), No 198, 15-22; No. 199, 53-60.
5. Högbom A. G. (1941), "Die Atlantisliteratur unserer Zeit" *Bulletin of the Geological Institute of the University of Uppsala*, 1940.
6. Saint-Michel L. (1953), *Aux sources de l'Atlantide*. Bourges
7. Sykes E. (1947), *A Bibliography of Classical References to Atlantis*, Rome.
8. Sykes E. (1950), "European Literature Since 1914", *Atlantis Research*, 2, No. 6, 81-84.
9. Zhirov N. Th. (1959), "Russian and Soviet Literature on Atlantis", *Atlantis* (London), 13, 3-7.

In addition, there are long lists of references in the works of Bessmertny (39), Donnelly and Sykes (57), Imbelloni and Vivante (69), and Sprague de Camp (102).

A comprehensive reference list is also to be found in the rare book: J. Leslie, *Submerged Atlantis Restored*, Rochester, 1911.

The oldest periodical on atlantology is the journal *Atlantis*, whose publication was started in Paris, France, in 1923. Today it has adopted a mystical-occultist trend. A bi-monthly journal devoted to Atlantis and atlantology generally is published in London, Britain, by Dr. E. Sykes. It began publication in 1948 under the name *Atlantean Bulletin*. In 1949 it was renamed *Atlantean Research*, and since 1951 it has been published under its present name as the organ of the international Atlantis Research Centre. Another journal of the same name, *Atlantis*, was published as a single issue in March 1963 in Genoa, Italy, by Leonardo Bettini and Alf Bajocco.* A journal named *Atlantida* was published in the Azores in 1957.

In the past there have been other attempts to start the publication of periodicals and semi-periodicals devoted to atlantology, but many of them degenerated into occultist magazines and printed very little on scientific atlantology. Of the scientific journals, mention must be made of *Atlantide in Italia*, which was published in Bari, Italy, in 1930-32 by Dr. Nikola Russo. Also meriting mention is the yearbook of Emile Chaouat *Lumière sur l'Atlantide* (1953-59). *Atlantide*, organ of the Tunisian atlantologists, published irregularly by A Giraud, ceased publication in 1958.

---

* A fourth journal of the same name, published in the Federal Republic of Germany, now has nothing to do with atlantology.

II. Literature Used in This Work
(up to 1964 inclusively)

A. Special Literature on Atlantology

10. Andreyeva E. V. (1961), *V poiskakh zateryannogo mira (Atlantida)* (*In Quest of the Lost World of Atlantis*), Leningrad.
11. Bashinsky S. (1914), *Atlantida (Atlantis)*, St Petersburg.
12. Berg L. S. (1928), "Atlantida i Egeida" ("Atlantis and Aegidus"), *Priroda*. No 4, 383-385.
13. Bogayevsky B L. (1926), "Atlantida i atlantskaya kultura" ("Atlantis and Atlantean Culture"), *Novy Vostok*, No. 15, 222-250.
14. Bogachev V. V. (1912), *Atlantida (Atlantis)*, Yuryev.
15. Bryusov V. Y. (1917), "Uchiteli uchitelei" ("Teachers of Teachers"), *Letopis*, Nos. 9-12, 157.
16. Grigoriev A. (1926), "Atlantida v noveishem osveshchenii" ("Atlantis in the Light of Modern Data"), *Priroda*, Nos. 3-4, 106-107.
17. Devigne R. (1924), *Un continent disparu, l'Atlantide, sixieme part du monde*, Paris; Russian translation, Moscow, 1926
18. Zhirov N. F (1957), *Atlantida (Atlantis)*, Moscow.
19. Zhirov N. F. (1959), "Strana na dne okeana", *Otvechayem na pisma rabochikh* ("Land on the Ocean Floor", *We Reply to Letters from Workers*), Issue 2, 83-95.
20. Karnozhitsky A N. (1897), "Atlantida" ("Atlantis"), *Nauchnoye obozreniye*, 4, No. 2, 12-39; No. 4, 42-53.
21. Doyle, A. Conan (1957), *The Maracot Deep*. Afterword by N. F. Zhirov, Moscow.
22. Knorozov Y. V. (1961), "N. F. Zhirov. Atlantida" ("N F. Zhirov. Atlantis"), 1957 (review), *Sovetskaya etnografia*, No. 4, pp. 213-218.
22a. Knorozov Y., Kondratov A. (1964), "Atlantidy ne bylo?" ("Atlantis, a Reality?"), *Znaniye-sila*, No. 4, 32-34.
23. Krestev K. (1959). *The Lost Continent of Atlantis*, Sofia, in the Bulgarian language
24. Norov A. S. (1854), *Atlantida po grecheskim i arabskim istochnikam (Atlantis from Greek and Arab Sources)*, St. Petersburg.
24a. Obruchev V. A. (1963), "Zagadka proshlogo" ("Riddle of the Past"), *Ogonyok*, No 47, 14-15.
25. Reshetov Y. G. (1963), "Taina Atlantidy" ("The Mystery of Atlantis"), *Semya i shkola*, No 4, 44-46.
26. Termier P (1913), "L'Atlantide", *Revue Scientifique*, No. 2, 33-41. Russian translation (1913) in the journal *Ezhegodnik geologii i mineralogii Rossii*, 15, 83.
27. Uzin S. V. (1954), "Atlantida" ("Atlantis"), *Znaniye-sila*, No. 8, 22.
28. Furman I Y. (1955), *Tainy dvukh okeanov (Mysteries of Two Oceans)*, Summary of a lecture for the Society for the Dissemination of Political and Scientific Knowledge, Voronezh
29. Furman I. Y. (1959), "Atlantida: mif ili realnost?" ("Atlantis: Myth Or Reality?"), *Literatura i zhizn*, No 95 (211), August 9, p 4
30 Hagemeister E F. (1955), "Lednikovy period i Atlantida" ("The Ice Age and Atlantis"), *Priroda*, No. 7, 92-94, With an afterword by Academician V. A. Obruchev.
31. Yanshin A. (1958), "Sushchestvovala li Atlantida?" ("Did Atlantis Exist?"), *Vechernaya Moskva*, No. 234 (10597), October 3, p. 3
32. Debate on the subject: "Did Atlantis Exist?" (1956). *Tekhnika molodezhi*, Nos. 9, 10, 11 and 12 Contributions by N. S. Vetchinkin, I A. Yefremov, N. F. Zhirov, M. Y. Plyam and E. F. Hagemeister; With excerpts from Plato and from essays by V. Y. Bryusov.

33. "Segodnya solntse zakhodit nad Atlantidoi" ("Today the Sun Sets Over Atlantis") (1956). *Inostrannaya literatura*, No. 9, 284. Review of a stage production by Vitezslav Nezval.

34. Andersen H. P. C (1949), "Atlantean Traces in the Cape Verde Islands", *Atlantean Research*, 2, No 1, 13.

35. Bac H. (1960), "Les atlantes furent-ils un peuple bleu?" *Atlantis* (Paris), No. 204, 68-72.

36 Baer P. C (1835), *Essai historique et critique sur l'Atlantique des ancient dans lequel on se propose se faire voir la conformité qu'il y a entre l'histoire des Atlantiques et celle des Hebres*, Avignon, 2-eme ed

37. Bellamy H. S. (1948), *The Atlantis Myth*, London.

38. Berlioux E F (1883), *Les Atlantes. Histoire de l'Atlantide et de l'Atlas primitif, ou l'introduction à l'histoire de l'Europe*, Lyon.

39. Bessmertny A. (1932), "Das Atlantisrätsel", *Geschichte und Erklarung der Atlantishypothesen*, Leipzig

40 Boneff N. (1948), "Une application de la theorie des marées aux problème de l'Atlantide", *Annuaire, Université*, facult. scientifique, 45, 1, 155-165, Sofia

41 Boneff N. (1949), "An Asteroid as the Possible Cause of the Atlantis Submersion", *Atlantean Research*, 2, No. 4, 50-52.

42 Boneff N. (1951), "The Theory of the Tides and the Problem of Atlantis", *Atlantis* (London), 4, 36-37.

43. Boneff N. (1959), "The Problem of Atlantis", *Atlantis* (London), 12, 63

44. Borchardt P. (1927), "Nordafrika und die Metallreichtümer von Atlantis", *Pettermanns Geographische Mitteilungen*, 73, 280-282

45 Borchardt P. (1927), "Nordafrika und die naturalichen Reichtümer von Atlantis", *Pettermanns Geographische Mitteilungen*, 73, 326

46 Borchardt P. (1927), "Die Messingstadt in 1001—Nacht—eine Erinnerung von Atlantis?" *Pettermanns Geographische Mitteilungen*, 73, 328

47 Bory de St. Vincent J.B.G M. (1803), *Essais sur les isles Fortunatae et l'antique Atlantide ou precis de l'histoire general de l'archipel des Canaries*, Paris

48 Braghin A. (1946), *Atlantis*, Stuttgart.

49. Bramwell J. (1937), *Lost Atlantis*, London.

50. Brandenstein W (1951), *Atlantis, Grosse und Untergang eines geheimnisvollen Inselreich*, Wien

51 Bryant G. J., Sykes E. (1953-55), "The Lost Atlantis", *Atlantis* (London), 7, 3-13; 23-29; 50-56; 63-89; 103-108; 8, 130-136; 154-159; 171-178; 189-198.

52 Bryant G. J. (1955), "Butavand's Atlantis", *Atlantis* (London), 8, 148-154.

53 Butavand F. (1925), *La véritable histoire de l'Atlantide*, Paris

54 Couissin P. (128), *L'Atlantide de Platon et les origines de la civilisation*, Aix-en-Provence

55 Daniel H. (1956), *La Atlantida fue conocida por el hombre*, Bol Inst. Atropol Medellin (Colombia), 1, No. 4, 323-331

55a Danizot G. (1934), *Sur la structure des isles Canaries, considerée dans des rapports avec le probleme de l'Atlantide*, CR Acad. Scien, Paris, 199, 372-373

56 Donnelly I. (1911), *Atlantis, die vorsintfluchtliche Welt*, Leipzig. Translated from the American publication: *Atlantis, the Antedeluvian World* (1882), New York

57. Donnelly I., Sykes E. (1949), *Atlantis, the Antedeluvian World*, revised edition, London-New York.

58 Filippoff L (1930), *Sur la determination astronomique de l'epoque de la disparition de l'Atlantide*, CR Ac. Sc, Paris, 191, 393-394

59 Filippoff L (1931), "Comment j'ai determiné la date de la disparition de l'Atlantide", *Atlantis* (Paris), IV, No 33.

60 Forrest H. E. (1935), *The Atlantean Continent, Its Bearing Upon the Great Ice Age and the Distribution of Species*, London, 2nd. ed

61 Galanopoulos A G (1960), *On the Location and Size of Atlantis*, Athens

62 Galanopoulos A G. (1960), *On the Origin of the Deluge of Deucalion and the Myth of Atlantis*, Athens.

63. Germain L. (1913), *Le problème de l'Atlantide et la zoologie*, Annal. Geograph , 22, No 123, 209-226.
64. Germain L. (1924), "L'Atlantide", *Revue Scientifique*, 62, 455-463, 481-491.
65 Germain L (1955), *L'Atlantide*, Paris
66. Giroff N. Th (1963), "L'Atlantide comme une realité scientifique", *Le musée vivant* 27 (3), Nos. 19-20, 425-429
67. Herrmann A. (1927), "Atlantis, Tartessos und die Saulen des Herakles", *Pettermanns Geographische Mitteilungen*, 73, 288
68. Hoffmann P. (1953), "Snorre Sturlasson and Atlantis", *Atlantis* (London), 5, 102-104.
69. Imbelloni J., Vivante A. (1942), *Le livre des Atlantides*, Paris. Translated from a publication in the Spanish language, 1939.
70. Jessen O (1925), *Tartessos—Atlantis*, Zeitsch. ges Erdkunde, 184.
71. Kamienski M (1956), "The Date of the Submersion of Poseidonia", *Atlantis* (London). 9, 43-48.
72. Le Cour P. (1950), *L'Atlantide. Origines des civilisations*, Paris
73. Malaise R. (1949), "The Possibility of the Egyptian and Atlantean Cultures Having Been Contemporary", *Atlantean Research*, 2, No. 4, 58-60.
74. Malaise R. (1951), *Atlantis en geologisk verklighet*, Stockholm.
75. Malaise R. (1956), "Sjunket land i Atlantes", *Ymer*, 2, 121-132.
76. Malaise R. (1957), "Oceanic Bottom Investigations and Their Bearings on Geology", *Geologiska Foreningen i Stockholm Forhandungar*, 79, 195-225.
77. Malaise R. (1961), "Atlantis and the Ice Age", *Atlantis (London)*, 14, 23-40.
78 Manzi M. (1922), *Le livre de l'Atlantide*, Paris.
79. Moreaux Th. (1924), *L'Atlantide a-t-elle existée?* Paris.
80 Muck O (1956), *Atlantis. Die Welt vor der Sintflut*, Olter—Freiburg, 2 Aufl.
81. Negris Ph. (1920), *L'Atlantide*, Paris.
82. Netolizky F. (1936), "Die Atlantiszeit", *Welt als Geschichte*, 1, 515.
83. Noroff A. S. (1854), *Die Atlantis nach griechischen und arabischen Quellen*, St. Petersburg.
83a. Overwijn T. F (1951), *That Oera Linda Bock*, Dorarecni, L-de druck.
84. Pettersson H. (1948), *Atlantis und Atlantik*, Vienna. Translated from the Swedish publication: *Atlantis och Atlanten* (1944), Stockholm.
85. Phelon W. P. (1903), *Our Story of Atlantis*. Written down for the Hermetic Brotherhood, San Francisco.
86. Poisson G. (1945), *L'Atlantide devant la science*, Paris.
87. Reshetov Y. G. (1961), "The Mythology of the Greeks in Relation to the Atlantis Legend", *Atlantis* (London), 14, 83-90.
88 Rousseau-Liesens A. (1956), *Les Colonnes d'Hercule et l'Atlantide*, Bruxelles.
89. Roux C. (1926), *Note sur la situation et la configuration probables de l'Atlantide de Platon*, Lyon.
90. Rudbeck O. (1675), *Atlantica, sive Manheim very Japhete posterorum sedes ac patria*, Uppsala.
91. Russo N. (1930), "Atlantide, Tirrenia e Tirrenia", *L'Atlantide in Italia*, 1, No. 11-12.
92. Russo Ph. (1960), "Atlantide et transgression flandrienne", *Atlantis* (Paris), No 204, 51-67.
93. Rutot A. (1920), *L'Atlantide*, Bruxelles.
94. Saurat D (1954), *L'Atlantide et la regne des géants*, Paris.
95. Scharff R. F. (1903), "Some Remarks on the Atlantis Problem", *Proceedings of the Royal Society of Ireland (Irish Academy)*, 24, Sect. B, 203-207.
96. Schuchert Ch. (1917), "Atlantis, the Lost Continent. A Review of Termier's Evidence", *Geographical Review*, III, 64.
97. Schuchert Ch. (1917), "Atlantis and the Permanency of the Atlantic Ocean", *Proceedings of the National Academy of Science*, Washington, 65-72.
98. Schulten A. (1927), "Tartessos und Atlantis", *Pettermanns Geographische Mitteilungen*, 73, 284
99. Scott-Elliot W. (1901), *L'Histoire de l'Atlantide*, Paris. Translated from the English publication: *The Story of Atlantis*, 1896, London.

100. Spanuth J. (1953), *Das entratselt Atlantis*, Stuttgart, 2-te Aufl.
101. Spence L. (1924), *The Problem of Atlantis*, London
102. Sprague de Camp L. (1954), *Lost Continents. The Atlantis Theme in History, Science and Literature*, New York
103. Steiner R. (1923), *Atlantis and Lemuria*, London.
104 Sykes E. (1950). "Orichalcum", *Atlantean Research*, 2, No 6, 85.
105. Sykes E. (1951). "The City of Brass", *Atlantis* (London), 4, 57-68.
106. Sykes E. (1952), "The Schliemann Mystery", *Atlantis* (London), 4, 81-82.
107 Sykes E (1952), "Some Atlantean Personalities", *Atlantis* (London), 4, 126-127.
108. Sykes E. (1952), "The Story of the Silver Belt", *Atlantis* (London), 5, 12-16
109. Sykes E. (1953), "Where Calypso May Have Lived", *Atlantis* (London), 5, 136-137.
110. Sykes E. (1958), "Two Operas on Atlantis in the News", *Atlantis* (London), 11, 57.
111. Sykes E. (1959), "Jules Verne and Atlantis", *Atlantis* (London), 12, 82-86.
112. Sykes E. (1962), "Three Atlantean News Items", *Atlantis* (London), 15, 2.
113. S(ykes) E (1963), More on the Fortunate Isles. *Atlantis* (London), 16, 35-37.
114 (E S.) (1963), "Summary of a Letter from Kamilla Abaturova", *Atlantis* (London), 16, 8-9.
115. Termier P (1913), "L'Atlantide", *Bulletin of the Institute of Oceanography*, Monaco, No 256.
116. Tournier I (1950), "The Orichalcum of the Atlanteans", *Atlantean Research*, 2, No, 6, 86-87.
117. Unger F. (1870), *Die verschwundene Insel Atlantis*, Wien, 2-te Aufl.
118. Wishaw E. M. (1929), *Atlantis in Andalusia. A Study of Folk Memory*, London.
119. Zajdler L. (1963), *Atlantida*, Warszawa; Russian translation (1966) edited by N. F. Zhirov, with an afterword by Professor O. K. Leontyev.
120 Zhirov N. Th. (1958). "The Paul Schliemann Mystery", *Atlantis* (London), 11, 23-24
121. Zhirov N. Th. (1958), "Short Notices on Atlantis Research", *Atlantis* (London), 11, 87-88
122. Zhirov N. Th. (1958), "The Destroyer of Atlantis", *Atlantis* (London), 11, 98-100.
123. Zhirov N. Th. (1958), "Odysseus, the Argonauts and Atlantis", *Atlantis* (London), 11, 112-115; 12, 6-10.
124. Zhirov N. Th. (1959), "Geographical Symbolism and Atlantis", *Atlantis* (London), 12, 51.
125. Zhirov N. Th. (1959), "The Topography of Atlantis of Plato", *Atlantis* (London), 12, 88-89
126. Zhirov N. Th. (1959), "The Two Ethiopias", *Atlantis* (London), 12. 89-91.
127. Zhirov N. Th. (1959), "Scientific Atlantology, Its Paths and Problems", *Atlantis* (London), 13, 103-113.
128. Zhirov N. Th. (1959), "Carolina Bays and Atlantis", *Atlantis* (London), 13, 10-15.
129. Zhirov N. Th (1960), "Erytheia, Tartessos and Atlantis", *Atlantis* (London), 13, 53-54.
130. Zhirov N. Th. (1961), "The Geological History of Atlantis", *Atlantis* (London), 14, 42-58
131. Zhirov N. Th. (1962), "A Critical Study of the Material Culture of Plato's Atlantis", *Atlantis* (London), 15, 3-15.
132. Zhirov N. Th (1962), "Chronological Data of Interest for Atlantology", *Atlantis* (London), 15, 23-27.
133. Zhirov N Th. (1963), ".. Comments on the Fortunate Isles", *Atlantis* (London), 16, 88-89
134. Bettini L. (1963), "Le probleme de l'Atlantide et la protohistoire egèenne", *Atlantis* (Genova), I, No 1, 3-7.

B. Sections and Chapters Devoted to Atlantis in Various Works

135. Andreyeva E. V. (1954), *Uekoviye zagadki (Age-old Riddles)*, Moscow, 53-92

136 Bashmakov A A. (1912), *Tripolitania i Kirenaika v otnosheni ikh istorii i etnografii (Tripolitania and Cyrenaica in Relation to Their History and Ethnography)*, St. Petersburg, 11-13.

137. Bauer N , Russian translation (1959) from the German *Mysteries of the Ocean Depths*, Moscow, 180-185.

138 Bobyr Z. (1962), "Zakhvachennaya planeta" ("A Captured Planet"), *Nauka i zhizn*, No. 12, 87-92

138a Vasilyev M , Gushchev S. (1960), *Tvoi tainy, priroda! (Your Secrets, Nature!)*, Moscow, 150-156

139 Golubev G (1960). *Nerazgadanniye tainy (Unravelled Mysteries)*, Moscow, 99-176

140. Plato's Dialogues "Timaeus" (or *On the Nature of Things*) and "Critias" (1886) Translated with commentaries by G V. Malevansky, Kiev.

141. Dobrynin B F. (1923), *Submerged Continents*, Moscow, 56 (Chapter 5)

142. Zhirov N. F. (1960), "Zagadki drevnikh kultur" ("Riddles of Ancient Cultures"), *On Land and at Sea*, Issue I, 530-539, Moscow

143. Kolubovsky I. (1927), *Potonuvshiye materiki (Sunken Continents)*, Moscow.

144 Lhote H (1959), *A la decouverte des fresques du Tassili*, Paris. Russian translation (1962), Moscow, 114-121

145 Plato, *Essays* (1879) Translation with commentaries by F G. Karpov, Moscow, Vol 6, "Timaeus", 377-385, "Critias", 500-519

146 Thomson J. O. (1948), *History of Ancient Geography*, Cambridge Russian translation (1953), Moscow, 139-143

147 Uzin S. V. (1958), *Zagadki materikov i okeanov (Riddles of Continents and Oceans)*, Moscow, 100-143

148 Chirvinsky P N (1912), "Peremeshcheniye polyusov kak osnovnaya prichina izmeneniya klimatov v tretichny i chetvertichny periody i glavnaya prichina takogo peremeshcheniya" ("Movement of Poles as the Basic Reason for the Climatic Changes in the Tertiary and Quaternary Periods and the Main Reason of This Movement"), *Yezhegodnik geologii i mineralogii Rossii*, 15, 78.

149 Babcock W H (1925), *Legendary Islands of the Atlantic. A Study of Medieval Geography*. American Geographical Society, Research Service, No. 2. New York, 2nd ed , 11-33

150 Beaumont C. (1946), *Riddle of Prehistoric Britain*, London

151. Blavatska H P., *Die Geheimlehre*, Bd 2, *Anthropogenesis*, Leipzig. Translation First publication in the English language (1888)

152 Carli G R (1788), *Lettre Americaine*, Paris

153. Churchward J. (1933), *The Lost Continent of Mu*, New York.

153a Frandsen M (1945), *Pyramide Viskom*, Copenhagen

154. Frost K T (1913), "The Critias and Minoan Crete", *Journal of Hellenic Studies*, 33, 189

155 Georg E. (1939), *Verschollene Kulturen Das Menschenheitserlebens Ablauf und Deutungsversuch*, Leipzig, 71-184.

156 Germain L (1935), "Le mer des Sargasses", *Bulletin of the Institute of Oceanography*, Monaco, No 671.

157 Guignard M. (1962), *Comment j'ai déchiffré la langue étrusque*, Puttelange les Thionville

158 Hennig R (1925), *Vor ratselhaften Lander*, Munchen, 7-64

159 Homet M. F. (1958), *Die Sohne der Sonne*, Olten, Freiburg, 175-179, 195-298

160 Hörbiger H , Fauth F (1925), *Glazialkosmogonie*, Leipzig.

161 Hutin S (1961), *Les civilisations inconnues*, Paris, 56-103.

162 Jacolliot L. (1874), *Histoire des Vierges. Les peuples et les continents disparus*, Paris

163. Kamienski M (1952), "The Past of Halley's Comet", *Atlantis* (London), 4, 95-98

164 Kowalska K. (1957), *Morze Sargasowe*, Warszawa, 144-153
165 Le Plongeon A. (1895), *Queen Moo and the Egyptian Sphynx*, London.
166 Malaise R. (1945), *Tenthredinoides of South-Eastern Asia*, London, 19-41.
167 Martin T H (1841), *Etudé sur le Timée de Platon*, Paris, Vol. I
168. Odhner N, Malaise R. (1960), "On the Last Theory of the Ice Age", *New World Antiquity*, 7, 147-156
169 Rhode E (1900), *Der griechische Roman und seine Vorlaufer*, Leipzig, 2-te Auf, 210-222
170 Rivaud A (1925), *Timée et Critias, aux Belles-Lettres*, Paris
171 Ruzo D. (1954), "La culture Masma", Lima
172 Ruzo D. (1956), "La culture Masma, *L'Ethnographie*, 45-53.
173 Ruzo D (1959) "La culture Masma", *L'Ethnographie*, 75-87
174 Sykes E (1960), "A Catastrophe Myth from Scandinavia", *Atlantis* (London), 14, 3-16
175 Sykes E (1961), "The Twilight of the Nordic Gods", *Atlantis* (London), 14, 63-72
176 Taylor A E. (1929), *The Timaeus and Critias*, London.
177 Termier P. (1924), *A la gloire de la Terre*, Paris 2-me ed., chap. V.
177a Wauchope R. (1963), *Lost Tribes and Sunken Continents*, Chicago and London, 2nd ed Russian translation (1966) edited by Y. V. Knorozov.
178 Zajdler L. (1956), *Dzieje zegara*, Warszawa, 51-57
179 (The anonyme critic) (1956), *New World Antiquity*, 3, 156

C. Other Utilised References

180 Avdiyev V. I. (1953), *Istoriya drevnego vostoka* (*History of the Ancient East*), Moscow, 2nd ed
181 Avien R. F. (1939), "Oera Maritima", *Bulletin of Ancient History*, No. 2, 227, translation.
182. Alimen H. (1955), *Prehistoire de l'Afrique*, Paris. Russian translation (1960), Moscow
183 Arkhangelsky A. D, Strakhov N M (1938), *Geologicheskoye stroyeniye i istoriya razvitiya Chernogo morya* (*Geological Structure and History of Development of the Black Sea*), Moscow
184 Arkhangelsky A D (1947), *Geologicheskoye stroyeniye i geologicheskaya istoriya SSSR* (*Geological Structure and Geological History of the USSR*), Moscow
185 Afanasyev G. D (1953), "K probleme granita" ("The Problem of Granite"). *News of the USSR Academy of Sciences*, Geology Series, No 1, 63-80.
186 Afanasyev G D. (1960), "O petrograficheskoi interpretatsii geofizicheskikh dannykh v stroyenii Zemli" ("Petrographic Interpretation of Geophysical Data on the Earth's Structure"), *News of the USSR Academy of Sciences*, Geology Series. No 7, 3-31
186a Balukhovsky N F (1963), "Geologicheskiye tsikly" ("Geological Cycles"), *Priroda*, No 2, 54-59.
187 Baranov V I, Serdyukova A. S (1959), "Radiogennoye teplo" ("Radiogenous Heat'). *Priroda*, No 3, 29-34
188 Barth T. F W Russian translation (1961) from the English "Composition and Evolution of the Magma of the Southern Mid-Atlantic Ridge', *Physical and Chemical Problems of the Formation of Rock*, Moscow, 31-55
189 Bashkirov S A (1947), *Antiseismizm drevnei arkhitektury* (*Antiseismism of Ancient Architecture*), Yaroslavl
190 Bekshtrem A (1911), "Zagadochny disk" ("An Enigmatic Disc"), *Journal of the Ministry of Education*, New Series 36, December. Department of Classical Philology, 549-602
191 Belov M. I (1960), "Oshibka ili umysel?" ("An Error or Design?") (The Maps of Piri Reis and Their American Interpreters), *Priroda*, No. 11, 89-95.
192 Belousov V V. (1942), "O geologicheskom stroyenii okeanov" ("The Geological Structure of Oceans"), *Priroda*, Nos. 5-6, 26.

193. Belousov V. V. (1952), "Tektonicheskoye razvitiye zemnogo shara" ("Tectonic Development of the Earth"), *Priroda*, No. 2, 49

194. Belousov V. V. (1954), *Osnovniye voprosy geotektoniki (Fundamental Problems of Geotectonics)*, Moscow

195 Belousov V. V. (1955), "O geologicheskom stroyenii i razvitii okeanicheskikh vpadin" ("The Geological Structure and Development of Ocean Hollows"), *News of the USSR Academy of Sciences*, Geology Series, Nos. 3, 3-18

196 Belousov V. V. (1960), "Razvitiye zemnogo shara i tektogenez" ("Development of the Earth and Tectogenesis"), *Sovetskaya geologiya*, No. 7, 3-27

197. van Bemmelen R. W. (1954), *Mountain-Building*, Hague Russian translation (1956), Moscow

198. Berg L S (1946), *Podvodniye doliny (Submarine Valleys)*, USSR Geographical Society, 73, 301.

199. Berg L. S. (1946), "Drevnost cheloveka v Amerike" ("Antiquity of Man in America"), *Priroda*, No. 12, 77.

200. Berg L. S. (1946), "O predpolagayemoi svyazi mezhdu velikim oledeneniyem i goroobrazovaniyem" ("The Surmised Link Between the Great Ice Age and Mountain-Building"), *Bulletin of Geography*, 1, 23-31.

201. Berg L. S. (1947), "Nekotoriye soobrazheniya o teorii peredvizheniya materikov" ("Some Considerations Regarding the Theory of the Movement of Continents"), *News of the USSR Geographical Society*, 74, 7-12.

202. Berg L. S (1947), *Klimat i zhizn (Climate and Life)*, Moscow. 2nd ed.

203. Berg L. S. (1948), "O predpolagayemom razdvizhenii materikov" ("The Surmised Separation of Continents"), *News of the USSR Academy of Sciences*, Geology Series, No 3, 3.

204. Berckhemer H. (1956), "Rayleigh-wave Dispersion and Crustal Structure in the East Atlantic Ocean Basin", *Bulletin of the Seismological Society of America*, 46, No. 2. Russian translation (1959) in *Structure of the Earth According to Seismic Data*, Moscow, 271-275.

205. Birch F. (1955), *Physics of the Crust of the Earth*, Baltimore. 101-118. Russian translation (1957) in *The Earth's Crust*, Moscow, 114-129.

206. Bodnarsky M. S. (1932), "Perviye russkiye geograficheskiye atlasy" ("First Russian Geographical Atlases"), *Zemlevedeniye*, 29, Issue I.

207. Brookes C. E. P. (1950), *Climates Through the Ages*, London. Russian translation (1952), Moscow

208. Bubnov S. N. (1960), *Osnovniye problemy geologii (Fundamental Problems of Geology)*, Moscow.

209 Bourcart J. (1949), *Geographie du fond des mers*, Paris Russian translation (1958), Moscow.

210. Bucher W. H. (1956), "Modellversuche und Gedanken über das Wesen der Orogenese", *Geotektonische Symposium zu Ehren von Hans Stille* Russian translation (1960) in *Problems of Modern Tectonics Abroad*, Moscow, 431-451.

211. Vaillant G. (1941), *Aztecs of Mexico*, New York. Russian translation (1949), Moscow.

212. Vallaux C. (1933), *La geographie generale des mers*, Paris. Russian translation (1948), Moscow

213. Wegener A. (1936), *Die Entstehung der Kontinente und Ozeane*, Braunschweig, 2-te Aufl. Russian translation (1924) from the 1st edition, Moscow.

214. Wegmann C. E. (1956), "Stockwerktektonik und Modelle von Gesteindifferentiation", *Geotektonische Symposium zu Ehren von Hans Stille*, Russian translation (1960) in *Problems of Modern Tectonics Abroad*, Moscow, 201-222

215. Vernadsky V. I. (1933), "Ob oblastyakh okhlazhdeniya v zemnoi kore" ("Regions of Cooling in the Earth's Crust"), *Proceedings of the State Institute of Hydrology*, 10, 5.

216. Vernadsky V. I. (1942), "O geologicheskikh obolochkakh Zemli kak planety" ("Geological Shells of the Earth as a Planet"), *Herald of the USSR Academy of Sciences*, Geography-Geophysics Series, No. 6, 258-259.

217. Wilson D. T. (1959), "Geophysics and the Growth of Continents", *Priroda*, No. 8, 41-52

218. Vinogradova P. S., Kislyakov A. G., Litvin V. M., Ponomarenko L. S.

(1959), "Rezultaty okeanograficheskikh issledovany v raione Farero-Islandskogo poroga v 1955-1956 gg." ("Results of Oceanographic Investigations in the Region of the Iceland-Faeroe Rise in 1955-1956"), *Proceedings of the Polar Institute of Deep-Sea Fishing and Oceanography*, XI, 106-133.

219. Vikhrenko M. M, Nikolayeva V. K. (1962), "Vzveshenniye veshchestva severnoi chasti Atlanticheskogo okeana, po dannym vtorogo i chetvertogo reisov e/s 'Mikhail Lomonosov'" ("Suspension Material in the North Atlantic According to Data of the 2nd and 4th Cruises of the *Mikhail Lomonosov*"), *Proceedings of the Institute of Oceanology*, 56, 87-122.

220. Voyeikov A. I. (1881), "Klimaticheskiye usloviya lednikovykh yavleny, nastoyashchikh i proshedshikh" ("Climatic Conditions of Glacial Phenomena, Past and Present"), *Proceedings of the St. Petersburg Mineralogical Society*, Series 2, 1, 16, 21

221. Voitkevich G. V. (1958), "Yedinaya geokhronologiya dokembriya' ("Single Geochronology of the Pre-Cambrian Period"), *Priroda*, No. 5, 77-79

222. E. V(ulf) (1926), "Rodina banana" ("Homeland of the Banana"), *Priroda*, No 7-8, 101

223. Vulf E. V. (1932), *Uvedeniye v istoricheskuyu geografiyu rasteny (Introduction to the Historical Geography of Plants)*, Moscow

224. Vulf E. V. (1937), "Geografiya rasteny i teoriya Vegenera" ("Geography of Plants and the Wegener Theory"), *Priroda*, No 3, 28

225. Vulf E. V. (1944), *Istoricheskaya geografiya rasteny (Historical Geography of Plants)*, Moscow.

226. Gagelyants A. A., Galperin E I., Kosminskaya I. P., Krakshina R. M. (1958), "Stroyeniye zemnoi kory tsentralnoi chasti Kaspiiskogo morya, po dannym glubinnogo seismicheskogo zondirovaniya" ("Structure of the Earth's Crust in the Central Caspian, According to Deep-Sea Seismic Soundings"), *Reports of the USSR Academy of Sciences*, 123, 520-522

227. Gakkel Y. Y. (1957), *Nauka i osvoyeniye Arktiki (Science and the Harnessing of the Arctic)*, Moscow.

228. Gakkel Y. Y. (1958), "Priznaki sovremennogo podvodnogo vulkanizma na khrebte Lomonosova" ("Evidence of Modern Submarine Volcanic Activity on the Lomonosov Ridge"), *Priroda*, No. 4, 87-90.

229. Gakkel Y. Y. (1961) "Sovremennoye predstavleniye o khrebte Lomonosova" ("Present-Day Notions About the Lomonosov Ridge"), *Materials on the Arctic and Antarctic*, Issue 1, Leningrad, 24-25

230. Gakkel Y. Y. (1961), "Podvodny khrebet Mendeleyeva" ("The Submarine Mendeleyev Ridge"), *Materials on the Arctic and Antarctic*, Issue 1, Leningrad, 41-42.

231. Caudio A. (1958), "The Riddle of the Guanches". Russian translation published in the magazine *V zashchitu mira*, 7, No. 80, 80-91, No. 82, 88-95.

232. "Geokhronologicheskaya shkala v absolutnom letoischislenii, po dannym laboratoriy SSSR v 1960g" ("Geochronological Scale in Absolute Dating, According to Soviet Laboratories in 1960" (1960), *News of the USSR Academy of Sciences*, Geology Series No. 10, 17-21.

233. Heezen B. C., Ewing M., Manzis P. (1958), *Submarine Turbidity Currents*. Russian translation in *Priroda*, No. 2, 100-104

234. Gilluly J. (1955), "Geologic Contrasts Between Continents and Ocean Basins", *Crust of the Earth*, Baltimore, 7-18, Russian translation (1957) in *The Earth's Crust*, Moscow, 19-31.

236. Gipp S. K. (1962), "Proyavleniye podvodnogo vulkanizma v raione Azorskikh ostrovov" ("Manifestations of Submarine Volcanic Activity Near the Azores"), *Proceedings of the Institute of Oceanology*, 56, 23-31.

237 Homer (1935), *Odysseus*, Translation by V. A. Zhukovsky, commentaries by I. M. Trotsky, Moscow.

237a. *Gondwana* (1964), A Collection, Moscow.

238. Goncharov V. P., Neprochnov Y. P. (1960), "Geomorfologiya dna i voprosy tektoniki Chernogo morya" ("Geomorphology of the Floor and Problems of Tectonics of the Black Sea"), in *Marine Geology*, Moscow, 94-104.

239. Gorbovsky A. (1962-63), "Zagadki drevnei istorii" ("Riddles of Ancient

History"), *Baikal*, 8, No. 4, 50-60, 63-84, No 5, 92-108; No 6 55-68, 77-82, 9, No 1, 65-86.

240 Gorbovsky A. (1963), "Stariye zagadki istorii i noviye gipotezy" ("Old Riddless of History and New Hypotheses"), *Nauka i zhizn*, Nos 1, 2, 3, 4, 6.

241 Gorsky N. N. (1960), *Tainy okeana (Mysteries of the Ocean)*, Moscow

242 Grabovsky N. A., Greku R. H., Metalnikov A. P. (1961), "Nekotoriye geomorfologicheskiye osobennosti relyefa dna Atlanticheskogo okeana po tridtsatomu meridianu ot Severnogo polyarnogo kruga do Yuzhnogo tropika" ("Some Geomorphological Features of the Atlantic Topography Along the 30th Meridian from the Arctic Circle to the Southern Tropics"), *Okeanologiya*, 1, 860-865.

243. Grabovsky N. A. (1962), "O geomorfologicheskikh osobennostyakh relyefa dna Severo-Vostochnoi Atlantiki" ("Geomorphological Features of the Floor Topography in the Northwestern Atlantic"), *Okeanologiya*, 2, 92-97

244. Gutenberg B., Richter C F (1939), "The Constitution of the Earth's Crust The Continents and Oceans", *International Constitution of the Earth*, ed. by B Gutenberg, New York-London. Russian translation (1949), in *Internal Structure of the Earth*, Moscow, 314-341.

245 Debets G. F, Trofimova T A., Cheboksarov P I. (1951), "Problemy zaseleniya Yevropy, po antropologicheskim dannym" ("The Settlement of Europe According to Anthropological Data"), *Proceedings of the Institute of Ethnography*, 16, 409

246 Demenitskaya R M (1958), "Zavisimost moshchnosti zemnoi kory ot vozrasta skladchatosti" ("Dependence of the Thickness of the Earth's Crust on the Age of Folding"), *Sovetskaya geologiya*, No. 1, 3-23.

247 Daly R A. (1933), *Igneous Rocks and the Depth of the Earth*, London-New York, Russian translation (1936), Moscow-Leningrad

247a. Yevteyev S. A, Lazukov G. I (1964), "Rol glyatsioizostazii v dvizheniyakh zemnoi kory oblastei sovremennogo i drevnego oledeneniya" ("Role of Glacial Isostasy in the Movements of the Earth's Crust in Regions of Modern and Ancient Glaciation"), *Transactions of the USSR Academy of Sciences*, Geography Series, No 2, 21-31.

248 Yelnitsky L. A. (1961), *Znaniya drevnikh o severnykh stranakh (The Ancients on Northern Countries)*, Moscow

249. Yelnitsky L A (1962), *Drevneishiye okeanskiye plavaniya (Navigation in Antique Times)*, Moscow

250 Yermolayev M M (1947), "Problema istoricheskoi gidrologii morei i okeanov" ("The Problem of Historical Hydrology of Seas and Oceans"), *Voprosy geographii*, 7, 32.

250a Yerofeyev P N (1963), "Stroyeniye banki Gorrindzh (Atlanticheskiy okean)' ["Structure of the Gorringe Bank (Atlantic Ocean)"], *Reports of the USSR Academy of Sciences*, 151, 1159-61.

251. Yefimenko P. P. (1938), *Pervobytnoye obshchestvo (Primitive Society)*, Leningrad, 2nd ed.

252. Zhivago A V. (1960), "Geomorfologiya morskogo dna na Mezhdunarodnom okeanograficheskom kongresse v Nyu-Yorke, 31 avgusta-11 sentyabrya 1959 g." ("Geomorphology of the Sea Floor at the International Oceanographic Congress in New York, August 31-September 11, 1959"), *News of the USSR Academy of Sciences*, Geography Series No 1, 136-140

253 Zhivago A. V., Udintsev G B (1960), "Sovremenniye problemy geomorphologii dna morei i okeanov" ("Modern Problems of the Geomorphology of the Floor of Seas and Oceans"), *Herald of the USSR Academy of Sciences*, Geography Series No. 1, 22-36.

254. Zhivago A V., Lisitsyn A. P, Udintsev G B (1962), "X Tikhookeansky nauchny kongress Voprosy morskoi geologii i geomorfologii" ("10th Pacific Scientific Congress. Problems of Marine Geology and Geomorphology"), *Okeanologiya*, 2, 469-488.

254a. Zhirov N F. (1963), "Ostrov istoricheskikh zagadok" ("Island of Historical Riddles"), *At Sea and On Land*, Issue 4, 570-582

255 Zhukovsky P. M. (1956), *Proiskhozhdeniye kulturnykh rasteny (Origin of Cultured Plants)*, Moscow

256 Zavaritsky A. N. (1944) *Uvedeniye v petrokhimiyu izverzhennykh gornykh porod (Introduction to the Petrochemistry of Igneous Rock)*, Sverdlovsk.
257. Zenkevich L. A , Lisitsyn A. P., Udintsev G. B. (1959), "Glubiny okeana kak obyekt izucheniya" Sb. *Itogi nauki. Dostizheniya okeanologii I. Uspekh v izucheni okeanicheskikh glubin* ("Ocean Depths as a Subject of Study" in *Results of Science. Achievements of Oceanology. I. Success in the Study of Ocean Depths*), Moscow, 7-26.
258. Zenkevich L. A. (1961), "Problemy, svyazanniye s izucheniyem glubin okeana" ("Problems Linked Up With the Study of Ocean Depths"), *Okeanologiya*, I, 382-398
259 Zenkevich L. A , Birshtein Y. A. (1961), "O geologicheskoi drevnosti glubokovodnoi fauny" ("Geological Antiquity of Deep-Sea Fauna"), *Okeanologiya*, 1, 111-124
260 Zubov N N. (1938), *Morskiye vody i ldy (Sea Water and Ice)*, Moscow.
261 Ilyin A V. (1959), "O nekotorykh chertakh geomorfologii Atlanticheskogo okeana k severo-zapadu ot Anglii" ("Some Features of the Geomorphology of the Atlantic Ocean Northwest of Britain"), *Reports of the USSR Academy of Sciences*, 127, 881-883.
262 Ilyin A. V (1960), "Geomorfologicheskiye issledovaniya v Severnoi Atlantike na e/s 'Mikhail Lomonosov' " ("Geomorphological Investigations in the North Atlantic by the *Mikhail Lomonosov*"), *Proceedings of the Institute of Marine Hydrophysics of the USSR Academy of Sciences*, 19, 115-135
263. Ilyin A V. (1961), "Rifovaya dolina v Atlanticheskom okeane" ("The Rift Valley in the Atlantic Ocean"), *Priroda*, No 3, 93-96
264. Eardley A. J. (1954), "Tectonic Relations of North and South America", *Bulletin of the American Association of Petrology and Geology*, 38, No 5 Russian translation (1960) in *Problems of Modern Tectonics Abroad*, Moscow, 343-432
265 Karlov N. N. (1960), "Vozrast kromanyonskogo cheloveka". ("Age of Cro-Magnon Man"), *Priroda*, No 6, 83.
266. Carter G. (1933), *The Tomb of Tutankhamon*. Russian translation (1959), Moscow.
267. Katterfeld G. H. (1962), *Lik Zemli (The Face of the Earth)*, Moscow.
268. Kennedy G. C , "The Origin of Continents and Mountain Ranges". Russian translation (1961), in *Physical and Chemical Problems of the Formation of Rock and Ore*, Moscow, 161-173
268a Kind N. V. (1962), "Nekotoriye noviye danniye ob absolyutnoi khronologii verkhnego pleistotsena i vozrast verkhnepaleoliticheskikh stoyanok Yevropy" ("Some New Data on the Absolute Chronology of the Upper Pleistocene and the Age of the Upper Paleolithic Settlements in Europe"), *Bulletin of the Commission of the USSR Academy of Sciences for the Study of the Quaternary Period*, No 27, 133-138.
268b Kind N. V. (1963), "Absolyutnaya khronologiya poslednei lednikovoi epokhi i vozrast paleolita Yevropy" ("Absolute Chronology of the Last Glaciation and the Age of the European Paleolithic"), *Absolute Geochronology of the Quaternary Period*, Moscow, 107-117.
269. Klenova M. V. (1948), *Geologiya morya (Geology of the Sea)*, Moscow.
270 Klenova M V. (1958), "Problemy geologii morya" ("Problems of Geology of the Sea"), *Priroda*, No 12, 39-42
271. Klenova M V. (1960), "Raboty po geologii morya v Atlanticheskom okeane" ("Works on Marine Geology in the Atlantic Ocean"), *News of the USSR Academy of Sciences*, Geology Series, No. 10, 77-81
272. Klenova M. V, Lavrov B. M. (1962), "Raboty po geologii morya v Atlanticheskom okeane" ("Works on Marine Geology in the Atlantic Ocean"), *Bulletin of the Oceanographic Commission of the USSR Academy of Sciences*, No 8, 38-45
273 Klenova M. V., Zenkevich N. L (1962), "Geologicheskiye raboty v zapadnoi chasti Severnoi Atlantiki" ("Geological Investigations in the Western North Atlantic"), *Proceedings of the Institute of Marine Hydrophysics of the USSR Academy of Sciences*, 25, 142-186
274 Klenova M. V., Lavrov V M , Nikolayeva V. K (1962), "Rasprostraneniye

vzvesi v Atlanticheskom okeane v svyazi s relyefom dna" ("Distribution of Suspension in the Atlantic in Connection with the Floor Topography"), *Reports of the USSR Academy of Sciences*, 144, 1153-1155

274a Knorozov Y. V. (1963), *Pismennost indeitsev maiya* (*Written Language of the Mayas*), Moscow-Leningrad.

275 Kort V. G (1962), "34i reis e/s 'Vityaz'" ("34th Cruise of the *Vityaz*"), *Okeanologiya*, 2, 564-571

276 Kosven M. (1947), "Amazonki" ("The Amazons"), *Sovetskaya etnografiya*, No 2. 33-59; No 3, 3-32

277. Kosven M. O. (1958), *Ocherki istorii pervobytnoi kultury* (*Essays on the History of Primitive Culture*), Moscow

278. Kokhnenko S. V. (1958), *Biologiya i rasprostraneniye ugrya* (*The Biology and Distribution of Eels*), Minsk

279. Krasilnikov N. A. (1958), "Pogloshcheniye yestestvenno-radioaktivnykh elementov pochvennymi mikroorganizmami" ("Absorption of Natural Radioactive Elements by Soil Microorganisms"), *Priroda*, No 9, 97-99

280 Kriss A. E. (1959), *Morskaya mikrobiologiya (glubokovodnaya)* [*Marine (Deep-Sea) Microbiology*], Moscow.

281. Kropotkin P. N. (1956), *Geologicheskaya istoriya i stroyeniye Zemli (The Geological History and Structure of the Earth)*, Moscow

282. Kropotkin P. N. (1956), "Proiskhozhdeniye materikov i okeanov" ("Origin of Continents and Oceans"), *Priroda*, No. 4, 31-42

283. Kropotkin P. N., Lyustikh E. N., Povalo-Shveikovskaya N. N. (1958), *Anomalii sily tyazhesti na materikakh i okeanakh i ikh znacheniye dlya tektoniki (Anomalies of the Force of Gravity in Continents and Oceans and Their Significance to Tectonics)*, Moscow.

284. Kropotkin P. N. (1960), "Paleomagnetizm i ego znacheniye dlya stratigrafii i geotektoniki" ("Paleomagnetism and Its Significance to Stratigraphy and Geotectonics"), *News of the USSR Academy of Sciences*, Geology Series, No. 12, 3-25.

285. Kuplyansky B. M (1948), "Vopros o proiskhozhdenii granitov v sovremennoi nauke" ("The Question of the Origin of Granites in Modern Science"), *Priroda*, No. 8, 12-18.

286. Lavrov V. M. (1962), "Kharakterniye cherty stratifikatsii osadkov Severo-Vostochnoi Atlantiki" ("Specific Features of the Stratification of Sediments in the Northeastern Atlantic"), *Proceedings of the Institute of Oceanology*, 56, 15-22.

286a Lavrov V. M. (1965), "O relyefe i tektonike ekvatorialnoi chasti Sredinnogo Atlanticheskogo khrebta" ("The Topography and Tectonics of the Equatorial Mid-Atlantic Ridge"), *Reports of the USSR Academy of Sciences*, 162, 1134-1137.

286b Lavrov V. M. (1966), "Podvodny vulkanizm Azorskogo gornogo uzla v Severnoi Atlantike" ("Submarine Volcanic Activity in the Azores Mountain System of the North Atlantic"), *Modern Volcanic Activity*, Vol. 1, 24-32, Moscow.

287. Lazarev P. P. (1950), "Ob odnoi prichine izmeneniya klimatov zemnogo shara v geologicheskiye epokhi" ("A Reason for the Change in the Earth's Climate During the Geological Epochs"), *Collected Works*, Vol. 3, 208-210.

288. Lazarev P.P. (1950), "O metode, pozvolyayushchem dokazat zavisimost okeanskikh techeny ot passatnykh vetrov, i o roli okeanskikh techeny v izmeneniyakh klimata v razlichniye geologicheskiye epokhi" ("A Method Proving the Dependence of Ocean Currents on the Trade Winds, and the Role of Ocean Currents in Climatic Changes During Different Geological Epochs"), *Collected Works*, Vol. 3, 216-228.

289. Laktionov A. F. (1959), "Relyef dna Grenlandskogo morya v raione poroga Nansena" ("Floor Topography of the Greenland Sea near the Nansen Ridge"), *Priroda*, No. 10, 95-97

290 De Landa Diego, *Relacion de las cosas Jucatan*. Russian translation (1955), Moscow.

291. Lapina N. N. (1961), "Istoriya razvitiya Severnogo Ledovitogo okeana v pozdnechetvertichnoye vremya" ("History of the Development of the Arctic Ocean in Late Quaternary Times"), *Materials on the Arctic and Antarctic*, Issue 1, Leningrad, 50-51.

292. Levin B. Y. (1959), "Razvitiye planetnoi kosmogonii" ("Development of Planetary Cosmogony"), *Priroda*, No 10, 19-26

293. Levin M. G., Okladnikov A. P. (1959), "Mezhdunarodnaya Konferentsiya v Kopengagene po arkheologii i antropologii Arktiki" ("Copenhagen International Conference on Arctic Archaeology and Anthropology, *Sovetskaya etnografia*, No. 2, 148-156

294 Levinson-Lessing F. Y. (1943), *Problema genezisa magmaticheskikh porod i puti k ee razresheniyu (The Problem of the Genesis of Magma Rock and Ways of Resolving This Problem)*, Moscow.

295. Lindberg G. U. (1955), *The Quaternary Period in the Light of Biogeographical Data*, Moscow-Leningrad

295a Lindberg G. U. (1962-63), "O svyazi kontinentov Yevropy i Ameriki" ("Relationship Between the Continents of Europe and America"), *Soviet Fishing Research in the Northwest Atlantic*, 69-82, Moscow (1962); "Svyaz yevropeiskikh rek s rekami Severnoi Ameriki" "Relationship Between European and North American Rivers"), *Proceedings of the USSR Geographical Society*, 2, 107-114 (1963). "Sovremenniye ryby rasskazyvayut o proshlom Zemli" ("Modern Fish Tell of the Past"), *Nauka i zhizn*, No. 11, 46-49 (1963).

296. Lees G. M. (1954), "Geological Evidence on the Nature of the Ocean Floor", *Proceedings of the Royal Society of London*, Series A, 222, 400-402.

297. Litvin V. M. (1957), "Noviye danniye po relyefu dna Norvezhskogo i Grenlandskogo morei" ("New Data on the Floor Topography of the Norwegian and Greenland Seas"), *Scientific-Technical Bulletin. Polar Institute of Deep-Sea Fishing and Oceanography*, No. 2, 17-21.

298. Litvin V. M. (1959), "Podvodniye doliny na yuzhnom sklone Islandii" ("Submarine Valleys on the Southern Slope of Iceland"), *News of the USSR Academy of Sciences*, Geography Series, No. 6, 115-117.

299. Litvin V. M. (1959), "Relyef dna v raione Datskogo proliva" ("Floor Topography in the Region of the Denmark Strait"), *Scientific-Technical Bulletin. Polar Institute of Deep-Sea Fishing and Oceanography*, No. 4 (8), 59-63.

300. Litvin V. M. (1962), "Geomorfologiya dna Norvezhskogo morya" ("Floor Geomorphology of the Norwegian Sea"), *Proceedings of the Oceanographic Commission of the USSR Academy of Sciences*, 10, No. 3, 79-86.

301. Litvin V. M. (1962), "Osnovniye rezultaty issledovany PINRO po geomorfologii dna Norvezhskogo morya" ("Principal Results of the Investigations of the Floor Geomorphology of the Norwegian Sea by the Polar Institute of Deep-Sea Fishing and Oceanography"), *Scientific-Technical Bulletin. Research and Design Institute of Deep-Sea Fishing and Oceanography*, No. 2-3 (20-21), 48-51

302. Lichkov B. L. (1940), "Sovremennaya geologicheskaya epokha i ee kharakterniye cherty" ("The Modern Geological Epoch and Its Specific Features"), *Priroda*, No. 9, 16

303 Lichkov B. L. (1956), "O svyazi mezhdu izmeneniyami struktury Zemli i izmeneniyami klimata" ("The Relationship Between the Earth's Structural Changes and Climatic Changes"), *Readings in Memory of Lev Semyonovich Berg*, I-III, 1952-54, Moscow-Leningrad, 112-211

304. Lukashevich I. D. (1915), "O prichinakh lednikovoi epokhi" ("Reasons for the Ice Age"), *Priroda*, No. 7-8, 959-980.

305. Lyubimova E. A. (1958), "Termicheskaya istoriya i temperatura Zemli" ("Thermal History and the Temperature of the Earth"), *Bulletin of the Moscow Society of Naturalists*, Geology Division, 33 (4).

306. Lyubimova E. A. (1962), "Ob istochnikakh vnutrennego tepla Zemli" ("Sources of the Earth's Inner Heat"), *Voprosy kosmogonii*, 8, 97-108.

307. Lyustikh E. N (1948), "Gravimetrichesky metod izucheniya prichin kolebatelnykh dvizheny zemnoi kory i nekotoriye rezultaty ego primeneniya" ("Gravimetrical Method of Studying the Reasons of the Oscillatory Movements of the Earth's Crust and Some Results of Applying This Method"), *News of the USSR Academy of Sciences*, Geology Series, No. 6

308. Lyustikh E. N. (1957), "Izostazia i izostaticheskiye gipotezy" ("Isostasy and Isostatic Hypotheses"), *Proceedings of the Institute of Geophysics of the USSR Academy of Sciences*, No. 35 (165).

309. Lyustikh E. N. (1959), "O gipotezakh talassogeneza i glybakh zemnoi kory" ("Hypotheses on Talassogenesis and Blocks of the Earth's Crust"), *News of the USSR Academy of Sciences*, Geophysics Series, No 11, 1542-1549

310 Lyustikh E. N, Saltykovsky A. Y. (1961), "O nekotorykh gipotezakh proiskhozhdeniya granitnogo sloya Zemli" ("Some Hypotheses on the Origin of the Earth's Granite Stratum"), *Geokhimiya*, No 4, 371-373

311. Magidovich I. P. (1949), *Ocherki po istorii geograficheskikh otkryty (Essays on the History of Geographical Discoveries)*, Issue 1, Moscow

312. Magnitsky V A. (1958), "K voprosu o proiskhozhdenii i putyakh razvitiya kontinentov i okeanov" ("Origin and Development of Continents and Oceans"), *Voprosy kosmogonii*, 6

313. Magnitsky V. A. (1961), *Vnutrenneye stroyeniye Zemli (Internal Composition of the Earth)*, Moscow.

314. Mazarovich A I. (1952), *Osnovy regionalnoi geologii materikov (Fundamentals of the Regional Geology of Continents)*, Part 2, Moscow

315 Mackay E (1948), *Early Indus Civilisation*, London; Russian translation (1951), Moscow.

316. Maksimov I. V. (1961), "Vekovoi tsikl solnechnoi deyatelnosti i Severo-Atlanticheskoye techeniye" ("Century Cycle of Solar Activity and the North Atlantic Current"), *Okeanologiya*, 1, 206-212.

317 Maksimova S. V. (1958), "Gipoteza peremeshcheniya materikov i zoogeografiya" ("Hypothesis of the Movement of Continents and Zoogeography"), *Priroda*, No 5, 21-30

318 K. M(arkov) (1946), "Obsuzhdeniye v amerikanskoi pechati problemy gorizontalnogo dvizheniya (drifta) materikov" ("Discussion in the American Press of the Problem of the Drift of Continents"), *Voprosy geografii*, 1, 195-199.

319. Markov K. K. (1943), *Osnovniye problemy geomorfologii (Fundamental Problems of Geomorphology)*, Moscow

320. Markov K. K. (1951), *Paleogeografiya (Paleogeography)*. Moscow, 1960

321. Markov K. K. (1953), "Noveishy geologichesky period—antropogen" ("The Latest Geological Period—Anthropogen"), *Priroda*, No. 3, 48-62

322 Martynov D. N. (1955), *Mezhzvezdnaya materiya (Interstellar Matter)*, Moscow

323. Machatschek F. (1955), *Das Relief der Erde*, 2nd ed , Berlin Russian translation (1961), Moscow.

324. Melnikov O. A. (1957), "Mezhzvezdnaya sreda" ("The Interstellar Environment"), *Priroda*, No 10, 11-22

325 Menzbir M. (1923), *Taina Veligoko okeana (Riddle of the Pacific Ocean)*, Moscow

326. Murray W. (1920, *The Ocean*. Russian translation (1923), Kiev

327 Meshcheryakov Y. A. (1955), "Sovremenniye tektonicheskiye dvizheniya Britanskikh ostrovov" ("Modern Tectonic Changes on the British Isles"), *Priroda*, No 2, 89.

328. Meshcheryakov Y. A. (1958), "Sovremenniye dvizheniya zemnoi kory" ("Modern Changes in the Earth's Crust"), *Priroda*, No 9, 15-24

329. Milankowitsch M (1930), *Mathematische und astronomische Theorie der Klimatschwankungen*, Berlin Russian translation (1939), Moscow.

330 Mishulin A. V. (1952), *Antichnaya Ispania do ustanovleniya rimskoi provintsialnoi sistemy (Antique Spain Prior to the Establishment of the Roman Provincial System)*, Moscow

331. Miroshnikov L. D (1953), "Ostatki drevesnoi lesnoi rastitelnosti na Taimyrskom poluostrove" ("Remains of Arboreal Vegetation on the Taimyr Peninsula"), *Priroda*, No. 5, 21-30.

332. Mikhalovich (1955), "The Geosyncline of the Pacific Ocean", *Geology on the Balkan Peninsula*, 23, 243-247. In the Bulgarian language.

333 de Morgan ((1921), *L'humanité prehistorique*, Paris. Russian translation (1926), Moscow-Leningrad

334 Morozov N. A. (1909), *V poiskakh filosofskogo kamnya (In Search of the Philosopher's Stone)*, Moscow

335 Moskvitin A I. (1959), "Sovremenniye predstavleniya o stratigraficheskom

delenii i dlitelnosti pleistotsena" ("Modern Notions of the Stratigraphic Division and Duration of the Pleistocene"), *Bulletin of the USSR Academy of Sciences, Commission for the Study of the Quaternary Period*, 23, 3-16.

336. Muratov M. V. (1957), "Problemy proiskhozhdeniya okeanicheskikh vpadin" ("Origin of Ocean Basins"), *Bulletin of the Moscow Society of Naturalists*, Geology Series, 32, No. 5, 55-70.

337. Mushketov D. I. (1935), *Regionalnaya geotektonika (Regional Geotectonics)*, Moscow.

338. Nalivkin D. V. (1958), "Geologicheskiye katastrofy" ("Geological Catastrophes"), *Priroda*, No. 6, 27-32.

339. Nalivkin D. V. (1960), "Yarkaya stranitsa geologicheskoi istorii Azii" ("A Bright Page in the Geological History of Asia"), *Priroda*, No. 8, 35-42.

340. Nevessky E. N. (1960), "O ritmichnosti morskikh transgressy" ("Rhythmic Nature of Sea Transgressions"), *Okeanologiya*, 1, 63-77.

341. Neiman B. N. (1962), *Rasshiryayushchayasya Zemlya (The Expanding Earth)*, Moscow.

342. Neprochnov Y. P. (1959), "Glubinnoye stroyeniye zemnoi kory pod Chernym morem k yugo-zapadu ot Kryma, po seismicheskim dannym" ("Depth Composition of the Earth's Crust Beneath the Black Sea Southwest of the Crimea According to Seismic Data"), *Reports of the USSR Academy of Sciences*, 125, 1119-1122.

343. Nesis K. N. (1961), "Sushchestvuyut li v Belom more tikhookeanskiye littorinoviye relikty?" ("Are There Pacific Littoral Relics in the White Sea?"), *Okeanologiya*, 1, 498-503.

344. Nesis K. N. (1961), "Puti i vremya formirovaniya razorvannogo areala u amfiborealnykh vidov morskikh donnykh zhivotnykh" ("The Ways and Time of the Formation of the Ruptured Areal of Amphiboreal Species of Sea Bottom Fauna"), *Okeanologiya*, 1, 893-903.

345. Nesis K. N. (1962), "Korally i morskiye perya—indikatory gidrologicheskogo rezhima" ("Corals and Pinnae as Indicators of the Hydrological Regime"), *Okeanologiya*, 2, 705-714.

346. Nikiforovsky V. A. (1962), *Ekspeditsiya na "Sedove" v Atlantichesky okean (The "Sedov" Expedition in the Atlantic Ocean)*, Moscow.

348. Nikolayev N. I. (1955), "Razvitiye struktury zemnoi kory i ee relyef, po dannym neotektoniki" ("Development of the Composition and Topography of the Earth's Crust According to Neotectonic Data"), *Sovetskaya geologiya*.

349. Obruchev V. A. (1947), *Osnovy geologii (Fundamentals of Geology)*, Moscow.

350. Obruchev V. A (1948), "Osnovniye cherty kinetiki i plastiki neotektoniki" ("Basic Features of the Kinetics and Plasticity of Neotectonics"), *News of the USSR Academy of Sciences*, Geology Series, No. 5.

351. Obruchev S. V. (1951), "Khronologia lednikovykh epokh, po probam morskikh gruntov" ("Chronology of the Glacial Epochs According to Marine Soil Cores"), *Priroda*, No. 12, 40-41.

352. Oliver J. E., Ewing J. I., Press F. (1955), "Crustal Structure and Surface-Wave Dispersion", Part IV, "Atlantic and Pacific Ocean Basins", *Bulletin of the Geological Society of America*, 66, 912-1956. Russian translation (1959) in *Structure of the Earth's Crust According to Seismic Data*, Moscow, 306-347.

353. Orlov P. (1935), "Bolsherogy olen (Megaceros euriceros) v istoricheskoye vremya" ("The Magaceros Euriceros in Historical Times"), *Priroda*, No. 7, 80.

354. Officer C. E., Ewing J. I, Edwards R. S, Johnson H. R. (1957), "Geophysical Investigations in the Eastern Caribbean: Venezuelan Basin, Antilles Island Arc and Puerto Rico Trench", *Bulletin of the Geological Society of America*, 66, No. 3. Russian translation (1960) in *Problems of Modern Tectonics Abroad*, Moscow, 129-161.

355. Panov D. G. (1941), "K chetvertichnoi istorii yugo-zapadnoi Islandii" ("Quaternary History of Southwest Iceland"), *News of the USSR Geographical Society*, 73, 484

356. Panov D. G. (1949), "O proiskhozhdenii i istorii razvitiya okeanov" ("Origin and History of Oceans"), *Voprosy geografii*, 12, 188.

357. Panov D. G. (1949), "Obzor osnovnoi literatury po voprosu proiskhozhdeniya i razvitiya okeanicheskikh vpadin" ("Review of Basic Literature on the Origin and Development of Ocean Basins"), *Voprosy geografii*, 1, 221.
358. Panov D. G. (1950), "Problema proiskhozdeniya materikov i okeanov v svete novykh issledovany" ("The Origin of Continents and Oceans in the Light of New Studies"), *Priroda*, No. 3, 10-24.
359. Panov D. G. (1955), "O tektonicheskikh usloviyakh tsentralnoi chasti Arktiki" ("Tectonic Conditions of the Central Arctic"), *Reports of the USSR Academy of Sciences*, 105, 339-342.
360. Panov D. G (1955), "Struktura i neotektonicheskoye razvitiye dna okeanov" ("Structure and Neotectonic Development of the Ocean Floor"), *Scientific Notes of the Rostov-on-Don State University*, 55; *Reports of the Department of Geology and Geography*, Issue 10.
361. Panov D G. (1958), "Geneticheskiye tipy ostrovov" ("Genetic Types of Islands"), *Scientific Reports of the Higher School. Geological-Geographical Sciences*, Issue 1, 34-41.
362. Panov D. G. (1959), "Geneticheskiye tipy podvodnykh dolin i podvodnykh kanyonov" ("Genetic Types of Abyssal Valleys and Canyons"), *News of the USSR Geographical Society*, 91, 457-464.
363. Panov D. G. (1959), "O drevnosti Tikhogo okeana" ("The Antiquity of the Pacific Ocean"), *Scientific Reports of the Higher School. Geological-Geographical Sciences*, Issue 2, 3-10.
364. Panov D. G. (1961), *Proiskhozhdeniye materikov i okeanov (Origin of Continents and Oceans)*, Moscow.
364a. Panov D. G. (1963), *Morfologiya dna Mirovogo okeana (Floor Morphology of the World Ocean)*, Moscow.
365. Pendlebury J. D. S. (1950), *Archaeology of Crete*, Moscow, translation.
366. Plass G. N. (1960), "Uglekislota i klimat" ("Carbon Dioxide and Climate"), *Priroda*, No. 12, 40-46.
367. (Pseudo-)Plutarch (1894), "Dialogue About the Person Visible in the Moon", *Philological Review*, 16, Books 1-2, translated by G. A. Ivanov.
368. Poborchaya L. V. (1962), "Mutyeviye (suspenzionniye) potoki" ["Turbidity (Suspension) Currents"], *Okeanologiya*, 2, 735-740.
369. Pokrovsky Y. M. (1936), *Ocherki po istorii metallurgii (Essays on the History of Metallurgy)*, Moscow-Leningrad.
370. Poldevaart A. (1955), "Chemistry of the Earth's Crust", *Crust of the Earth*, Baltimore. Russian translation (1957) in *The Earth's Crust*, Moscow, 130-157.
371. Polikarpov G. G. (1954), "Nakopleniye radioizotopov tseria presnovodnymi mollyuskami" ("Accumulation of Cerium Radioisotopes by Fresh-Water Mollusks"), *Priroda*, No. 5, 86-87.
372. Pushcharovsky Y. M. (1960, "Nekotoriye obshchiye problemy tektoniki Arktiki" ("Some General Problems of Arctic Tectonics"), *News of the USSR Academy of Sciences*, Geology Series, No. 9, 15-28.
373. Ravdonikas V. I. (1947), *Istoriya pervobytnogo obshchestva (History of Primitive Society)*, Part 2, Moscow.
374. Reder D. G. (1948), "Iz istorii odnogo drevneyegipetskogo goroda v svete poslednikh raskopok" ("History of an Ancient Egyptian Town in the Light of Latest Excavations"), *Bulletin of Ancient History*, No. 2, 141.
374a. Reder D. G. (1965), *Mify i legendy drevnego dvurechya (Myths and Legends of Ancient Mesopotamia)*, Moscow.
375. Rezanov I. A. (1960), "K voprosu o geologicheskoi interpretatsii dannykh glubinnogo seismicheskogo zondirovaniya" ("Geological Interpretation of Deep-Sea Seismic Soundings"), *Sovetskaya geologiya*, No. 6, 65-77.
376. Rezanov I. A. (1962), "V glub Zemli. Sostav i proiskhozhdeniye bazaltovogo sloya zemnoi kory" ("In the Depths of the Earth. Composition and Origin of the Basalt Stratum of the Earth's Crust"), *Priroda*, No. 6, 84-91.
377. Rainey F. (1957), "Problemy amerikanskoi arkheologii" ("Problems of American Archaeology"), *Sovetskaya etnografia*, No. 6, 31-37.
378. Raitt R. W., Fisher R. I., Mason R. G. (1955), "Tonga Trench", *Geolog-*

ical Society of America, Special Paper 62, 237-254 Russian translation (1957), in *The Earth's Crust*, Moscow, 251-270.

379 Raıtt R W (1956), "Seismic-Refraction Studies of the Pacific Ocean Basin Part I. Crustal Thickness of the Central Equatorial Pacific", *Bulletın of the Geological Society of America*, 67, 1623-1939. Russian translation (1959), in *Structure of the Earth's Crust According to Seismic Data*, Moscow, 284-305.

380. Reshetov Y. G. (1962), "Antropologicheskiye nakhodki v Azii i Afrike" ("Anthropological Finds in Asia and Africa"), *Priroda*, No. 6, 111-112.

381. Rubakin N. A (1919), *Podzemny ogon (Subterranean Fire)*.

382 Savarensky E. F, Solovyova O. N, Lazareva A. P (1960). "Dispersia voln Releya i stroyeniye zemnoi kory na severe Yevrazii i v Atlanticheskom okeane" ("Rayleigh-Wave Dispersion and the Structure of the Earth's Crust in the North of Eurasia and in the Atlantic Ocean"), *Bulletin of the Seismic Council of the USSR Academy of Sciences*, No. 10, 168-175.

383. Saidova H. M (1958), "Noviye danniye po ekologii foraminifer" ("New Data on the Ecology of Foraminifera"), *Priroda*, No. 10, 107-110

384. Saks V. N. (1947), "Klimaty proshlogo na severe SSSR" ("Past Climate in the North of the USSR"), *Priroda*, No 8, 9.

385. Saks V. N. (1948), "Zagadka podvodnykh dolin", ("The Riddle of Submarine Valleys"), *Priroda*, No. 9, 32-40

386 Saks V. N., Belov V. A., Lapina N N. (1955), "Sovremenniye predstavleniya o geologii tsentralnoi Arktiki" ("Modern Notıons of Central Arctic Geology"), *Priroda*, No. 7, 13

387. Seleshnıkov S. I. (1962), *Istoriya kalendarya i ego predstoyashchaya reforma (History of the Calendar and Its Impending Reform)*, Leningrad.

388. Serebryany L. R. (1960), "K razrabotke absolutnoi khronologicheskoi shkaly verkhnego pleistotsena i golotsena s pomoshchyu radiougolnogo metoda" ("Elaboration of an Absolute Chronological Scale for the Upper Pleistocene and Holocene by Radiocarbon Dating"), *Bulletin of the Commission for the Study of the Quaternary Period, USSR Academy of Sciences*, 24, 8-21.

389. Serebryany L. R. (1961), "K paleogeografii golotsena v raione Baltiki (v svete dannykh radiougolnogo metoda)" ["Paleogeography of the Holocene in the Baltic (in the Light of Radiocarbon Dating)"], *Problems of the Holocene*, Vilnius, 177-199

390 Smyslov A. A (1960), "Znacheniye dannykh o radioaktivnosti i teploprovodnosti gornykh porod pri metallogenicheskikh issledovaniyakh" ("Importance of Data on the Radioactivity and Thermal Conductivity of Rock to Metallogenic Investigations"), *News of the USSR Academy of Sciences*, Geology Series, No. 7, 32-45.

391. Stepanov V. N (1961), "Osnovniye razmery Mırovogo okeana i glavneishikh ego chastei" ("Prıncipal Dimensions of the World Ocean and of Its Major Regions"), *Okeanologiya*, 1, 213-219.

392. Strakhov N. M. (1930), "Posledniye stranitsy geologicheskoi istorii Chernogo morya" ("Latest Pages of the Geological History of the Black Sea"), *Pıiroda*, No. 11-12, 1090.

393. Strakhov N. M. (1948), *Osnovy istoricheskoi geologii, (Fundamentals of Historical Geology)*, Part 2, Moscow.

393a. Strakhov N. M. (1962), "Etapy razvitiya vneshnikh geosfer i osadochnogo porodoobrazovania v istorii Zemli" ("Stages of the Development of External Geospheres and Sediment-Formation in the History of the Earth"), *News of the USSR Academy of Sciences*, Geology Series, No. 12, 3-22.

394. Struve V. V. (1937), "Khronologia Manefona ı periody Sotisa" ("Chronology of Manetho and the Periods of Sothis"), *Ancillary Historical Discıplines*, Moscow-Leningrad, 19-66.

395. Struve V. V. (1952), "Khronologiya I v. do n.e. v trude Gerodota" ("Chronology of the 1st century B C. by Herodotus"), *Bulletin of Ancient History*, No. 12.

396. Sushkin P. P. (1928), "Vysokogorniye oblasti zemnogo shara i vopros o rodine pervobytnogo cheloveka" ("Mountainous Regions of the Earth and the Homeland of Primitive Man"), *Priroda*, No. 3, 249.

397. Tarasov B. V. (1961), "Novoye v relyefe dna Severnogo Ledovitogo okeana" ("New Data on Arctic Floor Topography"), *Problems of the Arctic and Antarctic*, Issue 8, 89-90

398. Tarasov N. I. (1939), "Sargassovo more" ("The Sargasso Sea"), *Priroda*, No. 5, 45.

399. Tikhomirov V. V. (1958), "K voprosu o razvitii zemnoi kory i prirode granita" ("The Development of the Earth's Crust and the Nature of Granite"), *News of the USSR Academy of Sciences*, Geology Series, No 8, 8-15.

400. Tochilin M. S. (1960), "Evolyutsia atmosfery Zemli" ("Evolution of the Earth's Atmosphere"), *Priroda*, No. 1, 26-32.

400a. Trapeznikov Y. A. (1963) "Referativny obzor i kritika sovremennykh gipotez rasshiryayushcheisya Zemli" ("Summary Review and Criticism of Modern Theories of the Expansion of the Earth"), *Bulletin of the Moscow Society of Naturalists*, Geology Division, 38, No 5, 65-74

401. Treshnikov A. F, Tolstikov E I (1956), *Dreifuyushchiye stantsii v tsentralnoi Arktike*. *"Severny polyus-3" i "Severny polyus-4" (Drifting Stations in the Central Arctic—North Pole-3 and North Pole-4)*, Moscow.

402. Treshnikov A. F. (1960), "Arktika raskryvayet svoi tainy" ("The Arctic Bares Its Mysteries"), *Priroda*, No. 2, 25-32

403. Turayev B. A. (1898), *Bog Tot (The God Thoth)*, Moscow.

404. Udintsev G B (1959), "Issledovaniya relyefa dna morei i okeanov" ("Investigations of Sea and Ocean Floot Topograyh"). In *Results of Science. Achievements of Oceanology I. Successes in the Study of Ocean Depths*, Moscow, 27-90.

405. Udintsev G. B. (1962), "Noviye danniye o relyefe glubokovodnykh zhelobov zapadnoi chasti Tikhogo okeana" ("New Data on the Topography of the Abyssal Trenches in the West Pacific"), *Marine Geology and Coast Dynamics*, Moscow, 45-65.

406. Uklonsky A. S. (1940), *Mineralogiya (Mineralogy)*, Moscow-Leningrad.

407. Umbgrove J. H. F. (1947), "The Pulse of the Earth", Chapter 7, *The Island Arcs*, New York, 144-216. Russian translation (1952) in *Island Arcs*, Moscow, 5-96.

408. Waters A. C. (1955), *Volcanic Rocks and the Tectonic Cycle*, Geological Society of America, Special Paper 62, 703-722. Russian translation (1957), in *The Earth's Crust*, Moscow

409. Fyodorov A. F. (1959), "Yestestvennaya radioaktivnost morskikh organizmov" ("Natural Radioactivity of Marine Organisms"), *Priroda*, No. 4, 86-89.

410. Fedynsky V. V. (1960), "Geofizicheskiye danniye o nekotorykh chertakh stroyeniya i razvitiya zemnoi kory" ("Geophysical Data on Some Features of the Structure and Development of the Earth's Crust"), *International Geological Congress, 21st Session. Papers of Soviet Geologists*; Problem 2, Section II, Moscow.

411. Filatova Z. A. (1962), "O paleogeografii tropicheskoi chasti Tikhogo okeana (po dokladu G. V. Menarda i E. L. Gamiltona)" ["Paleogeography of the Tropical Region of the Pacific (According to a Paper by V. G. Menard and E. L. Hamilton)"], *Okeanologiya*, 2, 489-492.

412. Flint R. F. (1963), "Lednikovy pokrov (issledovaniya amerikanskikh geologov" ["The Icecap (Studies by American Geologists)"] *Priroda*, No. 1, 34-38.

413. de Vries H. (1959), "Measurement and Use of the Natural Radiocarbon". *Researches in Geochemistry*, ed. by P. H. Abelson, New York Russian translation (1961), in *Geochemical Researches*, Moscow, 217-243.

414 Frolova N. V. (1951), "Ob usloviyakh osadkonakopleniya v arkheiskuyu eru" ("Sedimentation in the Archean Era"), *Proceedings of Irkutsk State University*, Geology Series, 5, Issue 2.

415. Khain V. E. (1961), *Proiskhozhdeniye materikov i okeanov (Origin of Continents and Oceans)*, Moscow.

416. Heyerdahl T. (1949), *Kon-Tiki*, Stockholm. Russian translation (1956), Moscow.

417. Heezen B C., Tharp M., Ewing M. (1959), *Floors of the Oceans I. North Atlantic. Part I. Physiographic Diagram of the North Atlantic. Part 2. Text to Accompany the Physiographic Diagram*, "Geological Society of America", Special Paper 65, Baltimore Russian translation (1962), Moscow.

418. Heezen B C (1960), "Rift Valley on the Ocean Bottom", *Scientific America*, 207, No. 10, 98-110. Russian translation (1963), *Okeanologiya* 3, No. 1, 60-70.
419. Hennig R. (1944-56), *Terrae Incognitae*, 2-te Aufl, Leiden. Russian translation (1961-63) in 4 vols., Moscow-Leningrad.
420. Hess H. H. (1948), "Major Structural Features of the Western North Pacific", *Bulletin of the Geological Society of America*, 59, 417-445. Russian translation (1952), in *Island Arcs*, Moscow, 135-170.
421. Hess H. H. (1955), "Serpentines, Orogeny and Epirogeny", *Crust of the Earth*, 391-408 Russian translation (1957) in *The Earth's Crust*, Moscow, 403-422.
422. Hess H. H. (1954), "Geological Hypotheses and the Earth's Crust Under the Ocean", *Proceedings of the Royal Society of London*, Series A, 222, 348. Russian translation (1959) in *Structure of the Earth's Crust According to Seismic Data*, Moscow, 17-27.
423. Khizanashvili G D. (1960), "Dinamika zemnoi osi vrashcheniya i urovnei okeana" ("Dynamics of the Earth's Axis of Rotation and the Ocean Level"), Tbilisi.
424. Khizanashvili G. D (1962), "O pereseleniyakh v chetvertichnoye vremya razlichnykh vidov zhivotnykh v svete dinamiki zemnoi osi vrashcheniya" ("Migration of Different Species of Animals in the Quaternary Period in the Light of the Dynamics of the Earth's Axis of Rotation"), *Okeanologiya*, 2, 735-740.
425. Hill M. N. (1952), "Seismic Shooting in the Area of the Eastern Atlantic", *Philosophical Transactions of the Royal Society of London*, Series A, 244, 561-596 Russian translation (1959) in *Structure of the Earth's Crust According to Seismic Data*, Moscow, 212-258.
426 Hill M. N., Laughton A S. (1954), "Seismic Observations in the Eastern Atlantic", *Proceedings of the Royal Society*, London, Series A, 222, 348-356 Russian translation (1959), in *Structure of the Earth's Crust According to Seismic Data*, Moscow, 259-270
427. Khramov A. N. (1958), *Paleomagnitnaya korrelyatsiya osadochnykh tolshch (Paleomagnetic Correlation of Sediments)*, Leningrad.
428. Child V. G (1947), *The Dawn of European Civilisation*, London Russian translation (1952), Moscow
429. Cherdyntsev V. V. (1961), "Opredeleniye absolutnogo vozrasta chetvertichnykh okamenelykh kostei po otnosheniyu izotopov tyazhelykh elementov" ("Determination of the Absolute Age of Quaternary Fossil Bones in Relation to Heavy Element Isotopes") in *Problems of Holocene Geology*, Moscow, 85-95
430. Shatsky N. S (1946), "Gipoteza Vegenera i geosinklinali" ("The Wegener Hypothesis and Geosynclines"), *News of the USSR Academy of Sciences*, Geology Series, No. 4.
431. Schwarzbach M. (1950) *Das Klima der Vorzeit*, 1-te Aufl, Stuttgart. Russian translation (1955), Moscow.
432. Sheinmann Y. M (1955), "Zametki k klassifikatsii struktury materikov" ("Notes on the Classification of the Structure of Continents"), *News of the USSR Academy of Sciences*, Geology Series, No. 3, 19-35.
433. Sheinmann Y. M. (1958), "Mesto Atlanticheskogo i Indiiskogo okeanov v formirovanii struktury Zemli" ("Place of the Atlantic and Indian Oceans in the Formation of the Earth's Structure"), *Reports of the USSR Academy of Sciences*, 119, 779-781.
433a. Sheinmann Y. M. (1963), "'Rasshiryayushchayasya Zemlya' i pospeshnaya populyarizatsiya" ("The 'Expanding Earth' and Hasty Popularisation"), *Priroda*, No. 6, 77-79
434 Shapley H, editor (1953), *Climatic Change, Evidence, Causes and Effects. A Symposium*, Cambridge. Russian translation (1958) in *Climatic Changes*, Moscow
435 Shifman I. S (1960), "Obyedineniye finikiiskikh koloniy v zapadnom Sredizemnomorye i vozniknoveniye karfagenskoi derzhavy" ("Unification of the Phoenician Colonies in the Western Mediterranean and the Emergence of Carthage"), *Bulletin of Ancient History*, No. 2, 3-46
436. Shmidt P. Y. (1947), *Migratsiya ryb (The Migration of Fish)*, Moscow.
438. Shokalsky Y. M. (1933), *Fizicheskaya okeanografiya (Physical Oceanography)*, Leningrad.

439. Shternfeld A. Y. (1937), *Uvedeniye v kosmonavtiku, (Introduction to Cosmonautics)*, Moscow.
440 Stille H (1955), "Recent Deformations of the Earth's Crust in the Light of Those of Earlier Epochs", *Crust of the Earth*, Baltimore, 171-192 Russian translation (1957) in *The Earth's Crust*, Moscow, 187-208
441. Shuleikin V V. (1949), *Ocherki po istorii morya (Essays on the History of the Sea)*, Moscow
442. Shcherbakov D A (1962), *Puchiny okeana (Depths of the Ocean)*, Moscow.
443. *The Gilgamesh Epic (1961)*, translation with commentaries by I M Dyakonov, Moscow-Leningrad
444 Ericson D B, Ewing M, Heezen B C, Wollin G. (1955), "Sediment Deposition in Deep Atlantic", *Crust of the Earth*, Baltimore, 205-220 Russian translation (1957) in *The Earth's Crust*, Moscow, 222-236.
445 Ewing J. I., Officer C. B., Edwards R S, Johnson H R. (1957), "Geophysical Investigations in the Eastern Caribbean: Trinidad Shelf, Tobago Trough, Barbados Ridge, Atlantic Ocean", *Bulletin of the Geological Society of America*. 69, No. 7. Russian translation (1960) in *Problems of Modern Tectonics Abroad*, Moscow, 162-189.
446. Yakovlev S V. (1959), "Voprosy chetvertichnoi geologii na XX sessii Mezhdunarodnogo geologicheskogo kongressa v Meksike 3-11 sentyabrya 1956" ("Problems of Quaternary Geology at the 20th Session of the International Geological Congress in Mexico, September 3-11, 1956"), *Bulletin of the USSR Academy of Sciences, Commission for the Study of the Quaternary Period*, 23, 116-120
447. "Zagadka podvodnykh skal" ("The Riddle of Submarine Cliffs") (1960), *Priroda*, No. 12, 113
448. *XI Generalnaya assambleya Mezhdunarodnogo geodezicheskogo i geofizicheskogo soyuza, 1957, XI General Assembly of the International Geodesical and Geophysical Union, 1957* (1959), Collection of Papers, Moscow
449. Agostinho J. (1936), "The Volcanoes of the Azores Islands", *Bulletin Volcanologique*, 8 (2), 123-138.
450. De Almeido F F. M. (1955), *Geology and Petrology of the Fernando de Noronha Archipelago*, Monograph, 13, 1-181
451. Arldt T. (1919-20), *Handbuch der Paleogeographie*, Leipzig.
452. Anders E, Limber D. N (1959), "Origin of the Worzel Deep-Sea Ash", *Nature*, Vol 184, No 4679, pp 44-45.
453. Arrhenius G (1961), "Geological Record on the Ocean Floor"; *Oceanography*, edited by Mary Sears, publication No. 67 of the American Association for the Advancement of Sciences, pp. 129-150
454. Axelrod D I (1962), "Post-Pliocene Uplift of the Sierra Nevada", California, *Bulletin of the Geological Society of America*, Vol. 73, No 2, pp 183-197.
455. Bac H. (1959), "A propos des 'Tables d'Emeraud'", *Atlantis*, (Paris), No 195, 79-82
456 Barendsen G W., Deevey E. S, Gralenski L. J. (1957), "Yale Natural Radiocarbon Measurements III", *Science*, Vol. 126, No. 3279, pp 908-919
457. Bath M. (1960), "Crustal Structure of Iceland", *Journal of Geophysical Research*, Vol 65, No 6, pp 1793-1807
458 Beck A E. (1961), "Energy Requirements of an Expanding Earth", *Journal of Geophysical Research*, Vol. 66, No 5, pp 1485-1490
459. Bellamy H. S, Allan P. (1956), *The Calendar of Tiahuanaco*, London
460 Bellamy H S, Allan P (1959), *The Great Idol of Tiahuanaco*, London
461. Belot B (1918), *Origine des formes de la Terre et des plantes*, Paris
462. Berthelot S (1879), *Antiquites canariennes*, Paris
463. Berthois L, Guilcher A. (1961), "Etudé de sediments de roches draguès sur le banc Porcupine et à ses abords, *Rev trav. Inst. peches maritimes*, 25, No. 3, 355-385.
464. Berthois L. (1962), "Morphologie et geologie sous-marine (Bathymetrie du section atlantique du banc Porcupine au Cap Finisterre), *Rev. trav. Inst. peches maritimes*, 26, No 2, 219-243
465. Birch F. (1960-61), "The Velocity of Compressional Waves in Rocks to

10 Kilobars", *Journal of Geophysical Research*, Vol. 65, No. 4, 1083-1102 (Part 1); Vol. 66, No. 7, 2199-2224 (Part 2).

465a. Black R. F., Langhein W.S. (1964), *Anangula: A Geologic Interpretation of the Oldest Archaeologic Sites in the Aleutians, Science* 143, 1321-1322.

466. Bonfanti N. (1957), "Una nuova ipotesi nella storia della terra", *L'Universo*, No. 4, 727-738.

467. Bontier P., Le Verrier J. (1872), *The Cananian or Book of the Conquest and Conversion of the Canarians in the Year 1402 by Messire Jean de Betencourt*, London (Hacluyt Society).

468. Bourdier F. (1958), "Rythme des variations climatiques du Quaternaire et nouvelle courbe de Milankowitsch", *Bull. Soc. prehistorique franc.*, 55, 552-553.

469. Bramlette M. N., Bradley W. H. (1942), "Geology and Biology of North Atlantic Deep-Sea Cores Between Newfoundland and Ireland", *US Geological Survey*, Prof. Papers, No. 196a

470. Brasseur de Bourbourg Ch. (1861), *Popol Vuh. Le livre sacré et les mythes de l'antiquité americaine avec les livres heroiques et historiques des Quiches*, Paris.

471. Brennan L. A. (1959), *No Stone Unturned. An Almanac of North American Prehistory*, New York.

472. Bretz J. H. (1960), "Bermuda: A Partially Drowned, Late Nature, Pleistocene Karst", *Bulletin of the Geological Society of America*, Vol. 71, No. 12, 1729-1754.

473. Breusing A. (1889), *Die Losung des Trierenratsel. Die Irrfahrten des Odysseus*, Bremen.

474. Broecker W. S., Kulp J. L. (1954), "Carbon 14 Age Research", *Bulletin of the Geological Society of America*, Vol. 65, No. 12, 1234.

475. Broecker W. S., Kulp J. L. (1957), "Lamont Natural Radiocarbon Measurements IV, *Science*, Vol. 126, No. 3287, 1324.

476. Beuchley R. W. (1959), *Glacier-Caused Variations in Ocean Salinity as a Parameter in the Theory of Ice Age*, Preprints of the International Oceanographical Congress, 1959, Washington, 88-90.

477. Buffington E. C. (1961), "Experimental Turbidity Currents on the Sea Floor", *Bulletin of the American Association of Petrologists and Geologists*, 45, 1392-1400.

478. Bullard E. C. (1961), "Forces and Processes at Work in Ocean Basins", *Oceanography*, edited by Mary Sears (Publications of the American Association for the Advancement of Sciences), No. 7, 39-50.

479. Burri C. (1960), *Petrocheme der Capverden und Vergleich der Capverdischen Vulkanismus mit demijenigen des Rheinlandes*, Schweizarische mineral. und petrograph. Mitteilungen, 40, 115-161.

480. Butterlin J. (1956), "Nouvelles indications au systeme de la constitution geologiques des fonds de la mer des Antilles", *Comptes Rendus Soc. geolog. France*, No. 1, 13-14.

481. Butterlin J. (1956). *La constitution geologique et structure des Antilles*, Paris.

482. Cailleux A. (1959), "Sur les galets dragués à 4225 m de profonder entre les Açores et Breste", *CR Acad. Scien.*, Paris, 249, 1128-1129.

483. Cailleux A. (1959), "Bilans de sedimentation et de petrogenese", *Cahiers geologiques*, No. 53, 511-513.

484. Carder D. S. (1959), *Seismic Waves from Nuclear Explosions and the Structure Under the Western Pacific*, Preprints of the International Oceanographical Congress, 1959, Washington, 13-14

485. Carr D. R., Kulp J. K. (1953), "Age of a Mid-Atlantic Ridge Basalt Boulder", *Bulletin of the Geological Society of America*, Vol. 64, No. 2, 253-255.

486. Chevalier A. (1935), "Les isles du Cap Verde. Flore de l'Archipel", *Revue botanique*, 15, 733.

487. Cloos H. (1939), "Zur Tektonik der Azoren", *Abhandl. d. Preuss. Akademie d. Wissensch., mathem-physik. Klasse*, No. 5, 59-64.

487a. Colinvaux P. (1964), "Origin of Ice Ages; Pollen Evidence from Arctic Alaska", *Science*, 145, No. 3433, 707-708.

488. Cortesao J. (1937), "The Pre-Columbian Discovery of America", *Geographical Journal*, 26-42.
489. Cotton Ch. (1961), "Growing Mountains and Infantile Islands on the Western Pacific Rim", *Geographical Journal*, 127, No. 2, 209-211.
490. Cotton Ch. (1962), "Dating Recent Mountain Growths by Fossil Pollen", *Tuatara*, 10, No. 1, 5-12.
491. Cox A., Doell R. R. (1960), "Review of Paleomagnetism", *Bulletin of the Geological Society of America*, Vol. 71, No. 6, 645-768.
492. Dahl E. (1955), "Biographic and Geologic Indications of Uglaciated Areas in Scandinavia During the Glacial Ages", *Bulletin of the Geological Society of America*, Vol. 66, No. 12, Part I, 1499-1520.
493. Daly R. A. (1936), "Origin of Submarine 'Canyons'", *American Journal of Science*, Vol. XXXI, 5th series, No. 186, 401-420.
494. Dana J. D. (1864), *Textbook of Geology*, New York.
495. Danzel Th. W. (1937), *Handbuch der prakolumbischen Kulturen in Latinamerika*, Hamburg.
495a. Davies D., Francis T. I. G. (1964), "The Crustal Structure of the Seychelles Bank", *Deep-Sea Research*, 11, 921-927.
496. Defant A. (1939), "Die Altair-Kuppe", *Abhandl. d. Preuss. Akademie d. Wissensch., mathemat-physik. Klasse*, No. 5, 40-45.
496a. Delporte H. (1963), "Le passage du Mousterien au paleolitique superieur", *Bull. Soc. meridion, spéol. et prehist.*, 1956-59, 6-9, 40-52.
497. Demortier G. (1955), "Théorie relative à la formation des plissements alpins et à la génèse des continents et des océans actuelle", *Bulletin de l'Institut agronomique et des stations de recherches de Gembloux*, Vol. XXIII, No. 4, 378-429
498. Dietrich G. (1959), "Zur Topographie und Morphologie des Meeresbodens im nordlichen Nordatlantischen Ozean", *Deutsch. Hydrograph. Zeit.*, 12-n Ergänzungsheft B, No. 3, 26-34.
499. Dietz R. S., Menard H. W. (1951), "Hawaiian Swell, Deep and Arch. The Subsidence of the Hawaiian Islands", *Bulletin of the Geological Society of America*, 62, 1431.
500. Dietz R. S. (1959), *Point d'impact des asteroides comme origine des bassins oceaniques; une hypothese. Topographie et geologie des profondeurs oceaniques*, Paris, 265-275.
501. Dietz R. S., Shumwey G. (1961), "Arctic Basin Geomorphology", *Bulletin of the Geological Society of America*, Vol. 72, No. 9, 1319-1330.
502. Dietz R. S. (1961), "Ocean Basin Evolution by Sea Floor Spreading". *Abstracts of Symposium Papers of Fourth Pacific Science Congress*, Honolulu, 357.
503. Doberer K. K. (1953), *Zum Problem der vorgeschichtlichen Fels—Schienenstrange auf Malta*, Urania (DDR), 16, 396-397.
504. Doell R. R., Cox A. V. (1960), "Paleomagnetism, Polar Wandering and Continental Drift", *Geological Survey*, Profes. Paper, No. 400b, 426-427.
504a. Dreimanis A. (1962), "Postglacial Mastodon Remains at Tufferville, Ontario", *Geological Society of America*, Special Papers, No. 68, 167.
504b. Drake Ch. L., Campbell N. J., Sander G., Nabe J. E. A. (1963), "A Mid-Labrador Sea Ridge", *Nature*, 200, 1085-1086.
505. Du Rietz E. (1940), "Problems of Bipolar Plant Distribution", *Acta phytogeographica Suecica*, 13, 215-282.
506. Eardley A. J., Gvosdetsky V. (1959), "Pleistocene (Saltair) Core from Great Salt Lake", *Bulletin of the Geological Society of America*, Vol. 70, No. 12, 1594-1595.
507. Edgerton W. F., Wilson J. (1936), *Historical Records of Ramses III. The Texts in Medinet Habu*, Chicago.
508. Ehara Shingo (1958), "Geotectonic Movements in the Pacific, Under Way Since the Beginning of the Miocene", *Journal of the Geological Society of Japan*, 64, No. 748, 13-28.
509. Elmendorf C. H., Heezen B. C. (1957), "Oceanographic Information for the Engineering Submarine Cable Systems", *The Bell System Technical Journal*, Vol. XXXVI, No. 5, 1047-1093.

510. Emiliani C. (1956), "Note on Absolute Chronology of Human Evolution", *Science*, Vol. 123, No. 3204, 924.
511. Emiliani C. (1957), "Temperature and Age Analysis of Deep-Sea Cores", *Science*, Vol. 125, No. 3244, 383-387.
512. Emiliani C. (1961), "The Temperature Decrease of Surface Sea-Waters in High Latitudes and of Abyssal-Hadal Water in Open Oceanic Basins During the Past 75 Million Years", *Deep-Sea Research*, Vol. 8, No. 2, 144-147.
513. Emiliani C. (1961), "Cenozoic Climatic Changes as Indicated by the Stratigraphy and Chronology of Deep-Sea Cores of Globigerina Ooze Facies", *Annals of the New York Academy of Sciences*, 95, 521-536.
513a. Emiliani C. (1964), "Upper Cenozoic Stratigraphy and the Evolution of the Hominidae", *Geological Society of America*, Special Paper, 73, 295.
514. Ericson D. B., Ewing M., Heezen B. C. (1951), "Deep-Sea Sands and Submarine Canyons", *Bulletin of the Geological Society of America*, Vol. 62, No. 8, 961-966.
515. Ericson D. B., Ewing M., Heezen B. C. (1952), "Turbidity Currents and Sediments in the North Atlantic", *Bulletin of the Association of Petrologists and Geologists*, 36, 489-511.
516. Ericson D. B., Wollin G., Wollin J. (1955), "Coiling Direction of Globorotalia Truncatulinoides in Deep-Sea Cores", *Deep-Sea Research*, Vol. 2, No. 2, 152-158.
517. Ericson D. B., Ewing M., Wollin G., Heezen B. C. (1961), "Atlantic Deep-Sea Sediment Cores", *Bulletin of the Geological Society of America*, Vol. 72, No. 2, 193-285.
517a. Ericson D. B., Ewing M., Wollin G. (1964), "The Pleistocene Epoch in Deep-Sea Sediments", *Science*, 146, No. 3645, 723-732.
517b. Ericson D. B., Kulp J. L. (1961), "Potassium-Argon Dates on Basaltic Rocks", *New York Academy of Sciences Ann.*, 91, 321-323.
518. Ewing J. I., Ewing M. (1959), "Seismic-Refraction Measurements in the Atlantic Ocean Basin, in the Mediterranean Sea, on the Mid-Atlantic Ridge and in Norwegian Sea", *Bulletin of the Geological Society of America*, Vol. 70, No. 3, 291-318.
519. Ewing M. (1948), "Exploring the Mid-Atlantic Ridge", *The National Geographic Magazine*, Vol. XCIV, No. 3, 275.
520. Ewing M. (1949), "New Discoveries of the Mid-Atlantic Ridge", *The National Geographic Magazine*, Vol. XCIV, No. 5, 611-640.
520a. Ewing M. (1952), "The Atlantic Ocean Basin", *Bulletin of the American Museum of Natural History*, Vol. 99, 87.
521. Ewing M., Ericson B. C., Northrop J., Dorman J. (1953), "Exploration of the Northwest Atlantic Mid-Ocean Canyon", *Bulletin of the Geological Society of America*, Vol. 64, No. 7, 865-868.
522. Ewing M., Donn W. L. (1956-58), "A Theory of Ice Age I-II", *Science*, Vol. 127, No. 3307, 1159-1162; Donn W. L., Ewing M. (1966), "A Theory of Ice Age III", *Science*, 152, No. 3730, 1706-1712.
523. Ewing M., Heezen B. C. (1956), "Oceanographic Research Programme of the Lamont Geological Observatory", *Geographical Review*, Vol. XLVI, No. 4, 508-535.
524. Ewing M., Heezen B. C., Ericson D. (1959), "Significance of the Worzel Deep-Sea Ash", *Proceedings of the National Academy of Sciences*, USA, 45, 355.
525. Ewing M., Landesman M. (1961), "Shape and Structure of Ocean Basins", *Oceanography*, edited by Mary Sears (American Association for the Advancement of Science, Publication No. 67), 3-38.
525a. Ewing M. (1964), "Comments on the Theory of Glaciation", *Problems Paleoclimatologic*, London-New York-Sydney, 348-353, 360-363.
525b. Ewing M., Ewing J. I., Talwani M. (1964), "Sediment Distribution in the Oceans: the Mid-Atlantic Ridge", *Bulletin of the Geological Society of America*, 75, 17-35.
526. Fairbridge R. W. (1959), *Periodicity of Eustatic Oscillation*, Preprints of the International Oceanographical Congress, 1959, Washington, 97-99.
527. Fairbridge R. W. (1961), *The Melanesian Border Plateau: A Zone of*

Crustal Shearing in the Southwest Pacific, Publicat. Bureau Centr. Seism Internat, A, No 22, 137-149.

528 Field H M (1936), "Recent Development in the Geophysical Study of Ocean Basins", *American Geophysical Union Transactions*, 20-23.

529 Fisher J (1956), *Rockall*, London

529a Fonjaz V. H. (1963), "Resumé geologico das Ilhas dos Açores", *GEA Rev. geol*, 2, No. 7, 28-29.

530. Fuglister F. G. (1960), *Atlantic Ocean Atlas of Temperature and Salinity and Data from the International Geophysical Year of 1957-58*, Woodhole, Mass., USA.

531 Furon R (1949), "Sur des trilobites dragués à 4255 m de profondeur par le 'Talisman' " (1883), *CR l'Académie des Sciences*, Paris, Vol. 228, No. 19, 1509

532 De Geer E. H. (1955), "La deglaciation scandinave selon la chronologie Der Geer", *Bull. Soc. geolog. France*, (6), 50, 169-192

533. Gellert J. F. (1958), "Kurze Bemerkungen zur Klimazonierung der Erde und zur planetarischen Zirkulation der Atmosphäre in der jungerer erdgeschichtlichen Vorzeit, ausgehen vom Tertiär, Wiss", *Zeit. Padag. Hochsch. Potsdam, math-naturw. Reihe 1956-57*, No. 2, 145-151

533a Heezen B. C., Bunce E. T., Hersey J. B, Tharp M. (1964), "Chain and Romanche Fracture Zones", *Deep-Sea Research*, 11, 11-13.

533b Heezen B C, Gerard R. D, Tharp M. (1964), "The Vema Fracture Zone in the Equatorial Atlantic", *Journal of Geological Research*, 69, 733-739.

534 Gentil L. (1910), "Les mouvements tertiaires dans le Haut-Atlas Marocain", *CR l'Académie des Sciences*, Paris, Vol 150, No. 22, 1465.

535. Gerard R, Lanseth M. G, Ewing M (1962), "Thermal Gradient Measurements in the Water and Bottom Sediment of the Western Atlantic", *Journal of Geophysical Research*, Vol. 67, No. 2, 785-803.

536 Gorceix Ch. (1924), *L'Origine des grands reliefs terrestres*, Paris

537. Gravenor O. P., Bayrock L A. (1961), "Glacial Deposits of Alberta", *Soils Canada*, Toronto, 33-50.

538 Gregory J. W. (1929), "The Geological History of the Atlantic Ocean", *Quarterly Journal of the Geological Society*, 85, 68-122.

539. Gregory J. W. (1930), "The Geological History of the Pacific Ocean", *Nature*, Vol. 125, No 3159, 750-751.

540. Gross H (1957), *Die geologische Gliederung und Chronologie des Jungpleistizens in Mitteleuropa und angrenzen Gebieten Quarter* 9, 3-39.

541. Gross H. (1959), "Noch einmal: Riss oder Würm?" *Gross Hugo Nachtrag. Eiszeitalter und Gegenwart* 10, 65-76.

542. Guilcher A. (1962), "Chronique océanographique, Norois, Vol. 33, No 9, 65-69.

543 Hallier H. (1912), *Uber fruhere Landbrucken, Pflanzen und Volkeranderungen zwieschen Australasien und Amerika*, Leiden

544. Hamilton E. L. (1960), "Ocean Basin Ages and Amounts of Original Sediments", *Journal of Sedimentary Petrology*, Vol 30, No. 3, 370-379

545. Harrison E R. (1960), "Origin of the Pacific Basin: A Meteorite Impact Hypothesis", *Nature*, Vol. 188, No. 4756, 1064-1067.

546 Hough J. L. (1953), "Pleistocene Climatic Record in a Pacific Ocean Core Sample", *The Journal of Geology*, Vol. 61, No. 3, 252.

547. Hausen H. (1956), *Contribution to the Geology of Tenerife (Canary Islands)*, Comment. Phys. Mathem 18, No. 1, 270.

548. Hawkis L (1938), "The Age of the Rocks and the Topography of the Middle Northern Iceland (Tertiary and Quaternary)", *Geological Magazine*, 75, No. 889, 289-296.

549. Heezen B C, Ewing M., Ericson D. B., Bentley C.R. (1954), "Flat-Topped Atlantis, Cruiser and Great Meteor Seamounts", *Bulletin of the Geological Society of America*, Vol. 65, No. 12, 1261.

550. Heezen B C (1955), "Turbidity Currents from the Magdalena River, Colombia", *Bulletin of the Geological Society of America*, Vol. 66, No. 12, 1572

551 Heezen B. C (1959), *Geologie sous-marine et deplacement des continents. Topographie et geologie des profondeurs oceaniques*, Paris, 302-304.

552. Heezen B. C. (1960), "The Rift in the Ocean Floor", *Scientific American*, Vol 203, No. 4, 99-110.
553. Heezen B. C., Coughlin R., Beckman W. C. (1960), "Equatorial Atlantic Mid-Ocean Canyon", *Bulletin of the Geological Society of America*, Vol. 71, No. 12, 1886.
554. Hennig R. (1927), "Die Karthager auf den Azoren", *Petermanns Geographische Mitteilungen*, 73, 208.
555 Hennig R. (1934), *Die Geographie des homerischen Epos*, Leipzig.
556 Henseling R. (1937), "Das Alter der Maya-Astronomie", *Forschungen und Fortschritte*, 13, No. 26/27, 318-320.
557. Henseling R. (1949), "Das Alter der Maya-Astronomie und die Oktaeteris", *Forschungen und Fortschritte*, 25, No. 3/4, 25-27.
558. Hess H. H. (1959), *Nature of the Great Oceanic Ridges*, Preprints of the International Oceanographical Congress, Washington, 33-34.
559. Heyerdahl T. (1952), *American Indians in the Pacific*, Stockholm-London-Oslo.
560. Hill M. N. (1960), "A Median Valley of the Mid-Atlantic Ridge", *Deep-Sea Research*, Vol. 6, No. 3, 193-205.
561. Hills L. D. (1956), "The Island of Captain Robson", *Atlantis* (London), 9, 72-75.
562. Hoffman P. (1952), "The Syriadic Columns and the Great Pyramid", *Atlantis* (London), 4, 119-126
563. Holdate M. (1958), *Mountains in the Sea. The Story of the Gough Island Expedition*, London-New York.
564. Holtedahl H. (1956), "On the Norwegian Continental Terrace, Primarily Outside More-Romsdal: Its Geomorphology and Sediments", *Univer i Bergen Arbok 1955, Naturvid. rekke*, 14.
565. Hooton E. A (1925), *The Ancient Inhabitants of the Canary Islands*, Harvard.
565a. Hubert J F (1964), "Textural Evidence for Deposition of Many Western North Atlantic Deep-Sea Sands by Ocean-Bottom Currents Rather Than Turbidity Currents", *Journal of Geology*, 72, 757-785
566 Ibarra Grasso D (1958), "Yacimientos paleoliticos eu Bolivia", *Estuarica*, 1 No 2, 75-78.
567. Ihering H. (1927), *Geschichte des Atlantischen Ozean*, Leipzig.
568 Jarke J. (1957), "Jahresversammlung der Geologischen Vereinigung vom 15, bis 18. März in Weisbaden· 'Das Meer in Gegenwart und Vergangenheit' ", *Deutsch Hydrograph. Zcit*, 10 No. 3, 109-111.
569. Jarke J. (1958), "Sedimente und Mikrofaunen in Bereich der Grenzschwelle zweier ozeanischer Raume, dargestellt an einem Schnitt über den Island-Faroer Rücken", *Geologische Rundschau*, 47, 234-249, 469, 476, 483.
569a. Jansen H. I. (1962-63), "Australia and the Pacific Ocean", *Queensland Geographic Journal*, 61, 31-37.
570. Jeffreys H. (1952), *The Earth*, 3rd ed., University Press, 392.
570a Jeffreys H (1964), "How Old is the Earth?", *Quarterly Journal of the Royal Astronomical Society*, 5, 10-22.
571. Joleaud L (1924), "L'histoire biogeographique de l'Amerique et la theorie de Wegener", *Jour. Soc. americanistes de Paris*, 16.
572. Joquel A. L (1955), "Captain Robson's Discovery", *Atlantis* (London), 9, 6-8.
573. Joquel A. L. (1956), "A Letter", *Atlantis* (London), 10, 16-17
574. Kamienski M. (1949), "Zodiacal Epochs", *Atlantean Research*, 2, No. 4, 52-54.
575. Kamienski M. (1961), "Orientational Chronological Table of Modern and Ancient Perhelion Passages of Halley's Comet 1910 A.D.—9541 B.C.", *Acta Astronomica*, 11, No. 4, 223-229.
576. Kenyon K. M. (1957), *Digging Up Jericho*, London.
577. Kolbe R. W. (1955), "Diatoms from Equatorial Atlantic Cores", *Reports of the Swedish Deep-Sea Expedition 1947-48*, Vol VII, fasc. 111, 947-948.

578. Kolbe R. W (1957), "Fresh-Water Diatoms from Atlantic Deep-Sea Sediments", *Science*, 126, 1053-1056.
579. Koczy F. F., Burri M. (1958), "Essai d'interpietation de quelques formes du terrain sous-marin", *Deep-Sea Research*, Vol. 5, No. 1, 7-17.
579a. Krause D. C. (1964), "Guinea Fracture Zone in the Equatorial Atlantic", *Science*, 146, 57-59.
580. Kreici-Graf K. (1962), "Vertikal Bewegungen der Makaronesien (Zur Geologie der Makaronesien)", *Geologische Rundschau*, 51, 73-122, 296, 299, 301.
581. Kuenen Ph. H., Migliorini C. I. (1950), "Turbidity Currents as a Cause of Graded Bedding", *Journal of Geology*, 56, 91-126.
582. Küllenberg B. (1954), "Remarks on the Grand Banks Turbidity Current", *Deep-Sea Research*, Vol. 1, No. 4, 203-210.
583. Kuno H., Fisher R, Nasu N. (1956), "Rock Fragments and Pebbles Dredged Near Simmu Seamount, Northwestern Pacific", *Deep-Sea Research*, Vol. 3, No. 2, p. 126.
584. Kurten B. (1960), "Faunal Turnover Dates for the Pleistocene and Late Pliocene", *Comment. Biol. Soc. Scient. Fennica*, 22, No. 5, 1-14.
584a. Laming A., Emperaire J. (1958), "Bilan de trois campagnies de fouilles archeologiques au Brazil meridional", *Journal of the Society of Americanists*, 47, 199-212.
585. Landes K. K. (1952), "Our Shrinking Globe", *Bulletin of the Geological Society of America*, Vol. 63, No. 3, 225-240.
586. Landes K. K. (1952), "Our Shrinking Globe: A Reply", *Bulletin of the Geological Society of America*, Vol. 63, No. 10, 1073-1074.
587. Lasareff P. (1929), "Sur une methode permettant de demontrer la dependance des courants oceaniques dans changement de climat aux epoque geologique", *Beitrage zur Geophysik*, 21.
588. Laughton A. S. (1957), "Exploring the Deep Ocean Floor", *Journal of the Royal Society of Arts*, 106, 39-56.
589. Laughton A. S. (1959), *The Exploration of an Interplain Deep-Sea Channel*, Preprints of the International Oceanographic Congress, 1959, Washington, 36-38.
590. Laughton A. S., Hill M. N., Allan T. D. (1960), "Geophysical Investigations of a Seamount 150 Miles North of Madeira", *Deep-Sea Research*, Vol. 7, No. 2, 117-141.
591. Le Danois E. (1938), *Atlantique, histoire et vie d'un ocean*, Paris.
592. Lee T. E. (1961), "The Question of Indian Origin", *Science of Man I*, No. 5, 159; *New World Antiquity*, 8, 82-96.
593. Lees G. M. (1953), "The Geological History of the Oceans", *Deep-Sea Research*, Vol. 1, No. 2, 67-71.
594. Le Maitre R. W. (1959), "The Geology of Gough Island, South Atlantic", *Overseas Geological and Mineralogical Researches*, London, Vol. 7. No. 4, 371-380.
595. Lhote H. (1958), *Peintures prehistoriques du Sahara*, Paris.
597. Locher F. W. (1953), "Ein Beitrag zum Problem der Tiefseesands in westlichen Teil des äquatorialen Atlantik", *Heidelberger Beiträge Miner. u. Petrographie*, 4, 135.
598. London J. (1957), "Carbon Dioxide of Climatic Control", *Techn. Rep. Inst. Solar-Terrestrial Research for 1956*, No. 1, 88-90.
599. Lovering J. F. (1958), "The Nature of the Mohorovicic Discontinuity", *Transactions of the American Geophysical Union*, 35, No. 5.
600. Lubimova H. A. (1960), "On Processes of Heat Transfer in the Earth's Mantle", *Journal of the Physics of the Earth*, 8, No. 2, 11-16.
601. Lutoslawski W. (1877), *The Origin and Growth of Plato's Logic*, London.
602. Macdonald G. A. (1960), "Dissimilarity of Continental and Oceanic Rock Types, *Journal of Petrology*, 1, 172-177.
603. MacGowan K. (1950), *Early Man in the New World*, New York.
604. Machado F. (1959), "Submarine Pits of the Azores Plateau", *Bulletin volcanologique*, Series II, Vol. XXI, 109-116.

605. Malaise R. (1950), "The Constriction Theory", *The Earth Science Digest*, 4, No. 8, 3-10.
606. Martin F. (1906), *Le livre d'Henoch, traduit sur le texte ethiopen*, Paris.
607. Mason R. G. (1959), "Geophysical Investigations of the Sea Floor", *Liverpool-Manchester Geological Journal*, 2, 389-410.
608. Mayr C. (1952), "The Problem of Land Connection Across the South Atlantic With Special Reference to the Mesozoic", *Bulletin of the American Museum of Natural History*, 99, 79-258. (A Symposium.)
609. Mellis O. (1955), "Volcanic Ash-Horizons in Deep-Sea Sediments from the Eastern Mediterranean", *Deep-Sea Research*, Vol. 2, No. 2, 89-92.
610. Mellis O. (1960), "Gesteinfragmente im roten Ton des Atlantische Ozeans", *Medd. Oceangr. Inst.* Goteborg, B. 8, No. 6, 173.
611. Melton F. A., Schriver W. (1933), "The Carolina Bays: Are They Meteorite Scars?", *Journal of Geology*, 41, 52-66.
612. Menard H. W. (1959), *Distribution et origine des zones plates abyssales. Topographie et geologie des profonders oceaniques*, Paris, 95-107.
612a. Menard H. W. (1960), "The East Pacific Rise", *Science*, 132, 7-16; Russian translation (1964) in *Topography and Geology of the Ocean Floor*, Moscow, 225-253.
613. Mendonca Dias A. A. de (1959), "A crustal Deforming Agent and the Mechanism of the Volcanic Activity in the Azores", *Bulletin volcanologique*, Series II, Vol. XXI, 94-102.
614. Menzis R. J., Imbrie J., Heezen B. C. (1961), "Further Considerations Regarding the Antiquity of the Abyssal Fauna with Evidence for a Changing Abyssal Environment", *Deep-Sea Research*, Vol. 8, No. 2, 79.
615. Meyer R. (1960), "Changes in Wisconsin Glacial Stage Chronology by C^{14} Dating", *Transactions of the American Geophysical Union*, 41, 288-289.
616. Mitchell R. C. (1956), "Association lithologique et tectonique dans le domaine Caraibe", Cahiers geologiques, No. 37, 365-368.
617. Moore D. (1961), "Submarine Slumps", *Journal of Sedimentation Petrology*, 31, 343-357.
618. Mori F. (1961), *IV mission paletnologica nall'Acacus, Saharal Fezzanese*, Roma.
619. Mori F. (1961), *Aspetti di cronologia Sahariana allo luce dei ritrovanoenti della V mission paletnologica nell'Acacus*, Roma.
620. Müller H. (1844), *Das nordische Griechentum und die urgeschichtliche Bedeutung des nordwestlichen Europas*, Mainz.
620a. Müller W. (1962), "Der Ablauf der hotozänen Meerestransgression an der südlichen Nordseeküste und Folgerungen in Bezug, auf eine geochronologische Holozäng liederung", *Eiszeitalter und Gegenwart*, 13, 197-226.
621. Neumann B. (1902), "Messing-Zeitsch", *Angew. Chemie*, 21, 511.
622. Newman W. S. (1959), *Geological Significance of Recent Borings in the Vicinity of Castle Harbor, Bermuda*, Preprints of the International Oceanographical Congress, 1959, Washington, 46-47.
623. Northrop J., Frosh R. A., Frasseto R. (1962), "Bermuda—New England Seamount Arc", *Bulletin of the Geological Society of America*, Vol. 73, No. 5, 587-594.
624. Odhner N. (1923), "Contribution of the Marine Mollusc Faunas of South and West Africa", *Medd. Goteborgs Mus. Goteb. K. Vet. o Vitt. Samh. Handl.*, 4, 26, 7.
625. Odhner N. (1934), "The Constriction Hypothesis", *Geografisk Annaler* (Stockholm), 16, 109-124.
626. Odhner N. (1948), "Les modifications des continents et leurs consequences biographiques." *CR somm. seans. Soc. biographique*, 25, 75.
627. Odhner N. (1958), "Fundamental Argument in Cenozoic Geology Dynamic Factors: Crustal Undulations, Thermal Dilatation and Constriction", *Arkiv f. Mineral. Geol.* (Kungl. Svenska Vetenskapakademiens), 2, No. 24.
628. Odhner N. (1962), "Bilateral Constriction in the Ocean", *Bull. Instit. Oceanographique, Monaco*, No. 1230.

629. Osborne F. F. (1960), *On Turbidities*, "Royal Society of Canada", Series 4, 54, June 1-9.
630. Oulianoff (1961), "Rides (Ripple Marks) sur les fonds oceaniques et courants sous-marins", *CR Acad. Sc.*, Paris, 255, 507-509
631. Parker R. H. (1961), "Speculations on the Origin of the Invertebrate Faunas of the Lower Continental Slope", *Deep-Sea Research*, Vol. 8, No. 3/4, 286-293.
632. Paulian P. (1959), "Le phoque moine des Antilles (Monachus monachus) interessant probleme de biogeographie", *Comptes Rendus biogeograph*, 1958, No. 308-310, 97-99
632a. Pericot G. L. (1963), "L'Aurignocien et le Perigordien en Espagne", *Bull. Soc. meridion, speleol et prehist. 1956-59*, 6-9, 85-92.
633. Pettersson H. (1954), *The Ocean Floor*, New Haven.
634. Phleger F. B. (1948), "Foraminifera of a Submarine Core from the Carribean Sea", *Göteborgs Kungl. Vetensk, od Vitterheds Samholler Hardl.*, 6 Fl. Ser. b., Bd. 5, No. 14.
635. Phleger F. B. (1949), "Submarine Geology and Pleistocene Research," *Bulletin of the Geological Society of America*, Vol 60, No. 9, 1457.
636. Phleger F. B., Parker F. L, Pierson J. E. (1953), *North Atlantic Foraminifera. Swedish Deep-Sea Expedition*, Reports, 7, No. 1, 122.
637. Piggot C. S., Bradley W. H, Cushman J. A. (1940), "Geology and Biology of North Atlantic Deep-Sea Cores Between Newfoundland and Ireland", *US Geological Survey*, Prof. Papers, No. 196, Washington.
638. Piggot C. S., Urry W. D. (1942), "Time Relations in Ocean Sediments", *Bulletin of the Geological Society of America*, Vol. 53, No. 8, 1187.
639. Pompa y Pompa A. (1958), *El circumpacifico y la cultura megalitica en America*, Mexico.
640. Pratt R. M. (1961), "Erratic Boulders from Great Meteor Seamount", *Deep-Sea Research*, Vol. 8, No. 2, 152-153.
641. Cloud Preston E. (1961), "Paleobiogeography of the Marine Realm". *Oceanography*, edited by Mary Sears (American Association for the Advancement of Science, Publication No. 67), 151-200.
642. Prouty W. F. (1952). "Carolina Bays and Their Origin", *Bulletin of the Geological Society of America*, Vol. 63, No. 2, 167-224.
642a. Putzer H (1957), "Eipirogene, Bewegungen in Quartär an den Sudost-Kuste Brasilens und das Sambaqui-Problem", *Beiheft zum geologischen Jahrbuch*, No. 25, 149-186.
642b. Rao S. R (1963), "A 'Persian Gulf' Seal from Lothal", *Antiquity*, 37, No. 146, 96-99
643. Ratcliffe E. H. (1960), "The Thermal Conductivities of Ocean Sediments", *Journal of Geophysical Research*, Vol. 65, No. 5, 1535-1541.
644. Reid C. (1913), *Submerged Forests*, London
645. Reitzel J. (1961), "Some Heat-Flow Measurements in the North Atlantic", *Journal of Geophysical Research*, Vol. 66, No 7, 2267-2268.
646 Reshetov Y. G. (1962), "How Civilisation Arose," *New World Antiquity*, 9, 131-139
647. Revelle R. (1951), "Evidence of Instability of Pacific Basin", *Bulletin of the Geological Society of America*, Vol. 62, No. 12, 1510.
648. Revelle R. (1955), "On the History of the Oceans", *Journal of Marine Research*, 14, 446-461.
649. Rey Pastor A. (1955), "Estudio morfo-tectonico de la falla del Guadalquivir", *Rev. Geofis.*, 14, No. 54, 101-137.
649a. Rezanov J. A. (1964), "Über die Beschaffenheit und die Entstehung der Basaltschicht der Erdkruste Veröff", *Inst. Bodendynamik und Erdbedenforschung*, Jena, No. 77, 109-112.
650. Rickard T. A. (1932), *Man and Metals*, New York-London, 2nd ed.
651. Ridley F. (1960), "Transatlantic Contacts of Primitive Man Eastern Canada and Northwestern Russia", *Pennsylvania Archaeologist. Bulletin of the Society for Pennsylvania Archaeology*, 30, No 2, 46-57.

652. Righby J. K., Burckle L. H., Kolbe R. W. (1958), "Turbidity Currents and Displaced Fresh-Water Diatoms", *Science,* Vol. 127, No 3313, 1504-1505
653 Riem J. (1925), *Die Sintflut in Sage und Wissenschaft,* Hamburg
654. Rigg J. B. (1960), "On the Possible Existence of a Submerged Shoreline at a Depth of 300 Metres in the Northeastern Atlantic", *Weather,* 15, No. 7, 226-231.
655. Rosholt J. N., Emiliani C., Geiss J., Koszy F. F., Wangersky P. J. (1961), "Absolute Dating of Deep-Sea Cores by the Pa^{231}/Th^{230} Method", *Journal of Geology,* 69, 162-185
656. Rothè J. P. (1951), "The Structure of the Bed of the Atlantic Ocean", *American Geophysical Union Transactions,* 32, 457-461.
656a. Rutten M. C., Wensink H. (1960), "Structure of the Central Graben of Iceland", *21st International Geological Congress 1960,* Part 18, Copenhagen, 81-88.
657. Sabine P. A. (1960), "The Geology of Rockall, North Atlantic", *Bulletin of Geological Survey of Great Britain,* No 16, 156-178.
658. Satterwaite L , Ralph E. K. (1960), "New Radiocarbon Dates and the Maya Correlation Problem," *American Antiquity,* 26, No. 2, 165-184.
659. Scheidegger A. E. (1953), "Examination of the Physics of Theories of Orogenesis, *Bulletin of the Geological Society of America,* Vol. 64, No. 2, 127-150.
660. Scheidegger A. E. (1961), *Theoretical Geomorphology,* Berlin.
660a. Scheidegger A. E. (1963), "On the Tectonic Stresses in the Vicinity of a Valley and a Mountain Range", *Proceedings of the Royal Society of Victoria,* 76, No. 1-2, 141-145.
661. Schott G. (1926), *Geographie des Atlantischen Ozeans,* Hamburg; 2-te Aufl , 3-te Aufl., 1942.
662 Schulten A. (1922), *Tartessos. Ein Beitrag zur altesten Geschichtes des Westens,* Hamburg, 2-te Aufl , 1950.
663. Schwarzbach M (1960), "Die Eiszeit—Hypothese von Ewing und Donn Zeitsch", *Deutsch. Geolog. Gesellschaft,* 112, No. 2, 309-315
664. Segota T. (1961), "Absolute Chronology of the Quaternary Period", *Bull. scient. Conseil Acad.,* RPFY 6, No 2, 39-41.
665. Segota T. (1961), "The Geographic Background of the Ice Ages", *Bull. scient. Conseil Acad.,* RPFY 6, No. 3, 75.
666 Shand J. (1949), "Rocks and the Mid-Atlantic Ridge", *Journal of Geology,* 57, 89-92.
667. Shell I. I. (1957), "Theory of Ice Age", *Science,* 125, 235.
668. Shepard F. P., Emery K. O. (1941), "Submarine Topography of the California Coast", *Geological Society of America,* Special Papers, No. 31, Baltimore.
669. Shepard F. P. (1951), "Submarine Erosion, a Discussion of Recent Papers", *Bulletin of the Geological Society of America,* Vol. 62, No. 12, 1407-1410.
670. Shepard F. P. (1952), "Composite Origin of Submarine Canyons", *Journal of Geology,* 60, 84-96
671. Shepard F. P. (1955), "Delta-Front Valleys Bordering the Mississippi Distributaries", *Bulletin of the Geological Society of America,* Vol. 66, No 12, 1480-1498.
672. Shepard F P. (1959), *Turbidity Currents and Erosion of the Deep-Sea Floor,* Preprints of the International Oceanographic Congress, Washington, 50-51.
673. Shepard F. P. (1959), *The Earth Beneath the Sea,* Baltimore
674. De Sitter L. U. (1961), "Compression and Tension in the Earth's Crust", *Geologische Rundschau,* 50, 219-225, 685, 708
674a. Skeels M A. (1961), "The Mastodon and Mammoths of Michigan", *Michigan Academy of Science, Arts and Letters,* 47, 101-133.
675. De Sonneville-Bordes (1956), "Contributions recentes à la connaissance du Magdalenien", *Anthropologie,* 60, 369-378
676. Staub W. (1961), "Wesentliche Phasen der Würmeiszeit und Nacheiszeit im Schweizerischen Mittelland", *Jahresber. Geograph. Gesellschaft,* Bern, 45, 41-43.
677. Stearns H. T. (1961), "Eustatic Shorelines in Pacific Islands", *10th Pacific Scientific Congress,* Pacific Scientific Association, Honolulu, 1961, 294.

678. Stehli F. G. (1957), "Possible Permian Climatic Zonation and Its Implications", *American Journal of Science*, 255, 607-618.
679. Stille H. (1948), "Ur-und Neuozeane", *Abhandl. Deutsch. Akad. Wissensch., mathem.-physik. Klasse fur*, 1945-1946, No. 6.
680. Stille H. (1957), "'Atlantische' und 'Pazifische' Tektonik", *Geologische Jahrebericht*, 74, 677-685.
681. Straka H. (1956), "Die pollenanalytische Datierung von jungeren Vulkanausbruchen", *Erdkunde*, 10, 204-216.
682. Sykes E. (1960), "Stagnation in Oceanography", *New World Antiquity*, 7, 67-79.
683. Talwani M., Sutton G. H., Worzel J. L. (1959), "Crustal Section Across the Puerto Rico Trench", *Bulletin of the Geological Society of America*, Vol. 70, No. 12, 1752.
684. Talwani M., Heezen B. C., Worzel J. L. (1961), *Gravity Anomalies and Crustal Structure in the Mid-Atlantic Ridge*, Publications Centre of the Seismological International, A22, 81-111.
685. Tatel H. E. (1956), "Structure of the Earth's Crust from Gravity Measurements", *Science*, Vol. 124, No. 3227, 941.
686. Tavernier R., Heinzelin J. (1957) "Chronologie du pleistocene superieur. plus particulierement en Belgique, *Geol. en mijnbouw*, 19, 306-309.
687. Taylor A. E. (1926), *Plato, the Man and His Work*, London.
688. Thorarinsson S., Tryggvason T. (1960), "Geology in Iceland", *Geotimes*, 4, No. 6, 8-10.
689. Tolstoy I., Ewing M. (1949), "North Atlantic Hydrography and the Mid-Atlantic Ridge", *Bulletin of the Geological Society of America*, Vol. 60, No. 10, 1527-1540.
690. Tolstoy I. (1951), "Submarine Topography in the North Atlantic", *Bulletin of the Geological Society of America*, Vol. 62, No. 5, 441-450.
692. Ulrich J. (1960), "Zur Topographie des Reykjanes-Rückens", *Kieler Meeresforschungen*, 16, No. 2, 155-163.
693. Umbgrove J. H. F. (1947), *The Pulse of the Earth*, New York.
694. Vening Meinesz F. A. (1948), "Gravity Expedition at Sea, 1923-1938 *Delftsche Uitgevers Maatshappay*, No. 4.
695 Verneau R. (1887), *Rapport sur une mission scientifique dans l'archipel Canarien*, Paris
696. Verril A. H., Ruth Verril (1953), *America's Ancient Civilisation*, New York, 2nd ed.
697. Wakeel K. E., Rieley J. P. (1961), "Chemical and Mineralogical Studies of Deep-Sea Sediments", *Geochimica et cosmochimica Acta*, 25, No. 2, 110-146.
698. Waldo J. H. (1960), "The Last Pleistocene Age As Seen Here", *Rocks and Minerals*, 35, No. 9-10, 454-459.
699. Weibull W. (1947), "The Thickness of Ocean Sediments Measured by a Reflection Method", *Medd. Oceangr. Inst.*, Göteborg, No. 12.
700. Von Wilamowitz-Mollendorf U. (1914), "Die Phäaken", *Inter. Monats. Wiss., Kunst. und Techn.*, Juni Heft.
701. Willet H. C. (1957), "Alternate Theories of Climatic Changes", *Techn. Rep. Inst. Solar-Terrestrial Res. for 1956*, No. 1, 91-94.
702. Willis B. (1910), "Principles of Paleography", *Science*, Vol. 31, No. 790, 241.
703. Winkler H. A. (1938), *Rock Drawings of Southern Upper Egypt*, London.
704. Wiseman J., Ovey C. (1950), "Recent Investigations of the Deep-Sea Floor", *Proceedings of the Geologists Association*, 61, 28-34.
705. Woldstedt P. (1960), "Die letzte Eiszeit in Nordamerika und Europa", *Eiszeitalter und Gegenwart*, 11, 148-165.
706. Woolard C. P. (1960), "Seismic Crustal Studies During the IGY, Part I, Marine Programme", *Trans. Americ. Geophys. Union*, 41, 107-113.
707. Worthington L. V., Metcalf W. G. (1961), "The Relationship Between Potential Temperature and Salinity in Deep Atlantic Waters", *Rapports et pro-*

cés-verbeaux des reunions. Conseil permanent international de l'exploration de mer, 149, 122-128.

708. Worzel J. L (1959), "Extensive Deep-Sea Sub-Bottom Reflection Identified as White Ash", Proceedings of the National Academy of Sciences of the USA, 45, 349.

709. Worzel J. L., Talwani M (1959), "Gravity Anomalies on Seamounts", Bulletin of the Geological Society of America, Vol. 70, No. 12, 1702-1703.

710 Wundt W. (1958-59), "Die Penk'sche Eiszeitgliederung und die Strahlungskurve", Quatär, 10-11, 15-26.

711. Wüst G. (1939) "Das submarine Relief bei den Azoren", Abhandl. d. Preuss. Akad. Wissensch., mathemat.-physikal. Klasse, No. 5, 46-58.

712. Young L. (1949), "Platonic Miscellany", Atlantean Research, 2, No. 3, 26-39.

713. Zeuner F F (1959), The Pleistocene Period: Its Climate, Chronology and Faunal Succession, London, 2nd revised edition.

714. Zhirov N. Th. (1958), The Cosmic Ice Theory Brought Up To Date, Atlantis (London), Vol. 10, 113-117, Vol. 11, No. 2, 28-30.

715. "The Geological and Geophysical Results of the Cruises of RRS 'Discovery 11' During May 1958-July 1959", Geophysical Journal of the Royal Astronomical Society, 2. 168-170.

716. "Informations" (1963), Cahiers oceanographiques, 14, 437-444.

717. Seismic Studies in the Western Caribbean (1959), Transact. Americ. Geophysic. Union, 40, 73-75

III. ADDITIONAL REFERENCES (1965-1967)

718. Abramova Z. A. (1966), "Lokalniye osobennosti paleoliticheskikh kultur Sibiri" ("Local Features of Siberian Paleolithic Cultures"), Seventh International Congress of Prehistorians and Protohistorians, Papers and Communications by Soviet Archaeologists, Moscow, 46-55.

719 Afanasyev B. L. (1966), "K problemam riftov i mobilizma" ("The Problem of Rifts and Mobilism"), News of the USSR Academy of Sciences, Geology Series, No. 8, 126-130.

720. Briggs J. C. (1966), "Okeanicheskiye ostrova, endemizm i morskiye paleotemperatury" ("Oceanic Islands, Endemism and Marine Paleotemperatures"), Second International Oceanographic Congress, Summary of Papers, Moscow, 60, 61.

721. Volarovich M. P. and others (1966), "Seria statei po izucheniyu skorosti rasprostraneniya prodolnykh voln v gornykh porodakh pri razlichnykh davleniyakh" ("Series of Papers on the Study of Latitudinal Wave Dispersion Velocities in Rock Under Various Pressures"). In Electrical and Mechanical Properties of Rocks Under High Pressures, Proceedings of the Institute of Physics of the Earth at the Academy of Sciences of the USSR, No. 37 (204), Moscow.

722. Volarovich M. P., Galdin N. E., Levykin A. I. (1966), "Issledovaniya skorostei prodolnykh voln v obraztsakh izverzhennykh i metamorficheskikh gornykh porod pri davlenii do 20,000 kg/sm^2" ("Studies of Longitudinal Wave Velocities in Igneous and Metamorphic Rocks under Pressures of up to 20,000 kg/cm^2"), Proceedings of the Academy of Sciences of the USSR, Physics of the Earth, No. 3, 15-23.

723. Gakkel Y. Y, Demenitskaya R. M., Karasik A. M., Isayev E. N., Ushakov S. A. (1966), "Morfologiya, fizicheskiye polya i glubinnaya struktura Arkticheskogo basseina" ("Morphology, Physical Field and Abyssal Structure of the Arctic Basin"), Second International Oceanographic Congress. Summary of Papers, Moscow, 106.

724 Demenitskaya R. M., Karasik A. M., Kiselev Y. G. (1967), "Noviye danniye o geologicheskom stroyenii dna Severnogo Ledovitogo okeana po materialam

geofizicheskikh issledovaniy" ("New Data on the Geological Structure of the Arctic Ocean Floor According to Geophysical Research") in *Method, Techniques and Results of Geophysical Exploration*, Moscow, 31, 38.

725. Dibner K. D. (1965), "Istoria formirovaniya pozdne-pleistotsenovykh i golotsenovykh otlozheniy Zemli Frantsa Iosifa" ("History of Formation of Late Pleistocene and Holocene Sediments in Franz Josef Land"), *Proceedings of the Institute of Arctic Geology*, 143, 300-318.

726. Zhivago A. V. (1966), "Voprosy stroyeniya zemnoi kory, tektoniki i geomorfologii dna okeanov i morei na 2-m Mezhdunarodnom Okeanograficheskom kongresse" ("Problems of the Crustal Structure, Tectonics and Geomorphology of the Floor of Oceans and Seas at the Second International Oceanographic Congress"), *Okeanologiya*, 6, 988-997.

727. Zhirov N. F. (1966), "Obrechennaya na gibel" ("Doomed to Destruction"), *Neman*, No. 11, 151-160.

729. Zhirov N. F. (1968), *Atlantida. Kratkaya istoriya problemy (Atlantis. A Brief Survey of the Problem)*, Moscow, expected in 1970.

730 Zolotnitsky N S (1966), "O vozmozhnosti obrazovaniya potokov muti v vodnykh basseinakh za schet massovogo vynosa rekami vzveshennogo oblomochnogo materiala" ("The Possibility of Turbidity Currents Forming in Water Basins Through the Mass Transportation of Suspended Clastic Material by Rivers"), *Bulletin of the Ivan Franko Branch of the Lvov Polytechnical Institute*, No. 6, 7-13.

731. Ilyin A. V. (1966), "O nekotorykh osobennostyakh morfologii sredinno-Atlanticheskogo khrebta" ("Some Features of the Morphology of the Mid-Atlantic Ridge"), *Second International Oceanographic Congress, Summary of Papers*, Moscow, 178-179.

732. Ilyin A. V. (1967), "O morfologicheskikh razlichiyakh v predelakh Sredinno-Atlanticheskogo khrebta" ("Morphological Distinctions in the Mid-Atlantic Ridge"), *Reports of the Academy of Sciences of the USSR*, 172, 913-916

733. Klenova M. V. (1966), "Noviye danniye po geologii Atlanticheskogo okeana" ("New Data on the Geology of the Atlantic Ocean"), *Okeanologicheskiye issledovaniya*, No. 15, 112-117.

734. Klenova M. V., Lavrov V. M. (1966), "Skhema tektoniki Atlanticheskogo okeana" ("Pattern of Tectonics in the Atlantic"), *Bulletin of the Moscow Society of Naturalists*, Geology Section, 41, No. 5, 139-140.

735. Krause D. C. (1966), "Svyaz Sredinno-Atlanticheskogo rifta s Azorskoi platformoi" ("Relationship Between the Mid-Atlantic Rift and the Azores Plateau"), *Second International Oceanographic Congress, Summary of Papers*, Moscow, 219-220.

736. Krestev K. (1966), *Atlantida (Atlantis)*, Varna, in the Bulgarian language.

737. Lavrov V. M. (1965), "O relyefe i tektonike ekvatorialnoi chasti Sredinnogo Atlanticheskogo khrebta" ("Topography and Tectonics of the Equatorial Mid-Atlantic Ridge"), *Reports of the Academy of Sciences of the USSR*, 162, 1134-1137.

738. Lavrov V. M. (1966), "Podvodny vulkanizm Azorskogo gornogo uzla v Severnoi Atlantike" ("Submarine Volcanic Activity in the Azores Mountain System in the North Atlantic"), *Present-day Volcanism*, Vol. I, 24-32.

739. Lavrov V. M. (1966), "O tektonicheskoi prirode vpadiny Romanche" ("Tectonic Nature of the Romanche Trench"), *Reports of the Academy of Sciences of the USSR*, 170, 695-698.

740. Laughton A. S., Matthews D. H. (1966), "Poperechniye struktury v vostochnoi chasti Severnoi Atlantiki" ("Transversal Structure on the Eastern North Atlantic"), *Second International Oceanographic Congress. Summary of Papers*, Moscow, 236-237

741 Leontyev O. K. (1965), "Nekotoriye zakonomernosti relyefa dna okeanov i planetarnaya sistema sredinno-okeanicheskikh khrebtov" ("Some Laws Governing the Ocean Floor Topography and the Planetary System of Mid-Ocean Ridges"), *At a Conference on Problems of Planetology*, Leningrad, 108-112.

742. Litvin V. M. (1966), "Geomorfologiya sredinno-okeanicheskogo khrebta v Norvezhskom i Grenlandskom moryakh i ego svyaz so Sredinno-Atlanticheskim

khrebtom" ("Geomorphology of the Mid-Ocean Ridge in the Norwegian and Greenland Seas and Its Relationship with the Mid-Atlantic Ridge"), *Second International Oceanographic Congress. Summary of Papers*, Moscow, 247-248.

743 Litvin V. M. (1966), "Noviye danniye po stroyeniyu shelfa i ostrovnogo sklona v raione yugo-zapadnoi Islandii" ("New Data on the Structure of the Shelf and Island Slope in Southwestern Iceland"), *Proceedings of a Session of the PINRO Scientific Council on the Results of Investigations in 1964*, Issue 6, Murmansk, 97-107.

744. Lyustikh E. N. (1965), "Neomobilizm i konvektsiya v mantii Zemli. Statya I-ya. Dovody storonnikov mobilizma i dovody i v polzu konvektsii" ("Neomobilism and Convection in the Earth's Mantle, Paper No. 1, Arguments of the Mobilists and Arguments in Favour of Convection"), *Bulletin of the Moscow Society of Naturalists*, Geology Section, 40, No. 1, 5-27; "Statya 2-ya (1965), Uvyazka gipotezy konvektsii i materikovogo dreifa" ["Paper No. 2 (1965)] Coordination Between the Theories of Convection and the Continental Shelf"), *Ibid.*, 40, No. 2, 5-21, (1965), "Konvektsia v mantii i sfericheskiye funktsii" ("Convection in the Mantle and Spherical Functions"), *News of the Academy of Sciences of the USSR, Physics of the Earth*, No 8, 100-110

745. Markov K. K., Suyetova I. A. (1965), "Evstaticheskiye kolebaniya urovnya okeana" ("Eustatic Fluctuations of the Ocean Level"), *Basic Problems of the Quaternary Period*, Moscow, 143-146

746 Pukhlyakov L. A. (1965), "K voprosu proiskhozhdeniya Tikhogo okeana" ("The Origin of the Pacific Ocean"), *News of the Tomsk Polytechnical Institute*, 127, No.2, 216-227.

747. Raznitsyn V. A. (1965), "K voprosu o proiskhozhdenii zemnoi kory i glavnykh etapakh ee razvitiya" ("The Origin of the Earth's Crust and the Principal Stages of Its Development"), *News of Institutions of Higher Learning; Geology and Surveying*, No. 10, 3-12.

748 Rassokho A I. Senchura L I, Demenitskaya R M, Karasik A. M, Kisilyov Y. G, Timoshenko N. K. (1967), "Podvodniy sredinniy Arktichesky khrebet i ego mesto v sisteme khrebtov Severnogo Ledovitogo okeana" ("The Submarine Arctic Ridge and Its Place in the System of Ridges in the Arctic Ocean"), *Reports of the Academy of Sciences of the USSR*, 172, 659-662.

749 Reder D. G. (1965), *Mify i legendy drevnego Dvurechya (Myths and Legends of Ancient Mesopotamia)*, Moscow.

750. Reshetov Y. (1966), "Fakty protiv legend" ("Facts Versus Legends"), *Tekhnika-molodezhi*, No. 7, 14.

751. Stovas M. V. (1966), "Sovremennoye voskhodyashcheye dvizheniye urovnya okeana v ekvatorialnoi zone" ("Modern Rise of the Ocean Level in the Equatorial Zone"), *Geophysics and Astronomy; Information Bulletin*, No. 9, 73-79.

752. Udintsev G. B. (1966), "Geomorfologiya i tektonika dna okeanov" ("Geomorphology and Tectonics of the Ocean Floor"), *Herald of the Academy of Sciences of the USSR*, No. 9, 98-103.

753. Sheinmann Y. M. (1965), "Ob odnoi osobennosti sredinnykh okeanicheskikh khrebtov" ("A Feature of the Mid-Oceanic Ridges"), *Geotektonika* 1, No. 4, 106-108.

754 Sheinmann Y. M (1966), "Yeshcho raz o mobilizme" ("Once More on Mobilism"), *Geotektonika* 2, No. 2, 110-121.

755 Sheinmann Y. M (1966), "O vozraste sovremennykh struktur dna okeana (na primere Atlantiki)" ["Age of Modern Structures of the Ocean Floor (on the Example of the Atlantic)"], *Second International Oceanographic Congress. Summary of Papers*, Moscow, 422-424.

756 Discussion in the magazine *Zemlya i Uselennaya* (1965-66): "Tonula li Atlantida?" ("Did Atlantis Sink?"): A. V. Ilyin (1965), No. 3, 94-95; N. F. Zhirov (1966), No. 2, 57-58; A V. Ilyin (1966), No. 2, 58-59; O K. Leontyev (1966), "Sovremenniye nauchniye danniye ne podtverzhdayut sushchestvovaniya Atlantidy" ("Modern Scientific Data Do Not Confirm the Existence of Atlantis"), No. 2, 59-61.

757 Arkhanguelski M. (1965), "On the Surface of Equal Pressure and the

Equilibrium of the World", *Rev. roumaine Sci. techn. Ser. Mec. appl.*, 10, No. 4, 1071-1080.

758. Amin B. S., Kharkar D. P. L. (1966), "Cosmogonic ^{10}Be and ^{26}Al in Marine Sediments", *Deep-Sea Research*, 13, 805-824.

759. Andel T. H. van, Bowen V. T., Sachs P., Siever R. (1965), "Morphology and Sediments of a Portion of the Mid-Atlantic Ridge", *Science*, 148, 1214-1216.

760. Belliar P. (1966), "Reflexions sur les glaciations", *Rev. Geograph. phys. et glob dynam*, 8, 335-341.

761. Berger R, Orr Ph. C. (1966), "The Fire Areas on Santa Rosa Island", California, *Proceedings of the National Academy of Sciences of the USA*, 56, 1678, 1682.

762. Bleton A. (1966), "Apercu geologique sur l'archipel des Canaries", *Jardins Maroc*, 51, No. 21, 19-21.

763. Bott M H. P. (1965), "The Upper Mantle Beneath Iceland", *Geophysical Journal of the Royal Astronomical Society*, No. 2-3, 275-277.

764. Bott M. H. P. (1966), "Formation of Oceanic Ridges", *Nature*, 207, 840-843.

765. Cann J. R., Funnel M. (1967), "Palmer Ridge: A Section Through the Upper Part of the Ocean Crust?", *Nature*, 213, 661-664.

766. Christensen N. I. (1965), "Compressional Wave Velocities in Metamorphic Rocks at Pressures to 10 Kilobars", *Journal of Geophysical Research*, 70, 6147-6164.

767. Connolly J. R, Ewing M. (1965), "Pleistocene Glacial Marine Zones in North Atlantic Deep-Sea Sediments", *Nature*, 208, 135-138.

768. Gorshkov G. S. (1965), "On the Relation of Volcanoes and the Upper Mantle", *Bulletin of Volcanology*, 28, 159-169.

769. Hedervari P. (1965), "Genetikai kapcsolat az oceani aknak es a guyotkepzdmenyek kózott", *Foldr. ert.*, 15, 497-502.

770. Heezen B. C., Tharp M. (1965), "Tectonic Fabric of the Atlantic and Indian Oceans and Continental Drift, A Symposium on Continental Drift", *Philosophical Transactions of the Royal Society of London*, A259, No. 1099, 227-239.

771. Hess H. H. (1965), "Mid-Oceanic Ridges and Tectonics of the Sea Floor", *Submarine Geology and Geophysics*, London, 317-333.

772. Hester J. J. (1966), "Late Pleistocene Environments and Early Man in South America", *American Naturalist*, 100, No. 914, 377-388.

773. Jeffrey F. P., Heezen B. C. (1965), "Sands of the Mid-Atlantic Ridge", *Science*, 149, 1367-1370.

774. Jones E. J. W., Laughton A. S., Hill M. N, Davies D. D. (1966), "A Geophysical Study of Part of the Western Boundary of the Madeira-Cape Verde Abyssal Plain", *Deep-Sea Research*, 13, 889-907.

775. Krause D. C. (1965), "East and West Azores Fracture Zones in the North Atlantic", *Golston Papers XVII*, Bristol, 163-173.

776 Le Pichon X, Houtz R. E., Drake Ch., Nafe J E. (1965), "Crustal Structure of the Mid-Oceanic Ridges, I. Seismic Refractions", *Journal of Geophysical Research*, 70, 319-339.

777. Le Pichon X. (1966), "Etude geophysique de la dorsale medio-Atlantique", *Cahiers oceanographiques*, 18. No 5, 327-349.

778. Loncarevic B. D., Mason C. S. (1966), "Mid-Atlantic Ridge Near 45°N. I. The Median Valley", *Canadian Journal of Earth Sciences*, 3, No. 3, 327-349.

779. Machado F. (1966), *Volcanismo das Ilhas de Cabo Verde e Des cutras ilhas Atlantidas*, Lisboa.

780. Matthews D. H., Davies D. (1966), *Geophysical Studies of the Seychelles Bank*, *Philosophical Transactions of the Royal Society of London*, A 259, 1099, 227-239.

781. Melson G. W., Bowen V. T., van Andel T. H., Siever R. (1966), "Greenstones from the Central Valley of the Mid-Atlantic Ridge", *Nature*, 209, 604-605.

782. Melson W G (1966), "Geologic Significance of St. Paul's Rocks", *Oceanus*, 12, No. 4, 8-11.

783. Ostenso N. A. (1966), "The Structure of the Arctic Ocean", *Transactions of the New York Academy of Sciences*, 28, 978-980.
784. Santo Tetsuo (1965), "Lateral Variation of the Rayleigh Wave Dispersion Character, Part I, Observational Data", *Pure and Applied Geophysics*, 62, No. 3, 49-66.
785. Vacquier V. (1965), "Transcurrent Faulting in the Ocean Floor", *Philosophical Transactions of the Royal Society of London*, A258, No. 1088, 77-81, 107-108.
786 Vogt P. R., Ostenso N. A. (1966), "Magnetic Survey of the Mid-Atlantic Ridge Between 42°N and 47°N", *Transactions of the American Geophysical Union*, 47, 122-123.
787. Walker G. P. I. (1965), "Evidence of Crustal Drift from Icelandic Geology", *Philosophical Transactions of the Royal Society of London*, A258, No. 1088, 199-215.
788. Wilson J. T. (1966), "Did the Atlantic Close and Then Re-open?", *Nature*, 211, 676-681.
789. Worzel J. L. (1965), "Deep Structure of Coastal Margins and Mid-Oceanic Ridges", *Submarine Geology and Geophysics*, London, 335-461.
790. Zhirov N. (1965), "L'Atlantide e possible?", *Sci. e vita*, 17, No. 198 20-25.
791. Thorarinsson S. (1966), "The Median Zone of Iceland", *Papers of the Geological Survey of Canada*, No. 14, 187-211.
792. Asada Toshi (1965), "Comparison of Continental Seismic Velocities from Explosion Results and Laboratory Measurements", *Journal of the Physics of the Earth*, 13, 1-4.
793. Gainanov A. G., Stroyev P. A. (1966), "Nekotoriye osobennosti gravitatsionnogo polya i stroyeniya zemnoi kory Atlanticheskogo, Indiiskogo i Tikhogo okeanov" ("Some Features of the Gravitational Field and Crustal Structure ot the Atlantic, Indian and Pacific Oceans"), Collection II, *Geophysical Research*, Moscow, 231-240.
794. Loncarevic B. D. (1967), "The Mid-Atlantic Ridge and North Atlantic Ocean", *Geological Survey of Canada*, Paper No. 41, Canadian Upper Mantle Report, 1967; Ottawa, 1967, 220-227.
795. Kerr J. W. (1967), "A Submerged Continental Remnant Beneath the Labrador Sea", *Earth and Planet. Sci. Letters*, 2, 283-89.
796. Laughton A. S. (1968), "New Evidence of Erosion on the Deep Ocean Floor", *Deep-Sea Research*, Vol. 15, No. 1, 21-29.
797. Litvin V. M. (1968), "Geomorfologiya sredinnogo okeanicheskogo khrebta v Norvezhskom i Grenlandskom moryakh" ("Geomorphology of the Mid-Oceanic Ridge in the Norwegian and Greenland Seas"), *Okeanologiya*, 8, 86-93.
798. Tjeerd H. van Andel, John B. Corliss, Vaughan T. Bowen (1967), "The Intersection Between the Mid-Atlantic Ridge and the Vema Fracture Zone in the North Atlantic", *Journal of Marine Research*, 24, 343-54; *Transactions of the American Geophysical Union*, 48, 133-34.
799. Ivanova I. K. (1967), "Voprosy arkheologii i istorii iskopayemogo cheloveka na VII kongresse" ("Problems of Archaeology and the History of Fossil Man at the 7th Congress"), *7th INQA Congress*, Moscow, 185-209.
800. Heirtzler J. R., Hayes D. E (1967), "Magnetic Boundaries in the North Atlantic Ocean", *Science*, 157, 185-87.
801. Rothe P. (1967), "Prävulkanische Sedimentgestein auf Fuerteventura (Kanarische Inseln)", *Naturwissenschaften*, 54, No. 14, 366-67.
802. Lyustikh E. N. (1967), Criticism of Hypotheses of Convection and Continental Drift, *Geophysical Journal of the Royal Astronomical Society*, 14, 347-52.
803. Ewing John, Ewing Maurice (1967), "Sediment Distribution on the Mid-Oceanic Ridges with Respect to Spreading of the Sea Floor", *Science*, 156, 1590-1592.
804. Berry W. B. N., Boncot A. J. (1967), "Continental Stability—A Silurian Point of View", *Journal of Geophysical Research*, 72, 2254-2256.
805. Johnson G. L. (1967), "North Atlantic Fracture Zones Near 53°", *Earth and Planet, Sci. Letters* 2, 445-446.
806. Matthews D. H, Batt J (1967), "Formation of Magnetic Anomaly Pattern

of Mid-Atlantic Ridge", *Geophysical Journal of the Royal Astronomical Society*, 13, 345-57.

807. Smiley C. (1967), "Paleoclimatic Interpretation of Some Mesozoic Floral Sequences", *Bulletin of the American Association of Petrologists and Geologists*, 51, No. 6, Part 1, 849-863.

808. Rybin A. M. (1967), "Szhimayetsya ili rasshiryaetsya Zemlya? Proiskhozhdeniye okeanicheskikh vpadin" ("Is the Earth Shrinking or Expanding? Origin of Oceanic Hollows"), *Priroda*, No. 4, 50-56.

809. Dzerdzeyevsky B. L. (1967), "Klimatologiya na VII Kongresse" ("Climatology at the 7th Congress"), *7th INQA Congress*, 1965, Moscow, 210-219.

810. Hospers J., van Andel S. I. (1967), "Paleomagnetism and the Hypothesis of an Expanding Earth", *Tectonophysics*, 5, 5-24.

811. Zavadovsky Y. N. (1967), *Berbersky yazyk (The Berber Language)*, Moscow.

812. Fedorova I. K. (1965), "Versions of Myths and Legends in Manuscripts from Easter Island", *Reports of the Norwegian Archaeological Expedition to Easter Island and the East Pacific*, Vol. 2, 397-98. Edited by Thor Heyerdahl and E. N. Ferdan, Stockholm.

813. Leontyev O. K. (1968), *Dno okeana (The Ocean Bottom)*, Moscow.

814 Dubois J. (1968), "Etude de la dispersion des ondes de Rayleigh dans la region de sud-ouest Pacifique", *Ann. Geophys*, 24, 359-360.

815. Gakkel Y. Y., Belov N. D., Dibner V. D., Lapina N. N. (1968), "Morphostruktura i donniye osadki Arkticheskogo basseina" ("Morphological Structure and Bottom Sediments of the Arctic Basin"), *Proceedings of the Arctic and Antarctic Research Institute*, 285, 15-27.

816 Govorukha L. S (1968), "Y. Y Gakkel ob Arktide" ("Y. Y. Gakkel on Arctis"), *Ibid.*, 37-51

817. Gakkel Y. Y, Dibner V. D., Litvin V. M. (1968), "Osnovniye cherty endogennoi geomorfologii i tektoniki Atlantichesko-Arkticheskoi provintsii Severnogo Ledovitogo okeana" ("Principal Features of the Endogenic Geomorphology and Tectonics of the Atlantic-Arctic Province of the Arctic Ocean"), *Ibid.*, 28-36.

818. Orlenok V. V., Gainanov A. G. (1967), "Geofizicheskiye issledovaniya struktury zemnoi kory Labradorskogo morya" ("Geophysical Investigations of the Structure of the Earth's Crust in the Labrador Sea"), *Herald of Moscow University, Geology*, No. 5, 146-157.

819. Schofield J. C. (1967), "Notes on the Geology of the Tonga Islands", *New Zealand Journal of Geology and Geophysics*, 10, 1424-1428.

820. Maok R. (1966), "Probleme des Gondwanalandes im Sinne tangentialen Krustenverschiebungen", *Bol. paran. geol.*, Nos. 18-20, 50-70.

821. Schmidt D. L. (1968), "Gondwana and Drift Symposium in South America", *Antarctic J.U S.*, 3, 1517.

822. Rezanov I. A. (1967), "Mezhdunarodny proekt 'Verkhnyaya mantiya'" ("International Project 'Upper Mantle'"), *The Earth and the Universe*, No. 6, pp. 82-84.

823. Johnson G. L., Paw J. A. (1968), "Extension of the Mid-Labrador Sea Ridge", *Nature*, 217, 1033-1034.

824. Zamyslova Y. A. (1967), "Drevniy chelovek v Severnoi Amerike (obzor literatury)" ["Ancient Man in North America (Review of Literature)"], *Bulletin of the Commission for the Study of the Quaternary Period*, No 34, 107-119.

825. Khazanov A. (1965), "Devyanosto vekov Khatal Kuyuka", ("Ninety Centuries of Khatal Kuyuk"), Almanac *Na sushe i na more*, Vol. 6, 574-581